ANCIENT AMERICANS

ANCIENT AMERICANS

Rewriting the History of the New World

CHARLES C. MANN

Granta Books
London

Granta Publications, 2/3 Hanover Yard, Noel Road, London N1 8BE

First published in Great Britain by Granta Books 2005

First published in the United States in 2005, under the title *1491: New Revelations of the Americas Before Columbus*, by Alfred A. Knopf, a division of Random House Inc., New York, and in Canada by Random House of Canada Limited, Toronto.

Portions of this book have appeared in different form in *The Atlantic Monthly*, *Harvard Design Magazine*, *Journal of the Southwest*, *The New York Times* and *Science*.

A CIP catalogue record for this book is available from the British Library.

1 3 5 7 9 10 8 6 4 2

ISBN-13: 978-1-86207-617-4
ISBN-10: 1-86207-617-0

Printed and bound in Great Britain
by William Clowes Limited, Beccles, Suffolk

For the woman in the next-door office—
Cloudlessly, like everything else

—*CCM*

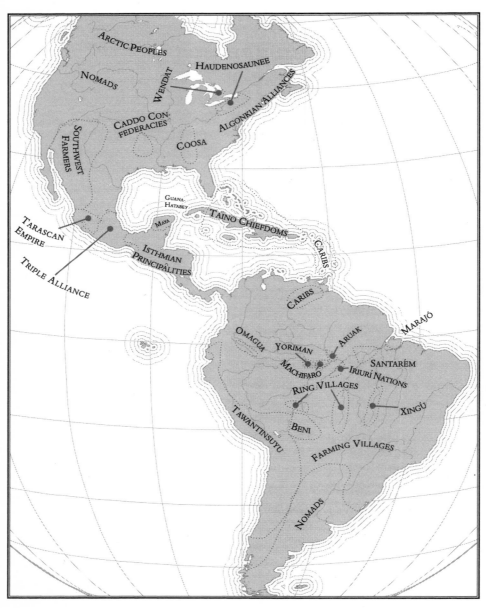

ARCTIC PEOPLES

NOMADS

WENDAT

HAUDENOSAUNEE

ALGONKIAN ALLIANCES

CADDO CON-
FEDERACIES

SOUTHWEST
FARMERS

COOSA

GUANA-
HATABEY

MAYA

TAINO CHIEFDOMS

CARIBS

TARASCAN
EMPIRE

ISTHMIAN
PRINCIPALITIES

TRIPLE ALLIANCE

CARIBS

MARAJÓ

OMAGUA

YORIMAN

ARUAK

MACHIFARO

SANTARÉM

IRIURÍ NATIONS

RING VILLAGES

XINGÚ

TAWANTINSUYU

BENI

FARMING VILLAGES

NOMADS

NATIVE AMERICA, 1491 A.D.

✻ CONTENTS ✻

Contents

CODA

❋ MAPS ❋

❋ PREFACE ❋

The seeds of this book date back, at least in part, to 1983, when I wrote an article for *Science* about a NASA program that was monitoring atmospheric ozone levels. In the course of learning about the program, I flew with a research team in a NASA plane equipped to sample and analyze the atmosphere at thirty thousand feet. At one point the group landed in Mérida, in Mexico's Yucatán Peninsula. For some reason the scientists had the next day off, and we all took a decrepit Volkswagen van to the Maya ruins of Chichén Itzá. I knew nothing about Mesoamerican culture—I may not even have been familiar with the term "Mesoamerica," which encompasses the area from central Mexico to Panama, including all of Guatemala and Belize, and parts of El Salvador, Honduras, Costa Rica, and Nicaragua, the homeland of the Maya, the Olmec, and a host of other indigenous groups. Moments after we clambered out of the van I was utterly enthralled.

On my own—sometimes for vacation, sometimes on assignment—I returned to Yucatán five or six times, three times with my friend Peter Menzel, a photojournalist. For a German magazine, Peter and I made a twelve-hour drive down a terrible dirt road (thigh-deep potholes, blockades of fallen timber) to the then-unexcavated Maya metropolis of Calakmul. Accompanying us was Juan de la Cruz Briceño, Maya himself, caretaker of another, smaller ruin. Juan had spent twenty years as a *chiclero*, trekking the forest for weeks on end in search of chicle trees, which have a gooey sap that Indians have dried and chewed for millennia and that in the late nineteenth century became the base of the chewing-gum industry. Around a night fire he told us about the ancient, vine-shrouded cities he had stumbled across in his rambles, and his amazement when scientists informed him that his ancestors had built them. That night we slept in hammocks amid tall, headstone-like carvings that had not been read for more than a thousand years.

My interest in the peoples who walked the Americas before Columbus only snapped into anything resembling focus in the fall of 1992. By chance one Sunday afternoon I came across a display in a college library of the special Columbian quincentenary issue of the *Annals of the Association of American Geographers*. Curious, I picked up the journal, sank into an armchair, and began to read an article by William Denevan, a geographer at the University of Wisconsin. The article opened with the question, "What was the New World like at the time of Columbus?" Yes, I thought, what *was* it like? Who lived here and what could have passed through their minds when European sails first appeared on the horizon? I finished Denevan's article and went on to others and didn't stop reading until the librarian flicked the lights to signify closing time.

I didn't know it then, but Denevan and a host of fellow researchers had spent their careers trying to answer these questions. The picture they have emerged with is quite different from what most Americans and Europeans think, and still little known outside specialist circles.

A year or two after I read Denevan's article, I attended a panel discussion at the annual meeting of the American Association for the Advancement of Science. Called something like "New Perspectives on the Amazon," the session featured William Balée of Tulane University. Balée's talk was about "anthropogenic" forests—forests *created* by Indians centuries or millennia in the past—a concept I'd never heard of before. He also mentioned something that Denevan had discussed: many researchers now believe their predecessors underestimated the number of people in the Americas when Columbus arrived. Indians were more numerous than previously thought, Balée said—much more numerous. Gee, someone ought to put all this stuff together, I thought. It would make a fascinating book.

I kept waiting for that book to appear. The wait grew more frustrating when my son entered school and was taught the same things I had been taught, beliefs I knew had long been sharply questioned. Since nobody else appeared to be writing the book, I finally decided to try it myself. Besides, I was curious to learn more. The book you are holding is the result.

Some things this book is not. It is not a systematic, chronological account of the Western Hemisphere's cultural and social development before 1492. Such a book, its scope vast in space and time, could not be written—by the time the author approached the end, new findings would have been made and the beginning would be outdated. Among those who assured me of this were the very researchers who have spent much of the last few decades wrestling with the staggering diversity of pre-Columbian societies.

Nor is this book a full intellectual history of the recent changes in perspective among the anthropologists, archaeologists, ecologists, geographers, and historians who study the first Americans. That, too, would be impossible, for the ramifications of the new ideas are still rippling outward in too many directions for any writer to contain them in one single work.

Instead, this book explores what I believe to be the three main foci of the new findings: Indian demography (Part I), Indian origins (Part II), and Indian ecology (Part III). Because so many different societies illustrate these points in such different ways, I could not possibly be comprehensive. Instead, I chose my examples from cultures that are among the best documented, or have drawn the most recent attention, or just seemed the most intriguing.

Throughout this book, as the reader already will have noticed, I use the term "Indian" to refer to the first inhabitants of the Americas. No question about it, Indian is a confusing and historically inappropriate name. Probably the most accurate descriptor for the original inhabitants of the Americas is Americans. Actually using it, though, would be risking worse confusion. In this book I try to refer to people by the names they call themselves. The overwhelming majority of the indigenous peoples whom I have met in both North and South America describe themselves as Indians. (For more about nomenclature, see Appendix A, "Loaded Words.")

In the mid-1980s I traveled to the village of Hazelton, on the upper Skeena River in the middle of British Columbia. Many of its inhabitants belong to the Gitksan (or Gitxsan) nation. At the time of my visit, the Gitksan had just lodged a lawsuit with the governments of both British Columbia and Canada. They wanted the province and the nation to recognize that the Gitksan had lived there a long time, had never left, had never agreed to give their land away, and had thus retained legal title to about eleven thousand square miles of the province. They were very willing to negotiate, they said, but they were not willing to not be negotiated with.

Flying in, I could see why the Gitksan were attached to the area. The plane swept past the snowy, magnificent walls of the Rocher de Boule Mountains and into the confluence of two forested river valleys. Mist steamed off the land. People were fishing in the rivers for steelhead and salmon even though they were 165 miles from the coast.

The Gitanmaax band of the Gitksan has its headquarters in Hazelton, but most members live in a reserve just outside town. I drove to the reserve, where Neil Sterritt, head of the Gitanmaax council, explained the litigation to me. A straightforward, level-voiced man, he had got his start as a mining engineer and then come back home with his shirtsleeves rolled up, ready for a lengthy bout of legal wrangling. After multiple trials and appeals, the Supreme Court of Canada ruled in 1997 that British Columbia had to negotiate the status of the land with the Gitksan. Talks were still ongoing in 2005, two decades after the lawsuit first began.

After a while Sterritt took me to see 'Ksan, a historical park and art school created in 1970. In the park were several re-created longhouses, their facades covered in the forcefully elegant, black-and-red arcs of Northwest Coast Indian art. The art school trained local Indians in the techniques of translating traditionally derived designs into silk-screen prints. Sterritt left me in a back room of the schoolhouse and told me to look around. There was more in the room than he may have realized, for I quickly found what looked like storage boxes for a number of old and beautiful masks. Beside them was a stack of modern prints, some of which used the same designs. And there were boxes of photographs, old and new alike, many of splendid artworks.

In Northwest Coast art the subjects are flattened and distorted—it's as if they've been reduced from three dimensions to two and then folded like origami. At first I found all the designs hard to interpret, but soon some seemed to pop right out of the surface. They had clean lines that cut space into shapes at once simple and complex: objects tucked into objects, creatures stuffed into their own eyes, humans who were half beast and beasts who were half human—all was metamorphosis and surreal commotion.

A few of the objects I looked at I understood immediately, many I didn't understand at all, some I thought I understood but probably didn't, and some maybe even the Gitksan didn't understand, in the way that most Europeans today can't truly understand the effect of Byzantine art on the spirits of the people who saw it at the time of its creation. But I was delighted by the boldly graphic lines and dazzled by the sense that I was peeking into a vibrant past that I had not known existed and that continued to inform the present in a way I had not realized. For an hour or two I went from object to object, always eager to see more. In assembling this book, I hope to share the excitement I felt then, and have felt many times since.

INTRODUCTION

Holmberg's Mistake

❋   I   ❋

A View from Above

IN THE BENI

The plane took off in weather that was surprisingly cool for central Bolivia and flew east, toward the Brazilian border. In a few minutes the roads and houses disappeared, and the only traces of human settlement were the cattle scattered over the savanna like sprinkles on ice cream. Then they, too, disappeared. By that time the archaeologists had their cameras out and were clicking away in delight.

Below us lay the Beni, a Bolivian province about the size of Illinois and Indiana put together, and nearly as flat. For almost half the year rain and snowmelt from the mountains to the south and west cover the land with an irregular, slowly moving skin of water that eventually ends up in the province's northern rivers, which are upper tributaries of the Amazon. The rest of the year the water dries up and the bright green vastness turns into something that resembles a desert. This peculiar, remote, often watery plain was what had drawn the researchers' attention, and not just because it was one of the few places on earth inhabited by some people who might never have seen Westerners with cameras.

Clark Erickson and William Balée, the archaeologists, sat up front. Erickson, based at the University of Pennsylvania, worked in concert with a Bolivian archaeologist, who that day was elsewhere, freeing up a seat in the plane for me. Balée, of Tulane, is actually an anthropologist, but as scientists have come to appreciate the ways in which past and present inform each other, the distinction between anthropologists and archaeologists has blurred. The two men differ in build, temperament, and scholarly proclivity, but they pressed their faces to the windows with identical enthusiasm.

Scattered across the landscape below were countless islands of forest, many of them almost-perfect circles—heaps of green in a sea of yellow grass. Each island rose as much as sixty feet above the floodplain, allowing trees to grow that otherwise could not endure the water. The forests were bridged by raised berms, as straight as a rifle shot and up to three miles long. It is Erickson's belief that this entire landscape—thirty thousand square miles or more of forest islands and mounds linked by causeways—was constructed by a technologically advanced, populous society more than a thousand years ago. Balée, newer to the Beni, leaned toward this view but was not yet ready to commit himself.

Erickson and Balée belong to a cohort of scholars that in recent years has radically challenged conventional notions of what the Western Hemisphere was like before Columbus. When I went to high school, in the 1970s, I was taught that Indians came to the Americas across the Bering Strait about thirteen thousand years ago, that they lived for the most part in small, isolated groups, and that they had so little impact on their environment that even after millennia of habitation the continents remained mostly wilderness. Schools still impart the same ideas today. One way to summarize the views of people like Erickson and Balée would be to say that they regard this picture of Indian life as wrong in almost every aspect. Indians were here far longer than previously thought, these researchers believe, and in much greater numbers. And they were so successful at imposing their will on the landscape that in 1492 Columbus set foot in a hemisphere thoroughly marked by humankind.

Given the charged relations between white societies and native peoples, inquiry into Indian culture and history is inevitably contentious. But the recent scholarship is especially controversial. To begin with, some researchers—many but not all from an older generation—deride the new theories as fantasies arising from an almost willful misinterpretation of data and a perverse kind of political correctness. "I have seen no evidence that large numbers of people ever lived in the Beni," Betty J. Meggers, of the Smithsonian Institution, told me. "Claiming otherwise is just wishful thinking." Indeed, two Smithsonian-backed archaeologists from Argentina have argued that many of the larger mounds are natural floodplain deposits; a "small initial population" could have built the remaining causeways and raised fields in as little as a decade. Similar criticisms apply to many of the new scholarly claims about Indians, according to Dean R. Snow, an anthropologist at Pennsylvania State University. The problem is that "you can make the meager evidence from the ethnohistorical record tell you anything you want," he says. "It's really easy to kid yourself." And some have charged that the claims advance the political agenda of those who seek to discredit European culture, because the high numbers seem to inflate the scale of native loss.

Disputes also arise because the new theories have implications for today's ecological battles. Much of the environmental movement is animated, consciously or not, by what geographer William Denevan calls "the pristine myth"—the belief that the Americas in 1491 were an almost untouched, even Edenic land, "untrammeled by man," in the words of the Wilderness Act of 1964, a U.S. law that is one of the founding documents of the global environmental movement. To green activists, as the University of Wisconsin historian William Cronon has written, restoring this long-ago, putatively natural state is a task that society is morally bound to undertake. Yet if the new view is correct and the work of humankind was pervasive, where does that leave efforts to restore nature?

The Beni is a case in point. In addition to building roads, causeways, canals, dikes, reservoirs, mounds, raised agricultural fields, and possibly ball courts, Erickson has argued, the Indians who lived there before Columbus trapped fish in the seasonally flooded grassland. The trapping was not a matter of a few isolated natives with nets, but a society-wide effort in which hundreds or thousands of people fashioned dense, zigzagging networks of earthen fish weirs (fish-corralling fences) among the causeways. Much of the savanna is natural, the result of seasonal flooding. But the Indians maintained and expanded the grasslands by regularly setting huge areas on fire. Over the centuries the burning created an intricate ecosystem of fire-adapted plant species dependent on indigenous pyrophilia. The Beni's current inhabitants still burn, although now it is mostly to maintain the savanna for cattle. When we flew over the region, the dry season had just begun, but mile-long lines of flame were already on the march. Smoke rose into the sky in great, juddering pillars. In the charred areas behind the fires were the blackened spikes of trees, many of them of species that activists fight to save in other parts of Amazonia.

The future of the Beni is uncertain, especially its most thinly settled region, near the border with Brazil. Some outsiders want to develop the area for ranches, as has been done with many U.S. grasslands. Others want to keep this sparsely populated region as close to wilderness as possible. Local Indian groups regard this latter proposal with suspicion. If the Beni becomes a reserve for the "natural," they ask, what international organization would let them continue setting the plains afire? Could any outside group endorse large-scale burning in Amazonia? Instead, Indians propose placing control of the land into their hands. Activists, in turn, regard that idea without enthusiasm—some indigenous groups in the U.S. Southwest have promoted the use of their reservations as repositories for nuclear waste. And, of course, there is all that burning.

HOLMBERG'S MISTAKE

"Don't touch that tree," Balée said.

I froze. I was climbing a low, crumbly hill and had been about to support myself by grasping a scrawny, almost vine-like tree with splayed leaves. "*Triplaris americana,*" said Balée, an expert in forest botany. "You have to watch out for it." In an unusual arrangement, he said, *T. americana* plays host to colonies of tiny red ants—indeed, it has trouble surviving without them. The ants occupy minute tunnels just beneath the bark. In return for shelter, the ants attack anything that touches the tree—insect, bird, unwary writer. The venom-squirting ferocity of their attack gives rise to *T. americana*'s local nickname: devil tree.

At the base of the devil tree, exposing its roots, was a deserted animal burrow. Balée scraped out some dirt with a knife, then waved me over, along with Erickson and my son Newell, who were accompanying us. The depression was thick with busted pottery. We could see the rims of plates and what looked like the foot of a teakettle—it was shaped like a human foot, complete with painted toenails. Balée plucked out half a dozen pieces of ceramic: shards of pots and plates, a chipped length of cylindrical bar that may have been part of a pot's support leg. As much as an eighth of the hill, by volume, was composed of such fragments, he said. You could dig almost anywhere on it and see the like. We were clambering up an immense pile of broken crockery.

The pile is known as Ibibate, at fifty-nine feet one of the tallest known forested mounds in the Beni. Erickson explained to me that the pieces of ceramic were probably intended to help build up and aerate the muddy soil for settlement and agriculture. But though this explanation makes sense on engineering grounds, he said, it doesn't make the long-ago actions of the moundbuilders any less mysterious. The mounds cover such an enormous area that they seem unlikely to be the byproduct of waste. Monte Testaccio, the hill of broken pots southeast of Rome, was a garbage dump for the entire imperial city. Ibibate is larger than Monte Testaccio and but one of hundreds of similar mounds. Surely the Beni did not generate more waste than Rome—the ceramics in Ibibate, Erickson argues, indicate that large numbers of people, many of them skilled laborers, lived for a long time on these mounds, feasting and drinking exuberantly all the while. The number of potters necessary to make the heaps of crockery, the time required for labor, the number of people needed to provide food and shelter for the potters, the organization of large-scale destruction and burial—all of it is evidence, to

Erickson's way of thinking, that a thousand years ago the Beni was the site of a highly structured society, one that through archaeological investigation was just beginning to come into view.

Accompanying us that day were two Sirionó Indians, Chiro Cuéllar and his son-in-law Rafael. The two men were wiry, dark, and nearly beardless; walking beside them on the trail, I had noticed small nicks in their earlobes. Rafael, cheerful almost to bumptiousness, peppered the afternoon with comments; Chiro, a local figure of authority, smoked locally made "Marlboro" cigarettes and observed our progress with an expression of amused tolerance. They lived about a mile away, in a little village at the end of a long, rutted dirt road. We had driven there earlier in the day, parking in the shade of a tumbledown school and some old missionary buildings. The structures were clustered near the top of a small hill—another ancient mound. While Newell and I waited by the truck, Erickson and Balée went inside the school to obtain permission from Chiro and the other members of the village council to tramp around. Noticing that we were idle, a couple of Sirionó kids tried to persuade Newell and me to look at a young jaguar in a pen, and to give them money for this thrill. After a few minutes, Erickson and Balée emerged with the requisite permission—and two chaperones, Chiro and Rafael. Now, climbing up Ibibate, Chiro observed that I was standing by the devil tree. Keeping his expression deadpan, he suggested that I climb it. Up top, he said, I would find some delicious jungle fruit. "It will be like nothing you have experienced before," he promised.

From the top of Ibibate we were able to see the surrounding savanna. Perhaps a quarter mile away, across a stretch of yellow, waist-high grass, was a straight line of trees—an ancient raised causeway, Erickson said. Otherwise the countryside was so flat that we could see for miles in every direction—or, rather, we could have seen for miles, if the air in some directions had not been filled with smoke.

Afterward I wondered about the relationship of our escorts to this place. Were the Sirionó like contemporary Italians living among the monuments of the Roman Empire? I asked Erickson and Balée that question during the drive back.

Their answer continued sporadically through the rest of the evening, as we rode to our lodgings in an unseasonable cold rain and then had dinner. In the 1970s, they said, most authorities would have answered my question about the Sirionó in one way. Today most would answer it in another, different way. The difference involves what I came to think of, rather unfairly, as Holmberg's Mistake.

Although the Sirionó are but one of a score of Native American groups in

the Beni, they are the best known. Between 1940 and 1942 a young doctoral
student named Allan R. Holmberg lived among them. He published his
account of their lives, *Nomads of the Longbow*, in 1950. (The title refers to the
six-foot bows the Siriónó use for hunting.) Quickly recognized as a classic,
Nomads remains an iconic and influential text; as filtered through countless
other scholarly articles and the popular press, it became one of the main
sources for the outside world's image of South American Indians.

The Sirionó, Holmberg reported, were "among the most culturally backward peoples of the world." Living in constant want and hunger, he said,
they had no clothes, no domestic animals, no musical instruments (not even
rattles and drums), no art or design (except necklaces of animal teeth), and
almost no religion (the Sirionó "conception of the universe" was "almost
completely uncrystallized"). Incredibly, they could not count beyond three
or make fire (they carried it, he wrote, "from camp to camp in a [burning]
brand"). Their poor lean-tos, made of haphazardly heaped palm fronds,
were so ineffective against rain and insects that the typical band member
"undergoes many a sleepless night during the year." Crouched over meager
campfires during the wet, buggy nights, the Sirionó were living exemplars of
primitive humankind—the "quintessence" of "man in the raw state of
nature," as Holmberg put it. For millennia, he thought, they had existed
almost without change in a landscape unmarked by their presence. Then
they encountered European society and for the first time their history
acquired a narrative flow.

Holmberg was a careful and compassionate researcher whose detailed
observations of Sirionó life remain valuable today. And he bravely sur-
mounted trials in Bolivia that would have caused many others to give up.
During his months in the field he was always uncomfortable, usually hungry,
and often sick. Blinded by an infection in both eyes, he walked for days
through the forest to a clinic, holding the hand of a Sirionó guide. He never
fully recovered his health. After his return, he became head of the anthropology department at Cornell University, from which position he led its celebrated efforts to alleviate poverty in the Andes.

Nonetheless, he was wrong about the Sirionó. And he was wrong about
the Beni, the place they inhabited—wrong in a way that is instructive, even
exemplary.

Before Columbus, Holmberg believed, both the people and the land had
no real history. Stated so baldly, this notion—that the indigenous peoples of
the Americas floated changelessly through the millennia until 1492—may
seem ludicrous. But flaws in perspective often appear obvious only after they
are pointed out. In this case they took decades to rectify.

The Bolivian government's instability and fits of anti-American and anti-European rhetoric ensured that few foreign anthropologists and archaeologists followed Holmberg into the Beni. Not only was the government hostile, the region, a center of the cocaine trade in the 1970s and 1980s, was dangerous. Today there is less drug trafficking, but smugglers' runways can still be seen, cut into remote patches of forest. The wreck of a crashed drug plane sits not far from the airport in Trinidad, the biggest town in the province. During the drug wars "the Beni was neglected, even by Bolivian standards," according to Robert Langstroth, a geographer and range ecologist in Wisconsin who did his dissertation fieldwork there. "It was a backwater of a backwater." Gradually a small number of scientists ventured into the region. What they learned transformed their understanding of the place and its people.

Just as Holmberg believed, the Sionó were among the most culturally impoverished people on earth. But this was not because they were unchanged holdovers from humankind's ancient past but because smallpox and influenza laid waste to their villages in the 1920s. Before the epidemics at least three thousand Sionó, and probably many more, lived in eastern Bolivia. By Holmberg's time fewer than 150 remained—a loss of more than 95 percent in less than a generation. So catastrophic was the decline that the Sionó passed through a genetic bottleneck. (A genetic bottleneck occurs when a population becomes so small that individuals are forced to mate with relatives, which can produce deleterious hereditary effects.) The effects of the bottleneck were described in 1982, when Allyn Stearman of the University of Central Florida became the first anthropologist to visit the Sionó since Holmberg. Stearman discovered that the Sionó were thirty times more likely to be born with clubfeet than typical human populations. And almost all the Sionó had unusual nicks in their earlobes, the traits I had noticed on the two men accompanying us.

Even as the epidemics hit, Stearman learned, the group was fighting the white cattle ranchers who were taking over the region. The Bolivian military aided the incursion by hunting down the Sionó and throwing them into what were, in effect, prison camps. Those released from confinement were forced into servitude on the ranches. The wandering people Holmberg traveled with in the forest had been hiding from their abusers. At some risk to himself, Holmberg tried to help them, but he never fully grasped that the people he saw as remnants from the Paleolithic Age were actually the persecuted survivors of a recently shattered culture. It was as if he had come across refugees from a Nazi concentration camp, and concluded that they belonged to a culture that had always been barefoot and starving.

Far from being leftovers from the Stone Age, in fact, the Sirionó are probably relative newcomers to the Beni. They speak a language in the Tupí-Guaraní group, one of the most important Indian language families in South America but one not common in Bolivia. Linguistic evidence, first weighed by anthropologists in the 1970s, suggests that they arrived from the north as late as the seventeenth century, about the time of the first Spanish settlers and missionaries. Other evidence suggests they may have come a few centuries earlier; Tupí-Guaraní–speaking groups, possibly including the Sirionó, attacked the Inka empire in the early sixteenth century. No one knows why the Sirionó moved in, but one reason may be simply that the Beni then was little populated. Not long before, the previous inhabitants' society had disintegrated.

To judge by *Nomads of the Longbow*, Holmberg did not know of this earlier culture—the culture that built the causeways and mounds and fish weirs. He didn't see that the Sirionó were walking through a landscape that had been shaped by somebody else. A few European observers before Holmberg had remarked upon the earthworks' existence, though some doubted that the causeways and forest islands were of human origin. But they did not draw systematic scholarly attention until 1961, when William Denevan came to Bolivia. Then a doctoral student, he had learned of the region's peculiar landscape during an earlier stint as a cub reporter in Peru and thought it might make an interesting topic for his thesis. Upon arrival he discovered that oil-company geologists, the only scientists in the area, believed the Beni was thick with the remains of an unknown civilization.

Convincing a local pilot to push his usual route westward, Denevan examined the Beni from above. He observed exactly what I saw four decades later: isolated hillocks of forest; long raised berms; canals; raised agricultural fields; circular, moat-like ditches; and odd, zigzagging ridges. "I'm looking out of one of these DC-3 windows, and I'm going berserk in this little airplane," Denevan said to me. "I *knew* these things were not natural. You just don't have that kind of straight line in nature." As Denevan learned more about the landscape, his amazement grew. "It's a completely humanized landscape," he said. "To me, it was clearly the most exciting thing going on in the Amazon and adjacent areas. It may be the most important thing in all of South America, I think. Yet it was practically untouched" by scientists. It is *still* almost untouched—there aren't even any detailed maps of the earthworks and canals.

Beginning as much as three thousand years ago, this long-ago society—. Erickson believes it was probably founded by the ancestors of an Arawak-speaking people now called the Mojo and the Bauré—created one of the largest, strangest, and most ecologically rich artificial environments on the

Flying over eastern Bolivia in the early 1960s, the young geographer William Denevan was amazed to see that the landscape (bottom)—home to nothing but cattle ranches for generations—still bore evidence that it had once been inhabited by a large, prosperous society, one whose very existence had been forgotten. Incredibly, such discoveries are still being made. In 2002 and 2003, Finnish and Brazilian researchers revealed the remains of dozens of geometrical earthworks (top) in the western Brazilian state of Acre where the forest had just been cleared for cattle ranches.

planet. These people built up the mounds for homes and farms, constructed the causeways and canals for transportation and communication, created the fish weirs to feed themselves, and burned the savannas to keep them clear of invading trees. A thousand years ago their society was at its height. Their villages and towns were spacious, formal, and guarded by moats and palisades. In Erickson's hypothetical reconstruction, as many as a million people may have walked the causeways of eastern Bolivia in their long cotton tunics, heavy ornaments dangling from their wrists and necks.

Today, hundreds of years after this Arawak culture passed from the scene, the forest on and around Ibibate mound looks like the classic Amazon of conservationists' dreams: lianas thick as a human arm, dangling blade-like leaves more than six feet long, smooth-boled Brazil nut trees, thick-bodied flowers that smell like warm meat. In terms of species richness, Balée told me, the forest islands of Bolivia are comparable to any place in South America. The same is true of the Beni savanna, it seems, with its different complement of species. Ecologically, the region is a treasure, but one designed and executed by human beings. Erickson regards the landscape of the Beni as one of humankind's greatest works of art, a masterpiece that until recently was almost completely unknown, a masterpiece in a place with a name that few people outside Bolivia would recognize.

"EMPTY OF MANKIND AND ITS WORKS"

The Beni was no anomaly. For almost five centuries, Holmberg's Mistake—the supposition that Native Americans lived in an eternal, unhistoried state—held sway in scholarly work, and from there fanned out to high school textbooks, Hollywood movies, newspaper articles, environmental campaigns, romantic adventure books, and silk-screened T-shirts. It existed in many forms and was embraced both by those who hated Indians and those who admired them. Holmberg's Mistake explained the colonists' view of most Indians as incurably vicious barbarians; its mirror image was the dreamy stereotype of the Indian as a Noble Savage. Positive or negative, in both images Indians lacked what social scientists call *agency*—they were not actors in their own right, but passive recipients of whatever windfalls or disasters happenstance put in their way.

The Noble Savage dates back as far as the first full-blown ethnography of American indigenous peoples, Bartolomé de Las Casas's *Apologética Historia Sumaria,* written mainly in the 1530s. Las Casas, a conquistador who repented of his actions and became a priest, spent the second half of his long life opposing European cruelty in the Americas. To his way of thinking, Indians were natural creatures who dwelt, gentle as cows, in the "terrestrial paradise." In their prelapsarian innocence, he believed, they had been quietly waiting—waiting for millennia—for Christian instruction. Las Casas's contemporary, the Italian commentator Pietro Martire d'Anghiera, shared these views. Indians, he wrote (I quote the English translation from 1556), "lyve in that goulden world of whiche owlde writers speake so much," existing "simplye and innocentlye without inforcement of lawes."

In our day, beliefs about Indians' inherent simplicity and innocence refer mainly to their putative lack of impact on the environment. This notion dates back at least to Henry David Thoreau, who spent much time seeking "Indian wisdom," an indigenous way of thought that supposedly did not encompass measuring or categorizing, which he viewed as the evils that allowed human beings to change Nature. Thoreau's ideas continue to be influential. In the wake of the first Earth Day in 1970, a group named Keep America Beautiful, Inc., put up billboards that portrayed a Cherokee actor named Iron Eyes Cody quietly weeping over polluted land. The campaign was enormously successful. For almost a decade the image of the crying Indian appeared around the world. Yet though Indians here were playing a heroic role, the advertisement still embodied Holmberg's Mistake, for it implicitly depicted Indians as people who never changed their environment from its original wild state. Because history is change, they were people without history.

Las Casas's anti-Spanish views met with such harsh attacks that he instructed his executors to publish the *Apologética Historia* forty years after his death (he died in 1566). In fact, the book did not appear in complete form until 1909. As the delay suggests, polemics for the Noble Savage tended to meet with little sympathy in the eighteenth and nineteenth centuries. Emblematic was the U.S. historian George Bancroft, dean of his profession, who argued in 1834 that before Europeans arrived North America was "an unproductive waste . . . Its only inhabitants were a few scattered tribes of feeble barbarians, destitute of commerce and of political connection." Like Las Casas, Bancroft believed that Indians had existed in societies without change—except that Bancroft regarded this timelessness as an indication of sloth, not innocence.

In different forms Bancroft's characterization was carried into the next century. Writing in 1934, Alfred L. Kroeber, one of the founders of American anthropology, theorized that the Indians in eastern North America could not develop—could have no history—because their lives consisted of "warfare that was insane, unending, continuously attritional." Escaping the cycle of conflict was "well-nigh impossible," he believed. "The group that tried to shift its values from war to peace was almost certainly doomed to early extinction."* Kroeber conceded that Indians took time out from fighting to grow crops, but insisted that agriculture "was not basic to life in the East; it was an auxiliary, in a sense a luxury." As a result, "Ninety-nine per cent or more of what [land] might have been developed remained virgin."

Four decades later, Samuel Eliot Morison, twice a Pulitzer Prize winner, closed his two-volume *European Discovery of America* with the succinct claim that Indians had created no lasting monuments or institutions. Imprisoned in changeless wilderness, they were "pagans expecting short and brutish lives, void of any hope for the future." Native people's "chief function in history," the British historian Hugh Trevor-Roper, Baron Dacre of Glanton, proclaimed in 1965, "is to show to the present an image of the past from which by history it has escaped."

Textbooks reflected academic beliefs faithfully. In a survey of U.S. history schoolbooks, the writer Frances Fitzgerald concluded that the characterization of Indians had moved, "if anything, resolutely backward" between the 1840s and the 1940s. Earlier writers thought of Indians as important, though uncivilized, but later books froze them into a formula: "lazy, childlike, and cruel." A main textbook of the 1940s devoted only a "few paragraphs" to Indians, she wrote, "of which the last is headed 'The Indians Were Backward.' "

These views, though less common today, continue to appear. The 1987 edition of *American History: A Survey,* a standard high school textbook by three well-known historians, summed up Indian history thusly: "For thousands of centuries—centuries in which human races were evolving, forming communities, and building the beginnings of national civilizations in Africa, Asia, and Europe—the continents we know as the Americas stood empty of mankind and its works." The story of Europeans in the New World, the book informed students, "is the story of the creation of a civilization where none existed."

It is always easy for those living in the present to feel superior to those who lived in the past. Alfred W. Crosby, a University of Texas historian, noted that many of the researchers who embraced Holmberg's Mistake lived in an era when the driving force of events seemed to be great leaders of European descent and when white societies appeared to be overwhelming nonwhite

---

*According to Joseph Conrad, the violence was of culinary origin. "The Noble Red Man was a mighty hunter," explained the great novelist, "but his wives had not mastered the art of conscientious cookery—and the consequences were deplorable. The Seven Nations around the Great Lakes and the Horse tribes of the plains were but one vast prey to raging dyspepsia." Because their lives were blighted by "the morose irritability which follows the consumption of ill-cooked food," they were continually prone to quarrels.

societies everywhere. Throughout all of the nineteenth and much of the twentieth century, nationalism was ascendant, and historians identified history with nations, rather than with cultures, religions, or ways of life. But the Second World War taught the West that non-Westerners—the Japanese, in this instance—were capable of swift societal change. The rapid disintegration of European colonial empires further adumbrated the point. Crosby likened the effects of these events on social scientists to those on astronomers from "the discovery that the faint smudges seen between stars on the Milky Way were really distant galaxies."

Meanwhile, new disciplines and new technologies were creating new ways to examine the past. Demography, climatology, epidemiology, economics, botany, and palynology (pollen analysis); molecular and evolutionary biology; carbon-14 dating, ice-core sampling, satellite photography, and soil assays; genetic microsatellite analysis and virtual 3-D fly-throughs—a torrent of novel perspectives and techniques cascaded into use. And when these were employed, the idea that the only human occupants of one-third of the earth's surface had changed little for thousands of years began to seem implausible. To be sure, some researchers have vigorously attacked the new findings as wild exaggerations. ("We have simply replaced the old myth [of untouched wilderness] with a new one," scoffed geographer Thomas Vale, "the myth of the humanized landscape.") But after several decades of discovery and debate, a new picture of the Americas and their original inhabitants is emerging.

Advertisements still celebrate nomadic, ecologically pure Indians on horseback chasing bison in the Great Plains of North America, but at the time of Columbus the great majority of Native Americans could be found south of the Río Grande. They were not nomadic, but built up and lived in some of the world's biggest and most opulent cities. Far from being dependent on big-game hunting, most Indians lived on farms. Others subsisted on fish and shellfish. As for the horses, they were from Europe; except for llamas in the Andes, the Western Hemisphere had no beasts of burden. In other words, the Americas were immeasurably busier, more diverse, and more populous than researchers had previously imagined.

And older, too.

THE OTHER NEOLITHIC REVOLUTIONS

For much of the last century archaeologists believed that Indians came to the Americas through the Bering Strait about thirteen thousand years ago at the tail end of the last Ice Age. Because the sheets of polar ice locked up huge amounts of water, sea levels around the world fell about three hundred feet. The shallow Bering Strait became a wide land bridge between Siberia and Alaska. In theory, paleo-Indians, as they are called, simply walked across the fifty-five miles that now separate the continents. C. Vance Haynes, an archae-ologist at the University of Arizona, put the crowning touches on the scheme in 1964, when he noted evidence that at just the right time—that is, about thirteen thousand years ago—two great glacial sheets in northwest Canada parted, leaving a comparatively warm, ice-free corridor between them. Down this channel paleo-Indians could have passed from Alaska to the more habitable regions in the south without having to hike over the ice pack. At the time, the ice pack extended two thousand miles south of the Bering Strait and was almost devoid of life. Without Haynes's ice-free corridor, it is hard to imagine how humans could have made it to the south. The combina-tion of land bridge and ice-free corridor occurred only once in the last twenty thousand years, and lasted for just a few hundred years. And it hap-pened just before the emergence of what was then the earliest known cul-ture in the Americas, the Clovis culture, so named for the town in New Mexico where its remains were first definitely observed. Haynes's exposition made the theory seem so ironclad that it fairly flew into the textbooks. I learned it when I attended high school. So did my son, thirty years later.

In 1997 the theory abruptly came unglued. Some of its most ardent parti-sans, Haynes among them, publicly conceded that an archaeological dig in southern Chile had turned up compelling evidence of human habitation more than twelve thousand years ago. And because these people lived seven thousand miles south of the Bering Strait, a distance that presumably would have taken a long time to traverse, they almost certainly arrived before the ice-free corridor opened up. (In any case, new research had cast doubt on the existence of that corridor.) Given the near impossibility of surpassing the glaciers without the corridor, some archaeologists suggested that the first Americans must have arrived twenty thousand years ago, when the ice pack was smaller. Or even earlier than that—the Chilean site had suggestive evi-dence of artifacts more than thirty thousand years old. Or perhaps the first Indians traveled by boat, and didn't need the land bridge. Or maybe they arrived via Australia, passing the South Pole. "We're in a state of turmoil," the consulting archaeologist Stuart Fiedel told me. "Everything we knew is now supposed to be wrong," he added, exaggerating a little for effect.

No consensus has emerged, but a growing number of researchers believe that the New World was occupied by a single small group that crossed the Bering Strait, got stuck on the Alaska side, and straggled to the rest of the

Americas in two or three separate groups, with the ancestors of most modern Indians making up the second group. Researchers differ on the details; some scientists have theorized that the Americas may have been hit with as many as five waves of settlement before Columbus, with the earliest occurring as much as fifty thousand years ago. In most versions, though, today's Indians are seen as relative latecomers.

Indian activists dislike this line of reasoning. "I can't tell you how many white people have told me that 'science' shows that Indians were just a bunch of interlopers," Vine Deloria Jr., a political scientist at the University of Colorado at Boulder, said to me. Deloria is the author of many books, including *Red Earth, White Lies,* a critique of mainstream archaeology. The book's general tenor is signaled by its index; under "science," the entries include "corruption and fraud and," "Indian explanations ignored by," "lack of proof for theories of," "myth of objectivity of," and "racism of." In Deloria's opinion, archaeology is mainly about easing white guilt. Determining that Indians superseded other people fits neatly into this plan. "If we're only thieves who stole our land from someone else," Deloria said, "then they can say, 'Well, we're just the same. We're all immigrants here, aren't we?' "

The moral logic of the we're-all-immigrants argument that Deloria cites is difficult to parse; it seems to be claiming that two wrongs make a right. Moreover, there's no evidence that the first "wrong" was a wrong—nothing is known about the contacts among the various waves of paleo-Indian migration. But in any case whether most of today's Native Americans actually arrived first or second is irrelevant to an assessment of their cultural achievements. In every imaginable scenario, they left Eurasia before the first whisper of the Neolithic Revolution.

The Neolithic Revolution is the invention of farming, an event whose significance can hardly be overstated. "The human career," wrote the historian Ronald Wright, "divides in two: everything before the Neolithic Revolution and everything after it." It began in the Middle East about eleven thousand years ago. In the next few millennia the wheel and the metal tool sprang up in the same area. The Sumerians put these inventions together, added writing, and in the third millennium B.C. created the first great civilization. Every European and Asian culture since, no matter how disparate in appearance, stands in Sumer's shadow. Native Americans, who left Asia long before agriculture, missed out on the bounty. "They had to do everything on their own," Crosby said to me. Remarkably, they succeeded.

Researchers have long known that a second, independent Neolithic Revolution occurred in Mesoamerica. The exact timing is uncertain—archaeologists keep pushing back the date—but it is now thought to have occurred about ten thousand years ago, not long after the Middle East's Neolithic Revolution. In 2003, though, archaeologists discovered ancient seeds from cultivated squashes in coastal Ecuador, at the foot of the Andes, which may be older than any agricultural remains in Mesoamerica—a *third* Neolithic Revolution. This Neolithic Revolution probably led, among many other things, to the cultures in the Beni. The two American Neolithics spread more slowly than their counterpart in Eurasia, possibly because Indians in many places had not had the time to build up the requisite population density, and possibly because of the extraordinary nature of the most prominent Indian crop, maize.*

The ancestors of wheat, rice, millet, and barley look like their domesticated descendants; because they are both edible and highly productive, one can easily imagine how the idea of planting them for food came up. Maize can't reproduce itself, because its kernels are securely wrapped in the husk, so Indians must have developed it from some other species. But there are no wild species that resemble maize. Its closest genetic relative is a mountain grass called teosinte that looks strikingly different—for one thing, its "ears" are smaller than the baby corn served in Chinese restaurants. No one eats teosinte, because it produces too little grain to be worth harvesting. In creating modern maize from this unpromising plant, Indians performed a feat so improbable that archaeologists and biologists have argued for decades over how it was achieved. Coupled with squash, beans, and avocados, maize provided Mesoamerica with a balanced diet, one arguably more nutritious than its Middle Eastern or Asian equivalent. (Andean agriculture, based on potatoes and beans, and Amazonian agriculture, based on manioc [cassava], had wide impact but on a global level were less important than maize.)

About seven thousand years elapsed between the dawn of the Middle Eastern Neolithic and the establishment of Sumer. Indians navigated the same path in somewhat less time (the data are too sketchy to be more precise). Pride of place must go to the Olmec, the first technologically complex culture in the hemisphere. Appearing in the narrow "waist" of Mexico about 1800 B.C., they lived in cities and towns centered on temple mounds. Strewn among them were colossal male heads of stone, many six feet tall or more, with helmet-like headgear, perpetual frowns, and somewhat African fea-

---

*In the United States and parts of Europe the name is "corn." I use "maize" because Indian maize—multicolored and mainly eaten after drying and grinding—is strikingly unlike the sweet, yellow, uniform kernels usually evoked in North America by the name "corn." In Britain, "corn" can mean the principal cereal crop in a region—oats in Scotland, for example, are sometimes referred to by the term.

tures, the last of which has given rise to speculation that Olmec culture was inspired by voyagers from Africa. The Olmec were but the first of many societies that arose in Mesoamerica in this epoch. Most had religions that focused on human sacrifice, dark by contemporary standards, but their economic and scientific accomplishments were bright. They invented a dozen different systems of writing, established widespread trade networks, tracked the orbits of the planets, created a 365-day calendar (more accurate than its contemporaries in Europe), and recorded their histories in accordion-folded "books" of fig tree bark paper.

Arguably their greatest intellectual feat was the invention of zero. In his classic account *Number: The Language of Science,* the mathematician Tobias Dantzig called the discovery of zero "one of the greatest single accomplishments of the human race," a "turning point" in mathematics, science, and technology. The first whisper of zero in the Middle East occurred about 600 B.C. When tallying numbers, the Babylonians arranged them into columns, as children learn to do today. To distinguish between their equivalents to 11 and 101, they placed two triangular marks between the digits: 1△△1, so to speak. (Because Babylonian mathematics was based on 60, rather than 10, the example is correct only in principle.) Curiously, though, they did not use the symbol to distinguish among their versions of 1, 10, and 100. Nor could the Babylonians add or subtract with zero, let alone use zero to enter the realm of negative numbers. Sanskrit mathematicians first used zero in its contemporary sense—a number, not a placeholder—sometime in the first few centuries A.D. It didn't appear in Europe until the twelfth century. Even then European governments and the Vatican resisted zero—a something that stood for nothing—as foreign and un-Christian. Meanwhile, the first recorded zero in the Americas occurred in a Maya carving from 357 A.D., possibly before the Sanskrit. And there are monuments from before the birth of Christ that do not bear zeroes themselves but are inscribed with dates in a calendrical system based on the existence of zero.

Does this mean that the Maya were then more advanced than their counterparts in, say, Europe? Social scientists flinch at this question, and with good reason. The Olmec, Maya, and other Mesoamerican societies were world pioneers in mathematics and astronomy—but they did not use the wheel. Amazingly, they had invented the wheel but did not employ it for any purpose other than children's toys. Those looking for a tale of cultural superiority can find it in zero; those looking for failure can find it in the wheel. Neither line of argument is useful, though. What is most important is that by 1000 A.D. Indians had expanded their Neolithic revolutions to create a panoply of diverse civilizations across the hemisphere.

Five hundred years later, when Columbus sailed into the Caribbean, the descendants of the world's Neolithic Revolutions collided, with overwhelming consequences for all.

A   G U I D E D   T O U R

Imagine, for a moment, an impossible journey: taking off in a plane from eastern Bolivia as I did, but doing so in 1000 A.D. and flying a surveillance mission over the rest of the Western Hemisphere. What would be visible from the windows? Fifty years ago, most historians would have given a simple answer to this question: two continents of wilderness, populated by scattered bands whose ways of life had changed little since the Ice Age. The sole exceptions would have been Mexico and Peru, where the Maya and the ancestors of the Inka were crawling toward the foothills of Civilization.

Today our understanding is different in almost every perspective. Picture the millennial plane flying west, from the lowlands of the Beni to the heights of the Andes. On the ground beneath as the journey begins are the causeways and canals one sees today, except that they are now in good repair and full of people. (Fifty years ago, the earthworks were almost completely unknown, even to those living nearby.) After a few hundred miles the plane ascends to the mountains—and again the historical picture has changed. Until recently, researchers would have said the highlands in 1000 A.D. were occupied by scattered small villages and one or two big towns with some nice stonework. But recent archaeological investigations have revealed that at this time the Andes housed two mountain states, each much larger than previously appreciated.

The state closest to the Beni was based around Lake Titicaca, the 120-mile-long alpine lake that crosses the Peru-Bolivia border. Most of this region has an altitude of twelve thousand feet or more. Summers are short; winters are correspondingly long. This "bleak, frigid land," wrote the adventurer Victor von Hagen, "seemingly was the last place from which one might expect a culture to develop." But in fact the lake is comparatively warm, and so the land surrounding it is less beaten by frost than the surrounding highlands. Taking advantage of the better climate, the village of Tiwanaku, one of many settlements around the lake, began after about 800 B.C. to drain the wetlands around the rivers that flowed into the lake from the south. A thousand years later the village had grown to become the center of a large polity, also known as Tiwanaku.

Less a centralized state than a clutch of municipalities under the com-

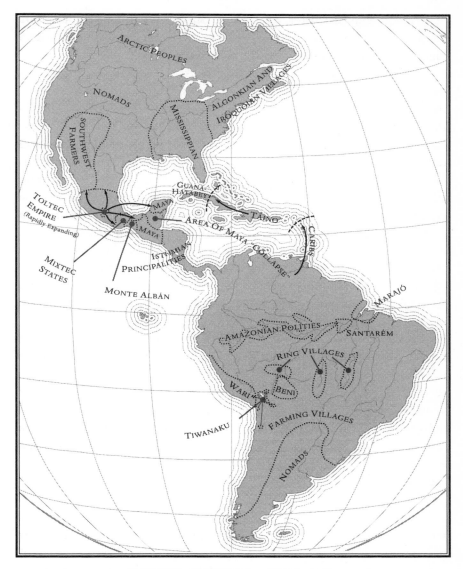

NATIVE AMERICA, 1000 A.D.

mon religio-cultural sway of the center, Tiwanaku took advantage of the extreme ecological differences among the Pacific coast, the rugged mountains, and the altiplano (the high plains) to create a dense web of exchange: fish from the sea; llamas from the altiplano; fruits, vegetables, and grains from the fields around the lake. Flush with wealth, Tiwanaku city swelled into a marvel of terraced pyramids and grand monuments. Stone breakwaters extended far out into Lake Titicaca, thronged with long-prowed boats made of reeds. With its running water, closed sewers, and gaudily painted walls, Tiwanaku was among the world's most impressive cities.

University of Chicago archaeologist Alan L. Kolata excavated at Tiwanaku during the 1980s and early 1990s. He has written that by 1000 A.D. the city had a population of as much as 115,000, with another quarter million in the surrounding countryside—numbers that Paris would not reach for another five centuries. The comparison seems fitting; at the time, the realm of Tiwanaku was about the size of modern France. Other researchers believe this population estimate is too high. Twenty or thirty thousand in the central city is more likely, according to Nicole Couture, a University of Chicago archaeologist who helped edit the definitive publication of Kolata's work in 2003. An equal number, she said, occupied the surrounding countryside.

Which view is right? Although Couture was confident of her ideas, she thought it would be "another decade" before the matter was settled. And in any case the exact number does not affect what she regards as the key point. "Building this enormous place up here is really remarkable," she said. "I realize that again every time I come back."

North and west of Tiwanaku, in what is now southern Peru, was the rival state of Wari, which then ran for almost a thousand miles along the spine of the Andes. More tightly organized and military minded than Tiwanaku, the rulers of Wari stamped out cookie-cutter fortresses and stationed them all along their borders. The capital city—called, eponymously, Wari—was in the heights, near the modern city of Ayacucho. Housing perhaps seventy thousand souls, Wari was a dense, alley-packed craze of walled-off temples, hidden courtyards, royal tombs, and apartments up to six stories tall. Most of the buildings were sheathed in white plaster, making the city sparkle in the mountain sun.

In 1000 A.D., at the time of our imaginary overflight, both societies were reeling from a succession of terrible droughts. Perhaps eighty years earlier, dust storms had engulfed the high plains, blackening the glaciers in the peaks above. (Ice samples, dug out in the 1990s, suggest the assault.) Then came a run of punishing dry spells, many more than a decade in duration, interrupted by gigantic floods. (Sediment and tree-ring records depict the sequence.) The disaster's cause is still in dispute, but some climatologists believe that the Pacific is subject to "mega-Niño events," murderously strong versions of the well-known El Niño patterns that play havoc with American weather today. Mega-Niños occurred every few centuries between 200 and 1600 A.D. In 1925 and 1926, a strong El Niño—not a mega-Niño, but one that was bigger than usual—blasted Amazonia with so much dry heat that sudden fires killed hundreds, perhaps thousands, of people in the forest. Rivers dried up, their bottoms carpeted with dead fish. A mega-Niño in the eleventh century may well have caused the droughts of those years. But whatever the cause of the climatic upheaval, it severely tested Wari and Tiwanaku society.

Here, though, one must be careful. Europe was racked by a "little ice age" of extreme cold between the fourteenth and nineteenth centuries, yet historians rarely attribute the rise and fall of European states in that period to climate change. Fierce winters helped drive the Vikings from Greenland and led to bad harvests that exacerbated social tensions in continental Europe, but few would claim that the little ice age caused the Reformation. Similarly, the mega-Niños were but one of many stresses on Andean civilizations at the time, stresses that in their totality neither Wari nor Tiwanaku had the political resources to survive. Soon after 1000 A.D. Tiwanaku split into flinders that would not be united for another four centuries, when the Inka swept them up. Wari also fell. It was succeeded and perhaps taken over by a state called Chimor, which oversaw an empire that sprawled over central Peru until it, too, was absorbed by the Inka.

Such newly discovered histories appear everywhere in the Americas. Take the plane north, toward Central America and southern Mexico, into the bulge of the Yucatán Peninsula, homeland of the Maya. Maya ruins were well known forty years ago, to be sure, but among them, too, many new things have been discovered. Consider Calakmul, the ruin that Peter Menzel and I visited in the early 1980s. Almost wholly unexcavated since its discovery, the Calakmul we came to lay swathed in dry, scrubby vegetation that crawled like a swarm of thorns up its two huge pyramids. When Peter and I spoke to William J. Folan of the Universidad Autónoma de Campeche, who was just beginning to work at the city, he recommended that we not try going to the ruin unless we could rent a heavy truck, and not even to try with the truck if it had rained. Our visit to Calakmul did nothing to suggest that Folan's advice was wrong. Trees enveloped the great buildings, their roots slowly ripping apart the soft limestone walls. Peter photographed a monument with roots coiled around it, boa constrictor style, five or six feet high. So overwhelming was the tropical forest that I thought Calakmul's history would remain forever unknown.

Happily, I was wrong. By the early 1990s Folan's team had learned that this long-ignored place covered as much as twenty-five square miles and had thousands of buildings and dozens of reservoirs and canals. It was the biggest-ever Maya polity. Researchers cleaned and photographed its hundred-plus monuments—and just in time, for epigraphers (scholars of ancient writing) had in the meantime deciphered Maya hieroglyphics. In 1994 they identified the city-state's ancient name: Kaan, the Kingdom of the Snake. Six years later they discovered that Kaan was the focus of a devastating war that convulsed the Maya city-state for more than a century. And Kaan is just one of the score of Maya settlements that in the last few decades have been investigated for the first time.

A collection of about five dozen kingdoms and city-states in a network of alliances and feuds as convoluted as those of seventeenth-century Germany, the Maya realm was home to one of the world's most intellectually sophisticated cultures. About a century before our imaginary surveillance tour, though, the Maya heartland entered a kind of Dark Ages. Many of the greatest cities emptied, as did much of the countryside around them. Incredibly, some of the last inscriptions are gibberish, as if scribes had lost the knowledge of writing and were reduced to meaningless imitation of their ancestors. By the time of our overflight, half or more of what once had been the flourishing land of the Maya was abandoned.

Some natural scientists attribute this collapse, close in time to that of Wari and Tiwanaku, to a massive drought. The Maya, packed by the millions into land poorly suited to intensive farming, were dangerously close to surpassing the capacity of their ecosystems. The drought, possibly caused by a mega-Niño, pushed the society, already so close to the edge, over the cliff.

Such scenarios resonate with contemporary ecological fears, helping to make them popular outside the academy. Within the academy skepticism is more common. The archaeological record shows that southern Yucatán was abandoned, while Maya cities in the northern part of the peninsula soldiered on or even grew. Peculiarly, the abandoned land was the wettest—with its rivers, lakes, and rainforest, it should have been the best place to wait out a drought. Conversely, northern Yucatán was dry and rocky. The question is why people would have fled from drought to lands that would have been even more badly affected.

And what of the rest of Mesoamerica? As the flight continues north, look west, at the hills of what are now the Mexican states of Oaxaca and Guerrero. Here are the quarrelsome, splintered city-states of the Mixtec, finally overwhelming the Zapotec, their ancient rivals based in the valley city of Monte Albán. Further north, expanding their empire in a hot-brained hurry, are the Toltec, sweeping in every direction from the mile-high basin that today houses Mexico City. As is often the case, the Toltec's rapid military success led to political strife. A Shakespearian struggle at the top, complete with accusations of drunkenness and incest, forced out the long-ruling king, Topiltzin Quetzalcoatl, in (probably) 987 A.D. He fled with boatloads of loyalists to the Yucatán Peninsula, promising to return. By the time of our plane trip,

Quetzalcoatl had apparently conquered the Maya city of Chichén Itzá and was rebuilding it in his own Toltec image. (Prominent archaeologists disagree with each other about these events, but the murals and embossed plates at Chichén Itzá that depict a Toltec army bloodily destroying a Maya force are hard to dismiss.)

Continue the flight to what is now the U.S. Southwest, past desert farms and cliff dwellings, to the Mississippian societies in the Midwest. Not long age archaeologists with new techniques unraveled the tragedy of Cahokia, near modern St. Louis, which was once the greatest population center north of the Río Grande. Construction began in about 1000 A.D. on an earthen structure that would eventually cover fifteen acres and rise to a height of about a hundred feet, higher than anything around it for miles. Atop the mound was the temple for the divine kings, who arranged for the weather to favor agriculture. As if to lend them support, fields of maize rippled out from the mound almost as far as the eye could see. Despite this apparent evidence of their power, Cahokia's rulers were setting themselves up for future trouble. By mining the forests upstream for firewood and floating the logs downriver to the city, they were removing ground cover and increasing the likelihood of catastrophic floods. When these came, as they later did, kings who gained their legitimacy from their claims to control the weather would face angry questioning from their subjects.

Continue north, to the least settled land, the realm of hunters and gatherers. Portrayed in countless U.S. history books and Hollywood westerns, the Indians of the Great Plains are the most familiar to nonscholars. Demographically speaking, they lived in the hinterlands, remote and thinly settled; their lives were as far from Wari or Toltec lords as the nomads of Siberia were from the grandees of Beijing. Their material cultures were simpler, too—no writing, no stone plazas, no massive temples—though Plains groups did leave behind about fifty rings of rock that are reminiscent of Stonehenge. The relative lack of material goods has led some to regard these groups as exemplifying an ethic of living lightly on the land. Perhaps, but North America was a busy, talkative place. By 1000 A.D., trade relationships had covered the continent for more than a thousand years; mother-of-pearl from the Gulf of Mexico has been found in Manitoba, and Lake Superior copper in Louisiana.

Or forgo the northern route altogether and fly the imaginary plane east from the Beni, toward the mouth of the Amazon. Immediately after the Beni, one encounters, in what is now the western Brazilian state of Acre, another society: a network of small villages associated with circular and square earthworks in patterns quite unlike those found in the Beni. Even less is known about these people; the remains of their villages were discovered only in 2003, after ranchers clearing the tropical forest uncovered them. According to the Finnish archaeologists who first described them, "it is obvious" that "relatively high population densities" were "quite common everywhere in the Amazonian lowlands." The Finns here are summing up the belief of a new generation of researchers into the Amazon: the river was much more crowded in 1000 A.D. than it is now, especially in its lower half. Dense collections of villages thronged the bluffs that line the shore, with their people fishing in the river and farming the floodplains and sections of the uplands. Most important were the village orchards that marched back from the bluffs for miles. Amazonians practiced a kind of agro-forestry, farming with trees, unlike any kind of agriculture in Europe, Africa, or Asia.

Not all the towns were small. Near the Atlantic was the chiefdom of Marajó, based on an enormous island at the mouth of the river. Marajó's population, recently estimated at 100,000, may have been equaled or even surpassed by a still-nameless agglomeration of people six hundred miles upstream, at Santarém, a pleasant town that today is sleeping off the effects of Amazonia's past rubber and gold booms. The ancient inhabitation beneath and around the modern town has barely been investigated. Almost all that we know is that it was ideally located on a high bluff overlooking the mouth of the Tapajós, one of the Amazon's biggest tributaries. On this bluff geographers and archaeologists in the 1990s found an area more than three miles long that was thickly covered with broken ceramics, much like Ibibate. According to William I. Woods, an archaeologist and geographer at the University of Kansas, the region could have supported as many as 400,000 inhabitants, at least in theory, making it one of the bigger population centers in the world.

And so on. Western scholars have written histories of the world since at least the twelfth century. As children of their own societies, these early historians naturally emphasized the culture they knew best, the culture their readership most wanted to hear about. But over time they added the stories of other places in the world: chapters about China, India, Persia, Japan, and other places. Researchers tipped their hats to non-Western accomplishments in the sciences and arts. Sometimes the effort was grudging or minimal, but the vacant reaches in the human tale slowly contracted.

One way to sum up the new scholarship is to say that it has begun, at last, to fill in one of the biggest blanks in history: the Western Hemisphere before 1492. It was, in the current view, a thriving, stunningly diverse place, a tumult of languages, trade, and culture, a region where tens of millions of people loved and hated and worshipped as people do everywhere. Much of this world vanished after Columbus, swept away by disease and subjugation. So thorough was the erasure that within a few generations neither conqueror nor conquered knew that this world had existed. Now, though, it is returning to view. It seems incumbent on us to take a look.

PART ONE

Numbers from Nowhere?

2

Why Billington Survived

THE FRIENDLY INDIAN

On March 22, 1621, an official Native American delegation walked through what is now southern New England to negotiate with a group of foreigners who had taken over a recently deserted Indian settlement. At the head of the party was an uneasy triumvirate: Massasoit, the sachem (political-military leader) of the Wampanoag confederation, a loose coalition of several dozen villages that controlled most of southeastern Massachusetts; Samoset, sachem of an allied group to the north; and Tisquantum, a distrusted captive, whom Massasoit had reluctantly brought along as an interpreter.

Massasoit was an adroit politician, but the dilemma he faced would have tested Machiavelli. About five years before, most of his subjects had fallen before a terrible calamity. Whole villages had been depopulated—indeed, the foreigners ahead now occupied one of the empty sites. It was all he could do to hold together the remnants of his people. Adding to his problems, the disaster had not touched the Wampanoag's longtime enemies, the Narragansett alliance to the west. Soon, Massasoit feared, they would take advantage of the Wampanoag's weakness and overrun them.

Desperate threats require desperate countermeasures. In a gamble, Massasoit intended to abandon, even reverse, a long-standing policy. Europeans had been visiting New England for at least a century. Shorter than the natives, oddly dressed, and often unbearably dirty, the pallid foreigners had peculiar blue eyes that peeped out of the masks of bristly, animal-like hair that encased their faces. They were irritatingly garrulous, prone to fits of chicanery, and often surprisingly incompetent at what seemed to Indians like basic tasks. But they also made useful and beautiful goods—copper kettles, glittering colored glass, and steel knives and hatchets—unlike anything else in New England. Moreover, they would exchange these valuable items for cheap furs of the sort used by Indians as blankets. It was like happening upon a dingy kiosk that would swap fancy electronic goods for customers' used socks—almost anyone would be willing to overlook the shopkeeper's peculiarities.

Over time, the Wampanoag, like other native societies in coastal New England, had learned how to manage the European presence. They encouraged the exchange of goods, but would only allow their visitors to stay ashore for brief, carefully controlled excursions. Those who overstayed their welcome were forcefully reminded of the limited duration of Indian hospitality. At the same time, the Wampanoag fended off Indians from the interior, preventing them from trading directly with the foreigners. In this way the shoreline groups put themselves in the position of classic middlemen, overseeing both European access to Indian products and Indian access to European products. Now Massasoit was visiting a group of British with the intent of changing the rules. He would permit the newcomers to stay for an unlimited time—provided they formally allied with the Wampanoag against the Narragansett.

Tisquantum, the interpreter, had shown up alone at Massasoit's home a year and a half before. He spoke fluent English, because he had lived for several years in Britain. But Massasoit didn't trust him. He seems to have been in Massasoit's eyes a man without anchor, out for himself. In a conflict, Tisquantum might even side with the foreigners. Massasoit had kept Tisquantum in a kind of captivity since his arrival, monitoring his actions closely. And he refused to use him to negotiate with the colonists until he had another, independent means of communication with them.

That March Samoset—the third member of the triumvirate—appeared, having hitched a ride from his home in Maine on an English ship that was plying the coast. Not known is whether his arrival was due to chance or if Massasoit had asked him to come down because he had picked up a few English phrases by trading with the British. In any case, Massasoit first had sent Samoset, rather than Tisquantum, to the foreigners.

Samoset had walked unaccompanied and unarmed into the circle of rude huts in which the British were living on March 17, 1621. The colonists saw a robust, erect-postured man wearing only a loincloth; his straight black hair was shaved in front but flowed down his shoulders behind. To their further amazement, this almost naked man greeted them in broken but understandable English. He left the next morning with a few presents. A day later he came back, accompanied by five "tall proper men"—the phrase is the colonist Edward Winslow's—with three-inch black stripes painted down the middle of their faces. The two sides talked inconclusively, each warily check-ing out the other, for a few hours. Now, on the 22nd, Samoset showed up again at the foreigners' ramshackle base, this time with Tisquantum in tow. Meanwhile Massasoit and the rest of the Indian company waited out of sight.

Samoset and Tisquantum spoke with the colonists for about an hour. Per-haps they then gave a signal. Or perhaps Massasoit was simply following a prearranged schedule. In any case, he and the rest of the Indian party appeared without warning at the crest of a hill on the south bank of the creek that ran through the foreigners' camp. Alarmed by Massasoit's sudden entrance, the Europeans withdrew to the hill on the opposite bank, where they had emplaced their few cannons behind a half-finished stockade. A standoff ensued.

Finally Winslow exhibited the decisiveness that later led to his selection as colony governor. Wearing a full suit of armor and carrying a sword, he waded through the stream and offered himself as a hostage. Tisquantum, who walked with him, served as interpreter. Massasoit's brother took charge of Winslow and then Massasoit crossed the water himself, followed by Tisquantum and twenty of Massasoit's men, all ostentatiously unarmed. The colonists took the sachem to an unfinished house and gave him some cushions to recline on. Both sides shared some of the foreigners' homemade moonshine, then settled down to talk, Tisquantum translating.

To the colonists, Massasoit could be distinguished from his subjects more by manner than by dress or ornament. He wore the same deerskin shawls and leggings and like his fellows had covered his face with bug-repelling oil and reddish-purple dye. Around his neck hung a pouch of tobacco, a long knife, and a thick chain of the prized white shell beads called wampum. In appear-ance, Winslow wrote afterward, he was "a very lusty man, in his best years, an able body, grave of countenance, and spare of speech." The Europeans, who had barely survived the previous winter, were in much worse shape. Half of the original colony now lay underground beneath wooden markers painted with death's heads; most of the survivors were malnourished.

Their meeting was a critical moment in American history. The foreigners called their colony Plymouth; they themselves were the famous Pilgrims.* As schoolchildren learn, at that meeting the Pilgrims obtained the services of Tisquantum, usually known as "Squanto." In the 1970s, when I attended high

---

*The *Mayflower* passengers are often called "Puritans," but they disliked the name. Instead they used terms like "separatists," because they separated themselves from the Church of England, or "saints," because their church, patterned on the early Christian church, was the "church of saints." "Pilgrims" is the title preferred by the Society of Mayflower Descendants.

school, a popular history text was *America: Its People and Values,* by Leonard C. Wood, Ralph H. Gabriel, and Edward L. Biller. Nestled among colorful illustrations of colonial life was a succinct explanation of Tisquantum's role:

> A friendly Indian named Squanto helped the colonists. He showed them how to plant corn and how to live on the edge of the wilderness. A soldier, Captain Miles Standish, taught the Pilgrims how to defend themselves against unfriendly Indians.

My teacher explained that maize was unfamiliar to the Pilgrims and that Tisquantum had demonstrated the proper maize-planting technique—sticking the seed in little heaps of dirt, accompanied by beans and squash that would later twine themselves up the tall stalks. And he told the Pilgrims to fertilize the soil by burying fish alongside the maize seeds, a traditional native technique for producing a bountiful harvest. Following this advice, my teacher said, the colonists grew so much maize that it became the centerpiece of the first Thanksgiving. In our slipshod fashion, we students took notes.

The story in *America: Its People and Values* isn't wrong, so far as it goes. But the impression it gives is entirely misleading.

Tisquantum *was* critical to the colony's survival, contemporary scholars agree. He moved to Plymouth after the meeting and spent the rest of his life there. Just as my teacher said, Tisquantum told the colonists to bury several small fish in each maize hill, a procedure followed by European colonists for two centuries. Squanto's teachings, Winslow concluded, led to "a good increase of Indian corn"—the difference between success and starvation.

Winslow didn't know that fish fertilizer may not have been an age-old Indian custom, but a recent invention—if it was an Indian practice at all. So little evidence has emerged of Indians fertilizing with fish that some archaeologists believe that Tisquantum actually picked up the idea from European farmers. The notion is not as ridiculous as it may seem. Tisquantum had learned English because British sailors had kidnapped him seven years before. To return to the Americas, he in effect had to escape *twice*—once from Spain, where his captors initially sold him into slavery, and once from England, to which he was smuggled from Spain, and where he served as a kind of living conversation piece at a rich man's house. In his travels, Tisquantum stayed in places where Europeans used fish as fertilizer, a practice on the Continent since medieval times.

Skipping over the complex course of Tisquantum's life is understandable in a textbook with limited space. But the omission is symptomatic of the complete failure to consider Indian motives, or even that Indians might *have* motives. The alliance Massasoit negotiated with Plymouth was successful from the Wampanoag perspective, for it helped to hold off the Narragansett. But it was a disaster from the point of view of New England Indian society as a whole, for the alliance ensured the survival of Plymouth colony, which spearheaded the great wave of British immigration to New England. All of this was absent not only from my high school textbooks, but from the academic accounts they were based on.

This variant of Holmberg's Mistake dates back to the Pilgrims themselves, who ascribed the lack of effective native resistance to the will of God. "Divine providence," the colonist Daniel Gookin wrote, favored "the quiet and peaceable settlement of the English." Later writers tended to attribute European success not to European deities but to European technology. In a contest where only one side had rifles and cannons, historians said, the other side's motives were irrelevant. By the end of the nineteenth century, the Indians of the Northeast were thought of as rapidly fading background details in the saga of the rise of the United States—"marginal people who were losers in the end," as James Axtell of the College of William and Mary dryly put it in an interview. Vietnam War–era denunciations of the Pilgrims as imperialist or racist simply replicated the error in a new form. Whether the cause was the Pilgrim God, Pilgrim guns, or Pilgrim greed, native losses were foreordained; Indians could not have stopped colonization, in this view, and they hardly tried.

Beginning in the 1970s, Axtell, Neal Salisbury, Francis Jennings, and other historians grew dissatisfied with this view. "Indians were seen as trivial, ineffectual patsies," Salisbury, a historian at Smith College, told me. "But that assumption—a whole continent of patsies—simply didn't make sense." These researchers tried to peer through the colonial records to the Indian lives beneath. Their work fed a tsunami of inquiry into the interactions between natives and newcomers in the era when they faced each other as relative equals. "No other field in American history has grown as fast," marveled Joyce Chaplin, a Harvard historian, in 2003.

The fall of Indian societies had everything to do with the natives themselves, researchers argue, rather than being religiously or technologically determined. (Here the claim is not that indigenous cultures should be blamed for their own demise but that they helped to determine their own fates.) "When you look at the historical record, it's clear that Indians were trying to control their own destinies," Salisbury said. "And often enough they succeeded"—only to learn, as all peoples do, that the consequences were not what they expected.

This chapter and the next will explore how two different Indian societies, the Wampanoag and the Inka, reacted to the incursions from across the sea. It may seem odd that a book about Indian life *before* contact should devote space to the period *after* contact, but there are reasons for it. First, colonial descriptions of Native Americans are among the few glimpses we have of Indians whose lives were not shaped by the presence of Europe. The accounts of the initial encounters between Indians and Europeans are windows into the past, even if the glass is smeared and distorted by the chroniclers' prejudices and misapprehensions.

Second, although the stories of early contact—the Wampanoag with the British, the Inka with the Spanish—are as dissimilar as their protagonists, many archaeologists, anthropologists, and historians have recently come to believe that they have deep commonalities. And the tales of other Indians' encounters with the strangers were alike in the same way. From these shared features, researchers have constructed what might be thought of as a master narrative of the meeting of Europe and America. Although it remains surprisingly little known outside specialist circles, this master narrative illuminates the origins of every nation in the Americas today. More than that, the effort to understand events after Columbus shed unexpected light on critical aspects of life *before* Columbus. Indeed, the master narrative led to such surprising conclusions about Native American societies before the arrival of Europeans that it stirred up an intellectual firestorm.

COMING OF AGE IN THE DAWNLAND

Consider Tisquantum, the "friendly Indian" of the textbook. More than likely Tisquantum was not the name he was given at birth. In that part of the Northeast, *tisquantum* referred to rage, especially the rage of *manitou*, the world-suffusing spiritual power at the heart of coastal Indians' religious beliefs. When Tisquantum approached the Pilgrims and identified himself by that sobriquet, it was as if he had stuck out his hand and said, Hello, I'm the Wrath of God. No one would lightly adopt such a name in contemporary Western society. Neither would anyone in seventeenth-century indigenous society. Tisquantum was trying to project something.

Tisquantum was not an Indian. True, he belonged to that category of people whose ancestors had inhabited the Western Hemisphere for thousands of years. And it is true that I refer to him as an Indian, because the label is useful shorthand; so would his descendants, and for much the same reason. But "Indian" was not a category that Tisquantum himself would have recognized, any more than the inhabitants of the same area today would call

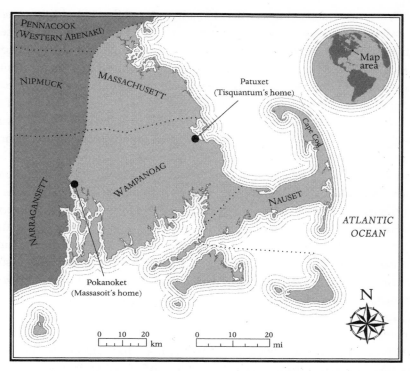

MASSACHUSETT ALLIANCE, 1600 A.D.

themselves "Western Hemisphereans." Still less would Tisquantum have claimed to belong to "Norumbega," the label by which most Europeans then referred to New England. ("New England" was coined only in 1616.) As Tisquantum's later history made clear, he regarded himself first and foremost as a citizen of Patuxet, a shoreline settlement halfway between what is now Boston and the beginning of Cape Cod.

Patuxet was one of the dozen or so settlements in what is now eastern Massachusetts and Rhode Island that comprised the Wampanoag confederation. In turn, the Wampanoag were part of a tripartite alliance with two other confederations: the Nauset, which comprised some thirty groups on Cape Cod; and the Massachusett, several dozen villages clustered around Massachusetts Bay. All of these people spoke variants of Massachusett, a member of the Algonquian language family, the biggest in eastern North America at the time. (Massachusett thus was the name both of a language and of one of the groups that spoke it.) In Massachusett, the name for the New England shore was the Dawnland, the place where the sun rose. The inhabitants of the Dawnland were the People of the First Light.

Ten thousand years ago, when Indians in Mesoamerica and Peru were inventing agriculture and coalescing into villages, New England was barely inhabited, for the excellent reason that it had been covered until relatively recently by an ice sheet a mile thick. People slowly moved in, though the area long remained cold and uninviting, especially along the coastline. Because rising sea levels continually flooded the shore, marshy Cape Cod did not fully lock into its contemporary configuration until about 1000 B.C. By that time the Dawnland had evolved into something more attractive: an ecological crazy quilt of wet maple forests, shellfish-studded tidal estuaries, thick highland woods, mossy bogs full of cranberries and orchids, fractally complex snarls of sandbars and beachfront, and fire-swept stands of pitch pine—"tremendous variety even within the compass of a few miles," as the ecological historian William Cronon put it.

In the absence of written records, researchers have developed techniques for teasing out evidence of the past. Among them is "glottochronology," the attempt to estimate how long ago two languages separated from a common ancestor by evaluating their degree of divergence on a list of key words. In the 1970s and 1980s linguists applied glottochronological techniques to the Algonquian dictionaries compiled by early colonists. However tentatively, the results indicated that the various Algonquian languages in New England all date back to a common ancestor that appeared in the Northeast a few centuries before Christ.

The ancestral language may derive from what is known as the Hopewell culture. Around two thousand years ago, Hopewell jumped into prominence from its bases in the Midwest, establishing a trade network that covered most of North America. The Hopewell culture introduced monumental earthworks and, possibly, agriculture to the rest of the cold North. Hopewell villages, unlike their more egalitarian neighbors, were stratified, with powerful, priestly rulers commanding a mass of commoners. Archaeologists have found no evidence of large-scale warfare at this time, and thus suggest that Hopewell probably did not achieve its dominance by conquest. Instead, one can speculate, the vehicle for transformation may have been Hopewell religion, with its intoxicatingly elaborate funeral rites. If so, the adoption of Algonquian in the Northeast would mark an era of spiritual ferment and heady conversion, much like the time when Islam rose and spread Arabic throughout the Middle East.

Hopewell itself declined around 400 A.D. But its trade network remained intact. Shell beads from Florida, obsidian from the Rocky Mountains, and mica from Tennessee found their way to the Northeast. Borrowing technology and ideas from the Midwest, the nomadic peoples of New England transformed their societies. By the end of the first millennium A.D., agriculture was spreading rapidly and the region was becoming an unusual patchwork of communities, each with its preferred terrain, way of subsistence, and cultural style.

Scattered about the many lakes, ponds, and swamps of the cold uplands were small, mobile groups of hunters and gatherers—"collectors," as researchers sometimes call them. Most had recently adopted agriculture or were soon to do so, but it was still a secondary source of food, a supplement to the wild products of the land. New England's major river valleys, by contrast, held large, permanent villages, many nestled in constellations of suburban hamlets and hunting camps. Because extensive fields of maize, beans, and squash surrounded every home, these settlements sprawled along the Connecticut, Charles, and other river valleys for miles, one town bumping up against the other. Along the coast, where Tisquantum and Massasoit lived, villages often were smaller and looser, though no less permanent.

Unlike the upland hunters, the Indians on the rivers and coastline did not roam the land; instead, most seem to have moved between a summer place and a winter place, like affluent snowbirds alternating between Manhattan and Miami. The distances were smaller, of course; shoreline families would move a fifteen-minute walk inland, to avoid direct exposure to winter storms and tides. Each village had its own distinct mix of farming and foraging—this one here, adjacent to a rich oyster bed, might plant maize purely for variety, whereas that one there, just a few miles away, might subsist almost entirely on its harvest, filling great underground storage pits each fall. Although these settlements were permanent, winter and summer alike, they often were not tightly knit entities, with houses and fields in carefully demarcated clusters. Instead people spread themselves through estuaries, sometimes grouping into neighborhoods, sometimes with each family on its own, its maize ground proudly separate. Each community was constantly "joining and splitting like quicksilver in a fluid pattern within its bounds," wrote Kathleen J. Bragdon, an anthropologist at the College of William and Mary—a type of settlement, she remarked, with "no name in the archaeological or anthropological literature."

In the Wampanoag confederation, one of these quicksilver communities was Patuxet, where Tisquantum was born at the end of the sixteenth century.

Tucked into the great sweep of Cape Cod Bay, Patuxet sat on a low rise above a small harbor, jigsawed by sandbars and shallow enough that children could walk from the beach hundreds of yards into the water before the waves went above their heads. To the west, maize hills marched across the sandy hillocks in parallel rows. Beyond the fields, a mile or more away from the sea, rose a forest of oak, chestnut, and hickory, open and park-like, the underbrush kept down by expert annual burning. "Pleasant of air and prospect," as one English visitor described the area, Patuxet had "much plenty both of fish and fowl every day in the year." Runs of spawning Atlantic salmon, shortnose sturgeon, striped bass, and American shad annually filled the harbor. But the most important fish harvest came in late spring, when the herring-like alewives swarmed the fast, shallow stream that cut through the village. So numerous were the fish, and so driven, that when mischievous boys walled off the stream with stones the alewives would leap the barrier—silver bodies gleaming in the sun—and proceed upstream.

Tisquantum's childhood *wetu* (home) was formed from arched poles lashed together into a dome that was covered in winter by tightly woven rush mats and in summer by thin sheets of chestnut bark. A fire burned constantly in the center, the smoke venting through a hole in the center of the roof. English visitors did not find this arrangement peculiar; chimneys were just coming into use in Britain, and most homes there, including those of the wealthy, were still heated by fires beneath central roof holes. Nor did the English regard the Dawnland *wetu* as primitive; its multiple layers of mats, which trapped insulating layers of air, were "warmer than our English houses," sighed the colonist William Wood. The *wetu* was less leaky than the typical English wattle-and-daub house, too. Wood did not conceal his admiration for the way Indian mats "deny entrance to any drop of rain, though it come both fierce and long."

Around the edge of the house were low beds, sometimes wide enough for a whole family to sprawl on them together; usually raised about a foot from the floor, platform-style; and always piled with mats and furs. Going to sleep in the firelight, young Tisquantum would have stared up at the diddering shadows of the hemp bags and bark boxes hanging from the rafters. Voices would skirl up in the darkness: one person singing a lullaby, then another person, until everyone was asleep. In the morning, when he woke, big, egg-shaped pots of corn-and-bean mash would be on the fire, simmering with meat, vegetables, or dried fish to make a slow-cooked dinner stew. Outside the *wetu* he would hear the cheerful thuds of the large mortars and pestles in which women crushed dried maize into *nokake*, a flour-like powder "so sweet, toothsome, and hearty," colonist Gookin wrote, "that an Indian will travel many days with no other but this meal." Although Europeans bemoaned the lack of salt in Indian cuisine, they thought it nourishing. According to one modern reconstruction, Dawnland diets at the time averaged about 2,500 calories a day, better than those usual in famine-racked Europe.

In the *wetu*, wide strips of bark are clamped between arched inner and outer poles. Because the poles are flexible, bark layers can be sandwiched in or removed at will, depending on whether the householder wants to increase insulation during the winter or let in more air during the summer. In its elegant simplicity, the *wetu's* design would have pleased the most demanding modernist architect.

Pilgrim writers universally reported that Wampanoag families were close and loving—more so than English families, some thought. Europeans in those days tended to view children as moving straight from infancy to adulthood around the age of seven, and often thereupon sent them out to work. Indian parents, by contrast, regarded the years before puberty as a time of playful development, and kept their offspring close by until marriage. (Jarringly, to the contemporary eye, some Pilgrims interpreted this as sparing the rod.) Boys like Tisquantum explored the countryside, swam in the ponds at the south end of the harbor, and played a kind of soccer with a small leather ball; in the summer and fall they camped out in huts in the fields, weeding the maize and chasing away birds. Archery practice began at age two. By adolescence boys would make a game of shooting at each other and dodging the arrows.

The primary goal of Dawnland education was molding character. Men and women were expected to be brave, hardy, honest, and uncomplaining. Chatterboxes and gossips were frowned upon. "He that speaks seldom and opportunely, being as good as his word, is the only man they love," Wood explained. Character formation began early, with family games of tossing naked children into the snow. (They were pulled out quickly and placed next to the fire, in a practice reminiscent of Scandinavian saunas.) When Indian boys came of age, they spent an entire winter alone in the forest, equipped only with a bow, a hatchet, and a knife. These methods worked, the awed Wood reported. "Beat them, whip them, pinch them, punch them, if [the Indians] resolve not to flinch for it, they will not."

Tisquantum's regimen was probably tougher than that of his friends, according to Salisbury, the Smith College historian, for it seems that he was selected to become a *pniese,* a kind of counselor-bodyguard to the sachem. To master the art of ignoring pain, future *pniese* had to subject themselves to such miserable experiences as running barelegged through brambles. And they fasted often, to learn self-discipline. After spending their winter in the woods, *pniese* candidates came back to an additional test: drinking bitter gentian juice until they vomited, repeating this bulimic process over and over until, near fainting, they threw up blood.

Patuxet, like its neighboring settlements, was governed by a sachem, who upheld the law, negotiated treaties, controlled foreign contacts, collected tribute, declared war, provided for widows and orphans, and allocated farm-land when there were disputes over it. (Dawnlanders lived in a loose scatter, but they knew which family could use which land—"very exact and punctu-all," Roger Williams, founder of Rhode Island colony, called Indian care for property lines.) Most of the time, the Patuxet sachem owed fealty to the great sachem in the Wampanoag village to the southwest, and through him to the sachems of the allied confederations of the Nauset in Cape Cod and the Massachusett around Boston. Meanwhile, the Wampanoag were rivals and enemies of the Narragansett and Pequots to the west and the many groups of Abenaki to the north. As a practical matter, sachems had to gain the consent of their people, who could easily move away and join another sachemship. Analogously, the great sachems had to please or bully the lesser, lest by the defection of small communities they lose stature.

Sixteenth-century New England housed 100,000 people or more, a figure that was slowly increasing. Most of those people lived in shoreline communities, where rising numbers were beginning to change agriculture from an option to a necessity. These bigger settlements required more centralized administration; natural resources like good land and spawning streams, though not scarce, now needed to be managed. In consequence, boundaries between groups were becoming more formal. Sachems, given more power and more to defend, pushed against each other harder. Political tensions

were constant. Coastal and riverine New England, according to the archaeologist and ethnohistorian Peter Thomas, was "an ever-changing collage of
personalities, alliances, plots, raids and encounters which involved every
Indian [settlement]."

Armed conflict was frequent but brief and mild by European standards. The *casus belli* was usually the desire to avenge an insult or gain
status, not the wish for conquest. Most battles consisted of lightning
guerrilla raids by ad hoc companies in the forest: flash of black-and-
yellow-striped bows behind trees, hiss and whip of stone-tipped arrows
through the air, eruption of angry cries. Attackers slipped away as soon
as retribution had been exacted. Losers quickly conceded their loss of
status. Doing otherwise would have been like failing to resign after losing
a major piece in a chess tournament—a social irritant, a waste of time
and resources. Women and children were rarely killed, though they were
sometimes abducted and forced to join the winning group. Captured
men were often tortured (they were admired, though not necessarily
spared, if they endured the pain stoically). Now and then, as a sign of victory, slain foes were scalped, much as British skirmishes with the Irish
sometimes finished with a parade of Irish heads on pikes. In especially
large clashes, adversaries might meet in the open, as in European battle-
fields, though the results, Roger Williams noted, were "farre less bloudy,
and devouring then the cruell Warres of Europe." Nevertheless, by
Tisquantum's time defensive palisades were increasingly common, especially in the river valleys.

Inside the settlement was a world of warmth, family, and familiar custom. But the world outside, as Thomas put it, was "a maze of confusing
actions and individuals fighting to maintain an existence in the shadow of
change."

And that was before the Europeans showed up.

TOURISM AND TREACHERY

British fishing vessels may have reached Newfoundland as early as the 1480s
and areas to the south soon after. In 1501, just nine years after Columbus's
first voyage, the Portuguese adventurer Gaspar Corte-Real abducted fifty-
odd Indians from Maine. Examining the captives, Corte-Real found to his
astonishment that two were wearing items from Venice: a broken sword and
two silver rings. As James Axtell has noted, Corte-Real probably was able to
kidnap such a large number of people only because the Indians were already

so comfortable dealing with Europeans that big groups willingly came aboard his ship.*

The earliest written description of the People of the First Light was by Giovanni da Verrazzano, an Italian mariner-for-hire commissioned by the king of France in 1523 to discover whether one could reach Asia by rounding the Americas to the north. Sailing north from the Carolinas, he observed that the coastline everywhere was "densely populated," smoky with Indian bon-fires; he could sometimes smell the burning hundreds of miles away. The ship anchored in wide Narragansett Bay, near what is now Providence, Rhode Island. Verrazzano was one of the first Europeans the natives had seen, perhaps even the first, but the Narragansett were not intimidated. Almost instantly, twenty long canoes surrounded the visitors. Cocksure and graceful, the Narragansett sachem leapt aboard: a tall, long-haired man of about forty with multicolored jewelry dangling about his neck and ears, "as beautiful of stature and build as I can possibly describe," Verrazzano wrote.

His reaction was common. Time and time again Europeans described the People of the First Light as strikingly healthy specimens. Eating an incredibly nutritious diet, working hard but not broken by toil, the people of New England were taller and more robust than those who wanted to move in—"as proper men and women for feature and limbes as can be founde," in the words of the rebellious Pilgrim Thomas Morton. Because famine and epi-demic disease had been rare in the Dawnland, its inhabitants had none of the pox scars or rickety limbs common on the other side of the Atlantic. Native New Englanders, in William Wood's view, were "more amiable to behold (though [dressed] only in Adam's finery) than many a compounded fantastic [English dandy] in the newest fashion."

The Pilgrims were less sanguine about Indians' multicolored, multitex-tured mode of self-presentation. To be sure, the newcomers accepted the practicality of deerskin robes as opposed to, say, fitted British suits. And the colonists understood why natives' skin and hair shone with bear or eagle fat (it warded off sun, wind, and insects). And they could overlook the Indians' practice of letting prepubescent children run about without a stitch on. But the Pilgrims, who regarded personal adornment as a species of idolatry, were dismayed by what they saw as the indigenous penchant for foppery. The robes were adorned with animal-head mantles, snakeskin belts, and bird-wing headdresses. Worse, many Dawnlanders tattooed their faces, arms, and

*The first Europeans known to have reached the Americas were the Vikings, who appeared off eastern Canada in the tenth century. Their short-lived venture had no known effect on native life. Other European groups may also have arrived before Columbus, but they, too, had no well-substantiated impact on the people they visited.

In 1585–86 the artist John White spent fifteen months in what is now North Carolina, returning with more than seventy watercolors of American people, plants, and animals. White's work, later distributed in a series of romanticized engravings (two of which are shown here), was not of documentary quality by today's standards—his Indians are posed like Greek statues. But at the same time his intent was clear. To his eye, the people of the Carolinas, cultural cousins to the Wampanoag, were in superb health, especially compared to poorly nourished, smallpox-scarred Europeans. And they lived in what White viewed as well-ordered settlements, with big, flourishing fields of maize.

legs with elaborate geometric patterns and totemic animal symbols. They wore jewelry made of shell and swans'-down earrings and chignons spiked with eagle feathers. If that weren't enough, both sexes painted their faces red, white, and black—ending up, Gookin sniffed, with "one part of their face of one color; and another, of another, very deformedly."

And the *hair!* As a rule, young men wore it long on one side, in an equine mane, but cropped the other side short, which prevented it from getting tangled in their bow strings. But sometimes they cut their hair into such wild patterns that attempting to imitate them, Wood sniffed, "would torture the wits of a curious barber." Tonsures, pigtails, head completely shaved but for a single forelock, long sides drawn into a queue with a raffish short-cut roach in the middle—all of it was prideful and abhorrent to the Pilgrims. (Not everyone in England saw it that way. Inspired by asymmetrical Indian coiffures, seventeenth-century London blades wore long, loose hanks of hair known as "lovelocks.")

As for the Indians, evidence suggests that they tended to view Europeans with disdain as soon as they got to know them. The Huron in Ontario, a chagrined missionary reported, thought the French possessed "little intelligence in comparison to themselves." Europeans, Indians told other Indians, were physically weak, sexually untrustworthy, atrociously ugly, and just plain smelly. (The British and French, many of whom had not taken a bath in their entire lives, were amazed by the Indian interest in personal cleanliness.) A Jesuit reported that the "savages" were disgusted by handkerchiefs: "They say, we place what is unclean in a fine white piece of linen, and put it away in our pockets as something very precious, while they throw it upon the ground." The Micmac in New Brunswick and Nova Scotia scoffed at the notion of European superiority. If Christian civilization was so wonderful, why were its inhabitants all trying to settle somewhere else?

For fifteen days Verrazzano and his crew were the Narragansett's honored guests—though the Indians, Verrazzano admitted, kept their women out of sight after hearing the sailors' "irksome clamor" when females came into view. Much of the time was spent in friendly barter. To the Europeans' confusion, their steel and cloth did not interest the Narragansett, who wanted to swap only for "little bells, blue crystals, and other trinkets to put in the ear or around the neck." On Verrazzano's next stop, the Maine coast, the Abenaki *did* want steel and cloth—demanded them, in fact. But up north the friendly welcome had vanished. The Indians denied the visitors permission to land; refusing even to touch the Europeans, they passed goods back and forth on a rope over the water. As soon as the crew members sent over the last items, the locals began "showing their buttocks and laughing." Mooned

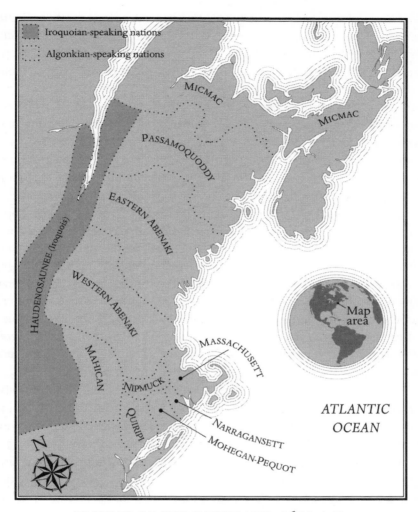

PEOPLES OF THE DAWNLAND, 1600 A.D.

by the Indians! Verrazzano was baffled by this "barbarous" behavior, but the reason for it seems clear: unlike the Narragansett, the Abenaki had long experience with Europeans.

During the century after Verrazzano Europeans were regular visitors to the Dawnland, usually fishing, sometimes trading, occasionally kidnapping natives as souvenirs. (Verrazzano had grabbed one himself, a boy of about eight.) By 1610 Britain alone had about two hundred vessels operating off Newfoundland and New England; hundreds more came from France, Spain, Portugal, and Italy. With striking uniformity, these travelers reported that

New England was thickly settled and well defended. In 1605 and 1606 Samuel de Champlain, the famous explorer, visited Cape Cod, hoping to establish a French base. He abandoned the idea. Too many people already lived there. A year later Sir Ferdinando Gorges—British, despite the name—tried to found a community in Maine. It began with more people than the Pilgrims' later venture in Plymouth and was better organized and supplied. Nonetheless, the local Indians, numerous and well armed, killed eleven colonists and drove the rest back home within months.

Many ships anchored off Patuxet. Martin Pring, a British trader, camped there with a crew of forty-four for seven weeks in the summer of 1603, gathering sassafras—the species was common in the cleared, burned-over areas at the edge of Indian settlements. To ingratiate themselves with their hosts, Pring's crew regularly played the guitar for them (the Indians had drums, flutes, and rattles, but no string instruments). Despite the entertainment, the Patuxet eventually got tired of the foreigners camping out on their land. Giving their guests a subtle hint that they should be moving on, 140 armed locals surrounded their encampment. Next day the Patuxet burned down the woodlands where Pring and his men were working. The foreigners left within hours. Some two hundred Indians watched them from the shore, politely inviting them to come back for another short visit. Later Champlain, too, stopped at Patuxet, but left before wearing out his welcome.

Tisquantum probably saw Pring, Champlain, and other European visitors, but the first time Europeans are known to have affected his life was in the summer of 1614. A small ship hove to, sails a-flap. Out to meet the crew came the Patuxet. Almost certainly the sachem would have been of the party; he would have been accompanied by his *pniese*, including Tisquantum. The strangers' leader was a sight beyond belief: a stocky man, even shorter than most foreigners, with a voluminous red beard that covered so much of his face that he looked to Indian eyes more beast than human. This was Captain John Smith of Pocahontas fame. According to Smith, he had lived an adventurous and glamorous life. As a youth, he claimed, he had served as a privateer, after which he was captured and enslaved by the Turks. He escaped and awarded himself the rank of captain in the army of Smith.* Later he actually became captain of a ship and traveled to North America several times. On this occasion he had sailed to Maine with two ships, intending to

---

*These preposterous tales may actually be true; other amazing Smith stories certainly are. While Smith was establishing a colony at Jamestown, for instance, Pocahontas likely did save his life, although little of the rest of the legend embodied in the Disney cartoon is true. The girl's name, for instance, was actually Mataoka—*pocahontas*, a teasing nickname, meant something like "little hellion." Mataoka was a priestess-in-training—a kind of *pniese*-to-be—in the

hunt whales. The party spent two months chasing the beasts but failed to catch a single one. Plan B, Smith wrote later, was "Fish and Furs." He assigned most of the crew to catch and dry fish in one ship while he puttered up and down the coast with the other, bartering for furs. In the middle of this perambulating he showed up in Patuxet.

Despite Smith's peculiar appearance, Tisquantum and his fellows treated him well. They apparently gave him a tour, during which he admired the gardens, orchards, and maize fields, and the "great troupes of well-proportioned people" tending them. At some point a quarrel occurred and bows were drawn, Smith said, "fortie or fiftie" Patuxet surrounding him. His account is vague, but one imagines that the Indians were hinting at a limit to his stay. In any case, the visit ended cordially enough, and Smith returned to Maine and then England. He had a map drawn of what he had seen, persuaded Prince Charles to look at it, and curried favor with him by asking him to award British names to all the Indian settlements. Then he put the maps in the books he wrote to extol his adventures. In this way Patuxet acquired its English name, Plymouth, after the city in England (it was then spelled "Plimoth").

Smith left his lieutenant, Thomas Hunt, behind in Maine to finish loading the other ship with dried fish. Without consulting Smith, Hunt decided to visit Patuxet. Taking advantage of the Indians' recent good experience with English visitors, he invited people to come aboard. The thought of a summer day on the foreigners' vessel must have been tempting. Several dozen villagers, Tisquantum among them, canoed to the ship. Without warning or pretext the sailors tried to shove them into the hold. The Indians fought back. Hunt's men swept the deck with small-arms fire, creating "a great slaughter." At gunpoint, Hunt forced the survivors belowdecks. With Tisquantum and at least nineteen others, he sailed to Europe, stopping only once, at Cape Cod, where he kidnapped seven Nauset.

---

central town of the Powhatan alliance, a powerful confederacy in tidewater Virginia. Aged about twelve, she may have protected Smith, but not, as he wrote, by interceding when he was a captive and about to be executed in 1607. In fact, the "execution" was probably a ritual staged by Wahunsenacawh, head of the Powhatan alliance, to establish his authority over Smith by making him a member of the group; if Mataoka interceded, she was simply playing her assigned role in the ritual. The incident in which she may have saved Smith's life occurred a year later, when she warned the English that Wahunsenacawh, who had tired of them, was about to attack. In the Disney version, Smith returns to England after a bad colonist shoots him in the shoulder. In truth, he did leave Virginia in 1609 for medical treatment, but only because he somehow blew up a bag of gunpowder while wearing it around his neck.

In Hunt's wake the Patuxet community raged, as did the rest of the Wampanoag confederacy and the Nauset. The sachems vowed not to let foreigners rest on their shores again. Because of the "worthlesse" Hunt, lamented Gorges, the would-be colonizer of Maine, "a warre [was] now new begunne between the inhabitants of those parts, and us." Despite European guns, the Indians' greater numbers, entrenched positions, knowledge of the terrain, and superb archery made them formidable adversaries. About two years after Hunt's offenses, a French ship wrecked at the tip of Cape Cod. Its crew built a rude shelter with a defensive wall made from poles. The Nauset, hidden outside, picked off the sailors one by one until only five were left. They captured the five and sent them to groups victimized by European kidnappers. Another French vessel anchored in Boston Harbor at about the same time. The Massachusett killed everyone aboard and set the ship afire.

Tisquantum was away five years. When he returned, everything had changed—calamitously. Patuxet had vanished. The Pilgrims had literally built their village on top of it.

THE PLACE OF THE SKULL

According to family lore, my great-grandmother's great-grandmother's great-grandfather was the first white person hanged in North America. His name was John Billington. He emigrated aboard the *Mayflower*, which anchored off the coast of Massachusetts on November 9, 1620. Billington was not among the company of saints, to put it mildly; within six months of arrival he became the first white person in America to be tried for sassing the police. His two sons were no better. Even before landing, one nearly blew up the *Mayflower* by shooting a gun at a keg of gunpowder while inside the ship. After the Pilgrims landed the other son ran off to live with some nearby Indians, leading to great consternation and an expedition to fetch him back. Meanwhile Billington père made merry with other non-Puritan lowlifes and haphazardly plotted against authority. The family was "one of the profanest" in Plymouth colony, complained William Bradford, its long-serving governor. Billington, in his opinion, was "a knave, and so shall live and die." What one historian called Billington's "troublesome career" ended in 1630 when he was hanged for shooting somebody in a quarrel. My family has always claimed that he was framed—but we *would* say that, wouldn't we?

Growing up, I was always tickled by this raffish personal connection to history: part of the Puritans, but not actually puritanical. As an adult, I decided to learn more about Billington. A few hours at the library sufficed to convince me that some aspects of our agreeable family legend were untrue. Although Billington was in fact hanged, at least two other Europeans were executed in North America before him. And one of them was convicted for the much more interesting offense of killing his pregnant wife and eating her. My ancestor was probably only No. 3, and there is a whisper of scholarly doubt about whether he deserves to be even that high on the list.

I had learned about Plymouth in school. But it was not until I was poking through the scattered references to Billington that it occurred to me that my ancestor, like everyone else in the colony, had voluntarily enlisted in a venture that had him arriving in New England without food or shelter six weeks before winter. Not only that, he joined a group that, so far as is known, set off with little idea of where it was heading. In Europe, the Pilgrims had refused to hire the experienced John Smith as a guide, on the theory that they could use the maps in his book. In consequence, as Smith later crowed, the hapless *Mayflower* spent several frigid weeks scouting around Cape Cod for a good place to land, during which time many colonists became sick and died. Landfall at Patuxet did not end their problems. The colonists had intended to produce their own food, but inexplicably neglected to bring any cows, sheep, mules, or horses. To be sure, the Pilgrims had intended to make most of their livelihood not by farming but by catching fish for export to Britain. But the only fishing gear the Pilgrims brought was useless in New England. Half of the 102 people on the *Mayflower* made it through the first winter, which to me seemed amazing. How did they survive?

In his history of Plymouth colony, Governor Bradford himself provides one answer: robbing Indian houses and graves. The *Mayflower* hove to first at Cape Cod. An armed company of Pilgrims staggered out. Eventually they found a deserted Indian habitation. The newcomers—hungry, cold, sick—dug open burial sites and ransacked homes, looking for underground stashes of food. After two days of nervous work the company hauled ten bushels of maize back to the *Mayflower,* carrying much of the booty in a big metal kettle the men had also stolen. "And sure it was God's good providence that we found this corn," Winslow wrote, "for else we know not how we should have done."

The Pilgrims were typical in their lack of preparation. Expeditions from France and Spain were usually backed by the state, and generally staffed by soldiers accustomed to hard living. English voyages, by contrast, were almost always funded by venture capitalists who hoped for a quick cash-out. Like Silicon Valley in the heyday of the Internet bubble, London was the center of a speculative mania about the Americas. As with the dot-com boom, a great deal of profoundly fractured cerebration occurred. Decades after first touching the Americas, London's venture capitalists still hadn't figured out that New England is colder than Britain despite being farther south. Even when they focused on a warmer place like Virginia, they persistently selected as colonists people ignorant of farming; multiplying the difficulties, the would-be colonizers were arriving in the middle of a severe, multiyear drought. As a result, Jamestown and the other Virginia forays survived on Indian charity—they were "utterly dependent and therefore controllable," in the phrase of Karen Ordahl Kuppermann, a New York University historian. The same held true for my ancestor's crew in Plymouth.

Inexperienced in agriculture, the Pilgrims were also not woodspeople; indeed, they were so incurious about their environment that Bradford felt obliged to comment in his journal when Francis Billington, my ancestor's son, climbed to the top of a tall tree to look around. As Thoreau noted with disgust, the colonists landed at Plymouth on December 16, but it was not until January 8 that one of them went as far away as two miles—and even then the traveler was, again, Francis Billington. "A party of emigrants to California or Oregon," Thoreau complained,

> with no less work on their hands,—and more hostile Indians,—would do as much exploring in the first afternoon, and the Sieur de Champlain would have sought an interview with the savages, and examined the country as far as the Connecticut [River, eighty miles away], and made a map of it, before Billington had climbed his tree.

Huddled in their half-built village that first terrible winter, the colonists rarely saw the area's inhabitants, except for the occasional shower of brass- or claw-tipped arrows. After February, glimpses and sightings became more frequent. Scared, the Pilgrims hauled five small cannons from the *Mayflower* and emplaced them in a defensive fortification. But after all the anxiety, their first contact with Indians went surprisingly easily. Within days Tisquantum came to settle among them. And then they heard his stories.

No record survives of Tisquantum's first journey across the Atlantic, but arithmetic gives some hint of the conditions in Hunt's ship. John Smith had arrived with two ships and a crew of forty-five. If the two ships had been of equal size, Hunt would have sailed with a crew of about twenty-two. Because Hunt, Smith's subordinate, had the smaller of the two vessels, the actual number was surely less. Adding twenty or more captured Indians thus meant that the ship was sailing with at least twice its normal complement. Tisquantum would have been tied or chained, to prevent rebellion, and jammed into whatever dark corner of the hull was available. Presumably he was fed from the ship's cargo of dried fish. Smith took six weeks to cross the Atlantic to England. There is no reason to think Hunt went faster. The only difference was that he took his ship to Málaga, on Spain's Mediterranean coast. There he intended to sell all of his cargo, including the human beings.

The Indians' appearance in this European city surely caused a stir. Not long before, Shakespeare had griped in *The Tempest* that the populace of the much bigger city of London "would not give a doit [a small coin] to a lame beggar, [but] will lay out ten to see a dead Indian." Hunt managed to sell only a few of his captives before local Roman Catholic priests seized the rest—the Spanish Church vehemently opposed brutality toward Indians. (In 1537 Pope Paul III proclaimed that "Indians themselves indeed are true men" and should not be "deprived of their liberty" and "reduced to our service like brute animals.") The priests intended to save both Tisquantum's body, by preventing his enslavement, and his soul, by converting him to Christianity. It is unlikely that Tisquantum was converted, though it's possible that he allowed the friars to *think* he had been. In any case, this resourceful man convinced them to let him return home—or, rather, to try to return. He got to London, where he stayed with John Slany, a shipbuilder with investments in Newfoundland. Slany apparently taught Tisquantum English while maintaining him as a curiosity in his townhouse. Meanwhile, Tisquantum persuaded him to arrange for passage to North America on a fishing vessel. He ended up in a tiny British fishing camp on the southern edge of Newfoundland. It was on the same continent as Patuxet, but between them were a thousand miles of rocky coastline and the Micmac and Abenaki alliances, which were at war with one another.

Because traversing this unfriendly territory would be difficult, Tisquantum began looking for a ride to Patuxet. He extolled the bounty of New England to Thomas Dermer, one of Smith's subordinates, who was then staying in the same camp. Dermer, excited by Tisquantum's promise of easy wealth, contacted Ferdinando Gorges. Gorges, a longtime, slightly dotty enthusiast about the Americas, promised to send over a ship with the men, supplies, and legal papers necessary for Dermer to take a crack at establishing a colony in New England. Dermer, with Tisquantum, was supposed to meet the ship when it arrived in New England.

One Edward Rowcraft captained the ship sent by Gorges from England. According to Gorges's principal biographer, Rowcraft "appears to have been unfit for such an enterprise." This was an understatement. In a bizarre episode, Rowcraft sailed to the Maine coast in early 1619; promptly spotted a French fishing boat; seized it for supposedly trespassing on British property (North America); placed its crew in chains aboard his own ship; sent that ship back to Gorges with the prisoners; continued his journey on the smaller French vessel, which led to a mutiny; quelled the mutiny; stranded the mutineers on the Maine coast; discovered that a) without the mutineers he didn't have enough people to operate the captured ship and b) it was slowly filling up with water from leaks; and decided to sail immediately for Britain's colony in Jamestown, Virginia, which had the facilities to repair the hull—a course that entailed skipping the promised rendezvous with Dermer. At Jamestown, Rowcraft managed, through inattentiveness, to sink his ship. Not long afterward he was killed in a brawl.

Incredibly, Dermer failed to execute *his* part of the plan, too. In orthodox comedy-of-errors style, he did not wait for Rowcraft in Maine, as he was supposed to, but sailed back to England, Tisquantum in tow. (The two ships more or less crossed paths in the Atlantic.) Dermer and Tisquantum met personally with Gorges.* Evidently they made an excellent impression, for despite Dermer's proven inability to follow instructions Gorges sent him back with Tisquantum and a fresh ship to meet Rowcraft, who was supposed to be waiting for them in New England. Dermer touched land in Maine and discovered that Rowcraft had already left. On May 19, 1619, still accompanied by Tisquantum, he set out for Massachusetts, hoping to catch up with Rowcraft (he didn't know that Rowcraft had sunk his own ship).

What Tisquantum saw on his return home was unimaginable. From southern Maine to Narragansett Bay, the coast was empty—"utterly void," Dermer reported. What had once been a line of busy communities was now a mass of tumbledown homes and untended fields overrun by blackberries. Scattered among the houses and fields were skeletons bleached by the sun. Slowly Dermer's crew realized they were sailing along the border of a cemetery two hundred miles long and forty miles deep. Patuxet had been hit with special force. Not a single person remained. Tisquantum's entire social world had vanished.

Looking for his kinsfolk, he led Dermer on a melancholy march inland. The settlements they passed lay empty to the sky but full of untended dead. Tisquantum's party finally encountered some survivors, a handful of families in a shattered village. These people sent for Massasoit, who appeared,

---

*Gorges may have met Tisquantum before. In 1605 the adventurer George Weymouth abducted five Indians, conning three into boarding his ship voluntarily and seizing the other two by the hair. According to Gorges's memoirs, Tisquantum was one of the five. He stayed with Gorges for nine years, after which he went to New England with John Smith. If this is correct, Tisquantum had barely come home before being kidnapped *again*. Historians tend to discount Gorges's tale, partly because his memoirs, dictated late in life, mix up details, and partly because the notion that Tisquantum was abducted twice just seems incredible.

Dermer wrote, "with a guard of fiftie armed men"—and a captive French sailor, a survivor of the shipwreck on Cape Cod. Massasoit asked Dermer to send back the Frenchman. And then he told Tisquantum what had happened.

One of the French sailors had learned enough Massachusett to inform his captors before dying that God would destroy them for their misdeeds. The Nauset scoffed at the threat. But the Europeans carried a disease, and they bequeathed it to their jailers. Based on accounts of the symptoms, the epidemic was probably of viral hepatitis, according to a study by Arthur E. Spiess, of the Maine Historic Preservation Commission, and Bruce D. Spiess, of the Medical College of Virginia. (In their view, the strain was, like hepatitis A, probably spread by contaminated food, rather than by sexual contact, like hepatitis B or C.) Whatever the cause, the results were ruinous. The Indians "died in heapes as they lay in their houses," the merchant Thomas Morton observed. In their panic, the healthy fled from the sick, carrying the disease with them to neighboring communities. Behind them remained the dying, "left for crows, kites, and vermin to prey upon." Beginning in 1616, the pestilence took at least three years to exhaust itself and killed as much as 90 percent of the people in coastal New England. "And the bones and skulls upon the severall places of their habitations made such a spectacle," Morton wrote, that the Massachusetts woodlands seemed to be "a new-found Golgotha," the Place of the Skull, where executions took place in Roman Jerusalem.

The religious overtones in Morton's metaphor are well placed. Neither the Indians nor the Pilgrims had our contemporary understanding of infectious disease. Each believed that sickness reflected the will of celestial forces. As the writer and historian Paula Gunn Allen put it,

> The idea that the realm of the spirits or the supernatural was powerfully engaged in the day-to-day life of nations as well as of villagers was commonly held on both sides of the Atlantic. . . . Both [Indians and Europeans] predicted events by the position of certain stars on the ecliptic plane around earth as much as by visionary techniques, and both assumed the reality of malicious as well as beneficent supernaturals.

The only real question in the minds of either side was whether Indian spiritual forces could affect Europeans, and vice versa. (As an experiment, Cotton Mather, a celebrated New England minister, tried to exorcise the "daemons in a possessed young woman" with incantations in Massachusett. To his satisfaction, the results demonstrated empirically that Indian magic had no effect on Christian devils.) Until the sickness Massasoit had directly ruled a community of several thousand and held sway over a confederation of as many as twenty thousand. Now his group was reduced to sixty people and the entire confederation to fewer than a thousand. The Wampanoag, wrote Salisbury, the Smith historian, came to the obvious logical conclusion: "their deities had allied against them."

The Pilgrims held similar views. Governor Bradford is said to have attributed the plague to "the good hand of God," which "favored our beginnings" by "sweeping away great multitudes of the natives . . . that he might make room for us." Indeed, more than fifty of the first colonial villages in New England were located on Indian communities emptied by disease. The epidemic, Gorges said, left the land "without any [people] to disturb or appease our free and peaceable possession thereof, from when we may justly conclude, that GOD made the way toe effect his work."

Much as the Lisbon earthquake of 1755, which killed tens of thousands in one of Europe's richest cities, prompted spiritual malaise across Europe, the New England epidemic shattered the Wampanoag's sense that they lived in balance with an intelligible world. On top of that, the massive death toll created a political crisis. Because the hostility between the Wampanoag and the neighboring Narragansett had restricted contact between them, the disease had not spread to the latter. Massasoit's people were not only beset by loss, they were in danger of subjugation.

After learning about the epidemic, the distraught Tisquantum first returned with Dermer to southern Maine. Apparently concluding he was never going to meet Rowcraft, Dermer decided in 1620 to make another pass at New England. Tisquantum returned, too, but not with Dermer. Instead he walked home—the long, risky journey he had wanted to avoid. In the interim, yet another English expedition had attacked the Wampanoag, killing several without apparent provocation. Understandably enraged, Indians attacked Dermer several times on his journey south; he was eventually slain on Martha's Vineyard by another former Indian abductee. For his part, Tisquantum was seized on his journey home, perhaps because of his association with the hated English, and sent to Massasoit as a captive.

As he had before, Tisquantum talked his way out of a jam. This time he extolled the English, filling Massasoit's ears with tales of their cities, their great numbers, their powerful technology. Tisquantum said, according to a colonist who knew him, that if the sachem "Could make [the] English his Friends then [any] Enemies yt weare to[o] strong for him"—in other words, the Narragansett—"would be Constrained to bowe to him." The sachem listened without trust. Within a few months, word came that a party of English

In this engraving taken from a John White watercolor of an East Coast village, the palisaded wall suggests that warfare was common enough to merit
the considerable labor of cutting down many trees with stone tools, but the
forces were not large enough to require moats, stone walls, earthen embank-
ments, or any other big defensive fortification.

had set up shop at Patuxet. The Wampanoag observed them suffer through
the first punishing winter. Eventually Massasoit concluded that he possibly
should ally with them—compared to the Narragansett, they were the lesser
of two evils. Still, only when the need for a translator became unavoidable
did he allow Tisquantum to meet the Pilgrims.

Massasoit had considerable experience with Europeans—his father had sent Martin Pring on his way seventeen years before. But that was before the epidemic, when Massasoit had the option of expelling them. Now he told the Pilgrims that he was willing to leave them in peace (a bluff, one assumes, since driving them away would have taxed his limited resources). But in return he wanted the colonists' assistance with the Narragansett.

To the Pilgrims, the Indians' motives for the deal were obvious. They wanted European technology on their side. In particular, they wanted guns. "He thinks we may be [of] some strength to him," Winslow said later, "for our pieces [guns] are terrible to them."

In fact Massasoit had a subtler plan. It is true that European technology dazzled Native Americans on first encounter. But the relative positions of the two sides were closer than commonly believed. Contemporary research suggests that indigenous peoples in New England were *not* technologically inferior to the British—or, rather, that terms like "superior" and "inferior" do not readily apply to the relationship between Indian and European technology.

Guns are an example. As Chaplin, the Harvard historian, has argued, New England Indians were indeed disconcerted by their first experiences with European guns: the explosion and smoke, the lack of a visible projectile. But the natives soon learned that most of the British were terrible shots, from lack of practice—their guns were little more than noisemakers. Even for a crack shot, a seventeenth-century gun had fewer advantages over a longbow than may be supposed. Colonists in Jamestown taunted the Powhatan in 1607 with a target they believed impervious to an arrow shot. To the colonists' dismay, an Indian sank an arrow into it a foot deep, "which was strange, being that a Pistoll could not pierce it." To regain the upper hand, the English set up a target made of steel. This time the archer "burst his arrow all to pieces." The Indian was "in a great rage"; he realized, one assumes, that the foreigners had cheated. When the Powhatan later captured John Smith, Chaplin notes, Smith broke his pistol rather than reveal to his captors "the awful truth that it could not shoot as far as an arrow could fly."

At the same time, Europeans were impressed by American technology. The foreigners, coming from a land plagued by famine, were awed by maize, which yields more grain per acre than any other cereal. Indian moccasins were so much more comfortable and waterproof than stiff, moldering English boots that when colonists had to walk for long distances their Indian companions often pitied their discomfort and gave them new footwear. Indian birchbark canoes were faster and more maneuverable than any small European boat. In 1605 three laughing Indians in a canoe literally paddled circles round the lumbering dory paddled by traveler George Weymouth and seven other men. Despite official disapproval, the stunned British eagerly exchanged knives and guns for Indian canoes. Bigger European ships with sails had some advantages. Indians got hold of them through trade and shipwreck, and trained themselves to be excellent sailors. By the time of the epidemic, a rising proportion of the shipping traffic along the New England coast was of indigenous origin.

Reading Massasoit's motives at this distance is a chancy business. But it seems likely that he did not want to ally with the foreigners primarily for their guns, as they believed. Although the sachem doubtless relished the possibility of additional firepower, he probably wanted more to confront the Narragansett with the unappetizing prospect of attacking one group of English people at the same time that their main trading partners were other English people. Faced with the possibility of disrupting their favored position as middlemen, the Narragansett might think twice before staging an incursion. Massasoit, if this interpretation is correct, was trying to incorporate the Pilgrims into the web of native politics. Not long before Massasoit had expelled foreigners who stayed too long in Wampanoag territory. But with the entire confederation now smaller than one of its former communities, the best option seemed to be allowing the Pilgrims to remain. It was a drastic, even fatal, decision.

MACHINATIONS

Tisquantum worked to prove his value to the Pilgrims. He was so successful that when some anti-British Indians abducted him the colonists sent out a military expedition to get him back. They did not stop to ask themselves why he might be making himself essential, given how difficult it must have been to live in the ghost of his childhood home. In retrospect, the answer seems clear: the alternative to staying in Plymouth was returning to Massasoit and renewed captivity.

Recognizing that the Pilgrims would be unlikely to keep him around forever, Tisquantum decided to gather together the few survivors of Patuxet and reconstitute the old community at a site near Plymouth. More ambitious still, he hoped to use his influence on the English to make this new Patuxet the center of the Wampanoag confederation, thereby stripping the sachemship from Massasoit, who had held him captive. To accomplish these goals, he intended to play the Indians and English against each other.

The scheme was risky, not least because the ever-suspicious Massasoit sent one of his *pniese,* Hobamok, to Plymouth as a monitor. (Hobamok, like

Tisquantum, apparently adopted a new name in his dealings with the British; "Hobamok" was the source of evil in Wampanoag cosmology.) Sometimes the two men were able to work together, as when Hobamok and Tisquantum helped the Pilgrims negotiate a treaty with the Massachusett to the north. They also helped establish a truce with the Nauset of Cape Cod after Bradford promised to pay back the losses caused by their earlier grave robbing.

By fall the settlers' situation was secure enough that they held a feast of thanksgiving. Massasoit showed up with ninety people, most of them young men with weapons. The Pilgrim militia responded by marching around and firing their guns in the air in a manner intended to convey menace. Gratified, both sides sat down, ate a lot of food, and complained about the Narragansett. *Ecce* Thanksgiving.

All the while, Tisquantum covertly tried to persuade other Wampanoag that he was better able to protect them against the Narragansett than Massasoit. In case of attack, Tisquantum claimed, he could respond with an equal number of Indian troops—and the Pilgrims, who might be able to intimidate the enemy. He evidently believed that the Narragansett did not have enough experience with European guns to know that they were not as fearsome as they first appeared. To advance his case, Tisquantum told other Indians that the foreigners had hidden away casefuls of the agent that caused the epidemic, and that he could manipulate them into unleashing it.

Even as Tisquantum attempted to foment Indian distrust of Massasoit, he told the colonists that Massasoit was going to double-cross them by leading a joint attack on Plymouth with the Narragansett. And he attempted to trick the Pilgrims into attacking the sachem.

In the spring of 1622 Tisquantum accompanied a delegation to the Massachusett in Boston Harbor. Minutes after they left, Bradford later recalled, one of the surviving Patuxet "came running in seeming great fear" to inform the settlers that the Narragansett "and he thought also Massasoit" were planning to attack. The idea clearly was that the colonists, enraged by the putative assault, would rise up and smite Massasoit. Tisquantum would be away, so his hands would seem clean. Instead everything went awry. In Indian villages people could only be summoned by shouting; once a canoe had gone a few hundred yards, it could not readily be called back. But when the news came of the impending attack, Bradford ordered the Pilgrims to fire a cannon to order back the expedition and Tisquantum. Meanwhile Hobamok, who had acquired some English, indignantly denied the story. In a move that Tisquantum apparently had not anticipated, Bradford dispatched Hobamok's wife to Massasoit's home to find out what the sachem was doing. She reported that "all was quiet." Actually, this wasn't entirely true. Massasoit was furious—at Tisquantum. He demanded that the Pilgrims send their translator to him for a quick execution.

Bradford refused; Tisquantum's language skills were too vital. Tisquantum is one of my subjects, Massasoit said. You Pilgrims have no jurisdiction over him. And he offered a cache of fur to sweeten the deal. When the colony still would not surrender Tisquantum, Massasoit sent a messenger with a knife and told Bradford to lop off Tisquantum's hands and head. To make his displeasure manifest, he summoned Hobamok home and cut off contact with the Pilgrims. Nervous, the colonists began building defensive fortifications. Worse, almost no rain fell between mid-May and mid-July, withering their crops. Because the Wampanoag had stopped trading with them, the Pilgrims would not be able to supplement their harvest.

Tisquantum, afraid of Massasoit's wrath, was unable to take a step outside of Plymouth without an escort. Nonetheless, he accompanied Bradford on a trip to southeast Cape Cod to negotiate another pact. They were on the way home when Tisquantum suddenly became sick. He died in a few days, his hopes in ruins. In the next decade tens of thousands of Europeans came to Massachusetts. Massasoit shepherded his people through the wave of settlement, and the pact he signed with Plymouth lasted for more than fifty years. Only in 1675 did one of his sons, angered at being pushed around by colonists' laws, launch what was perhaps an inevitable attack. Indians from dozens of groups joined in. The conflict, brutal and sad, tore through New England.

The Europeans won. Historians attribute part of the victory to Indian unwillingness to match the European tactic of massacring whole villages. Another reason for the newcomers' triumph was that by that time they outnumbered the natives. Groups like the Narragansett, which had been spared by the epidemic of 1616, were crushed by a smallpox epidemic in 1633. A third to half of the remaining Indians in New England died. The People of the First Light could avoid or adapt to European technology but not European disease. Their societies were destroyed by weapons their opponents could not control and did not even know they had.

3

In the Land of Four Quarters

In the early 1960s, Henry F. Dobyns, a young anthropologist working on a rural-aid project in Peru, dispatched assistants to storehouses of old records throughout the country. Dobyns himself traveled to the central cathedral in Lima. Entering the nave, visitors passed by a chapel on the right-hand side that contained the mummified body of Francisco Pizarro, the romantic, thuggish Spaniard who conquered Peru in the sixteenth century. Or, rather, they passed by a chapel that was *thought* to contain the conqueror's mummified body; the actual remains turned up years later, stashed inside two metal boxes beneath the main altar. Dobyns was not visiting the cathedral as a sightseer. Instead, he descended into the structure's basement—cold, dank, poorly lighted—to inspect birth and death registers kept there.

Dobyns belonged to a research team led by his doctoral advisor, Allan R. Holmberg of Cornell, the Holmberg after whom I have unkindly named Holmberg's Mistake. Holmberg had persuaded Cornell to let him lease an old colonial estate in rural Peru (the Carnegie Corporation, a charitable foundation despite its name, provided the funds). The estate included an entire village, whose inhabitants, most of them Indian, were its sharecroppers. "It was really a form of serfdom," Dobyns told me. "The villagers were just heartbreakingly poor." Holmberg planned to test strategies for raising their incomes. Because land tenure was a contentious issue in Peru, he had asked Dobyns to finalize the lease and learn more about the estate's history. With his adjutants, Dobyns visited a dozen archives, including those in the cathedral.

Dobyns had been dipping his toe into archival research for more than a decade, with results he found intriguing. His first foray into the past occurred in 1953, while he was visiting his parents in Phoenix, Arizona, during a school break. A friend, Paul H. Ezell, asked him for some help with his doctoral thesis. The thesis concerned the adoption of Spanish culture by the Pima Indians, who occupy a 372,000-acre reservation south of Phoenix. Many of the region's colonial-era records survived in the Mexican town of Altar, in the border state of Sonora. Ezell wanted to examine those records, and asked Dobyns to come along. One weekend the two men drove from Phoenix to Nogales, on the border. From Nogales, they went south, west, and up into the highlands, often on dirt roads, to Altar.

Then a huddle of small houses surrounding a dozen little stores, Altar was, Dobyns said, "the end of the earth." Local women still covered their heads with shawls. Gringo visitors, few in number, tended to be prospectors chasing rumors of lost gold mines in the mountains.

After surprising the parish priest by their interest in his records, the two young men hauled into the church their principal research tool: a Contura portable copier, an ancestor to the Xerox photocopier that required freshly stirred chemicals for each use. The machine strained the technological infrastructure of Altar, which had electricity for only six hours a day. Under flickering light, the two men pored through centuries-old ledgers, the pages beautifully preserved by the dry desert air. Dobyns was struck by the disparity between the large number of burials recorded at the parish and the far smaller number of baptisms. Almost all the deaths were from diseases brought by Europeans. The Spaniards arrived and then Indians died—in huge numbers, at incredible rates. It hit him, Dobyns told me, "like a club right between the eyes."

At first he did nothing about his observation. Historical demography was not supposed to be his field. Six years later, in 1959, he surveyed more archives in Hermosilla and found the same disparity. By this point he had almost finished his doctorate at Cornell and had been selected for Holmberg's project. The choice was almost haphazard: Dobyns had never been to Peru.

Peru, Dobyns learned, was one of the world's cultural wellsprings, a place as important to the human saga as the Fertile Crescent. Yet the area's significance had been scarcely appreciated outside the Andes, partly because the Spaniards so thoroughly ravaged Inka culture, and partly because the Inka themselves, wanting to puff up their own importance, had actively concealed the glories of the cultures before them. Incredibly, the first full history of the fall of the Inka empire did not appear until more than three hundred years after the events it chronicled: William H. Prescott's *History of the Conquest of Peru,* published in 1847. Prescott's thunderous cadences remain a pleasure to read, despite the author's firmly stated belief, typical for his time, in the moral inferiority of the natives. But the book had no successor. More than a century later, when Dobyns went to Lima, Prescott's was still the only complete account. (A fine history, John Hemming's *Conquest of the Incas,* appeared in 1970. But it, too, has had no successor, despite a wealth of new information.) "The Inka were largely ignored because the entire continent of South America was largely ignored," Patricia Lyon, an anthropologist at the Institute for Andean Studies, in Berkeley, California, explained to me. Until the end of colonialism, she suggested, researchers tended to work in their own countries' possessions. "The British were in Africa, along with the Germans and French. The Dutch were in Asia, and nobody was in South America," because most of its nations were independent. The few researchers who did examine Andean societies were often sidetracked into ideological warfare. The Inka practiced a form of central planning, which led scholars into a sterile Cold War squabble about whether they were actually socialists *avant la lettre* in a communal Utopia or a dire precursor to Stalinist Russia.

Given the lack of previous investigation, it may have been inevitable that when Dobyns traced births and deaths in Lima he would be staking out new ground. He collected every book on Peruvian demography he could find. And he dipped into his own money to pay Cornell project workers to explore the cathedral archives and the national archives of Peru and the municipal archives of Lima. Slowly tallying mortality and natality figures, Dobyns continued to be impressed by what he found. Like any scholar, he eventually wrote an article about what he had learned. But by the time his article came out, in 1963, he had realized that his findings applied far beyond Peru.

The Inka and the Wampanoag were as different as Turks and Swedes. But Dobyns discovered, in effect, that their separate battles with Spain and England followed a similar biocultural template, one that explained the otherwise perplexing fact that *every* Indian culture, large or small, eventually succumbed to Europe. (Shouldn't there have been *some* exceptions?) And then, reasoning backward in time from this master narrative, he proposed a new way to think about Native American societies, one that transformed not only our understanding of life before Columbus arrived, but our picture of the continents themselves.

TAWANTINSUYU

In 1491 the Inka ruled the greatest empire on earth. Bigger than Ming Dynasty China, bigger than Ivan the Great's expanding Russia, bigger than Songhay in the Sahel or powerful Great Zimbabwe in the West Africa tablelands, bigger than the cresting Ottoman Empire, bigger than the Triple

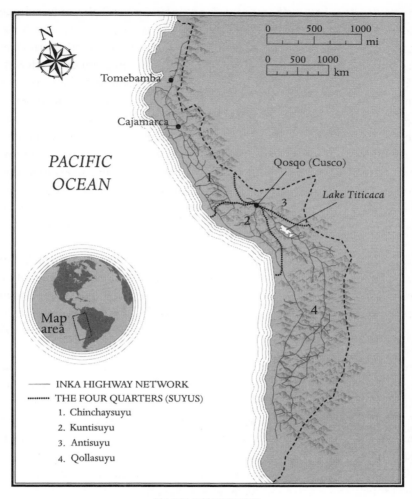

PACIFIC
OCEAN

Tomebamba

Cajamarca

Qosqo (Cusco)

Lake Titicaca

Map
area

------ INKA HIGHWAY NETWORK
······· THE FOUR QUARTERS (SUYUS)
   1. Chinchaysuyu
   2. Kuntisuyu
   3. Antisuyu
   4. Qollasuyu

TAWANTINSUYU
The Land of the Four Quarters, 1527 A.D.

Alliance (as the Aztec empire is more precisely known), bigger by far than any European state, the Inka dominion extended over a staggering thirty-two degrees of latitude—as if a single power held sway from St. Petersburg to Cairo. The empire encompassed every imaginable type of terrain, from the rainforest of upper Amazonia to the deserts of the Peruvian coast and the twenty-thousand-foot peaks of the Andes between. "If imperial potential is judged in terms of environmental adaptability," wrote the Oxford historian Felipe Fernández-Armesto, "the Inka were the most impressive empire buiders of their day."

The Inka goal was to knit the scores of different groups in western South America—some as rich as the Inka themselves, some poor and disorganized, all speaking different languages—into a single bureaucratic framework under the direct rule of the emperor. The unity was not merely political: the Inka wanted to meld together the area's religion, economics, and arts. Their methods were audacious, brutal, and efficient: they removed entire populations from their homelands; shuttled them around the biggest road system on the planet, a mesh of stone-paved thoroughfares totaling as much as 25,000 miles; and forced them to work with other groups, using only Runa Sumi, the Inka language, on massive, faraway state farms and construction projects.* To monitor this cyclopean enterprise, the Inka developed a form of writing unlike any other, sequences of knots on strings that formed a binary code reminiscent of today's computer languages (see Appendix B, "Talking Knots"). So successful were the Inka at remolding their domain, according to the late John H. Rowe, an eminent archaeologist at the University of California at Berkeley, that Andean history "begins, not with the Wars of [South American] Independence or with the Spanish Conquest, but with the organizing genius of [empire founder] Pachakuti in the fifteenth century."

Highland Peru is as extraordinary as the Inka themselves. It is the only place on earth, the Cornell anthropologist John Murra wrote, "where millions [of people] insist, against all apparent logic, on living at 10,000 or even 14,000 feet above sea level. Nowhere else have people lived for so many thousands of years in such visibly vulnerable circumstances." And nowhere else have people living at such heights—in places where most crops won't grow, earthquakes and landslides are frequent, and extremes of weather are the norm—repeatedly created technically advanced, long-lasting civilizations. The Inka homeland, uniquely high, was also uniquely steep, with slopes of more than sixty-five degrees from the horizontal. (The steepest street in San Francisco, famed for its nearly undrivable hills, is thirty-one-and-a-half degrees.) And it was uniquely narrow; the distance from the Pacific shore to the mountaintops is in most places less than seventy-five miles and in many less than fifty. Ecologists postulate that the first large-scale human societies tended to arise where, as Jared Diamond of the University of California at Los Angeles put it, geography provided "a wide range of altitudes and topographies within a short distance." One such place is the Fertile Crescent, where the mountains of western Iran and the Dead Sea, the lowest place on

*Runa Sumi (Quechua, to the Spanish) is the language of all Inka names, including "Inka." I use the standard Runa Sumi romanization, which means that I do not use the Spanish "Inca."

earth, bracket the Tigris and Euphrates river systems. Another is Peru. In the short traverse from mountain to ocean, travelers pass through twenty of the world's thirty-four principal types of environment.

To survive in this steep, narrow hodgepodge of ecosystems, Andean communities usually sent out representatives and colonies to live up- or downslope in places with resources unavailable at home. Fish and shellfish from the ocean; beans, squash, and cotton from coastal river valleys; maize, potatoes, and the Andean grain quinoa from the foothills; llamas and alpacas for wool and meat in the heights—each area had something to contribute. Villagers in the satellite settlements exchanged products with the center, sending beans uphill and obtaining llama jerky in return, all the while retaining their citizenship in a homeland they rarely saw. Combining the fruits of many ecosystems, Andean cultures both enjoyed a better life than they could have wrested from any single place and spread out the risk from the area's

Highland Peru, captured in this image of the Inka ruin Wiñay Wayna by the indigenous Andean photographer Martín Chambi (1891–1973), is the only place on earth where people living at such inhospitable altitudes repeatedly created materially sophisticated societies.

frequent natural catastrophes. Murra invented a name for this mode of existence: "vertical archipelagoes."

Verticality helped Andean cultures survive but also pushed them to stay small. Because the mountains impeded north-south communication, it was much easier to coordinate the flow of goods and services east to west. As a result the region for most of its history was a jumble of small- and medium-scale cultures, isolated from all but their neighbors. Three times, though, cultures rose to dominate the Andes, uniting previously separate groups under a common banner. The first period of hegemony was that of Chavín, which from about 700 B.C. to the dawn of the Christian era controlled the central coast of Peru and the adjacent mountains. The next, beginning after Chavín's decline, was the time of two great powers: the technologically expert empire of Wari, which held sway over the coastline previously under Chavín; and Tiwanaku, centered on Lake Titicaca, the great alpine lake on the Peru-Bolivia border. (I briefly discussed Wari and Tiwanaku earlier, and will return to them—and to the rest of the immense pre-Inka tradition—later.) After Wari and Tiwanaku collapsed, at the end of the first millennium, the Andes split into sociopolitical fragments and with one major exception remained that way for more than three centuries. Then came the Inka.

The Inka empire, the greatest state ever seen in the Andes, was also the shortest lived. It began in the fifteenth century and lasted barely a hundred years before being smashed by Spain.

As conquerors, the Inka were unlikely. Even in 1350 they were still an unimportant part of the political scene in the central Andes, and newcomers at that. In one of the oral tales recorded by the Spanish Jesuit Bernabé Cobo, the Inka originated with a family of four brothers and four sisters who left Lake Titicaca for reasons unknown and wandered until they came upon what would become the future Inka capital, Qosqo (Cusco, in Spanish). Cobo, who sighed over the "extreme ignorance and barbarity" of the Indians, dismissed such stories as "ludicrous." Nonetheless, archaeological investigation has generally borne them out: the Inka seem indeed to have migrated to Qosqo from somewhere else, perhaps Lake Titicaca, around 1200 A.D.

The colonial account of Inka history closest to indigenous sources is by Juan de Betanzos, a Spanish commoner who rose to marry an Inka princess and become the most prominent translator for the colonial government. Based on interviews with his in-laws, Betanzos estimated that when the Inka showed up in the Qosqo region "more than two hundred" small groups were already there. Qosqo itself, where they settled, was a hamlet "of about thirty small, humble straw houses."

Archaeological evidence suggests that the Inka gradually became more powerful. The apparent turning point in their fortunes occurred when they somehow made enemies of another group, the Chanka, who eventually attacked them. This unremarkable provincial squabble had momentous consequences.

According to a widely quoted chronology by the sixteenth-century cleric Miguel Cabello Balboa, the Chanka offensive took place in 1438. The Inka leader at that time was Wiraqocha Inka.* "A valiant prince," according to Cobo, Wiraqocha Inka had a "warlike" nature even as a young man and vowed that after taking the throne "he would conquer half the world." Perhaps so, but he fled the Chanka attack with three of his four sons, including his designated successor, Inka Urqon. A younger son, Inka Cusi Yupanki, refused to run. Instead he fought the Chanka with such bravery that (according to the legend) the very stones rose up to join the fray. Inka Yupanki won the battle, capturing many Chanka leaders. Later he skinned them in celebration—Pizarro saw the trophies on display. But first Inka Yupanki presented the captives to his father, so that Wiraqocha Inka could perform the victory ritual of wiping his feet on their bodies.

Fearing that Inka Yupanki was becoming too big for his britches, Wiraqocha Inka chose that moment to remind his younger son of his subordinate status. The foot-wiping honor, he proclaimed, actually belonged to the next Inka: Inka Urqon. "To this," Betanzos wrote, "Inka Yupanki answered that he was begging his father to tread on the prisoners, that he had not won the victory so that such women as Inka Urqon and the rest of his brothers could step on them." A heated argument led to a standoff. In a Shakespearian move, Wiraqocha Inka decided to settle the issue by murdering his inconvenient younger son. (It was "a crazy impulse," one of Wiraqocha Inka's generals later explained.) Inka Yupanki was tipped off and the scheme failed. The humiliated Wiraqocha Inka went into exile while Inka Yupanki returned in triumph to Qosqo, renamed himself Pachakuti ("Worldshaker"), and proclaimed that the ruling Inka families were descended from the sun. Then he went about conquering everything in sight.

Hey, wait a minute! the reader may be saying. This family story makes such terrific melodrama that it seems reasonable to wonder whether it actually happened. After all, every known written account of the Inka was set down after the conquest, a century or more after Pachakuti's rise. And these

*The Inka sovereign had the title of "Inka"—he was *the* Inka—but he could also include "Inka" in his name. In addition, Inka elites changed their names as they went through their lives. Each Inka was thus known by several names, any of which might include "Inka."

differ from each other, sometimes dramatically, reflecting the authors' biases and ignorance, and their informants' manipulation of history to cast a flattering light on their family lines. For these reasons, some scholars dismiss the chronicles entirely. Others note that both the Inka and the Spaniards had long traditions of record-keeping. By and large the chroniclers seem to have been conscious of their roles as witnesses and tried to live up to them. Their versions of events broadly agree with each other. As a result, most scholars judiciously use the colonial accounts, as I try to do here.

After taking the reins of state, Pachakuti spent the next twenty-five years expanding the empire from central highland Peru to Lake Titicaca and beyond. His methods were subtler and more economical with direct force than one might expect, as exemplified by the slow takeover of the coastal valley of Chincha. In about 1450 Pachakuti dispatched an army to Chincha under Qhapaq Yupanki (Ka-*pok* Yu-pan-ki, meaning roughly "Munificent Honored One"), a kind of adopted brother. Marching into the valley with thousands of troops, Qhapaq Yupanki informed the fearful local gentry that he wanted nothing from Chincha whatsoever. "He said that he was the son of the Sun," according to the report of two Spanish priests who investigated the valley's history in the 1550s. "And that he had come for their good and for everyone's and that he did not want their silver nor their gold nor their daughters." Far from taking the land by force, in fact, the Inka general would give them "all that he was carrying." And he practically buried the Chincha leadership under piles of valuables. In return for his generosity, the general asked only for a little appreciation, preferably in the form of a large house from which the Inka could operate, and a staff of servants to cook, clean, and make the things needed by the outpost. And when Qhapaq Yupanki left, he asked Chincha to keep expressing its gratitude by sending craftspeople and goods to Qosqo.

A decade later Pachakuti sent out another army to the valley, this one led by his son and heir, Thupa Inka Yupanki ("Royal Honored Inka"). Thupa Inka closeted himself with the local leadership and laid out many inspired ideas for the valley's betterment, all of which were gratefully endorsed. Following the Inka template, the local leaders drafted the entire populace into service, dividing households by sex and age into cohorts, each with its own leader who reported to the leader of the next larger group. "Everything was in order for the people to know who was in control," the Spanish priests wrote. Thupa Inka delegated tasks to the mobilized population: hewing roads to link Chincha to other areas controlled by the Inka, building a new palace for the Inka, and tending the fields set aside for the Inka. Thupa Inka apparently left the area in charge of his brother, who continued managing its gratitude.

The next visit came from Pachakuti's grandson, probably in the 1490s. With him came escalating demands for land and service—the veneer of reciprocity was fading. By that point the Chincha had little alternative but to submit. They were surrounded by Inka satrapies; their economy was enmeshed with the imperial machinery; they had hundreds or thousands of people doing the empire's bidding. The Chincha elite, afraid to take on the Inka army, always chose compliance over valor, and were rewarded with plum positions in the colonial government. But their domain had ceased to exist as an independent entity.

In 1976 Edward N. Luttwak, now at the Center for Strategic and International Studies, in Washington, D.C., published a short, provocative book about imperial Rome that distinguished between *territorial* and *hegemonic* empires. Territorial empires directly occupy territories with their armies, throw out the old rulers, and annex the land. In hegemonic empires, the internal affairs of conquered areas remain in the hands of their original rulers, who become vassals. Territorial empires are tightly controlled but costly to maintain; hegemonic empires are inexpensive to maintain, because the original local rulers incur the costs of administration, but the loose tie between master and vassal encourages rebellion. Every conquest-minded state is a mixture of both, but all Native American empires leaned toward the hegemonic. Without horses, Indian soldiers unavoidably traveled slower than European or Asian soldiers. If brigades were tied up as occupiers, they could not be reassigned quickly. As a result, the Inka were almost forced to co-opt local rulers instead of displacing them. They did so with a vengeance.

Pachakuti gave command of the military to his son Thupa Inka in 1463 and turned his attention to totally rebuilding Qosqo in imperial style, in the process becoming one of history's great urban planners. Although he drew on Andean aesthetic traditions, Pachakuti put his own stamp on Inka art and architecture. Whereas the buildings of Sumer and Assyria were covered with brilliant mosaics and splendid pictorial murals, the Inka style was severe, abstract, stripped down to geometric forms—startlingly contemporary, in fact. (According to the Peruvian critic César Paternosto, such major twentieth-century painters as Josef Albers, Barnett Newman, and Mark Rothko were inspired by Inka art.)

At the heart of the new Qosqo was the plaza of Awkaypata, 625 feet by 550 feet, carpeted almost in its entirety with white sand carried in from the Pacific and raked daily by the city's army of workers. Monumental villas and temples surrounded the space on three sides, their walls made from immense blocks of stone so precisely cut and fit that Pizarro's younger cousin Pedro, who accompanied the conqueror as a page, reported "that the point of a pin could not have been inserted in one of the joints." Across their

Inka masonry amazed the conquistadors, who could not understand how they put together such enormous stones without mortar or draft animals. And it was astonishingly durable—the U.S. explorer Hiram Bingham photographed the fortress of Saqsawaman in 1913, and found it in near-perfect condition despite four centuries of neglect.

facades ran enormous plates of polished gold. When the alpine sun filled Awkaypata, with its boldly delineated horizontal plain of white sand and sloping sheets of gold, the space became an amphitheater for the exaltation of light.

In Pachakuti's grand design, Awkaypata was the center of the empire—and the cosmos. From the great plaza radiated four highways that demarcated the four asymmetrical sectors into which he divided the empire, Tawantinsuyu, "Land of the Four Quarters." To the Inka, the quarters echoed the heavenly order. The Milky Way, a vast celestial river in Andean cosmology, crosses the Peruvian sky at an angle of about twenty-eight degrees to the earth's orbit. For six months the stream of stars slants across the sky from, so to speak, northeast to southwest; the other six months it slants from southeast to northwest. The transition roughly coincides with the transition between dry and wet seasons—the time when the Milky Way releases life-giving water to Pacha Mama, Mother Earth—and divides the heavens into four quarters. Awkaypata, reflecting this pattern, was the axis of the universe.

Not only that, Qosqo was the center of a *second* spiritual pattern. Radiating out from Awkaypata was a drunken spiderweb of forty-one crooked, spiritually powerful lines, known as *zeq'e,* that linked holy features of the landscape: springs, tombs, caves, shrines, fields, stones. About four hundred of these *wak'a* (shrines, more or less) existed around Qosqo—the landscape around the capital was charged with telluric power. (The *zeq'e* also played a role in the Inka calendar, which apparently consisted of forty-one eight-day weeks.) So complexly interrelated was the network of *wak'a* and *zeq'e*, Columbia University archaeologist Terence D'Altroy has written, "that many otherwise diligent scholars have been reduced to scratching their heads and trusting someone else's judgement." Each *wak'a* had its own meaning, relative status, social affiliation, and set of ceremonial uses. One big stone outside town was believed to be the petrified body of one of the original Inka brothers; Inka armies often carried it with them, dressed in fine togs, as a kind of good-luck talisman. To keep track of the florid abundance of shrines and lines, Cobo observed, the empire "had more than a thousand men in the city of Qosqo who did nothing but remember these things."

Not only did Pachakuti reconfigure the capital, he laid out the institutions that characterized Tawantinsuyu itself. For centuries, villagers had spent part of their time working in teams on community projects. Alternately bullying and cajoling, Pachakuti expanded the service obligation unrecognizably. In Tawantinsuyu, he decreed, all land and property belonged to the state (indeed, to the Inka himself). Peasants thus had to work periodically for the empire as farmers, herders, weavers, masons, artisans, miners, or soldiers. Often crews spent months away from home. While they were on the road, the state fed, clothed, and housed them—all from goods supplied by other work crews. Conscripts built dams, terraces, and irrigation canals; they grew crops on state land and raised herds on state pastures and made pots in state factories and stocked hundreds of state warehouses; they paved the highways and supplied the runners and llamas carrying messages and goods along them. Dictatorially extending Andean verticality, the imperium shuttled people and materiel in and out of every Andean crevice.

Around the Inka capital of Qosqo (modern Cusco) were more than four hundred *wak'a*, places in the landscape charged with spiritual power. Many of these were stones, some carved in elaborate representations, perhaps of the areas they influenced.

Not the least surprising feature of this economic system was that it functioned without money. True, the lack of currency did not surprise the Spanish invaders—much of Europe did without money until the eighteenth century. But the Inka did not even have *markets*. Economists would predict that this nonmarket economy—vertical socialism, it has been called—should produce gross inefficiencies. These surely occurred, but the errors were of surplus, not want. The Spanish invaders were stunned to find warehouses overflowing with untouched cloth and supplies. But to the Inka the brimming coffers signified prestige and plenty; it was all part of the plan. Most important, Tawantinsuyu "managed to eradicate hunger," the Peruvian novelist Mario Vargas Llosa noted. Though no fan of the Inka, he conceded that "only a very small number of empires throughout the whole world have succeeded in achieving this feat."

When Tawantinsuyu swallowed a new area, the Inka forcibly imported settlers from other, faraway areas, often in large numbers, and gave them land. The newcomers were encouraged to keep their own dress and customs rather than integrate into the host population. To communicate, both groups were forced to use Ruma Suni, the language of their conquerors. In the short run this practice created political tensions that the Inka manipulated to control both groups. In the long term it would have (if successful) eroded the distinctions among cultures and forged a homogeneous new nation in the imprint of Tawantinsuyu. Five centuries later the wholesale reshuffling of populations became an infamous trademark of Stalin and Mao. But the scale on which the Inka moved the pieces around the ethnic checkerboard would have excited their admiration. Incredibly, foreigners came to outnumber natives in many places. It is possible that ethnic clashes would eventually have caused Tawantinsuyu to implode, Yugoslavia-style. But if Pizarro had not interrupted, the Inka might have created a monolithic culture as enduring as China.

THE GILDED LITTER OF THE INKA

How did Pizarro do it? Sooner or later, everyone who studies the Inka confronts this question. Henry Dobyns wondered about it, too. The empire was as populous, rich, and well organized as any in history. But no other fell before such a small force: Pizarro had only 168 men and 62 horses. Researchers have often wondered whether the Inka collapse betokens a major historical lesson. The answer is yes, but the lesson was not grasped until recently.

The basic history of the empire was known well enough by the time and

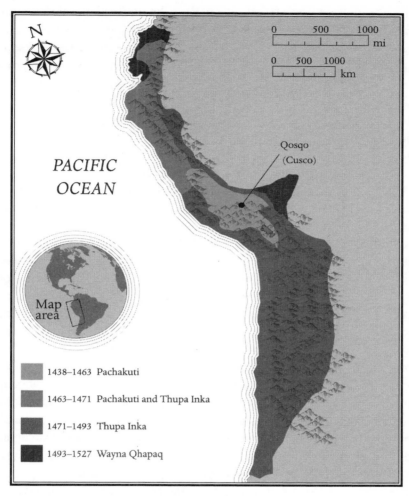

TAWANTINSUYU
Expansion of the Inka Empire, 1438–1527 A.D.

Tawantinsuyu is known to have risen and fallen with breathtaking rapidity, but the exact chronology of its trajectory is disputed. Most researchers regard the account of Miguel Cabello Balboa as approximately correct. It is the source for this map, though the reader is cautioned against regarding it as either exact or universally accepted.

Dobyns began reading the old colonial accounts. According to Cabello Balboa's chronology, Pachakuti died peacefully in 1471. His son Thupa Inka, long the military commander, now took the imperial "crown"—a multicolored braid, twisted around the skull like a headband, from which hung a red tasseled fringe that fell across the forehead. Carried on a golden litter—the Inka did not walk in public—Thupa Inka appeared with such majesty, according to the voyager Pedro Sarmiento de Gamboa, that "people left the roads along which he had to pass and, ascending the hills on either side, worshipped and adored" him by "pulling out their eyebrows and eyelashes." Minions collected and stored every object he touched, food waste included, to ensure that no lesser persons could profane these objects with their touch. The ground was too dirty to receive the Inka's saliva so he always spat into the hand of a courtier. The courtier wiped the spittle with a special cloth and stored it for safekeeping. Once a year everything touched by the Inka—clothing, garbage, bedding, saliva—was ceremonially burned.

Thupa Inka inaugurated the Inka custom of marrying his sister. In fact, Thupa Inka may have married *two* of his sisters. The practice was genetically unsound but logically consistent. Only close relatives of the Inka were seen as of sufficient purity to produce his heir. As Inkas grew in grandeur, more purity was required. Finally only a sister would do. The Inka's sister-wives accompanied him on military forays, along with a few hundred or thousand of his subordinate wives. The massive scale of these domestic arrangements seems not to have impeded his imperial progress. By his death in 1493, Thupa Inka had sent his armies deep into Ecuador and Chile, doubling the size of Tawantinsuyu again. In terms of area conquered during his lifetime, he was in the league of Alexander the Great and Genghis Khan.

Thupa Inka's death set off a fight for the royal fringe. Tawantinsuyu did not have strict succession rules. Instead the Inka selected the son he thought most qualified. Thupa Inka had more than sixty sons from all of his wives, according to Sarmiento de Gamboa, so he had a lot of choice. Alas, Thupa Inka apparently selected one son but then changed his mind on his deathbed and selected another. Factions formed around each son, leading to a melée. The first son was banished or killed and the second took the name Wayna Qhapaq (*Why*-na Ka-*pok*) and became the Inka. Because the new Inka was still a teenager (his name means "Munificent Youth"), two of his uncles served as regents. One uncle tried to usurp power but was killed by the other. Eventually the Inka grew old enough to take the reins. Among his first official acts was killing two of his own brothers to avoid future family problems. Then he, like his father, married his sister.

Wayna Qhapaq was not a military adventurer like his father. He initially seems to have viewed his role mainly as one of consolidation, rather than conquest, perhaps because Tawantinsuyu was approaching the geographic limits of governability—communication down the long north-south spine of the empire was stretched to the limit. Much of Wayna Qhapaq's time was devoted to organizing the empire's public works projects. Often these were more political than practical. Because the Inka believed that idleness

Wiraqocha Inka,
the Eighth Inka

Pachakuti,
the Ninth Inka

Thupa Inka,
the Tenth Inka

Wayna Qhapaq,
the Eleventh Inka

Washkar,
the Twelfth Inka

Atawallpa
(meeting Pizarro)

In 1615, the Inka writer Felipe Guamán Poma de Ayala presented his life's work, a massive history of Inka society with four hundred drawings, to King Philip II of Spain, hoping that the king would use it to learn more about his new subjects. Whether Philip ever saw the manuscript is unknown, but Poma de Ayala's work—one of the few non-European accounts of Inka life—is now a fundamental scholarly source. Although the portraits here are not taken from life, they hint at how the Inka viewed and remembered their leaders.

fomented rebellion, the Spanish traveler Pedro Cieza de León reported, he ordered unemployed work brigades "to move a mountain from one spot to another" for no practical purpose. Cieza de León once came upon three different highways running between the same two towns, each built by a different Inka.

Consolidation was completed in about 1520. Wayna Qhapaq then marched to Ecuador at the head of an army, intending to expand the empire to the north. It was a journey of return: he had been born in southern Ecuador during one of his father's campaigns. He himself brought with him one of his teenage sons, Atawallpa. When Wayna Qhapaq came to his birthplace, the city now called Cuenca, Cobo reported, "he commanded that a magnificent palace be constructed for himself." Wayna Qhapaq liked his new quarters so much that he stayed on while Atawallpa and his generals went out to subjugate a few more provinces.

They did not meet with success. The peoples of the wet equatorial forests did not belong to the Andean culture system and were not interested in joining. They fought ferociously. Caught by an ambush, Atawallpa was forced to retreat. Enraged by this failure, Cobo wrote, Wayna Qhapaq "prepared himself as quickly as possible to go in person and avenge this disgrace." He left his pleasure palace and publicly berated Atawallpa at the front. In a renewed offensive, the army advanced under the Inka's personal command. Bearing clubs, spears, bows, lances, slings, and copper axes, brilliant in cloaks of feathers and silver breastplates, their faces painted in terrifying designs, the Inka army plunged into the forests of the northern coast. They sang and shouted in unison as they fought. The battle seesawed until a sudden counterattack knocked Wayna Qhapaq out of his litter—a humiliation. Nearly captured by his foes, he was forced to walk like a plebe back to his new palace. The Inka army regrouped and returned. After prolonged struggle it subjugated its foes.

Finding the warm Ecuadorian climate more to his liking than that of chilly Qosqo, Wayna Qhapaq delayed his triumphal return for six years. Wearing soft, loose clothing of vampire-bat wool, he swanned around his palaces with a bowl of palm wine or *chicha*, a sweet, muddy, beer-like drink usually made from crushed maize. "When his captains and chief Indians asked him how, though drinking so much, he never got intoxicated," reported Pizarro's younger cousin and page, Pedro, "they say that he replied that he drank for the poor, of whom he supported many."

In 1525 Wayna Qhapaq suddenly got sick and expired in his Ecuadorian retreat. Once again the succession was contested and bloody. Details are murky, but on his deathbed the Inka seems to have passed over Atawallpa, who had not distinguished himself, and designated as his heir a son named Ninan Cuyuchi. Unluckily, Ninan Cuyuchi died of the same illness right before Wayna Qhapaq. The Inka's next pick was a nineteen-year-old son who had stayed behind in Qosqo. As was customary, high priests subjected this choice to a divination. They learned that this son would be dreadfully unlucky. The priest who reported this unhappy result to Wayna Qhapaq found him dead. In consequence, the court nobles were left to choose the emperor. They settled on the teenager who had been the Inka's final choice.

The teenager's principal qualification for the post was that his mother was Wayna Qhapaq's sister. Nonetheless, he had no doubts about crowning himself immediately—he didn't even wait to find out if Wayna Qhapaq had left any instructions or last wishes. The new Inka took the name Washkar Inka ("Golden Chain Inka"). Atawallpa remained in Ecuador, ostensibly because he was unable to show his face after being berated by his father, but presumably also because he knew that the life expectancy of Inka brothers tended to be short.

Meanwhile, Wayna Qhapaq's mummified body was dressed in fine clothing and taken back to Qosqo on a gold litter bedecked with feathers. Along the way, the dead emperor's executors, four high-ranking nobles, schemed to depose and murder Washkar and install yet another son in his place. Something aroused Washkar's suspicions as the party neared Qosqo—perhaps his discovery that Atawallpa had stayed in Ecuador with most of the Inka army, perhaps a tipoff from a loyal uncle whom the conspirators had approached. After staging a grand funeral for his father, Washkar ordered the executors to meet him one at a time, which provided the occasion to arrest them. Torture and execution followed.

The plot circumvented, Washkar went to work eliminating any remaining objections to his accession. Because Wayna Qhapaq had not actually married Washkar's mother—the union was properly incestuous but not properly legitimate—the new Inka demanded that his mother participate ex post facto in a wedding ceremony with his father's mummy. Even for the Andes this was an unusual step. Washkar further solidified his credentials as ruler by marrying his sister. According to the unsympathetic account of Cabello Balboa, Washkar's mother, who was apparently willing to marry her dead brother, objected to her son's plan to marry her daughter. The ceremony took place only after "much begging and supplication."

Civil war was probably unavoidable. Egged on by scheming courtiers and generals, relations between Atawallpa and Washkar spent several years swinging through the emotional valence from concealed suspicion to overt hostility. Washkar, in Qosqo, had the machinery of the state at his disposal; in addition, his claim to the fringe was generally accepted. Atawallpa, in Ecuador, had a war-tested army and the best generals but a weaker claim to the throne (his mother was merely his father's cousin, not his sister). The war lasted for more than three years, seesawed across the Andes, and was spectacularly brutal. Washkar's forces seized the initial advantage, invading Ecuador and actually capturing Atawallpa, almost tearing off one of his ears in the process. In a sequence reminiscent of Hollywood, one of Atawallpa's wives supposedly smuggled a crowbar-like tool into his improvised battlefield prison (his intoxicated guards permitted a conjugal visit). Atawallpa dug his way out, escaped to Ecuador, reassembled his army, and drove his foes south. On a plateau near today's Peru-Ecuador border the northern forces person-ally led by Atawallpa shattered Washkar's army. A decade later Cieza de León saw the battleground and from the wreckage and unburied remains thought the dead could have numbered sixteen thousand. The victors captured and beheaded Washkar's main general. Atawallpa mounted a bowl atop the skull, inserted a spout between the teeth, and used it as a cup for his *chicha*.

With the momentum of war turning against him, Washkar left Qosqo to lead his own army. Atawallpa sent his forces ahead to meet it. After a horrific battle (Cieza de León estimated the dead at thirty-five thousand), Washkar was captured in an ambush in the summer of 1532. Atawallpa's generals took the Inka as a captive to Qosqo and executed his wives, children, and relatives in front of him. Meanwhile, Atawallpa's triumphant cavalcade, perhaps as many as eighty thousand strong, slowly promenaded to Qosqo. In October or November 1532, the victors stopped outside the small city of Cajamarca, where they learned that pale, hairy people who sat on enormous animals had landed on the coast.

No matter how many times what happened next has been recounted, it has not lost its power to shock: how the curious Atawallpa decided to wait for the strangers' party to arrive; how Pizarro, for it was he, persuaded Atawallpa to visit the Spaniards in the central square of Cajamarca, which was surrounded on three sides by long, empty buildings (the town appar-ently had been evacuated for the war); how on November 16, 1532, the emperor-to-be came to Cajamarca in his gilded and feather-decked litter, pre-ceded by a squadron of liveried men who swept the ground and followed by five or six thousand troops, almost all of whom bore only ornamental, parade-type weapons; how Pizarro hid his horses and cannons just within the buildings lining the town square, where the 168 Spanish awaited the Inka with such fear, Pedro Pizarro noted, that many "made water without know-ing it out of sheer terror"; how a Spanish priest presented Atawallpa with a travel-stained Christian breviary, which the Inka, to whom it literally meant nothing, impatiently threw aside, providing the Spanish with a legal fig leaf for an attack (desecrating Holy Writ); how the Spanish, firing cannons, wear-ing armor, and mounted on horses, none of which the Indians had ever seen, suddenly charged into the square; how the Indians were so panicked by the smoke and fire and steel and charging animals that in trying to flee hundreds trampled each other to death ("they formed mounds and suffocated one another," one conquistador wrote); how the Spanish took advantage of the soldiers' lack of weaponry to kill almost all the rest; how the native troops who recovered from their initial surprise desperately clustered around

Atawallpa, supporting his litter with their shoulders even after Spanish broadswords sliced off their hands; how Pizarro personally dragged down the emperor-to-be and hustled him through the heaps of bodies on the square to what would become his prison.

Pizarro exulted less in victory than one might imagine. A self-made man, the illiterate, illegitimate, neglected son of an army captain, he ached with dreams of wealth and chivalric glory despite the fortune he had already acquired in the Spanish colonies. After landing in Peru he realized that his tiny force was walking into the maw of a powerful empire. Even after his stunning triumph in Cajamarca he remained torn between fear and ambition. For his part, Atawallpa observed the power of Inka gold and silver to cloud European minds.* Precious metals were not valuable in the same way in Tawantinsuyu, because there was no currency. To the Inka ruler, the foreigners' fascination with gold apparently represented his best chance to manipulate the situation to his advantage. He offered to fill a room twenty-two feet by seventeen feet full of gold objects—and two equivalent rooms with silver—in exchange for his freedom. Pizarro quickly agreed to the plan.

Atawallpa, still in command of the empire, ordered his generals to strip Qosqo of its silver and gold. Not having lived in the city since childhood, he had little attachment to it. He also told his men to slay Washkar, whom they still held captive; all of Washkar's main supporters; and, while they were at it, all of Atawallpa's surviving brothers. After his humiliating captivity ended, Atawallpa seems to have believed, the ground would be clear for his rule.

Between December 1532 and May 1533, caravans of precious objects—jewelry, fine sculptures, architectural ornamentation—wended on llama-back to Cajamarca. As gold and silver slowly filled the rooms, all of Tawantinsuyu seemed frozen. It was as if someone had slipped into the Kremlin in 1950 and held Stalin at gunpoint, leaving the nation, accustomed to obeying a tyrant, utterly rudderless. Meanwhile, the waiting Spanish, despite their unprecedented success, grew increasingly fearful and suspicious. When Atawallpa fulfilled his half of the bargain and the ransom was

---

*Because of their obsession with gold, the conquistadors are often dismissed as "gold crazy." In fact they were not so much gold crazy as status crazy. Like Hernán Cortés, who conquered Mexico, Pizarro was born into the lower fringes of the nobility and hoped by his exploits to earn titles, offices, and pensions from the Spanish crown. To obtain these royal favors, their expeditions had to bring something back for the king. Given the difficulty and expense of transportation, precious metals—"nonperishable, divisible, and compact," as historian Matthew Restall notes—were almost the only goods that they could plausibly ship to Europe. Inka gold and silver thus represented to the Spaniards the intoxicating prospect of social betterment.

complete Pizarro melted everything into ingots and shipped them to Spain. The conquistadors did not follow through on their part of the deal. Rather than releasing Atawallpa, they garroted him. Then they marched to Qosqo.

Almost at a stroke, just 168 men had dealt a devastating blow to the greatest empire on earth. To be sure, their victory was nowhere near complete: huge, bloody battles still lay ahead. Even after the conquistadors seized Qosqo, the empire regrouped in the hinterlands, where it fought off Spanish forces for another forty years. Yet the scale of Pizarro's triumph at Cajamarca cannot be gainsaid. He had routed a force fifty times larger than his own, won the greatest ransom ever seen, and vanquished a cultural tradition that had lasted five millennia—all without suffering a single casualty.

VIRGIN SOIL

I have just pulled a fast one. The Inka history above is as contemporary scholars understand it. They disagree on which social factors to emphasize and on how much weight to assign individual Spanish chronicles, but the outline seems not in serious dispute. The same is not true of my rendering of Pizarro's conquest. I presented what is more or less the account current when Dobyns arrived in Peru. But in his reading he discovered a hole in this version of events—a factor so critical that it drastically changed Dobyns's view of native America.

Why did the Inka lose? The usual answer is that Pizarro had two advantages: steel (swords and armor, rifles and cannons) and horses. The Indians had no steel weapons and no animals to ride (llamas are too small). They also lacked the wheel and the arch. With such inferior technology, Tawantinsuyu had no chance. "What could [the Inka] offer against this armory?" asked John Hemming, the conquest historian. "They were still fighting in the bronze age." The Inka kept fighting after Atawallpa's death. But even though they outnumbered the Europeans by as much as a hundred to one, they always lost. "No amount of heroism or discipline by an Inka army," Hemming wrote, "could match the military superiority of the Spaniards."

But just as guns did not determine the outcome of conflict in New England, steel was not the decisive factor in Peru. True, anthropologists have long marveled that Andean societies did not make steel. Iron is plentiful in the mountains, yet the Inka used metal for almost nothing useful. In the late 1960s, Heather Lechtman, an archaeologist at the MIT Center for Materials Research in Archaeology and Ethnology, suggested to "an eminent scholar of Andean prehistory that we take a serious and careful look at Andean metallurgy." He responded, "But there wasn't any." Lechtman went and looked anyway. She discovered that Inka metallurgy was, in fact, as refined as European metallurgy, but that it had such different goals that academic experts had not even recognized it.

According to Lechtman, Europeans sought to optimize metals' "hardness, strength, toughness, and sharpness." The Inka, by contrast, valued "plasticity, malleability, and toughness." Europeans used metal for tools. Andean societies primarily used it as a token of wealth, power, and community affiliation. European metalworkers tended to create metal objects by pouring molten alloys into shaped molds. Such foundries were not unknown to the Inka, but Andean societies vastly preferred to hammer metal into thin sheets, form the sheets around molds, and solder the results. The results were remarkable by any standard—one delicate bust that Lechtman analyzed was less than an inch tall but made of twenty-two separate gold plates painstakingly joined.

If a piece of jewelry or a building ornament was to proclaim its owner's status, as the Inka desired, it needed to shine. Luminous gold and silver were thus preferable to dull iron. Because pure gold and silver are too soft to hold their shape, Andean metalworkers mixed them with other metals, usually copper. This strengthened the metal but turned it an ugly pinkish-copper color. To create a lustrous gold surface, Inka smiths heated the copper-gold alloy, which increases the rate at which the copper atoms on the surface combine with oxygen atoms in the air—it makes the metal corrode faster. Then they pounded the hot metal with mallets, making the corrosion flake off the outside. By repeating this process many times, they removed the copper atoms from the surface of the metal, creating a veneer of almost pure gold. Ultimately the Inka ended up with strong sheets of metal that glittered in the sun.

Andean cultures did make tools, of course. But rather than making them out of steel, they preferred fiber. The choice is less odd than it may seem. Mechanical engineering depends on two main forces: compression and tension. Both are employed in European technology, but the former is more common—the arch is a classic example of compression. By contrast, tension was the Inka way. "Textiles are held together by tension," William Conklin, a research associate at the Textile Museum in Washington, D.C., told me. "And they exploited that tension with amazing inventiveness and precision."

In the technosphere of the Andes, Lechtman explained, "people solved basic engineering problems through the manipulation of fibers," not by creating and joining hard wooden or metal objects. To make boats, Andean cultures wove together reeds rather than cutting up trees into planks and nailing them together. Although smaller than big European ships, these vessels were not puddle-muddlers; Europeans first encountered Tawantinsuyu in the form of an Inka ship sailing near the equator, three hundred miles from its home port, under a load of fine cotton sails. It had a crew of twenty and was easily the size of a Spanish caravelle. Famously, the Inka used foot-thick cables to make suspension bridges across mountain gorges. Because Europe had no bridges without supports below, they initially terrified Pizarro's men. Later one conquistador reassured his countrymen that they could walk across these Inka inventions "without endangering themselves."

Andean textiles were woven with great precision—elite garments could have a thread count of five hundred per inch—and structured in elaborate layers. Soldiers wore armor made from sculpted, quilted cloth that was almost as effective at shielding the body as European armor and much lighter. After trying it, the conquistadors ditched their steel breastplates and helmets wholesale and dressed like Inka infantry when they fought.

Although Andean troops carried bows, javelins, maces, and clubs, their most fearsome weapon, the sling, was made of cloth. A sling is a woven pouch attached to two strings. The slinger puts a stone or slug in the pouch, picks up the strings by the free ends, spins them around a few times, and releases one of the strings at the proper moment. Expert users could hurl a stone, the Spanish adventurer Alonso Enríquez de Guzmán wrote, "with such force that it will kill a horse. . . . I have seen a stone, thus hurled from a sling, break a sword in two pieces when it was held in a man's hand at a distance of thirty paces." (Experimenting with a five-foot-long, Andean-style sling and an egg-sized rock from my garden, I was able, according to my rough calculation, to throw the stone at more than one hundred miles per hour. My aim was terrible, though.)

In a frightening innovation, the Inka heated stones in campfires until they were red hot, wrapped them in pitch-soaked cotton, and hurled them at their targets. The cotton caught fire in midair. In a sudden onslaught the sky would rain burning missiles. During a counterattack in May 1536 an Inka army used these missiles to burn Spanish-occupied Qosqo to the ground. Unable to step outside, the conquistadors cowered in shelters beneath a relentless, weeks-long barrage of flaming stone. Rather than evacuate, the Spanish, as brave as they were greedy, fought to the end. In a desperate, last-ditch counterattack, the Europeans eked out victory.

More critical than steel to Pizarro's success was the horse. The biggest animal in the Andes during Inka times was the llama, which typically weighs three hundred pounds. Horses, four times as massive, were profoundly, terribly novel. Add to this the shock of observing humans somehow astride their

The conquistadors disparaged steep Inka highways because they had been designed for sure-footed llamas rather than horses. But they were beautifully made—this road, photographed in the 1990s, had lasted more than five hundred years without maintenance.

backs like half-bestial nightmare figures and it is possible to imagine the dismay provoked by Pizarro's cavalry. Not only did Inka infantrymen have to overcome their initial stupefaction, their leaders had to reinvent their military tactics while in the midst of an invasion. Mounted troops were able to move at rates never encountered in Tawantinsuyu. "Even when the Indians had posted pickets," Hemming observed, "the Spanish cavalry could ride past them faster than the sentries could run back to warn of danger." In clash after clash, "the dreaded horses proved invincible." But horses are not *inherently* unbeatable; the Inka simply did not discover quickly enough where they had an advantage: on their roads.

European-style roads, constructed with horses and cars in mind, view flatness as a virtue; to go up a steep hill, they use switchbacks to make the route as horizontal as possible. Inka roads, by contrast, were built for llamas. Llamas prefer the coolness of high altitudes and, unlike horses, readily go up and down steps. As a result, Inka roads eschewed valley bottoms and used long stone stairways to climb up steep hills directly—brutal on horses' hooves, as the conquistadors often complained. Traversing the foothills to Cajamarca, Francisco Pizarro's younger brother Hernando lamented that the route, a perfectly good Inka highway, was "so bad" that the Spanish "could not use horses on the roads, not even with skill." Instead the conquistadors had to dismount and lead their reluctant animals through the steps. At that point they were vulnerable. Late in the day, Inka soldiers learned to wait above and roll boulders on their foes, killing some of the animals and frightening others into running away. Men left behind could be picked off at leisure. Multiple ambushes cost the lives of many Spanish troops and animals.

To be sure, horses confer an advantage on flat ground. But even on the plains the Inka could have won. Foot soldiers have often drubbed mounted troops. At the battle of Marathon in 490 B.C., the outnumbered, outarmored Athenian infantry destroyed the cavalry of the Persian emperor Darius I. More than six thousand Persians died; the Greeks lost fewer than two hundred men. So dire had the situation initially appeared that before the fight Athens sent a messenger to Sparta, its hated rival, to beg for aid. In the original marathon, the courier ran more than a hundred miles in two days to deliver his message. But by the time the Spartan reinforcements arrived, there was nothing to see but dead Persians.

The Inka losses were not foreordained. Their military was hampered by the cult of personality around its deified generals, which meant both that leaders were not easily replaced when they were killed or captured and that innovation in the lower ranks was not encouraged. And the army never learned to bunch its troops into tight formations, as the Greeks did at Marathon, forming human masses that can literally stand up to cavalry. Nonetheless, by the time of the siege of Qosqo the Inka had developed an effective anti-cavalry tactic: bolas. The Inka bola consisted of three stones tied to lengths of llama tendon. Soldiers threw them, stones a-whirl, at charging horses. The weapons wrapped themselves around the animals' legs and brought them down to be killed by volleys of sling missiles. Had the bolas come in massed, coordinated onslaughts instead of being wielded by individual soldiers as they thought opportune, Pizarro might well have met his match.

If not technology or the horse, what defeated the Inka? As I said, some of the blame should be heaped on the overly centralized Inka command structure, a problem that has plagued armies throughout time. But another, much larger part of the answer was first stated firmly by Henry Dobyns. During his extracurricular reading about Peru, he came across a passage by Pedro Cieza de León, the Spanish traveler who observed three roads between the same two cities. Entranced by the first exhibition of Inka booty in Spain, Cieza de

León had crossed the Atlantic as a teenager and spent fifteen years in Peru, Bolivia, Ecuador, and Colombia, traveling, fighting, and taking notes for what would become a massive, three-volume survey of the region. Only the first part was printed in his lifetime, but by the twentieth century historians had found and published most of the rest. Dobyns learned something from Cieza de León that was not mentioned in Prescott's history, in the Smithsonian's official *Handbook of South American Indians,* or in any of the then-standard descriptions of Tawantinsuyu. According to Cieza de León, Wayna Qhapaq, Atawallpa's father, died when "a great plague of smallpox broke out [in 1524 or 1525], so severe that more than 200,000 died of it, for it spread to all parts of the kingdom."

Smallpox not only killed Wayna Qhapaq, it killed his son and designated heir—and his brother, uncle, and sister-wife. The main generals and much of the officer corps died, wrote the Inka chronicler Santacruz Pachacuti Yamqui Salcamayhua, "all their faces covered with scabs." So did the two regents left in Qosqo by Wayna Qhapaq to administer the empire. After the dying Wayna Qhapaq locked himself away so that nobody could see his pustulous face, Salcamayhua reported, he was visited by a terrifying midnight vision. Surrounding him in his dream were "millions upon millions of men." The Inka asked who they were. "Souls of the lost," the multitude told him. All of them "would die from the pestilence," each and every one.

The story is probably apocryphal, but its import isn't. Smallpox has an incubation period of about twelve days, during which time sufferers, who may not know they are sick, can infect anyone they meet. With its fine roads and great population movements, Tawantinsuyu was perfectly positioned for a major epidemic. Smallpox radiated throughout the empire like ink spreading through tissue paper. Millions of people simultaneously experienced its symptoms: high fever, vomiting, severe pain, oozing blisters everywhere on the body. Unable to number the losses, the Jesuit Martín de Murúa said only that the toll was "infinite thousands."

The smallpox virus is thought to have evolved from a cattle virus that causes cowpox; a now-extinct equine virus responsible for horsepox; or, perhaps most likely, the camelpox virus, which affects camels, as the name suggests. People who survive the disease become immune to it. In Europe, the virus was such a constant presence that most adults were immune. Because the Western Hemisphere had no cows, horses, or camels, smallpox had no chance to evolve there. Indians had never been exposed to it—they were "virgin soil," in epidemiological jargon.

Virgin-soil death rates for smallpox are hard to establish because for the last century most potential research subjects have been vaccinated. But a study in the early 1960s of seven thousand unvaccinated smallpox cases in southern India found that the disease killed 43 percent of its victims. Noting the extreme vulnerability of Andean populations—they would not even have known to quarantine victims, as Europeans had—Dobyns hypothesized that the empire's population "may well have been halved during this epidemic." In about three years, that is, as many as one out of two people in Tawantinsuyu died.

The human and social costs are beyond measure. Such overwhelming traumas tear at the bonds that hold cultures together. The epidemic that struck Athens in 430 B.C., Thucydides reported, enveloped the city in "a great degree of lawlessness." The people "became contemptuous of everything, both sacred and profane." They joined ecstatic cults and allowed sick refugees to desecrate the great temples, where they died untended. A thousand years later the Black Death shook Europe to its foundations. Martin Luther's rebellion against Rome was a grandson of the plague, as was modern anti-Semitism. Landowners' fields were emptied by death, forcing them either to work peasants harder or pay more to attract new labor. Both choices led to social unrest: the Jacquerie (France, 1358), the Revolt of Ciompi (Florence, 1378), the Peasants' Revolt (England, 1381), the Catalonian Rebellion (Spain, 1395), and dozens of flare-ups in the German states. Is it necessary to spell out that societies mired in fratricidal chaos are vulnerable to conquest? To borrow a trope from the historian Alfred Crosby, if Genghis Khan had arrived with the Black Death, this book would not be written in a European language.

As for Tawantinsuyu, smallpox wiped out Wayna Qhapaq and his court, which led to civil war as the survivors contested the spoils. The soldiers who died in the battle between Atawallpa and Washkar were as much victims of smallpox as those who died from the virus itself.

The ferocity of the civil war was exacerbated by the epidemic's impact on a peculiarly Andean institution: royal mummies. People in Andean societies viewed themselves as belonging to family lineages. (Europeans did, too, but lineages were more important in the Andes; the pop-cultural comparison might be *The Lord of the Rings,* in which characters introduce themselves as "X, son of Y" or "A, of B's line.") Royal lineages, called *panaqa,* were special. Each new emperor was born in one *panaqa* but created a new one when he took the fringe. To the new *panaqa* belonged the Inka and his wives and children, along with his retainers and advisers. When the Inka died his *panaqa* mummified his body. Because the Inka was believed to be an immortal deity, his mummy was treated, logically enough, as if it were still living. Soon after arriving in Qosqo, Pizarro's companion Miguel de Estete saw a parade of defunct emperors. They were brought out on litters, "seated on their thrones and surrounded by pages and women with flywhisks in their hands, who ministered to them with as much respect as if they had been alive."

Because the royal mummies were not considered dead, their successors obviously could not inherit their wealth. Each Inka's *panaqa* retained all of his possessions forever, including his palaces, residences, and shrines; all of his remaining clothes, eating utensils, fingernail parings, and hair clippings; and the tribute from the land he had conquered. In consequence, as Pedro Pizarro realized, "the greater part of the people, treasure, expenses, and vices [in Tawantinsuyu] were under the control of the dead." The mummies spoke through female mediums who represented the *panaqa*'s surviving courtiers or their descendants. With almost a dozen immortal emperors jostling for position, high-level Inka society was characterized by ramose political intrigue of a scale that would have delighted the Medici. Emblematically, Wayna Qhapaq could not construct his own villa on Awkaypata—his undead ancestors had used up all the available space. Inka society had a serious mummy problem.

After smallpox wiped out much of the political elite, each *panaqa* tried to move into the vacuum, stoking the passions of the civil war. Different mummies at different times backed different claimants to the Inka throne. After Atawallpa's victory, his *panaqa* took the mummy of Thupa Inka from its palace and burned it outside Qosqo—burned it alive, so to speak. And later Atawallpa instructed his men to seize the gold for his ransom as much as possible from the possessions of another enemy *panaqa*, that of Pachacuti's mummy.

Washkar's *panaqa* kept the civil war going even after his death (or, rather, nondeath). While Atawallpa was imprisoned, Washkar's *panaqa* sent one of his younger brothers, Thupa Wallpa, to Cajamarca. In a surreptitious meeting with Pizarro, Thupa Wallpa proclaimed that he was Washkar's legitimate heir. Pizarro hid him in his own quarters. Soon afterward, the lord of Cajamarca, who had backed Washkar in the civil war, told the Spanish that Atawallpa's army was on the move, tens of thousands strong. Its generals planned to attack Pizarro, he said, and free the emperor. Atawallpa denied the charge, truthfully. Pizarro nonetheless ordered him to be bound. Some of the Spaniards most sympathetic to Atawallpa asked to investigate. Soon after they left, two Inka ran to Pizarro, claiming that they had just fled from the invading army. Pizarro hurriedly convoked a military tribunal, which quickly sentenced the Inka to execution—the theory apparently being that the approaching army would not attack if its leader were dead. Too late the Spanish expedition came back to report that no Inka army was on the move. Thupa Wallpa emerged from hiding and was awarded the fringe as the new Inka.

The execution, according to John Rowe, the Berkeley archaeologist, was the result of a conspiracy among Pizarro, Thupa Wallpa, and the lord of Cajamarca. By ridding himself of Atawallpa and taking on Thupa Wallpa, Rowe argued, Pizarro "had exchanged an unwilling hostage for a friend and ally." In fact, Thupa Wallpa openly swore allegiance to Spain. To him, the oath was a small price to pay; by siding with Pizarro, Washkar's *panaqa,* "which had lost everything, had a chance again." Apparently the new Inka hoped to return with Pizarro to Qosqo, where he might be able to seize the wheel of state. After that, perhaps, he could wipe out the Spaniards.

On the way to Qosqo, Pizarro met his first important resistance near the river town of Hatun Xauxa, which had been overrun by Atawallpa's army during the civil war. The same force had returned there to battle the Spanish. But the Inka army's plan to burn down the town and prevent the invaders from crossing the river was foiled by the native Xauxa and Wanka populace, which had long resented the empire. Not only did they fight the Inka, they followed the old adage about the enemy of my enemy being my friend and actually furnished supplies to Pizarro.

After the battle Thupa Wallpa suddenly died—so suddenly that many Spaniards believed he had been poisoned. The leading suspect was Challcochima, one of Atawallpa's generals, whom Pizarro had captured at Cajamarca and brought along on his expedition to Qosqo. Challcochima may not have murdered Thupa Wallpa, but he certainly used the death to try to persuade Pizarro that the next Inka should be one of Atawallpa's sons, not anyone associated with Washkar. Meanwhile, Washkar's *panaqa* sent out yet another brother, Manqo Inka. He promised that if he were chosen to succeed Thupa Wallpa he would swear the same oath of allegiance to Spain. In return, he asked Pizarro to kill Challcochima. Pizarro agreed and the Spaniards publicly burned Challcochima to death in the main plaza of the next town they came to. Then they rode toward Qosqo.

To Dobyns, the moral of this story was clear. The Inka, he wrote in his 1963 article, were not defeated by steel and horses but by disease and factionalism. In this he was echoing conclusions drawn centuries before by Pedro Pizarro. Had Wayna Qhapaq "been alive when we Spaniards entered this land," the conquistador remarked, "it would have been impossible for us to win it. . . . And likewise, had the land not been divided by the [smallpox-induced civil] wars, we would not have been able to enter or win the land."

Pizarro's words, Dobyns realized, applied beyond Tawantinsuyu. He had studied demographic records in both Peru and southern Arizona. In both, as in New England, epidemic disease arrived *before* the first successful colonists. When the Europeans actually arrived, the battered, fragmented cultures

Although Andean societies have been buffeted by disease and economic exploitation since the arrival of Europeans, indigenous tradition remained strong enough that this *chicha* seller in Cuzco, photographed by Martín Chambi in 1921, might have seemed unremarkable in the days of the Inka.

could not unite to resist the incursion. Instead one party, believing that it was about to lose the struggle for dominance, allied with the invaders to improve its position. The alliance was often successful, in that the party gained the desired advantage. But its success was usually temporary and the culture as a whole always lost.

Between the sixteenth and eighteenth centuries, this pattern occurred again and again in the Americas. It was a kind of master narrative of post-contact history. In fact, Europeans routinely lost when they could not take

advantage of disease and political fragmentation. Conquistadors tried to take
Florida half a dozen times between 1510 and 1560—and failed each time. In
1532 King João III of Portugal divided the coast of Brazil into fourteen
provinces and dispatched colonists to each one. By 1550 only two settlements
survived. The French were barely able to sustain trading posts in the St.
Lawrence and didn't even try to plant their flag in pre-epidemic New England. European microorganisms were slow to penetrate the Yucatán Peninsula, where most of the Maya polities were too small to readily play off
against each other. In consequence, Spain never fully subdued the Maya. The
Zapatista rebellion that convulsed southern Mexico in the 1990s was merely
the most recent battle in an episodic colonial war that began in the sixteenth
century.

All of this was important, the stuff of historians' arguments and doctoral
dissertations, but Dobyns was thinking of something else. If Pizarro had
been amazed by the size of Tawantinsuyu *after* the terrible epidemic and
war, how many people had been living there to begin with? Beyond that,
what was the population of the Western Hemisphere in 1491?

AN ARITHMETICAL PROGRESSION

Wayna Qhapaq died in the *first* smallpox epidemic. The virus struck Tawantinsuyu again in 1533, 1535, 1558, and 1565. Each time the consequences were
beyond the imagination of our fortunate age. "They died by scores and hundreds," recalled one eyewitness to the 1565 outbreak. "Villages were depopulated. Corpses were scattered over the fields or piled up in the houses or
huts. . . . The fields were uncultivated; the herds were untended [and] the
price of food rose to such an extent that many persons found it beyond their
reach. They escaped the foul disease, but only to be wasted by famine." In
addition, Tawantinsuyu was invaded by other European pestilences, to
which the Indians were equally susceptible. Typhus (probably) in 1546,
influenza in 1558 (together with smallpox), diphtheria in 1614, measles in
1618—all flensed the remains of Inka culture. Taken as a whole, Dobyns
thought, the epidemics must have killed nine out of ten of the inhabitants of
Tawantinsuyu.

Dobyns was not the first to arrive at this horrific conclusion. But he was
the first to put it together with the fact that smallpox visited before anyone in
South America had even *seen* Europeans. The most likely source of the virus,
Dobyns realized, was the Caribbean. Smallpox was recorded to have
appeared on the island of Hispaniola in November or December 1518. It

killed a third of the native population before jumping to Puerto Rico and Cuba. Spaniards, exposed in childhood to the virus, were mostly immune. During Hernán Cortés's conquest of Mexico, an expedition led by Pánfilo de Narváez landed on April 23, 1520, near what is today the city of Veracruz. According to several Spanish accounts, the force included an African slave named Francisco Eguía or Baguía who had smallpox. Other reports say that the carriers were Cuban Indians whom Narváez had brought as auxiliaries. In any case, *someone* brought the virus—and infected a hemisphere.

The disease raced to Tenochtitlán, leading city of the Mexica (Aztecs), where it laid waste to the metropolis and then the rest of the empire. From there, Dobyns discovered, colonial accounts show smallpox hopscotching through Central America to Panama. At that point it was only a few hundred miles from the Inka frontier. The virus seemingly crossed the gap, with catastrophic consequences.

Then Dobyns went further. When microbes arrived in the Western Hemisphere, he argued, they must have swept from the coastlines first visited by Europeans to inland areas populated by Indians who had never seen a white person. Colonial writers knew that disease tilled the virgin soil of the Americas countless times in the sixteenth century. But what they did not, could not, know is that the epidemics shot out like ghastly arrows from the limited areas they saw to every corner of the hemisphere, wreaking destruction in places that never appeared in the European historical record. The first whites to explore many parts of the Americas therefore would have encountered places that were *already* depopulated.

As a result, Dobyns said, all colonial population estimates were too low. Many of them, put together just after epidemics, would have represented population nadirs, not approximations of precontact numbers. From a few incidents in which before and after totals are known with relative certainty, Dobyns calculated that in the first 130 years of contact about 95 percent of the people in the Americas died. To estimate native numbers before Columbus, one thus had to multiply census figures from those times by a factor of twenty or more. The results obtained by this procedure were, by historical standards, stunningly high.

Historians had long wondered how many Indians lived in the Americas before contact. "Debated since Columbus attempted a partial census at Hispaniola in 1496," Denevan, the Beni geographer, has written, "it remains one of the great inquiries of history." Early researchers' figures were, to put it mildly, informally ascertained. "Most of them weren't even ballpark calculations," Denevan told me. "No ballpark was involved." Only in 1928 did the first careful estimate of the indigenous population appear. James Mooney, a distinguished ethnographer at the Smithsonian Institution, combed through colonial writings and government documents to conclude that in 1491 North America had 1.15 million inhabitants. Alfred L. Kroeber, the renowned Berkeley anthropologist, built upon Mooney's work in the 1930s. Kroeber cut back the tally still further, to 900,000—a population density of less than one person for every six square miles. Just 8.4 million Indians, Kroeber suggested, had lived in the entire hemisphere.

Recognizing that his continent-wide estimate did not account for regional variation, Kroeber encouraged future scholars to seek out and analyze "sharply localized documentary evidence." As he knew, some of his Berkeley colleagues were already making those analyses. Geographer Carl Sauer published the first modern estimate of northwest Mexico's pre-Columbian population in 1935. Meanwhile, physiologist Sherburne F. Cook investigated the consequences of disease in the same area. Cook joined forces with Woodrow W. Borah, a Berkeley historian, in the mid-1950s. In a series of publications that stretched to the 1970s, the two men combed through colonial financial, census, and land records. Their results made Kroeber uneasy. When Columbus landed, Cook and Borah concluded, the central Mexican plateau alone had a population of 25.2 million. By contrast, Spain and Portugal together had fewer than ten million inhabitants. Central Mexico, they said, was the most densely populated place on earth, with more than twice as many people per square mile than China or India.

"Historians and anthropologists did not, however, seem to be paying much attention" to Cook and Borah, Dobyns wrote. Years later, his work, coupled with that of Denevan, Crosby, and William H. McNeill, finally made them take notice. Based on their work and his own, Dobyns argued that the Indian population in 1491 was between 90 and 112 million people. Another way of saying this is that when Columbus sailed more people lived in the Americas than in Europe.

According to a 1999 estimate from the United Nations, the earth's population in the beginning of the sixteenth century was about 500 million. If Dobyns was right, disease claimed the lives of 80 to 100 million Indians by the first third of the seventeenth century. All these numbers are at best rough approximations, but their implications are clear: the epidemics killed about one out of every five people on earth. According to W. George Lovell, a geographer at Queen's University in Ontario, it was "the greatest destruction of lives in human history."

Dobyns published his conclusions in the journal *Current Anthropology* in 1966. They spawned rebuttals, conferences, even entire books. (Denevan assembled one: *The Native Population of the Americas in 1492.*) "I always felt guilty about the impact of my *Current Anthropology* article," Dobyns told me, "because I thought and still think that Cook and Borah and Sauer had all said this in print earlier, but people weren't listening. I'm *still* puzzled by the reaction, to tell you the truth. Maybe it was the time—people were prepared to listen in the 1960s."

Listen—and attack. Dobyns's population projections were quickly seen by some as politically motivated—self-flagellation by guilty white liberals or, worse, a push to inflate the toll of imperialism from the hate-America crowd. "No question about it, some people want those higher numbers," Shepard Krech III, an anthropologist at Brown, told me. These people, he said, were thrilled when Dobyns revisited the subject in a 1983 book, *Their Number Become Thinned*, and revised his estimates upward.

Perhaps the most vehement critic was David Henige, an African studies and Near East bibliographer at the University of Wisconsin, whose book, *Numbers from Nowhere*, published in 1998, is a landmark in the literature of demographic vilification. "Suspect in 1966, it is no less suspect nowadays," Henige charged of Dobyns's work. "If anything, it is worse." Henige stumbled across a seminar on Indian demography taught by Denevan in 1976. An "epiphanic moment" occurred when he read that Cook and Borah had "uncovered" the existence of eight million people in Hispaniola. Can you just *invent* millions of people? he wondered. "We can make of the historical record that there was depopulation and movement of people from internecine warfare and diseases," he said to me. "But as for how much, who knows? When we start putting numbers to something like that—applying large figures like 95 percent—we're saying things we shouldn't say. The number implies a level of knowledge that's impossible."

Indian activists reject this logic. "You always hear white people trying to minimize the size of the aboriginal populations their ancestors personally displaced," according to Lenore Stiffarm, an ethnologist at the University of Saskatchewan. Dismissing the impact of disease, in her view, is simply a way to reduce the original population of the Americas. "Oh, there used to be a few people there, and disease killed some of them, so by the time we got here they were almost all gone." The smaller the numbers of Indians, she said, the easier it is to regard the continent as empty, and hence up for grabs. "It's perfectly acceptable to move into unoccupied land," Stiffarm told me. "And land with only a few 'savages' is the next best thing."

When Henige wrote *Numbers from Nowhere*, the fight about pre-Columbian population had already consumed forests' worth of trees—his bibliography is ninety pages long. Four decades after Dobyns's article appeared, his colleagues "are still struggling to get out of the crater that paper left in anthropology," according to James Wilson, author of *Their Earth Shall Weep,* a history of North America's indigenous peoples after conquest. The dispute shows no sign of abating. This is partly because of the inherent fascination with the subject. But it is also due to the growing realization of how much is at stake.

4

Frequently Asked Questions

NOT ENOUGH FOR YANKEE STADIUM

On May 30, 1539, Hernando De Soto landed his private army near Tampa Bay in Florida. De Soto was a novel figure: half warrior, half venture capitalist. He grew very rich very young in Spanish America by becoming a market leader in the nascent slave trade. The profits helped to fund the conquest of the Inka, which made De Soto wealthier still. He accompanied Pizarro to Tawantinsuyu, burnishing his reputation for brutality—he personally tortured Challcochima, Atawallpa's chief general, before his execution. Literally looking for new worlds to conquer, De Soto returned to Spain soon after his exploits in Peru. In Charles V's court he persuaded the bored monarch to let him loose in North America with an expedition of his own. He sailed to Florida with six hundred soldiers, two hundred horses, and three hundred pigs.

From today's perspective, it is difficult to imagine the ethical system that could justify De Soto's subsequent actions. For four years his force wandered through what are now Florida, Georgia, North and South Carolina, Tennessee, Alabama, Mississippi, Arkansas, Texas, and Louisiana, looking for gold and wrecking most everything it touched. The inhabitants often fought back vigorously, but they were baffled by the Spaniards' motives and astounded by the sight and sound of horses and guns. De Soto died of fever with his expedition in ruins. Along the way, though, he managed to rape, torture, enslave, and kill countless Indians. But the worst thing he did, some researchers say, was entirely without malice—he brought pigs.

According to Charles Hudson, an anthropologist at the University of Georgia who spent fifteen years reconstructing De Soto's path, the expedition built barges and crossed the Mississippi a few miles downstream from the present site of Memphis. It was a nervous time: every afternoon, one of the force later recalled, several thousand Indian soldiers approached in canoes to within "a stone's throw" of the Spanish and mocked them as they labored. The Indians, "painted with ochre," wore "plumes of many colors, having feathered shields in their hands, with which they sheltered the oarsmen on either side, the warriors standing erect from bow to stern, holding bows and arrows." Utterly without fear, De Soto ignored the taunts and occasional volleys of arrows and poled over the river into what is now eastern Arkansas, a land "thickly set with great towns," according to the account, "two or three of them to be seen from one." Each city protected itself with earthen walls, sizable moats, and deadeye archers. In his brazen fashion, De Soto marched right in, demanded food, and marched out.

After De Soto left, no Europeans visited this part of the Mississippi Valley for more than a century. Early in 1682 white people appeared again, this time Frenchmen in canoes. In one seat was René-Robert Cavelier, Sieur de la Salle. La Salle passed through the area where De Soto had found cities cheek by jowl. It was deserted—the French didn't see an Indian village for two hundred miles. About fifty settlements existed in this strip of the Mississippi when De Soto showed up, according to Anne Ramenofsky, an archaeologist at the University of New Mexico. By La Salle's time the number had shrunk to perhaps ten, some probably inhabited by recent immigrants. De Soto "had a privileged glimpse" of an Indian world, Hudson told me. "The window opened and slammed shut. When the French came in and the record opened up again, it was a transformed reality. A civilization crumbled. The question is, how did this happen?"

Today most historians and anthropologists believe the culprit was disease. In the view of Ramenofsky and Patricia Galloway, an anthropologist at the University of Texas, the source of contagion was very likely not De Soto's army but its ambulatory meat locker: his three hundred pigs. De Soto's company was too small to be an effective biological weapon. Sicknesses like measles and smallpox would have burned through his six hundred men long before they reached the Mississippi. But that would not have been true for his pigs.

Pigs were as essential to the conquistadors as horses. Spanish armies traveled in a porcine cloud; drawn by the supper trough, the lean, hungry animals circled the troops like darting dogs. Neither species regarded the arrangement as novel; they had lived together in Europe for millennia. When humans and domesticated animals share quarters, they are constantly exposed to each other's microbes. Over time mutation lets animal diseases jump to people: avian influenza becomes human influenza, bovine rinderpest becomes human measles, horsepox becomes human smallpox. Unlike Europeans, Indians did not live in constant contact with many animals. They domesticated only the dog; the turkey (in Mesoamerica); and the llama, the alpaca, the Muscovy duck, and the guinea pig (in the Andes). In some ways this is not surprising: the New World had fewer animal candidates for taming than the Old. Moreover, few Indians carry the gene that permits adults to digest lactose, a form of sugar abundant in milk. Non-milk drinkers, one imagines, would be less likely to work at domesticating milk-giving animals. But this is guesswork. The fact is that what scientists call zoonotic disease was little known in the Americas. By contrast, swine, mainstays of European agriculture, transmit anthrax, brucellosis, leptospirosis, trichinosis, and tuberculosis. Pigs breed exuberantly and can pass diseases to deer and turkeys, which then can infect people. Only a few of De Soto's pigs would have had to wander off to contaminate the forest.

The calamity wreaked by the De Soto expedition, Ramenofsky and Galloway argued, extended across the whole Southeast. The societies of the Caddo, on the Texas-Arkansas border, and the Coosa, in western Georgia, both disintegrated soon after. The Caddo had a taste for monumental architecture: public plazas, ceremonial platforms, mausoleums. After De Soto's army left the Caddo stopped erecting community centers and began digging community cemeteries. Between the visits of De Soto and La Salle, according to Timothy K. Perttula, an archaeological consultant in Austin, Texas, the Caddoan population fell from about 200,000 to about 8,500—a drop of nearly 96 percent. In the eighteenth century, the tally shrank further, to 1,400. An equivalent loss today would reduce the population of New York City to 56,000, not enough to fill Yankee Stadium. "That's one reason whites think of Indians as nomadic hunters," Russell Thornton, an anthropologist at the University of California at Los Angeles, said to me. "Everything else—all the heavily populated urbanized societies—was wiped out."

Could a few pigs truly wreak this much destruction? Such apocalyptic scenarios have invited skepticism since Henry Dobyns first drew them to wide attention. After all, no eyewitness accounts exist of the devastation—none of the peoples in the Southeast had any form of writing known today. Spanish and French narratives cannot be taken at face value, and in any case say nothing substantial about disease. (The belief that epidemics swept through the Southeast comes less from European accounts of the region than from the disparities among those accounts.) Although the archaeological record is suggestive, it is also frustratingly incomplete; soon after the Spaniards visited, mass graves became more common in the Southeast, but there is yet no solid proof that a single Indian in them died of a pig-transmitted disease. Asserting that De Soto's visit caused the subsequent collapse of the Caddo and Coosa may be only the old logical fallacy of *post hoc ergo propter hoc.*

Not only do archaeologists like Dobyns, Perttula, and Ramenofsky argue that unrecorded pandemics swept through the Americas, they claim that the diseases themselves were of unprecedented deadliness. As a rule, viruses, microbes, and parasites do not kill the majority of their victims—the pest that wipes out its host species has a bleak evolutionary future. The influenza epidemic of 1918, until AIDS the greatest epidemic of modern times, infected tens of millions around the world but killed fewer than 5 percent of its victims. Even the Black Death, a symbol of virulence, was not as deadly as these epidemics are claimed to be. The first European incursion of the Black Death, in 1347–51, was a classic virgin-soil epidemic; mutation had just created the pulmonary version of the bacillus *Yersinia pestis.* But even then the disease killed perhaps a third of its victims. The Indians in De Soto's path, if researchers are correct, endured losses that were anomalously greater. How could this be true? the skeptics ask.

Consider, too, the Dobynsesque procedure for recovering original population numbers: applying an assumed death rate, usually 95 percent, to the observed population nadir. According to Douglas H. Ubelaker, an anthropologist at the National Museum of Natural History, the population nadir for Indians north of the Río Grande was around 1900, when their numbers fell to about half a million. Assuming a 95 percent death rate (which Ubelaker, a skeptic, does not), the precontact population of North America would have been 10 million. Go up 1 percent to a 96 percent death rate and the figure jumps to 12.5 million—creating more than two million people arithmetically from a tiny increase in mortality rates. At 98 percent, the number bounds to 25 million. Minute changes in baseline assumptions produce wildly different results.

Worse, the figures have enormous margins of error. Rudolph Zambardino, a statistician at North Staffordshire Polytechnic, in England, has pointed out that the lack of direct data forces researchers into salvos of extrapolation. To approximate the population of sixteenth-century Mexico, for example, historians have only the official counts of *casados* (householders) in certain areas. To calculate the total population, they must adjust that number by the estimated average number of people in each home, the estimated number of homes not headed by a *casado* (and thus not counted), the estimated number of *casados* missed by the census takers, and so on. Each one of these factors has a margin of error. Unfortunately, as Zambardino noted, "the errors multiply each other and can escalate rapidly to an unacceptable magnitude." If researchers presented their estimates with the proper error bounds, he said, they would see that the spread is far too large to constitute "a meaningful quantitative estimate."

Extraordinary claims require extraordinary evidence, scientists say. Other episodes of mass fatality are abundantly documented: the Black Death in Europe, the post-collectivization famine in the Soviet Union, even the traffic in African slaves. Much less data support the notion that Old World bacteria and viruses turned the New World into an abattoir.* Such evidence as can be found lies scribbled in the margins of European accounts—it is, as Crosby admitted, "no better than impressionistic."

"Most of the arguments for the very large numbers have been theoretical," Ubelaker told me. "But when you try to marry the theoretical arguments to the data that are available on individual groups in different regions, it's hard to find support for those numbers." Archaeologists, he said, keep searching for the settlements in which those millions of people supposedly lived. "As more and more excavation is done, one would expect to see more evidence for [dense populations] than has thus far emerged." Dean R. Snow, of Pennsylvania State, repeatedly examined precontact sites in eastern New York and found "no support for the notion that ubiquitous pandemics swept the region." In the skeptics' view, Dobyns, and other High Counters (as proponents of large pre-Columbian numbers have been called) are like people who discover an empty bank account and claim from its very emptiness that it once contained millions of dollars. Historians who project large Indian populations, Low Counter critics say, are committing the intellectual sin of arguing from silence.

Given these convincing rebuttals, why have the majority of researchers nonetheless become High Counters? In arguing that Indians died at anomalously high rates from European diseases, are researchers claiming that they were somehow uniquely vulnerable? Why hypothesize the existence of vast, super-deadly pandemics that seem unlike anything else in the historical record? The speed and scale of the projected losses "boggle the mind," observed Colin G. Calloway, a historian at Dartmouth—one reason, he suggested, that researchers were so long reluctant to accept them. Indeed, how *can* one understand losses of such unparalleled scope? And if the European entrance into the Americas five centuries ago was responsible for them, what moral reverberations does this have today?

---

*Just one major disease, syphilis, is believed to have spread the other way, from the Americas to Europe, though this has long been controversial. See Appendix C, "The Syphilis Exception."

THE GENETICS OF VULNERABILITY

In August 1967 a missionary's two-year-old daughter came down with measles in a village on the Toototobi River in Brazil, near the border with Venezuela. She and her family had just returned from the Amazonian city of Manaus and had been checked and cleared by Brazilian doctors before departure. Nonetheless the distinctive spots of measles emerged a few days after the family's arrival on the Toototobi. The village, like many others in the region, was populated mainly by Yanomami Indians, a forest society on the Brazil-Venezuela border that is among the least Westernized on earth. They had never before encountered the measles virus. More than 150 Yanomami were in the village at the time. Most or all caught the disease. Seventeen died despite the horrified missionaries' best efforts. And the virus escaped and spread throughout the Yanomami heartland, carried by people who did not know they had been exposed.

Partly by happenstance, the U.S. geneticist James Neel and the U.S. anthropologist Napoleon Chagnon flew into Yanomami country in the midst of the epidemic. Neel, who had long been worried about measles, was carrying several thousand doses of vaccine. Alas, the disease had preceded them. They frantically tried to create an epidemiological "firebreak" by vaccinating ahead of the disease. Despite their efforts, the affected villages had a mean death rate of 8.8 percent. Almost one out of ten people died from a sickness that in Western societies was just a childhood annoyance.

Later Neel concluded that the high death rate was in part due to grief and despair, rather than the virus itself. Still, the huge toll was historically unprecedented. The implication, implausible at first glance, was that Indians in their virgin-soil state were more vulnerable to European diseases than virgin-soil Europeans would have been. Perhaps surprisingly, there is some scientific evidence that Native Americans *were* for genetic reasons unusually susceptible to foreign microbes and viruses—one reason that researchers believe that pandemics of Dobynsian scale and lethality could have occurred.

Here I must make a distinction between two types of susceptibility. The first is the lack of acquired immunity—immunity gained from a previous exposure to a pathogen. People who have never had chicken pox are readily infected by the virus. After they come down with the disease, their immune system trains itself, so to speak, to fight off the virus, and they never catch it again, no matter how often they are exposed. Most Europeans of the day had been exposed to smallpox as children, and those who didn't die were immune. Smallpox and other European diseases didn't exist in the Americas, and so every Indian was susceptible to them in this way.

In addition to having no acquired immunity (the first kind of vulnerability), the inhabitants of the Americas had immune systems that some researchers believe were much more restricted than European immune systems. If these scientists are correct, Indians as a group had less innate ability to defend themselves against epidemic disease (the second kind of vulnerability). The combination was devastating.

The second type of vulnerability stems from a quirk of history. Archaeologists dispute the timing and manner of Indians' arrival in the Americas, but almost all researchers believe that the initial number of newcomers must have been small. Their gene pool was correspondingly restricted, which meant that Indian biochemistry was and is unusually homogeneous. More than nine out of ten Native Americans—and almost all South American Indians—have type O blood, for example, whereas Europeans are more evenly split between types O and A.

Evolutionarily speaking, genetic homogeneity by itself is neither good nor bad. It can be beneficial if it means that a population lacks deleterious genes. In 1491, the Americas were apparently free or almost free of cystic fibrosis, Huntington's chorea, newborn anemia, schizophrenia, asthma, and (possibly) juvenile diabetes, all of which have some genetic component. Here a limited gene pool may have spared Indians great suffering.

Genetic homogeneity can be problematic, too. In the 1960s and 1970s Francis L. Black, a virologist at Yale, conducted safety and efficacy tests among South American Indians of a new, improved measles vaccine. During the tests he drew blood samples from the people he vaccinated, which he later examined in the laboratory. When I telephoned Black, he told me that the results were "thought-provoking." Every individual person's immune system responded robustly to the vaccine. But the native population as a whole had a "very limited spectrum of responses." And that, he said, "could be a real problem in the right circumstances." For Indians, those circumstances arrived with Columbus.

Black was speaking of human leukocyte antigens (HLAs), molecules inside most human cells that are key to one of the body's two main means of defense. Cells of all sorts are commonly likened to biochemical factories, busy ferments in which dozens of mechanisms are working away in complex sequences that are half Rube Goldberg, half ballet. Like well-run factories, cells are thrifty; part of the cellular machinery chops up and reuses anything that is floating around inside, including bits of the cell and foreign invaders such as viruses. Not all of the cut-up pieces are recycled. Some are passed on to HLAs, special molecules that transport the snippets to the surface of the cell.

Outside, prowling, are white blood cells—leukocytes, to researchers. Like minute scouts inspecting potential battle zones, leukocytes constantly scan cell walls for the little bits of stuff that HLAs have carried there, trying to spot anything that doesn't belong. When a leukocyte spots an anomaly—a bit of virus, say—it destroys the infected or contaminated cell immediately. Which means that unless an HLA lugs an invading virus to where the leukocyte can notice it, that part of the immune system cannot know it exists, let alone attack it.

HLAs carry their burdens to the surface by fitting them into a kind of slot. If the snippet doesn't fit into the slot, the HLA can't transport it, and the rest of the immune system won't be able to "see" it. All people have multiple types of HLA, which means that they can bring almost every potential problem to the attention of their leukocytes. Not *every* problem, though. No matter what his or her genetic endowment, no one person's immune system has enough different HLAs to identify every strain of every virus. Some things will always escape notice. Imagine someone sneezing in a crowded elevator, releasing into the air ten variants of a rhinovirus, the kind of virus that causes the common cold. (Viruses mutate quickly and are commonly present in the body in multiple forms, each slightly different from the others.) For simplicity's sake, suppose that the other elevator passengers inhale all ten versions of the virus. One man is lucky: he happens to have HLAs that can lock onto and carry pieces of all ten variants to the cell surface. Because his white blood cells can identify and destroy the infected cells, this man doesn't get sick. Not so lucky is the woman next to him: she has a different set of HLAs, which are able to pick up and transport only eight of the ten varieties. The other two varieties escape the notice of her leukocytes and go on to give her a howling cold (eventually other immune mechanisms kick in and she recovers). These disparate outcomes illustrate the importance to a population of having multiple HLA profiles; one person's HLAs may miss a particular bug, but another person may be equipped to combat it, and the population as a whole survives.

Most human groups are a scattershot mix of HLA profiles, which means that almost always some people in the group will not get sick when exposed to a particular pathogen. Indeed, if laboratory mice have too much HLA diversity, Black told me, researchers can't use them to observe the progress of an infectious disease. "You get messy results—they don't all get sick." The opposite is true as well, he said. People with similar HLA profiles fall victim to the same diseases in the same way.

In the 1990s Black reviewed thirty-six studies of South American Indians. Not to his surprise, he discovered that overall Indians have fewer HLA types than populations from Europe, Asia, and Africa. European populations have at least thirty-five main HLA classes, whereas Indian groups have no more than seventeen. In addition, Native American HLA profiles are dominated by an unusually small number of types. About one third of South American Indians, Black discovered, have identical or near-identical HLA profiles; for Africans the figure is one in two hundred. In South America, he estimated, the minimum probability that a pathogen in one host will next encounter a host with a similar immune spectrum is about 28 percent; in Europe, the chance is less than 2 percent. As a result, Black argued, "people of the New World are unusually susceptible to diseases of the Old."*

Actually, some Old World populations were just as vulnerable as Native Americans to those diseases, and likely for the same reason. Indians' closest genetic relatives are indigenous Siberians. They did not come into substantial contact with Europeans until the sixteenth century, when Russian fur merchants overturned their governments, established military outposts throughout the region, and demanded furs in tribute. In the train of the Russian fur market came Russian diseases, notably smallpox.

The parallels with the Indian experience are striking. In 1768 the virus struck Siberia's Pacific coast, apparently for the first time. "No one knows how many have survived," confessed the governor of Irkutsk, the Russian base on Lake Baikal, apparently because officials were afraid to travel to the affected area. A decade later, in 1779, the round-the-globe expedition of Captain James Cook reached Kamchatka, the long peninsula on the Pacific coast. The shoreline, the British discovered, was a cemetery. "We every where met with the Ruins of large Villages with no Traces left of them but the Foundation of the Houses," lamented David Samwell, the ship's surgeon. "The Russians told us that [the villages] were destroyed by the small Pox." The explorer Martin Sauer, who visited Kamchatka five years after Cook's expedition, discovered that the Russian government had at last ventured into the former epidemic zone. Scarcely one thousand natives remained on the peninsula, according to official figures; the disease had claimed more than five thousand lives. The tally cannot be taken as exact, but the fact remains: a single epidemic killed more than three of every four indigenous Siberians in that area.

After a few such experiences, the natives tried to fight back. "As soon as [indigenous Siberians] learn that smallpox or other contagious diseases are in

*Because the point is persistently misunderstood, it bears repeating that Indians' relative genetic homogeneity does *not* imply genetic inferiority. Even a champion of Indians like historian Francis Jennings got this wrong: "The Europeans' capacity to resist certain diseases," he wrote in his polemical *Invasion of America*, "made them superior, in the pure Darwinian sense, to the Indians." No: Spaniards simply represented a wider genetic array. Asserting their superiority is like saying that the motley mob at a football game is somehow intrinsically superior to the closely related attendees of a family reunion.

town," the political exile Heinrich von Füch wrote, "they set up sentries along all the roads, armed with bows and arrows, and they will not allow anyone to come into their settlements from town. Likewise, they will not accept Russian flour or other gifts, lest these be contaminated with small-pox." Their efforts were in vain. Despite extreme precautions, disease cut down native Siberians again and again.

After learning about this sad history I again telephoned Francis Black. Being genetically determined, Indian HLA homogeneity cannot be changed (except by intermarriage with non-Indians). Did that mean that the epidemics were unavoidable? I asked. Suppose that the peoples of the Americas had, in some parallel world, understood the concept of contagion and been prepared to act on it. Could the mass death have been averted?

"There have been lots of cases where individual towns kept out epidemics," Black said. During plague episodes, "medieval cities would barricade themselves behind their walls and kill people who tried to come in. But whole countries—that's much harder. England has kept out rabies. That's the biggest success story that comes to mind, offhand. But rabies is primarily an animal disease, which helps, because you only have to watch the ports—you don't have many undocumented aliens sneaking in with sick dogs. And rabies is not highly contagious, so even if it slips through it is unlikely to spread."

He stopped speaking for long enough that I asked him if he was still on the line.

"I'm trying to imagine how you would do it," he said. "If Indians in Florida let in sick people, the effects could reach all the way up to here in Connecticut. So all these different groups would have had to coordinate the blockade together. And they'd have to do it for centuries—four hundred years—until the invention of vaccines. Naturally they'd want to trade, furs for knives, that kind of thing. But the trade would have to be conducted in antiseptic conditions."

The Abenaki sent goods to Verrazzano on a rope strung from ship to shore, I said.

"You'd have to have the entire hemisphere doing that. And the Europeans would presumably have to cooperate, or most of them, anyway. I can't imagine that happening, actually. Any of it."

Did that mean the epidemics were inevitable and there was nothing to be done?

The authorities, he replied, could "try to maintain isolation, as I was saying. But that ends up being paternalistic and ineffective. Or they can endorse marriage and procreation with outsiders, which risks destroying the society they supposedly are trying to preserve. I'm not sure what I'd recommend.

Except getting these communities some decent health care, which they almost never have."

Except for death, he went on, nothing in medicine is *inevitable*. "But I don't see how it [waves of epidemics from European diseases] could have been prevented for very long. That's a terrible thought. But I've been working with highly contagious diseases for forty years, and I can tell you that in the long run it is almost impossible to keep them out."*

"OUR EYES WERE APPALLED WITH TERROR"

A second reason historians believe that epidemics tore through Native American communities before Europeans arrived is that epidemics also did it *after* Europeans arrived. In her book *Pox Americana* (2001), the Duke University historian Elizabeth Fenn meticulously pieced together evidence that the Western Hemisphere was visited by two smallpox pandemics shortly before and during the Revolutionary War. The smaller of the two apparently began outside Boston in early 1774 and lurked in the area for the next several years like a sniper, picking off victims at the rate of ten to thirty a day. In Boston the Declaration of Independence was overshadowed by the previous day's proclamation of a citywide campaign of inoculation (an early, risky form of vaccination in which people deliberately infected themselves with a mild dose of smallpox to produce immunity).

Even as it besieged Boston, the virus also spread down the eastern seaboard, laying waste as far as Georgia. It wreaked havoc on the Tsalagi (the group often called the Cherokee, which is a mildly insulting name coined by their enemies, the Creek confederation) and the Haudenosaunee (the indigenous name for the six nations that made up what Europeans called the Iro-

---

*In 2004 two U.S. anthropologists and a Venezuelan medical researcher proposed that Native American susceptibility to infectious disease might have a *second* cause: helper-T cells, which like HLAs help the immune system recognize foreign objects. To simplify considerably, helper-T cells occur in two main types, one that targets microorganisms and one that targets parasites. The body cannot sustain large numbers of both, and hence adult immune systems tend to be skewed toward one or the other, usually depending on whether as children they were more often exposed to microorganisms or parasites. Indians have historically been burdened by flukes, tapeworms, and nematodes, so they have long had majorities of parasite-fighting helper-T cells. Europeans, who grew up in germ-filled environments, usually lean the other way. As a result, the three researchers suggested, adult Indians were—and possibly still are—more vulnerable to infectious diseases than adult Europeans. Conversely, Europeans would be comparatively more vulnerable to parasites. If further research supports this hypothesis, preventing childhood parasite infections might allow Indian immune systems to orientate themselves toward bacteria and viruses, possibly reducing future deaths.

quois League). Both were important allies of the British, and after the epidemic neither was able to fight the colonists successfully. Smallpox also ruined the British plan to raise an army of slaves and indentured servants by promising them freedom after the war—the disease killed off most of the "Ethiopian regiment" even as it assembled.

An equal-opportunity killer, smallpox ravaged the rebels, too. The virus had been endemic in Europe for centuries, which meant that most Europeans were exposed to it before adulthood. But it was only an occasional, terrible visitor in the Americas, which meant that most adult colonists had not acquired childhood immunity. On an individual level, they were almost as vulnerable as Indians. On a group level, though, they were less genetically homogeneous, which conferred some relative advantage; the virus would sweep through them, but not kill quite so many. Still, so many soldiers in the Continental army fell during the epidemic that revolutionary leaders feared that the disease would bring an end to their revolt. "The small Pox! The small Pox!" John Adams wrote to his wife, Abigail. "What shall We do with it?" His worries were on target: the virus, not the British, stopped the Continental army's drive into Quebec in 1776. In retrospect, Fenn told me, "One of George Washington's most brilliant moves was to inoculate the army against smallpox during the Valley Forge winter of '78." Without inoculation, she said, the smallpox epidemic could easily have handed the colonies back to the British.

Even as the first outbreak faded, Fenn wrote, a second, apparently unrelated epidemic burned through Mexico City. The first cases occurred in August 1779. By year's end perhaps eighteen thousand had died in the city area and the disease was racing through the countryside in every direction. Communications in those days were too poor to permit us to document a transmission chain, but records show smallpox flaring in separate explosions to the south like a chain of firecrackers: Guatemala (1780–81), Colombia (1781–83), Ecuador (1783). Was the virus retracing a journey to Tawantinsuyu it had taken before? "It seems likely," decided Calloway, the Dartmouth historian. Fenn tried to trace the virus as it went north. Like Dobyns, she examined parish burial records. In 1780 a telltale surge of mortality traveled north along the heavily traveled road to Santa Fe. From there, smallpox apparently exploded into most of western North America.

First to suffer, or so the sketchy evidence suggests, were the Hopi. Already reeling from a drought, they were blasted by smallpox—as many as nine out of ten may have died. When the Spanish governor tried to recruit the Hopi to live in missions, their leaders told him not to bother: the epidemic soon would expunge them from the earth. As if drought and conta-

gion were not enough, the Hopi were constantly under attack by the Nermernuh (or Nemene), a fluid collection of hunting bands known today as the
Comanche (the name, awarded by an enemy group, means "people who
fight us all the time"). Originally based north of Santa Fe, the Nermernuh
were on their way to dominating the southern plains; they had driven away
their Apache and Hopi rivals with trip-hammer ambushes and deadly incursions and were bent on doing the same to any European colonists who ventured in. In 1781 the raiding abruptly stopped. Silence for eighteen months.
Was the ceasefire due to Mexico City smallpox that had been transmitted by
the Hopi? Four years afterward, a traveler noted in his diary that the Nermernuh lived in fear of disease because they had been recently struck by
smallpox—tenuous but suggestive evidence.

What is certain is that both Hopi and Nermernuh were part of a network
of exchange that had hummed with vitality since ancient times and had
recently grown more intense with the arrival of horses, which sped up communication. Smallpox raced along the network through the Great Plains and
the Rocky Mountains, ricocheting among the Mandans, Hidatsas, Ojibwes,
Crows, Blackfoot, and Shoshone, a helter-skelter progress in which a virus
leapfrogged from central Mexico to the shore of Hudson Bay in less than two
years. Indians in the northern Great Plains kept "winter counts," oral
chronologies of the most important events in each year. Often the counts
were accompanied by a spiraling sequence of drawings on a hide, with each
year summarized by a drawing as an aide-mémoire. In several Lakota (Sioux)
counts 1780–81 was bleakly summed as the year of Smallpox Used Them Up;
and the Lakota were not the only ones affected.

In 1781 a company of Blackfoot stumbled across a Shoshone camp at
dawn near the Red Deer River in Alberta. The Blackfoot were a tightly organized confederation of groups that inhabited the plains between the Missouri and Saskatchewan Rivers. Equipped with guns and horses from French
traders, they had pushed their southern neighbors, the Shoshone—left at a
disadvantage because they had no access to the French and their goods, and
the Spanish, whom they did have access to, tried to block Indian access to
weapons—from the plains into the mountains of what are now Wyoming
and Colorado. When the Shoshone finally obtained guns—they traded with
their linguistic cousins, the Nermernuh, who took the weapons as booty
from defeated Spaniards—open warfare broke out. In this bellicose context,
the Blackfoot party knew exactly what to do when it happened upon a slum-
bering Shoshone encampment. With "sharp flat daggers and knives," one of
the raiders later remembered, they silently sliced open the Shoshone tents
"and entered for the fight; but our war whoops instantly stopt, our eyes were

appalled with terror; there was no one to fight with but the dead and the dying, each a mass of corruption." The Blackfoot did not touch the bodies, but were infected anyway. When the company returned home, the raider lamented, smallpox "spread from one tent to another as if the Bad Spirit carried it."

According to Fenn, "the great preponderance of the evidence" indicates that the Shoshone also transmitted smallpox down the Columbia River into the Pacific Northwest. Calloway suggests the Crow as a plausible alternative. Whoever passed on the virus, its effects were still visible a decade later in 1792, when the British navigator George Vancouver led the first European expedition to survey Puget Sound. Like Cook's crew in Kamchatka, he found a charnel house: deserted villages, abandoned fishing boats, human remains "promiscuously scattered about the beach, in great numbers." Everything they saw suggested "that at no very remote period this country had been far more populous than at present." The few suffering survivors, noted Second Lieutenant Peter Puget, were "most terribly pitted . . . indeed many have lost their Eyes."

Europeans were well versed in the brutal logic of quarantine. When plague appeared, they boarded up houses and fled to the countryside. By contrast, the historian Neal Salisbury observed, family and friends in Indian New England gathered at the sufferer's bedside to wait out the illness, a practice that "could only have served to spread the disease more rapidly." Even the idea of contagion itself was novel. "We had no belief that one Man could give [a disease] to another," the Blackfoot raider remembered, "any more than a wounded Man could give his wound to another." Because they knew of no protective measures, the toll was even higher than it would have been.

Living in the era of antibiotics, we find it difficult to imagine the simultaneous deaths of siblings, parents, relatives, and friends. As if by a flash of grim light, Indian villages became societies of widows, widowers, and orphans; parents lost their children, and children were suddenly alone. Rare is the human spirit that remains buoyant in a holocaust. "My people have been so unhappy for so long they wish to *disincrease,* rather than to multiply," a Paiute woman wrote in 1883. A Lakota winter count memorialized the year 1784 with a stark image: a pox-scarred man, alone in a tipi, shooting himself.

Disease not only shattered the family bonds that were the underlying foundation of Indian societies, it wiped out the political superstructure at the top. King Liholiho Kamehameha II and Queen Kamamalu of Hawai'i visited Great Britain on a diplomatic mission in 1824. While staying in a posh London hotel and attending the theater in the English king's own box, the royal couple and most of the rest of their party came down with measles. It killed the queen on July 8. The grieving king died six days later, at the age of twenty-seven. The death of the royal couple ushered in a time of social chaos. It was as catastrophic for Hawai'i as the death of Wayna Qhapaq for Tawantinsuyu.

A particularly poignant loss occurred in the summer of 1701, when the leaders of forty native nations convened in Montreal to negotiate an end to decades of war among themselves and the French. Death stalked the congress in the form of influenza. By then the Indians of the Northeast knew such diseases all too well: sickness had carried off so many members of the Haudenosaunee that the alliance was forced to replenish itself by adopting abductees and prisoners of war. At the time of the conference at least a quarter of the Haudenosaunee were former captives. At great personal risk, many Indian leaders attended the conference even after they knew that influenza was in Montreal. Dozens died. Among them was the Huron leader Kondiaronk, a famed orator who had, more than any other, convened the gathering as a last-ditch effort to avoid internecine conflict. His body was placed on a bed of beaver pelts, covered by a scarlet cloth, and surrounded by a copper pot, a rifle, and a sword. In their diversity, the objects symbolized the peaceful mixing of cultures that Kondiaronk hoped lay in the future.

Nobody knows how many died during the pandemics of the 1770s and 1780s, but even if one had a number it wouldn't begin to tally the impact. Disease turned whole societies to ash. Six Cree groups in western Canada disappeared after 1781; the Blackfoot nation, blasted by smallpox, sent peace emissaries to Shoshone bands, only to find that all had vanished. "The country to the south was empty and silent," Calloway wrote. So broken were the Omaha by disease that according to tradition they launched a deliberately suicidal attack against their enemies. Those who did not die quit their villages and became homeless wanderers.

Cultures are like books, the anthropologist Claude Lévi-Strauss once remarked, each a volume in the great library of humankind. In the sixteenth century, more books were burned than ever before or since. How many Homers vanished? How many Hesiods? What great works of painting, sculpture, architecture, and music vanished or never were created? Languages, prayers, dreams, habits, and hopes—all gone. And not just once, but over and over again. In our antibiotic era, how can we imagine what it means to have entire ways of life hiss away like steam? How can one assay the total impact of the unprecedented calamity that gave rise to the world we live in? It seems important to try. I would submit that the best way to come near to encompassing the scale and kind of the loss, and its causes, is to look at the single case where the intellectual life of a Native American society is almost as well documented as its destruction.

FLOWERS AND SONG

In 1524, according to colonial accounts, an extraordinary face-off took place in one of the great buildings of Tenochtitlán, capital of the Triple Alliance—the Aztec empire, as it is better known—which Hernán Cortés had conquered three years before.* Facing each other across a room, two delegations of elite clerics battled over the nature of God. On one side were twelve eminent Franciscan monks, who had traveled from Europe in a mission authorized by Pope Hadrian VI. On the other were twelve high priests from the Triple Alliance, men who had wielded immense spiritual and political power until Cortés shuttered the grand temples and brought down the clerisy. Although the pope in Rome had authorized the friars' mission, all twelve were Spanish, because Spain had conquered the empire, and because Spain, which had spent centuries extracting itself from the rule of African Muslims, had experience with powerful alien ideologies. Analogously, the priests of the Triple Alliance were probably all Mexica. The Mexica were the dominant partner in the Alliance, and they had founded and populated Tenochtitlán, the empire's biggest city.

The Franciscans' mission had begun with a request by Cortés. Cortés believed that the military conquest of the Alliance had to be accompanied and justified by an equivalent spiritual conquest. The Indians, he said, must be led to salvation. And he asked King Charles V of Spain for some priests to do the job. In turn the king turned to the pope for his blessing and advice. Cortés did not want "bishops and pampered prelates," wrote historian William H. Prescott, "who too often squandered the substance of the Church in riotous living, but . . . men of unblemished purity of life, nourished with the learning of the cloister, [who] counted all personal sacrifices as little in the cause to which they were devoted."

Led by the intellectual Martín de Valencia, a man so dedicated to ascetic faith that he ended his days as a hermit in the Mexican desert, the friars intended to guide Spain's new subjects along the exhilarating path to Christendom. The monks understood that the Mexica already *had* a church—a false church intended to snare their souls for the devil, but a church nonethe-

*Historians increasingly shy away from the term "Aztec," because the nineteenth-century naturalist Alexander von Humboldt coined it in a misapprehension. Humboldt's "Aztecs" were actually the people of three nations, the members of the Triple Alliance.

less. And they knew that the Indians were too numerous to be reached by even the most zealous missionaries. Valencia's plan was conversion by proxy: he and the rest of the twelve would open the eyes of the Indian priesthood to the beauties of the true faith, gaining their adherence by reasoned theological discussion, and then the priests would fan out and spread the Gospel in their native tongue.

The sole record of the discussions between the monks and the Mexica was compiled four decades later by another Franciscan, Bernardino de Sahagún. Sahagún knew ten of the twelve Spaniards at the meeting, interviewed four of the Mexica priests, and filled in gaps by extrapolating from similar theological discussions in which he had participated. Written in dialogue verse, an *opera seria* exchange of long recitatives, his reconstruction does not individually identify the speakers—perhaps, some historians believe, because the great meeting did not actually take place, Sahagún's account being a distillation of many smaller encounters. Only part of the original manuscript survives, written in Nahuatl, the Mexica language, which Sahagún learned to speak fluently. Still, what remains is enough to indicate how the Mexica viewed their position vis-à-vis the Spanish: defeated, but not unequal.

In Sahagún's reconstruction, the Franciscans speak first, their interpreters struggling to make European concepts clear in Nahuatl verse, the language of high discourse. The monks explain that they have been sent by "the one who on the earth is the greater speaker of divine things," the pope, to bring the "venerable word / of the One Sole True God" to New Spain. By worshipping at false altars, the friars say, "you cause Him an injured heart, / by which you live in His anger, His ire." So infuriated was the Christian God by the Indians' worship of idols and demons that he sent out "the Spaniards, / . . . those who afflicted you with tormenting sorrow, / by which you were punished / so that you ceased / these not few injuries to His precious heart." The Triple Alliance was subjugated, in other words, because its people had failed to recognize the One True God. By accepting the Bible, the priests explain, the Mexica "will be able to cool the heart / of He by Whom All Live, / so He will not completely destroy you."

The Mexica respond immediately. Not wanting to join Christendom, they also know that they cannot prevail in a direct confrontation with their conquerors. Shrewdly, they try to shift the terms of the argument to more congenial rhetorical ground—an approach that will force the friars to treat them as equals. "What now, immediately, will we say?" the lead cleric asks. "We are those who shelter the people, / We are mothers to the people, fathers to the people." Translation: We priests are in the same business as you

Franciscans. We are high-ranking clerics, elite intellectuals, just like you. And just like you we have a function: providing comfort and meaning to the common folk. To disavow their faith, the Mexica say, would tear apart their lives. For this reason and others, the priests explain, "we cannot yet agree to [Christianity] ourselves / We do not yet make it true for ourselves." Behind the priests' refusal is an implied request: You know what it is like to be in our shoes. You carry the same responsibilities. As one group of highly placed religious functionaries to another, don't do this to us!

Having expected childlike natives, empty vessels waiting to be filled by the Word, the Franciscans instead found themselves fencing with skilled rhetoricians, proud of their intellectual traditions. In the end the friars resorted to a crude but effective argument: the Indians had to pledge fealty to the Christian god, because their own "gods were not powerful enough to liberate them from the hands of the Spaniards." In a sober ceremony, the Mexica abjured their old religion and embraced Christianity.

For more than a decade, Sahagún and other religious authorities regarded the conversion as a triumph. He initially began his reconstruction of the debate to commemorate it. But he never published the manuscript, because he was slowly coming to believe that the Church's efforts in New Spain had been a failure. Despite lip-service devotion to the Gospel, the Mexica remained outside Christendom, as do some of their descendants to this day.

Sahagún is known as the first American anthropologist, for he labored for decades to understand the Indians he sought to convert. With other missionaries, he amassed an archive on the Mexica and their neighbors—dynastic histories, dictionaries of native languages, descriptions of customs, collections of poetry and drama, galleries of paintings and sculpture—unequaled by that on any other Indian group, even the Inka. From it emerges, in almost full detail, a group portrait of a kind that is usually obscured by loss.

Masters of power politics, engineers of genius, the Mexica were also upstarts and pretenders, arrivistes who falsely claimed a brilliant line of descent. They are best known for assembling the greatest empire ever seen in Mesoamerica. But their finest accomplishment may have been the creation of a remarkable intellectual tradition, one that like the Greeks began with the questions of lyric poets and then went on to distinct schools of inquiry associated with elite academies.

Mexica histories begin by relating their migration to the Basin of Mexico. Fringed by mountains, the basin was about a hundred miles long from north to south and perhaps half that size from east to west. At its center was Lake Texcoco, a fifty-mile-long volcanic lake with exceptionally clear, clean water. Around the time of Christ, a small village on its northeast periphery named Teotihuacán emerged as a military power. During the next four centuries its realm steadily expanded until it ruled directly over much of central Mexico and indirectly, through puppet governments, as far south as Guatemala. Its eponymous capital then may have had 200,000 inhabitants, enormous at the time; its ruins, an hour by bus from Mexico City, are among the few remnants of the ancient world that today don't seem *small*.

The city was organized around the Avenue of the Dead, a miles-long, north-south boulevard that cut straight as an ax stroke across the landscape. From the northern end of the avenue rose the Pyramids of the Sun and Moon, each as big as the biggest Egyptian pyramids. To their south sprawled the Temple of the Feathered Serpent, where the empire's rulers, as ruthless and preoccupied with national glory as so many Bismarcks, considered what to do with their soldiers. Despite the empire's fame and power, its history is still little known; archaeologists do not know what language its people spoke, or even its proper name ("Teotihuacán" was coined centuries later). It had writing of some kind, though it seems not to have been used much; in any case the script has not been deciphered.

Teotihuacán fell in the eighth century for reasons yet unknown, but left an enduring mark in central Mexico. Three hundred years afterward the rising Toltec styled themselves its heirs. They, too, built an empire, which fell amid internal dissension in about 1200 A.D. The collapse of the Toltec created an opening in the warm, fertile basin. Into it moved half a dozen groups from the northern and western desert, the Mexica among them.

The Mexica were an unlikely choice for heir to the imperial tradition of Teotihuacán and the Toltecs. Poor and unsophisticated, they probably came to Lake Texcoco about 1250 A.D. and became vassals of more important groups. Eventually some enemies drove them away from the fertile shore. The Mexica fled to a swampy, uninhabited island. According to an account by Hernando Álvaro Tezozómoc, grandson of the last Mexica ruler, the refugees stumbled about the island for days, looking for food and a place to settle, until one of the priests had a vision in a dream. In the dream, the Mexica's patron deity instructed his people to look in the swamp for a cactus. Standing on the cactus, the god promised, "you shall see an eagle . . . warming itself in the sun."

> And [the next morning], once more, they went in among the
>   rushes, in among the reeds, to the edge of the spring.
> And when they came out into the reeds,
> There at the edge of the spring was the *tenochtli* [a fruit-
>   bearing cactus],
> And they saw an eagle on the *tenochtli,* perched on it,
>   standing on it.

At about 200 feet tall and 700 feet on a side, the Pyramid of the Sun in Teotihuacán is the world's third-largest pyramid. It was built in stages in the second and third centuries A.D. atop a deep, 300-foot cave created by a lava tube that may have represented the place where humankind emerged onto the earth. The pyramid and the rest of the city are oriented on a rectilinear grid 15° 25″ from true north, a direction that may have aligned with the cave mouth.

It was eating something, it was feeding,
It was pecking at what it was eating.
And when the eagle saw the Mexica, he bowed his head low.
Its nest, its pallet, was of every kind of precious feather—
Of lovely cotinga feathers, roseate spoonbill feathers, quetzal
    feathers.
And they also saw strewn about the heads of sundry birds,
The heads of precious birds strung together,
And some birds' feet and bones.

And the god called out to them, he said to them,
"Oh Mexica, it shall be there!"
(But the Mexica did not see who spoke.)
It was for this reason that they call it Tenochtitlán.
And the Mexica wept, they said,
"Oh happy, oh blessed are we!
We have beheld the city that shall be ours!
Let us go now, let us rest. . . ."
This was in the year . . . 1325.

In this way came into being Tenochtitlán, sole rival, in size and opulence, to Teotihuacán.

Among the Mexica, a council of clan elders chose the overall ruler. Or, rather, chose the overall *rulers*—the Mexica divided authority between a *tlatoani* (literally, "speaker"), a diplomatic and military commander who controlled relations with other groups, and a *cihuacoatl* (literally, "female serpent"), who supervised internal affairs. For a century after Tenochtitlán's birth, the *tlatoani*'s position was unenviable. The Mexica were subordinated by a nearby city-state on the shore, and the *tlatoani* was forced to send Mexica men as conscripts for its wars. Only in 1428 did Itzacóatl, a newly selected *tlatoani*, ally with two other small vassal states to overthrow their mutual overlords. In victory, the three groups officially formed the Triple Alliance, with the Mexica the most powerful leg of the tripod. Like Tawantinsuyu, the empire grew rapidly. Its presiding genius was not Itzacóatl, though, but his nephew Tlacaélel (1398–1480).

During his long life Tlacaélel was twice offered the position of *tlatoani* but turned it down both times. Preferring the less glorious and supposedly less influential position of *cihuacoatl,* head of internal affairs, he ruled from behind the scenes, dominating the Alliance for more than fifty years and utterly reengineering Mexica society. Born to an elite family, Tlacaélel first became known at the age of thirty, when he inspired the Mexica to revolt against their masters, supervised the gestation of the Alliance, and served as Itzacóatl's general during the assault. After the victory he met with Itzacóatl and the Mexica clan leaders. In addition to taking slaves and booty, wartime victors in central Mexico often burned their enemies' codices, the hand-painted picture-texts in which priests recorded their people's histories. Tlacaélel insisted that in addition to destroying the codices of their former oppressors the Mexica should set fire to their *own* codices. His explanation for this idea can only be described as Orwellian: "It is not fitting that our people / Should know these pictures. / Our people, our subjects, will be lost / And our land destroyed, / For these pictures are full of lies." The "lies" were the inconvenient fact that the Mexica past was one of poverty and humiliation. To motivate the people properly, Tlacaélel said, the priesthood should rewrite Mexica history by creating new codices, adding in the great deeds whose lack now seemed embarrassing and adorning their ancestry with ties to the Toltecs and Teotihuacán.

A visionary and patriot, Tlacaélel believed that the Mexica were destined to rule a vast empire. But because ambition succeeds best when disguised by virtue, he wanted to furnish the Alliance with an animating ideology—a manifest destiny, as it were, or *mission civilisatrice.* He came up with a corker: a theogony that transformed the Mexica into keepers of the cosmic order.

At its center was Huitzilopochtli, a martial god who wore a helmet shaped like a hummingbird's head and carried a fire-breathing serpent as a weapon. Huitzilopochtli had long been the Mexica's patron deity. It was he who had entered the Mexica priest's dream to explain where to found Tenochtitlán. After the formation of the Triple Alliance, Tlacaélel "went about persuading the people," as one Mexica historian wrote, that Huitzilopochtli was not a mere tutelary deity, but a divinity essential to the fate of humankind.

At the apex of the celestial hierarchy stood Ométeotl, the omnipresent sustainer of the cosmos, "the Lord of the Close Vicinity" in Nahuatl. In Tlacaélel's vision, Ométeotl had four sons, one of whom was Huitzilopochtli. These four sons had been vying for supremacy since the beginning of time; the history of the universe was mainly a record of their endless struggle. At intervals the brothers would wrestle themselves into a precarious equilibrium, like sumo giants straining motionlessly against each other in the ring, with one brother on top and the other three in a temporary, isometric balance below. In these interregnums of order, Tlacaélel explained, the topmost brother linked himself to the sun, on which all living creatures depend.

In some versions of the story, the brother became the sun; in others, he merely supervised its workings. Either way, life could exist only when one brother held sway and the cosmic battle quieted and the sun was able to shine. But when the balance came apart, as it always did, the brothers would resume their strife. The sun would go dark, sinking the cosmos into an endless, lethal night. Eventually the sons would arrive at a new transitory order and reignite the sun, letting existence begin anew. This apocalyptic cycle had occurred four times before. The Mexica lived during the Fifth Sun, when the sun was identified with Huitzilopochtli.

The sun's role was hellishly difficult, Tlacaélel said. Even when the strife among Ométeotl's sons quieted enough to allow the sun to shine, it still had to battle the stars and moon every day as it rose in the sky—a literal struggle of light against darkness. Each day of sunlight was a victory that must be fought and won again the next day. Because the sun could not hold out forever against its foes, one sixteenth-century Nahuatl account explained, it would one day inevitably lose—there was no getting around it. "In this Sun it shall come to pass / That the earth shall move, / That there shall be famine, / And that we all shall perish." But the calamity could be postponed, at least for a while, if the sun was fortified for its battles with the stars. To gain strength, the sun needed *chalchíhuatl*—the mysterious, ineffable fluid of life-energy. The sacred mission of the Triple Alliance, Tlacaélel proclaimed, was to furnish this vital substance to Huitzilopochtli, who would then use it for the sun, postponing the death of everyone on the planet.

There was but one method for obtaining this life-energy: ritual human sacrifice. To obtain the victims, Tlacaélel said (according to one of Sahagún's contemporaries), the sun needed a "marketplace" where he could "go with his army [that is, the army of the Triple Alliance] to buy victims, men for him to eat. . . . And this will be a good thing, for it will be as if he had his maize cakes hot from the griddle—tortillas from a nearby place, hot and ready to eat whenever he wishes them." Occasionally the victims were slaves and criminals, but mainly they were prisoners of war. In this way the sacred mission of the Triple Alliance became translated into a secular mission: to obtain prisoners to sacrifice for the sun, the Alliance had to take over the world. In Tlacaélel's scheme, imperial conquests were key to "the moral combat against evil," explained Miguel León-Portilla, a Mexican anthropologist who has devoted much of his career to analyzing Mexica thought. "The survival of the universe depended on them."

Human sacrifice is such a charged subject that its practice by the Triple Alliance has inevitably become shrouded in myths. Two are important here. The first is that human sacrifice was never practiced—the many post-conquest accounts of public death-spectacles are all racist lies. It was indeed in the Spanish interest to exaggerate the extent of human sacrifice, because ending what Cortés called this "most horrid and abominable custom" became a post hoc rationale for conquest. But the many vividly depicted ceremonies in Mexica art and writing leave little doubt that it occurred—and on a large scale. (Cortés may well have been correct when he estimated that sacrifice claimed "three or four thousand souls" a year.)

The second myth is that in its penchant for public slaughter the Triple Alliance was fundamentally different from Europe. Criminals beheaded in Palermo, heretics burned alive in Toledo, assassins drawn and quartered in Paris—Europeans flocked to every form of painful death imaginable, free entertainment that drew huge crowds. London, the historian Fernand Braudel tells us, held public executions eight times a year at Tyburn, just north of Hyde Park. (The diplomat Samuel Pepys paid a shilling for a good view of a Tyburn hanging in 1664; watching the victim beg for mercy, he wrote, was a crowd of "at least 12 or 14,000 people.") In most if not all European nations, the bodies were impaled on city walls and strung along highways as warnings. "The corpses dangling from trees whose distant silhouettes stand out against the sky, in so many old paintings, are merely a realistic detail," Braudel observed. "They were part of the landscape." Between 1530 and 1630, according to Cambridge historian V. A. C. Gatrell, England executed seventy-five thousand people. At the time, its population was about three million, perhaps a tenth that of the Mexica empire. Arithmetic suggests that if England had been the size of the Triple Alliance, it would have executed, on average, about 7,500 people per year, roughly twice the number Cortés estimated for the empire. France and Spain were still more bloodthirsty than England, according to Braudel.

In their penchant for ceremonial public slaughter, the Alliance and Europe were more alike than either side grasped. In both places the public death was accompanied by the reading of ritual scripts. And in both the goal was to create a cathartic paroxysm of loyalty to the government—in the Mexica case, by recalling the spiritual justification for the empire; in the European case, to reassert the sovereign's divine power after it had been injured by a criminal act. Most important, neither society should be judged—or in the event judged each other—entirely by its brutality. Who today would want to live in the Greece of Plato and Socrates, with its slavery, constant warfare, institutionalized pederasty, and relentless culling of surplus population? Yet Athens had a coruscating tradition of rhetoric, lyric drama, and philosophy. So did Tenochtitlán and the other cities in the Triple Alliance. In fact, the corpus of writings in classical Nahuatl, the language of the Alliance, is even larger than the corpus of texts in classical Greek.

The Nahuatl word *tlamatini* (literally, "he who knows things") meant something akin to "thinker-teacher"—a philosopher, if you will. The *tlamatini*, who "himself was writing and wisdom," was expected to write and maintain the codices and live in a way that set a moral example. "He puts a mirror before others," the Mexica said. In what may have been the first large-scale compulsory education program in history, every male citizen of the Triple Alliance, no matter what his social class, had to attend one sort of school or another until the age of sixteen. Many *tlamatinime* (the plural form of the word) taught at the elite academies that trained the next generation of priests, teachers, and high administrators.

Like Greek philosophy, the teachings of the *tlamatinime* were only tenuously connected to the official dogma of Tlacaélel. (True, Plato does have Socrates subtly "correct" Homer, because the gods supposedly couldn't have behaved in the immoral way described by the poet. But by and large the Greek pantheon on Mount Olympus plays no role in either Plato or Aristotle.) But the *tlamatinime* shared the religion's sense of the evanescence of existence. "Truly do we live on Earth?" asked a poem or song attributed to Nezahual-cóyotl (1402–72), a founding figure in Mesoamerican thought and the *tlatoani* of Texcoco, one of the other two members of the Triple Alliance. His lyric, among the most famous in the Nahuatl canon, answers its own question:

> Not forever on earth; only a little while here.
> Be it jade, it shatters.

Be it gold, it breaks.
Be it a quetzal feather, it tears apart.
Not forever on earth; only a little while here.

In another verse assigned to Nezahualcóyotl this theme emerged even more baldly:

Like a painting, we will be erased.
Like a flower, we will dry up here on earth.
Like plumed vestments of the precious bird,
That precious bird with the agile neck,
We will come to an end.

Contemplating mortality, thinkers in many cultures have drawn solace from the prospect of life after death. This consolation was denied to the Mexica, who were agonizingly uncertain about what happened to the soul. "Do flowers go to the region of the dead?" Nezahualcóyotl asked. "In the Beyond, are we still dead or do we live?" Many if not most *tlamatinime* saw existence as Nabokov feared: "a brief crack of light between two eternities of darkness."

In Nahuatl rhetoric, things were frequently represented by the unusual device of naming two of their elements—a kind of doubled Homeric epithet. Instead of directly mentioning his body, a poet might refer to "my hand, my foot" (*noma nocxi*), which the savvy listener would know was a synecdoche, in the same way that readers of English know that writers who mention "the crown" are actually talking about the entire monarch, and not just the headgear. Similarly, the poet's speech would be "his word, his breath" (*itlatol ihiyo*). A double-barreled term for "truth" is *neltilitztli tzintliztli,* which means something like "fundamental truth, true basic principle." In Nahuatl, the words almost shimmer with connotation: what was true was well grounded, stable and immutable, enduring above all.

Because we human beings are transitory, our lives as ephemeral as dreams, the *tlamatinime* suggested that immutable truth is by its nature beyond human experience. On the ever-changing earth, wrote León-Portilla, the Mexican anthropologist, "nothing is 'true' in the Nahuatl sense of the word." Time and again, the *tlamatinime* wrestled with this dilemma. How can beings of the moment grasp the perduring? It would be like asking a stone to understand mortality.

According to León-Portilla, one exit from this philosophical blind alley was seen by the fifteenth-century poet Ayocuan Cuetzpaltzin, who described it metaphorically, as poets will, by invoking the *coyolli* bird, known for its bell-like song:

He goes his way singing, offering flowers.
And his words rain down
Like jade and quetzal plumes.
Is this what pleases the Giver of Life?
Is that the only truth on earth?

Ayocuan's remarks cannot be fully understood out of the Nahuatl context, León-Portilla argued. "Flowers and song" was a standard double epithet for poetry, the highest art; "jade and quetzal feathers" was a synecdoche for great value, in the way that Europeans might refer to "gold and silver." The song of the bird, spontaneously produced, stands for aesthetic inspiration. Ayocuan was suggesting, León-Portilla said, that there *is* a time when humankind can touch the enduring truths that underlie our fleeting lives. That time is at the moment of artistic creation. "From whence come the flowers [the artistic creations] that enrapture man?" asks the poet. "The songs that intoxicate, the lovely songs?" And he answers: "Only from His [that is, Ométeotl's] home do they come, from the innermost part of heaven." Through art alone, the Mexica said, can human beings approach the real.

Cut short by Cortés, Mexica philosophy did not have the chance to reach as far as Greek or Chinese philosophy. But surviving testimony intimates that it was well on its way. The stacks of Nahuatl manuscripts in Mexican archives depict the *tlamatinime* meeting to exchange ideas and gossip, as did the Vienna Circle and the French philosophes and the Taisho-period Kyoto school. Their musings of the *tlamatinime* occurred in intellectual neighborhoods frequented by philosophers from Brussels to Beijing, but the mix was entirely the Mexica's own. Voltaire, Locke, Rousseau, and Hobbes never had a chance to speak with these men or even know of their existence—and here, at last, we begin to appreciate the enormity of the calamity, for the distintegration of native America was a loss not just to those societies but to the human enterprise as a whole.

Having grown separately for millennia, the Americas were a boundless sea of novel ideas, dreams, stories, philosophies, religions, moralities, discoveries, and all the other products of the mind. Few things are more sublime or characteristically human than the cross-fertilization of cultures. The simple discovery by Europe of the existence of the Americas caused an intellectual ferment. How much grander would have been the tumult if Indian societies had survived in full splendor!

Here and there we see clues to what might have been. Pacific Northwest Indian artists carved beautiful masks, boxes, bas-reliefs, and totem poles within the dictates of an elaborate aesthetic system based on an ovoid shape that has no name in European languages. British ships in the nineteenth century radically transformed native art by giving the Indians brightly colored paints that unlike native pigments didn't wash off in the rain. Indians incorporated the new pigments into their traditions, expanding them and in the process creating an aesthetic *nouvelle vague.* European surrealists came across this colorful new art in the first years of the twentieth century. As artists will, they stole everything they could, transfiguring the images further. Their interest helped a new generation of indigenous artists to explore new themes.

Now envision this kind of fertile back-and-forth happening in a hundred ways with a hundred cultures—the gifts from four centuries of intellectual exchange. One can hardly imagine anything more valuable. Think of the fruitful impact on Europe and its descendants from contacting Asia. Imagine the effect on these places and people from a *second* Asia. Along with the unparalleled loss of life, that is what vanished when smallpox came ashore.

ASSIGNING BLAME

Weighing loss of such scale, one naturally wants to identify and denounce the responsible party. In the case of the Mexica, the obvious target is Hernán Cortés, who landed near what is now the city of Veracruz on April 22, 1519. An astute politician, Cortés studied the Triple Alliance with a view to dismembering it. The empire, he quickly understood, was anything but unified. Like Tawantinsuyu, it was a patchwork of satrapies rather than a unified state; indeed, several large groups within the Alliance had managed to hang on to their independence despite being surrounded by hostile forces. Although the empire left the original elites of conquered lands in place, it humiliated them. The people, forced to disgorge ever-increasing tribute to Tenochtitlán, were resentful and bitter. Cortés divined the discontent beneath the Alliance's martial display and would later benefit from it.

Marching inland from the sea, the Spanish at first fought repeatedly with Tlaxcala, a confederation of four small kingdoms that had maintained its independence despite repeated Alliance incursions. Thanks to their guns, horses, and steel blades, the foreigners won every battle, even with Tlaxcala's huge numerical advantage. But Cortés's force shrank with every fight. He was on the verge of losing everything when the four Tlaxcala kings abruptly reversed course. Concluding from the results of their battles that they could wipe out the Europeans, though at great cost, the Indian leaders offered what seemed a win-win deal: they would stop attacking Cortés, sparing his

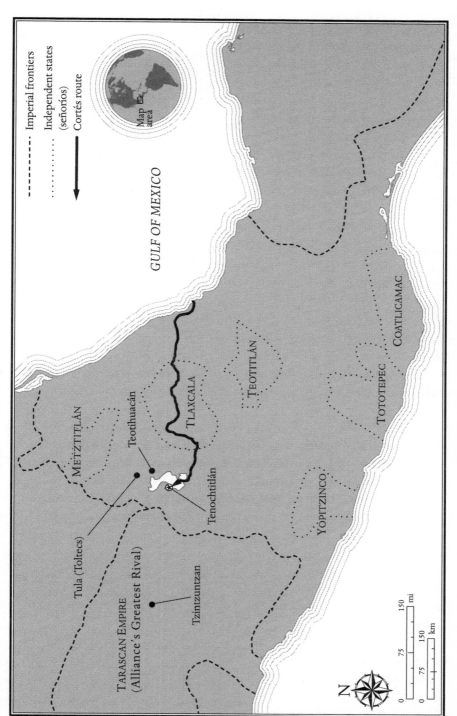

Imperial frontiers
Independent states (señoríos)
Cortés route

Map area

GULF OF MEXICO

TARASCAN EMPIRE
(Alliance's Greatest Rival)

Tzintzuntzan

Tula (Toltecs)

METZTITLÁN

Teotihuacán

Tenochtitlán

TLAXCALA

TEOTITLÁN

YOPITZINCO

TOTOTEPEC

COATLICAMAC

N

0   75   150
km
0   75   150
mi

TRIPLE ALLIANCE, 1519 A.D.

life, the lives of the surviving Spaniards, and those of many Indians, if he
in return would join with Tlaxcala in a united assault on the hated Triple
Alliance. To seal the partnership, one of the four kings—Tlaxcala's main military leader—betrothed his daughter to Pedro de Alvarado, Cortés's second-
in-command. Mounted on their strange, monstrous beasts, the Spanish rode
at the forefront of an army of perhaps twenty thousand Tlaxcalans. In
November 1519, they entered Tenochtitlán, brushing by the objections of the
startled and indecisive *tlatoani,* the famous Motecuhzoma (better known,
inaccurately, as Montezuma).

Tenochtitlán dazzled its invaders—it was bigger than Paris, Europe's
greatest metropolis. The Spaniards gawped like yokels at the wide streets,
ornately carved buildings, and markets bright with goods from hundreds of
miles away. Boats flitted like butterflies around the three grand causeways
that linked Tenochtitlán to the mainland. Long aqueducts conveyed water
from the distant mountains across the lake and into the city. Even more
astounding than the great temples and immense banners and colorful prom-
enades were the botanical gardens—none existed in Europe. The same novelty attended the force of a thousand men that kept the crowded streets
immaculate. (Streets that weren't ankle-deep in sewage! The conquistadors
had never conceived of such a thing.)

And the whole of this wealth and power, Cortés subsequently explained
to the Spanish king, flowed into the hands of Motecuhzoma.

> Can there be anything more magnificent than that this barbarian lord
> should have all the things to be found under the heavens in his domain,
> fashioned in gold and silver and jewel and feathers? And so realistic in
> gold and silver that no smith in the world could have done better? And
> in jewels so fine that it is impossible to imagine with what instruments
> they were cut so perfectly? . . . In Spain there is nothing to compare
> with it.

Dazzled as he was, Cortés was also aware that with a single command Motecuhzoma could order his army "to obliterate all memory of us." The
Spaniards counteracted this threat by inventing a pretext to seize the *tlatoani*
in his own palace, making him first their captive and then their puppet.

In both Europe and Mesoamerica kings ruled by the dispensation of the
heavens. The Mexica reacted to the sacrilegious abduction of their leader with
the same baffled horror with which Europeans later reacted to Cromwell's
execution of Charles I in 1649. Not wanting to act in a way that could result
in Motecuhzoma's death, the Mexica took seven months to mount a coun-

An enormous, opulent city of canals and (mostly) artificial islands in the middle of a great mountain lake, the Mexica capital of Tenochtitlán stunned the conquistadors when they first saw it. This reconstruction, a mural by the artist Miguel Covarrubias, in Mexico City's great archaeology museum, underplays the busyness of the city; eyewitness accounts report that clouds of boats darted around its edges and through its canals.

terattack. Fearing the worst, the debased *tlatoani* made a begging public appearance on behalf of the Spanish. He soon died, either murdered by the Spaniards (according to Mexica accounts) or slain by his own countrymen (as Spanish chronicles tell it). Soon after came the long-delayed assault. Under the leadership of a vigorous new *tlatoani*, Cuitlahuac, the Indians forced the invaders into narrow alleys where horses were of little advantage. Under a pitiless hail of spears, darts, and arrows, Cortés and his men retreated down the long causeways that linked the island city to the mainland. In a single brutal night more than eight hundred Spaniards died—three-fourths of Cortés's force. Although the Alliance destroyed the causeways in front of the Spaniards, the surviving Europeans were able to cross the gaps because they were so choked with the dead that the men could walk on the bodies of their countrymen. Because the Mexica did not view the goal of warfare as wiping out enemies to the last man, they did not hunt down the last Spaniards. A costly mistake: Cortés was among the escapees.

A man of unfathomable determination, Cortés never thought of giving up. He persuaded several other vassal states to join his anti-Alliance alliance with Tlaxcala. Negotiating furiously, he assembled a force of as many as 200,000 men and built thirteen big ships in an audacious plan to assault Tenochtitlán from the water. He followed this plan and ever after has been identified by history as the city's conqueror. But all of his bold resolve would

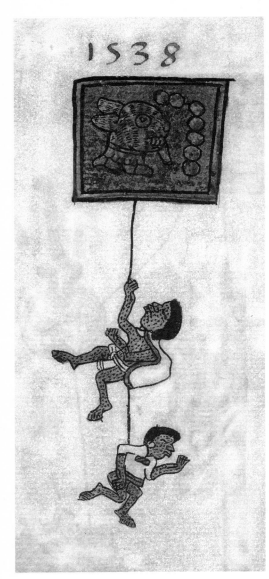

1538

Sixteenth-century Mexica drawings of smallpox, the disease that destroyed the empire by crippling the defenders of Tenochtitlán in the battle against Cortés and his native allies. "An epidemic broke out, a sickness of pustules," begins the account in Bernardino de Sahagún's *General History of the Things of New Spain* (ca. 1575, in James Lockhart's translation). "Large bumps spread on people, some were entirely covered. They spread everywhere, on the face, the head, the chest, etc. . . . [Victims] could no longer walk about, but lay in their dwellings and sleeping places, no longer able to move or stir. They were unable to change position, to stretch out on their sides or face down, or raise their heads. . . . The pustules that covered people caused great desolation; very many people died of them, and many just starved to death; starvation reigned, and no one took care of others any longer." The drawing at left, from a sixteenth-century codex, is a winter-count-like depiction of a year dominated by smallpox; two men lie dying or dead, their bodies spotted with pustules. The drawing below, from the *General History,* shows cries of pain escaping from victims' lips.

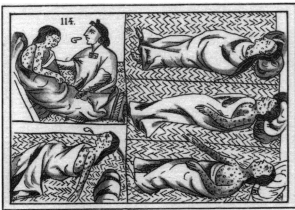

have come to nothing without the vast indigenous army whose leaders believed they could use the Spanish presence to catalyze the destruction of the Triple Alliance. And even this enormous force might not have overcome the empire if while Cortés was building his ships Tenochtitlán had not been swept by smallpox in the same pandemic that later wiped out Tawantinsuyu. Without any apparent volition by Cortés, the great city lost at least a third of its population to the epidemic, including Cuitlahuac.

When Cortés and his Indian allies finally attacked, the Mexica resisted so fiercely despite their weakness that the siege has often been described as the costliest battle in history—casualty estimates range up to 100,000. Absent smallpox, it seems likely that Cortés would have lost. In the event, he was able to take the city only by systematically destroying it. The Alliance capitulated on August 21, 1521. It was the end of an imperial tradition that dated back to Teotihuacán a millennium before.

Cortés was directly responsible for much of the carnage in Tenochtitlán, but the war was only a small part of a larger catastrophe for which blame is harder to assign. When Cortés landed, according to the Berkeley researchers Cook and Borah, 25.2 million people lived in central Mexico, an area of about 200,000 square miles. After Cortés, the population of the entire region collapsed. By 1620–25, it was 730,000, "approximately 3 percent of its size at the time that he first landed." Cook and Borah calculated that the area did not recover its fifteenth-century population until the late 1960s.

From Bartolomé de Las Casas on, Europeans have known that their arrival brought about a catastrophe for Native Americans. "We, Christians, have destroyed so many kingdoms," reflected Pedro Cieza de León, the traveler in postconquest Peru. "For wherever the Spaniards have passed, conquering and discovering, it is as though a fire had gone, destroying everything in its path." And since Las Casas historians, clerics, and political activists have debated whether Europeans and their descendants in the Americas are morally culpable for the enormous Indian losses. Indeed, some writers have employed the loaded term "holocaust" to describe the contact and its aftermath. Following in its train, inevitably, has come an even more potent label: genocide.

Europe's defenders argue that the mass deaths cannot be described as genocide. The epidemics often were not even known to Europeans, still less deliberately caused by them. For that reason, they fall into a different moral class than the Jewish Holocaust, which was a state policy of mass murder. "Very probably the greatest demographic disaster in history, the depopulation of the New World, for all its terror and death, was largely an *unintended* tragedy," wrote Steven Katz in his monumental *Holocaust in Historical Context*. The wave of Indian deaths, in his view, was "a tragedy that occurred

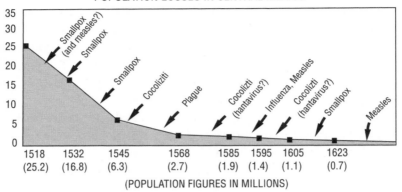

POPULATION LOSSES IN CENTRAL MEXICO

(POPULATION FIGURES IN MILLIONS)

Berkeley researchers Cook and Borah spent decades reconstructing the population of the former Aztec realm in the wake of the Spanish conquest. By combining colonial-era data from many sources, the two men estimated that the number of people in the region fell from 25.2 million in 1518, just before Cortés arrived, to about 700,000 in 1623—a 97 percent drop in little more than a century. (Each marked date is one for which they presented a population estimate.) Using parish records, Mexican demographer Elsa Malvido calculated the sequence of epidemics in the region, portions of which are shown here. Dates are approximate, because epidemics would last several years. The identification of some diseases is uncertain as well; for example, sixteenth-century Spaniards lumped together what today are seen as distinct maladies under the rubric "plague." In addition, native populations were repeatedly struck by "cocoliztli," a disease the Spanish did not know but that scientists have suggested might be a rat-borne hantavirus—spread, in part, by the postconquest collapse of Indian sanitation measures. Both reconstructions are tentative, but the combined picture of catastrophic depopulation has convinced most researchers in the field.

despite the sincere and indisputable desire of the Europeans to keep the Indian population alive."

Katz overstates his case. True, the conquistadors did not want the Indians to die off en masse. But that desire did not stem from humanitarian motives. Instead, the Spanish wanted native peoples to use as a source of forced labor. In fact, the Indian deaths were such a severe financial blow to the colonies that they led, according to Borah, to an "economic depression" that lasted "more than a century." To resupply themselves with labor, the Spaniards began importing slaves from Africa.

Later on, some of the newcomers indeed campaigned in favor of eradicating natives. The poet-physician Oliver Wendell Holmes Sr., for instance, regarded the Indian as but "a sketch in red crayon of a rudimental manhood." To the "problem of his relation to the white race," Holmes said, there was one solution: "extermination." Following such impulses, a few Spanish—and a few French, Portuguese, and British—deliberately spread disease. Many more treated Indians cruelly, murderously so, killing countless thousands. But the pain and death caused from the deliberate epidemics, lethal cruelty, and egregious racism pale in comparison to those caused by the great waves of disease, a means of subjugation that the Europeans could not control and in many cases did not know they had. How can they be morally culpable for it?

Not so fast, say the activists. Europeans may not have known about microbes, but they thoroughly understood infectious disease. Almost 150 years before Columbus set sail, a Tartar army besieged the Genoese city of Kaffa. Then the Black Death visited. To the defenders' joy, their attackers began dying off. But triumph turned to terror when the Tartar khan catapulted the dead bodies of his men over the city walls, deliberately creating an epidemic inside. The Genoese fled Kaffa, leaving it open to the Tartars. But they did not run away fast enough; their ships spread the disease to every port they visited.

Coming from places that had suffered many such experiences, Europeans fully grasped the potential consequences of smallpox. "And what was their collective response to this understanding?" asked Ward Churchill, a professor of ethnic studies at the University of Colorado at Boulder.

> Did they recoil in horror and say, "Wait a minute, we've got to halt the process, or at least slow it down until we can get a handle on how to prevent these effects"? Nope. Their response pretty much across-the-board was to accelerate their rate of arrival, and to spread out as much as was humanly possible.

But this, too, overstates the case. Neither European nor Indian had a secular understanding of disease. "Sickness was the physical manifestation of the will of God," Robert Crease, a philosopher of science at the State University of New York at Stony Brook, told me. "You could pass it on to someone, but doing that was like passing on evil, or bad luck, or a bad spirit—the transmission also reflected God's will." The conquistadors knew the potential impact of disease, but its *actual* impact, which they could not control, was in the hands of God.

The Mexica agreed. In all the indigenous accounts of the conquest and its aftermath, the anthropologist J. Jorge Klor de Alva observed, the Mexica lament their losses, but, "the Spaniards are rarely judged in moral terms, and Cortés is only sporadically considered a villain. It seems to be commonly understood"—at least by this bleakly philosophical, imperially minded group—"that the Spaniards did what any other group would have done or would have been expected to do if the opportunity had existed."

Famously, the conquistador Bernal Díaz de Castillo ticked off the reasons he and others joined Cortés: "to serve God and His Majesty [the king of Spain], to give light to those who were in darkness, and to grow rich, as all men desire to do." In Díaz's list, spiritual and material motivations were equally important. Cortés was constantly preoccupied by the search for gold, but he also had to be restrained by the priests accompanying him from promulgating the Gospel in circumstances sure to anger native leaders. After the destruction of Tenochtitlán, the Spanish court and intellectual elite were convulsed with argument for a century about whether the conversions were worth the suffering inflicted. Many believed that even if Indians died soon after conversion, good could still occur. "Christianity is not about getting healthy, it's about getting saved," Crease said, summarizing. Today few Christians would endorse this argument, but that doesn't make it any easier to assign the correct degree of blame to their ancestors.

In an editorial about Black's analysis of Indian HLA profiles, Jean-Claude Salomon, a medical researcher at France's Centre National de la Recherche Scientifique, asked if the likely inevitability of native deaths could "reduce the historical guilt of Europeans." In a sense it does, Salomon wrote. But it did not let the invaders off the hook—they caused huge numbers of deaths, and knew that they had done it. "Those who carried the microbes across the Atlantic were responsible, but not guilty," Salomon concluded. Guilt is not readily passed down the generations, but responsibility can be. A first step toward satisfying that responsibility for Europeans and their descendants in North and South America would be to treat indigenous people today with respect—something that, alas, cannot yet be taken for granted. Recognizing and obeying past treaties wouldn't be a bad idea, either.

ISN'T THIS ALL JUST REVISIONISM?

Yes, of course—except that it's more like *re*-revisionism. The first European adventurers in the Western Hemisphere did not make careful population counts, but they repeatedly described indigenous America as a crowded, jostling place—"a beehive of people," as Las Casas put it in 1542. To Las Casas, the Americas seemed so thick with people "that it looked as if God has placed all of or the greater part of the entire human race in these countries."

So far as is known, Las Casas never tried to enumerate the original native population. But he did try to calculate how many died from Spanish disease and brutality. In Las Casas's "sure, truthful estimate," his countrymen in the first five decades after Columbus wiped out "more than twelve million souls, men and women and children; and in truth I believe, without trying to deceive myself, that it was more than fifteen million." Twenty years later, he raised his estimate of Indian deaths—and hence of the initial population—to forty million.

Las Casas's successors usually shared his ideas—the eighteenth-century Jesuit Francisco Javier Clavijero, for example, asserted that the pre-Columbian population of Mexico alone was thirty million. But gradually a note of doubt crept in. To most historians, the colonial accounts came to seem exaggerated, though exactly why was not often explained. ("Sixteenth-century Europeans," Cook and Borah dryly remarked, "did indeed know how to count.") Especially in North America, historians' guesses at native numbers kept slipping down. By the 1920s they had dwindled to forty or fifty million in the entire hemisphere—about the number that Las Casas believed had died in Mesoamerica alone. Twenty years after that, the estimates had declined by another factor of five.

Today the picture has reversed. The High Counters seem to be winning the argument, at least for now. No definitive data exist, but the majority of the extant evidentiary scraps indicate it. "Most of the arrows point in that direction," Denevan said to me. Zambardino, the computer scientist who decried the margin of error in these estimates, noted that even an extremely conservative extrapolation of known figures would still project a precontact population in central Mexico alone of five to ten million, "a very high population, not only in terms of the sixteenth century, but indeed on any terms." Even Henige, of *Numbers from Nowhere,* is no Low Counter. When I asked him what he thought the population of the Americas was before Columbus, he insisted that any answer would be speculation and made me promise not to print what he was going to say next. Then he named a figure that thirty years ago would have caused a commotion, a figure that to me suggested Las Casas may have been right all along.

To Fenn, the smallpox historian, the squabble over the number of deaths and the degree of blame obscures something more important. In the long run, Fenn says, the consequential finding of the new scholarship is not that many people died but that many people *lived*. The Americas were filled with an enthusiastically diverse assortment of peoples who had knocked about the continents for millennia. "We are talking about enormous numbers of people," she told me. "You have to wonder, Who were all these people? And what were they doing?"

PART TWO

Very Old Bones

❋ 5 ❋

Pleistocene Wars

The last time I spoke with Sérgio D. J. Pena, he was hunting for ancient Indians in modern blood. The blood was sealed into thin, rodlike vials in Pena's laboratory at the Federal University of Minas Gerais, in Belo Horizonte, Brazil's third-largest city. To anyone who has seen a molecular biology lab on the television news, the racks of refrigerating tanks, whirling DNA extractors, and gene-sequencing machines in Pena's lab would look familiar. But what Pena was doing with them would not. One way to describe Pena's goal would be to say that he was trying to bring back a people who vanished thousands of years ago. Another would be to say that he was wrestling with a scientific puzzle that had resisted resolution since 1840.

In that year Peter Wilhelm Lund, a Danish botanist, found thirty skeletons in caves twenty miles north of Belo Horizonte. The caves were named Lagoa Santa, after a nearby village. Inside them were a jumble of remains from people and big, extinct beasts. If the human and animal bones were from the same time period, as their proximity suggested, the implication was that people had been living in the Americas many thousands of years ago, much longer than most scientists then believed. Who were these ancient hunters? Regarding Europe as the world's intellectual capital, the intrigued Lund sent most of the skeletons to a museum in his native Copenhagen. He was certain that researchers there would quickly study and identify them. Instead the bones remained in boxes, rarely disturbed, for more than a century.

Scientists finally examined the Lagoa Santa skeletons in the 1960s. Laboratory tests showed that the bones could be fifteen thousand years old—possibly the oldest human remains in the Western Hemisphere. Lund had noted the skulls' heavy brows, which are rare in Native Americans. The new measurements confirmed that oddity and suggested that these people were in many ways physically quite distinct from modern Indians, which indicated, at least to some Brazilian archaeologists, that the Lagoa Santa people could not have been the ancestors of today's native populations. Instead the earliest inhabitants of the Americas must have been some other kind of people.

North American researchers tended to scoff at the notion that some mysterious non-Indians had lived fifteen thousand years ago in the heart of Brazil, but South Americans, Pena among them, were less dismissive. Pena had studied and worked for twelve years overseas, mainly in Canada and the United States. He returned in 1982 to Belo Horizonte, a surging, industrial city in the nation's east-central highlands. In Brazilian terms, it was like abandoning a glamorous expatriate life in Paris to come back to Chicago. Pena had become interested while abroad in using genetics as a historical tool—studying family trees and migrations by examining DNA. At Belo Horizonte, he joined the university faculty and founded, on the side, Brazil's first DNA-fingerprinting company, providing paternity tests for families and forensic studies for the police. He taught, researched, published in prestigious U.S. and European journals, and ran his company. In time he became intrigued by the Lagoa Santa skeletons.

The most straightforward way to discover whether the Lagoa Santa people were related to modern Indians, Pena decided, would be to compare DNA from their skeletons with DNA from living Indians. In 1999 his team tried to extract DNA from Lagoa Santa bones. When the DNA turned out to be unusable, Pena came up with a second, more unorthodox approach: he decided to look for Lagoa Santa DNA in the Botocudo.

The Botocudo were an indigenous group that lived a few hundred miles north of what is now Rio de Janeiro. (The name comes from *botoque*, the derogatory Portuguese term for the big wooden discs that the Botocudo inserted in their lower lips and earlobes, distending them outward.) Although apparently never numerous, they resisted conquest so successfully that in 1801 the Portuguese colonial government formally launched a "just war against the cannibalistic Botocudo." There followed a century of intermittent strife, which slowly drove the Botocudo to extinction.

With their slightly bulging brows, deepset eyes, and square jaws, the Botocudo were phenotypically different (that is, different in appearance) from their neighbors—a difference comparable to the difference between West Africans and Scandinavians. More important, some Brazilian scientists believe, the Botocudo were phenotypically similar to the Lagoa Santa people. If the similarity was due to a genetic connection—that is, if the Botocudo were a remnant of an early non-Indian population at Lagoa Santa—studying

Botocudo DNA should provide clues to the genetic makeup of the earliest Americans. To discover whether that genetic connection existed, Pena would first have to obtain some Botocudo DNA. This requirement would have seemed to doom the enterprise, because the Botocudo no longer exist. But Pena had an idea—innovative or preposterous, depending on the point of view—of how one might find some Botocudo DNA anyway.

All human beings have two genomes. The first is the genome of the DNA in chromosomes, the genome of the famous human genome project, which proclaimed its success with great fanfare in 2000. The second and much smaller genome is of the DNA in mitochondria; it was mapped, to little public notice, in 1981. Mitochondria are minute, bean-shaped objects, hundreds of which bob about like so much flotsam in the warm, salty envelope of the cell. The body's chemical plants, they gulp in oxygen and release the energy-rich molecules that power life. Mitochondria are widely believed to descend from bacteria that long ago somehow became incorporated into one of our evolutionary ancestors. They replicate themselves independently of the rest of the cell, without using its DNA. To accomplish this, they have their own genome, a tiny thing with fewer than fifty genes, left over from their former existence as free-floating bacteria. Because sperm cells are basically devoid of mitochondria, almost all of an embryo's mitochondria come from the egg. Children's mitochondria are thus in essence identical to their mother's.*

More than that, every woman's mitochondrial DNA is identical not only to her mother's mitochondrial DNA, but to that of her mother's mother's mitochondrial DNA, and her mother's mother's mother's mitochondrial DNA, and so on down the line for many generations. The same is not true for men. Because fathers don't contribute mitochondrial DNA to the embryo, the succession occurs only through the female line.

In the late 1970s several scientists realized that an ethnic group's mitochondrial DNA could provide clues to its ancestry. Their reasoning was complex in detail, but simple in principle. People with similar mitochondria have, in the jargon, the same "haplogroup." If two ethnic groups share the same haplogroup, it is molecular proof that the two groups are related; their members belong to the same female line. In 1990 a team led by Douglas C. Wallace, now at the University of California at Irvine, discovered that just four

---

*I use the hedge words "basically," "almost," and "in essence" because sperm actually have 50 to 100 mitochondria, just enough to power them through their short lives. By contrast, the egg has as many as 100,000 mitochondria. When the sperm joins the egg, the egg eliminates sperm mitochondria. Every now and then, though, a few escape destruction and end up in the embryo's cells.

mitochondrial haplogroups account for 96.9 percent of Native Americans—
another example of Indians' genetic homogeneity, but one without any
known negative (or positive) consequences. Three of the four Indian haplogroups are common in southern Siberia. Given the inheritance rules for
mitochondrial DNA, the conclusion that Indians and Siberians share common ancestry seems, to geneticists, inescapable.

Wallace's research gave Pena a target to shoot at. Even as the Brazilian
government was wiping out the Botocudos, some Brazilian men of European descent were marrying Botocudo women. Generations later, the
female descendants of those unions should still have mitochondria identical
to the mitochondria of their female Botocudo ancestors. In other words,
Pena might be able to find ancient American DNA hidden in Brazil's European population.

Pena had blood samples from people who believed their grandparents or
great-grandparents were Indians and who had lived in Botocudo territory.
"I'm looking for, possibly, a very odd haplogroup," he told me. "One that is
not clearly indigenous or clearly European." If such a haplogroup turned up
in Pena's assays, it could write a new chapter in the early history of Native
Americans. He expected to be searching for a while, and anything he found
would need careful confirmation.

Since the sixteenth century, the origins of Native Americans have been
an intellectual puzzle.* Countless amateur thinkers took a crack at the problem, as did anthropologists and archaeologists when those disciplines were
invented. The professionals made no secret of their disdain for the amateurs,
whom they regarded as annoyances, cranks, or frauds. Unfortunately for the
experts, in the 1920s and 1930s their initial theories about the timing of Indians' entrance into the Americas were proven wrong, and in a way that
allowed the crackpots to claim vindication. Thirty years later a new generation of researchers put together a different theory of Native American origins that gained general agreement. But in the 1980s and 1990s a gush of new
information about the first Americans came in from archaeological digs,
anthropological laboratories, molecular biology research units, and linguists'
computer models. The discoveries once again fractured the consensus about
the early American history, miring it in dispute. "It really does seem sometimes that scientific principles are going out the window," the archaeologist
C. Vance Haynes said to me, unhappily. "If you listen to [the dissenting
researchers], they want to throw away everything we've established."

---

*A puzzle to Europeans, anyway—Indians seem to have been, as a rule, satisfied with tra-
ditional explanations of their origins.

Haynes was waxing rhetorical—the critics don't want to jettison *every-thing* from the past. But I could understand the reason for his dour tone. Again the experts were said to have been proved wrong, opening a door that until recently was bolted against the crackpots. A field that had seemed unified was split into warring camps. And projects like Pena's, which not long ago would have seemed marginal, even nutty, now might have to be taken seriously.

In another sense, though, Haynes's unhappy view seemed off the mark. The rekindled dispute over Indian origins has tended to mask a greater archaeological accomplishment: the enormous recent accumulation of knowledge about the American past. In almost every case, Indian societies have been revealed to be older, grander, and more complex than was thought possible even twenty years ago. Archaeologists not only have pushed back the date for humanity's entrance into the Americas, they have learned that the first large-scale societies grew up earlier than had been believed—almost two thousand years earlier, and in a different part of the hemisphere. And even those societies that had seemed best understood, like the Maya, have been placed in new contexts on the basis of new information.

At one point I asked Pena what he thought the reaction would be if he discovered that ancient Indians were, in fact, not genetically related to modern Indians. He was standing by a computer printer that was spewing out graphs and charts, the results of another DNA comparison. "It will seem impossible to believe at first," he said, flipping through the printout. "But if it is true—and I am not saying that it is—people will ultimately accept it, just like all the other impossible ideas they've had to accept."

LOST TRIBES

So various were the peoples of the Americas that continent-wide generalizations are risky to the point of folly. Nonetheless, one can say that for the most part the initial Indian-European encounter was less of an intellectual shock to Indians than to Europeans. Indians were surprised when strange-looking people appeared on their shores, but unlike Europeans they were not surprised that such strange people *existed*.

Many natives, seeking to categorize the newcomers, were open to the possibility that they might belong to the realm of the supernatural. They often approached visitors as if they might be deities, possibly calculating, in the spirit of Pascal's wager, that the downside of an erroneous attribution of celestial power was minimal. The Taino Indians, Columbus reported after his first voyage, "firmly believed that I, with my ships and men, came from

the heavens. . . . Wherever I went, [they] ran from house to house, and to the
towns around, crying out, 'Come! come! and see the men from the heavens!' " On Columbus's later voyages, his crew happily accepted godhood—
until the Taino began empirically testing their divinity by forcing their heads
underwater for long periods to see if the Spanish were, as gods should be,
immortal.

Motecuhzoma, according to many scholarly texts, believed that Cortés
was the god-hero Quetzalcoatl returning home, in fulfillment of a prophecy.
What historian Barbara Tuchman called the emperor's "wooden-
headedness, in the special variety of religious mania" is often said to be why
he didn't order his army to wipe out the Spaniards immediately. But the
anthropologist Matthew Restall has noted that none of the conquistadors'
writings mention this supposed apotheosis, not even Cortés's lengthy
memos to the Spanish king, which go into detail about every other wonderful thing he did. Instead the Quetzalcoatl story first appears decades later.
True, the Mexica apparently did call the Spaniards *teteoh,* a term referring
both to gods and to powerful, privileged people. The ambiguity captures the
indigenous attitude toward the hairy, oddly dressed strangers on their shores:
recognition that their presence was important, plus a willingness to believe
that such unusual people might have qualities unlike those of ordinary men
and women.

Similarly, groups like the Wampanoag, Narragansett, and Haudenosaunee in eastern North America also thought at first that Europeans might
have supernatural qualities. But this was because Indians north and south
regarded Europeans as human beings exactly like themselves. In their view
of the world, certain men and women, given the right circumstances, could
wield more-than-human powers. If the Wampanoag and Mexica had
shamans who could magically inflict sickness, why couldn't the British? (The
Europeans, who themselves believed that people could become witches and
magically spread disease, were hardly going to argue.)

As a rule, Indians were theologically prepared for the existence of Europeans. In Choctaw lore, for example, the Creator breathed life into not one
but many primeval pairs of human beings scattered all over the earth. It
could not have been terribly surprising to Choctaw thinkers that the descendants of one pair should show up in the territory of another. Similarly, the
Zuñi took the existence of Spaniards in stride, though not their actions. To
the Zuñi, whose accounts of their origins and early history are as minutely
annotated as those in the Hebrew Bible, all humankind arose from a small
band that faded into existence in a small, dark, womb-like lower world. The
sun took pity on these bewildered souls, gave them maize to eat, and distrib-

uted them across the surface of the earth. The encounter with Europeans was thus a meeting of long-separated cousins.

Contact with Indians caused Europeans considerably more consternation. Columbus went to his grave convinced that he had landed on the shores of Asia, near India. The inhabitants of this previously unseen land were therefore Asians—hence the unfortunate name "Indians." As his successors discovered that the Americas were not part of Asia, Indians became a dire anthropogonical problem. According to Genesis, all human beings and animals perished in the Flood except those on Noah's ark, which landed "upon the mountains of Ararat," thought to be in eastern Turkey. How, then, was it possible for humans and animals to have crossed the immense Pacific? Did the existence of Indians negate the Bible, and Christianity with it?

Among the first to grapple directly with this question was the Jesuit educator José de Acosta, who spent a quarter century in New Spain. Any explanation of Indians' origins, he wrote in 1590, "cannot contradict Holy Writ, which clearly teaches that all men descend from Adam." Because Adam had lived in the Middle East, Acosta was "forced" to conclude "that the men of the Indies traveled there from Europe or Asia." For this to be possible, the Americas and Asia "must join somewhere."

> If this is true, as indeed it appears to me to be, . . . we would have to say that *they crossed not by sailing on the sea, but by walking on land.* And they followed this way quite unthinkingly, changing places and lands little by little, with some of them settling in the lands already discovered and others seeking new ones. [Emphasis added]

Acosta's hypothesis was in basic form widely accepted for centuries. For his successors, in fact, the main task was not to discover whether Indians' ancestors had walked over from Eurasia, but which Europeans or Asians had done the walking. Enthusiasts proposed a dozen groups as the ancestral stock: Phoenicians, Basques, Chinese, Scythians, Romans, Africans, "Hindoos," ancient Greeks, ancient Assyrians, ancient Egyptians, the inhabitants of Atlantis, even straying bands of Welsh. But the most widely accepted candidates were the Lost Tribes of Israel.

The story of the Lost Tribes is revealed mainly in the Second Book of Kings of the Old Testament and the apocryphal Second (or Fourth, depending on the type of Bible) Book of Esdras. At that time, according to scripture, the Hebrew tribes had split into two adjacent confederations, the northern kingdom of Judah, with its capital in Jerusalem, and the southern kingdom of Israel, with its capital in Samaria. After the southern tribes took to behaving sinfully, divine retribution came in the form of the Assyrian king Shal-maneser V, who overran Israel and exiled its ten constituent tribes to Mesopotamia (today's Syria and Iraq). Now repenting of their wickedness, the Bible explains, the tribes resolved to "go to a distant land never yet inhab-ited by man, and there at last to be obedient to their laws." True to their word, they walked away and were never seen again.

Because the Book of Ezekiel prophesizes that in the final days God "will take the children of Israel from among the heathen . . . and bring them into their own land," Christian scholars believed that the Israelites' descendants—Ezekiel's "children of Israel"—must still be living in some remote place, waiting to be taken back to their homeland. Identifying Indians as these "lost tribes" solved two puzzles at once: where the Israelites had gone, and the ori-gins of Native Americans.

Acosta weighed the Indians-as-Jews theory but eventually dismissed it because Indians were not circumcised. Besides, he blithely explained, Jews were cowardly and greedy, and Indians were not. Others did not find his refu-tation convincing. The Lost Tribes theory was endorsed by authorities from Bartolomé de Las Casas to William Penn, founder of Pennsylvania; the famed minister Cotton Mather; and the Book of Mormon. It explained both who had crossed over from Asia—and when they had done so. In 1650 James Ussher, archbishop of Armagh, calculated from Old Testament genealogical data that God created the universe on Sunday, October 23, 4004 B.C. So august was Ussher's reputation, wrote historian Andrew Dickson White, that "his dates were inserted in the margins of the authorized version of the English Bible, and were soon practically regarded as equally inspired with the sacred text itself." According to Ussher's chronology, the Lost Tribes left Israel in 721 B.C. Presumably they began walking to the Americas soon thereafter. Even allowing for a slow passage, the Israelites must have arrived by around 500 B.C. When Columbus landed, the Americas therefore had been settled for barely two thousand years.

The Lost Tribes theory held sway until the nineteenth century, when it was challenged by events. As Lund had in Brazil, British scientists discovered some strange-looking human skeletons jumbled up with the skeletons of extinct Pleistocene mammals. The find, quickly duplicated in France, caused a sensation. To supporters of Darwin's recently published theory of evolu-tion, the find proved that the ancestors of modern humans had lived during the Ice Ages, tens or hundreds of thousands of years ago. Others attacked this conclusion, and the skeletons became one of the *casus belli* of the evolu-tion wars. Indirectly, the discovery also stimulated argument about the set-tlement of the Americas. Evolutionists believed that the Eastern and

Western Hemispheres had developed in concert. If early humans had inhabited Europe during the Ice Ages, they must also have lived in the Americas at the same time. Indians must therefore have arrived before 500 B.C. Ussher's chronology and the Lost Tribes scenario were wrong.

The nineteenth century was the heyday of amateur science. In the United States as in Europe, many of Darwin's most ardent backers were successful tradespeople whose hobby was butterfly or beetle collecting. When these amateurs heard that the ancestors of Indians must have come to the Americas thousands of years ago, a surprising number of them decided to hunt for the evidence that would prove it.

"BLIND LEADERS OF THE BLIND"

In 1872 one such seeker—Charles Abbott, a New Jersey physician—found stone arrowheads, scrapers, and axheads on his farm in the Delaware Valley. Because the artifacts were crudely made, Abbott believed that they must have been fashioned not by historical Indians but by some earlier, "ruder" group, modern Indians' long-ago ancestors. He consulted a Harvard geologist, who told him that the gravel around the finds was ten thousand years old, which Abbott regarded as proof that Pleistocene Man had lived in New Jersey at least that far in the past. Indeed, he argued, Pleistocene Man had lived in New Jersey for so many millennia that he had probably *evolved* there. If modern Indians *had* migrated from Asia, Abbott said, they must have "driven away" these original inhabitants. Egged on by his proselytizing, other weekend bone hunters soon found similar sites with similar crude artifacts. By 1890 amateur scientists claimed to have found traces of Pleistocene Americans in New Jersey, Indiana, Ohio, and the suburbs of Philadelphia and Washington, D.C.

Unsurprisingly, Christian leaders rejected Abbott's claims, which (to repeat) contradicted both Ussher's chronology and the theologically convenient Lost Tribes theory. More puzzling, at least to contemporary eyes, was the equally vehement objections voiced by professional archaeologists and anthropologists, especially those at the Smithsonian Institution, which had established a Bureau of American Ethnology in 1879. According to David J. Meltzer, a Southern Methodist University archaeologist who has written extensively about the history of his field, the bureau's founders were determined to set the new disciplines on a proper scientific footing. Among other things, this meant rooting out pseudoscience. The bureau dispatched William Henry Holmes to scrutinize the case for Pleistocene proto-Indians.

Holmes was a rigorous, orderly man with, Meltzer told me, "no sense of

C. C. Abbott

William Henry Holmes

humor whatsoever." Although Holmes in no way believed that Indians were descended from the Lost Tribes, he was also unwilling to believe that Indians or anyone else had inhabited the Americas as far back as the Ice Ages. His determined skepticism on this issue is hard to fathom. True, many of the ancient skeletons in Europe were strikingly different from those of contemporary humans—in fact, they were Neanderthals, a different subspecies or species from modern humans—whereas all the Indian skeletons that archaeologists had seen thus far looked anatomically modern. But why did this lead Holmes to assume that Indians must have migrated to the Americas in the recent past, a view springing from biblical chronology? Underlying his actions may have been bureau researchers' distaste for "relic hunters" like Abbott, whom they viewed as publicity-seeking quacks.

Holmes methodically inspected half a dozen purported Ice Age sites, including Abbott's farm. In each case, he dismissed the "ancient artifacts" as much more recent—the broken pieces and cast-asides of Indian workshops from the colonial era. In Holmes's sardonic summary, "Two hundred years of aboriginal misfortune and Quaker inattention and neglect"—this was a shot at Abbott, a Quaker—had transformed ordinary refuse that was at most a few centuries old into a "scheme of cultural evolution that spans ten thousand years."

The Bureau of American Ethnology worked closely with the United States Geological Survey, an independent federal agency founded at the same time. Like Holmes, Geological Survey geologist W. J. McGee believed it was his duty to protect the temple of Science from profanation by incompetent and overimaginative amateurs. Anthropology, he lamented, "is particularly attractive to humankind, and for this reason the untrained are constantly venturing upon its purlieus; and since each heedless adventurer leads a rabble of followers, it behooves those who have at heart the good of the science . . . to bell the blind leaders of the blind."

To McGee, one of the worst of these "heedless adventurers" was Abbott, whose devotion to his purported Pleistocene Indians seemed to McGee to exemplify the worst kind of fanaticism. Abbott's medical practice collapsed because patients disliked his touchy disposition and crackpot sermons about ancient spear points. Forced to work as a clerk in Trenton, New Jersey, a town he loathed, he hunted for evidence of Pleistocene Indians during weekends on his farmstead. (In truth, the Abbott farm *had* a lot of artifacts; it is now an official National Historic Landmark.) Bitterly resenting his marginal position in the research world, he besieged scientific journals with angry denunciations of Holmes and McGee, explanations of his own theories, and investigations into the intelligence of fish ("that this class of animals is more 'knowing' than is generally believed is, I hold, unquestionable"), birds ("a high degree of intelligence"), and snakes ("neither among the scanty early references to the serpents found in New Jersey, nor in more recent herpetological literature, are there to be found statements that bear directly upon the subject of the intelligence of snakes").

Unsurprisingly, Abbott detested William Henry Holmes, W. J. McGee, and the "scientific men of Washington" who were conspiring against the truth. "The stones are inspected," he wrote in one of the few doggerel poems ever published in *Science,*

> And Holmes cries, "rejected,
> They're nothing but Indian chips."
> He glanced at the ground,
> Truth, fancied he found,
> And homeward to Washington skips. . . .
>
> So dear W.J.,
> There is no more to say,
> Because you'll never agree
> That anything's truth,
> But what issues, forsooth,
> From Holmes or the brain of McGee.

Abbott was thrilled when his associate Ernest Volk dug up a human femur deep in the gravel of the farm. Volk had spent a decade searching for Ice Age humans in New Jersey. Gloating that his new discovery was "the key to it all," Volk sent the bone for examination to a physical anthropologist named Aleš Hrdlička. (The name, approximately pronounced A-*lesh* Herd-*lish*-ka, was a legacy of his birth in Bohemia.) Hrdlička had seen the Neanderthal skeletons, which did not resemble those of modern humans. Similarly, he believed, ancient Indian skeletons should also differ from those of their descendants. Volk's femur looked anatomically contemporary. But even if it *had* looked different, Hrdlička said, that wouldn't be enough to prove that the ancestors of Indians walked New Jersey thousands of years ago. Volk and Abbott would also have to prove that the bone was old. Even if a bone looked just like a Neanderthal bone, it couldn't be classified as one if it had been found in modern construction debris. Only if the archaeological context—the dirt and rock around the find—was established as ancient could the bone be classified as ancient too.

In the next quarter century amateur bone hunters discovered dozens of what they believed to be ancient skeletons in what they believed to be ancient sediments. One by one Hrdlička, who had moved to the Smithsonian and become the most eminent physical anthropologist of his time, shot them down. *The skeletons are completely modern,* he would say. And the sediments around them were too disturbed to ascertain their age. *People dig graves,* he reminded the buffs. *You should assume from the outset that if you find a skeleton six feet deep in the earth that the bones are a lot newer than the dirt around them.*

With his stern gaze, scowling moustache, and long, thick hair that swept straight back from the forehead, Hrdlička was the very image of celluloid-collar Authority. He was an indefatigably industrious man who wrote some four hundred articles and books; founded the *American Journal of Physical Anthropology;* forcefully edited it for twenty-four years; and collected, inspected, and cataloged more than 32,000 skeletons from around the world, stuffing them into boxes at the Smithsonian. By temperament, he was suspicious of anything that smacked of novelty and modishness. Alas, the list of things that he dismissed as intellectual fads included female scientists, genetic analysis, and the entire discipline of statistics—even such simple statistical measures as standard deviations were notably absent from the *American Journal of Physical Anthropology.* Hrdlička regarded himself as the conscience of physical anthropology and made it his business to set boundaries. So thoroughly did he discredit all purported findings of ancient Indians that a later director of the Bureau of American Ethnology admitted that for decades it was a career-killer for an archaeologist to claim to have "discovered indications of a respectable antiquity for the Indian."

In Europe, every "favorable cave" showed evidence "of some ancient man," Hrdlička proclaimed in March 1928. And the evidence they found in those caves was "not a single implement or whatnot," but of artifacts in "such large numbers that already they clog some of the museums in Europe." Not in the Americas, though. "Where are any such things in America?" he taunted the amateurs. "Where are the implements, the bones of animals upon which these old men have fed? . . . Where is the explanation of all this? What is the matter?"

Aleš Hrdlička

FOLSOM AND THE GRAYBEARDS

Twenty years before Hrdlička's mockery, a flash flood tore a deep gully into a ranch in the northeast corner of New Mexico, near the hamlet of Folsom. Afterward ranch foreman George McJunkin checked the fences for damage. Walking along the new gully, he spotted several huge bones projecting from its sides. Born a slave before the Civil War, McJunkin had no formal education—he had only learned to read as an adult. But he was an expert horseman, a self-taught violinist, and an amateur geologist, astronomer, and natural historian. He instantly recognized that the bones did not belong to any extant species and hence must be very old. Believing that his discovery was important, he tried over the years to show the bones to local Folsomites. Most spurned his entreaties. Eventually a white blacksmith in a nearby town came, saw, and got equally excited. McJunkin died in 1922. Four years later, the blacksmith persuaded Jesse D. Figgins, head of the Colorado Museum of Natural History, to send someone to Folsom.

Figgins wanted to display a fossil bison in his museum, especially if he could get one of the big varieties that went extinct during the Pleistocene. When he received a favorable report from Folsom, he dispatched a work crew to dig out the bones. Its members quickly stumbled across two artifacts—not crude, Abbott-style arrowheads, but elegantly crafted spear points. They also found that a piece from one of the spear points was pressed into the dirt surrounding a bison bone. Since this type of mammal had last existed thousands of years ago, the spear point and its owner must have been of equivalent antiquity.

The spear points both intrigued and dismayed Figgins. His museum had discovered evidence that the Americas had been inhabited during the Pleistocene, a major scientific coup. But this also put Figgins, who knew little about archaeology, in the crosshairs of Aleš Hrdlička.

Early in 1927 Figgins took the spear points to Washington, D.C. He met both Hrdlička and Holmes, who, to Figgins's relief, treated him courteously. Hrdlička told Figgins that if more spear points turned up, he should not excavate them, because that would make it difficult for others to view them in their archaeological and geological context. Instead, he should leave them in the ground and ask the experts to supervise their excavation.

Figgins regarded Hrdlička's words as a friendly suggestion. But according to Meltzer, the Southern Methodist University anthropologist, the great man's motives were less charitable. Figgins had sent excavation teams to several areas in addition to Folsom, and had also found implements in them. Encouraged by the increasing number of discoveries, Figgins's estimation of their import was growing almost daily. Indeed, he was now claiming that the artifacts were half a million years old. *Half a million years!* One can imagine Hrdlička's disgust—*Homo sapiens* itself wasn't thought to be half a million years old. By asking Figgins to unearth any new "discoveries" only in the presence of the scientific elite, Hrdlička hoped to eliminate the next round of quackery before it could take hold.

In August 1927 Figgins's team at Folsom came across a spear point stuck between two bison ribs. He sent out telegrams. Three renowned scientists promptly traveled to New Mexico and watched Figgins's team brush away the dirt from the point and extract it from the gully. All three agreed, as they quickly informed Hrdlička, that the discovery admitted only one possible explanation: thousands of years ago, a Pleistocene hunter had speared a bison.

After that, Meltzer told me, "the whole forty-year battle was essentially over. [One of three experts, A. V.] Kidder said, 'This site is real,' and that was it." Another of the experts, Barnum Brown of the American Museum of Natural History in New York City, took over the excavations, shouldering Figgins aside. After spending the next summer at Folsom, he introduced the site to the world at a major scientific conference. His speech did not even mention Figgins.

Hrdlička issued his caustic "where are any such things" speech months after learning about Folsom—a disingenuous act. But he never directly challenged the spear points' antiquity. Until his death in 1943, in fact, he avoided the subject of Folsom, except to remark that the site wasn't *conclusive* proof that the Americas were inhabited during the Pleistocene. "He won every battle but lost the war," Meltzer said. "Every one of the sites that he discredited was, in fact, not from the Pleistocene. He was completely right about them. And he was right to insist that Figgins excavate the Folsom points in front of experts. But Abbott and the rest of the 'nutcases' were right that people came much earlier to the Americas."

THE CLOVIS CONSENSUS

Early in 1929, the Smithsonian received a letter from Ridgely Whiteman, a nineteen-year-old in the village of Clovis, New Mexico, near the state border with Texas. Whiteman had graduated from high school the previous summer and planned to make his living as a carpenter and, he hoped, as an artist. Wandering in the basins south of Clovis, he observed what looked like immense bones protruding from the dry, blue-gray clay. Whiteman, who was part Indian, was fascinated by Indian lore and had been following the archaeological excitement in Folsom, two hundred miles to the north. He sent a letter to the Smithsonian, informing the staff that he, too, had found "extinct elephant bones" and that someone there should take a look. Surprisingly, the museum responded. Paleontologist Charles Gilmore took the train to Clovis that summer.

Clovis is at the southern end of the Llano Estacado (the "Staked Plain"), fifty thousand square miles of flat, almost featureless sand and scrub. Whiteman's bones were in Blackwater Draw, which during the Pleistocene served as a wide, shallow regional drainage channel, a kind of long, slow-moving lake. As the Ice Ages ended, Blackwater Draw slowly dried up. The continuous flow of water turned into isolated ponds. Game animals congregated around the water, and hunters followed them there. By the time of Gilmore's visit, Blackwater Draw was an arid, almost vegetation-free jumble of sandy drifts and faces of fractured caliche. In one of archaeology's great missed opportunities, Gilmore walked around the area for an hour, decided that it was of no interest, and took the train back to Washington.

The thumbs-down response stupefied Whiteman, who had already turned up dozens of fossils and artifacts there. On and off, he continued his efforts to attract scholarly interest. In the summer of 1932 a local newspaper reporter put him into contact with Edgar B. Howard, a graduate student at the University of Pennsylvania, who had, one of his assistants later wrote, a "driving mania" to discover a Folsom-like site of his own. Howard had already spent three years combing the Southwest for ancient bones, crawling into rattlesnake caves and taking a pickax to rock faces. Intrigued by White-man's curios, he asked if he could examine them that winter during his down time. Howard took them back to Philadelphia but had no chance to inspect them. A few weeks after his return a construction project near Clovis unearthed more huge bones. Locals gleefully took them away—one bowl-ing-ball-size mammoth molar ended up as a doorstop. After hearing the news, Howard raced back to see what he could salvage. He telegrammed his supervisors on November 16:

EXTENSIVE BONE DEPOSIT AT NEW SITE. MOSTLY BISON, ALSO HORSE & MAMMOTH. SOME EVIDENCE OF HEARTHS ALONG EDGES. WILL TIE UP PERMISSIONS FOR FUTURE WORK.

Howard returned to Clovis in the summer of 1933 and systematically sur-veyed Blackwater Draw, looking for areas in which, like Folsom, human arti-facts and extinct species were mixed together. He quickly found several and set to digging. Once again, the telegrams went out. A parade of dignitaries from the East trooped out to inspect the excavations. Howard worked at Clo-vis for four years, each time staffing the field crews with a mix of sunburned locals in boots and jeans and well-tailored Ivy League college students on vacation. "One greenhorn was heard upbraiding his Massachusetts friend for not having perceived at once, as did he," Howard's chief assistant later recalled, "that the purpose of a [local farmer's] windmill was for fanning heat-exhausted cattle." Windmills were not the only surprise in store for the students. The temperature in the digging pits sometimes hit 130°F.

Slowly peeling away the geological layers, Howard's workers revealed that Blackwater Draw had hosted not one, but *two* ancient societies. One had left relics just like those at Folsom. Below the dirt strata with these objects, though, was a layer of quite different artifacts: bigger, thicker, and not as beautifully made. This second, earlier culture became known as the Clovis culture.

Because Clovis was so dry, its stratigraphy—the sequence of geological layers—had not been jumbled up by later waterflow, a common archaeolog-ical hazard. Because of this unusual clarity and because Howard meticu-lously documented his work there, even the most skeptical archaeologists quickly accepted the existence and antiquity of the Clovis culture. To trum-pet his findings, Howard arranged for the Academy of Natural Sciences, in Philadelphia, to sponsor an international symposium on Early Man. More than four hundred scientists migrated to Philadelphia from Europe, Asia, Africa, and Australia. The symposium featured a full-scale reproduction, fifteen feet wide and thirty-four feet long, complete with actual artifacts and bones, of a particularly profitable section of Howard's excavation. (Whiteman was not invited; he died in Clovis in 2003 at the age of ninety-one.)

The most prominent speaker in Philadelphia was Aleš Hrdlička, then sixty-eight. Hrdlička gave Clovis the ultimate accolade: silence. Before one of the biggest archaeological audiences in history, Hrdlička chose to discuss the skeletal evidence for Indians' early arrival in the Americas. He listed every new find of old bones in the last two decades, and scoffed at them all. "So far as human skeletal remains are concerned," he concluded, "there is to this moment no evidence that would justify the assumption of any great, i.e., geological antiquity" for American Indians. Every word Hrdlička said was true—but irrelevant. By focusing on skeletons, he was able to avoid discussing Clovis, the focus of the conference, because Howard had found no skeletons there.*

Clovis culture had a distinctive set of tools: scrapers, spear-straighteners, hatchetlike choppers, crescent-moon-shaped objects whose function remains unknown. Its hallmark was the "Clovis point," a four-inch spearhead with a slightly cut-in, concave tail; in silhouette, the points somewhat resemble those goldfish-shaped cocktail crackers. Folsom points, by contrast, are smaller and finer—perhaps two inches long and an eighth of an inch thick—and usually have a less prominent tail. Both types have wide, shallow grooves or channels called "flutes" cut into the two faces of the head. The user apparently laid the tip of the spear shaft in the flute and twisted hide or sinew repeatedly around the assembly to hold it together. When the point broke, inevitable with stone tools, the head could be loosened and slid forward on the shaft, letting the user chip a new point. A paleo-Indian innovation, this type of fluting exists only in the Americas.

With Blackwater Draw as a pattern, scientists knew exactly what to look for. During the next few decades, they discovered more than eighty large paleo-Indian sites throughout the United States, Mexico, and southern

*Hrdlička's complaint about the lack of skeletal evidence was unfair for another reason: paleo-Indian skeletons are extremely rare. In Europe, archaeologists have discovered scores of skeletons ten thousand years old or more. By contrast, only nine reasonably complete skeletons of similar age have been found in North America (a few more exist in South America, although, as with the Lagoa Santa skeletons, their provenance is often unclear). "It's a big mystery why we don't find the burials," the University of Vermont archaeologist James Petersen told me. "Some Indians will tell you that their dead all moved to a spiritual plane, and that's about as good as any answer that we've got."

Clovis (left) and Folsom points (shown to scale;
fluting at bases)

Canada. All of them had either Folsom or Clovis points, which convinced many archaeologists that the Clovis people, the earlier of the two, must have been the original Americans.

Nobody really knew how old the Clovis people were, though, because geological strata can't be dated precisely. Figgins surmised that Folsom had been inhabited fifteen to twenty thousand years ago, which meant that Clovis must be a little before that. More precise dates did not come in until the 1950s, when Willard F. Libby, a chemist at the University of Chicago, invented carbon dating.

Libby's research began in the global scientific race during the 1930s and 1940s to understand cosmic rays, the mysterious, ultrahigh-velocity subatomic particles that continually rain onto the earth from outer space. Like so many bullets, the particles slam into air molecules in the upper atmosphere, knocking off fragments that in turn strike other air molecules. Along the way, Libby realized, the cascade of interactions creates a trickle of carbon-14 (C^{14}), a mildly radioactive form of carbon that over time disintegrates—*decays*, as scientists say—back into ordinary, nonradioactive carbon. Libby determined that the rate at which cosmic rays create C^{14} is roughly equal to the rate at which it decays. As a result, a small but steady percentage of the carbon in air, sea, and land consists of C^{14}. Plants take in C^{14} through photosynthesis, herbivores take it in from the plants, and carnivores take it in from them. In consequence, every living cell has a consistent, low level of C^{14}—they are all very slightly radioactive, a phenomenon that Libby first observed empirically.

When people, plants, and animals die, they stop assimilating C^{14}. The C^{14} already inside their bodies continues to decay, and as a result the percentage of C^{14} in the dead steadily drops. The rate of decline is known precisely; every 5,730 years, half of the C^{14} atoms in nonliving substances become regular carbon atoms. By comparing the C^{14} level in bones and wooden implements to the normal level in living tissues, Libby reasoned, scientists should be able to determine the age of these objects with unheard-of precision. It was as if every living creature had an invisible radioactive clock in its cells.

In 1949 Libby and a collaborator ascertained the C^{14} level in, among other things, a mummy coffin, a piece of Hittite floor, an Egyptian pharaoh's funerary boat, and the tomb of Sneferu of Meydum, the first Fourth Dynasty pharaoh. Archaeologists already knew their dates of construction, usually from written records; the scientists wanted to compare their estimates to the known dates. Even though Libby and his collaborator were still learning how to measure C^{14}, their estimates were rarely more than a century off—a level of agreement, they wrote dryly, that was "seen to be satisfactory."

Libby won a well-deserved Nobel Prize in 1960. By that time, carbon dating was already revolutionizing archaeology. "You read books and find statements that such and such a society or archaeological site is 20,000 years old," he remarked. "We learned rather abruptly that these numbers, these ancient ages, are not known." Archaeologists had been making inferences from limited, indirect data. With radiocarbon, these numbers, these ancient ages, *could* be known, and with ever-increasing accuracy.

One of the first tasks assigned to the new technique was determining the age of the Clovis culture. Much of the work occurred at the University of Arizona, in Tucson, which in 1958 established the world's first major archaeological carbon-dating laboratory. At the new lab was a doctoral student named C. Vance Haynes. Haynes was a mining engineer who became fascinated by archaeology during a stint in the air force. While serving at a base in the Southwest, he began collecting arrowheads, a hobby that ultimately led to his abandoning geology and coming to the University of Arizona as a graduate student in archaeology. As the Clovis-culture dates crossed his lab bench, Haynes was struck by their consistency. No matter what the location of a site, carbon dating showed that it was occupied between 13,500 and

12,900 years ago.* To Haynes, with his geologist's training, the dates were auspicious. The Clovis culture arose just after the only time period in which migration from Siberia seemed to have been possible.

During the Ice Ages so much of the world's water was frozen into glaciers that sea levels fell as much as four hundred feet. The strait between Siberia's Chukotsky Peninsula and Alaska's Seward Peninsula is now only 56 miles wide and about 120 feet deep, shallower than many lakes. The decline in sea levels let the two peninsulas join up. What had been a frigid expanse of whale habitat became a flat stretch of countryside more than a thousand miles wide. Beringia, as this land is called, was surprisingly temperate, sometimes even warmer than it is today; masses of low flowers covered it every spring. The relative salubriousness of the climate may seem incredible, given that Beringia is on the Arctic Circle and the world was still in the throes of the Ice Ages, but many lines of evidence suggest that it is true. In Siberia and Alaska, for instance, paleoentomologists—scientists who study ancient insects—have discovered in late-Pleistocene sediments fossil beetles and weevils of species that live only in places where summer temperatures reach the fifties.

Beringia was easily traversable. Western Canada was not, because it was buried beneath two massive, conjoined ice sheets, each thousands of feet deep and two thousand miles long. Even today, crossing a vast, splintered wilderness of ice would be a risky task requiring special vehicles and a big support staff. For whole bands to walk across it with backpacks full of supplies would be effectively impossible. (In any case, why would they want to do it?

There was a short period, though, when the barrier could be avoided—or at least some scientists so believed. The Ice Ages drew to a close about fifteen thousand years ago. As the climate warmed, the glaciers slowly melted and sea levels rose; within three thousand years, Beringia had again disappeared

---

*Here and throughout I give the currently accepted dates, which are made with better techniques and more grasp of the vagaries of carbon dating than were then available to Haynes. Scientists discovered in the 1960s that the rate of C^{14} formation and intake varied more than Libby had thought. As a result, raw C^{14} dates must be corrected ("calibrated," in the jargon) to obtain calendar dates, something archaeologists do not always make clear. In addition, they often write dates not as years A.D. or B.C. but as years B.P. (Before Present), with the present set by convention at 1950 A.D. Thus 2000 B.P. is 50 B.C. In an attempt to reduce confusion, all dates in this book are ordinary calendar dates—that is, radiocarbon dates corrected by the most recent calibration. Scientists usually report C^{14} dates with their potential error, as in 3000 ± 150 B.P. (1050 ± 150 B.C.). To avoid typographical clutter, I do not include the error spread, believing that readers understand the unavoidable uncertainties in measuring minute levels of residual radioactivity.

beneath the waves. In the 1950s some geologists concluded that between the beginning of the temperature rise and the resubmergence of the land bridge the inland edges of the two great ice sheets in western Canada shrank, forming a comparatively hospitable pathway between them. This ice-free corridor ran down the Yukon River Valley and along the eastern side of the Canadian Rockies. Even as the Pacific advanced upon Beringia, these geologists said, plant and animal life recolonized the ice-free corridor. And it did so just in time to let paleo-Indians through.

C. Vance Haynes

In a crisply argued paper in *Science* in 1964, Haynes drew attention to the correlation between the birth of "an ice-free, trans-Canadian corridor" and the "abrupt appearance of Clovis artifacts some 700 years later." Thirteen thousand to fourteen thousand years ago, he suggested, a window in time opened. During this interval—and, for all practical purposes, *only* during this interval—paleo-Indians could have crossed Beringia, slipped through the ice-free corridor, and descended into southern Alberta, from where they would have been able to spread throughout North America. The implication was that every Indian society in the hemisphere was descended from Clovis. The people at Blackwater Draw were the ancestral culture of the Americas.

Haynes was the first to put together this picture. The reaction, he told me, was "pretty gratifying." The fractious archaeological community embraced his ideas with rare unanimity; they rapidly became the standard model for the peopling of the Americas. On the popular level, Haynes's scenario made so much intuitive sense that it rapidly leapt from the pages of *Science* to high school history textbooks, mine among them. Three years later, in 1967, the picture was augmented with overkill.

If time travelers from today were to visit North America in the late Pleistocene, they would see in the forests and plains an impossible bestiary of lumbering mastodon, armored rhinos, great dire wolves, sabertooth cats, and ten-foot-long glyptodonts like enormous armadillos. Beavers the size of armchairs; turtles that weighed almost as much as cars; sloths able to reach tree branches twenty feet high; huge, flightless, predatory birds like rapacious ostriches—the tally of Pleistocene monsters is long and alluring.

At about the time of Clovis almost every one of these species vanished.

So complete was the disaster that most of today's big American mammals, such as caribou, moose, and brown bear, are immigrants from Asia. The die-off happened amazingly fast, much of it in the few centuries between 11,500 and 10,900 B.C. And when it was complete, naturalist Alfred Russell Wallace wrote, the Americas had become "a zoologically impoverished world, from which all of the hugest, and fiercest, and strangest forms [had] recently disappeared."

The extinctions permanently changed American landscapes and American history. Before the Pleistocene, the Americas had three species of horse and at least two camels that might have been ridden; other mammals could have been domesticated for meat and milk. Had they survived, the consequences would have been huge. Not only would domesticated animals have changed Indian societies, they might have created new zoonotic diseases. Absent the extinctions, the encounter between Europe and the Americas might have been equally deadly for both sides—a world in which *both* hemispheres experienced catastrophic depopulation.

Researchers had previously noted the temporal coincidence between the paleo-Indians' arrival and the mass extinction, but they didn't believe that small bands of hunters could wreak such ecological havoc. Paul Martin, a paleontologist who was one of Haynes's Arizona colleagues, thought otherwise. Extinction, he claimed, was the nigh-inevitable outcome when beasts with no exposure to *Homo sapiens* suddenly encountered "a new and thoroughly superior predator, a hunter who preferred killing and persisted in killing animals as long as they were available."

Imagine, Martin said, that an original group of a hundred hunters crossed over Beringia and down the ice-free corridor. Historical records show that frontier populations can increase at astonishing rates; in the early nineteenth century, the annual U.S. birthrate climbed as high as 5 percent. If the first paleo-Indians doubled in number every 20 years (a birthrate of 3.4 percent), the population would hit 10 million in only 340 years, a blink of an eye in geological terms. A million paleo-Indians, Martin argued, could easily form a wave of hunters that would radiate out from the southern end of the ice-free corridor, turning the continent into an abattoir. Even with conservative assumptions about the rate of paleo-Indian expansion, the destructive front would reach the Gulf of Mexico in three to five centuries. Within a thousand years it would strike Tierra del Fuego. In the archaeological record, Martin pointed out, this hurricane of slaughter would be visible only as the near-simultaneous appearance of Clovis artifacts throughout North America—and "the swift extermination of the more conspicuous native American large mammals." Which, in fact, is exactly what one sees.

Not everyone was convinced by Martin's model. Paleontologists noted

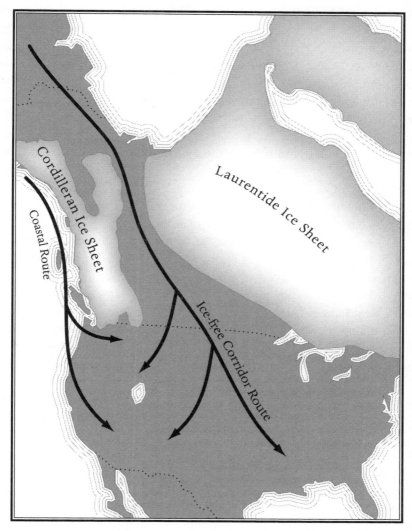

PALEO-INDIAN MIGRATION ROUTES
North America, 10,000 B.C.

that many non-game species vanished, too, which in their view suggests that the extinction wave was more likely due to the abrupt climatic changes at the end of the Pleistocene; Martin pointed out that previous millennia had experienced equally wild shifts with no extinction spasm. In addition, similar extinctions occurred when human beings first invaded Madagascar, Australia, New Zealand, and the Polynesian Islands.

Despite overkill's failure to enjoy full acceptance, it helped set in stone what became the paradigmatic image of the first Americans. Highly mobile, scattered in small bands, carnivorous to a fault, the paleo-Indians conjured by archaeologists were, above all, "stout-hearted, daring, and voracious big-game hunters," in the skeptical summary of Norman Easton, an anthropologist at Yukon College, in White Horse. Clovis people were thought to have a special yen for mammoth: great ambulatory meat lockers. Sometimes they herded the hairy creatures en masse into gullies or entangling bogs, driving the animals to their doom with shouts, dogs, torches, and, possibly, shamanic incantations. More often, though, hunters stalked individual beasts until they were close enough to throw a spear in the gut. "Then you just follow them around for a day or two until they keel over from blood loss or infection," Charles Kay, an ecological archaeologist at Utah State University, told me. "It's not what we think of as sporting, but it's very effective and a hell of a lot safer than hand-to-hand combat with a mammoth."

Shifting location to follow game, the Clovis people prowled roughly circular territories that could have been two hundred miles in diameter (the size would vary depending on the environmental setting). With any luck, the territory would contain flint, jasper, or chalcedony, the raw material for spear points, meat scrapers, and other hunting tools. Bands may have had as many as fifty members, with girls going outside the group to marry. At camp, women and girls made clothes, gathered food—wild plums, blackberries, grapes—and tended babies. Men and boys went hunting, possibly as a group of fathers and sons, probably for days at a time.

As the extinctions proceeded, the Clovis people switched from mammoths to the smaller, more numerous bison. The spear points grew smaller, the hunting more systematic (with prey becoming scarcer, it needed to be). Bands camped on ridges overlooking ponds—the men wanted to spot herds when they came to drink. When the animals plunged their muzzles into the water, hunting parties attacked, forcing the startled bison to flee into a dead-end gully. The beasts bellowed in confusion and pain as the paleo-Indians moved in with jabbing spears. Sometimes they slaughtered a dozen or more at once. Each hunter may have gobbled down as much as ten pounds of bison flesh a day. They came back staggering under the load of meat. Life in this vision of early America was hard but pleasant; in most ways, archaeologists said, it was not that different from life elsewhere on the planet at the time.

Except that it may not have been like that at all.

CONTINENTAL DIVIDE

In the early 1980s a magazine asked me to report on a long-running legal battle over Pacific Northwest salmon. A coalition of Indian tribes had taken

Washington State to court over a treaty it had signed with them in 1854, when the state was still part of the Oregon Territory. In the treaty, the territory promised to respect the Indians' "right of taking fish, at all usual and accustomed grounds and stations," which the tribes interpreted as guaranteeing them a share of the annual salmon harvests. Washington State said that the treaty did not mean what the Indians claimed, and in any case that circumstances had changed too much for it still to be binding. The courts repeatedly endorsed the Indian view and the state repeatedly appealed, twice reaching the U.S. Supreme Court. As the Indians approached final victory, tension rose in the fishing industry, then almost entirely controlled by whites. The magazine wanted me to write about the fight.

To learn more about the dispute, I visited the delta of the Nisqually River, at the southern tip of Puget Sound. Housing the Nisqually tribe, the sliver of land that is their reservation, and the riverbank meadow on which the treaty was signed, the delta is passed through, unnoticed, every day by the thousands of commuters on the interstate highway that slices through the reservation. At the time of my visit, the Nisqually had been annoying state authorities for decades, tenaciously pursuing what they believed to be their right to fish on their ancestral fishing grounds. I met the Franks, the stubborn, charismatic father-and-son team who then more or less ran the tribe, in a cluttered office that in my recollection occupied half of a double-wide trailer. Both had been arrested many times for "protest fishing"—fishing when the state said they couldn't—and were the guiding spirits behind the litigation. After we spoke, Billy Frank, the son, told me I should visit Medicine Creek, where the Nisqually and eight other tribes had negotiated the treaty. And he asked someone who was hanging around to give me a tour.

That someone introduced himself as Denny. He was slim and stylish with very long black hair that fell unbound over the shoulders of his Levi jacket. Sewn on the back of the jacket was a replica of the American eagle on the dollar bill. A degree in semiotics was not required to see that I was in the presence of an ironist. He was not a Nisqually, he said, but from another Northwest group—at this remove, I can't recall which. We clambered into an old truck with scraped side panels. As we set off, Denny asked, "Are you an archaeologist?"

Journalist, I told him.

"Good," he said, slamming the truck into gear.

Because journalists rarely meet with such enthusiasm, I guessed—correctly—that his approval referred to my non-archaeological status. In this way I learned that archaeologists have aroused the ire of some Native American activists.

We drove to a small boat packed with fishing gear that was tied down on the edge of the Nisqually. Denny got the motor running and we puttered downstream, looking for harbor seals, which he said sometimes wandered up the river. Scrubby trees stood out from gravel banks, and beneath them, here and there, were the red-flushed, spawned-out bodies of salmon, insects happy around them. Freeway traffic was clearly audible. After half an hour we turned up a tributary and made land on a muddy bank. A hundred yards away was a tall snag, the dead stalk of a Douglas fir, standing over the meadow like a sentinel. The treaty negotiations had been conducted in its shelter. From under its branches the territorial governor had triumphantly emerged with two sheets of paper which he said bore the X marks of sixty-two Indian leaders, some of whom actively opposed the treaty and apparently were not at the signing.

Throughout our little excursion Denny talked. He told me that the claw holding the arrows on the back of the one-dollar bill was copied by Benjamin Franklin from an incident in Haudenosaunee lore; that the army base next door sometimes fired shells over the reservation; that Billy Frank once had been arrested with Marlon Brando; that a story Willie Frank, Billy's father, had told me about his grandparents picking up smallpox-infected blankets on the beach was probably not true, but instead was an example of Willie's fondness for spoofing gullible journalists; that Denny knew a guy who also had an eagle on the back of his jean jacket, but who, unlike Denny, could make the eagle flex its wings by moving his shoulders in a certain way that Denny admired; that most Indians hate the Internal Revenue Service even more than they hate the Bureau of Indian Affairs, because they believe that they paid taxes for all time when the federal government forced them to give up two billion acres of land; and that if I really wanted to see a crime against nature, I should visit the Quinault reservation, on the Olympic Peninsula, which had been plundered by loggers in the 1950s (I did, a few weeks afterward; Denny was right). He also explained to me why he and some other Indians had it in for archaeologists. The causes were many, in his telling, but two of them seemed especially pertinent: Aleš Hrdlička and the overkill hypothesis.

Hrdlička's zeal for completeness made him accumulate as many Indian skeletons as possible. Unfortunately, his fascination with the bones of old Indians was not matched by an equivalent interest in the sensibilities of living Native Americans. Both his zeal and his indifference were gaudily on display on Kodiak Island, Alaska, where he exhumed about a thousand skeletons between 1932 and 1936 at Larsen Bay, a village of Alutiiq Indians. Many of the dead were two thousand years old, but some were ripped from recent Alutiiq graves, and a few were not Alutiiq at all—the wife of a local salmon-cannery

manager, eager to help Science, shipped Hrdlička the cadavers of Chinese
workers when they died.

Larsen Bay was the single most productive excavation of Hrdlička's long
career. Confronted with what he viewed as an intellectual treasure trove, this
precise, meticulous, formal man was to all appearances overcome by enthusiasm and scholarly greed. In his pop-eyed hurry to pull bones out of the
ground, he tore open the site with a bulldozer and didn't bother taking notes,
sketching maps, or executing profile drawings. Without documentation,
Hrdlička was unable afterward to make head or tail of the houses, storage
pits, hearths, and burial wells he uncovered. He pored through old Russian
and American accounts of the area to find answers, but he never asked the
people in Larsen Bay about their own culture. Perhaps his failure to approach
the Alutiiq was a good thing. Hrdlička's excavation, made without their permission, so angered them that they were still steaming when Denny was
there on a salmon boat fifty years later. (In 1991 the Smithsonian gave back
the skeletons, which the townspeople reburied.)

Overkill was part of the same mindset, Denny told me. As the environmental movement gathered steam in the 1960s, he said, white people had discovered that Indians were better stewards of the land. Indigenous peoples
were superior to them—horrors! The archies—that was what Denny called
archaeologists—had to race in and rescue Caucasian self-esteem. Which they
did with the ridiculous conceit that the Indians had been the authors of an
ecological mega-disaster. Typical, Denny thought. In his view, archaeologists' main function was to make white people feel good about themselves—
an opinion that archaeologists have learned, to their cost, is not Denny's
alone.

"Archaeologists are trapped in their own prejudices," Vine Deloria Jr., the
Colorado political scientist, told me. The Berkeley geographer Carl Sauer
first brought up overkill in the 1930s, he said. "It was immediately knocked
down, because a lot of shellfish and little mammals also went extinct, and
these mythical Pleistocene hit men wouldn't have wiped them out, too. But
the supposedly objective scientific establishment likes the picture of Indians
as ecological serial killers too much to let go of it."

To Deloria's way of thinking, not only overkill but the entire Clovis-first
theory is a theoretical Rube Goldberg device. "There's this perfect moment
when the ice-free corridor magically appears just before the land bridge is
covered by water," he said. "And the paleo-Indians, who are doing fine in
Siberia, suddenly decide to *sprint* over to Alaska. And then they *sprint*
through the corridor, which just in time for them has been replenished with
game. And they keep sprinting so fast that they overrun the hemisphere even

faster than the Europeans did—and this even though they didn't have horses, because they were so busy killing them all." He laughed. "And these are the same people who say traditional origin tales are improbable!"

Activist critiques like those from Denny and Deloria have had relatively little impact on mainstream archaeologists and anthropologists. In a sense, they were unnecessary: scientists themselves have launched such a sustained attack on the primacy of Clovis, the existence of the ice-free corridor, and the plausibility of overkill that the Clovis consensus has shattered, probably irrecoverably.

In 1964, the year Haynes announced the Clovis-first model, archaeologist Alex D. Krieger listed fifty sites said to be older than Clovis. By 1988 Haynes and other authorities had shot them all down with such merciless dispatch that victims complained of persecution by the "Clovis police." Haynes, the dissenters said, was a new Hrdlička (minus the charge of insensitivity to living Native Americans). As before, archaeologists became gun-shy about arguing that Indians arrived in the Americas before the canonical date. Perhaps as a result, the most persuasive scientific critiques on Clovis initially came from fields that overlapped archaeology, but were mainly outside of it: linguistics, molecular biology, and geology.

From today's vantage, the attack seems to have begun, paradoxically, with the publication in 1986 of a landmark *pro*-Clovis paper in *Current Anthropology* by a linguist, a physical anthropologist, and a geneticist. The linguistic section attracted special attention. Students of languages had long puzzled over the extraordinary variety and fragmentation of Indian languages. California alone was the home of as many as 86 tongues, which linguists have classified into between 5 and 15 families (the schemes disagree with one another). No one family was dominant. Across the Americas, Indians spoke some 1,200 separate languages that have been classified into as many as 180 linguistic families. By contrast, all of Europe has just 4 language families—Indo-European, Finno-Ugric, Basque, and Turkic—with the great majority of Europeans speaking an Indo-European tongue. Linguists had long wondered how Indians could have evolved so many languages in the thirteen thousand years since Clovis when Europeans had evolved many fewer in the forty thousand years since the arrival of humans there.

In the first part of the 1986 article, Joseph H. Greenberg, a linguist at Stanford, proclaimed that the profusion of idioms was more apparent than real. After four decades of comparing Native American vocabularies and grammars, he had concluded that Indian languages belonged to just three main linguistic families: Aleut, spoken by northern peoples in a broad band from Alaska to Greenland; Na-Dené, spoken in western Canada and the U.S.

Southwest; and Amerind, much the biggest family, spoken everywhere else, including all of Central and South America. "The three linguistic stocks," Greenberg said, "represent separate migrations."

According to Greenberg's linguistic analysis, paleo-Indians had crossed over Beringia not once, but thrice. Using glottochronology he estimated that the ancestors of Aleuts had crossed the strait around 2000 B.C. and that the ancestors of Na-Dené had made the journey around 7000 B.C. As for Amerind, Greenberg thought, "we are dealing with a time period probably greater than eleven thousand years." But it was not *that* much greater, which indicated that the ancestors of Amerind-speaking peoples came over at just about the time that Clovis showed up in the archaeological record. Clovis-first, yes, but Clovis the first of three.

In the same article, Christy G. Turner II, a physical anthropologist at Arizona State, supported the three-migrations scheme with dental evidence. All humans have the same number and type of teeth, but their characteristics—incisor shape, canine size, molar root number, the presence or absence of grooves on tooth faces—differ slightly in ways that are consistent within ethnic groups. In a fantastically painstaking process, Turner measured "28 key crown and root traits" in more than 200,000 Indian teeth. He discovered that Indians formed "three New World dental clusters" corresponding to Greenberg's Aleut, Na-Dené, and Amerind. By comparing tooth variation in Asian populations, Turner estimated the approximate rate at which the secondary characteristics in teeth evolved. (Because these factors make no difference to dental function, anthropologists assume that any changes reflect random mutation, which biologists in turn assume occurs at a roughly constant rate.) Applying his "worldwide rate of dental microevolution" to the three migrations, Turner came up with roughly similar dates of emigration. Amerinds, he concluded, had split off from northeast Asian groups about fourteen thousand years ago, which fit well "with the widely held view that the first Americans were the Clovis-culture big-game-hunting paleo-Indians."

The article provoked vigorous reaction, not all of the sort that its authors wished. In hindsight, a hint of what was to come lay in its third section, in which Arizona State geneticist Stephen L. Zegura conceded that the "tripartite division of modern Native Americans is still without strong confirmation" from molecular biology. To the authors' critics, the lack of confirmation had an obvious cause: the whole three-migrations theory was wrong. "Neither their linguistic classification nor their dental/genetic correlation is supported," thundered Lyle Campbell, of the State University of New York at Buffalo. Greenberg's three-family division, Campbell thought, "should be shouted down in order not to confuse nonspecialists." The Amerind-language family was so enormous, Berkeley linguist Johanna Nichols complained, that the likelihood of being able to prove it actually existed was "somewhere between zero and hopeless."

Although the three-migrations theory was widely attacked, it spurred geneticists to pursue research into Native American origins. The main battleground was mitochondrial DNA, the special DNA with which Pena, the Brazilian geneticist, hoped to find the Botocudo. As I mentioned before, a scientific team led by Douglas Wallace found in 1990 that almost all Indians belong to one of four mitochondrial haplogroups, three of which are common in Asia (mitochondria with similar genetic characteristics, such as a particular mutation or version of a gene, belong to the same haplogroup). Wallace's discovery initially seemed to confirm the three-migrations model: the haplogroups were seen as the legacy of separate waves of migration, with the most common haplogroup corresponding to the Clovis culture. Wallace came up with further data when he began working with James Neel, the geneticist who studied the Yanomami response to measles.

In earlier work, Neel had combined data from multiple sources to estimate that two related groups of Central American Indians had split off from each other eight thousand to ten thousand years before. Now Neel and Wallace scrutinized the two groups' mitochondrial DNA. Over time, it should have accumulated mutations, almost all of them tiny alterations in unused DNA that didn't affect the mitochondria's functions. By counting the number of mutations that appeared in one group and not the other, Neel and Wallace determined the rate at which the two groups' mitochondrial DNA had separately changed in the millennia since their separation: .2 to .3 percent every ten thousand years. In 1994 Neel and Wallace sifted through mitochondrial DNA from eighteen widely dispersed Indian groups, looking for mutations that had occurred since their common ancestors left Asia. Using their previously calculated rate of genetic change as a standard, they estimated when the original group had migrated to the Americas: 22,414 to 29,545 years ago. Indians had come to the Americas ten thousand years before Clovis.

Three years later, Sandro L. Bonatto and Francisco M. Bolzano, two geneticists at the Federal University of Rio Grande do Sul, in the southern Brazilian city of Pôrto Alegre, analyzed Indian mitochondrial DNA again— and painted a different picture. Wallace and Neel had focused on the three haplogroups that are also common in Asia. Instead, the Brazilians looked at the fourth main haplogroup—Haplogroup A is its unimaginative name— which is almost completely absent from Siberia but found in every Native American population. Because of its rarity in Siberia, the multiple-migrations theory had the implicit and very awkward corollary that the tiny minority of people with Haplogroup A just happened to be among the small bands that crossed Beringia—not just once, but several times. The two men argued it was more probable that a single migration had left Asia, and that some people in Haplogroup A were in it.

By tallying the accumulated genetic differences in Haplogroup A members, Bonatto and Bolzano calculated that Indians had left Asia thirty-three thousand to forty-three thousand years ago, even earlier than estimated by Wallace and Neel. Not only that, the measurements by Bonatto and Bolzano suggested that soon after the migrants arrived in Beringia they split in two. One half set off for Canada and the United States. Meanwhile, the other half remained in Beringia, which was then comparatively hospitable. The paleo-Indians who went south would not have had a difficult journey, because they arrived a little bit *before* the peak of the last Ice Age—before, that is, the two glacial sheets in Canada merged together. When that ice barrier closed, though, the Indians who stayed in Beringia were stuck there for the duration: almost twenty thousand years. Finally the temperatures rose, and some of them went south, creating a second wave and then, possibly, a third. In other words, just one group of paleo-Indians colonized the Americas, but it did so two or three times.

As other measurements came in, the confusion only increased. Geneticists disagreed about whether the totality of the data implied one or more migrations; whether the ancestral population(s) were small (as some measure of mitochondrial DNA diversity suggested) or large (as others indicated); whether Indians had migrated from Mongolia, the region around Lake Baikal in southern Siberia, or coastal east Asia, even possibly Japan.

Everything seemed up for grabs—or, anyway, almost everything. In the welter of contradictory data, University of Hawaii geneticist Rebecca L. Cann reported in 2001, "only one thing is certain": scientists may argue about everything else, she said, but they all believe that "the 'Clovis First' archaeological model of a late entry of migrants into North America is unsupported by the bulk of new archaeological and genetic evidence."

COAST TO COAST

The "new archaeological evidence" to which Cann referred was from Monte Verde, a boggy Chilean riverbank excavated by Tom Dillehay of the University of Kentucky; Mario Pino of the University of Chile in Valdivia; and a team of students and specialists. They began work in 1977, finished excavation in 1985, and published their final reports in two massive volumes in 1989 and 1997. In the twenty years between the first shovelsful of dirt and the final errata sheets, the scientists concluded that paleo-Indians had occupied Monte Verde at least 12,800 years ago. Not only that, they turned up suggestive indications of human habitation more than 32,000 years ago. Monte Verde, in southern Chile, is ten thousand miles from the Bering Strait. Archaeologists have tended to believe that paleo-Indians would have needed millennia to walk from the north end of the Americas to the south. If Monte Verde was a minimum of 12,800 years old, Indians must have come to the Americas thousands of years before that.

For the most part, archaeologists had lacked the expertise to address the anti-Clovis evidence from genetics and linguistics. But Monte Verde was *archaeology*. Dillehay had dug up something like a village, complete with tent-like structures made from animal hides, lashed together by poles and twisted reeds—a culture that he said had existed centuries before Clovis, and that may have been more sophisticated. Skepticism was forceful, even rancorous; arguments lasted for years, with critics charging that Dillehay's evidence was too low-quality to accept. "People refused to shake my hand at meetings," Dillehay told me. "It was like I was killing their children."

In 1997 a dozen prominent researchers, Haynes among them, flew to Chile to examine the site and its artifacts. The hope was to settle the long-standing dispute by re-creating the graybeards' visit to Folsom. After inspecting the site itself—a wet, peaty bank strikingly unlike the sere desert home of Folsom and Clovis—the archaeologists ended up at a dimly lighted cantina

Tom Dillehay

with the appropriate name of La Caverna. Over a round of beers an argument erupted, prompted, in part, by Haynes's persistent skepticism. Dillehay told Haynes his experience with stone tools in Arizona was useless in evaluating wooden implements in Peru, and then stomped outside with a supporter. But despite the heated words, a fragile consensus emerged. The experts wrote an article making public their unanimous conclusion. "Monte Verde is real," Alex W. Barker, now at the Milwaukee Public Museum, told the *New York Times*. "It's a whole new ball game."

Not everyone wanted to play. Two

years later Stuart J. Fiedel, a consulting archaeologist in Alexandria, Virginia, charged that Dillehay's just-published final Monte Verde report was so poorly executed—"bungled" and "loathsome" were among the descriptors he provided when we spoke—that verifying the original location "of virtually every 'compelling,' unambiguous artifact" on the site was impossible. Stone tools, which many archaeologists regard as the most important artifacts, have no organic carbon and therefore cannot be carbon-dated. Researchers must reckon their ages by ascertaining the age of the ground they are found in, which in turn requires meticulously documenting their provenance. Because Dillehay's team had failed to identify properly the location of the stone tools in Monte Verde, Fiedel said, their antiquity was up to question; they could have been in a recent sediment layer. Haynes, who had authenticated Monte Verde in 1997, announced in 1999 that the site needed "further testing."

The dispute over the Clovis model kept growing. In the 1990s geologists laid out data indicating that the ice sheets were bigger and longer lasting than had been thought, and that even when the ice-free corridor existed it was utterly inhospitable. Worse, archaeologists could find no traces of paleo-Indians (or the big mammals they supposedly hunted) in the corridor from the right time. Meanwhile, paleontologists learned that about two-thirds of the species that vanished did so a little *before* Clovis appears in the archaeological record. Finally, Clovis people may not have enjoyed hunting that much. Of the seventy-six U.S. paleo-Indian camps surveyed by Meltzer and Donald K. Grayson, an archaeologist at the University of Washington at Seattle, only fourteen showed evidence of big-game hunting, all of it just two species, mastodon and bison. "The overkill hypothesis lives on," the two men sneered, "not because of [support from] archaeologists and paleontologists who are expert in the area, but because it keeps getting repeated by those who are not."

Clovis defenders remained as adamant as their critics. Regarding Monte Verde, Haynes told me, "My comment is, where are the photographs of these 'artifacts' when they were in place? If you're trying to prove that site to other archaeologists and you find an unequivocal stone artifact in situ in a site that's twelve thousand years old, everyone should run over with a camera. It wasn't until after we brought this up that they dug up some photographs. And they were fuzzy! I really became a doubter then." Such putative pre-Clovis sites are "background radiation," he said. "I'm convinced that a hundred years from now there will still be these 'pre-Clovis' sites, and this will go on ad infinitum."

"Some of our colleagues seem to have gone seriously wrong," lamented

Thomas F. Lynch of Texas A&M in the *Review of Archaeology* in 2001. Proudly claiming that he had helped "blow the whistle" on other Clovis challengers, Lynch described the gathering support for pre-Clovis candidates as a manifestation of "political correctness." He predicted that Monte Verde would eventually "fade away."

For better or worse, most archaeologists with whom I have spoken act as if the Clovis-first model were wrong, while still accepting that it might be correct. Truly ardent Clovisites, like Low Counters, are "in a definite minority now," according to Michael Crawford, a University of Kansas anthropologist—a conclusion that Fiedel, Haynes, and other skeptics ruefully echo. Following Monte Verde, at least three other pre-Clovis sites gained acceptance, though each continued to have its detractors.

The ultimate demise of the Clovis dogma is inevitable, David Henige, author of *Numbers from Nowhere,* told me. "Archaeologists are always dating something to five thousand years ago and then saying that this must be the first time it occurred because they haven't found any earlier examples. And then, incredibly, they defend this idea to the death. It's logically indefensible." Clovis-first, he said, is "a classic example of arguing from silence. Even in archaeology, which isn't exactly rocket science"—he chuckled—"there's only so long you can get away with it."

HUGGING THE SHORE

Since Holmes and Hrdlička, archaeologists and anthropologists have tried to separate themselves from Abbott's modern descendants: the mob of sweaty-palmed archaeology buffs who consume books about Atlantis and run Web sites about aliens in Peru and medieval Welsh in Iowa. The consensus around Clovis helped beat them back, but the confused back-and-forth ushered in by the genetic studies has provided a new opening. Unable to repel the quacks with a clear theory of their own, archaeologists and anthropologists found themselves enveloped in a cloud of speculation.

The most notorious recent example of this phenomenon is surely Kennewick Man. A 9,400-year-old skeleton that turned up near Kennewick, Washington, in 1997, Kennewick Man became a center of controversy when an early reconstruction of the skeleton's face suggested that it had Caucasian features (or, more precisely, "Caucasoid" features). The reconstruction, published in newspapers and magazines around the world, elicited assertions that Indians had European ancestry. Archaeologists and Indian activists, for once united, scoffed at this notion. Indian and European mitochondrial DNA

are strikingly different. How could Indians descend from Europeans if they did not inherit their genetic makeup?

Yet, as Fiedel conceded to me, the collapse of the Clovis consensus means that archaeologists must consider unorthodox possibilities, including that some other people preceded the ancestors of today's Indians into the Americas. Numerous candidates exist for these pre-paleo-Indians, among them the Lagoa Santa people, whose skulls more resemble the skulls of Australian aborigines than those of Native Americans. Skull gauging is, at best, an inexact science, and most archaeologists have dismissed the notion of an Australian role in American prehistory. But in the fall of 2003 an article in the journal *Nature* about ancient skulls in Baja California revived this possibility. Aborigines, in one scenario, may have traveled from Australia to Tierra del Fuego via Antarctica. Or else there was a single ancestral population split, with the ancestors of Australians heading in one direction and the ancestors of Indians heading in another. In either version of the scenario the ancestors of today's Indians crossed the Bering Strait to find the Americas already settled by Australians. Migration across Antarctica!—exactly the sort of extravagant notion that the whitecoats sought to consign to the historical dustbin. Now they may all be back. If Clovis was not first, the archaeology of the Americas is wide open, a prospect variously feared and welcomed. "Anything goes now, apparently," Fiedel told me. "The lunatics have taken over the asylum."

Despite such misgivings, one can see, squinting a little, the outlines of an emerging theory. In the last few years researchers have focused more and more on a proposal linked to the name of Knut Fladmark, an archaeologist at Simon Fraser University, in British Columbia. As a graduate student in the mid-1970s, Fladmark was so surprised to learn of the paucity of evidence for the ice-free corridor that he wondered if paleo-Indians had instead gone down the Pacific coast by boat. After all, aborigines had reached Australia by boat tens of thousands of years ago. Nonetheless, most archaeologists pooh-poohed the idea, because there was no substantiation for it.

By examining pollen in the ocean sediments near the Pacific coastline, researchers have recently learned that even in the depths of the Ice Age warm southern currents created temperate refuges along the shore—islands of trees and grass in a landscape of ice. Hopping from refuge to refuge, paleo-Indians could have made their way down the coast at any time in the last forty thousand years. "Even primitive boats," Fladmark has written, "could traverse the entire Pacific coast of North and South America in less than 10–15 years."

Evidence for the coastal route is sparse, not least because archaeologists have never looked for paleo-Indian settlements on the shoreline. Future searches will be difficult: thousands of years ago, the melting glaciers raised the seas, inundating coastal settlements, if they existed. Coastal-route proponents like to point out that Clovis-firsters believed in the existence of the ice-free corridor without much supporting data. The coastal route has equally little empirical backing, but in their view makes more sense. Most important, the image of a seagoing people fits into a general rethinking of paleo-Indian life.

Because the first-discovered Clovis site was a hunting camp, archaeologists have usually assumed that Clovis society was focused on hunting. Indeed, Clovisites were thought to have entered the ice-free corridor by pursuing game—"follow the reindeer," as skeptics refer to this scheme. In contemporary hunting and gathering societies, anthropologists have learned, gathering by women usually supplies most of the daily diet. The meat provided by male hunters is a kind of luxury, a special treat for a binge and celebration, the Pleistocene equivalent of a giant box of Toblerone. Compared to its brethren around the world, Clovis society, with its putative focus on massive, exterminating hunts, would have been an anomaly. A coastal route helps bring the paleo-Indians back in line.

Then as now, the Northwest Coast, thick with fruit and *fruits de mer*, was a gatherer's paradise: wild strawberries, wild blueberries, soapberries, huckleberries, thimbleberries, salmonberries; clams, cockles, mussels, oysters; flounder, hake, salmon. (To get breakfast, the local saying says, take a walk in the forest; to get dinner, wait for low tide.) Perhaps the smell of candlefish fat, ubiquitous in later Northwest Coast Indian cookery, even then hovered over the first visitors' fires. One can guess that their boats were not made of wood, because they had long lived on the almost treeless plains of Beringia. Instead they may have been made from animal skin, a readily available resource; though soft beneath the foot, fragile-looking hide vessels have been known to traverse hundreds of miles of open water. A visitor to the Northwest twenty thousand years ago might have seen such a craft bobbing over the waves like a long, floating balloon, ten or twenty men lining its sides, chasing minke whales with stone-tipped spears.

All of this is speculative, to say the least, and may well be wrong. Next year geologists may decide the ice-free corridor was passable, after all. Or more hunting sites could turn up. What seems unlikely to be undone is the awareness that Native Americans may have been in the Americas for twenty thousand or even thirty thousand years. Given that the Ice Age made Europe north of the Loire Valley uninhabitable until some eighteen thousand years ago, the Western Hemisphere should perhaps no longer be described as the "New World." Britain, home of my ancestor Billington, was empty until about 12,500 B.C., because it was still covered by glaciers. If Monte Verde is correct, as most believe, people were thriving from Alaska to Chile while much of northern Europe was still empty of mankind and its works.

6

Cotton (or Anchovies) and Maize

(Tales of Two Civilizations, Part I)

BIG BUILDING

"Would you like to hold a four-thousand-year-old textile?"

Without waiting for my assent, Jonathan Haas slid the fabric into my hand. It was about two inches on a side, little more than a scrap, and aged to the color of last season's straw. To my eye, it seemed carefully made: a warp of fine cotton threads, ten or fifteen to the inch, crossed at half-inch intervals by paired weft threads in a basket-like pattern known as "weft-twining." Haas, an archaeologist at the Field Museum of Natural History, in Chicago, had plucked the fabric from the earth minutes before, two graduate students immortalizing the operation with digital cameras. Thousands of years ago it had been handled or worn by other people; bits of their DNA might still adhere to the fibers. (If so, I was contaminating it.) To be the first person in two hundred generations to see or touch an object—to reach across time with eye and hand—is one of the reasons why people like Haas spend their days sifting through ancient soil.

Ordinarily, archaeologists label and store such artifacts immediately. But just as Haas removed the cloth from the ground, he was distracted by the excited shouts of a group of workers a hundred feet away. Haas clambered over the rough ground to take a look. Poking through the earth at the workers' feet was something that resembled the edge of a dinner plate. Haas knelt to inspect it. When he came back to his feet, his eyebrows had shot up like a pair of circumflexes. "What's *this* doing here?" Haas asked the air. "It looks like unfired ceramics." The site was supposed to be very old—well

"Would you like to hold a four-thousand-year-old textile?"

before the local invention of pottery. "Better have a look at it." Reaching for the trowel in his back pocket, he had realized that the textile was still in his hand, and asked if I would mind hanging on to it.

Haas was standing midway up a sixty-foot hummock in a valley along the central coast of Peru, about 130 miles north of Lima. The valley was desert, withered and yellow-gray except for the crooked band of green that marked the course of the Fortaleza River. In the late 1990s Haas and Winifred Creamer—his wife and co-teamleader, an archaeologist at Northern Illinois University—assisted a research team led by a Peruvian archaeologist, Ruth Shady Solis, that had spent years investigating an ancient ceremonial center fifteen miles to the south. By carbon-dating some of Shady's material, they helped establish that the Peruvuans had uncovered the oldest known city in the Americas.

Afterward, Haas, Creamer, and a Peruvian archaeologist, Álvaro Ruiz, drove a four-by-four through the back roads of the area between that excavation and the Fortaleza Valley. Called the Norte Chico, the region is studded with isolated knolls, twenty to fifty feet high and as much as two hundred feet long. These mounds had been flagged as possible ruins for nearly a century but never excavated because they seemed to have no valuable gold or ceramic objects. The Pan-American Highway had been laid right through them without causing an outcry. Haas, Creamer, and Ruiz had decided to drive through the area because they suspected that the mounds might be more interesting and numerous than had been realized. Ultimately, the three researchers determined that the Norte Chico held the remains of at least twenty-five cities, all of which they wanted to explore. On the day I visited, the team was unburying a city they called Huaricanga, after a nearby hamlet. Here the Pan-American Highway had, as it turned out, sliced through some of the oldest public architecture anywhere on earth.

"You mean to tell me there's no dental picks *at all?*" Haas was saying. "All these people and not one has a dental pick? I'd really like a pick for this thing."

"Nobody can find one," Creamer said. She left to supervise the second part of the dig, two hundred yards away, on the other side of the highway.

Haas sighed, pushed back his wide-brimmed straw hat, and leaned into the dirt with jackknife and paintbrush. Despite the low clouds—an almost featureless carpet a thousand feet above our heads—perspiration stippled his temples. With Ruiz documenting the work with a digital camera, Haas silently plucked out dead insects, bits of leaf, and lengths of *shicra,* a kind of thick twine made from reeds. When he had cleared enough, he sat back and stared at the now-exposed object. "I have no idea what this is," he announced. "Got any tweezers?" Ruiz produced a caliper-sized pair from his backpack.

"Bravo," Haas said. "We have tweezers."

Although the Huaricanga mound resembled an ancient sandhill, the soft, shifting, slightly gritty surface was not sand but the fine, windblown soil geologists call "loess." Fertile stuff, if it can somehow be irrigated, the loess blanketed the underlying structure like a heavy tarpaulin tossed over a piece of machinery. Here and there the archaeologists had scooped it away to reveal granite walls that had once been smoothly plastered. Over time, weather and earthquakes and perhaps human malice had buckled most of the walls, but their overall layout had been preserved. Behind them the team had removed some of the fill: bags of stones, created by knotting *shicra* into mesh sacks, filling the sacks with chunks of granite, and laying the results like fifty-pound bricks in the foundation.

Moving slowly, Haas tweezered out the pieces—they looked like the remnants of a serving platter—and passed them to Ruiz, who dropped them into a resealable plastic bag.

"Are all of those from a single object?" I asked.

"I'd guess so, but your guess is good as mine," Haas said. With his wide face, gray goatee, and merry smile, he resembled, for the moment, an aging folk singer. "All I can say is, this is *really* strange."

Almost twenty people were working on the Huaricanga mound, shoveling away the obscuring loess. Half of them were local workers; Peru has so many ruins from so many cultures that in many small towns archaeological labor is a flourishing blue-collar trade. The others were graduate students from Peru and the United States. After two days of labor, workers and students were halfway through clearing off the top platform and the staircases leading to it; the layout of the structure was visible enough to map. The temple, for the mound was surely built for religious reasons, was laid out in a wide, shallow U about 150 feet long and 60 feet high, with a sunken plaza between the arms. In its day its grandeur would have overwhelmed the visitor. Little wonder: at the time of its construction, the Huaricanga temple was among the world's biggest buildings.

In college I read a one-volume history of the world by the distinguished historian William H. McNeill. Called, simply enough, *A World History,* and published in 1967, it began with what McNeill and most other historians then considered the four wellsprings of human civilization: the Tigris-Euphrates Valley, in modern Iraq, home of Sumer, oldest of all complex polities; the Nile Delta, in Egypt; the Indus Valley, in Pakistan; and, in east central China, the valley of the Huang He, more familiar to Westerners as the Yellow River. If McNeill were writing *A World History* today, discoveries like those at Huari-canga would force him to add two more areas to the book. The first and bet-ter known is Mesoamerica, where half a dozen societies, the Olmec first among them, rose in the centuries before Christ. The second is the Peruvian littoral, home of a much older civilization that has come to light only in the twenty-first century.*

Mesoamerica would deserve its place in the human pantheon if its inhab-itants had only created maize, in terms of harvest weight the world's most important crop. But the inhabitants of Mexico and northern Central Amer-ica also developed tomatoes, now basic to Italian cuisine; peppers, essential to Thai and Indian food; all the world's squashes (except for a few domesti-cated in the United States); and many of the beans on dinner plates around the world. One writer has estimated that Indians developed three-fifths of the crops now in cultivation, most of them in Mesoamerica. Having secured their food supply, Mesoamerican societies turned to intellectual pursuits. In a millennium or less, a comparatively short time, they invented their own writ-ing, astronomy, and mathematics, including the zero.

A few decades ago, many researchers would have included jump-starting Andean civilization on the honor roll of Mesoamerican accomplishments. The Olmec, it was proposed, visited Peru, and the locals, dutiful students, copied their example. Today we know that technologically sophisticated societies arose in Peru first—the starting date, to archaeologists' surprise, keeps getting pushed back. Between 3200 and 2500 B.C., large-scale public buildings, the temple at Huaricanga among them, rose up in at least seven settlements on the Peruvian coast—an extraordinary efflorescence for that time and place. When the people of the Norte Chico were building these cities, there was only one other urban complex on earth: Sumer.

In the last chapter, I described how archaeologists have spent the last cen-tury pushing back their estimates of when Indians were first present in the Americas. Now I turn to a parallel intellectual journey: the growth in under-

---

*I am not criticizing McNeill for failing to include the Americas on his list of civilizations; he was simply reflecting the beliefs of his time. I would criticize *World History: Patterns of Change and Continuity*, a high school text published two decades later, in time for my son to encounter it. Referring exclusively to the "four initial centers" of civilization, this "world his-tory" allocated just nine pages to the pre-Columbian Americas. The thesis of the book in your hands is that Native American history merits more than nine pages.

standing of the antiquity, diversity, complexity, and technological sophistication of Indian societies. Much as historians of early Eurasia focus on the Tigris-Euphrates, Nile, Indus, and Huang He Valleys, historians of the Americas focus on Mesoamerica and the Andes.

Like the Eurasian centers of civilization, Mesoamerica and the Andes were places where complex, long-lasting cultural traditions began. But there was a striking difference between the Eastern and Western Hemispheres: the degree of interaction between their great cultural centers. A constant traffic in goods and ideas among Eurasian societies allowed them to borrow or steal each other's most interesting innovations: algebra from Islam, paper from China, the spinning wheel (probably) from India, the telescope from Europe. "In my lectures, I put this very baldly," Alfred Crosby told me. "I say that nobody in Europe or Asia ever invented anything—they got it from somebody else." He added, "When you think of the dozen most important things ever invented—the wheel, the alphabet, the stirrup, metallurgy—none of them were invented in Europe. But they all got used there."

By contrast, there was very little exchange of people, goods, or ideas between Mesoamerica and the Andes. Travelers on the Silk Road between China and the Mediterranean had to cross desert and the Hindu Kush, both formidable obstacles. But there was no road whatsoever across the two thousand miles of jagged mountains and thick rainforest between Mesoamerica and the Andes. In fact, there *still* isn't any road. The section of the Pan-American Highway that runs between them remains unfinished, because engineers can neither go around nor bulldoze through the swamps and mountains at the narrow Panama-Colombia border. Almost entirely by themselves for thousands of years, these two centers of civilization were so different that researchers today have difficulty finding a conceptual vocabulary that applies to both. Nonetheless, the tale of their mostly separate progress through time deserves prominent placement in any history of the world.

THE COTTON AGE

Peru is the cow-catcher on the train of continental drift. Leading South America's slow, grinding march toward Australia, its coastline hits the ocean floor and crumples up like a carpet shoved into a chairleg. Just offshore the impact pushes the plate on the bottom of the Pacific down and under the advancing coast, creating a trench almost five miles deep. Inland the impact thrusts up the two parallel mountain ranges that make up the Peruvian

Andes: the high Cordillera Negra, the Black Range, to the west, and the still higher Cordillera Blanca, the White Range, to the east. (The White Range has snow; the Black rarely does. Hence the names.) In northern Peru a third range rises between them; the altiplano, a scoop of high plains some five hundred miles long, fills the gap in the south. Taken together, the cordilleras and the altiplano make up the Andes, the second-biggest chain of mountains in the world.

Sandwiched between the Andes and the Pacific, Peru's coastland is a skinny gray-brown ribbon. From a geographer's point of view, it is a splendid anomaly, commencing with its extreme aridity. Over most of the South American landmass, the prevailing winds come from the east, across Brazil. As the warm, wet Amazonian air hits the towering Andes, it cools and sheds its moisture in the form of snow. Almost nothing is left for the Peruvian coast, which sits in the mountains' rain shadow. Surprisingly, the coast is also walled off from moisture on the Pacific side, where the trade winds create a *second* rain shadow. Blowing from the southwest, the trades push the warm surface waters northeast, pulling frigid water from the deep offshore trench to the surface. The upwelling, known as the Humboldt Current, chills the air above it. Coming from the west, the Pacific trade winds hit the cold air from the Humboldt Current and are forced upward in a classic temperature inversion of the sort common in southern California. In temperature inversions, air movement is inhibited—the cold air can't rise and the warm air doesn't fall—which in turn inhibits rainfall. Walled off from wet air by both the Andes and the Humboldt Current, the Peruvian littoral is astonishingly dry: the average annual precipitation is about two inches. The Atacama Desert, just south of Peru on the Chilean shore, is the driest place on earth—in some places rain has literally never been recorded. Space researchers use the Atacama as a model for the sands of Mars.

Pizarro's pilot once explained how to navigate from Mexico's Pacific shore to Peru: Sail south along the coast until you no longer see trees. Then you are in Peru. Yet the coast is not a classic, Sahara-style desert of sand dunes and scorching sun. It is punctuated by more than fifty rivers, which channel Andes snowmelt to the sea. The lines of vegetation along their banks are like oases, fertile places where people can farm in an otherwise almost lifeless land. For much of the year the ocean air is cold enough on winter mornings to make fog roll into the valleys a hundred feet deep. People wear sweatshirts and futilely wipe at the mist on their windshields. By noon the fog lifts, having deposited a few hundredths of an inch of moisture (summed over the year, the fog gives the desert most of its annual two inches of precipitation).

If the anti-Clovis arguments are correct, paleo-Indians walked or paddled to Peru fifteen thousand years ago or more. But Peru's first known inhabitants appear in the archaeological record sometime before 10,000 B.C. According to two studies in *Science* in 1998, these people apparently lived part of the year in the foothills, gathering and hunting (for the latter, no traces of Clovis points have been found). When winter came, they hiked to the warmer coast. At Quebrada Jaguay, a dry streambed on the nation's southern coast that was one of the two sites described in *Science,* they dug up wedge clams and chased schools of six-inch drumfish with nets. They carried their catch to their base, which was about five miles from the shore. (*Quebrada* means "ravine" and often refers to the gullies caused by flash floods.) Quebrada Tacahuay, the other *Science* site, was closer to the shore but even drier: its average annual rainfall is less than a quarter inch. The site, exposed by the construction of a road, is an avian graveyard. On their annual travels between the foothills and the shore, paleo-Indians seem to have visited the area periodically to feast on the cormorants and boobies that nested on the rocks by the beach.

By 8000 B.C., paleo-Indians had radiated throughout western South America. Their lives were similar enough to contemporary hunter-gatherers that perhaps they should now be simply called Indians. Whatever the name, they were varied enough to have pleased Walt Whitman. Some groups had settled into mountain caves, skewering deer-size vicuña on spears; others plucked fish from mangrove swamps; still others stayed on the beach as their forebears had, weaving nets and setting them into the water. In the parched Atacama Desert, the Chinchorro created history's first mummies.

Mummies were first discovered in the Atacama at the beginning of the twentieth century. But the Chinchorro attracted sustained attention only in 1983, when ninety-six superbly preserved cadavers were discovered beneath a massif that rises above downtown Arica, Chile. About 90 percent of their diet was seafood—fish, shellfish, marine mammals, and seaweed—the Chinchorro ate almost no fruit, vegetables, or land animals. Sometime before 5000 B.C. they began mummifying bodies—children at first, adults later on. Nobody knows why. They peeled off the skin from the limbs like so many socks, covered the result with white clay, painted it to resemble the deceased, and fitted the head with a wig made from its own hair. Such was the skill of the Chinchorro at preserving human flesh that scientists have been able to extract intact DNA from cadavers thousands of years older than the Egyptian pyramids.

Many of the child mummies exhibit signs of severe anemia, surprising in people who lived on seafood. In the preserved cadavers paleoparasitologists (scientists who study ancient parasites) have discovered eggs from *Diphyl-*

lobothrium pacificum, a marine tapeworm that usually afflicts fish and sea lions but can slip into human beings who eat raw seafood. The parasite clamps onto the intestines and siphons nutrients from the body. Some grow to lengths of sixteen feet. If the tapeworm attaches to the right place in the gut, it can leech vitamin B_{12} from the victim, instigating a lethal form of anemia. The Chinchorro, it seems, were beset by parasites.

The Chinchorro mummies were often repainted, indicating that they were not quickly interred but kept on display, perhaps for years. One can speculate that grieving parents were unable to let go of their children's bodies in a society that viewed the spirit as adhering to the flesh. What is certain is that the Chinchorro mummies are the first known manifestation of a phenomenon that marked Andean society all the way up to the Inka: the belief that the venerated, preserved dead could exert a powerful impact on the living.

Sometime before 3200 B.C., and possibly before 3500 B.C., something happened in the Norte Chico. On a world level, the eruption at the Norte Chico was improbable, even aberrant. The Tigris-Euphrates, Nile, Indus, and Huang He Valleys were fertile, sunny, well-watered breadbaskets with long stretches of bottomland that practically invited farmers to stick seeds in the soil. Because intensive agriculture has been regarded a prerequisite for complex societies, it has long been claimed that civilizations can arise only in such farm-friendly places. The Peruvian littoral is an agronomical no-go zone: barren, cloudy, almost devoid of rain, seismically and climatically unstable. Except along the rivers, nothing grows but lichen. "It looks like the last place you'd want to start up something major," Creamer said to me. "There doesn't seem to be anything there to build it on."

Nonetheless, they built it. "The complex of sites in the Norte Chico region is nothing short of extraordinary," Haas and Creamer wrote in 2005.

> While a very small number of moderate sites with communal architecture . . . are found in other parts of the Andes, the concentration of at least 25 large ceremonial/residential sites in the valleys of the Norte Chico is unique. Metaphorically, most of the Andes is covered with granules of sand [between 3000 B.C. and 1800 B.C.]. In a few spots, there are anthills that clearly stand out from the loose granules. Then in the Norte Chico, there is a volcano.

The Norte Chico consists of four narrow river valleys: from south to north, the Huaura, Supe, Pativilca, and Fortaleza. They converge on a slice of coastline less than thirty miles long. The first full-scale archaeological investigation of the area took place in 1941, when Gordon R. Willey and John M. Corbett of Harvard worked at Aspero, a salt marsh at the mouth of the Supe.

They found a big trash heap and a multiroomed building with no pottery and a few maize cobs under the pounded clay floor. They didn't know what to make of it. Why was there no pottery, when all previously examined large settlements in Peru had pottery? Why only a handful of maize cobs in the whole site, when maize, at least for the elite, was a staple food? How did they

Indian cities in Peru are some of the most heavily looted archaeological sites in the world. The looting dates back millennia, with the Inka having ravaged the centers of their predecessors, sometimes reusing art and stonework. The Spanish sack of Tawantinsuyu calamitously expanded on this tradition of plunder, which has greatly accelerated in modern times, fueled by the desperate poverty of Peru's Indian population. Here in the Fortaleza Valley, graverobbers—almost certainly local farmers—have ripped apart thousand-year-old tombs in a futile search for golden artifacts. Others gathered the remains into shrines for secretive, candlelit prayers to the dead, whose powers are recognized by alcohol and cigarettes.

grow maize in a salt marsh, anyway? How could they have agriculture but no pottery? Working before the invention of carbon dating, they had no way to determine Aspero's age. The puzzled archaeologists took thirteen years to publish their data.

Among Aspero's many curiosities, Willey and Corbett noted, were a half-dozen mounds, some of them nearly fifteen feet tall. These "knolls, or hillocks," the two men wrote, were "natural eminences of sand." Thirty years after his initial excavation, Willey revisited Aspero with Michael E. Moseley, an archaeologist now at the University of Florida. To his chagrin, Willey quickly recognized that the natural "knolls" were, in truth, human-made "temple-type platform mounds," evidence of a more materially advanced culture than he had imagined possible for the era. Indeed, Aspero may have had as many as *seventeen* artificial mounds, all of which Willey missed the first time round. "It is an excellent, if embarrassing, example," he remarked, "of not being able to find what you are not looking for."

At about the same time, one of Moseley's graduate students wrote his doctoral dissertation about Aspero. He had enough grant money to pay for seven radiocarbon dates. According to one of them, Aspero went back to 3000 B.C. The student also had a smaller, nearby site called As8 tested and got a date of 4900 B.C. *Ridiculous,* he in effect thought. *These dates are too old— obviously something went wrong. Maybe the samples were contaminated.* And he tossed the dates out.

That may have been a mistake. In 1994 Ruth Shady Solis, of the National University of San Marcos in Lima, began working fourteen miles inland from Aspero, at a site known as Caral. From the sandy soil emerged an imposing, 150-acre array of earthworks: six large platform mounds, one sixty feet tall and five hundred feet on a side; two round, sunken ceremonial plazas; half a dozen complexes of mounds and platforms; big stone buildings with residential apartments. Haas and Creamer worked with the project in 2000 and helped establish Caral's antiquity: it was founded before 2600 B.C. While Shady continued work on Caral, Haas, Creamer, and Ruiz split off to investigate the Pitivilca, the next river to the north, and the Fortaleza, just north of the Pitivilca. They found, Haas told me, "major urban centers on a par with Caral in terms of monumental architecture, ceremonial structures, and residential architecture. And some of them were older."

Examination of Huaricanga and the surrounding communities is far from complete—Haas, Creamer, and Ruiz published their first findings in December 2004. They found evidence of people living inland from the coast as early as 9210 B.C. But the oldest date securely associated with a city is about 3500 B.C., at Huaricanga. (There are hints of earlier dates.) Other urban sites

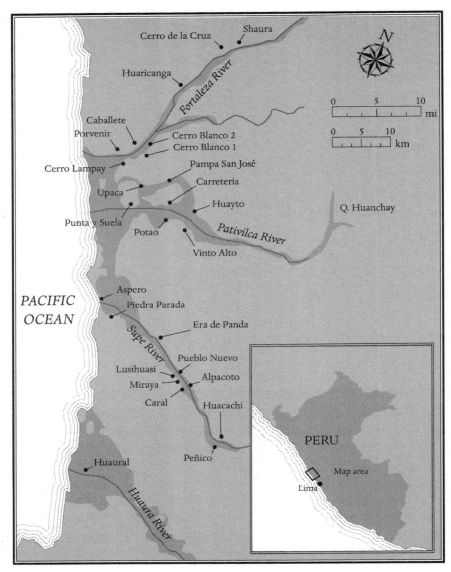

NORTE CHICO
The Americas' First Urban Complex, 3000–1800 B.C.

followed apace: Caballete in 3100 B.C., Porvenir and Upaca in 2700 B.C. Taken individually, none of the twenty-five Norte Chico cities rivaled Sumer's cities in size, but the totality was bigger than Sumer. Egypt's pyramids were larger, but they were built centuries later. I asked Haas and Creamer where a race of alien visitors in, say, 3000 B.C. would have landed if they were searching for earth's most sophisticated society. "I hate questions like that," Haas said, because they ask scientists to engage in the dubious enterprise of ranking cultures against each other on a scale.

"Wouldn't it depend on what the aliens thought was sophisticated?" Creamer asked. "I mean, who knows what they would think."

I asked them to indulge me.

"I know what you're getting at," Haas said, reluctantly. "In 3000 B.C. your aliens would have had a very limited number of options on the menu. And one of those options would have been the Norte Chico."

Because human beings rarely volunteer to spend their days loading baskets with heavy rocks to build public monuments, Haas, Creamer, and Ruiz argued that these cities must have had a centralized government that instigated and directed the work. In the Norte Chico, in other words, *Homo sapiens* experienced a phenomenon that at that time had occurred only once before, in Mesopotamia: the emergence, for better or worse, of leaders with enough prestige, influence, and hierarchical position to induce their subjects to perform heavy labor. It was humankind's second experiment with *government*.

"Where does government come from?" Haas asked. "What makes people decide to surrender some of their personal liberty to it? What did they gain from it? Philosophers have been asking this question for centuries. But archaeology should have something to contribute. In the Norte Chico, we may be able to provide some answers. It's one of only two places on earth— three, if you count Mesoamerica—where government was an *invention*. Everywhere else it was inherited or borrowed. People were born into societies with governments or saw their neighbors' governments and copied the idea. Here, people came up with it themselves."

Haas's enthusiasm seems hyperbolic to some of his colleagues. "What about Amazonian chiefdoms, North American Mississippian societies, and so on?" James Petersen, an archaeologist at the University of Vermont, asked me. "Plus Africa. 'Government' was independently invented there, too." But Haas argues that these peoples knew of the existence of hierarchical, structured societies with strong central leaders, and could pattern their societies after them. Only in a very few places, he says, Norte Chico among them, were cultures proceeding without a map.

In the Norte Chico, Haas told me, government seems not to have arisen from the need for mutual defense, as philosophers have often speculated. The twenty-five cities were not sited strategically and did not have defensive walls; no evidence of warfare, such as burned buildings or mutilated corpses, has been found. Instead, he said, the basis of the rulers' power was the collective economic and spiritual good. Norte Chico was the realm of King Cotton.

To feed Norte Chico's burgeoning population, Shady discovered, the valley folk learned how to irrigate the soil. Not given an environment that favored the development of intensive agriculture, that is, they shaped the landscape into something more suitable to their purposes. Luckily for their purposes, the area is geographically suited for irrigation. The peril of irrigation for farmers is evaporation. Just as water evaporating in a glass leaves behind a film of salts and minerals, water evaporating from irrigation channels leaves deposits in the soil. In a surprisingly short time, the salty deposits can build up to toxic levels, making the land unusable. Because the Cordillera Negra bulges especially close to the coast in the Norte Chico, the valleys are short and steeply walled; almost hurled from the heights, the rivers shoot toward the sea at high velocity. Even after diversion, the water gushes through irrigation channels so quickly that it can't evaporate and build up salts in the soil. To this day, one can only reach many archaeological sites in the Norte Chico by navigating around surging, brim-full irrigation ditches, some of them probably laid out originally by the same farmers who built the mounds.

The most important product of irrigation was cotton. Almost forty species of cotton exist worldwide, of which four have been domesticated, two in the Americas, two in the Middle East and South Asia. Cotton was known in Europe by the thirteenth century but not common until the eighteenth; Columbus and his men wore sturdy flax and coarse wool.* South American cotton (*Gossypium barbadense*) once grew wild along the continent's Pacific and Atlantic coasts. It may first have been domesticated in Amazonia, presumably near the river's mouth. Today it has been supplanted by Mexican cotton (another species, *Gossypium hirsutum*), which provides most of the world's harvest. But in the Andean past, the long, puffy bolls of South American cotton, some varieties naturally tinted pink, blue, or yellow, were the soft underpinning of Andean culture. "In the Norte Chico we see almost no visual arts," Ruiz told me after I gave him the scrap of cloth. "No sculpture, no carving or bas-relief, almost no painting or drawing—the interiors are completely bare. What we do see are these huge mounds—and textiles."

*Given the choice between their own scratchy wool and the Indians' smooth cotton, the conquistadors threw away their clothes and donned native clothing. Later this preference was mirrored in Europe. When cotton became readily available there in the eighteenth century, it grabbed so much of the textile market that French woolmakers persuaded the government to ban the new fiber. The law failed to stem the cotton tide. As the historian Fernand Braudel noted, some woolmakers then thought outside the box: they proposed sending prostitutes in cotton clothing to wander Paris streets, where police would publicly strip them naked. In theory, bourgeois women would then avoid cotton for fear of being mistaken for prostitutes and forcibly disrobed. This novel form of protectionism was never put into place.

Cotton was a key element in regional trade. People in shoreline settlements like Aspero could catch vast quantities of anchovies and sardines; Caral, Huaricanga, and the other inland towns had irrigation-produced cotton, fruit, and vegetables. The countless fish bones in inland Caral and Huaricanga and the fruit seeds and cotton nets in shoreline Aspero are evidence that they swapped one for the other. According to Haas, the inland centers must have controlled the exchange, because the fishers needed their cotton for nets. Cotton was both needed and easily stored, which made it useful as a medium of exchange or status. At Upaca, on the Pativilca, Haas's team discovered the ruins of stone warehouses. If they were for storing cotton, as Haas surmises, they would have been, in this textile-mad society, an emblem of state power and wealth, the ancient equivalent of Fort Knox.

By making these claims, Haas and Creamer were staking out a position in a long-running theoretical dispute. In 1975 Michael Moseley, the Florida archaeologist, drew together his own work in Aspero and earlier research by Peruvian and other researchers into what has been called the MFAC hypothesis: the maritime foundations of Andean civilization. He proposed that there was little subsistence agriculture around Aspero because it was a center of fishing, and that the later, highland Peruvian cultures, including the mighty Inka, all had their origins not in the mountains but in the great fishery of the Humboldt Current. Rather than being founded on agriculture, the ancient cities of coastal Peru drew their sustenance from the sea.

The MFAC hypothesis—that societies fed by fishing could have founded a civilization—was "radical, unwelcome, and critiqued as an economic impossibility," Moseley later recalled. Little wonder! The MFAC was like a brick through the window of archaeological theory. Archaeologists had always believed that in fundamental respects all human societies everywhere were alike, no matter how different they might appear on the surface. If one runs the tape backwards to the beginning, so to speak, the stories are all the same: foraging societies develop agriculture; the increased food supply leads to a population boom; the society grows and stratifies, with powerful clerics at the top and peasant cultivators at the bottom; massive public works ensue, along with intermittent social strife and war. If the MFAC hypothesis was true, early civilization in Peru was in one major respect strikingly unlike early civilization in Mesopotamia, Egypt, India, and China. Farming, the cornerstone of the complex societies in the rest of the world, was in Peru an afterthought. (In Chapter 1, I called Peru the site of an independent Neolithic Revolution, which I defined, following archaeological practice, as beginning with the invention of agriculture. If the MFAC is correct, the definition will have to be changed.)

The MFAC hypothesis was radical, its supporters conceded, but the supporting evidence could not be dismissed. Bone analyses show that late-Pleistocene coastal foragers "got 90 percent of their protein from the sea—anchovies, sardines, shellfish, and so on," said Susan deFrance, an archaeologist at the University of Florida. And the pattern continued for thousands of years and archaeological dig after archaeological dig. "Later sites like Aspero are just full of fish bones and show almost no evidence of food crops." The MFAC hypothesis, she told me, can be summarized as the belief "that these huge numbers of anchovy bones are telling you something." That "something" is that, according to Daniel H. Sandweiss of the University of Maine, "the incredibly rich ocean off this incredibly impoverished coast was the critical factor."

Further evidence both for and against the MFAC hypothesis emerged in the mid-1990s, with Shady's pathbreaking work on the Supe River. (Aspero, one recalls, sat at the river's mouth.) Shady's team uncovered seventeen riverside settlements, the second-biggest of which was Caral. In her view, monumental buildings implied a large resident population, but again there were plenty of anchovy bones and little evidence that locals farmed anything but cotton. To Moseley, the fish bones suggested that the ample protein on the coast allowed people to go inland and build irrigation networks to produce the cotton needed to expand fishing production. The need for nets, in Haas's view, gave the inland cities the whip hand—Norte Chico was based on farming, like all other complex societies, although not on farming for food. Besides, he says, so many more people lived along the four rivers than on the shore that they had to have been dominant. Moseley believes that Aspero, which has never been fully excavated, is older than the other cities, and set the template for them. "For archaeology," deFrance said, "what may be important" in the end is not the scope of the society "but where it emerged from and the food supply. You can't eat cotton." Evidence one way or the other may emerge if Moseley and Shady, as planned, return to Aspero. If they are correct, and Aspero turns out to be substantially older than now thought, it might win the title of the world's oldest city—the place where human civilization began. "Maybe we might actually stop people calling it the 'New World,'" Moseley joked.

Norte Chico chiefdoms were almost certainly theocratic, though not brutally so; leaders induced followers to obey by a combination of ideology, charisma, and skillfully timed positive reinforcement. Scattered almost randomly around the top of the mounds are burned, oxidized chunks of rock—hearth stones—in drifts of fish bones and ash. To Haas and Creamer, these look like the remains of feasts. The city rulers encouraged and rewarded the workforce during construction and maintenance of the mound by staging celebratory roasts of fish and achira root right on the worksite. Afterward they mixed the garbage into the mound, incorporating the celebration into the construction. At these feasts, alcohol in some form was almost certainly featured. So, perhaps, was music, both vocal and instrumental; excavating Caral, Shady discovered thirty-two flutes made of pelican wingbones tucked into a recess in the main temple.

What was it like building these first great structures? In June 1790, a year after the French Revolution swept away a corrupt and ineffectual monarchy, thousands of Parisians from every social class united to create the enormous Champ de Mars as a monument to the new society. Working in heavy rainfall without coercion or pay, they dug out the entire enormous space to a depth of four feet and then filled it up with enough sand and gravel to make an out-door amphitheater suitable for half a million people. The whole huge effort took only three weeks. Something analogous—an awed, wondering celebration of a new mode of existence—may have occurred at the Norte Chico.

Even today, the contrast is startling between the desert and the irrigated land, with its lush patchwork of maize, sugar, and fruit trees. Beyond the reach of the water the barrens instantly commence; the line of demarcation is sharp enough to cross with a step. To people born into a landscape of rock and fog, the conflagration of green must have been a dazzlement. Of course they would exalt the priests and rulers who promised to maintain this miracle. The prospect of a drunken feast afterward would be a bonus.

The only known trace of the Norte Chico deities may be a drawing etched into the face of a gourd. It depicts a sharp-toothed, hat-wearing figure who faces the viewer frontally and holds a long stick or rod vertically in each hand. When Creamer found the gourd in 2002, the image shocked Andeanists. It looked like an early version of the Staff God, a fanged, staff-wielding deity who is one of the main characters in the Andean pantheon. Previously the earliest manifestation of the Staff God had been thought to be around 500 B.C. According to radiocarbon tests, the Norte Chico gourd was harvested between 2280 and 2180 B.C. The early date implies, Haas and Creamer argued, that the principal Andean spiritual tradition originated in the Norte Chico, and that this tradition endured for at least four thousand years, millennia longer than had been previously suspected.

Many researchers reacted skeptically to the finding. According to Krzysztof Makowski, an archaeologist at the Pontifical Catholic University of Peru in Lima, the image is so anomalous—Creamer found it in a strata dating between 900 and 1300 A.D.—that a more likely explanation is that the figure was carved onto an ancient gourd that had been preserved by the

A recently discovered etched drawing on a gourd (left) has led some researchers to posit that the fanged Staff God was a central figure in an Andean religious tradition that lasted almost four thousand years. (Right, a Staff God from the first millennium A.D.)

extremely arid climate. Such reuse of old materials is not unknown, though nobody has ever seen it with a gourd three thousand years old. More important, Makowski says, researchers have little evidence that ancient Peruvians actually believed in a single overarching deity called the Staff God. "What we describe as the 'Staff God' is a convention," he explained to me, a standardized pose reminiscent in its way of the standardized poses in Byzantine art. The religious tradition of Peru, in his view, was an overlapping sequence of related faiths that has barely begun to be unraveled; it is as if archaeologists from the far future were excavating in Europe, and mulling over the ubiquitous image of the man on the cross. Was this one man? Many men depicted in a similar fashion? One man whose meaning changed over time?

What is known is that the tradition evolved, as religions will, with the circumstances of its believers. As Andean societies grew richer, their temples and the images in them grew grander and more refined, though the former stayed true to the U-shape-and-sunken-plaza pattern I saw in the Norte Chico and the latter, depicted often in the "Staff God" pose, never lost their erect postures, gnashing fangs, and brandished staffs. Over the millennia, this god or gods transmuted into Wiraqocha, the Inka creator deity, whose worship was brutally suppressed by Spain.

Whether on the coast or in the river valleys, Moseley said, the Norte Chico lighted a cultural fire. During the next three thousand years, Peru hosted so many diverse cultures that the archaeological timelines in textbooks, with their multiple arrows and switchbacks, are as impenetrable as the family trees of European kings. Despite their variousness, Haas says, all seem to have drawn in their diverse ways from the well of Norte Chico. Characterizing the similarities is as difficult as nailing down a blob of mercury, because exceptions abound and human behavior is always multifaceted. Nonetheless, visitors to Andean history note certain ways of doing things that recur in ways striking to the outsider, sometimes in one variant, sometimes in another, like the themes in a jazz improvisation. The primacy of exchange over a wide area, the penchant for collective, festive civic work projects, the high valuation of textiles and textile technology—Norte Chico, it seems possible to say, set the template for all of them.

And *only* Norte Chico. For the next four thousand years, Andean civilization was influenced by only one major import from the world outside: maize. A few other minor crops made the trip later, including tobacco, domesticated in Amazonia, then exported north to become the favorite vice of Indians from Mesoamerica to Maine. But it is a mark of maize's social, cultural, and even political centrality that it was the first—and for centuries the only—phenomenon to pass from Mexico to the Andes. The next major import, alas, was smallpox.

TINY COBS

Although it was just after dawn, several people were already waiting outside the small store. When the metal grating rolled up, I followed them inside. The shop was in a middle-class neighborhood of Oaxaca city, in southern Mexico. Behind the low counter, half a dozen women hovered over waist-high stoves made of concrete block. Recessed into the dome-shaped top of each stove were two shallow clay dishes that served as burners. With expert motions the women slipped tortillas—thin discs of cream-colored flour perhaps nine inches in diameter—onto the hot burners. In seconds the tortilla dried and puffed up like a soufflé. And from the storefront floated the aroma of toasting maize, which has permeated Mexico and Central America for thousands of years.

Established in 2001, the tortilla store is an innovative attempt to preserve one of earth's greatest cultural and biological assets: the many local varieties of maize in the narrow "waist" of southern Mexico. The isthmus is a medley of mountains, beaches, wet tropical forests, and dry savannas, and is the most ecologically diverse area in Mesoamerica. "Some parts of Oaxaca go up nine thousand feet," T. Boone Hallberg, a botanist at the Oaxaca Institute of Technology, told me. "Other parts are at sea level. Sometimes the soil is very acid, sometimes it's quite basic—all within a few hundred feet. You can go on either side of a highway, and the climate will be different on the east side than on the west side." The area's human geography is equally diverse: it is the home of more than a dozen major Indian groups, who have a long and fractious history. Despite the strife among them, all of them played a role in the region's greatest achievement, the development of Mesoamerican agriculture, arguably the world's most ecologically savvy form of farming, and of its centerpiece, *Zea mays*, the crop known to agronomists as maize.

I was visiting Amado Ramírez Leyva, the entrepreneur behind the tortilla store. Born in Oaxaca and trained as an agronomist, Ramírez Leyva had established a consortium of traditional farmers, Indians like himself (Ramírez Leyva is Mixtec, the second most numerous Indian group in the region). The farmers supply eight different varieties of dried maize to his shop, Itanoní, where the kernels are carefully ground, hand-pressed into tortillas, and cooked fresh for customers. Itanoní means "maize flower" in Mixtec, and refers to a flower that blooms in maize fields. It is one of the few tortillerías in Mexico—perhaps even the only one—to sell what might be described as "estate" tortillas: proudly labeled as being made from maize of one variety, from one area.

"Everyone in Mexico knows the rules for making a true tortilla," Ramírez Leyva told me. "But you can't get them that way now, except maybe in your grandmother's kitchen." First soak the dried maize kernels in a bath of lime and water to remove their thin, translucent skins (a process with its own special verb, *nixtamalizar*). Then stone-grind the kernels into *masa*, a light, slightly sticky paste with a distinct maize fragrance. Made without salt, spices, leavening, or preservatives, *masa* must be cooked within a few hours of being ground, and the tortilla should be eaten soon after it is cooked. Hot is best, perhaps folded over with mushrooms or cheese in a *tlacoya*. Like a glass of wine, he said, a tortilla should carry the flavor of its native place. "You want to try some?"

I did. The smells in the shop—dry-toasted maize, melting farm cheese, squash flowers sautéing in home-pressed oil—were causing my stomach to direct urgent messages to my brain.

Ramírez Leyva gave me a plateful of *tlacoyas*. "This is exactly what you would have eaten here ten thousand years ago," he said.

In his enthusiasm, he was overstating, but not by much. Indians didn't have cheese, for one thing. And they didn't eat tortillas ten thousand years ago, though tortillas are indeed ancient. It is known that 11,500 years ago paleo-Indians were hunting from caves in what is now Puebla, the state northwest of Oaxaca. These were not mastodon and mammoth hunters—

A gourmet tortilla shop in Oaxaca, Itanoní is an attempt to preserve southern Mexico's hundreds of varieties of maize, a Mesoamerican tradition that
has survived for thousands of years.

both species were already extinct. Instead they preyed on deer, horse, ante-
lope, jackrabbit, and, now and then, giant turtle, as well as several species of
rodent. Within the next two thousand years all of these animals except deer
vanished, too, done in either by a local variant of overkill, the onset of hot-
ter, drier conditions that shrank the available grassland, or both. Responding
to the lack of game, people in Oaxaca and Puebla focused more on gathering. Shifting among productive locations, individual families, living on their
own, ate seeds and fruit during the spring and fall and hunted during the winter. During the summer they joined together in bands of twenty-five to
thirty—cactus leaves, a local favorite, were plentiful enough in that season to
support larger groups.

All the while their store of knowledge about the environment increased.
People learned how to make agave plants edible (roast them), how to remove
the tannic acid from acorns (grind them to a powder, then soak), how to

make tongs to pick spiny cactus fruit, how to find wild squash flowers in the undergrowth, and other useful things. Along the way, perhaps, they noticed that seeds thrown in the garbage one year would sprout spontaneously in the next. The sum of these questions led to full-fledged agriculture—not just in the Tehuacán Valley, but in many places in southern Mexico. Squashes, gourds, peppers, and chupandilla plums were among the initial crops. The first cereal was probably millet—not the millet eaten today, which originated in Africa, but a cousin species, knotweed bristlegrass, which is no longer farmed. And then came maize.

At the DNA level, all the major cereals—wheat, rice, maize, millet, barley, and so on—are surprisingly alike. But despite their genetic similarity, maize looks and acts different from the rest. It is like the one redheaded early riser in a family of dark-haired night owls. Left untended, other cereals are capable of propagating themselves. Because maize kernels are wrapped inside a tough husk, human beings must sow the species—it cannot reproduce on its own. The uncultivated ancestors of other cereals resemble their domesticated descendants. People can and do eat their grain; in the Middle East, for example, the wild barley harvest from a small piece of land can feed a family. By contrast, no wild maize ancestor has ever been found, despite decades of search. Maize's closest relative is a mountain grass called teosinte that looks nothing like it (teosinte splits into many thin stems, whereas maize has a single thick stalk). And teosinte, unlike wild wheat and rice, is not a practical food source; its "ears" are scarcely an inch long and consist of seven to twelve hard, woody seeds. An entire ear of teosinte has less nutritional value than a single kernel of modern maize.

The grain in wild grasses develops near the top of the stem. As it matures, the stem slowly breaks up—shatters, in the jargon—letting the seed dribble to the ground. In wild wheat and barley, a common single-gene mutation blocks shattering. For the plant the change is highly disadvantageous, but it facilitates harvest by humans—the grain waits on the stem to be collected. The discovery and planting of nonshattering grain is thought to have precipitated the Neolithic revolution in the Middle East. Like other grasses, teosinte shatters, but there is no known nonshattering variant. (At least sixteen genes control teosinte and maize shattering, a situation so complex that geneticists have effectively thrown up their hands after trying to explain how a nonshattering type might have appeared spontaneously.) No known wild ancestor, no obvious natural way to evolve a nonshattering variant, no way to propagate itself—little wonder that the Mexican National Museum of Culture claimed in a 1982 exhibition that maize "was not domesticated, but *created*"—almost from scratch.

In the 1960s Richard S. MacNeish, of Phillips Academy, in Andover, Massachusetts, led an archaeological team that meticulously combed Puebla's Tehuacán Valley for signs of early agriculture. Like the Peruvian littoral, the Tehuacán Valley lies in a double rain shadow, sandwiched between two mountain ranges. The aridity similarly helps preserve archaeological evidence. MacNeish's team sifted through fifty caves before they found anything. In site No. 50, a rockshelter near the village of Coxcatlán, the team found maize cobs the size of a cigarette butt.

Ultimately, MacNeish's team found 23,607 whole or partial maize cobs in five caves in the Tehuacán Valley. This ancient refuse became ammunition in a long-running academic battle between Harvard botanist Paul C. Mangelsdorf and George Beadle, a geneticist who worked at Stanford, Caltech, and the University of Chicago. In the late 1930s both men proposed theories about the origin of maize. Mangelsdorf said that it descended from the mix of a now-vanished wild ancestor of maize and wild grasses from the genus *Tripsacum*. Teosinte, he said, played no role in its development. Beadle had a simpler theory: maize was directly descended from teosinte. Mangelsdorf treated this idea with disbelieving scorn. By now the reader will not be surprised to learn that an apparently arcane debate about the distant past could become vehemently personal. Relations between the two men became cold, then bitter, then explosive. Botanists chose sides and wrote caustic letters about each other.

Mangelsdorf worked with MacNeish and classified the 23,607 ancient maize cobs. The smallest and oldest, he proclaimed, were maize's true wild ancestor, which Indians had then crossed with *Tripsacum* to make modern maize. So powerful did the evidence of Mangelsdorf's tiny cobs seem that in the 1960s it buried the teosinte hypothesis, even though the latter's champion, Beadle, had for other research won a Nobel Prize. Beadle's ideas were taken up in revamped form by University of Wisconsin botanist Hugh Iltis in 1970. Maize originated, Iltis postulated, in a strange, wholesale mutation of teosinte, to which Indians added and subtracted features through intensive breeding. Mangelsdorf's side found itself on the defensive; Iltis had gleefully pointed out that the "wild maize" cobs from the Tehuacán Valley were identical to those of an unusual, fully domesticated variety of popcorn from Argentina. By then the dispute over the origin of maize had filled almost as much paper—and became as acrimonious—as the battle over Clovis.

In 1997 Mary W. Eubanks, a Duke University biologist, resuscitated the hybridization theory in a new variant. Maize, she suggested, might have been created by repeatedly crossing *Zea diploperennis,* a rare maize relative, and another cousin species, Eastern gamagrass. When species from different genera hybridize, the result can be what the biologist Barbara McClintock called "genomic shock," a wholesale reordering of DNA in which "new species can arise quite suddenly." In Eubanks's theory, Indians came upon a chance combination of *Zea diploperennis* and gamagrass and realized that by mixing these two species they could shape an entirely new biological entity. As proof, she announced the creation of a *Zea diploperennis*–gamagrass hybrid in the laboratory that displayed the attributes of ancient maize.

The teosinte faction remained skeptical. A consortium of twelve maize scientists harshly attacked Eubanks's work in 2001 for, in their view, failing to demonstrate that her hybrid was actually a *Zea diploperennis*–gamagrass mix and not an accidental blend of *Zea diploperennis* and modern maize. (Such errors are a constant threat; in a busy lab, it is all too easy for biologists to use the wrong pollen, mislabel a tray, or mistake one analysis for another.) Meanwhile other geneticists pinpointed teosinte mutations that could have led to modern maize, including *sugary 1,* a variant gene that alters maize starch in a way that gives tortillas the light, flaky texture celebrated at Itanoní.

Because maize is many steps removed from teosinte, these scientists argued that the modern species had to have been consciously developed by a small group of breeders who hunted through teosinte stands for plants with desired traits. Geneticists from Rutgers University, in New Brunswick, New Jersey, estimated in 1998 that determined, aggressive, knowledgeable plant breeders—which Indians certainly were—might have been able to breed maize in as little as a decade by seeking the right teosinte mutations.

From the historian's point of view, the difference between the two models is unimportant. In both, Indians took the first steps toward modern maize in southern Mexico, probably in the highlands, more than six thousand years ago. Both argue that modern maize was the outcome of a bold act of conscious biological manipulation—"arguably man's first, and perhaps his greatest, feat of genetic engineering," Nina V. Federoff, a geneticist at Pennsylvania State University, wrote in 2003. Federoff's description, which appeared in *Science,* intrigued me. It makes twenty-first-century scientists sound like pikers, I said when I contacted her. "That's right," she said. "To get corn out of teosinte is so—you couldn't get a grant to do that now, because it would sound so crazy." She added, "Somebody who did that today would get a Nobel Prize! If their lab didn't get shut down by Greenpeace, I mean."

To people accustomed to thinking of maize in terms of dark or light yellow kernels of corn on the cob, the variety in Mexican maize is startling. Red, blue, yellow, orange, black, pink, purple, creamy white, multicolored—the jumble of colors in Mesoamerican maize reflects the region's jumble of cultures and ecological zones. One place may have maize with cobs the size of a baby's hand and little red kernels no bigger than grains of rice that turn into tiny puffs when popped; in another valley will be maize with two-foot-long cobs with great puffy kernels that Mexicans float in soup like croutons.

"Every variety has its own special use," Ramírez Leyva explained to me. "This one is for holidays, this one makes tortillas, this one for *niquatole* [a kind of maize gelatin], this one for *tejate*," a cold drink in which maize flour, mamey pits, fermented white cacao beans, and other ingredients are marinated in water overnight and then sweetened and whipped to a froth. As a rule domesticated plants are less genetically diverse than wild species, because breeders try to breed out characteristics they don't want. Maize is one of the few farm species that is *more* diverse than most wild plants.

More than fifty genetically distinguishable maize "landraces" have been identified in Mexico, of which at least thirty are native to Oaxaca, according to Flavio Aragón Cuevas, a maize researcher at the Oaxaca office of the National Institute for Forestry, Agriculture, and Fisheries Research. A landrace is a family of local varieties, each of which may have scores of "cultivars," or cultivated varieties. As many as five thousand cultivars may exist in Mesoamerica.

Maize is open pollinated—it scatters pollen far and wide. (Wheat and rice discreetly pollinate themselves.) Because wind frequently blows pollen from one small maize field onto another, varieties are constantly mixing. "Maize is terribly promiscuous," Hugo Perales, an agronomist at the think tank Ecosur, in Chiapas, told me. Uncontrolled, open pollination would, over time, turn the species into a single, relatively homogeneous entity. But it does not, because farmers carefully sort through the seed they will sow in the next season and generally do not choose obvious hybrids. Thus there is both a steady flow of genes among maize landraces and a force counteracting that flow. "The varieties are not like islands, carefully apart," Perales explained. "They are more like gentle hills in a landscape—you see them, they are clearly present, but you cannot specify precisely where they start."

San Juan Chamula, a mountain town in central Chiapas, near the border with Guatemala, is an example. Located outside the colonial city of San Cristóbal de Las Casas, it has a sixteenth-century church with a brilliant blue interior that is a popular tourist destination. But beyond the souvenir kiosks in the cathedral square, most of the 44,000 inhabitants of Chamula scratch a living from the dry mountain slopes outside town. Almost all are Tzotzil, a southwestern branch of the Maya; in 1995, the most recent date for which census data are available, about 28,000 did not speak Spanish. According to a survey by Perales, 85 percent of the farmers plant the same maize landraces as their fathers, varieties that have been passed on and maintained for generations. The crop in the field today is the sum of thousands of individual choices made by community members in the past.

Indian farmers grow maize in what is called a *milpa*. The term means "maize field," but refers to something considerably more complex. A *milpa* is

Landrace maize from Oaxaca

a field, usually but not always recently cleared, in which farmers plant a dozen crops at once, including maize, avocados, multiple varieties of squash and bean, melon, tomatoes, chilis, sweet potato, jicama (a tuber), amaranth (a grain-like plant), and mucuna (a tropical legume). In nature, wild beans and squash often grow in the same field as teosinte, the beans using the tall teosinte as a ladder to climb toward the sun; below ground, the beans' nitrogen-fixing roots provide nutrients needed by teosinte. The *milpa* is an elaboration of this natural situation, unlike ordinary farms, which involve single-crop expanses of a sort rarely observed in unplowed landscapes.

Milpa crops are nutritionally and environmentally complementary. Maize lacks the amino acids lysine and tryptophan, which the body needs to make proteins and niacin; diets with too much maize can lead to protein deficiency and pellagra, a disease caused by lack of niacin. Beans have both lysine and tryptophan, but not the amino acids cysteine and methionine, which are provided by maize. As a result, beans and maize make a nutritionally complete meal. Squashes, for their part, provide an array of vitamins; avocados, fats. The *milpa*, in the estimation of H. Garrison Wilkes, a maize researcher at the University of Massachusetts in Boston, "is one of the most successful human inventions ever created."

Wilkes was referring to the ecological worries that beset modern agribusiness. Because agricultural fields are less diverse than natural ecosystems, they cannot perform all their functions. As a result, farm soils can rapidly become exhausted. In Europe and Asia, farmers try to avoid stressing the soil by rotating crops; they may plant wheat one year, legumes the next, and let the field lie fallow in the year following. But in many places this only works for a while, or it is economically unfeasible not to use the land for a year. Then farmers use artificial fertilizer, which at best is expensive, and at worst may inflict long-term damage on the soil. No one knows how long the system can continue. The *milpa,* by contrast, has a long record of success. "There are places in Mesoamerica that have been continuously cultivated for four thousand years and are still productive," Wilkes told me. "The *milpa* is the only system that permits that kind of long-term use." Likely the *milpa* cannot be replicated on an industrial scale. But by studying its essential features, researchers may be able to smooth the rough ecological edges of conventional agriculture. "Mesoamerica still has much to teach us," Wilkes said.

To Wilkes's way of thinking, ancient Indian farming methods may be the cure for some of modern agriculture's ailments. Beginning in the 1950s, scientists developed hybrid strains of wheat, rice, maize, and other crops that were vastly more productive than traditional varieties. The combination of the new crops and the greatly increased use of artificial fertilizer and irrigation led to the well-known Green Revolution. In many ways, the Green Revolution was a tremendous boon; harvests in many poor countries soared so fast that despite burgeoning populations the incidence of hunger fell dramatically. Unfortunately, though, the new hybrids are almost always more vulnerable to disease and insects than older varieties. In addition to being too costly for many small farmers, the fertilizer and irrigation can, if used improperly, damage the soil. Worst, perhaps, in the long run, the exuberant spread of the Green Revolution has pushed many traditional cultivars toward extinction, which in turn reduces the genetic diversity of crops. Wilkes believes that some or all of these difficulties may be resolved by reproducing features of the *milpa* in a contemporary setting. If this occurs, it will be the second time that the dissemination of Mesoamerican agricultural techniques will have had an enormous cultural impact—the first time being, of course, when they originated.

From today's vantage it is difficult to imagine the impact maize must have had in southern Mexico at the beginning, but perhaps a comparison will help. "Almost pure stands" of einkorn wheat covered "dozens of square kilometers" in Turkey, Iraq, Syria, and other parts of the Middle East, according to Jack R. Harlan and Daniel Zohary, two agronomists who pored over the area in the 1960s to determine the distribution of wild cereals. "Over many thousands of hectares" in those countries, they wrote in *Science,* "it would be possible to harvest wild wheat today from natural stands almost as dense as a cultivated wheat field." In the Middle East, therefore, the impact of agriculture was thus less a matter of raising the productivity of wheat, barley, and other cereals than of extending the range in which they could be grown, by developing varieties that could flourish in climates and soils that daunt the wild plant. By contrast, the Americas had no wild maize, and thus no wild maize harvest. Stands of teosinte have been seen in the wild, but because the "ears" are tiny and constantly shattering they are difficult to harvest. Thus before agriculture the people of Mesoamerica had never experienced what it was like to stand in a field of grain. Grain fields—landscapes of food!—were part of the mental furniture of people in Mesopotamia. They were an astounding novelty in Mesoamerica. Indians not only created a new species, they created a new environment to put it in. Unsurprisingly, the reverberations sounded for centuries.

Maize in the *milpa*, the Yale archaeologist Michael D. Coe has written, "is the key . . . to the understanding of Mesoamerican civilization. Where it flourished, so did high culture." The statement may be more precise than it seems. In the 1970s the geographer Anne Kirkby discovered that Indian farmers in Oaxaca considered it not worth their while to clear and plant a *milpa* unless it could produce more than about two hundred pounds of grain per acre. Using this figure, Kirkby went back to the ancient cobs excavated from Tehuacán Valley and tried to estimate how much grain per acre they would have yielded. The cob sizes steadily increased as they approached the present. In Kirkby's calculation, the harvest broke the magic two-hundred-pound line sometime between 2000 and 1500 B.C. At about that time, the first evidence of large-scale land clearing for *milpas* appears in the archaeological record. And with it appeared the Olmec, Mesoamerica's first great civilization.

Based on the Gulf Coast side of Mexico's waist, on the other side of a range of low mountains from Oaxaca, the Olmec clearly understood the profound changes wreaked by maize—indeed, they fêted them in their art. Like the stained-glass windows in European cathedrals, the massive Olmec sculptures and bas-reliefs were meant both to dazzle and instruct. A major lesson is the central place of maize, usually represented by a vertical ear with two leaves falling to the side, a talismanic symbol reminiscent of a fleur-de-lys. In sculpture after sculpture, ears of maize spring like thoughts from the skulls of supernatural beings. Olmec portraits of living rulers were often engraved on stelae (long, flat stones mounted vertically in the ground and carved on the face with images and writing). In these stela portraits, the king's clothes, chosen to represent his critical spiritual role in the society's prosperity, generally included a headdress with an ear of maize emblazoned on the front like a star. So resonant was the symbol, according to Virginia M. Fields, curator of pre-Columbian art at the Los Angeles County Museum of Art, that in later Maya hieroglyphics "it became the semantic equivalent of the highest royal title, *ahaw.*" In the Maya creation story, the famous *Popul Vuh,* humans were literally created from maize.

Maize and the *milpa* slowly radiated throughout the Americas, stopping their advance only where the climate grew too cold or dry. By the time of the Pilgrims, fields of mixed maize, beans, and squash lined the New England coast and in many places extended for miles into the interior. To the south, maize reached to Peru and Chile. Maize was a high-status food there even though Andean cultures had developed their own agricultural system, with potatoes occupying the central role. (Amazonia seems to have been an exception; most but not all researchers believe maize there was eclipsed by manioc.)

Maize had an equivalent impact on much of the rest of the world after Columbus introduced it to Europe. Central Europeans became especially hooked on it; by the nineteenth century, maize was the daily bread of Serbia, Rumania, and Moldavia. So dependent did northern Italy and southwestern France become on polenta, a type of cornmeal mush, that pellagra (the disease caused by maize's lack of niacin) became widespread. "I know little, if anything, pleasing to say about the people," wrote Goethe, who visited northern Italy in 1786. The women's "features indicated misery, and the children were just as pitiful to behold; the men are little better. . . . The cause of this sickly condition is found in the continued use of Turkish and heath corn."

Even greater was the impact in Africa, where maize was transforming agriculture by the end of the sixteenth century. "The probability is that the population of Africa was greatly increased because of maize and other American Indian crops," Alfred Crosby told me. "Those extra people helped make the slave trade possible." ("Other American Indian crops" included peanuts and manioc, both now African staples.) Maize swept into Africa as introduced disease was leveling Indian societies. Faced with a labor shortage, the Europeans turned their eyes to Africa. The continent's quarrelsome societies helped them siphon off millions of people. The maize-fed population boom, Crosby believes, let the awful trade continue without pumping the well dry.

THE STUPIDEST QUESTION IN THE WORLD

A few days after I met Ramírez Leyva, the tortilla entrepreneur, we went to Soledad Aquablanca, a clump of small farms two hours southeast of Oaxaca City. Waiting for us at the side of the road was Héctor Díaz Castellano, one of the farmers who supplied Ramírez Leyva's store. Díaz Castellano had a pencil moustache and a rakish straw hat. His Spanish was so heavily salted

Héctor Díaz Castellano

with Zapotec, the language of Oaxaca's biggest Indian group, that I could
not make out a word of it; Ramírez Leyva had to translate. The maize field
was at the end of a long, rutted dirt road that led up a rise. Although we had
left just after dawn, the sun was hot enough by our arrival to make me wish
for a hat. Díaz Castellano walked along the rows, his gaze taking in every
stalk as he passed. For an hour he spoke, almost without stopping, about his
maize and the market for his maize. He was not, I suspected, a naturally
loquacious man, but that morning he had a subject that interested him.

Díaz Castellano's maize field was one of the 340,000 farms in Oaxaca. His
farm, like about two-thirds of the farms in the state, occupied less than ten
acres—unviably small by the standards of developed nations. Most landrace
maize is grown on these farms, partly because of tradition and partly
because they are usually in areas that are too high, dry, steep, or exhausted to
support high-yield varieties (or owned by farmers too poor to afford the necessary fertilizer). As if being grown on tiny farms in bad conditions weren't
enough, landrace maize is usually less productive than modern hybrids; a
typical yield is .4 to .8 tons per acre, whereas Green Revolution varieties in
Oaxaca reap between 1.2 and 2.5 tons per acre when properly fertilized, a
crippling advantage. The meager harvests may be enough for subsistence but
can rarely be brought to market because farm villages are often hours away
on dirt roads from the nearest large town. But even when farmers try, it is

often little use: modern hybrids are so productive that despite the distances involved U.S. corporations can sell maize for less in Oaxaca than can Díaz Castellano. Landrace maize, he said, tastes better, but it is hard to find a way to make the quality pay off. He was lucky, he said, that Ramírez Leyva was trying to market his crop.

We went to Díaz Castellano's house for breakfast. His wife, Angelina, round and short-haired in a tight plaid dress, was cooking tortillas in an outdoor shed with corrugated aluminum walls. A wood fire burned beneath a concave clay griddle called a *comale*. The *comale* was propped above the flames on three rocks—a cooking method as old as Mesoamerican culture. By the fire, in a three-legged stone bowl, was a lump of fresh *masa* twice the size of a toaster. The stereotype is that rural Mexicans are generous to strangers. Piling my plate high, Angelina did nothing to dispel this impression.

I asked her husband what he was. I had wanted to find out which Indian group he was born into, but he took the question another way.

"*Somos hombres de maíz,*" he said, enunciating clearly for my benefit. *We are men of maize.*

I wasn't sure what to make of this gnomic utterance. Was he pulling my leg?

"Everybody says that," Ramírez Leyva said, observing my confusion. "It's an idiom." A little while later I visited a Danish anthropologist at the International Maize and Wheat Improvement Center (CIMMYT), outside Mexico City. Watching films of her interviews with Oaxacans, I saw two old women explain to the young anthropologist that they, too, were *hombres de maíz*. So Ramírez Leyva was right, I thought. A day later a CIMMYT biologist gave me a paperback book, describing it as "the best novel ever written about Mesoamerica." It was *Hombres de maíz*, by Miguel Angel Asturias. All right already, I thought. I get it.

Meanwhile Angelina had come out from behind the *comale* and joined her husband. In the Oaxacan countryside, they explained to me, a house without maize growing in the backyard is like a house without a roof or walls. You would never not have maize, they said. They were speaking matter-of-factly, as if telling me how to take the bus. Even in the city, they said, where people cannot grow maize, nobody would even think of passing a day without eating it.

Curious, I asked what they thought would happen if they didn't have maize every day. Díaz Castellano looked at me as if I had asked the stupidest question in the world.

"Why should I want to be somebody else?" he said.

7

Writing, Wheels, and Bucket Brigades

(Tales of Two Civilizations, Part II)

"LIKE GRAPES THEY FALL OFF"

On January 16, 1939, Matthew W. Stirling took an early-morning walk through the wet, buggy forest of Veracruz state, on the Gulf Coast side of Mexico's southern isthmus. Eighty years before his walk, a villager traipsing through the same woods had stumbled across a buried, six-foot-tall stone sculpture of a human head. Although the find was of obvious archaeological importance, the object was so big and heavy that in the intervening eight decades it had never been pulled out of the ground. Stirling, director of the Smithsonian Bureau of American Ethnology, had gone to Mexico the year before, in early 1938, to see the head for himself. He found it, sunk to the eyebrows in mud, after an eight-hour horseback ride from the nearest town. The head was in the midst of about fifty large, artificial earthen mounds—the ruins, Sterling concluded with excitement, of a previously unknown Maya civic center. He had decided to assemble a research team and explore the area in more detail the next year, and persuaded the National Geographic Society to foot the bill. When he returned to Veracruz, he and his team cleared the dirt around the great head, admiring its fine, naturalistic workmanship, so unlike the stiff, stylized sculpture common elsewhere in Mesoamerica. Nearby, they found a stela, its wide, flat face covered with bas-relief figures. Hoping to turn up others, Stirling was walking that January morning to the far end of the mounded area, where a workman had noticed a large, flat, partly submerged rock: a second stela.

Accompanying him were twelve workers from the nearby hamlet of Tres Zapotes. They pried the stela from the ground with wooden poles, but it was blank. Disappointed, Stirling took the crew to yet a third fallen stela. They scraped away the covering dirt and found that it, like the first, was covered with intricate images. Alas, the carvings were now too weathered to be deciphered. The frustrated Stirling asked the workers to expose the back of the slab by digging beneath it and levering up the stone with poles. Several of the men, he later recounted, "were on their knees in the excavation, cleaning the mud from the stone with their hands, when one of them spoke up in Spanish: 'Chief! Here are numbers!' "

Across the back of the stela were clumps of dots and bars, a notation familiar to Stirling from the Maya. The Maya used a dot to signify one and a horizontal bar to signify five; the number nineteen would thus be three bars and four dots. Stirling copied the dots and bars and "hurried back to camp, where we settled down to decipher them." The inscription turned out to be a date: September 3, 32 B.C, in today's calendar.

Stirling already knew that Tres Zapotes was anomalous—it was at least 150 miles west of any previously discovered Maya settlement. The date deepened the puzzle. If, as seemed likely, it recorded when the stela was put on display, this implied that Tres Zapotes had been a going concern in 32 B.C.—centuries before any other known Maya site. The date thus seemed to imply that the Maya had originated well to the west of what was thought of as their traditional homeland, and much earlier than had been thought. Stirling didn't believe it. Surely the Maya had not sprung up in Tres Zapotes and then moved en masse hundreds of miles to the east. But the alternative explanation—that Tres Zapotes was not a Maya community—seemed equally improbable. The Maya were universally regarded as the oldest advanced society in Mesoamerica. Whoever had carved the stela had some knowledge of writing and mathematics. If they were not Maya, the implication was that someone else had launched the project of civilization in Mesoamerica.

Learning from local people that Tres Zapotes was only one of many mound sites in Veracruz, Stirling decided to return in 1940 to survey them all. The task was daunting even for a cigar-chomping, whisky-drinking, adventure addict like Stirling. Most of the mound centers were in the middle of trackless mangrove swamps or up narrow, unmapped rivers choked with water hyacinth. Ticks and mosquitoes were indefatigable and present in huge numbers; the ticks were worse than the mosquitoes, Stirling remarked, because they had to be dug out of the flesh with a knife. At one point Stirling and a colleague hitched a ride in a pepper truck to one of the smaller sites. After jolting down a road with deep ruts "designed to test the very souls of motorcars," the two men were let off in a nondescript meadow. Stirling went to talk with the driver.

"The ticks are not bad, are they?" I asked him hopefully, viewing the tall grass and underbrush between the road and the mounds. "No," said the driver, beaming. "When full, like grapes they fall off and no harm is done. There are millions of them here, however."

In La Venta, a dry, raised "island" in the coastal swamp, Stirling's team discovered four more colossal heads. Like the first, they had no necks or bodies and wore helmets that vaguely resembled athletic gear. All were at least six feet tall and fifteen feet round and made from single blocks of volcanic basalt. How, Stirling wondered, had their makers transported these ten-ton blocks from the mountains and across the swamp? Whoever these people were, he eventually concluded, they could not be Maya; their ways of life seemed too different. Instead they must have belonged to another culture altogether. La Venta was filled with mounds and terraces, which told Stirling that many people had lived there. The city, he wrote in 1940, "may well be the

Curious villagers surround the great Olmec head excavated in 1939 by archaeologist Matthew Stirling in the Mexican state of Veracruz.

basic civilization out of which developed such high art centers as those of the Maya, Zapotecs, Toltecs, and Totonacs." He called its "mysterious people" the Olmec.

Stirling's account set the template for decades to follow. Ever since his day, the Olmec have been known by two Homeric epithets: they were "mysterious," and they were the "mother culture" of Mesoamerica. (Tourists are told by Frommer's 2005 Mexico guide, for example, to visit the ruins of the "enigmatic people" who created the "mother culture of Mesoamerica.") But in recent years many archaeologists have come to believe that neither description is correct.

The Olmec's purported mysteriousness is related to their emergence. To Stirling and many of his successors, the Olmec seemed to have no peers or ancestors; they appeared fully formed, apparently from nowhere, like Athena springing from the brow of Zeus. First there was a jungle with a few indistinguishable villages; then, suddenly, a sophisticated empire with monumental architecture, carved stelae, earthwork pyramids, hieroglyphic writing, ball courts, and fine artworks—all of it conjured into existence with the suddenness of a magician's trick. The Olmec, wrote Smithsonian archaeologist Betty Meggers, were a "quantum change." Their status as precursors led archaeologists to believe that the subsequent emergence of other complex societies was due to their example—or their conquest. Even the mighty Maya did little more than continue down the path set by the Olmec. "There is now little doubt," Yale archaeologist Michael Coe wrote in 1994, "that all later civilizations in Mesoamerica, whether Mexican or Maya, ultimately rest on an Olmec base."

Strictly speaking, Coe was mistaken. By the time he wrote, many of his colleagues strongly doubted that the Olmec either emerged alone or were the mother culture. They did emerge abruptly, these researchers say, but they were only the first of the half-dozen complex societies—"sister cultures"—that sprang up in southern Mexico after the development of maize agriculture. Focusing on the Olmec's chronological primacy, they believe, obscures the more important fact that Mesoamerica was the home of a remarkable multisociety ferment of social, aesthetic, and technical innovation.

RUBBER PEOPLE

Nobody knows the right name for the Olmec, but "Olmec" is the wrong one. They spoke a language in the Mixe-Zoquean language family, some members of which are still used in isolated pockets of southern Mexico. "Olmec," though, is a word in Nahuatl, the language of the Mexica to the north. It means, more or less, "people of the land of rubber." The problem with the name is not so much that the Olmec did not use it for themselves—nobody knows what that name was, and they have to be called something. Nor is the problem the rubber, which the Olmec used, and may have invented (scientists discovered in the 1990s that they made rubber by chemically treating the latex-containing sap of a tropical tree, *Castilla elastica*). The problem is that the Mexica did not actually use the name to refer to the putative mother culture in Veracruz, but to another, completely unrelated culture in Puebla to the west, a culture that, unlike the ancient Olmec, still existed at the time of the Spanish conquest. The confusion between the Mexica's Olmec and Stirling's Olmec led some archaeologists to propose that the latter should be called the "La Venta Culture," after the site he investigated. Almost everyone agreed that the new name was a big improvement, logically speaking. Unfortunately, nobody used it. Not for the first time in Native American history, the confusing, incorrect name prevailed.

The Olmec heartland was the coastal forests of Veracruz. Compared to the Norte Chico, the area is promising. Like the Peruvian littoral, it is bracketed by sea and mountains, but it catches, rather than misses, the prevailing winds, and the rain that comes with them. The shoreline itself is swampy, but not far from the coast the country rises into a lush, fertile plateau. Further inland are the Tuxtla Mountains, with many rivers cascading down their flanks. The rivers flood in the rainy season, enriching the land, Nile Delta style. During the rest of the year, the climate is drier, and farmers plant and tend their *milpas* on the alluvial soil.

The first traces of the people who would become the Olmec date back to about 1800 B.C. At that time there was little to distinguish them from groups elsewhere in Mesoamerica. But something happened in Veracruz, some spark or incitement, a cultural quickening, because within the next three centuries the Olmec had built and occupied San Lorenzo, the first large-scale settlement in North America—it covered 2.7 square miles. On a plateau commanding the Coatzacoalcos river basin, San Lorenzo proper was inhabited mainly by the elite; everyone else lived in the farm villages around it. The ceremonial center of the city—a series of courtyards and low mounds, the latter probably topped with thatch houses—sat on a raised platform 150 feet high and two-thirds of a mile to a side. The platform was built of almost three million cubic yards of rock, much of it transported from mountain quarries fifty miles away.

Scattered around the San Lorenzo platform were stone monuments: massive thrones for living kings, huge stone heads for dead ones. Rulers helped to mediate between supernatural forces in the air above and the watery place below where souls went after life. When kings died, their thrones were sometimes transformed into memorials for their occupants: the colossal heads. The features of these enormous portraits are naturalistically carved and amazingly expressive—thoughtful or fiercely proud, mirthful or dismayed. It is assumed they were placed like so many stone sentinels for maximum Orwellian impact: the king is here, the king is watching you.*

Like the carvings and stained-glass windows in European cathedrals, the art in San Lorenzo and other Olmec cities consisted mainly of powerful, recurring images—the crucifixions and virgins, so to speak, of ancient Mesoamerica. Among these repeated subjects is a crouched, blobby figure with a monstrously swollen head. Puzzled researchers long described these sculptures as "dwarves" or "dancers." In 1997 an archaeologist and a medical doctor with archaeological leanings identified them as human fetuses. Their features were portrayed accurately enough to identify their stage of development. Researchers had not recognized them because artistic renditions of fetuses are almost unheard of in European cultures (the first known drawing of one is by Leonardo). Other frequent themes included lepers, the pathologically obese, and people with thyroid deficiencies, all portrayed with a cool eye for anatomical detail. Perhaps the best-known subject is a man or boy gingerly holding a "were-jaguar": a limp, fat, sexless baby with a flattened nose and a snarling jaguar mouth. Often the baby has a deeply cloven skull.

The denizens of San Lorenzo are unlikely to have shared Europeans' dismay at the physical deformity portrayed in these images. Indeed, by contemporary standards high-born Olmec were deformed themselves. By binding small, flat pieces of wood to newborns' foreheads, they pushed up the soft infant bones, making the skull longer and higher than normal. To further proclaim their status, wealthy Olmec carved deep grooves into their teeth and pierced their nasal septums with bone awls, plugging the holes with ornamental jade beads. (Because no Olmec skeletons have been found, no direct proof of these practices exists; instead archaeologists base their beliefs on the portrayal of Olmec nobles in figurines and sculptures.)

Swanning about the elite precincts, the rich and powerful wore finely

---

*The statues' broad lips and flat noses have led "Africanist" historians like Clyde Winters and Ivan Van Sertima to claim that the Olmecs either were visited by Africans or had actually migrated from Africa. The African knowledge gained thereby explains the Olmec's rapid rise. These views are not widely endorsed. Surprisingly, several noted archaeologists, including Betty Meggers and Gordon Ekholm, have suggested the geographical opposite: that Olmec society was inspired by China. Visitors from the Shang Dynasty are said to have crossed the Pacific to teach the ancient Olmec how to write, build monuments, and worship a feline god. This hypothesis, too, has failed to stir enthusiasm.

woven clothing, but only below the waist—breechclouts for men, skirts and belts for women. Veracruz was too hot for anything more. On public occasions, nobles bedizened themselves with bracelets, anklets, many-stranded necklaces, bejeweled turbans, and big, hiphop-style pendants. Some of the last were concave mirrors made from beautifully polished magnetite. Precisely ground, the mirrors were able to start fires and project images onto flat surfaces, *camera lucida* fashion. Presumably they were used to dazzle hoi polloi. As for the poor, it is likely that they went naked, except possibly for sandals.

San Lorenzo fell in about 1200 B.C., victim of either revolution or invasion. Or perhaps it was abandoned and sacked for religious reasons—archaeologists have advanced several hypotheses for the city's demise. What is certain is that the site was vacated and the stelae defaced and the sculptures decapitated. The colossal heads being, so to speak, pre-decapitated, they were smashed with hammers and systematically buried in long lines. Vegetation overran the red-ocher floors and the workshops that manufactured ceramic figurines and iron beads and rubber ax-head straps.

Olmec society was surprisingly unaffected by the collapse of its greatest polity. A much bigger city, La Venta, was going up on a swamp island about forty miles away.

Today La Venta is partly buried by an oil refinery, but in its heyday—roughly speaking, 1150 B.C. to 500 B.C.—it was a large community with a ring of housing that surrounded a grand ceremonial center. The city's focus, its Eiffel Tower or Tiananmen Square, was a 103-foot-tall clay mound, a bulging, vertically fluted cone somewhat resembling a head of garlic. The mound rose at the south end of a rectangular, hundred-yard-long pavilion that was bordered by two knee-high berms. At the north end of the pavilion was a sunken rectangular courtyard fenced on three sides by a row of seven-foot basalt columns atop a low red and yellow adobe wall. The fourth, northern side opened onto a third mound, larger than the small mound but nowhere near the size of the big one. The pavilion and courtyard had painted walls and floors of colored sand and clay; heavy sculptural objects, including several of the trademark heads, studded the area. This central part of the city was reserved, archaeologists believe, for clerics and rulers. It was Buckingham Palace and the Vatican rolled into one.

La Venta, too, was destroyed, perhaps deliberately, around 350 B.C. But its eight-hundred-year existence spanned one of the most exciting times in American history. At La Venta's height, Olmec art and technical innovations could be found throughout Mesoamerica. So widespread was Olmec iconography—jaguar babies, carved stelae, distinctively shaped ceramics—that many archaeologists believed its very ubiquity was evidence that the Olmec "not only engendered Mesoamerica but also brought forth the first Mesoamerican empire." The description is from Ignacio Bernal, once director of Mexico's famed National Museum of Anthropology. Bernal, who died in 1992, envisioned an imperium that spanned much of southern Mexico, proselytizing its religion and forcing other groups to send their finest works to its heartland. The Olmec, he thought, were the Romans of Mesoamerica, a magisterial society that "established the pattern which, through the centuries, was to be followed by other expansionist Mesoamerican cultures."

Since Bernal's death many researchers have come to view the Olmec differently. According to the University of Michigan anthropologists Kent Flannery and Joyce Marcus, the Olmec heartland was but one of four regional power centers: the Central Basin to the north, where settlements like Tlatilco and Tlapacoya laid the groundwork for the empires of Teotihuacán and the Toltecs; in the isthmus, the chiefdoms of Oaxaca; the Olmec, along the Gulf Coast; and, later, the Maya polities in Yucatán and northern Guatemala. Some believe that there was a fifth power: Chalcatzingo, an important chiefdom between the Central Basin and Oaxaca.

In the first millennium B.C., all four (or five) were making the transition from individual fortified villages to groups of chiefdoms to states with centralized authority. Although the Olmec preceded the others, they did not set the template for them. Instead they all influenced each other, sometimes by trade, sometimes by violence, each one developing new techniques, exporting unique goods, and swiping ideas from the others. In this world of "competitive interaction," all parties hustled for advantage. Trade in goods was important, but it was the trade in ideas that mattered.

By making this argument, I am endorsing one side in the long-running dispute between mother- and sister-culture proponents. In other words, as one sister-culture advocate put it, I am "swallowing Marcus's [nonsense] whole." He may be right. But I would argue that there is a difference between *inheriting* a cultural tradition, as the Norte Chico culture's successors apparently did, and *copying* one, as the Olmec's proponents argue. Nobody disputes that Han Chinese society arose long before its neighbors in Asia, but Asian archaeologists don't refer to China as Asia's "mother culture," because China's neighbors used part of its intellectual legacy to build up their own distinct and different writing systems, agricultural technologies, imperial practices, and much else. Given the evidence available now, the same seems to be true for the Olmec and ancient Mesoamerica. (To me, anyway—many researchers disagree.)

Emblematic of this rocketing growth were the Olmec's neighbors in Oaxaca, the Zapotec, whom Flannery and Marcus have studied for more than two decades. The Zapotec were based across the mountains from the

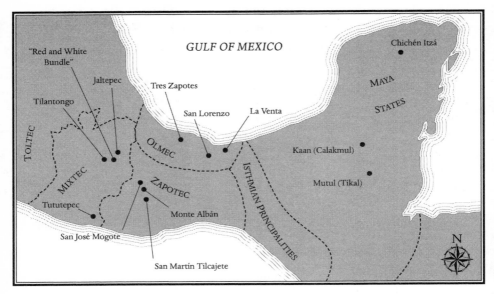

MESOAMERICA, 1000 B.C.—1000 A.D.

For thousands of years Mesoamerica was a wellspring of cultural innovation and growth. This map does not depict it accurately, because these societies were not contemporaries—the Olmec vanished centuries before the Mixtec and Zapotec began to reach their height, for example. Nonetheless, it should give some idea of each society's heartland.

Olmec, in Oaxaca's high Central Valley—three forty-to-sixty-mile-long bowls that intersect in a ragged Y. By about 1550 B.C., they were abandoning the life of hunting and gathering to live in villages with defensive palisades.* These early villages had wattle-and-daub houses, fine pottery, and some public architecture. They were controlled by "big men," the social scientist's term for the alpha male who is able in such informal settings to enforce his will through persuasion or force. Within a few hundred years, the big men acquired *rank*—that is, they began to wield power not only because of their personal charisma, but also because their societies had given them an elevated official position. It is the difference between the leading spirit on a pickup basketball team and the officially selected captain of a college squad. After this, political consolidation proceeded apace. Soon the valley was dominated by three main chiefdoms, one at each endpoint of the Y. They did not get along; a thirty-square-mile buffer zone in the middle, Flannery and Marcus noted, was "virtually unoccupied."

*Here, as elsewhere in this book, I am being chronologically inexact. The oldest Zapotec palisade Flannery and Marcus excavated yielded calibrated radiocarbon dates in the range between 1680 and 1410 B.C., which for brevity's sake I render as "about 1550 B.C."

The biggest of the three chiefdoms was located near today's village of San José Mogote. Around 750 B.C. it was attacked and its temple razed in a fire so intense that the clay walls melted. San José Mogote quickly rebuilt the temple a few yards away.

Across the new threshold artisans laid a carved stone. Splayed across its face, suitable for stomping on, was a bas-relief of a naked, disemboweled male corpse, apparently a defeated enemy, blood welling from his side. The carving, to my taste, is beautifully done, as graphically elegant, despite the gory subject matter, as a Matisse. What matters most to researchers, though, is not the design but the two curious marks between the cadaver's feet. The two marks are glyphs: the oldest firmly dated writing in the Americas. Despite their brevity, they are full of information, both because of the nature of written language, and because of the special way Mesoamerican people chose their names.

COUNTING AND WRITING

Writing begins with counting. When a culture grows big enough, it acquires an elite, which needs to monitor things it considers important: money, stored goods, births and deaths, the progression of time. In Mesopotamia, Sumerian accountants began keeping records with clay tokens around 9000 B.C. As the need for precision grew, they scratched marks on the tokens as mnemonic devices. For example, they might have distinguished a count of sheep from one of wheat by drawing a sheep on one and a wheat stalk on the other. Gradually the information on each record increased. The bureaucrats were not intending to create writing. Instead they were simply adding useful features as they became necessary. By 3200 B.C. Sumerian scribes had progressed to inscribing on clay tablets with sharpened reeds. A tablet might contain, say, two hash marks, a box, a circle with a cross in the middle, an asterisk-like shape, and an arrangement of three triangles. Scribes would know that the hash marks meant "two," the box was a "temple," the circle stood for "cattle," an asterisk meant "goddess," and the triangles were "Inanna"—two cattle owned by the goddess Inanna's temple. (Here I am lifting an example from Gary Urton, a Harvard anthropologist.) They had no way to indicate verbs or adjectives, no way to distinguish subject from object, and only a limited vocabulary. Nonetheless, Sumerians were moving toward something like writing.

In Mesoamerica, timekeeping provided the stimulus that accounting gave to the Middle East. Like contemporary astrologers, the Olmec, Maya, and Zapotec believed that celestial phenomena like the phases of the moon and

Venus affect daily life. To measure and predict these portents requires careful sky watching and a calendar. Strikingly, Mesoamerican societies developed *three* calendars: a 365-day secular calendar like the contemporary calendar; a 260-day sacred calendar that was like no other calendar on earth; and the equally unique Long Count, a one-by-one tally of the days since a fixed starting point thousands of years ago. Establishing these three calendars required advances in astronomy; synchronizing them required ventures into mathematics.

The 260-day ritual calendar may have been linked to the orbit of Venus; the 365-day calendar, of course, tracked the earth's orbit around the sun. Dates were typically given in both notations. For example, October 12, 2004, is 2 Lamat 11 Yax, where 2 Lamat is the date in the ritual calendar and 11 Yax the date in the secular calendar. Because the two calendars do not have the same number of days, they are not synchronized; the next time 2 Lamat occurs in the sacred calendar, it will be paired with a different day in the secular calendar. After October 12, 2004, in fact, 2 Lamat and 11 Yax will not coincide again for another 18,980 days, about fifty-two years.

Mesoamerican cultures understood all this, and realized that by citing dates with both calendars they were able to identify every day in this fifty-two-year period uniquely. What they couldn't do was distinguish one fifty-two-year period from another. It was as if the Christian calendar referred to the year only as, say, '04—one would then be unable to distinguish between 1904, 2004, and 2104. To prevent confusion, Mesoamerican societies created the third calendar, the Long Count. The Long Count tracks time from a starting point, much as the Christian calendar begins with the purported birth date of Christ. The starting point is generally calculated to have been August 13, 3114, B.C., though some archaeologists put the proper date at August 10 or 11, or even September 6. Either way, Long Count dates consisted of the number of days, 20-day "months," 360-day "years," 7,200-day "decades," and 144,000-day "millennia" since the starting point. Archaeologists generally render these as a series of five numbers separated by dots, in the manner of Internet Protocol addresses. Using the August 13 starting date, October 12, 2006, would be written in the Long Count as 12.19.13.12.18. (For a more complete explanation, see Appendix D.)

Because it runs directly from 1 B.C. to 1 A.D., the Christian calendar was long a headache for astronomers. Scientists tracking supernovae, cometary orbits, and other celestial phenomena would still have to add or subtract a year manually when they crossed the A.D.-B.C. barrier if a sixteenth-century astronomer named Joseph Scaliger hadn't got sick of the whole business and devised a calendar for astronomers that doesn't skip a year. The Julian calendar, which Scaliger named after his father, counts the days since Day 0. Scaliger chose Day 0 as January 1, 4713, B.C.; Day 1 was January 2. In this system, October 12, 2006, is Julian Day 2,454,021.

The Long Count calendar began with the date 0.0.0.0.0.* Mathematically, what is most striking about this date is that the zeroes are true zeroes. Zero has two functions. It is a number, manipulated like other numbers, which means that it is differentiated from nothing. And it is a placeholder in a positional notation system, such as our base-10 system, in which a number like 1 can signify a single unit if it is in the digits column or ten units if it is in the adjacent column.

That zero is not the same as nothing is a concept that baffled Europeans as late as the Renaissance. How can you calculate with nothing? they asked. Regarding zero as a dangerous idea, the Catholic Church banned Hindu-Arabic numerals—the 0 through 9 used today—in much of Italy until the fourteenth century. A classic demonstration of zero's status as a number, according to science historian Dick Teresi, is grade point average:

In a four-point system, an A equals 4, B equals 3, and so on, down to E, which equals 0. If a student takes four courses and gets A's in two but fails the other two, he receives a GPA of 2.0, or a C average. The two zeroes drag down the two A's. If zero were nothing, the student could claim that the grades for the courses he failed did not exist, and demand a 4.0 average. His dean would laugh at such logic.

Without a positional notation system, arithmetic is tedious and hard, as schoolchildren learn when teachers force them to multiply or subtract with Roman numerals. In Roman numerals, CLIV is 154, whereas XLII is 42. Maddeningly, both numbers have L (50) as the second symbol, but the two L's aren't equivalent, because the second is modified by the preceding X, which subtracts ten from it to make forty. Even though both CLIV and XLII are four-digit numbers, the left-hand symbol in the first number (C) cannot be directly compared with the left-hand symbol in the second (X). Positional notation symbols take the aggravation out of arithmetic.

*Actually, it didn't. Inexplicably, the biggest unit, the 144,000-day "millennium," began with 1, rather than 0. The first day in the calendar was thus 1.0.0.0.0. When I remarked on the peculiarity of this exception to a mathematician, he pointed out societies whose timekeeping systems are so irregular that children have to learn rhymes to remember the number of days in the months ("Thirty days hath September . . .") are in no position to scoff at the calendrical eccentricities of other cultures. At least all the "months" in the Mesoamerican calendar had the same number of days, he said.

Stirling's stela in Tres Zapotes bore a Long Count date of 7.16.6.16.18. The implication is that by 32 B.C. the Olmec already had all three calendars and zero to boot. One can't be sure, because the date does not include a zero or a reference to the other calendars. But it is hard to imagine how one could have a Long Count without them. Tentatively, therefore, archaeologists assign the invention of zero to sometime before 32 B.C., centuries ahead of its invention in India.

How long before 32 B.C.? The carved cadaver in San José Mogote may give a hint. In Mesoamerican cultures, the date of one's birth was such an important augury of the future that people often acquired that day as their name. It was as if coming into the world on New Year's Day were such a sign of good fortune that children born on that day would be named "January 1." This seems to have been the case for the man whose death was celebrated in the San José Mogote temple. Between his feet are two glyphs, one resembling a stovepipe hat with a U painted across the front, the other looking vaguely like a smiling pet monster from a Japanese cartoon. According to Marcus, the Michigan anthropologist, the glyphs correspond to 1-Earthquake, the Zapotec name for the seventeenth day of the 260-day sacred calendar. Because the carving depicts a man instead of an event, the date is generally thought to be the dead man's name. If so, 1-Earthquake is the first named person in the history of the Americas. Even if the date is not a name, the two glyphs indicate that by 750 B.C., when the slab was carved, the Zapotec were not only on the way to some form of writing, but had also assembled some of the astronomical and mathematical knowledge necessary for a calendar.

To judge by the archaeological record, this development took place in an astonishingly compressed period; what took the Sumerians six thousand years apparently occurred in Mesoamerica in fewer than a thousand. Indeed, Mesoamerican societies during that time created more than a dozen systems of writing, some of which are known only from a single brief text. The exact chronology of their evolution remains unknown, but could be resolved by the next object that a farmer discovers in a field. The earliest known Olmec writing, for example, is on a potsherd from Chiapas that dates from about 300 B.C. For a long time nobody could read it. In 1986 a workcrew building a dock on the Acula River in Veracruz pulled out a seven-foot stela covered with Olmec symbols. Thought to have been written in 159 A.D., the twenty-one columns of glyphs were the first Olmec text long enough to permit linguists to decipher the language. Two linguists did just that in 1993. The stela recounted the rise of a warrior-king named Harvest Mountain Lord who celebrated his ascension to the throne by decapitating his main rival during the

Discovered in 1975, this prone, disemboweled man was carved onto the stone threshold of a temple in San José Mogote, near the city of Oaxaca. Between the corpse's feet is the oldest certainly dated writing in the Americas: two glyphs (shaded in drawing) that probably represent his name, 1-Earthquake. The ornate scroll issuing from his side is blood. According to Joyce Marcus, the first archaeologist to examine this bas-relief, the Zapotec words for "flower" and "sacrificial object" are similar enough that the flowery blood may be a visual pun.

coronation. This information in hand, the linguists went back to the writing on the potsherd. Disappointingly, it turned out to be some banal utterances about dying and cutting cloth.

FROM 1-EARTHQUAKE TO 8-DEER

The development of writing in Zapotec society went hand-in-hand with growing urbanization. In about 500 B.C., San José Mogote seems to have transplanted itself to Monte Albán, in the middle of the buffer zone. About half an hour by bus from Oaxaca City, Monte Albán is today a decorous sprawl of walls and pyramids enveloped by a lush lawn (this last is an import from Europe; lawn grass did not exist in the Americas prior to Columbus). Arriving tourists are hailed by "guides" with backpacks full of phony ancient figurines and ethnically incorrect souvenirs of Mexica drawings. Their ministrations do not diminish the lonely dignity of the ruins. Monte Albán is atop a steep, 1,500-foot hill that overlooks the valley of Oaxaca. The Zapotec reconfigured the entire hill to build the city, slicing out terraces and platforms. By leveling the entire summit, they created a fifty-five-acre terrace half the size of the Vatican. At its zenith, Monte Albán housed seventeen thousand people and was by a considerable margin the biggest and most powerful population center in Mesoamerica.

The rationale for its construction is the subject of yet another lengthy archaeological dispute. One side proposes that Monte Albán formed because maize agriculture allowed the Oaxaca Valley's population to grow so much that the rural villages naturally clustered into something resembling cities. For most of its history Monte Albán was thus a huge village, not a true city, and certainly not a hierarchical state. Others argue that warfare had grown so devastating, as shown by the destruction of San José Mogote, that the main valley chiefdoms formed a defensive confederation headquartered at Monte Albán. Yet a third theory is that the Zapotec of Monte Albán—not the Olmec of La Venta—consolidated to form North America's first imperialist power, an aggressive state that subjugated dozens of other villages.

Among the strongest evidence for the last view are the nearly three hundred carved stone slabs at Monte Albán that depict slain, mutilated enemies: the rulers, Marcus believes, of communities conquered by Monte Albán. Some of the stones are labeled with enemy names, as with the unfortunate 1-Earthquake. These may commemorate victories in Monte Albán's grinding battle for supremacy with its local rival, San Martín Tilcajete, in the southern arm of the Central Valley. When San José Mogote founded Monte Albán, Tilcajete responded by gathering people from its surrounding villages, doubling in size, and erecting its own ceremonial buildings. War was the inevitable result. Monte Albán sacked Tilcajete in about 375 B.C. Undiscouraged, Tilcajete rebuilt itself on a better defensive position and acquired larger armies. When it again became a threat, Monte Albán attacked for the second time in 120 B.C. This time its forces finished the job. They burned the king's palace to the ground and emptied the rest of Tilcajete, leaving Monte Albán firmly in control of the entire valley.

With nothing to impede it, Monte Albán swept out and established a domain of almost ten thousand square miles. For centuries it stood on equal ground with its neighbors, the rising Maya states to the east and Teotihuacán to the north. It enjoyed relatively peaceful relations with both but had continual trouble in Mixteca, a constellation of petty principalities immediately to the west. By contrast with Monte Albán, these were minuscule entities; most were clusters of rustic villages covering ten to twenty square miles. Yet they were amazingly troublesome. Monte Albán repeatedly overran the Mixtec statelets, but never managed to eliminate them. These tiny, fractious domains endured for more than a thousand years. Meanwhile the much stronger and more centralized Zapotec empire collapsed completely in about 800 A.D.

Mixtec writing survives in eight codices, the deerskin or bark "books" whose painted pages could be folded like screens or hung on the wall like a mural. (The Spaniards destroyed all the rest.) More purely pictorial than Zapotec or Maya script, the texts were arranged almost randomly on the page; red lines directed the reader's eye from image to image. The symbols included drawings of events, portraits labeled by name (the king 4-Wind, for example, being shown by symbolic wind and four little bubbles in a line), and even punning rebuses. Enough writing has survived to give, when coupled with archaeological studies, a vivid picture of Mixtec life.

Like medieval Italian city-states, Mixtec principalities were rigidly stratified, with the king and a small group of kinspeople and noble advisers gobbling up much of the wealth and land. They constantly shifted configuration, some expanding by swarming over their neighbors, others imploding when their constituent villages seceded and joined other polities. More commonly, two states joined when their rulers married. Alliance through royal marriage was as common in eleventh-century Mixteca as it was in seventeenth-century Europe. In both, royal family trees formed an intricate network across national boundaries, but in Mixteca the queen's lands stayed in her line—the king's heir wasn't necessarily the queen's heir. Another difference: primogeniture was not expected. If the queen did not think her eldest son was fit for the crown, she could pass it to another child, or even to a nephew or cousin.

No fewer than four of the codices treat the story of 8-Deer Jaguar Claw, a wily priest-general-politician with a tragic love for the wife of his greatest enemy. Born in 1063 A.D., 8-Deer was a shirttail cousin to the ruling family of Tilantongo, which had been engaged for decades in a dynastic struggle with the kingdom of Red and White Bundle. (The name, a modern invention, comes from its name-glyph, which pictures the cloth wrapping used by the Mixtec to wrap holy objects; its exact location is still not nailed down.) Like his father, a high cleric, 8-Deer was trained for the priesthood, but political events and his own overweening ambition stopped him from following that path.

After an unprovoked attack on Red and White Bundle by Tilantongo raised hostilities to a fever, the warring parties agreed to meet in a sacred mountain cave with the Priestess of the Dead, a powerful oracle who had stripped away the flesh from her jaw, giving her a terrifying, skull-like appearance. Tilantongo's representative was 8-Deer, who attended the meeting in place of his recently deceased father. To his dismay, the priestess sided with Tilantongo's enemies and ordered 8-Deer, Tilantongo's champion, to exile himself a hundred miles away, in a jerkwater town on the Pacific called Tututepec.

Tucked away in Tututepec, 8-Deer assembled a private army, staffed it with many relatives, and in a series of swift campaigns seized dozens of neighboring villages and city-states. In addition to assembling the greatest empire ever seen in Mixteca, the conquests managed to kill off most of the siblings and cousins above him in the line of royal succession. After six years of war he returned home to Tilantongo. During this visit, according to John M. D. Pohl, the archaeologist whose interpretations I am mostly following here, 8-Deer accidentally encountered 6-Monkey, the young wife of the much older king of Red and White Bundle. Despite the long enmity between the two kingdoms, 8-Deer and 6-Monkey secretly became lovers.

In 1096 Tilantongo's sovereign died in mysterious circumstances. The Priestess of the Dead selected 8-Deer's beloved elder half brother to be the regent—that is, the half brother became the last person between 8-Deer and the throne of Tilantongo. Three years later, unknown assailants stabbed the half brother to death in a sweatbath. The inconsolable 8-Deer took the throne of Tilantongo and declared war on Red and White Bundle, which he claimed had orchestrated the murder.

Red and White Bundle's royal palace was built on a cliff over a bend in the river. Guarded by sheer walls on three sides, its soldiers had only to watch the fourth side, across which was an earthen berm. Leading an army of a thousand, 8-Deer threw up ladders, swarmed over the berm with his men, and entered the palace. As befit a conqueror, 8-Deer was wearing elaborate cotton armor, a ceremonial beard wig, and a cowl made from the head of a jaguar. Gold-and-jade necklaces dangled across his naked chest. In the palace he found 6-Monkey and her husband, the king of Red and White Bundle. Both were mortally wounded. In Pohl's account, 8-Deer held 6-Monkey as she died.

Captured with the royal couple were their two sons, the elder of whom, 4-Wind, was heir to the throne. Seizing him by the hair, 8-Deer forced the teenager to grovel before him. But he also made what seems to have been a sentimental decision: he spared the life of his lover's son. The folly of this action became apparent when 4-Wind and his brother escaped from confinement.

In this fragment from a Mixtec codex, the jaguar-cowled Lord 8-Deer (right) captures 4-Wind, son of his former lover, by the hair. As in other Mixtec codices, the characters' names are indicated by the accompanying circles-plus-head symbols.

Seeking revenge, 4-Wind approached the Zapotec empire for help. With Zapotec backing, he linked rebels in Red and White Bundle and a host of other cities defeated by 8-Deer. They besieged Tilantongo in 1115. The battle lasted six months and ended in total defeat for Tilantongo. In a mirror image of the past, the captured 8-Deer was forced to bow to 4-Wind. He was fifty-five years old and had six official kingships and dozens of petty states under his control. Victorious and vengeful, 4-Wind personally disemboweled him. Then he married 8-Deer's daughter.

In 4-Wind's first exercise of statecraft, he abandoned the Zapotec allies who had helped him achieve the throne, aligned Tilantongo with the Toltec empire to the north, and attacked the Zapotec. Ultimately the Mixtec under his lead took over much of Oaxaca, forcing the Zapotec states to pay tribute. The empire he established, far bigger than 8-Deer's, lasted until the fifteenth century, when the Mexica invaded. And then came Cortés.

W H E E L E D   I N T E R L U D E

As Matthew Stirling and his team were dodging ticks and unearthing stelae in Tres Zapotes, they found a cache of fifteen upside-down pottery bowls tucked into the ground six feet below the surface. The bowls protectively covered thirty-five toy-size, decorated figurines and twelve small, painted clay discs. Among the figurines were two dogs and a jaguar, each of which had thin tubes joining its two front feet and its two back feet. The discs lay beside them. Similar finds have been made further north, near Mexico City.

In the 1980s I saw the Tres Zapotes animals, or ones like them, at a museum in the Yucatán Peninsula. I was there with an Italian engineer whom I had met by chance a few hours before. Well before me, the engineer figured out the significance of the tubes between the figurines' feet. "Those are for axles," he said. "And those"—pointing to the discs—"must be the wheels." Looking at the little figures, it seemed obvious that they had been equipped with wheels in precisely the form he suggested.

The engineer scrunched up his face with incredulity. Tres Zapotes dated back to at least 1000 B.C. So the Olmec and their successors must have had the wheel for more than two thousand years. "Why didn't they use it for anything other than little toys?" he asked in Italian. "How could they not have understood that you could make bigger wheels and put them on carts? *Hanno fatto proprio una stupidaggine, quei tipi.*"

The word *stupidaggine* (an absurdity), similar enough in Italian and Spanish, rang out in the room, drawing stares. The engineer seemed not to care. He looked positively offended at the Olmec failure to see the world in the same way as a contemporary European engineer.

I'm giving my acquaintance a hard time, but his bafflement was easy for me to understand. In Mesopotamia, the wheel dates back to at least the time of Sumer. It was a basic part of life throughout Eurasia. Chariot wheels, water wheels, potter's wheels, millstone wheels—one can't imagine Europe or China without them. The only thing more mysterious than failing to invent the wheel would be inventing the wheel and then failing to use it. But that is exactly what the Indians did. Presumably countless thousands of people rolled the toylike figurines back and forth. How could none of them have thought of making their wheels bigger and more useful?

Some reasons are apparent. Because of the Pleistocene extinctions, the Americas lacked animals suitable for domestication into beasts of burden; without animals to haul carts, individuals on rough terrain can use skids almost as effectively. Even with animals, though, the Olmec would not have had much use for wheeled vehicles. Their country is so wet and boggy that Stirling's horses sank to their chests in mud; boats were a primary means of transportation until recently. In addition one might note that Mesoamerican societies were not alone in their wheel-blindness. Although Mesopotamia had the wheel in about 4000 B.C., nearby Egypt did not use the wheel until two thousand years later, despite being in close contact. Still, none of this explains why no Mesoamerican society ever used wheels to make ceramics and grind maize. After all, every society in Eurasia eventually employed pottery wheels and mill wheels.

A better answer might be one implicit in Robert Temple's book, *The Genius of China,* a history of Chinese science and technology published in 1998. According to Temple, the Chinese invented the moldboard plow by the third century B.C. Made of cast iron, the plowshare was shaped like a V, with the blade carving into the ground and the two arms arcing away like gull wings. Because the arms were curved, they turned the earth away from the blade, which both reduced friction and more effectively plowed the soil. (The "moldboard" is the curved plowshare; the name comes from *mold,* the Old German word for soil.)

The design of the moldboard plow is so obvious that it seems incredible that Europeans never thought of it. Until the Chinese-style plow was imported in the seventeenth century, farmers in France, Germany, Italy, the Netherlands, and other states labored to shove what amounted to a narrow slab of metal through the earth. "The increased friction meant that huge multiple teams of oxen were required, whereas Chinese plows could make do with a single ox," Temple explained. The European failure to think up the moldboard, according to science historian Teresi, was "as if Henry Ford designed the car without an accelerator, and you had to put the car in neutral, brake, and go under the hood to change speed. And then we did this for 2,000 years."

European agricultural production exploded after the arrival of the moldboard plow. The prosperity this engendered was one of the cushions on which the Enlightenment floated. "So inefficient, so wasteful of effort, and so utterly exhausting" was the old plow, Temple wrote, "that this deficiency of plowing may rank as mankind's single greatest waste of time and energy." Millions of Europeans spent centuries behind the plow, staring at the blade as it ineffectively mired itself in the earth. How could none of them have thought of changing the design to make the plow more useful?

The complexity of a society's technology has little to do with its level of social complexity—something that we, in our era of rapidly changing, seemingly overwhelming technology, have trouble grasping. Every society, big or little, misses out on "obvious" technologies. The lacunae have enormous impact on people's lives—imagine Europe with efficient plows or the Maya with iron tools—but not much effect on the scale of a civilization's endeavors, as shown by both European and Maya history. The corollary is that widespread and open trade in ideas is the best way to make up for the lacunae. Alas, Mesoamerica was limited in this respect. Like Europe, it was an extraordinarily diverse place with a shared cultural foundation. But where Europe had the profoundly different civilizations of China and Islam to steal from, Mesoamerica was alone in the world.

Or seemed to be, anyway.

A SLICE OF PERU

About a hundred miles north of the Peru-Chile border, the coastal highway passes by an uninhabited beach ringed by a tall chain-link fence. The fence has an entrance with a gigantic, stylized statue of a woman with huge earrings. By the statue hangs a faded banner: *Bolivia Mar.*

When Bolivia declared its independence it had a territorial pseudopod that extended southwest from its Andean heartland through the Atacama Desert to the sea. The land was useless for agriculture but had four plausible seaports and huge underground deposits of prehistoric guano, which Chilean companies mined and shipped to Europe for fertilizer. (Bolivia, then as now impoverished, didn't have the capital for this industry.) In 1878, Hilarion Daza, the illegitimate son of an Italian acrobat, seized power in Bolivia. Immediately he raised taxes on the Chilean-owned guano mines, which the previous Bolivian government had promised not to do. Outraged, Chile rolled its army into the area. In vain did Bolivia counterattack with its ally, Peru; Chile simply repelled their incompetently led forces and took over the entire territory, as well as a chunk of southern Peru. Ejected in an outburst of popular anger, Daza fled to Europe, taking most of Bolivia's treasury with him.

Chile finally returned most of Peru's territory in 1929 but never gave back any land to Bolivia—an outcome that nation has never accepted. To this day, Bolivia's parliament has a representative from the lost maritime province. The Miss Bolivia contest always includes a contestant ostensibly from the coast. Maps are sold in which the conquered land is still part of Bolivia.

In a gesture to its longtime, long-suffering ally, Peru symbolically gave two miles of its shoreline to Bolivia in 1992. Bolivia Mar—Bolivia-by-the-Sea—is a little island of Bolivia entirely surrounded by Peru. It has no facilities of any kind, so far as I could tell when I passed by. Private enterprise was supposed to build an industrial duty-free port in Bolivia Mar. Thus far the free market has not accepted the challenge. Every now and then parties of Bolivians drive down to Bolivia Mar to swim—a political gesture.

The main highway from Bolivia Mar to Bolivia itself follows the Osmore Valley, cutting a perfect sectional slice through Peru on the way. For the first fifteen miles the road climbs through a desert landscape almost devoid of settlement and prone to fog. Then the road hits a plateau and the fog dissipates. The landscape that comes into view is so dry that in most years the Osmore River simply disappears into the desert.

Around the small city of Moquegua the river hoves back into view and the highway abruptly pitches into the Cordillera Negra. The windshield fills with enough canyons, bluffs, mesas, and cliffs for a dozen *Road Runner* cartoons. Standing higher than its neighbors, at an altitude of about eight thousand feet, is a wide pillar of rock with a rounded, convoluted top that vaguely resembles the rounded, convoluted top of a human brain. The pillar is called Cerro Baúl. For about two hundred years, it was the sole meeting ground of two of the Americas' largest societies—societies similar in scale to, say, the Maya realm, but much less well known.

The two states, Wari and Tiwanaku, were probably the greatest of the Inkas' forerunners, and certainly the predecessors from whom they took the most. In their separate ways, both were children of Norte Chico. They worshipped figures in Staff God poses, lived in networks of vertical exchange, and had public architecture with designs based on templates from the coast. But in other ways they were as different from each other as Sicily and Scandinavia. Of the two, Wari was the more conventional, centralized state. Based east of Lima in the Andes heights, it first became prominent in the sixth century A.D.—a bad time to be launching a nation on the Pacific side of South America. At about that time, Andean societies were assailed by the first of several decades-long droughts, paradoxically interrupted by El Niño–induced floods. Some polities may have disintegrated beneath the climatic assault, but Wari thrived. The principal reason for its success was its innovative techniques of terracing and irrigation, the latter being used to implement the former. Surprisingly, Peru has more arable land above nine thousand feet than below. By diverting snowmelt from the ever-present Andes icecaps to high farm terraces, Wari was able literally to rise above the drought and flooding of lower elevations.

The staple crop of the highlands was the potato, which unlike maize regularly grows at altitudes of 14,000 feet; the tubers, cultivated in hundreds of varieties, can be left in the ground for as long as a year (if the weather

An anomaly in the southern Andes foothills, the great stone of Cerro Baúl dominates the neighboring slopes. On its summit are the remains of a Wari city.

remains cold), to be dug up and cooked when needed. (The potato's cold tolerance spurred its embrace by European peasants. Not only did potatoes grow in places where other crops could not, the plant was an ally in smallholders' ceaseless struggle against the economic and political elite. A farmer's barnful of wheat, rye, or barley was a fat target for greedy landlords and marauding armies; buried in the soil, a crop of potatoes could not be easily seized.) Maize, though, was what people wanted, the grain of choice for the elite—it was what you made *chicha* from. Its prestige was another reason for Wari's success. Because terraces soak up more sunlight than steep slopes, maize can be grown at higher than usual altitudes on them; irrigation similarly increases the area available for maize farming.

In a process that Michael Moseley has likened to "patenting and marketing a major invention," the Wari passed on their reclamation techniques to their neighbors, bringing a thousand-mile-long swath of the Peruvian Andes under their cultural sway. A sign of their influence was the spread of the

Wari religion, in which the figure archaeologists call Staff God was dominant—though the Wari transformed the staff, as if to remind others of their agricultural beneficence, into a stalk of maize. By the end of the first millennium A.D., Wari techniques had reclaimed more than a million acres of cropland from mountainsides that almost anywhere else would have been regarded as impossibly dry, steep, and cold. Today three-quarters of the terraces are abandoned, and the alpine landscape has not regained the productivity it had a thousand years ago. But until the Spanish conquest Andean valleys were so thoroughly punctuated by Wari-inspired terraces that to the Jesuit Bernabé Cobo they looked "as if they were covered with flights of stairs."

Wari's capital city, also named Wari, occupied an alpine plateau near the modern city of Ayacucho. Construction began in the first few centuries A.D. The city ultimately spread across two square miles, an array of two- and three-story buildings in compounds behind massive walls. Both peasant homes and great palaces were built in similar styles, according to William H. Isbell, an anthropologist at the State University of New York at Binghamton, and Alexei Vranich, an archaeologist at the University of Pennsylvania Museum of Archaeology and Anthropology. Everything was enclosed behind high, white walls, in what the two researchers described in 2004 as a hive of "repetitive, modular cells organized in high-walled geometric blocks." There were no standout public buildings, no great public spaces, no spectacular vistas—only a thicket of walls and narrow streets strewn with garbage (archaeologists have turned up so few clean floors and surfaces, Isbell and Vranich wrote, "that it is apparent that Wari people experienced domestic refuse as benign and unthreatening"). Apparently the walls ringing and crisscrossing the city were intended for privacy, not protection; Wari was not located in an easily defended spot. Along the spine of the Andes the empire set up a string of a dozen administrative centers that were like smaller versions of the capital. These were not built with defense in mind, either. Indeed, there is little record of Wari warfare. Its supremacy was commercial and intellectual; it was based less on infantry troops than on innovative technology. All of which may explain some of its behavior in Cerro Baúl.

Wari emissaries arrived in Moquegua around 600 A.D., according to Patrick Ryan Williams and Donna V. Nash, Field Museum archaeologists who have been working there since the early 1990s. A simpler culture had already staked out the best farmland in the area. The Wari neither aggressively threw them out nor withdrew in dismay. Guided, one imagines, by instructions from headquarters, they quickly set up living quarters on Cerro

Baúl itself. The big mesa is to this day regarded as an *apu*, an ancient spirit transfigured into rock. Thus putting a city directly on top of it was an arresting statement: *Here we are.*

On a practical level, living on a five-hundred-yard-long mesa was a daunting task. To supply water, the Wari carved a fifteen-mile canal through the mountains from the peaks to the bottom of Cerro Baúl, an engineering feat that would be a challenge today. "And even that got water only to the bottom of the hill," Williams told me. "After that, it was bucket brigades." As I huffed and puffed on the wickedly steep, thirty-minute hike to the summit, he invited me to imagine a continuous line of servants exchanging ceramic jugs (slopping, brimful ones going up; light, empty ones going down) along the path, working day in and day out to provide water for the priests and princes above.

Small, rudely fashioned models of farmhouses and farmyards covered the top of the butte. Most of the models simply outlined walls, fences, and doors with loose stones, but some were elaborate constructions complete with plastic model cars, toy animals, and thatch roofs. People were climbing Cerro Baúl, building their maquettes, and praying that the heavens would give them the real-life equivalents. The miniature farms extended for hundreds of yards in all directions. Here and there, makeshift crosses and pictures of saints added a veneer of Catholicism to indigenous Andean belief. Some of the ruined Wari walls were covered with ruined model walls. "This is getting out of hand," Williams said. "I don't want to knock down somebody's dream house to get to an archaeological site."

In about 750 A.D., about a century after Wari came to Cerro Baúl, Tiwanaku groups infiltrated the region around it. In most places on earth, this encounter would have been fraught with tension. And perhaps if Tiwanaku had been more like Wari there would have been immediate war. But Tiwanaku was so different in so many ways that ordinary expectations rarely apply to it. The celebrated anthropologist Clifford Geertz has half-jokingly suggested that all states can be parceled into four types: pluralist, in which the state is seen by its people as having moral legitimacy; populist, in which government is viewed as an expression of the people's will; "great beast," in which the rulers' power depends on using force to keep the populace cowed; and "great fraud," in which the elite uses smoke and mirrors to convince the people of its inherent authority. Every state is a mix of all of these elements, but in Tiwanaku, the proportion of "great fraud" may have been especially high. Nonetheless, Tiwanaku endured for many centuries.

Tiwanaku's capital, Tiwanaku city, was at the southwest end of Lake Titicaca. Situated at 12,600 feet, it was the highest city in the ancient world.

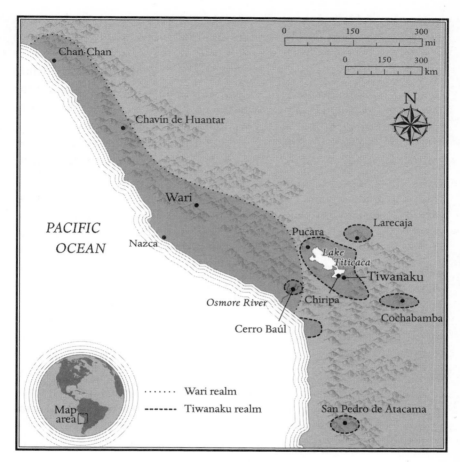

WARI AND TIWANAKU, 700 A.D.

Today visitors from lower altitudes are constantly warned that the area is very cold. "Bring warm clothing," Williams advised me in Cerro Baúl. "You're going to freeze." The warnings puzzled me, because Lake Titicaca, which is big enough to stay at a near-constant 51 degrees Fahrenheit, moderates the local climate (this is one reason why agriculture is possible at such height). On winter nights the average temperature is a degree below freezing—cold, but not any colder than New England, and considerably warmer than one would expect at 12,600 feet. Only when I traveled there did I realize that this was the temperature *indoors*. The modern town of Tiwanaku is a poor place and few of its buildings have any heating. One night there I attended a performance at a family circus that was touring the Andes. It was so cold inside the tent that for the first few minutes the audience was shrouded in a cloud of its own breath. My host that night was an American archaeologist. When I woke the next morning in her spare bedroom, my host, in parka, hat, and gloves, was melting water on her stove. The cold does not detract from the area's beauty: Tiwanaku sits in the middle of a plain ringed by ice-capped mountains. From the ruin's taller buildings the great lake, almost ten miles to the northwest, is just visible. The wide expanse of water seems to merge into the sky without a welt.

The first important settlement around Titicaca was likely Chiripa, on a little peninsula on the lake's southwest coast. Its ceremonial center, which may date to 900 B.C., was built around a Norte Chico–style sunken plaza. Chiripa was one of half a dozen small, competitive centers that emerged around the lake in that time. Most depended on raised-field agriculture, in which farmers grow crops on flat, artificially constructed surfaces created for the same reason that home gardeners grow vegetables on raised beds. (Similar but even larger expanses of raised fields are found in the Beni, the Mexican basin, and many other places.) By the time of Christ's birth, two of these early polities had become dominant: Pukara on the northern, Peruvian edge of the lake and Tiwanaku on the opposite, Bolivian side. In the third century A.D., Pukara rather abruptly disintegrated politically. People still lived there, but the towns dispersed into the countryside; pottery making, stela carving, and monument building ceased. No one is certain why.

Although Tiwanaku has been occupied since at least 800 B.C., it did not become an important center until about 300 B.C. and did not expand out from southern Titicaca until about two hundred years after Pukara's decline. But when it did reach out to its south and west, Tiwanaku transformed itself to become what Alan Kolata, an archaeologist at the University of Chicago, has called a "predatory state." It was not the centrally administered military power that term conjures. Instead, it was an archipelago of cities that acknowledged Tiwanaku's religious preeminence. "State religion and imperial ideology," Kolata argued, "performed much the same work as military conquest, but at significantly lower cost." Awed by its magnificence, fearful of the supernatural powers controlled by its priesthood, local rulers subordinated themselves.

Central to this strategy of intimidation was Tiwanaku city. A past wonder of the world, it is badly damaged today. In the last two centuries, people have literally carted away many of its buildings, using the stones for churches, homes, bridges, public buildings, and even landfill. At one point the Bolivian government drove a railroad through the site (recently it laid a road through another part). Hands more enthusiastic than knowledgeable reconstructed many of the remaining buildings. Still, enough remains to get a sense of the ancient city.

The Andean cross

Dominating its skyline was a seven-tiered pyramid, Akapana, laid out in a pattern perhaps inspired by the Andean cross. Ubiquitous in highlands art, the Andean cross is a stepped shape that some claim is inspired by the Southern Cross constellation and others believe represents the four quarters of the world. Whatever the case, Akapana's builders planned with a sense of drama. They constructed its base walls with sandstone blocks, the array interrupted every ten feet by rectangular stone pillars that are easily ten feet tall. So massive are the pillars that the first European to see Tiwanaku, Pedro Cieza de León, later confessed himself unable to "understand or fathom what kind of instruments or tools were used to work them." Rising from the center of a large moat, Akapana mimicked the surrounding mountains. A precisely engineered drainage system added to the similarity by channeling water from a cistern-like well at the summit down and along the sides, a stylized version of rainwater plashing down the Andes.

Atop an adjacent, somewhat smaller structure, a large, walled enclosure called Kalasasaya, is the so-called Gateway of the Sun, cut from a single block of stone (now broken in two and reassembled). Covered with a fastidiously elaborate frieze, the twelve-foot gateway focuses the visitor's eye on the image of a single deity whose figure projects from the lintel: the Staff God.

Today the Gateway of the Sun is the postcard emblem of Tiwanaku. During the winter solstice (June, in South America) hundreds of camera-toting European and American tourists wait on Kalasasaya through the entire freezing night for the sunrise, which is supposed to shine through the Gateway on that date alone. Guides in traditional costume explain that the reliefs on the lintel form an intricate astronomical calendar that may have been brought to earth by alien beings. To keep themselves warm during the inevitable longueurs, visitors sing songs of peace and harmony in several languages. Invariably the spectators are stunned when the first light of sunrise appears well to the side of the Gateway. Only afterward do they discover that the portal is not in its original location, and may have had nothing to do with astronomy or calendars.

If those tourists had come to Tiwanaku at its height, walking through the miles of raised fields surrounding it to the city's carefully fitted stone walls, they would have been delighted by its splendor. But it might also have seemed curiously incomplete, with half the city falling down and in need of repairs and the other half under construction. Modern drawings of ancient cities tend to show them at an imagined apogee, the great monuments all splendidly arrayed together, perfect as architectural models. But this is not what Tiwanaku looked like, nor even what it was *meant* to look like, according to Isbell and Vranich. From the very beginning, the two men wrote in 2004, the city was partly in ruins—intentionally so, because the fallen walls bequeathed on Tiwanaku the authority of the past. Meanwhile, other parts of the city were constantly enveloped in construction projects, which testified to the continued wealth and vitality of the state. Sometimes these projects acquired construction materials by cannibalizing old monuments, thereby hastening the process of creating ruins. In the Andean tradition, labor was probably contributed by visiting work parties. Periodically ritual feasts that included much smashing of pottery interrupted the hubbub of construction. But it always continued. "They build their monuments as if their intent was never to finish them," the Spanish academic Polo de Ondegardo marveled in 1571. Exactly right, Isbell and Vranich said. Completion was not the object. The goal was a constant buzz of purposeful activity.

As our hypothetical modern visitors wandered through the hurly-burly of construction and deconstruction, they might have felt that despite the commotion something was missing. Unlike Western cities, Tiwanaku had no *markets*—no bazaars full of shouting, bargaining, conniving entrepreneurs; no street displays of produce, pottery, and plonk; no jugglers and mimes trying to attract crowds; no pickpockets. In Africa, Asia, and Europe, Kolata wrote, "a city was a place of meeting and of melding for many different kinds of people. . . . Through trade and exchange, through buying and selling of every conceivable kind, the city was made and remade." Tiwanaku was utterly different. Andean societies were based on the widespread exchange of goods and services, but kin and government, not market forces, directed the flow. The citizenry grew its own food and made its own clothes, or obtained them through their lineages, or picked them up in government warehouses. And the city, as Kolata put it, was a place for "symbolically concentrating the political and religious authority of the elite." Other Andean cities, Wari among them, shared this quality. But Tiwanaku carried it to an extreme.

Tiwanaku has been excavated for a century, and the more archaeologists delve into it the less there seems to be. To Vranich, the capital's lack of resemblance to European imperial cities extends well beyond the absence of marketplaces. Far from being the powerful administrative center envisioned by earlier researchers, he says, Tiwanaku was a combination of the Vatican

On Lake Titicaca, the reed boats known as *totora* are still in use, as they have been for two thousand years. This replica of a large *totora* was built in 2001 to prove the vessels could have hauled the big stones used in Tiwanaku's walls.

The so-called Gateway of the Sun attracts pilgrims by the thousands who seek astronomical meaning in its location. Unfortunately, it was moved to its present site in the twentieth century.

and Disneyland, a religious show capital with a relatively small population—almost a *staff*—that attracted pilgrims by the thousand. Like the tourists at the solstice today, visitors came to this empire of appearances to be dazzled and awed. "In the central city, buildings and monuments went up and down, up and down, at an incredible rate," Vranich told me at Tiwanaku, where he had been working since 1996. "Nothing ever got finished completely, because they were just concerned with the facades. They had to keep changing the exhibits to keep the crowds coming."

The encounter between Tiwanaku and Wari at Cerro Baúl seems to have gone remarkably smoothly. At any rate, a study of more than a thousand Wari and Tiwanaku graves found no evidence of the trauma associated with violence. Instead, the two societies split the region between them. Wari camped atop Cerro Baúl and a neighboring hillock, Cerro Mejía. Between them was a steep valley with Tiwanaku settlements scattered throughout. Because Wari and Tiwanaku pottery differed, Williams and Nash have been able to map which group lived in which neighborhood by the distribution of ceramic fragments. The Wari canal provided drinking water, but had to pass through Tiwanaku territory at the base of Cerro Baúl. Tiwanaku let the water through, but took enough to irrigate more than seven hundred acres of terraces.

At the same time, Wari and Tiwanaku kept themselves separate. Although they shared resources, there is little evidence that people from one culture visited the other often, or had friendships across the political lines. Wari homes were furnished with Wari goods; Tiwanaku homes, Tiwanaku goods. Despite living next to each other, people continued to speak their different languages and wear their different clothing and look for inspiration and instruction from their different capitals. The social-science word for such intermingling without intermixing is "interdigitization." For two centuries at Cerro Baúl, Wari and Tiwanaku were like people in parallel worlds, sharing the same time and space but implacably separate from each other. It is a small reminder that Indians were neither the peaceful, love-thy-neighbor types envisioned by some apologists or the brutal, ceaselessly aggressive warriors decried by some political critics.

Wari abandoned Cerro Baúl in about 800 A.D., ceremoniously burning its buildings and smashing pottery. The retreat was part of a general fall, soon followed by Tiwanaku. Both declines have been laid to drought, but this is contested. The Wari had already survived drought. As for Tiwanaku, Vranich said, "How much would drought matter to Disneyland?" Its ability to retain its audience would be far more important.

The successors to both Wari and Tiwanaku combined the former's organizational skills and the latter's sense of design and razzle-dazzle. First came Chimor, then the greatest empire ever seen in Peru. Spread at its greatest extent over seven hundred miles of the coastline, Chimor was an ambitious state that grew maize and cotton by irrigating almost fifty thousand acres around the Moche River (all of modern Peru only reached that figure in 1960). A destructive El Niño episode in about 1100 A.D. made irrigation impossible for a while. In response, the government forced gangs of captive laborers to build a fifty-three-mile, masonry-lined canal to channel water from the Chicama River, in the next valley to the north, to farmland in the Moche Valley. The canal was a flop: some parts ran uphill, apparently because of incompetent engineering, and the rest lost nine-tenths of its water to evaporation and seepage. Some archaeologists believe that the canal was never meant to function. It was a PR exercise, they say, a Potemkin demonstration by the Chimor government that it was actively fighting El Niño.

When the bad weather ended, Chimor looked outside its borders. Armies went out and returned victorious to Chan Chan, the Chimor capital, a seaside metropolis with a dense center that covered four square miles. Dominated by nine high-walled imperial palace-tombs and five cathedral-like ceremonial complexes, the city was both exemplary in its grandeur and oddly empty, because its streets were restricted to the elite. Commoners were barred, except for a few specialized technicians and craftworkers. Each palace was hundreds of feet on a side and many were three stories tall. They were filled with storage space—living quarters were almost an afterthought. Their great beams adorned with splendidly worked gold and silver, the huge structures were jammed together around the center of town like people huddling in the shelter of an awning.

Chan Chan suffered a palace surfeit because dead rulers were regarded as divine figures. As with the Inka, the kings' mummified bodies continued to live opulently in their own homes and could not be displaced; indeed, the mummies were necessary presences at important state occasions. As a result, each new ruler had to build his own palace and acquire the riches necessary to maintain it till the end of time. The system almost guaranteed imperial ambitions and exuberant construction plans.

The biggest of Chan Chan's surviving palaces may have belonged to Minchaçaman—the eleventh king in the Chimor dynasty, according to one Spanish account—who reputedly conquered much of the coastline. Minchaçaman was a powerful figure who could have taken over even more land than he did. Unfortunately for him, he lived at the same time that a previously little-known group, the Inka, acquired a new ruler, Pachakuti. In about 1450 the Inka army, led by Qhapaq Yupanki, Pachakuti's brother, besieged the

In this rare aerial photograph—taken in 1931, before modern looting blasted the site—the ruined Moche capital of Chan Chan sprawls across the northern Peruvian coast. One of the wonders of the fifteenth-century world, Chan Chan abruptly fell to the Inka in about 1450; eighty years later, Spanish diseases and Spanish soldiers destroyed much of what had survived the Inka.

city-state of Cajamarca, in the foothills east of Chimor. Cajamarca's leader had allied himself with Minchaçaman, who rushed to his aid with an army. He does not seem to have known what he was in for, possibly because he viewed the Inka as a gang of rustic thugs. Qhapaq Yupanki awaited him in an ambush. Minchaçaman and his army were forced to flee as Cajamarca fell to the Inka. Qhapaq Yupanki covered himself with so much glory that when he returned home to Qosqo his brother, sensing future trouble, promptly executed him.

A decade or so later—in 1463, if Spanish chronicles are correct—the emperor sent out another army led by his son and designated successor,

Thupa Inka Yupanki. By that time nobody thought of the Inkas as hicks. Thupa Inka descended the Moche River and paralyzed Chimor's defenses by the simple expedient of threatening to destroy its water supply. Minchaçaman was captured, taken to Qosqo, and forced to watch Thupa Inka's victory celebration. Chimor's conquerors were quick studies. Liking the courtly magnificence of Chan Chan, they hauled away what they could and, more important, forced the city's gold, silver, and gem workers to accompany them to Qosqo. They were instructed to transform the city into a new Chan Chan, only more impressive. Seven decades later, when Pizarro held *his* victory celebration in Qosqo, it was more lushly opulent than any city in Europe.

MAKING THE *WAK'A*

Jonathan Haas and Winifred Creamer took me to Caballete, a narrow, dusty bowl, perhaps half a mile long and a quarter mile wide, a few miles up the Fortaleza River from the Peruvian coast. At the mouth of the bowl were three mounds in a rough semicircle that faced a fourth mound. In front of one mound, like a one-eighth scale model of Stonehenge, was a ragged circle of *wak'a*: sacred stones. Not far from the *wak'a* looters had dug up an ancient graveyard, pulling out the bodies and unwinding them from their sheets in a search for gold and jewels. When they didn't find any, they threw the bones down in disgust. In a square perhaps fifty yards on a side the ground was carpeted with broken human bones and scraps of thousand-year-old fabric.

We walked a little further and were greeted by a curious sight: skulls from the cemetery, gathered into several small piles. Around them were beer cans, cigarette butts, patent-medicine bottles, half-burned photographs, and candles shaped like naked women. These last had voodoo pins stuck in their heads and vaginas. Local people came to these places at night and either dug for treasure or practiced witchcraft, Haas said. In the harsh afternoon light they seemed to me tacky and sad. I imagined that the families of the people who had been buried at Caballete so long ago would have been outraged if they could have known what would happen to the bodies of their loved ones.

But then it occurred to me that my views may not have been shared by either the present or the past inhabitants of Norte Chico. I had no idea what people in Wari or Chimor would have thought of the scene before me. So far in this section, I have mainly described the economic and political history of Andean Indians. But people live also in the realm of the affective and aesthetic—that's why they bury bodies and sometimes dig them up and pour love potions on them. Despite all the knowledge gained by scientists in the last few decades, this emotional realm remains much harder to reach.

An obvious example on the southern coast is the Nazca, famous for the huge patterns they set into the ground. Figures of animals and plants, almost a thousand geometric symbols, arrow-straight lines many miles long—what were they for? Peruvian anthropologist Toribio Mejía Xesspe first brought these famous drawings to the attention of the outside world in 1927. Four decades later, the Swiss writer Erich von Däniken set off an international furor by claiming that the Nazca Indians could not have made these symbols, because they were too big for such "primitive" people to construct, and because they are visible only from the air. Instead, he said, the giant figures were landing signals for space travelers; the whole plain was a sort of gigantic extraterrestrial airport. Expanded in a series of best-selling books, this notion turned the lines into a major tourist attraction. Exasperated scientists pointed out that a) small groups could have constructed the images by moving the dark surface stone to expose the lighter-colored earth beneath, and b) the Nazca did not have to see the figures to experience them, for they can be understood by walking the lines, which it is believed the Indians did. The prevailing theory today is that the straight lines mapped out the area's many underground faults, which channel water. But nobody knows why the Nazca made the animal and plant figures, which seem less likely to have a direct function. What were the Nazca thinking as they created them? How did they feel when they walked them? To this day, the answers remain frustratingly far away.

Or consider the Moche, leaders of a military state that overran much of the northern coast, submerging the identities of its victims in its own. Huaca del Sol, the Moche capital, contains the largest adobe structure in the Andes, still hauntingly evocative despite centuries of systematic looting. (Unwilling to laboriously dig their way through the palace's tombs, the Spaniards diverted the Moche River through it, washing out the riches in orthodox Augean-stable style; contemporary thieves have contented themselves with picks and shovels.) After about 300 A.D., Moche artists confined themselves to perhaps half a dozen subjects, painting stories of supernatural figures on pottery and murals with ever more naturalistic technique. Actors reenacted the same stories in grand pageants and ritual celebrations. Individual combat is a common theme; losers were formally stripped of their garments and forced to parade naked. Another oft-repeated tale involves the death and burial of a regal figure. Many of the people in the paintings are sharply individuated. Great effort has gone into studying the Moche, but as Moseley says, their identities and motives often remain "elusive." The Moche polity broke up around 800 A.D., taking with it our chance to understand.

The history of Andean societies is so rich and complex that it often leaves archaeologists feeling overwhelmed—there is so much to learn that they can never keep up. A single example: scientists did not confirm the existence of the Great Wall of Peru, a forty-mile stone rampart across the Andes, until the 1930s. And it still has never been fully excavated.

One of the few moments when I imagined I could encompass something of the inner lives of these long-ago people occurred in Chavín de Huantar, a city of several thousand people that existed between about 800 B.C. and 200 A.D. Its most important feature, a ceremonial temple shaped in a Norte Chico–style U, was a masterpiece of architectural intimidation. Using a network of concealed vents and channels, priests piped loud, roaring sounds at those who entered the temple. Visitors walked up three flights of stairs, growls echoing around them, and into a long, windowless passageway. At the end of the corridor, in a cross-shaped room that flickered with torchlight, was a fifteen-foot-high stone figure with a catlike face, taloned fingers, fierce tusks, and Medusa hair. Nobody today is sure of the god's identity. Immediately above it, hidden from visitors' eyes, sat a priestly functionary, who provided the god's voice. After the long, torchlit approach, walking straight into the gaze of the snarling deity, mysterious bellows reverberating off the stone, the oracular declamation from above must have been spine-chilling.

Most of the complex is open to tourists. Many of the sculptures have

been put into museums; others presumably have been looted. Yet walking
into the temple still felt to me like entering a mountain of solid rock. Over
and over again, Andean stories tell of spirits embodied in stones and giants
transformed into natural features. The landscape has an intricate numinous
geography; it is charged with meaning that must be respected and heeded.
The earth, in this view, is not something to be left alone; the *wak'a* that litter
Peruvian anthropological sites are often partly sculpted, as if they had
needed some human attention to manifest their sacred qualities. Thus the
human-made tunnels into the temple were part of what made it embody the
power of a mountain. As I walked down the dimly lighted corridor toward
where the torchlit deity had stood, my fingers ran along the walls created by
Chavín craftworkers. They were fit beautifully into place and as cold and
hard as the mountains they came from. But they did not gain their power
without my hand to close the circuit. The natural world is incomplete without the human touch.

PART THREE

Landscape with Figures

❄ 8 ❄

Made in America

ENTERING THE WATER

At some point, Chak Tok Ich'aak must have realized that January 14, 378 A.D., would be his last day on earth. The king of Mutal, the biggest and most cosmopolitan city-state in the Maya world, he lived and worked in a sprawling castle a few hundred yards away from the great temples at the city's heart. (Now known as Tikal, the ruins of Mutal have become an international tourist attraction.) Audience seekers entered the castle through a set of three richly carved doors in its eastern wall. Inside was a receiving room where petitioners waited for the king's attention. An inner portal led to a torch-lit chamber, where Chak Tok Ich'aak, flanked by counselors and minions, reclined on an ornate bench. On that bench is, quite possibly, where he met his fate.*

Like most Maya rulers, Chak Tok Ich'aak spent a lot of his time luxuriating in his court while dwarf servants attended to his whims and musicians played conch shells and wooden trumpets in the background. But he also excelled at such regal duties as performing ritual public dances, sending out trade expeditions in search of luxury goods, and fighting wars—a celebratory stela has Chak Tok Ich'aak personally stomping a manacled POW. In another portrait, a bas-relief, the king is depicted as an alert man with a long breech-clout and a jeweled mass of necklaces, bracelets, anklets, and pendants click-

---

*Chak Tok Ich'aak's name, like most Maya names, is easier to pronounce than it looks. In most transliterations, all letters are pronounced much as they are in English, except that x is "sh." Thus the small ruin of Xpuhil is "Shpoo-heel." The only difficulty is the glottal stop, the constriction of the throat that occurs when someone with a classic Brooklyn accent pronounces "bottle." In Maya, the glottal stop is indicated by an apostrophe, as in Ich'aak. Chak Tok Ich'aak, incidentally, meant something like "Great True Jaguar Claw."

Mutal (modern Tikal) and the huge city-empire of Teotihuacán had trade relations—peaceful, so far as is known—that dated back to 200 A.D. Matters abruptly changed in January 378, when a force led by the Teotihuacán general Siyaj K'ak' arrived in the court of the Mutal king Chak Tok Ich'aak. As depicted on a painting wrapped around a Mutal vase, the foreign

ing and clattering about his person. Towering a foot over his skull was an elaborate headdress in the shape of a bird of prey, complete with swirling plumage. Like most Maya art, the portrait is too stylized to regard as a naturalistic rendering. Nonetheless, it effectively makes its point: Chak Tok Ich'aak was a major historical figure.

By combining scraps of data on several inscriptions, archaeologists have calculated that Chak Tok Ich'aak probably acceded to the throne in 360 A.D. At the time, the Maya realm consisted of sixty or so small, jostling statelets scattered across what is now northern Belize and Guatemala and the Yucatán Peninsula. Mutal was older and wealthier than most, but otherwise not strikingly different. Chak Tok Ich'aak changed that. During the eighteen years of his reign, the city acquired diplomatic stature and commercial clout; its population grew to perhaps ten thousand and it established trade contacts throughout Mesoamerica. As it prospered, Mutal attracted considerable attention—which, in the end, may have been the king's undoing.

Marching toward him that January day was an armed force from Teotihuacán, 630 miles to the west. Already in control of most of central Mexico, Teotihuacán was looking for new lands to dominate. Leading the expedition was one Siyaj K'ak', apparently a trusted general or counselor to the ruler of Teotihuacán. Four Maya cities along Siyaj K'ak''s path recorded his progress in murals, panel paintings, and stelae. Texts and images depict the Teotihuacanos as gaudily martial figures with circular mirrors strapped to their backs and squared-off helmets sweeping protectively in front of the jaw. They were bare-chested but wore fringed leggings and heavy shell necklaces and highstrapped sandals. In their hands were atlatls and obsidian darts to throw with them. Painted panels in one city show Maya soldiers in jaguar uniforms rush-

soldiers, shown with bundles of spears and atlatls, marched away from a Teotihuacán-style building (above) and confronted the lightly clad Mutal king on the steps of his palace (near left). The outcome of the meeting—Chak Tok Ich'aak's death—may be hinted at in the final image (far left), in which longhaired Maya pay their respects to an empty pyramid.

ing to attack the visitors, but in fact it seems unlikely that any of the small settlements between Teotihuacán and Mutal would have dared to harass them.

No detailed description of the encounter between Siyaj K'ak' and Chak Tok Ich'aak exists, but it is known that discussion did not go on for long. They two men met on January 14, 378 A.D. On that same day Chak Tok Ich'aak "entered the water," according to an account carved on a later stela. The Maya saw the afterworld as a kind of endless, foggy sea. "Entering the water" was thus a euphemism on the order of "passed on to a better place." Readers of the stela would understand that Chak Tok Ich'aak's old heart had quietly stopped beating after Siyaj K'ak' or one of his troops slipped a blade into it. Likely the rest of his family perished, as well as anyone else who objected. In any case no one seems to have complained when Siyaj K'ak' established a new dynasty at Mutal by installing the son of his Teotihuacán master on the vacant throne.

Chak Tok Ich'aak's death began a tumultuous period in Mesoamerican history. The new, Teotihuacán-backed dynasty at Mutal drove the city to further heights of power and prestige. Inevitably, its expansion was resented. A northern city-state, Kaan (now known as Calakmul), conscripted an army from its client states and launched a series of attacks. The ensuing strife lasted 150 years, spread across the Maya heartland, and resulted in the pillage of a dozen city-states, among them both Mutal and Kaan. After suffering repeated losses, Mutal unexpectedly defeated the superior forces of Kaan, possibly killing its king to boot. The beaten, humiliated Kaan lost the support of its vassals and was reduced to penury.

Mutal once again reclaimed its heritage from imperial Teotihuacán. But its triumph, though long sought, was short-lived. In one of archaeology's most enduring mysteries, Maya civilization crumbled around it within a century. After a final flash of imperial splendor, the city joined Kaan and most central Maya cities in obscurity and ruin. By about 900 A.D., both Mutal and Kaan stood almost empty, along with dozens of other Maya cities. And soon even the few people who still lived there had forgotten their imperial glories.

"GETTING ALONG WITH NATURE"

Why did the Maya abandon all their cities?

"No words are more calculated to strike dismay in the hearts of Maya archaeologists," the Maya archaeologist David Webster confessed in 2002. Webster, a researcher at Pennsylvania State University, admitted that during his "incautious younger years" he often told fellow airplane passengers that he was flying to work "at some ancient Maya center. Then, with utter predictability, [would come] the dreaded question. Nowadays, older and wiser, I usually mutter something vague about 'business' and then bury my nose in the airline magazine."

One reason Webster avoided the question is its scope. Asking what happened to the ancient Maya is like asking what happened in the Cold War—the subject is so big that one hardly knows where to begin. At the same time, that very sweep is why the Maya collapse has fascinated archaeologists since the 1840s, when the outside world first learned of the abandoned cities in Yucatán. Today we know that the fall was not quite as rapid, dramatic, and widespread as earlier scholars believed. Nevertheless, it was an extraordinary event: the disintegration of an entire social order, followed by a massive emptying-out of a once-populous and once-prosperous land. Rare is its equal in world history. What happened?

In the 1930s, Sylvanus G. Morley of Harvard, probably the most celebrated Mayanist of his day, espoused what is still the best-known theory: The Maya collapsed because they overshot the carrying capacity of their environment. They exhausted their resource base, began to die of starvation and thirst, and fled their cities en masse, leaving them as silent warnings of the perils of ecological hubris.

When Morley proposed his theory, it was little more than a hunch. Since then, though, scientific measurements, mainly of pollen in lake sediments, have shown that the Maya *did* cut down much of the region's forest, using the wood for fuel and the land for agriculture. The loss of tree cover would have caused large-scale erosion and floods. With their fields disappearing beneath their feet and a growing population to feed, Maya farmers were forced to exploit ever more marginal terrain with ever more intensity. The tottering system was vulnerable to the first good push, which came in the form of a century-long dry spell that hit Yucatán between about 800 and 900 A.D. Social disintegration followed soon thereafter.

Recounted in numberless articles and books, the Maya collapse has become an ecological parable for green activists; along with Pleistocene overkill, it is a favorite cautionary tale about surpassing the limits of Nature. The Maya "were able to build a complex society capable of great cultural and intellectual achievements, but they ended up destroying what they created," Clive Ponting wrote in his influential *Green History of the World* (1991). Following the implications of the Maya fall, he asked, "Are contemporary societies any better at controlling the drive toward ever greater use of resources and heavier pressure on the environment? Is humanity too confident about its ability to avoid ecological disaster?" The history of these Indians, Ponting and others have suggested, has much to teach us today.

Curiously, though, environmentalists also describe Native American history as embodying precisely the opposite lesson: how to live in a spiritual balance with Nature. Bookstore shelves groan beneath the weight of titles like *Sacred Ecology, Guardians of the Earth, Mother Earth Spirituality,* and *Indigenous Traditions and Ecology: The Interbeing of Cosmology and Community.* So strongly endorsed is this view of Native Americans that checklists exist to judge whether books correctly depict their environmental values. The Native Cultures Authenticity Guideline, for instance, assesses the portrayal of the "Five Great Values" shared by all "the major Native cultures" (including, one assumes, the Maya), one of which is "Getting Along with Nature"—"respecting the sacred natural harmony of and with Nature." To be historically accurate, according to the guidelines, major native cultures must be shown displaying "a proper reverence for the gift of life."

Indians as poster children for eco-catastrophe, Indians as green role models: the two images contradict each other less than they seem. Both are variants of Holmberg's Mistake, the idea that Indians were suspended in time, touching nothing and untouched themselves, like ghostly presences on the landscape. The first two sections of this book were devoted to two different ways that researchers have recently repudiated this perspective. I showed that they have raised their estimates of indigenous populations in 1492, and their reasons for it; and then why most researchers now believe that Indian societies have been here longer than had been imagined, and grew more complex and technologically accomplished than previously thought. In this section I treat another facet of Holmberg's Mistake: the idea that native cultures did not or could not control their environment. The view that Indians left no footprint on the land is an obvious example. That they marched heedlessly to tragedy is a subtler one. Both depict indigenous people as passively accepting whatever is meted out to them, whether it is the fruits of undisturbed ecosystems or the punishment for altering them.

Native Americans' interactions with their environments were as diverse as Native Americans themselves, but they were always the product of a specific historical process. Occasionally researchers can detail that process with some precision, as in the case of the Maya. More often one can see only the outlines of history, as in the reconfiguration of the eastern half of the United States. These two paradigmatic examples are the subjects I turn to now. In both, Indians worked on a very large scale, transforming huge swathes of the landscape for their own ends. Sifting through the evidence, it is apparent that many though not all Indians were superbly active land managers—they did not live lightly on the land. And they *do* have lessons to teach us, but they are not what are commonly supposed.

FIRE PLACE

Adriaen van der Donck was a lawyer who in 1641 transplanted himself to the Hudson River Valley, then part of the Dutch colony of New Amsterdam. He became a kind of prosecutor and bill collector for the Dutch West India Company, which owned and operated the colony as a private fiefdom. Whenever possible, van der Donck ignored his duties and tramped around the forests and valleys upstate. He spent a lot of time with the Haudenosaunee, whose insistence on personal liberty fascinated him. They were, he wrote, "all free by nature, and will not bear any domineering or lording over them."

When a committee of settlers decided to complain to the government about the Dutch West India Company's dictatorial behavior, it asked van der Donck, the only lawyer in New Amsterdam, to compose a protest letter and travel with it to The Hague. His letter set down the basic rights that in his view belonged to everyone on American soil—the first formal call for liberty in the colonies. It is tempting to speculate that van der Donck drew inspiration from the attitudes of the Haudenosaunee.

The Dutch government responded to the letter by taking control of New Amsterdam from the Dutch West India Company and establishing an independent governing body in Manhattan, thereby setting into motion the creation of New York City. Angered by their loss of power, the company directors effectively prevented van der Donck's return for five years. While languishing in Europe, he wrote a nostalgic pamphlet extolling the land he had come to love.

Every fall, he remembered, the Haudenosaunee set fire to "the woods, plains, and meadows," to "thin out and clear the woods of all dead substances and grass, which grow better the ensuing spring." At first the wildfire had scared him, but over time van der Donck had come to relish the spectacle of the yearly burning. "Such a fire is a splendid sight when one sails on the [Hudson and Mohawk] rivers at night while the forest is ablaze on both banks," he recalled. With the forest burning to the right and the left, the colonists' boats passed through a channel of fire, their passengers as goggle-eyed at the blaze as children at a video arcade. "Fire and flames are seen everywhere and on all sides . . . a delightful scene to look on from afar."

Van der Donck believed that North America was only "several hundred miles" across, and apparently assumed that all its inhabitants were exactly like the Haudenosaunee. He was wrong about the first belief, but in a sense correct about the second: from the Atlantic to the Pacific, from Hudson's Bay to the Río Grande, the Haudenosaunee and almost every other Indian group shaped their environment, at least in part, by fire.

Early in the last century, ecologists discovered the phenomenon of "succession," the more or less well-defined sequence by which ecosystems fill in open land. A textbook example occurred after the eruption in 1980 of Mount St. Helens, in southern Washington State, which inundated more than two hundred square miles with magma, volcanic ash, and mud. Surviving plants sprang quickly to life, sometimes resprouting within weeks. Then colonizing species like lupine appeared, preparing the ground for the return of the grasses. Fifteen years after the eruption, the ravaged slopes were dotted with trees and woody shrubs: red alder, lodgepole pine, willow bush. Here and there gleamed the waxy red boles of madrone. Forest giants like hemlock, Douglas fir, and Sitka spruce waited in the wings. In the classic successional course, each suite of plants replaces its predecessor, until the arrival of the final, "climax" ecosystem, usually tall forest.

If ecological succession were unstoppable, the continents would be covered by climax-stage vegetation: a world of great trees, dark and silent. Early-succession species would have vanished. Luckily for these species, succession is often interrupted—Nature does not move in lockstep. Windstorms, lightning fires, landslides, volcanic eruptions, and other natural calamities knock down trees and open up the forest, or prevent open country from turning into forestland. A few years or decades of tranquility may see grasses replaced by shrubs and trees which are in turn flattened by a violent thunderstorm, permitting the grass to thrive again. After a while, the shrubs and trees return, only to be wiped out by a flood. And so on. Different types of disturbance shape different ecosystems: floods in the Nile, landslides on the steep pitches of the Andes, hurricanes in the Yucatán Peninsula. For more than ten thousand years, most North American ecosystems have been dominated by fire.

In the Greek myth of Prometheus the gift of fire forever severs humankind from the natural world—the burning torch is the icon of the constructed and artificial. On the mundane, factual level, though, this resonant tale is wrong: Nature has always used fire as a mallet to beat landscapes into other forms. Prometheus only helped human beings to pick up the handle. "The earth," wrote the pioneering fire ecologist Edward V. Komarek, "born in fire, baptized by lightning, since before life's beginning has been and is, a fire planet." Set off by lightning, wildfires reset the ecological clock, dialing the array of plants and animals back a few successional stages. Fire benefits plants that need sunlight, while inhibiting those that love the cool gloaming of the forest floor; it encourages the animals that need those plants even as it discourages others; in turn, predator populations rise and fall. In this way fire regulates ecological character.

Fire is a dominating factor in many if not most terrestrial landscapes. It has two main sources: lightning and *Homo sapiens*. In North America, lightning fire is most common in the western mountains. Elsewhere, though, Indians controlled it—at least until contact, and in many places long after. In the Northeast, Indians always carried a deerskin pouch full of flints, Thomas Morton reported in 1637, which they used "to set fire of the country in all places where they come." The flints ignited torches, which were as important to the hunt as bows and arrows. Deer in the Northeast; alligators in the Everglades; buffalo in the prairies; grasshoppers in the Great Basin; rabbits in California; moose in Alaska: all were pursued by fire. Native Americans made big rings of flame, Thomas Jefferson wrote, "by firing the leaves fallen on the ground, which, gradually forcing animals to the center, they there slaughter them with arrows, darts, and other missiles." Not that Indians always used fire for strictly utilitarian purposes. At nightfall tribes in the Rocky Mountains entertained the explorers Meriwether Lewis and William Clark by applying torches to sap-dripping fir trees, which then exploded like Roman candles.

Rather than domesticate animals for meat, Indians retooled ecosystems to encourage elk, deer, and bear. Constant burning of undergrowth increased the numbers of herbivores, the predators that fed on them, and the people who ate them both. Rather than the thick, unbroken, monumental snarl of trees imagined by Thoreau, the great eastern forest was an ecological kaleidoscope of garden plots, blackberry rambles, pine barrens, and spacious groves of chestnut, hickory, and oak. The first white settlers in Ohio found woodlands that resembled English parks—they could drive carriages through the trees. Fifteen miles from shore in Rhode Island, Giovanni da Verrazzano found trees so widely spaced that the forest "could be penetrated even by a large army." John Smith claimed to have ridden through the Virginia forest at a gallop.

Incredible to imagine today, bison roamed from New York to Georgia. A creature of the prairie, *Bison bison* was imported to the East by Native Americans along a path of indigenous fire, as they changed enough forest into fallows for it to survive far outside its original range. When the Haudenosaunee hunted these animals, the historian William Cronon observed, they

> were harvesting a foodstuff which they had consciously been instrumental in creating. Few English observers could have realized this. People accustomed to keeping domesticated animals lacked the conceptual tools to recognize that the Indians were practicing a more distant kind of husbandry of their own.

Indian fire had its greatest impact in the middle of the continent, which Native Americans transformed into a prodigious game farm. Native Americans burned the Great Plains and Midwest prairies so much and so often that they increased their extent; in all probability, a substantial portion of the giant grassland celebrated by cowboys was established and maintained by the people who arrived there first. "When Lewis and Clark headed west from [St. Louis]," wrote ethologist Dale Lott, "they were exploring not a wilderness but a vast pasture managed by and for Native Americans."

In 1792 the surveyor Peter Fidler examined the plains of southern Alberta systematically, the first European to do so. Riding with several groups of Indians in high fire season, he spent days on end in a scorched land. "Grass all burnt this day," he reported on November 12. "Not a single pine to be seen three days past." A day later: "All burnt ground this Day." A day later: "The grass nearly burnt all along this Day except near the Lake." A month later: "The Grass is now burning [with] very great fury."

> Every fall & spring, & even in the winter when there is no snow, these large plains either in one place or other is constantly on fire, & when the Grass happens to be long & the wind high, the sight is grand & awful, & it drives along with amazing swiftness.

Fidler acknowledged that the fires could be "very dangerous" but understood their purpose. "These fires burning off the old grass," he observed, "in the ensuing Spring & Summer makes excellent fine sweet feed for the Horses & Buffalo, &c."

When Indian societies disintegrated from disease and mistreatment, forest invaded savanna in Wisconsin, Illinois, Kansas, Nebraska, Wyoming, and the Texas hill country. Europeans forgot what the landscape had looked like before and why. Captain John Palliser, traveling through the same lands as Fidler six decades later, lamented the Indians' "disastrous habit of setting the prairie on fire for the most trivial and worse than useless reasons." Afterward even the memory of indigenous fire faded. By the twentieth century biologists were stoutly denying its existence. The "open, park-like woods" seen by early settlers, Harvard naturalist Hugh Raup asserted in 1937, were not caused by fire; they "have been, from time immemorial, characteristic of vast areas in North America." Raup's summary description of the idea that they were due to regular, wide-scale Indian burning? "Inconceivable." "It is at least a fair assumption," a widely used college forestry textbook remarked in 1973, "that no habitual or systematic burning was carried out by Indians." In the western United States, the geographer Thomas R. Vale wrote in 2002, the "modest" Indian population "modified only a tiny fraction of the total landscape for their everyday living needs."

Vale is in the minority now. Spurred in part by historians like Cronon, most scientists have changed their minds about Indian fire. Using clever laboratory techniques, they have convinced themselves that in most cases the tribal lore and old chronicles were right all along: Indian embers were sparkling in the American night for centuries before the Sumerians climbed their ziggurats.

Carrying their flints and torches, Native Americans *were* living in balance with Nature—but they had their thumbs on the scale. Shaped for their comfort and convenience, the American landscape had come to fit their lives like comfortable clothing. It was a highly successful and stable system, if "stable" is the appropriate word for a regime that involves routinely enshrouding miles of countryside in smoke and ash. And it was a system that Indians were abandoning in ever-rising numbers at the time when Europeans came.

TEN THOUSAND MOUNDS

Anyone who traveled up the Mississippi in 1100 A.D. would have seen it looming in the distance: a four-level earthen mound bigger than the Great Pyramid of Giza. Around it like echoes were as many as 120 smaller mounds, some topped by tall wooden palisades, which were in turn ringed by a network of irrigation and transportation canals; carefully located fields of maize; and hundreds of red-and-white-plastered wood homes with high-peaked, deeply thatched roofs like those on traditional Japanese farms. Located near the confluence of the Missouri, Illinois, and Mississippi Rivers, the Indian city of Cahokia was a busy port. Canoes flitted like hummingbirds across its waterfront: traders bringing copper and mother-of-pearl from far-away places; hunting parties bringing such rare treats as buffalo and elk; emissaries and soldiers in long vessels bristling with weaponry; workers ferrying wood from upstream for the ever hungry cookfires; the ubiquitous fishers with their nets and clubs. Covering five square miles and housing at least fifteen thousand people, Cahokia was the biggest concentration of people north of the Río Grande until the eighteenth century.

Away from the riverside, Cahokia was hardly less busy and imposing. Its focal point was the great mound—Monks Mound, it is now called, named after a group of Trappists who lived nearby in the eighteenth and nineteenth centuries. Around its sides rushed a flow of men, their body paint and tattoos obscured by dust from the hardened, brick-like mud that lay underneath the entire city. Some built new mounds or maintained the old; others hauled wood for fuel and houses or carried water in leather pouches or weeded the maize fields with stone hoes. Women carried stacks of woven mats, baskets of fish and produce, yowling children. Cooksmoke chimneyed to the sky. Standards made of painted animal skins flapped everywhere. Anyone who has visited Siena or Venice knows how surprisingly noisy a city without engines can be. At peak times, given the right wind conditions, Cahokia must have been audible for miles.

Monks Mound opens onto a plaza a thousand feet long. In its southwest corner is a pair of mounds, one conical, one square. One day I climbed up their grassy sides at sunset. Hardly any other visitors were there. The humped outline of the vast heap of earth emerged from the empty green like a powerful prairie ship. The sun was low and the great mound was casting a shadow that looked long enough to reach the Allegheny Mountains. For a moment I saw no sign of contemporary life; St. Louis, just across the river, had not yet switched on its lights. Around me was the mound city and nothing but the mound city. To we moderns the sensation of being in a constructed environment is so ubiquitous as to be invisible—in the cocoon of our strip malls and automobiles, we are like the fish that cannot feel the water through which they swim. In Cahokia's day it was different. A thousand years ago it was the only place for a thousand miles in which one could be completely enveloped in an artificial landscape.

To visitors today it seems obvious that Cahokia and the many other

mound sites in the Midwest and Southeast are the remains of Indian settlements. It did not seem so clear in the past. Nineteenth-century writers attributed the mound complexes to, among others, the Chinese, the Welsh, the
Phoenicians, the lost nation of Atlantis, and various biblical personages. A
widely touted theory assigned authorship to Scandinavian émigrés, who later
picked up stakes, moved to Mexico, and became the Toltecs. The science-
fiction writer and archaeology buff Robert Silverberg devoted an entire
entertaining book to the back-and-forth over the origin of the mounds,
which intermittently preoccupied American intellectuals for a century.
Thomas Jefferson removed a slice from a mound on his estate, examined the
stratigraphic layers, and announced that Indians had made it. George Bancroft, one of the founders of American history, disagreed: the mounds, he
wrote in 1840, were purely natural formations.

Charitably, one could say that Bancroft was correct: Cahokia *was* a product of its geography, which in turn was a product of the Ice Age. When the
glaciers melted, water gushed south, creating the Mississippi River and the
Illinois and Missouri Rivers that funnel into it. They met in a roil of water
eighty miles wide. When the rivers receded, they exposed a wide strip of bottomland. Into this land a group of Indians coalesced sometime before 800 A.D.

Nobody knows what these people called themselves or which language
they spoke. They were not "Cahokians"—that name, itself a linguistic gar-
ble, comes from an unrelated group that migrated to the area almost a thousand years later. Archaeologists are unlikely to find a better name, though.
According to William Woods, the geographer and archaeologist at the University of Kansas, Monks Mound completely covers whatever habitation
these people had before they built Cahokia. To see the remaining traces of
this early settlement, scientists would have to jack up the whole enormous
pile and dig underneath. Almost all that can be known with certainty about
this initial group is that it belonged to a diverse, four-thousand-year-old tradition characterized by the construction of large earthen mounds.

Based around the Mississippi and its associated rivers, these societies scattered tens of thousands of mounds from southern Canada and the Great
Plains to the Atlantic coast and the Gulf of Mexico. They were especially
concentrated in the Ohio Valley, but nearly as many are found in the Southeast. Highways, farms, and housing developments have destroyed most of
them, and scientists have investigated only a small fraction of the survivors.
Most of the earthworks were shaped like big cones and stepped pyramids,
but some were sculpted into enormous birds, lizards, bears, long-tailed "alligators," and, in Peebles, Ohio, a 1,330-foot-long serpent.

The earliest known examples appeared in northeastern Lousiana about

5,400 years ago, well before the advent of agriculture. For reasons unknown, Indians heaved up a ring of eleven irregularly sized mounds, most of them connected by a ridge, on a hill overlooking the course of the Ouachita River. The biggest was as tall as a two-story house. About a dozen similar sites are known, of which the Ouachita ring is the oldest and biggest. None of the mounds in any of these places cover burials or contain artifacts or show signs of use. Indeed, they seem to have so little purpose that archaeologist Joe Saunders of Northeast Louisiana University, whose team excavated the Ouachita mounds in 1997, half-jokingly speculated to *Science* that the motive for building them could have been the act of construction itself. "I know it sounds awfully Zen-like," he conceded.

Because modern-day hunter-gatherers in Africa live in egalitarian bands that constantly move from place to place, archaeologists assumed that Native American hunter-gatherers must also have done so. Discovering the Louisiana mounds upset this view: they suggest that at least some early Indians were stay-at-homes. More important, they testify to levels of public authority and civic organization rarely associated with nomads. Building a ring of mounds with baskets or deerskins full of dirt is a long-term enterprise. During construction the workers must eat, which in turn means that other people must provide their food. Such levels of planning are ordinarily

The Ouachita mounds as they may have appeared at their creation, 5,400 years ago.

thought to kick in with the transition to agriculture. When people till and sow the land, anthropologists say, they set up systems to protect their investment. Eventually somebody ends up in charge of allocating goods and services. But the mound builders in Louisiana built these massive constructions at a time when agriculture was barely under way—it was like the whiff in the air from a faraway ocean. In the central river valleys of North America, people had a way of life without known analogue.

After these first mounds the record is sparse. After the Ouachita mounds, there is a gap in the record of more than a millennium. The curtain parts again in about 1500 B.C., when an archipelago of villages, the largest known as Poverty Point, grew up in the northeast corner of Louisiana. Located fifty-five miles from the Ouachita site, Poverty Point had as a focus a structure resembling an amphitheater: six concentric, C-shaped ridges, each five feet tall, on a bluff facing the river. The jaws of the widest C are 3,950 feet apart, an expanse so big that scientists did not recognize the ridges as constructions until they took aerial photographs of the site in the 1950s.

Now another gap: seven hundred years. The next major sequence occurs mainly in the Ohio Valley, hundreds of miles north. Here was a group known as the Adena—the name is that of a well-known site. Because Adena mounds served as tombs, researchers know more about their deaths than their lives. Accompanying the noble few in the tombs to the world of the deceased were copper beads and bracelets, stone tablets and collars, textiles and awls, and, sometimes, stone pipes in the shape of surreal animals. The head of the creature faced the user, who sucked in tobacco smoke from its mouth. It is widely believed that Adena tobacco was much stronger than today's tobacco—it was psychoactive.

Tobacco was only one of the crops grown at Adena villages. The Mississippi and Ohio Valleys and much of the U.S. Southeast were home to what is known as the Eastern Agricultural Complex. A full-fledged agricultural revolution with a multifarious suite of crops, the complex is an example of a major cultural innovation that has completely disappeared. Its crops were such unfamiliar plants as marshelder, knotweed, maygrass, and little barley. All of these species still exist; one could stock a specialty restaurant with them. (Sample menu: maygrass patties, steamed knotweed beans, and buffalo tongue.) No one seems to be doing that, though. In fact, farmers today treat several of these crops as weeds—they routinely blast little barley with herbicides. Archaeologists have tentative indications of early domestication in spots from Illinois to Alabama by 1000 B.C. But agriculture did not begin to flower, so to speak, until the Adena.

Adena influence in customs and artifacts can be spotted in archaeological sites from Indiana to Kentucky and all the way north to Vermont and even

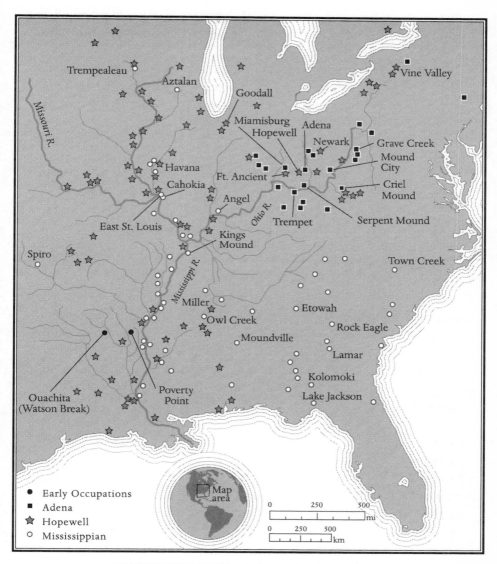

MOUNDBUILDERS, 3400 B.C.—I400 A.D.

New Brunswick. For a long time researchers believed this indicated that the Adena had conquered other groups throughout this area, but many now believe that the influence was cultural: like European teenagers donning baggy pants and listening to hip-hop, Adena's neighbors adopted its customs. Archaeologists sometimes call the area in which such cultural flows occur an "interaction sphere." Both less and more than a nation, an interaction sphere is a region in which one society disseminates its symbols, values, and inventions to others; an example is medieval Europe, much of which fell under the sway of Gothic aesthetics and ideas. The Adena interaction sphere lasted from about 800 B.C. to about 100 B.C.

Textbooks sometimes say that the Adena were succeeded by the Hopewell, but the relation is unclear; the Hopewell may simply have been a later stage of the same culture. The Hopewell, too, built mounds, and like the Adena seem to have spoken an Algonquian language. ("Hopewell" refers to the farmer on whose property an early site was discovered.) Based in southern Ohio, the Hopewell interaction sphere lasted until about 400 A.D. and extended across two-thirds of what is now the United States. Into the Midwest came seashells from the Gulf of Mexico, silver from Ontario, fossil shark's teeth from Chesapeake Bay, and obsidian from Yellowstone. In return the Hopewell exported ideas: the bow and arrow, monumental earthworks, fired pottery (Adena pots were not put into kilns), and, probably most important, the Hopewell religion.

The Hopewell apparently sought spiritual ecstasy by putting themselves into trances, perhaps aided by tobacco. In this enraptured state, the soul journeys to other worlds. As is usually the case, people with special abilities emerged to assist travelers through the portal to the numinous. Over time these shamans became gatekeepers, controlling access to the supernatural realm. They passed on their control and privileges to their children, creating a hereditary priesthood: counselors to kings, if not kings themselves. They acquired healing lore, mastered and invented ceremonies, learned the numerous divinities in the Hopewell pantheon. We know little of these gods today, because few of their images have endured to the present. Presumably shamans recounted their stories to attentive crowds; almost certainly, they explained when and where the gods wanted to build mounds.

In the context of the village, the mound, visible everywhere, was as much a beacon as a medieval cathedral. As with Gothic churches, which had plazas for the outdoor performance of sacred mystery plays, the mounds had greens before them: ritual spaces for public use. Details of the performances are lost, but there is every indication that they were exuberant affairs. "There is a stunning vigor about the Ohio Hopewell . . . ," Silverberg wrote,

> a flamboyance and fondness for excess that manifests itself not only in the intricate geometrical enclosures and the massive mounds, but in these gaudy displays of conspicuous consumption [in the tombs]. To envelop a corpse from head to feet in pearls, to weigh it down in many pounds of copper, to surround it with masterpieces of sculpture and pottery, and then to bury everything under tons of earth—this betokens a kind of cultural energy that numbs and awes those who follow after.

Vibrant and elaborate, perhaps a little vulgar in its passion for display, Hopewell religion spread through most of the eastern United States in the first four centuries A.D. As with the expansion of Christianity, the new converts are unlikely to have understood the religion in the same way as its founders. Nonetheless, its impact was profound. In a mutated form, it may well have given impetus to the rise of Cahokia.

THE RISE AND FALL OF THE AMERICAN BOTTOM

Cahokia was one big piece in the mosaic of chiefdoms that covered the lower half of the Mississippi and the Southeast at the end of the first millennium A.D. Known collectively as "Mississippian" cultures, these societies arose several centuries after the decline of the Hopewell culture, and probably were its distant descendants. At any one time a few larger polities dominated the dozens or scores of small chiefdoms. Cahokia, biggest of all, was preeminent from about 950 to about 1250 A.D. It was an anomaly: the greatest city north of the Río Grande, it was also the *only* city north of the Río Grande. Five times or more bigger than any other Mississippian chiefdom, Cahokia's population of at least fifteen thousand made it comparable in size to London, but on a landmass without Paris, Córdoba, or Rome.

I call Cahokia a city so as to have a stick to beat it with, but it was not a city in any modern sense. A city provides goods and services for its surrounding area, exchanging food from the countryside for the products of its sophisticated craftspeople. By definition, its inhabitants are urban—they aren't farmers. Cahokia, however, was a huge collection of farmers packed cheek by jowl. It had few specialized craftworkers and no middle-class merchants. On reflection, Cahokia's dissimilarity to other cities is not surprising; having never seen a city, its citizens had to invent every aspect of urban life for themselves.

Despite the nineteenth-century fascination with the mounds, archaeologists did not begin to examine Cahokia thoroughly until the 1960s. Since then studies have gushed from the presses. By and large, they have only confirmed Cahokia's status as a statistical outlier. Cahokia sat on the eastern side of the American Bottom. Most of the area has clayey soil that is hard to till and prone to floods. Cahokia was located next to the largest stretch of good farmland in the entire American Bottom. At its far edge, a forest of oak and hickory topped a line of bluffs. The area was little settled until as late as 600 A.D., when people trickled in and formed small villages, groups of a few hundred who planted gardens and boated up and down the Mississippi to other villages. As the millennium approached, the American Bottom had a resident population of several thousand. Then, without much apparent warning, there was, according to the archaeologist Timothy R. Pauketat of the University of Illinois at Urbana-Champaign, what has been called a "Big Bang"—a few decades of tumultuous change.

Cahokia's mounds emerged from the Big Bang, along with the East St. Louis mound complex a mile away (the second biggest, after Cahokia, though now mostly destroyed) and the St. Louis mounds just across the Mississippi (the fourth biggest). Monks Mound was the first and most grandiose of the construction projects. Its core is a slab of clay about 900 feet long, 650 feet wide, and more than 20 feet tall. From an engineering standpoint, clay should never be selected as the bearing material for a big earthen monument. Clay readily absorbs water, expanding as it does. The American Bottom clay, known as smectite clay, is especially prone to swelling: its volume can increase by a factor of eight. Drying, it shrinks back to its original dimensions. Over time the heaving will destroy whatever is built on top of it. The Cahokians' solution to this problem was discovered mainly by Woods, the University of Kansas archaeologist and geographer, who has spent two decades excavating Monks Mound.

To minimize instability, he told me, the Cahokians kept the slab at a constant moisture level: wet but not too wet. Moistening the clay was easy—capillary action will draw up water from the floodplain, which has a high water table. The trick is to stop evaporation from drying out the top. In an impressive display of engineering savvy, the Cahokians encapsulated the slab, sealing it off from the air by wrapping it in thin, alternating layers of sand and clay. The sand acts as a shield for the slab. Water rises through the clay to meet it, but cannot proceed further because the sand is too loose for further capillary action. Nor can the water evaporate; the clay layers atop the sand press down and prevent air from coming in. In addition, the sand lets rainfall drain away from the mound, preventing it from swelling too much. The final result covered almost fifteen acres and was the largest earthen structure in the Western Hemisphere; though built out of unsuitable material in a floodplain, it has stood for a thousand years.

Because the slab had to stay moist, it must have been built and covered quickly, a task requiring a big workforce. Evidence suggests that people moved from miles around to the American Bottom to be part of the project. If the ideas of Pauketat, the University of Illinois archaeologist, are correct, the immigrants probably came to regret their decision to move. To his way of thinking, the Big Bang occurred after a single ambitious person seized power, perhaps in a coup. Although his reign may have begun idealistically, Cahokia quickly became an autocracy; in an Ozymandiac extension

Reconstructions of Cahokia, the greatest city north of the Río Grande, ca. 1250 A.D.

of his ego, the supreme leader set in motion the construction projects. Loyalists forced immigrants to join the labor squads, maintaining control with the occasional massacre. Burials show the growing power of the elite: in a small mound half a mile south of Monks Mound, archaeologists in the late 1960s uncovered six high-status people interred with shell beads, copper ornaments, mica artworks—and the sacrificed bodies of more than a hundred retainers. Among them were fifty young women who had been buried alive.

Woods disagrees with what he calls the "proto-Stalinist work camp" scenario. Nobody was *forced* to erect Monks Mound, he says. Despite the intermittent displays of coercion, he says, Cahokians put it up "because they wanted to." They "were proud to be part of these symbols of community identity." Monks Mound and its fellows were, in part, a shout-out to the world—Look at us! We're doing something different! It was also the construction of a landscape of sacred power, built in an atmosphere of ecstatic religious celebration. The American Bottom, in this scenario, was the site of one of the world's most spectacular tent revivals. Equally important, Woods says, the mound city was in large part an outgrowth of the community's previous adoption of maize.

Before Cahokia's rise, people were slowly hunting the local deer and bison populations to extinction. The crops in the Eastern Agricultural Complex could not readily make up the difference. Among other problems, most had small seeds—imagine trying to feed a family on sesame seeds, and you have some idea of what it would have been like to subsist on maygrass. Maize had been available since the first century B.C. (It would have arrived sooner, but Indians had to breed landraces that could tolerate the cooler weather, shorter growing seasons, and longer summer days of the north.) The Hopewell, however, almost ignored it. Somewhere around 800 A.D. their hungry successors took another look at the crop and liked what they saw. The American Bottom, with its plenitude of easily cleared, maize-suitable land, was one of the best places to grow it for a considerable distance. The newcomers needed to store their harvests for the winter, a task most efficiently accomplished with a communal granary. The granary needed to be supervised—an invitation to develop centralized power. Growth happened fast and may well have been hurried along by a charismatic leader, Woods said, but something like Cahokia probably would have happened anyway.

Maize also played a role in the city's disintegration. Cahokia represented the first time Indians north of the Río Grande had tried to feed and shelter fifteen thousand people in one place, and they made beginner's mistakes. To obtain fuel and construction material and to grow food, they cleared trees and vegetation from the bluffs to the east and planted every inch of arable land. Because the city's numbers kept increasing, the forest could not return. Instead people kept moving further out to get timber, which then had to be carried considerable distances. Having no beasts of burden, the Cahokians themselves had to do all the carrying. Meanwhile, Woods told me, the city began outstripping its water supply, a "somewhat wimpy" tributary called Canteen Creek. To solve both of these problems at once, the Cahokians apparently changed its course, which had consequences that they cannot have anticipated.

Nowadays Cahokia Creek, which flows from the north, and Canteen Creek, which flows from the east, join together at a point about a quarter mile northeast of Monks Mound. On its way to the Mississippi, the combined river then wanders, quite conveniently, within two hundred yards of the central plaza. Originally, though, the smaller Canteen Creek alone occupied that channel. Cahokia Creek drained into a lake to the northwest, then went straight to the Mississippi, bypassing Cahokia altogether. Sometime between 1100 and 1200 A.D., according to Woods's as-yet unpublished

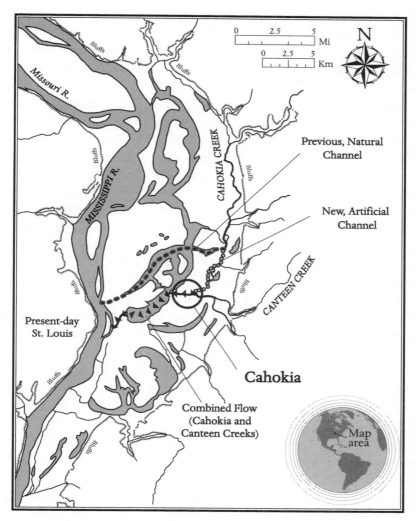

THE AMERICAN BOTTOM, 1300 A.D.

research, Cahokia Creek split in two. One fork continued as before, but the second, larger fork dumped into Canteen Creek. The combined river provided much more water to the city—it was about seventy feet wide. And it also let woodcutters upstream send logs almost to Monks Mound. A natural inference, to Woods's way of thinking, is that the city, in a major public works project, "intentionally diverted" Cahokia Creek.

In summer, heavy rains lash the Mississippi Valley. With the tree cover stripped from the uplands, rainfall would have sluiced faster and heavier into the creeks, increasing the chance of floods and mudslides. Because the now-combined Cahokia and Canteen Creeks carried much more water than had Canteen Creek alone, washouts would have spread more widely across the American Bottom than would have been the case if the rivers had been left alone. Beginning in about 1200 A.D., according to Woods, Cahokia's maize fields repeatedly flooded, destroying the harvests.

The city's problems were not unique. Cahokia's rise coincided with the spread of maize throughout the eastern half of the United States. The Indians who adopted it were setting aside millennia of tradition in favor of a new technology. In the past, they had shaped the landscape mainly with fire; the ax came out only for garden plots of marshelder and little barley. As maize swept in, Indians burned and cleared thousands of acres of land, mainly in river valleys. As in Cahokia, floods and mudslides rewarded them. (How do archaeologists know this? They know it from sudden increases in river sedimentation coupled with the near disappearance of pollen from bottomland trees in those sediments.) Between about 1100 and 1300 A.D., cataclysms afflicted Indian settlements from the Hudson Valley to Florida.

Apparently the majority learned from mistakes; after this time, archaeologists don't see this kind of widespread erosion, though they do see lots and lots of maize. A traveler in 1669 reported that six square miles of maize typically encircled Haudenosaunee villages. This estimate was very roughly corroborated two decades later by the Marquis de Denonville, governor of New France, who destroyed the annual harvest of four adjacent Haudenosaunee villages to deter future attacks. Denonville reported that he had burned 1.2 million bushels of maize—42,000 tons. Today, as I mentioned in Chapter 6, Oaxacan farmers typically plant roughly 1.25–2.5 acres to harvest a ton of landrace maize. If that relation held true in upstate New York—a big, but not ridiculous assumption—arithmetic suggests that the four villages, closely packed together, were surrounded by between eight and sixteen square miles of maize fields.

Between these fields was the forest, which Indians were subjecting to parallel changes. Sometime in the first millennium A.D., the Indians who had burned undergrowth to facilitate grazing began systematically replanting large belts of woodland, transforming them into orchards for fruit and mast (the general name for hickory nuts, beechnuts, acorns, butternuts, hazelnuts, pecans, walnuts, and chestnuts). Chestnut was especially popular—not the imported European chestnut roasted on Manhattan street corners in the fall, but the smaller, soft-shelled, deeply sweet native American chestnut, now almost extinguished by chestnut blight. In colonial times, as many as one out of every four trees in between southeastern Canada and Georgia was a chestnut—partly the result, it would seem, of Indian burning and planting.

Hickory was another favorite. Rambling through the Southeast in the 1770s, the naturalist William Bartram observed Creek families storing a hundred bushels of hickory nuts at a time. "They pound them to pieces, and then cast them into boiling water, which, after passing through fine strainers, preserves the most oily part of the liquid" to make a thick milk, "as sweet and rich as fresh cream, an ingredient in most of their cookery, especially hominy and corncakes." Years ago a friend and I were served hickory milk in rural Georgia by an eccentric backwoods artist named St. EOM who claimed Creek descent. Despite the unsanitary presentation, the milk was ambrosial—fragrantly nutty, delightfully heavy on the tongue, unlike anything I had encountered before.

Within a few centuries, the Indians of the eastern forest reconfigured much of their landscape from a patchwork game park to a mix of farmland and orchards. Enough forest was left to allow for hunting, but agriculture was an increasing presence. The result was a new "balance of nature."

From today's perspective, the *success* of the transition is striking. It was so sweeping and ubiquitous that early European visitors marveled at the number of nut and fruit trees and the big clearings with only a dim apprehension that the two might be due to the same human source. One reason that Bartram failed to understand the artificiality of what he saw was that the surgery was almost without scars; the new landscape functioned smoothly, with few of the overreaches that plagued English land management. Few of the overreaches, but not none: Cahokia was a glaring exception.

A friend and I visited Cahokia in 2002. Woods, who lived nearby, kindly agreed to show us around. The site is now a state park with a small museum. From Monks Mound we walked halfway across the southern plaza and then stopped to look back. From the plaza, Woods pointed out, the priests at the summit could not be seen. "There was smoke and noise and sacred activity constantly going on up there, but the peasants didn't know what they were doing." Nonetheless, average Cahokians understood the intent: to assure the city's continued support by celestial forces. "And *that* justification fell apart with the floods," Woods said.

There is little indication that the Cahokia floods killed anyone, or even led to widespread hunger. Nonetheless, the string of woes provoked a crisis of legitimacy. Unable to muster the commanding vitality of their predecessors, the priestly leadership responded ineffectively, even counterproductively. Even as the flooding increased, it directed the construction of a massive, two-mile-long palisade around the central monuments, complete with bastions, shielded entryways, and (maybe) a catwalk up top. The wall was built in such a brain-frenzied hurry that it cut right through some commoners' houses.

Cahokia being the biggest city around, it seems unlikely that the palisade was needed to deter enemy attack (in the event, none materialized). Instead it was probably created to separate elite from hoi polloi, with the goal of emphasizing the priestly rulers' separate, superior, socially critical connection to the divine. At the same time the palisade was also intended to welcome the citizenry—anyone could freely pass through its dozen or so wide gates. Constructed at enormous cost, this porous architectural folly consumed twenty thousand trees.

More consequential, the elite revamped Monks Mound. By extending a low platform from one side, they created a stage for priests to perform ceremonies in full view of the public. According to Woods's acoustic simulations, every word should have been audible below, lifting the veil of secrecy. It was the Cahokian equivalent of the Reformation, except that the Church imposed it on itself. At the same time, the nobles hedged their bets. Cahokia's rulers tried to bolster their position by building even bigger houses and flaunting even more luxury goods like fancy pottery and jewelry made from exotic semiprecious stones.

It did no good. A catastrophic earthquake razed Cahokia in the beginning of the thirteenth century, knocking down the entire western side of Monks Mound. In 1811 and 1812 the largest earthquakes in U.S. history abruptly lifted or lowered much of the central Mississippi Valley by as much as twelve feet. The Cahokia earthquake, caused by the same fault, was of similar magnitude. It must have splintered many of the city's wood-and-plaster buildings; fallen torches and scattered cooking fires would have ignited the debris, burning down most surviving structures. Water from the rivers, shaken by the quake, would have sloshed onto the land in a mini-tsunami.

Already reeling from the floods, Cahokia never recovered from the earthquake. Its rulers rebuilt Monks Mound, but the poorly engineered patch promptly sagged. Meanwhile the social unrest turned violent; many houses went up in flames. "There was a civil war," Woods said. "Fighting in the streets. The whole polity turned in on itself and tore itself apart."

For all their energy, Cahokia's rulers made a terrible mistake: they did not attempt to fix the problem directly. True, the task would not have been easy. Trees cannot be replaced with a snap of the fingers. Nor could Cahokia Creek readily be reinstalled in its original location. "Once the water starts flowing in the new channel," Woods said, "it is almost impossible to put it back in the old as the new channel rapidly downcuts and establishes itself."

Given Cahokia's engineering expertise, though, solutions were within reach: terracing hillsides, diking rivers, even moving Cahokia. Like all too many dictators, Cahokia's rulers focused on maintaining their hold over the people, paying little attention to external reality. By 1350 A.D. the city was almost empty. Never again would such a large Indian community exist north of Mexico.

HUNDRED YEARS' WAR

In the early 1980s I visited Chetumal, a coastal city on the Mexico-Belize border. A magazine had asked me to cover the intellectual ferment caused by the decipherment of Maya hieroglyphics. In researching the article, the photographer Peter Menzel and I became intrigued by the then little-known site of Calakmul, whose existence had been first reported five decades before. Although it was the biggest of all Maya ruins, it had never felt an archaeologist's trowel. Its temples and villas, enveloped in thick tropical forest, were as close to a lost city as we would ever be likely to see. Before visiting Calakmul, though, Peter wanted to photograph it from the air. Chetumal had the nearest airport, which was why we went there.

The town was unpromising in those days. We arrived late in the night, and the only restaurant we could find served a single platter: octopus with pureed beef liver. I am, as a rule, a member of the Clean Plate Club. Looking at the rubbery white octopus chunks bobbing in the tarry mass of liver, I rejected an entire meal for the first time since childhood. Soon afterward the electricity went out everywhere in town. For that reason we did not discover until we retired that our hotel beds were full of little hungry creatures. I was peevish the next morning when we met our pilot.

At first we flew over Highway 186, which arrows west from Chetumal across the Maya heartland. Every so often the pilot tapped my shoulder and pointed to an anonymous, tree-covered hummock. *"Ruinas,"* he said. Otherwise there was little to report. After a while we turned south, toward the border with Guatemala. The Yucatán Peninsula grows wetter as one heads south. The vegetation beneath the plane quickly became thicker, lusher, higher, more aggressive.

All at once we came upon Calakmul. The city proper, built on a low ridge, had once housed as many as fifty thousand people and sprawled across an area as big as twenty-five square miles. (The city-state's total population may have been 575,000.) The downtown area alone had six thousand masonry structures: homes, temples, palaces, and granaries, even an eighteen-foot-high defensive wall. Lacing through the buildings was a tracework of canals and reservoirs, many apparently stocked with fish. Thousands of acres of farmland extended beyond. Little of this was known then—I am quoting from later reports—and none of it was visible from the plane. From our vantage the only visual testament to Calakmul's past majesty was its two great central pyramids, each wrapped to the shoulders in vegetation.

Peter asked the pilot to fly low circles around the pyramids while he put together the perfect match of light, lens, angle, and shutter speed. He swapped lenses and cameras and window views in a dozen different combinations. At a certain point, he asked, peering through the shutter, *"¿Cuánta gasolina tenemos?"* How much gas do we have?

The pilot squinted at the fuel gauge: three-quarters full. A puzzled look spread over his face. I leaned over to watch as he tapped the gauge's foggy plastic cover with his forefinger. The needle plunged almost to empty—it had been pinned.

Peter put down his cameras.

Eventually the blood returned to our heads, permitting cerebration. We had to decide whether to take the shortest path to the airport, straight across the forest, or turn to the north and then fly east along Highway 186, which we could try to land on if we ran out of gas. The trade-off was that the highway route was so much longer that choosing it would greatly increase our chances of a forced touchdown. Soon we realized the decision boiled down to one question: How scary was the prospect of landing in the forest?

I recall looking down at the trees. They had engulfed the great buildings and were slowly ripping apart the soft limestone with their roots. Circling above the city, I had thought, *Nobody will ever find out anything about this place. The forest is too overpowering.* Calakmul's inhabitants had cut a little divot into its flanks for their city, but now the vegetation, massive and indifferent, was smothering every trace of their existence. From the plane the trees seemed to march to the horizon without interruption.

We flew over the highway. I tried not to stare at the fuel gauge. Still, I couldn't help noticing as, one after another, warning lights blinked on. The plane had so little gas that the engine quit a moment after our wheels hit the tarmac. When we rolled silently to a stop, the pilot leapt out and kissed the ground. I sat back and regarded Chetumal with new affection.

OPPOSITE: As late as the 1980s, the Maya city of Kaan (now Calakmul) was encased in vegetation (top). Excavations have now revealed the pyramids beneath the trees (the right-hand mound in the top photo is the pyramid at bottom), exemplifying the recent explosion of knowledge about the Maya.

In the mid-1990s the Mexican government paved a road to the site, which is now the center of the 1.7-million-acre Calakmul Biosphere Reserve. Aerial views of the ruins are now spectacular; archaeologists have cleared most of the central city. Along the way, contrary to my initial impression, they have managed to learn a great deal about Calakmul, the landscape it occupied, and the collapse that led to the forest's return. To begin with, they deciphered Calakmul's proper name: Kaan, the Kingdom of the Snake. Impressively, they learned it from the best possible source, the ancient Maya themselves.

Maya scribes wrote in codices made of folded fig-bark paper or deerskin. Not one of these "books" has survived time and the Spaniards (four postconquest books exist). What remains are texts on monuments, murals, and pottery—about fifteen thousand samples of writing, according to one estimate. Piecing together events from these sources is like trying to understand the U.S. Civil War from the plaques on park statues: possible, but tricky. Combining literal interpretation with an understanding of context, epigraphers (decipherers of ancient writing) have spent the last thirty years hauling submerged chunks of Maya history to the surface. David Stuart, a Mayanist at Harvard, decoted the encounter between Chak Tok Ich'aak and the Teotihuacán expedition in 2000. And Simon Martin and Nikolai Grube, respectively of University College London and the University of Bonn, first put the history of the great Mutal-Kaan war together in 1996.

Most of the stelae at Kaan were made from soft stone that has eroded too much to be readable. Martin and Grube thus had to rely on inscriptions at other sites that mention Kaan and its rulers. These are surprisingly numerous. Too numerous, in a way: archaeologists have turned up at least eleven versions of Kaan's early dynastic history painted on big vases. Exasperatingly, none of the eleven tells exactly the same story. The chronological list of rulers differs on different lists, some lists do not include known kings, and some include kings who probably were mythological—as if a tally of English rulers matter-of-factly included King Arthur and his father, Uther Pendragon. The dates are inconsistent, too. Kaan's origins may reach back as far as 400 B.C. But the city-state does not unambiguously enter the historical record until about 500 A.D., when it had a king named Yuknoom Ch'een. The city was already dominating its neighbors; in 546, Yuknoom Ch'een's apparent successor supervised the coronation of a five-year-old monarch in nearby Naranjo.

This supervision, recorded on a stela erected seventy years afterward, is the first known example in Yucatán of a Mesoamerican specialty: the chaperoned coronation. For much of the last century most Mayanists believed that at its height—200 to 900 A.D., roughly speaking—the Maya realm was divided into a hugger-mugger of more or less equivalent city-states. Critics pointed out that this theory failed to account for an inconvenient fact: Kaan, Mutal, and a few other cities were much bigger and more imposing than their neighbors, and therefore, one would usually assume, more powerful. According to the skeptics, Maya society was divided into a small number of blocs, each controlled by a dominant city, each striving to achieve some semblance of empire.

Compelling evidence for this view did not emerge until the mid-1980s, when several epigraphers figured out that the Maya glyph *ahaw*, which means "sovereign" or "lord," had a possessive form, *y-ahaw*, "his lord," meaning a lord who "belongs" to another lord: that is, a vassal king. Another glyph, *u-kahi*, turned out to mean "by the action of." They were only two words, but enough to make dozens of texts speak. In the stela, the five-year-old *ahaw* in Naranjo was crowned "by the action of" the *ahaw* of Kaan. Naranjo's young king "belonged" to Kaan. (Naranjo is the name scientists gave to the city; its original name may have been Saal.)

"The political landscape of the Classic Maya resembles many in the Old World—Classical Greece or Renaissance Italy are worthy comparisons— where a sophisticated and widely shared culture flourished among perpetual division and conflict," Martin and Grube wrote in *Chronicles of the Maya Kings and Queens* (2000), their remarkable summary of the epigraphic discoveries of the last three decades. It was a "world criss-crossed by numerous patron-client relationships and family ties, in which major centers vied with one another in enmities that could endure for centuries." As Martin put it to me, Maya civilization indeed bore striking similarities to that of ancient Greece. The Greeks were divided into numerous fractious communities, some of which were able to dominate others by threats of force, unequal alliance, or commerce. And just as the conflicted relationship among Athens and Sparta was a leitmotif of Greek life, so Maya society resounded for centuries with the echoes of the struggle between Mutal and Kaan.

Sometime before 561 A.D., a ruler known only as "Sky Witness" took the throne of Kaan. A major figure despite his obscurity, Sky Witness set out to destroy Mutal. The motive for his hatred is uncertain, though it may have been rooted in the invasion from Teotihuacán. The new rulers of Mutal had aggressively thrown their weight around and by Sky Witness's time controlled as much as eight thousand square miles. (Mutal city itself had an estimated population of sixty thousand, plus many more in its hinterland.) Particularly important, the Teotihuacán-backed dynasty took over several outposts on the Usumacinta River system, Yucatán's most important trade route. Shipments of luxury goods from faraway regions usually had to travel up or down the Usumacinta; Mutal's ability to tax and supervise the trade must have been terribly vexing, even if it had little practical import. Sky Witness may have thought that Mutal was becoming a dangerous neighbor and decided to take preemptive action. Or he may have wanted to control the Usumacinta and its tributaries himself. A dynastic dispute may have been involved. Grube told me that he thought the kings of Kaan, never allied with Teotihuacán, may have wanted to stamp out pernicious foreign influences— xenophobia is a powerful motive in every culture. No matter what the motive, Sky Witness's plan to dismantle Mutal was brilliant—in the short run, anyway. In the long run, it helped set in motion the Maya collapse.

Kaan and Mutal had a lot at stake. The Yucatán Peninsula is like a gigantic limestone wharf projecting into the Caribbean. Roughly speaking, the northwest-southeast line on which it joins the mainland runs through the middle of the Maya heartland. Despite receiving three to five feet of precipitation in an average year, this area is prone to drought. Almost all the rain falls during the May-to-December rainy season and rapidly sinks hundreds of feet into the porous limestone, from where it cannot easily be extracted. Little is available during the five hot, dry months between January and April. The region does have permanently water-filled swamps, sinkholes, and lakes, but often these are too salty to drink or use for irrigation. So toxic is the groundwater, a U.S.-Mexican research team remarked in 2002, that the Maya realm was "geochemically hostile" to urban colonization. Its occupation "more resembled settlement on the moon or Antarctica than most other terrestrial habitats."

Most of the salt occurred in the sediments on the swamp bottoms. To make the water potable, the Maya laid a layer of crushed limestone atop the sediments, effectively paving over the salt. As the researchers noted, the work had to be done before the Maya could move in and set up their *milpas* and gardens. "Permanent, year-round populations could be established only in the presence of an anticipatory engineering of water supplies." The Maya heartland, in other words, was a network of artificially habitable terrestrial islands.

As Maya numbers grew, so did the islands beneath them. North of Kaan, half a dozen small cities improved agricultural conditions by lifting up entire fields and carving out rain-retaining terraces on dry hillsides. Kaan itself dug out a series of reservoirs, established neighborhoods around each one, and linked the ensemble with a network of canals. Central Mutal was ringed by a chain of seven reservoirs, with another central reservoir reserved for royalty. And so on.

Revamping the landscape both allowed Maya cities to expand and made them more vulnerable. Despite constant maintenance erosion silted up reservoirs, hurricanes destroyed terraces, and weeds and sediment choked irrigation networks. Over time the Maya found themselves simultaneously maintaining existing systems and pushing out to cover past mistakes. If war damage made it impossible for a city's inhabitants to keep up, they would be in trouble; island dwellers who wreck their homes have no place to move. One can speculate that the losers' fear of having their backs to the wall generated the extraordinary tenacity of the Kaan-Mutal conflict.

Sky Witness's strategy was to ring Mutal with a chain of client states and allies and then strangle it, boa constrictor–style. In this way Kaan would both acquire a dominant position in the Maya realm and destroy its enemy. The first step was to suborn Mutal's most important vassal, the king of Oxwitza' (now known as Caracol). With 115,000 people, Oxwitza' was twice as populous as Mutal and controlled almost as much territory. Yet it had become Mutal's vassal soon after Teotihuacán installed the new dynasty. No concrete evidence exists that the first event caused the second, but the coincidence in timing is hard to dismiss. Sky Witness seems to have divined or inspired resentment in Oxwitza'. The king of Oxwitza' took the throne "by the action of" Mutal in 553 A.D. Within three years Sky Witness had persuaded the new ruler of Oxwitza' to betray his masters.

Maya polities were not large enough to maintain standing armies; instead both Kaan and Oxwitza' mustered short-term militiamen to fight wars. Wearing cotton armor and wooden helmets, brandishing lances, hatchets, and maces, and carrying great painted litters with effigies of their gods, the two militias marched on Mutal. Kaan is some sixty miles north of Mutal; Oxwitza' is fifty miles south of it. The two cities planned to crush Mutal between them. They carefully chose the day of the attack. Maya priests tracked the movements of Venus, which they regarded as a powerful portent. Its day of emergence in the morning sky was considered an occasion on which warfare and violence was likely to be rewarded—an optimal day to attack a city. On April 29, 562, in what archaeologists call a *Star Wars* assault, the two celestially guided armies overran Mutal, sacked its precincts, and probably killed its king (the relevant glyphs are too worn to read).

Kaan did not directly occupy Mutal; victorious Maya cities rarely had the manpower to rule their rivals directly. Instead, in the by-now familiar hegemonic pattern, they tried to force the rulers of the vanquished state to become their vassals. If an enemy sovereign was slain, as apparently happened in Mutal, the conquerors often didn't emplace a new one; kings were divine, and thus by definition irreplaceable. Instead the victorious force sim-

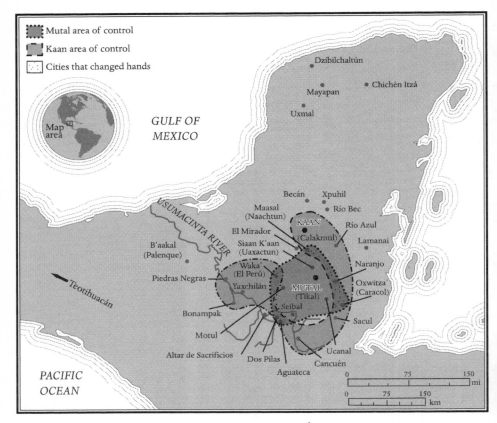

Mutal area of control
Kaan area of control
Cities that changed hands

Map area

GULF OF MEXICO

Dzibilchaltún
Chichén Itzá
Mayapan
Uxmal

USUMACINTA RIVER

Becán   Xpuhil
Maasal   Río Bec
(Naachtun)
KAAN
El Mirador   (Calakmul)   Río Azul
Siaan K'aan   Lamanai
B'aakal   (Uaxactun)
(Palenque)
Waka'   Naranjo
(El Perú)
Piedras Negras   Oxwitza'
Yaxchilán   MUTAL   (Caracol)
(Tikal)
Teotihuacán
Bonampak   Seibal
Sacul
Motul
Ucanal
Altar de Sacrificios   Cancuén
Dos Pilas
Aguateca   0   75   150
mi
PACIFIC   0   75   150
OCEAN   km

THE HUNDRED YEARS' WAR
Kaan and Mutal Battle to Control the Maya Heartland, 526–682 A.D.

The war between Kaan and Mutal lasted more than a century and consumed much of the Maya heartland. Kaan's strategy was to surround Mutal and its subordinate city-states with a ring of enemies. By conquest, negotiation, and marriage alliance, Kaan succeeded in encircling its enemy—but not in winning the war.

ply quit the scene, hoping that any remaining problems would disappear in the ensuing chaos. This strategy was partly successful in Mutal—not a single dated monument was erected in the city for a century. Because the city's postattack rulers had (at best) distant connections to the slain legitimate king, they struggled for decades to get on their feet. Unhappily for Kaan, they eventually did it.

The agent for Mutal's return was its king, Nuun Ujol Chaak. Taking the helm of the city in 620 A.D., he was as determined to reestablish his city's former glory as Kaan's rulers were to prevent it. He suborned Kaan's eastern neighbor, Naranjo, which attacked Mutal's former ally, Oxwitza'. The ensuing conflict spiraled out to involve the entire center of the Maya realm. Decades of conflict, including a long civil war in Mutal, led to the formation of two large blocs, one dominated by Mutal, the other by Kaan. As cities within the blocs traded attacks with each other, half a dozen cities ended up in ruins, including Naranjo, Oxwitza', Mutal, and Kaan. The story was not revealed in full until 2001, when a storm uprooted a tree in the ruin of Dos Pilas, a Mutal outpost. In the hole from its root ball archaeologists discovered a set of steps carved with the biography of B'alaj Chan K'awiil, a younger brother or half brother to Mutal's dynasty-restoring king, Nuun Ujol Chaak. As deciphered by the epigrapher Stanley Guenter, the staircase and associated monuments reveal the turbulent life of a great scalawag who spent his life alternately running from the armies of Kaan and Mutal and trying to set them against each other.

Eventually an army under Nuun Ujol Chaak met the forces of Kaan on April 30, 679. Maya battles rarely involved massive direct engagements. This was an exception. In an unusual excursion into the high-flown, the inscriptions on the stairway apostrophized the gore: "the blood was pooled and the skulls of the Mutal people were piled into mountains." B'alaj Chan K'awiil was carried into battle in the guise of the god Ik' Sip, a deity with a black-painted face. In this way he acquired its supernatural power. The technique worked, according to the stairway: "B'alaj Chan K'awiil brought down the spears and shields of Nuun Ujol Chaak." Having killed his brother, the vindicated B'alaj Chan K'awiil took the throne of Mutal.

In a celebration, B'alaj Chan K'awiil joined the rulers of Kaan in a joyous ceremonial dance on May 10, 682. But even as he danced with his master, a counterrevolutionary coup in Mutal placed Nuun Ujol Chaak's son onto the throne, from where he quickly became a problem. On August 5, 695, Kaan soldiers once again went into battle against Mutal. Bright with banners, obsidian blades gleaming in the sun, the army advanced on the long-term enemy it had routed so many times before—and was utterly defeated. In a psychological blow, Mutal captured the effigy of a Kaan patron deity—an enormous supernatural jaguar—that its army carried into battle. A month later, in a mocking ceremonial pageant, the king of Mutal paraded around with the effigy strapped to the back of his palanquin.

Kaan's loss marks the onset of the Maya collapse. Kaan never recovered from its defeat; Mutal lasted another century before it, too, sank into oblivion. Between 800 and 830 A.D., most of the main dynasties fell; cities winked out throughout the Maya heartland. Mutal's last carved inscription dates to

Maya "books" consisted of painted bark folded accordion-style into sheaves known as codexes. Time and the Spanish destroyed all but four codexes, and even those are fragmentary (above, a detail from the Paris codex, somewhat reconstructed; right, a piece of the Grolier codex).

869; soon after, its great public spaces were filled with squatters. In the next hundred years, the population of most southern areas declined by at least three-quarters.

The disaster was as much cultural as demographic; the Maya continued to exist by the million, but their central cities did not. Morley, the Harvard archaeologist, documented the cultural disintegration when he discovered that Maya inscriptions with Long Count dates rise steadily in number from the first known example, at Mutal in 292 A.D.; peak in about 790; and cease

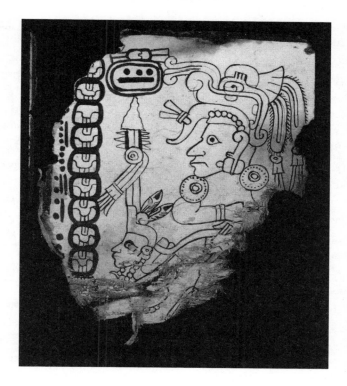

altogether in 909. The decline tracks the Maya priesthood's steady loss of the scientific expertise necessary to maintain its complex calendars.

The fall has been laid at the door of overpopulation, overuse of natural resources, and drought. It is true that the Maya were numerous; archaeologists agree that more people lived in the heartland in 800 A.D. than today. And the Maya indeed had stretched the meager productive capacity of their homeland. The evidence for drought is compelling, too. Four independent lines of evidence—ethnohistoric data; correlations between Yucatán rainfall and measured temperatures in western Europe; measurements of oxygen variants in lake sediments associated with drought; and studies of titanium levels in the Caribbean floor, which are linked to rainfall—indicate that the Maya heartland was hit by a severe drought at about the time of its collapse. Water levels receded so deeply, the archaeologist Richardson Gill argued in 2000, that "starvation and thirst" killed millions of Maya. "There was nothing they could do. There was nowhere they could go. Their whole world, as they knew it, was in the throes of a burning, searing, brutal drought. . . . There was nothing to eat. Their water reservoirs were depleted, and there was nothing to drink."

The image is searing: a profligate human swarm unable to overcome the anger of Nature. Yet Gill's critics questioned whether this view bore any resemblance to reality. The Maya realm had been thickly settled for a thousand years, and the Maya had wrung a living from its unpromising soils for even longer, weathering many dry spells along the way. The notion that they would have folded before the first severe drought seems implausible.

Moreover, the collapse did not occur in the pattern one would expect if drought were the cause: in general, the wetter southern cities fell first and hardest. Meanwhile, northern cities like Chichén Itzá, Uxmal, and Coba not only survived the dearth of rain, they prospered. In the north, in fact, the areas with the poorest natural endowments and the greatest susceptibility to drought were the most populous and successful. "How and why, then," asked Bruce H. Dahlin, an archaeologist at Howard University, "did the onset of prolonged drought conditions simultaneously produce a disaster in the southern and central lowlands—where one would least expect it—and continued growth and development in the north, again where one would least expect it?"

Dahlin argued in 2002 that Chichén Itzá had adapted to the drought by instituting "sweeping economic, military, political, and religious changes." Previous Maya states had been run by all-powerful monarchs who embodied the religion and monopolized trade. Almost all public announcements and ceremonies centered on the figure of the paramount ruler; in the stelae that recount royal deeds, the only other characters are, almost always, the king's family, other kings, and supernatural figures. Beginning in the late ninth or early tenth century A.D., public monuments in Chichén Itzá deemphasized the king, changing from official narratives of regal actions to generalized, nontextual images of religion, commerce, and war.

In the new regime, economic power passed to a new class of people: merchants who exchanged salt, chocolate, and cotton from Chichén Itzá for a host of goods from elsewhere in Mesoamerica. In previous centuries trade focused on symbolic goods that directly engaged the king, such as jewelry for the royal family. During the drought, something like markets emerged. Dahlins calculated that the evaporation pans outside a coastal satellite of Chichén Itzá would have produced at least three thousand tons of salt for export every year; in return, the Maya acquired tons of obsidian for blades, semiprecious stones for jewelry, volcanic ash for tempering pottery, and, most important, maize. Like Japan, which exports consumer electronics and imports beef from the United States and wheat from Australia, Chichén Itzá apparently traded its way through the drought.

The contrast between north and south is striking—and instructive. The obvious difference between them was the century and a half of large-scale warfare in the south. Both portions of the Maya realm depended on artificial landscapes that required constant attention. But only in the south did the Maya elite, entranced by visions of its own glory, take its hands off the switch. Drought indeed stressed the system, but the societal disintegration in the south was due not to surpassing inherent ecological limits but the political failure to find solutions. In our day the Soviet Union disintegrated after drought caused a series of bad harvests in the 1970s and 1980s, but nobody argues that climate ended Communist rule. Similarly, one should grant the Maya the dignity of assigning them responsibility for their failures as well as their successes.

Cahokia and the Maya, fire and maize: all exemplify the new view of indigenous impacts on the environment. When scholars first increased their estimates of Indians' ecological management they met with considerable resistance, especially from ecologists and environmentalists. The disagreement, which has ramifying political implications, is encapsulated by Amazonia, the subject to which I will now turn. In recent years a growing number of researchers has argued that Indian societies there had enormous environmental impacts. Like the landscapes of Cahokia and the Maya heartland, some anthropologists say, the great Amazon forest is also a cultural artifact—that is, an artificial object.

9

Amazonia

WHAT ORELLANA SAW

The biggest difficulty in reconstructing the pre-Colombian past is the absence of voices from that past. Mesoamerican peoples left behind texts that are slowly giving up their secrets, but in other areas the lack of written languages has left a great silence. Hints of past events can be found in Native American oral traditions, to be sure, but these are concerned more with interpreting eternal truths than the details of journalism and history. The Bible has much to teach, yet professors must use it judiciously, supplementing it with other sources, when they teach ancient Middle Eastern history. In the same way, preserved Indian lore throws a brilliantly colored but indirect light on the past. To understand long-ago Indian lives, one cannot avoid the accounts of the first literate people who saw them: European swashbucklers, fortune hunters, and missionaries.

As historical sources, colonial reports leave much to be desired. Their authors often were adversaries of the Indians they wrote about, usually did not speak the necessary languages, and almost always had an agenda other than empathetic description of indigenous folkways. Some wrote to further their careers; others, to score political points. Nevertheless these chronicles cannot be dismissed out of hand for these reasons. Used carefully, they can corroborate, even illuminate.

Consider Gaspar de Carvajal, author of the first written description of the Amazon, an account reviled for its inaccuracies and self-serving descriptions almost since the day it was released. Born in about 1500 in the Spanish town of Estremadura, Carvajal joined the Dominican order and went to South America to convert the Inka. He arrived in 1536, four years after Atawallpa's fall. Francisco Pizarro, now governor of Peru, was learning that to avoid outbreaks of feckless violence he needed to keep his men occupied at all times. One of the worst troublemakers was his own half brother, Gonzalo Pizarro. At the time, conquistador society was abuzz with stories of El Dorado, a native king said to possess so much gold that in an annual ritual he painted his body with gold dust and then rinsed off the brilliant coating in a special lake. After centuries of these baths, gold dust carpeted the lake floor. A lake of gold! To twenty-first-century ears the story sounds preposterous, but it did not to Gonzalo Pizarro, who had already helped seize an empire laden with jewels and precious metals. When he decided to search for El Dorado, Francisco encouraged him—he practically shoved Gonzalo out the door. In 1541 Gonzalo left the high Andean city of Quito at the head of an expedition of 200 to 280 Spanish soldiers (accounts differ), 2,000 pigs, and 4,000 highland Indians, the latter slaves in all but name. Accompanying the troops as chaplain was Gaspar de Carvajal.

Gonzalo's quest descended rapidly from the quixotic to the calamitous. Having no idea where to find El Dorado, he blundered randomly for months about the eastern foothills of the Andes, then as now a country of deep forest. Because the mountains catch all the moisture from the Amazon winds, the terrain is as wet as it is steep. It is also pullulatingly alive: howling with insects, hot and humid as demon's breath, perpetually shaded by mats of lianas and branches. Within weeks most of the horses died, their hooves rotting in the mire. So did most of the Indian laborers, felled by being worked to exhaustion in a hot, humid land twelve thousand feet below their cool mountain home. Having lost their beasts of burden, animal and human, the conquistadors painfully cobbled together a crude boat and floated their guns and heavy equipment down the Napo River, an upper tributary of the Amazon. Meanwhile, the soldiers slogged along the banks, a parallel but more laborious course.

The forest grew yet thicker, the countryside less inhabited. Soon they were utterly alone. "Not a bark dimpled the waters," William H. Prescott wrote in his *History of the Conquest of Peru*. "No living thing was to be seen but the wild tenants of the wilderness, the unwieldy boa, and the loathsome alligator basking on the borders of the stream." With no Indian villages to rob for supplies, the expedition ran short of food. The forest around them had plenty of food, but the Spaniards didn't know which plants were edible. Instead they ate all the surviving pigs, then the dogs, and then turned to spearing lizards. More and more men were sick. Having previously heard vague tales of a wealthy country further down the Napo, Francisco de Orellana, Gonzalo Pizarro's second-in-command and cousin, suggested that he split off part of the expedition to see if he could obtain supplies. Pizarro agreed, and Orellana set off in the expedition's prized boat on December 26, 1541, with a crew of fifty-nine, Carvajal among them.

Nine days and six hundred miles down the Napo, Orellana found villages with food—a society he called Omagua. His men gorged themselves and then considered their options. They did not relish the prospect of ferrying supplies back up the river to Gonzalo Pizarro and the rest of the expedition; rowing against the current would be difficult, and, as they knew all too well, there was nothing to eat along the way. Orellana decided instead to leave the starving Gonzalo to his fate and take the boat to the mouth of the river, which he correctly believed emptied into the Atlantic (incorrectly, he believed that the river was not too long).

Knowing that Gonzalo, in the unlikely event that he survived, would regard Orellana's actions as treasonous, Carvajal took upon himself the task of creating a justificatory paper trail: an account "proving" that the choice to abandon Gonzalo had been forced on them. To satisfy Spanish legal requirements, Orellana made a show of resigning his temporary command rather than leave Gonzalo. The crewmen, Carvajal claimed, then swore "by God . . . by the sign of the Cross, [and] by the four sacred Gospels" that they wanted Orellana to return as leader. Bowing to pressure, Orellana accepted the post. Then they built a second vessel and set off downstream.

Their worries about Gonzalo's reaction were well-founded. Half a year after Orellana's departure, the surviving members of his expedition staggered in rags into Quito. Gonzalo was among them. He wasted no time in demanding Orellana's arrest and execution. In taking the boat, most of the canoes, and some of the weapons from his famished troops, Orellana had displayed, Gonzalo said, "the greatest cruelty that ever faithless men have shown."

Meanwhile, Orellana and his men had spent five months floating down the Amazon, Carvajal recording every moment. It is inconceivable that their surroundings did not induce awe. Vastly bigger than any river in Europe or Asia, the Amazon contains a fifth of the earth's above-ground fresh water. It has islands the size of countries and masses of floating vegetation the size of islands. Half a dozen of its tributaries would be world-famous rivers anywhere else. A thousand miles up from the Atlantic, the river is still so broad that at high water the other side is only a faint dark line on the horizon. Ferries take half an hour to make the crossing. Seagoing vessels travel all the way up to Iquitos, Peru, 2,300 miles from the river's mouth, the furthest inland deep-ocean port in the world.

The prospect of a mutiny trial constantly in mind, Carvajal wrote rela-

The conventional view of Amazonia: endless untouched forest. The forest indeed exists, but humankind has long been one of its essential components.

tively little about his extraordinary surroundings. Instead he focused on creating a case for the value and necessity of Orellana's journey. To the contemporary eye, he didn't have much to work with. His case had three main elements: (1) the forcing of Orellana's hand (see above); (2) the crew's devotion to the Holy Virgin; and (3) the degree to which they suffered en route. In truth, the last does not seem feigned. In Carvajal's account, pain and sickness alternate with starvation. "We were eating leather from the seats and bows of saddles," runs one all-too-typical reminiscence. "Not to mention the soles and even whole shoes [with] no sauce other than hunger itself."

Encounters with the river's inhabitants were frequent and often hostile. Passing the native domains strung along the river was like passing a line of angry hives. Forewarned of the visitors' arrival by drum and messenger, Indians awaited them behind trees and in concealed canoes, shot fusillades of poisoned arrows, then withdrew. A few miles downriver would be the next group of Indians, and the next attack. Except when demanding food, the expedition navigated as far as possible from every village. Nonetheless three

Spaniards died in battle. An arrow hit Carvajal in the face, blinding him in one eye.

Carvajal wrote little about the peoples who spent so much time trying to kill him. But the small amount he did write depicts a crowded and prosperous land. Approaching what is now the Peru-Brazil border, he noted that "the farther we went the more thickly populated and the better did we find the land." One 180-mile stretch was "all inhabited, for there was not from village to village a crossbow shot." The next Indians down the river had "numerous and very large settlements and very pretty country and very fruitful land." And just beyond them were villages crowded cheek by jowl— "there was one day when we passed more than twenty." In another place Carvajal saw a settlement "that stretched for five leagues without there intervening any space from house to house."

Near the mouth of the Tapajós, about four hundred miles from the sea, Orellana's ragtag force came across the biggest Indian settlement yet—its homes and gardens lined the riverbank for more than a hundred miles. "Inland from the river, at a distance of one or two leagues . . . there could be seen some very large cities." A floating reception force of more than four thousand Indians—two hundred war canoes, each carrying twenty or thirty people—greeted the Spanish. Hundreds or thousands more stood atop the bluffs on the south bank, waving palm leaves in synchrony to create a kind of football wave that Carvajal clearly found peculiar and unnerving. His attention riveted to the scene, he for once noted some details. Approaching in their great canoes, the Indian soldiers wore brilliant feather cloaks. Behind the canoe armada was a floating orchestra of horns, pipes, and rebecs like three-stringed lutes. When the music played, the Indians attacked. Only the tremendous surprise created by the Spaniards' firearms provided the opportunity to escape.

Orellana died in 1546 on a second, failed voyage to the Amazon. Carvajal went on to achieve modest renown as a priest in Lima, dying peacefully at the age of eighty. Neither Orellana's journey nor Carvajal's account of it received the attention they merited; indeed, Carvajal's work was not formally published until 1894. Part of the reason for the lack of attention is that Orellana didn't conquer anything—he simply managed to emerge with his life. But another part is that few people believed Carvajal's description of the Amazon.

The main cause for skepticism was his notorious claim that halfway down the river the Spaniards were attacked by tall, topless women who fought without quarter and lived without men. When these "Amazons" wanted to reproduce, Carvajal explained, they captured males. After the women's "caprice [had] been suited," they returned the spent abductees to their homes. Any bravo who saw the prospect of some caprice-suiting as inviting enough to visit the Amazons himself, Carvajal solemnly warned, "would go a boy and return an old man." This absurd story was viewed as proof of Carvajal's untrustworthiness and Orellana's faithlessness. *"Mentirosa* [full of lies]," historian Francisco López de Gómara scoffed soon after Carvajal finished his manuscript.

Physical scientists were especially unwilling to accept his depiction of the Amazon. To ecologists, the great tropical forest in South America was and is the planet's greatest wilderness, primeval and ancient, an Edenic zone touched by humankind lightly if at all. Constrained by its punishing climate, poor soil, and lack of protein, these scientists argue, large-scale societies have never existed—*can* never exist—in the river basin. Amazonia thus could not have been the jostling, crowded place described by Carvajal.

As anthropologists have learned more about the vagaries of fieldwork, they have treated Carvajal more kindly. "He may not have been making up the Amazons out of whole cloth," William Balée, the Tulane anthropologist, told me. "It is possible that he saw female warriors, or warriors whom he believed were female. If he asked Indians about them, he could have misunderstood their answers. Or he could have understood them correctly, but not understood that his informants were pulling his leg. We now understand that ethnography is complex, and it's easy to go wrong." In recent years, these blanket dismissals have been challenged.

More important, anthropologists, archaeologists, geographers, and historians who were reassessing the environmental impact of indigenous cultures in North and Central America inevitably turned to the tropical forest. And in growing numbers researchers came to believe that the Amazon basin, too, bears the fingerprints of its original inhabitants. Far from being the timeless, million-year-old wilderness portrayed on calendars, these scientists say, today's forest is the product of a historical interaction between the environment and human beings—human beings in the form of the populous, long-lasting Indian societies described by Carvajal.

Such claims raise the hackles of many conservationists and ecologists. Amazonia, activists warn, is sliding toward catastrophe so rapidly that saving it must become a global priority. With bulldozers poised to destroy one of the planet's last great wild places, environmentalists say, claiming that the basin comfortably housed large numbers of people for millennia is so irresponsible as to be almost immoral—it is tantamount to giving developers a green light.

The Amazon is *not* wild, archaeologists and anthropologists retort. And claiming that it is will, in its ignorance, worsen the ecological ailments that activists would like to cure. Like their confreres elsewhere in the Americas, Indian societies had built up a remarkable body of knowledge about how to manage and improve their environment. By denying the very possibility of such practices, these researchers say, environmentalists may hasten, rather than halt, the demise of the forest.

GREEN PRISON

The nineteenth-century naturalist Thomas Belt may have said it best. In what Darwin called "the best of all natural history journals," Belt set down what has become the classic image of the tropical forest: a gigantic, teeming expanse, wildly diverse biologically but otherwise undifferentiated. "A ceaseless round of ever-active life weaves the forest scenery of the tropics into one monotonous whole," as he put it. And since Belt's day, terms like "Amazonia" and "Amazon basin" are often used as if they referred to a single, homogeneous entity.

This practice irritates professional geographers no end. Strictly speaking, "Amazon basin" refers to the drainage of the Amazon and its tributaries. "Amazonia," by contrast, refers to the bigger region bounded by the Andes to the west, the Guiana Shield to the north, and the Brazilian Shield to the south. And neither is coterminous with the "Amazonian rainforest." To begin with, not all of the "Amazonian rainforest" is rainy—parts of it receive little more precipitation per year than New York City. On top of that, about a third of Amazonia is not forest but savanna—the Beni, in Bolivia, is the biggest chunk. The river's floodplain and that of its tributaries take up another 5 to 10 percent of the basin. Only about half of Amazonia is upland forest—vines overhead in a tangle like sailing ships rigged by drunks; tree branches in multiple layers; beetles the size of butterflies and butterflies the size of birds—the ecosystem that people outside the region usually mean when they say "Amazon."

To biologists, the apparent fertility of the upland forest is a sham. This thesis was laid out clearly in Paul Richards's classic 1952 study, *The Tropical Rain Forest*. To be sure, Richards said, the Amazon forest is uniquely diverse and beautiful. But its exuberant canopy is a mask covering an impoverished base. The base is the region's poor soil. No matter what its original condition, the intense rain and heat of the forest have eroded its surface, washed out all its minerals, and decomposed vital organic compounds. As a result, much of the red Amazonian soil is weathered, harshly acid, and almost bereft of essential nutrients—one reason ecologists refer to the tropical forest as a "wet desert."

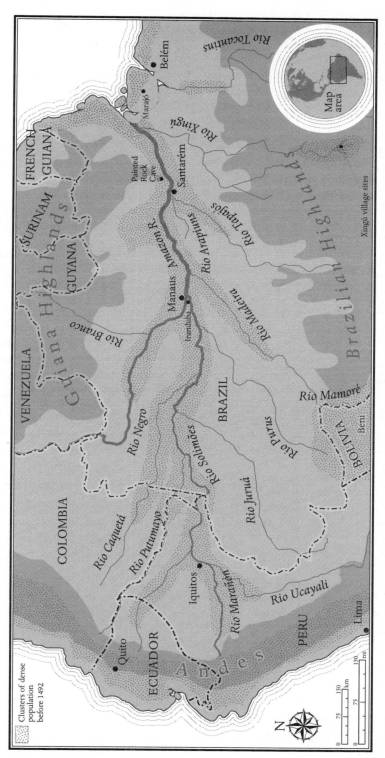

Clusters of dense population before 1492

French Guiana

Surinam

Guyana

Venezuela

Guiana Highlands

Colombia

Ecuador

Quito

Peru

Lima

Iquitos

Rio Caquetá

Rio Putumayo

Rio Negro

Rio Branco

Rio Solimões

Rio Marañón

Rio Ucayali

Rio Juruá

Rio Purus

Rio Madeira

Bolivia

Beni

Rio Mamoré

Brazil

Brazilian Highlands

Amazon R.

Manaus

Itanduba

Rio Arapiuns

Rio Tapajós

Santarém

Painted Rock Cave

Rio Xingu

Rio Tocantins

Marajó

Belém

Xingú village sites

Map area

N

0   75   150 km
0   75   150 mi

AMAZON BASIN

Correspondingly, most nutrients in tropical forests are stored not in the soil, as in temperate regions, but in the vegetation that covers it. When leaves or branches fall, the carbon and nitrogen in the debris are rapidly reabsorbed by the hyperefficient root systems of tropical plants. If loggers or farmers clear away the vegetation, they also remove the local supply of nutrients. Normally the forest quickly fills in bare spots, such as those created when big trees fall, and damage is kept to a minimum. But if the opening is too large or the ground is kept clear too long, the sun and rain decompose whatever organic matter remains and bake the surface into something resembling brick in both color and impermeability. In short order, the land becomes almost incapable of sustaining life. Thus the tropical forest, despite its fabulous vitality, exists on a knife edge.

These views were picked up and amplified in *Amazonia: Man and Culture in a Counterfeit Paradise,* by Betty J. Meggers, the Smithsonian archaeologist. Published in 1971, it may be the most influential book ever written about the Amazon. Agriculture, Meggers pointed out, depends on extracting the wealth of the soil. With little soil wealth to extract, she said, Amazonian farmers face inherent ecological limitations. The only form of agriculture they can practice for a long time is "slash-and-burn," or "swidden," as it is sometimes known. Farmers clear small fields with axes and machetes, burn off the chaff and refuse, and plant their seeds. The ash gives the soil a quick shot of nutrients, giving the crop a chance. As the crops grow, the jungle rapidly returns—weeds first, then fast-growing tropical trees. In the few years before forest recovers the plot, farmers can eke something out of the land.

Slash-and-burn, Meggers told me, is "a superb response to ecological limits." Farmers grab a few harvests, but the soil is not bared to rain and sun long enough to incur permanent damage. Switching from field to field to field, swidden farmers live in the forest without destroying the ecosystems they depend on: a supple, balanced harmony. This ancient lifeway survives today, according to this theory, in the ring-shaped compounds of the Yanomamo. (Most of the Yanomamo actually live around South America's *other* huge river system, the Orinoco, but they are seen as emblematic of Amazonia as well.) Gliding nearly nude beneath the trees, cultivating their temporary gardens, the Yanomamo are often said to be windows into the past, living much the same lives as their great-great-great-grandparents. Their long-term existence has not damaged the forest, Meggers told me, a testament to slash-and-burn's power to keep human groups sustainably within the rigid ecological limits of the tropics.

A second reason that slash-and-burn is required, Meggers told me, is the

Ethnographic celebrities, the Yanomamo are often portrayed as windows into the past, inhabitants of a forest wilderness they have inhabited, almost unchanged, for millennia. Recent studies have cast doubt on this picture. Indeed, the Yanomamo are relative newcomers to their homeland, many of them moving there only in the seventeenth century as they fled European diseases and cruelty further south. Some scholars believe their societies were originally so much larger and more materially complex that what is often pictured as an almost idyllic, "natural" existence is in fact a life in poor exile.

region's propensity for suffering "mega-Niño events"—super-strong El Niño climate swings that occur every three hundred to five hundred years. In the archaeological record, she said, "We're able to pick up severe droughts related to these mega-Niño events. What these did was reduce the food supply. The 1998 El Niño was a small example—they saw droughts, forest fires, and reduction of resources from when trees don't flower." Forest fires in the northern state of Roraima that year claimed such a huge area that Brazil requested aid from the United Nations. In the past, Meggers said, "the well-established groups that were sitting in one territory for several hundred years couldn't survive [the droughts], so they broke up. We see this repeated at least four times in the last two millennia." In other words, any Indians who tried to go beyond slash-and-burn to permanent cultivation would be knocked back to slash-and-burn by a mega-Niño. Slash-and-burn, she said, "avoids the risks, including the risk of growth—it's the smart thing to do."

Swidden, Meggers admitted, has a major drawback: it cannot yield enough to support a complex society. More intensive farming might produce the requisite surplus, but cannot be sustained; the plowed land, exposed to the elements, is destroyed in as little as a decade. Even with slash-and-burn, ecologists say, the forest can take as much as a hundred years to return completely to its previous state. European-style agriculture would not only fall victim to mega-Niños, it would permanently ruin the forest soils.

Carvajal therefore misunderstood what he saw, Meggers told me. Or else he had simply made up *everything*, and not just the Amazons. Caught in a lush, green trap, Indian villages could not possibly have grown as large as he reported—indeed, Meggers once proposed an upper limit of a thousand on their population. And the villages could not have been the sophisticated places he described, with their chiefly rulers, social classes, and specialized laborers (those military musicians on the Tapajós, for example). That was why archaeologists and anthropologists had come across the ruins of complex societies throughout Mesoamerica and the Andes, but saw only hunter-gatherers and slash-and-burners in Amazonia.

"The basic thing about the Amazon is that these people had a long-term period to learn about and experience and benefit from their knowledge of the environment," Meggers said. "Any group that overexploited their environment was going to be dead. The ones that survived, the knowledge got built into their ideology and behavior with taboos and other kinds of things." Having reached the optimal cultural level for their environment, she explained, Amazon Indian lives changed little, if at all, for at least two thousand years.

As proof, Meggers pointed to Marajó, an island more than twice the size of New Jersey that sits like a gigantic stopper in the mouth of the Amazon. The island, low and often swampy, is created by the collision of the Amazon with the sea, which forces the river to disgorge dissolved sediments. Much of the island is submerged during the rainy season, and even in the dry summer pieces of the mazy shoreline are constantly calving off like icebergs and falling into the water. Yet despite the unpromising setting, the Marajóara created a sophisticated society there from about 800 to 1400 A.D.

The island's pottery, some of it very large, has long been celebrated for its painted and incised representations of animals and plants, which are ornately entangled in a profusion that recalls the forest itself. The skillful pottery indicated that Marajó was a large-scale society—the only one then known in all of Amazonia. In the late 1940s Meggers and her husband, archaeologist Clifford J. Evans, decided to learn more.

The decision was ambitious. Archaeologists have traditionally avoided tropical forests, because the climate destroys all wood, cloth, and organic material—except for ceramics and stone, there is little left to dig up. And the Amazon basin, essentially an astoundingly large river valley made of deposited mud, has almost no stone, so archaeologists wouldn't even find that. (Because the nearest deposits of metal ore were in the Andes, thousands of miles upstream, Amazonian peoples had no metal.)

At Marajó, Meggers and Evans soon noticed an oddity: the earliest traces of Marajóara culture were the most elaborate. As the centuries advanced, the quality of the ceramics inexorably declined. The designs became cruder, the repertoire of themes reduced, the technical skill diminished. At the beginning, some grave sites were more elaborate than others, a testament to social stratification. Later on, all the dead were treated in the same mundane way. Early in their history, the Marajóara must have sneered at the lowly cultures on their borders. But as the forest, in a process out of *Heart of Darkness,* stripped away the layers of civilization, they became indistinguishable from their neighbors. A hundred years before Columbus, Meggers told me, they were blasted by a mega-Niño and then overrun by one of their erstwhile inferiors. The history of Marajó was all fall and no rise.

In a boldly written article in *American Anthropologist* in 1954, Meggers proclaimed the implications:

There is a force at work to which man through his culture must bow. This determinant operates uniformly regardless of time, place (within the forest), psychology or race. Its leveling effect appears to be inescapable. Even modern efforts to implant civilization in the South American tropical forest have met with defeat, or survive only with constant assistance from the outside. In short, the environmental potential of the tropical forest is sufficient to allow the evolution of culture to proceed only to the level represented by [slash-and-burn farmers]; further indigenous evolution is impossible, and any more highly evolved culture attempting to settle and maintain itself in the tropical forest environment will inevitably decline to the [slash-and-burn] level.

The impossibility of passing beyond slash-and-burn, Meggers said, was a consequence of a more general "law of environmental limitation of culture." And she stated the law, italicizing its importance: *"The level to which a*

Betty Meggers

culture can develop is dependent upon the agricultural potentiality of the environment it occupies."

How did Marajó escape, even temporarily, the iron grasp of its environment? And why was there no sign of its initial climb past ecological limits, only of its subsequent collapse before them? Meggers and Evans provided the answers three years later in an influential monograph. Marajó, they said, was not actually an Amazonian society. In fact, it was a failed cutting from a more sophisticated culture in the Andes, a cousin of Wari or Tiwanaku. Stranded in the wet desert of the Amazon, the culture struggled to gain its footing, tottered a few steps, and died.

Counterfeit Paradise was the product of more than twenty years of research. But that was not the sole reason for the book's influence. Meggers's message of limitation, published within a year of the first Earth Day, resonated in the ears of readers newly converted to the ecological movement. Since then countless campaigns to save the rainforest have driven home its lesson: development in tropical forests destroys both forests and their developers. Promulgated in ecology textbooks, Meggers's argument became a wellspring of the campaign to save rainforests, one of the few times in recent history that humankind has actually tried to profit from the lessons of the past.

Yet even as the themes of *Counterfeit Paradise* spread to the worlds of natural science and political activism, Meggers's ideas exerted ever-diminishing influence in archaeology itself. From her distinguished post at the Smithsonian, she battled on behalf of the law of environmental limitation. But her main accomplishment may have been inadvertently to keep new ideas about Amazonian history from the public eye—ideas about its past that may, according to their advocates, play a role in safeguarding its future.

PAINTED ROCK CAVE

"Rather than admiration or enthusiasm," the great Brazilian writer Euclides da Cunha wrote at the end of the nineteenth century, "the feeling that overtakes one when first encountering the Amazon is foremost one of disappointment." Like today's ecotourism brochures, the accounts of the great river basin in da Cunha's time celebrated its immensity but rarely dwelled on its extreme flatness—in the Amazon's first 2,900 miles the vertical drop is only 500 feet. "It is as though the place lacks vertical lines," da Cunha complained. "In a few hours the observer gives in to the fatigue of the unnatural monotony." Every year the river floods—not a disaster, but a season. A channel that is one mile wide in the dry season can become thirty miles wide in the wet. After five months the water recedes, leaving behind a layer of rich sediment. From the air, the river seems to ooze like dirty metal through a wash of green utterly devoid of the romantic crags, arroyos, and heights that signify wildness and natural spectacle to most people of European descent.

The area around the lower-Amazon city of Santarém is an exception. West of town, the Tapajós pours into the Amazon from the south, creating an inland bay that at high water is fifteen miles wide and a hundred miles long. The flood rises high enough to cover low river islands in knee-deep water, leaving their trees to stand out like miracles in mid-channel. Fishers from town ride their bicycles into little boats, parking the bikes while working by hanging them in the offshore trees. The bay is lined with bluffs high enough to cast long shadows. Almost five hundred years ago, Indians lined the edge of the rise, taunting Orellana by waving palm fronds.

On the opposite, northern side of the river are a series of sandstone ridges that reach down from the Guiana Shield in the north, halting close to the water's edge. Five hundred feet high and more, they rise above the canopy like old tombstones. Many of the caves in the buttes are splattered with ancient pictographs—rock paintings of hands, stars, frogs, and human figures, all reminiscent of Joan Miró, in overlapping red and yellow and brown. In the 1990s one of these caves, Caverna da Pedra Pintada—Painted Rock Cave—drew considerable attention in archaeological circles.

Wide and shallow and well lighted, Painted Rock Cave is less thronged with bats than some of the other caves. The arched entrance is twenty feet high and electric with gaudy imagery. Out front is a sunny natural patio, suitable for picnicking, that is edged by a few big rocks. During my visit I ate a sandwich atop a particularly inviting stone and looked through a stand of peach palms over the treetops to the water seven miles away. The people who created the petroglyphs, I thought, must have done about the same thing.

Painted Rock Cave has attracted scientists since the mid-nineteenth century, when Alfred Russel Wallace visited it. Wallace, a naturalist, was more interested in the palm trees outside the caves than the people who had lived inside them. The latter were left to an archaeologist, Anna C. Roosevelt, then at the Field Museum. To her exasperation, press accounts of Roosevelt's work often stress her descent from Theodore Roosevelt (she is his great-granddaughter), as if her lineage were more noteworthy than her accomplishments. In truth, though, she has demonstrated something of her ancestor's flare for drama and controversy.

Roosevelt first came to public attention when she reexcavated Marajó in the 1980s. By using a battery of new remote-sensing techniques—including total-station topographic mapping, ground-penetrating radar, and scanning for slight variations in magnetic field strength, electrical conductivity, and electrical resistance—she was able to build up a picture of Marajó far more detailed than Meggers and Evans could have in the 1940s and 1950s, when they worked there. Detailed—and different.

Published in 1991, Roosevelt's initial report on Marajó was like the anti-matter version of *Counterfeit Paradise*. A few scientists had challenged Meggers's ideas; Roosevelt excoriated them from top to bottom. Far from being a failed offshoot of another, higher culture, she concluded, Marajó was "one of the outstanding indigenous cultural achievements of the New World," a powerhouse that lasted for more than a thousand years, had "possibly well over 100,000" inhabitants, and covered thousands of square miles. Rather than damaging the forest, Marajó's "large population, highly intensive subsistence, [and] major systems of public works" had *improved* it: the places formerly occupied by the Marajóara showed the most luxuriant and diverse growth. "If you listened to Meggers's theory, these places should have been ruined," Roosevelt told me.

Rather than pressing down on Marajó, she said, the river and forest opened up possibilities. In highland Mexico, "it wasn't easy to get away from other people. With all those rocky hillsides and deserts, you couldn't readily start over. But in the Amazon, you *could* run away—strike off in your canoe and be gone."

As in *Huckleberry Finn?* I asked.

"If you like," she said. "You could go [along the river] where you wanted and homestead—the forest gives you all kinds of fruit and animals, the river gives you fish and plants. That was very important to societies like Marajó. They had to be much less coercive, much more hang-loose, much more socially fluid, or people wouldn't stay there." Compared with much of the rest of the world at that time, people in the Amazon "were freer, they were healthier, they were living in a really wonderful civilization."

Marajó never had the grand public monuments of a Tenochtitlán or a

Qosqo, Roosevelt noted, because its leaders "couldn't compel the labor." Nonetheless, she said, Marajó society was "just as orderly and beautiful and complex. The eye-opener was that you didn't need a huge apparatus of state control to have all that. And this had been entirely missed by Meggers, who couldn't see past her environmental-determinist theories. And I said so much in my book."

Meggers reacted to Roosevelt's critiques by sneering at her "polemical tone" and "extravagant claims." In concluding that large areas of Marajó had been continuously inhabited, Roosevelt had (according to Meggers) committed the beginner's error of confusing a site that had been occupied many times by small, unstable groups for a single, long-lasting society. Cultural remains, Meggers explained to me, "build up on areas of half a kilometer or so, because [shifting Indian groups] don't land exactly on the same spot. The decorated types of pottery don't change much over time, so you can pick up a bunch of chips and say, 'Oh, look, it was all one big site!' Unless you know what you're doing, of course." From her point of view, claiming that Amazonian societies could escape their environmental constraints was little more than a display of scientific ignorance, the archaeological version of trying to design perpetual-motion machines.

To Meggers's critics, the ecological-limits argument was not only wrong, but *familiar*—and familiar in an uncomfortable way. From the first days of contact, Europeans have perceived the Indians of the tropics as living in timeless stasis. Michel de Montaigne admiringly claimed in 1580 that the inhabitants of the Amazon had "no knowledge of numbers, no terms for gover-

In this reconstruction based on archaeologist Anna Roosevelt's view of Marajóara society, houses cluster on artificial platforms above the wet ground while farm fields stretch into the island's interior.

nor or political superior, no practice of
subordination or of riches or
poverty . . . no clothing, no agriculture, no metals." They abided, he said,
"without toil or travail" in a "boun-
teous" forest that "furnishes them
abundantly with all they need. . . .
They are still in that blessed state of
desiring nothing beyond what is
ordained by their natural necessities:
for them anything further is merely
superfluous."

Montaigne's successors quickly
turned his views upside-down. Like
him, they viewed Amazonians as existing outside history, but they now
regarded this as a bad thing. The

Anna Roosevelt

French natural historian Charles Marie de la Condamine retraced Orellana's
journey in 1743. He emerged with great regard for the forest—and none for
its inhabitants. The peoples of the Peruvian Amazon were nothing more
than "forest animals," he said. "Before making them Christians, they must
first be made human." In softened form, Condamine's views persisted into
the twentieth century. "Where man has remained in the tropics, with few
exceptions, he has suffered arrested development," the prominent geographer Ellen Churchill Semple remarked in 1911. "His nursery has kept him a
child." To be sure, advocates of environmental limitations today do not
endorse the racist views of the past, but they still regard the original inhabitants of the Amazon as trapped in their environment like flies in amber.
Meggers's "law of environmental limitation of culture," her critics in essence
say, is nothing but a green variant of Holmberg's Mistake.

Over time, the Meggers-Roosevelt dispute grew bitter and personal;
inevitable in a contemporary academic context, it featured charges of colonialism, elitism, and membership in the CIA. Particularly vexing to Meggers
was that some of the same people who demanded minutely detailed proof
for pre-Clovis sites had cheerfully accepted Roosevelt's revisionism about
Marajó. A big, prosperous city rising up on its own in the stifling Amazon
forest? Meggers could not contain her disbelief. "I wish a psychologist would
look into this," she said to me.

Meanwhile, Roosevelt went on to Painted Rock Cave. On the cave floor
what looked to me like nothing in particular turned out to be an ancient

midden: a refuse heap. Roosevelt's team slowly scraped away sediment, traveling backward in time with every inch. Even when the traces of human occupation ceased, they kept digging down. ("You always go a meter past sterile," she told me.) A few inches below what she had thought would be the last layer of human habitation she hit another—a culture, Roosevelt said later, that wasn't supposed to be there. It was as much as thirteen thousand years old.

Painted Rock Cave was occupied at roughly the same time that the Clovis culture was thriving to the north. But Amazon paleo-Indians didn't live in the same way as their northern counterparts, Roosevelt said. They didn't make or use Clovis points. They didn't hunt big game (almost none exists in the Amazon). Instead they plucked wild fruits from the forest, painted handprints on the walls, and ate the Amazon's 1,500 species of fish, especially the 500-pound piraruçu, the world's biggest freshwater fish. And then, after 1,200 years, these early people left the cave for good.

Painted Rock Cave became inhabited again in about 6000 B.C. Probably it was no more than temporary shelter, a refuge when floodwaters got too high. People could have brought in loads of turtles and shellfish, built a fire in the shelter of the cave, and enjoyed the feel of dry land. In any case these people—Roosevelt called them the Paituna culture, after a nearby village—had ceramic bowls, red- to gray-brown. Found at Painted Rock Cave and other places in the area, it is the oldest known pottery in the Americas.

And so there were two occupations: one very old, with ceramics; the other even older, without them. To Roosevelt, the first settlement of Painted Rock Cave demonstrated that the Amazon forest was not settled by a copy or offshoot of Clovis. This early culture was a separate entity—another nail in the coffin of the Clovis-as-template theory, to her way of thinking. The second occupation, with its early and apparently independent development of ceramics, demonstrated something equally vital: Amazonia was not a dead end where the environment ineluctably strangled cultures in their cradles. It was a source of social and technological innovation of continental importance.

By about four thousand years ago the Indians of the lower Amazon were growing crops—at least 138 of them, according to a recent tally. The staple then as now was manioc (or cassava, as it is sometimes called), a hefty root that Brazilians roast, chop, fry, ferment, and grind into an amazing variety of foods. To this day, no riverside table is complete without a bowl of *farofa*: crunchy, toasted manioc meal, vaguely resembling grated Parmesan cheese, which Amazonians sprinkle on their food with abandon. To farmers, manioc has a wonderful advantage: it can grow practically anywhere, in any conditions. In Santarém I met a woman who told me that the asphalt street in front of her home had just been ripped up by the municipal authorities. Underneath the pavement, which had been laid down years before, was a crop of manioc.

Manioc has always been *the* Amazonian staple. To this day, it is ubiquitous in the slash-and-burn plots that surround every riverside hamlet. These little, shifting farms look like unchanged remnants of the past. But that idea apparently is mistaken. Rather than being the timeless indigenous adaptation portrayed in ecology textbooks, many archaeologists now view slash-and-burn agriculture as a relatively modern technique whose spread was driven by European technology. The main reason is the stone ax.

Living in the world's thickest forest, the inhabitants of the Amazon basin had to remove a lot of trees if they wanted to accomplish practically anything. For this task the stone ax was their basic tool. Unfortunately, stone axes are truly wretched tools. With a stone ax, one does not so much cut down a tree as use the ax to beat a section of the trunk to pulp, weakening the base until the tree can no longer support itself. In the outskirts of the central Amazonian city of Manaus, a researcher let me whack at a big Brazil nut tree with a locally made replica of a traditional stone ax. After repeated blows I had created a tiny dent in the cylindrical wall of the bole. It was like attacking a continent. "Those things suck," the researcher said, shaking his head.

In the 1970s Robert Carneiro, of the American Museum of Natural History, measured the labor required to clear a field before the advent of steel. He set people to work with stone axes in thickly forested parts of Peru, Brazil, and Venezuela. Many of the trees were four feet in diameter or more. In Carneiro's experiments, felling a single four-foot tree with an indigenous stone ax took *115 hours*—nearly three weeks of eight-hour days. With a steel ax, his workers toppled trees of similar size in less than three hours. Carneiro's team used stone axes to clear about an acre and a half, a typical slash-and-burn plot, in the equivalent of 153 eight-hour days. Steel axes did the job in the equivalent of eight workdays—almost twenty times faster. According to surveys by Stephen Beckerman, an anthropologist at Pennsylvania State University, Amazonian slash-and-burners are able to work their plots for an average of three years before they are overwhelmed. Given that farmers also must hunt, forage, build houses and trails, maintain their existing gardens, and perform a hundred other tasks, Carneiro wondered how they could have been able to spend months on end banging on trees to clear new fields every three years.

Unsurprisingly, people with stone implements wanted metal tools as soon as they encountered them—the prospective reduction in workload was staggering. When Columbus landed, according to William Balée, the Yanomamo lived in settled villages in the Amazon basin. Battered by European diseases and slave raiding, many fled to the Orinoco, becoming wandering foragers. In the seventeenth century they acquired steel tools, and used them to make the return journey from seminomadic hunter-gatherers to agriculturalists who lived in more or less permanent villages. So precious did European axes become during this time, according to Brian Ferguson, an anthropologist at Rutgers University, that when a source appeared the Yanomami would relocate whole villages to be near it. Steel tools, he told me, "had a major, transformative effect on all the trade and marriage relations in a whole area. They led to new trade networks, they led to new political alliances, they even led to war." Researchers have often described the Yanomamo as "fierce," aggressive sorts whose small villages are constantly at violent odds with one another. In Ferguson's estimation, one cause of the endemic conflict observed by Western anthropologists and missionaries was the anthropologists and missionaries themselves, who gave their subjects "literally boatloads" of steel tools—axes, hatchets, machetes—to ingratiate themselves. At a stroke, the village hosting the Westerners would gleam with wealth; its neighbors would seek a share of the undeserved bounty; conflict would explode. "Steel to the Yanomamo was like gold for the Spanish," Ferguson said. "It could push fairly ordinary people to do things that they wouldn't consider doing otherwise." (The anthropologists and missionaries there vehemently deny Ferguson's claims. But so far as I am aware they did not call his scenario impossible. Rather, they said that to avoid unhappy consequences they had carefully controlled the amount of gift giving.)

Metal tools largely created slash-and-burn agriculture, William M. Denevan, the Wisconsin geographer, told me. "This picture of swidden as this ancient practice by which Indians kept themselves in a timeless balance with Nature—that is mostly or entirely a myth, I think. At least there's no evidence for it, and a fair amount of evidence against it, including the evidence of simple logic." Slash-and-burn, supposedly a quintessentially Amazonian trait, "is a modern intrusion."

A similar phenomenon seems to have taken place in North America, where Indians were widely said to have practiced slash-and-burn as part of their habit of living lightly on the land. Dismissing the data to back up these claims as "gossamer," the geographer William E. Doolittle of the University of Texas noted in 2000 that most colonial accounts showed Indians clearing their fields permanently, even ripping stumps out to prevent them from

sprouting. "Once fields were cleared, the intent was to cultivate them permanently, or at least for very long periods of time." As populations rose,
"farmers cleared new fields from the remaining forests." Slash-and-burn was
a product of European axes—and European diseases, which so shrank Indian
groups that they adopted this less laborious but also less productive method
of agriculture.

In the Amazon, the turn to swidden was unfortunate. Slash-and-burn cultivation has become one of the driving forces behind the loss of tropical forest. Although swidden does permit the forest to regrow, it is wildly inefficient
and environmentally unsound. The burning sends up in smoke most of the
nutrients in the vegetation—almost all of the nitrogen and half the phosphorus and potassium. At the same time, it pours huge amounts of carbon dioxide into the air, a factor in global warming. (Large cattle ranches are the
major offenders in the Amazon, but small-scale farmers are responsible for
up to a third of the clearing.) Fortunately, it is a relatively new practice, which
means it has not yet had much time to cause damage. More important, the
very existence of so much healthy forest after twelve thousand years of use
by large populations suggests that whatever Indians did *before* swidden must
have been ecologically more sustainable.

RAINDROP PHYSICS

The papaya orchard was so robust and healthy that it looked like an advertisement—the background image behind a celebrity endorser of a new
papaya drink. Sweating in the equatorial sun, some of the researchers admiringly fingered the plump, pendulous green fruit, each the size of a baby's
head, wrapped in clusters around the trees' sturdy trunks. Other scientists
bent down and with equal approbation scooped up handfuls of dirt. The
road to the plantation had been cut into the Amazon's famously poor soil—
it was the blaring orange-red of cheap makeup, almost surreally bright
against the great dark green leaves of the forest. But in the shade of the
papaya trees the soil was dark brown, with the moist, friable feel that gardeners seek.

At first glance, the soil seemed similar to what one would find in, say, the
grain belts of North America or Europe. After a more careful inspection,
though, it looked entirely different, because it was full of broken ceramics.
The combination of good soil, successful agriculture, and evidence of past
Indian inhabitation was what had brought the scientists to the farm. I had
been invited to tag along.

The orchard was about a thousand miles up the Amazon, two hours by ferry and bus from Manaus. Manaus, the biggest city on the river, is situated on the north bank of the Amazon, hard by its junction with the Negro River, a major tributary.* Between the two rivers is a tongue of land that, depending on your point of view, is either almost destroyed by development or quite lightly inhabited considering its proximity to a city of a million people. Near the tip of the tongue is the small village of Iranduba: a bush-pilot airport, a half-dozen lackadaisical stores, some bars with jukeboxes loud enough to knock birds from the trees, and docks for loading local farmers' produce. A few miles outside Iranduba, on a bluff above the Amazon, stood the papaya orchard. It was one of the many small riverside farms operated by the descendants of Japanese immigrants.

In 1994 Michael Heckenberger, now at the University of Florida in Gainesville, and James B. Petersen, now at the University of Vermont in Burlington, decided to look for potential archaeological sites in the central Amazon. With a team of Brazilian scientists, Meggers had surveyed much of the river and its tributaries in the 1970s and 1980s and concluded there was little of archaeological relevance—further proof of the inescapability of ecological constraints. Believing that Meggers's survey had been too coarse-grained, Heckenberger and Petersen decided to search a single area intensively. Joined by Eduardo Goés Neves of the University of São Paulo, several dozen of Neves's students, and, later, Robert N. Bartone, of the University of Maine at Farmington, they found more than thirty sites at the Amazon-Negro junction, four of which they excavated fully. The papaya farm was one of the four. Now Neves, Petersen, and Bartone were leading a score of visiting researchers and a journalist on a tour of the site.

From the shade of a doorway, the father of the family watched us mill around with a tolerant smile. A teenage girl stood outside, listlessly sweeping at a cloud of yellow butterflies. Through the loosely placed boards in the wall floated the bark and jabber of a talk-radio show about the latest soccer perfidy from Argentina, Brazil's hated rival. Although it was winter, the midday sun was hot enough to make sweat start out from the skin.

At the edge of the papaya grove were ten low earthen mounds that the team had identified as human-made. Carbon dating indicated that they were constructed in about 1000 A.D. The archaeologists had begun opening up the

*The river's main channel is in this area called the Solimões. English-language maps usually put Manaus at the meeting of the Negro and the Solimões, with the latter changing its name back to Amazon upstream. Brazilian maps say that the Amazon begins at the conjunction of the Negro and Solimões.

largest of the mounds. Already they had discovered nine burials, one body placed in a big funerary urn, all apparently interred at the same time. Because the scientists were unlikely to have uncovered the area's only concentration of human remains in their first, exploratory test pit, they believed that the entire mound was likely to be full of burials—hundreds of them. "That suggests thousands of people lived here," Neves said. "In 1000 A.D., that's a big place."

Shoving back his baseball cap, Neves levered himself into the excavation site, a six-foot, rectangular hole with the right-angled corners and precisely vertical walls that are a hallmark of archaeological investigation. One of the visiting researchers passed down a Munsell soil-color chart. Resembling strips of paint-color samples, these are used by pedologists (soil scientists) to classify soils. Neves scraped the wall lightly, exposing fresh earth, and pinned the chart to the wall with a big-headed nail. From the top of the dig he dangled a measuring tape—alternating ten-centimeter strips of red, white, and green—to indicate depth. Digital cameras ratcheted and whined. It was a vest-pocket version of the inspection of Folsom by the graybeards.

Neves had a little trouble hanging the tape because he couldn't find a place where it wouldn't get snagged on the broken ceramics protruding from the walls. They bristled from the side of the dig in a profusion that reminded me of the Beni mounds, hundreds of miles upstream. Some of the pieces seemed to form horizontal layers. As in the Beni, the ceramics had apparently been smashed deliberately, perhaps to build up the surface.

I asked Petersen, a ceramics specialist, how many plates and bowls and cups were in the mounds. He pulled out a scrap of paper and a pen and scribbled some numbers. In a minute or two he looked up. "This is a rough, back-of-the-envelope-type estimate," he warned, showing me the result: the single mound we were standing on might contain more than forty million potsherds. "Think of the industry required to produce that much pottery," Neves said. "Then they just smash it. Look at the way they piled up this good soil [to make the burial mound]—it's all wasteful behavior. I don't think scarcity was a problem here."

The ecological constraints on tropical soils are in large part due to the gravitational energy of raindrops. Rainfall, drumming down day in and day out, pounds the top few inches of earth into slurry from which nutrients are easily leached and which itself easily washes away. In uncut forest, the canopy intercepts precipitation, absorbing the physical impact of its fall from the clouds. The water eventually spills from the leaves, but it hits the ground less violently. When farmers or loggers clear the tree cover, droplets shoot at the ground with more than twice as much force.

Slash-and-burn minimizes the time in which the ground is unprotected. Intensive agriculture is much more productive but maximizes the land's exposure. This painful trade-off is why ecologists argue that any attempt by tropical forest societies to grow beyond small villages has always been doomed to fail.

According to Charles R. Clement, an anthropological botanist at the Brazilian National Institute for Amazon Research (INPA) in Manaus, though, the first Amazonians *did* avoid the Dilemma of Rainfall Physics. Speaking broadly, their solution was not to *clear* the forest but to *replace* it with one adapted to human use. They set up shop on the bluffs that mark the edge of high water—close enough to the river to fish, far enough to avoid the flood. And then, rather than centering their agriculture on annual crops, they focused on the Amazon's wildly diverse assortment of trees.

In his view, the Amazon's first inhabitants laboriously cleared small plots with their stone axes. But rather than simply planting manioc and other annual crops in their gardens until the forest took them over, they planted selected tree crops along with the manioc and managed the transition. Of the 138 known domesticated plant species in the Amazon, more than half are trees. (Depending on the definition of "domesticated," the figure could be as high as 80 percent.) Sapodilla, calabash, and tucumá; babaçu, açai, and wild pineapple; cocopalm, American-oil palm, and Panama-hat palm—the Amazon's wealth of fruits, nuts, and palms is justly celebrated. "Visitors are always amazed that you can walk in the forest here and constantly pick fruit from trees," Clement said. "That's because people *planted* them. They're walking through old orchards."

Peach palms—the trees through which I looked at the Amazon from Painted Rock Cave—are Clement's favorite example. Giddily tall and straight, they have up to a dozen stalks, with a protective mat of spikes wrapped around the bottom of the tree. The protection is little needed; peach palm wood is hard enough that in the Beni it was used for saw blades. Bundles of orange or red fruit hang like clusters of bocce balls from the base of the fronds. The fruit is soaked with oil and rich in beta-carotene, vitamin C, and, surprisingly, protein. When dried, the white or pink pulp makes flour for thin, tortilla-like cakes; when boiled and smoked, it becomes hors d'oeuvres; when cooked and fermented, it makes beer. (The sap also makes a kind of wine.) Two crops a year are not uncommon; in terms of yield per acre, peach palms are typically much more productive than rice, beans, or maize. Trees begin producing fruit after three to five years and can continue for another seventy years. Like strawberries, peach palm throws out adventitious shoots. With a little care, these can be harvested for heart-of-palm—very tasty heart-of-palm, in my experience. *Bactris gasipaes,* as scientists call it, has more than two hundred common names: pupunha, cahipay, tembe, pejibaye, chontaduro, pijuayo. To Clement, the proliferation of names suggests the plant was used for many purposes by many cultures.

In the 1980s and early 1990s Clement measured peach palms throughout the Amazon basin. He learned that several physical characteristics, including fruit size, lay on a gradient with those apparently closest to the wild state in western Amazonia, near the Beni; the implication was that the tree might first have been cultivated there. Using a different method, Jorge Mora-Urpí, one of Clement's collaborators, concluded that Indians might have bred the modern peach palm by hybridizing palms from several areas, including the Peruvian Amazon. Whatever the origin, people domesticated the species thousands of years ago and then spread it rapidly, first through Amazonia and then up into the Caribbean and Central America. *Bactris gasipaes* was in Costa Rica 1,700 to 2,300 years ago and probably earlier. By the time of Columbus, one seventeenth-century observer wrote, Native Americans valued it so highly "that only their wives and children were held in higher regard."

Unlike maize or manioc, peach palm can thrive with no human attention. Tragically, this quality has proven to be enormously useful. In the seventeenth and eighteenth centuries many Amazonian Indians, the Yanomamo among them, abandoned their farm villages, which had made them sitting ducks for European diseases and slave trading. They hid out in the forest, preserving their freedom by moving from place to place; in what Balée calls "agricultural regression," these hunted peoples necessarily gave up farming and kept body and soul together by foraging. The "Stone Age tribespeople in the Amazon wilderness" that captured so many European imaginations were in large part a European creation and a historical novelty; they survived because the "wilderness" was largely composed of their ancestors' orchards. "These old forests, called fallows, have traditionally been classified as high forest (pristine forest on well-drained ground) by Western researchers," Balée wrote in 2003. But they "would not exist" without "human agricultural activities." Indeed, Amazonians typically do not make the distinction between "cultivated" and "wild" landscapes common in the West; instead they simply classify landscapes into scores of varieties, depending on the types of species in each.

After we had spoken for a while Clement took me out of his office and into INPA's experimental forest. To my untrained eye, it looked much the same as the forests around the lodges outside Manaus that attract eco-tourists, except that INPA staffers kept down the undergrowth. There was the same cool green light from the canopy, the same refulgent smell, the same awe-inspiring sense of variety. The air vibrated with the same inharmonic racket of squealing, burbling, croaking, and cheeping birds. Dribbling down some of the tree trunks were little runnels that looked like dried sap. On a previous visit to the Amazon I had seen runnels just like these on a rubber tree in an abandoned plantation. Thinking it was a drip of latex sap, I plucked at one. It was the cover for a termite superhighway. Termites boiled out of the little tunnel and all over my hand. Termites *bite*. Flapping my hand wildly, I leapt back from the tree. My sandaled foot landed on a ground-wasp nest. In this way I learned why some Amazonians have a jaundiced view of biodiversity. On Clement's tour I kept my hands to myself.

It was July—winter in the Amazon, the worst time of the year for fruit. Nevertheless, Clement was able to find yellow bacuri and purple açai. He plucked what looked like a four-foot version of a string bean from a branch, split it lengthwise, and showed me flattened, shiny seeds arrayed along its length like teeth in a jaw. Each seed was the size of a thumb bone and nestled in a fluffy white coating. "Try this," he said. "It's the ice-cream bean." I put a seed in my mouth and sucked on it. The coating did taste quite like vanilla ice cream, and was just as refreshing. Three or four more fruits followed, each equally strange to me. (This is what people like about biodiversity.) Peach palm was not in season, but he found another member of the same genus. The fruit, when peeled, was unappetizing—quite like soggy cardboard in color, texture, and flavor. Clement squeezed some pulp. Oil dribbled from his fingers to the ground. "This'll put some calories into you," he said.

Planting their orchards for millennia, the first Amazonians slowly transformed large swaths of the river basin into something more pleasing to human beings. In the country inhabited by the Ka'apor, on the mainland southeast of Marajó, centuries of tinkering have profoundly changed the forest community. In Ka'apor-managed forests, according to Balée's plant inventories, almost half of the ecologically important species are those used by humans for food. In similar forests that have not recently been managed, the figure is only 20 percent. Balée cautiously estimated, in a widely cited article published in 1989, that at least 11.8 percent, about an eighth, of the non-flooded Amazon forest was "anthropogenic"—directly or indirectly created by humans.

Some researchers today regard this figure as conservative. "I basically think it's all human created," Clement told me. So does Erickson, the University of Pennsylvania archaeologist who told me in Bolivia that the lowland tropical forests of South America are among the finest works of art on the planet. "Some of my colleagues would say that's pretty radical," he said. According to Peter Stahl, an anthropologist at the State University of New York in Binghamton, "lots" of researchers believe that "what the eco-imagery would like to picture as a pristine, untouched Urwelt [primeval world] in fact has been managed by people for millennia." The phrase "built environment," Erickson argued, "applies to most, if not all, Neotropical landscapes."

GIFT FROM THE PAST

"Landscape," in this case, is meant exactly—Amazonian Indians literally created the ground beneath their feet. According to Susanna Hecht, a geographer at the University of California at Los Angeles, researchers into upland Amazonia took most of their soil samples along the region's highways, which indeed passed through areas with awful soil—some regions were so saturated with toxic aluminum that they are now being mined for bauxite. A few scientists, though, found patches of something better. "In part because of the empty-Amazon model," Hecht told me, these were "seen as anomalous and insignificant." But in the 1990s researchers began studying these unusual regions of *terra preta do Índio*—rich, fertile "Indian dark earth" that anthropologists believe was made by human beings.

Throughout Amazonia, farmers prize *terra preta* for its great productivity; some have worked it for years with minimal fertilization. Among them are the owners of the papaya orchard I visited, who have happily grown crops on their *terra preta* for two decades. More surprising still, the ceramics in the farm's *terra preta* indicate that the soil has retained its nutrients for as much as a millennium. On a local level, *terra preta* is valuable enough for locals to dig it up and sell as potting soil, an activity that, alas, has already destroyed countless artifacts. To the consternation of archaeologists, long planters full of ancient *terra preta,* complete with pre-Columbian potsherds, greet visitors to the Santarém airport. Because *terra preta* is subject to the same punishing conditions as the surrounding bad soils, "its existence is very surprising," according to Bruno Glaser, a chemist at the Institute of Soil Science and Soil Geography at the University of Bayreuth, Germany. "If you read the textbooks, it shouldn't be there."*

Terra preta exists in two forms: *terra preta* itself, a black soil thick with pottery, and *terra mulata,* a lighter dark brown soil with much less pottery. A number of researchers believe that although Indians made both, they deliberately created only the *terra mulata. Terra preta* was the soil created directly around homes by charcoal kitchen fires and organic refuse of various types. I use *terra preta* loosely to cover both.

Because careful surveys of Amazon soils have never been taken, nobody knows the amount and distribution of *terra preta*. Woods has guessed that *terra preta* might represent as much as 10 percent of the Amazon basin, an area the size of France. A recent, much more conservative estimate is that it covers .1 to .3 percent of the basin, a few thousand square miles. The big difference between these numbers matters less than one might expect: a few thousand square miles of farmland was enough to feed the millions in the Maya heartland.

Most big *terra preta* sites are on low bluffs at the edge of the floodplain. Typically, they cover five to fifteen acres, but some encompass seven hundred or more. The layer of black soil is generally one to two feet deep but can reach more than six feet. According to a recent study led by Dirse Kern, of the Museu Goeldi in Belém, *terra preta* is "not associated with a particular parent soil type or environmental condition," suggesting that it was not produced by natural processes. Another clue to its human origin is the broken ceramics with which it is usually mixed. "They practiced agriculture here for centuries," Glaser told me. "But instead of destroying the soil, they *improved* it, and that is something we don't know how to do today" in tropical soils.

As a rule, *terra preta* has more "plant-available" phosphorus, calcium, sulfur, and nitrogen than is common in the rain forest; it also has much more organic matter, better retains moisture and nutrients, and is not rapidly exhausted by agricultural use when managed well. The key to *terra preta*'s long-term fertility, Glaser says, is charcoal: *terra preta* contains up to sixty-four times more of it than surrounding red earth. Organic matter "sticks" to charcoal, rather than being washed away or attaching to other, nonavailable compounds. "Over time, it partly oxidizes, which keeps providing sites for nutrients to bind to." But simply mixing charcoal into the ground is not enough to create *terra preta*. Because charcoal contains few nutrients, Glaser argued, "high-nutrient inputs—excrement and waste such as turtle, fish, and animal bones—are necessary." Special soil microorganisms are also likely to play a role in its persistent fertility, in the view of Janice Thies, a soil ecologist who is part of a Cornell University team studying *terra preta*. "There are indications that microbial biomass is higher in *terra preta* than in other forest soils," she told me, which raises the possibility that scientists might be able to create a "package" of charcoal, nutrients, and microfauna that could be used to transform bad tropical soil into *terra preta*.

Despite the charcoal, *terra preta* is not a by-product of slash-and-burn agriculture. To begin with, slash-and-burn simply does not produce enough charcoal to make *terra preta*—the carbon mostly goes into the air in the form of carbon dioxide. Instead, Indians apparently made *terra preta* by a process that Christoph Steiner, a University of Bayreuth soil scientist, has dubbed "slash-and-char." Instead of completely burning organic matter to ash, ancient farmers burned it incompletely to make charcoal, then stirred the charcoal into the soil. In addition to its benefits to the soil, slash-and-char releases much less carbon into the air than slash-and-burn, which has large potential implications for climate change. Trees store vast amounts of carbon in their trunks, branches, and leaves. When they die or people cut them down, the carbon is usually released into the atmosphere, driving global warming. Experiments by Makoto Ogawa of the Kansai Environmental Engineering Center, near Kyoto, Japan, demonstrated that charcoal retains its carbon in the soil for up to fifty thousand years. "Slash-and-char is very clever," Ogawa told me. "Nobody in Europe or Asia that I know of ever understood the properties of charcoal in soil."

Indians are still making *terra preta* in this way, according to Hecht, the UCLA geographer. Hecht spent years with the Kayapó, in central Amazonia, watching them create "low-biomass" fires "cool enough to walk through" of pulled-up weeds, cooking waste, crop debris, palm fronds, and termite mounds. Burning, she wrote, is constant: "To live among the Kayapó is to live in a place where parts of the landscape smolder." Hecht regards Indian fire as an essential part of the Amazonian landscape, as it was in the forests of eastern North America. "We've got to get over this whole Bambi syndrome," she told me, referring to the movie's forest-fire scene, which has taught generations of children that burning wildlands is evil. "Let the Kayapó burn the rainforest—they know what they're doing."

In a preliminary test run at creating *terra preta*, Steiner, Wenceslau Teixeira of the Brazilian Agricultural Research Enterprise, and Wolfang Zech of the University of Bayreuth applied a variety of treatments involving charcoal and fertilizers for three years to rice and sorghum plots outside Manaus. In the first year, there was little difference among the treatments (except for the control plots, in which almost nothing grew). By the second year, Steiner said, "the charcoal was really making a difference." Plots with charcoal alone grew little, but those treated with a combination of charcoal and fertilizer yielded as much as 880 percent more than plots with fertilizer alone. His "*terra preta*" was this productive, Steiner told me, despite making no attempt to re-create the ancient microbial balance.

Beginning a little more than two thousand years ago, the central and lower Amazon were rocked by extreme cultural change. Arawak-speaking groups migrated in from the south and west, sometimes apparently driving Tupí-speaking groups north and east. Sedentary villages appeared. And so

Because Amazonia lacks stone and metal and its hot, wet climate rapidly destroys wood and cloth, material traces of past societies are hard to find. The main exception is pottery, striking examples of which survive, such as the highly decorative vessels from the Santarém area (right, this one probably made in the seventeenth century). Stone, being rare, was reserved for special items such as the mortars used to grind the hallucinagenic snuff *yobo*.

did *terra preta*. No one yet knows if or how these events were related. By about the time of Christ the central Amazon had at least some large, settled villages—Neves, Petersen, and Bartone excavated one on a high bank about thirty miles up the Río Negro. Judging by carbon dating and the sequence of ceramics, they believe the site was inhabited in two waves, from about 360 B.C., when *terra preta* formation began, to as late as 1440 A.D. "We haven't finished working, but there seems to be a central plaza and some defensive ditches there," Petersen told me. The plaza was at least a quarter mile long; the ditch, more than three hundred feet long and up to eighteen feet wide and six feet deep: "a big, permanent settlement."

Terra preta showed up at the papaya plantation between 620 and 720 A.D. By that time it seems to have been underneath villages throughout the central Amazon. Several hundred years later it reached the upper Xingú, a long Amazon tributary with its headwaters deep in southern Brazil. People had lived around the Xingú for a long time, but around 1100 or 1200 A.D., Arawak-speaking people appear to have moved in, jostling shoulders with people who spoke a Tupí-Guaraní language. In 2003 Heckenberger, who had worked with Petersen and Neves, announced in *Science* that in this area he and his colleagues had turned up remains of nineteen large villages linked by a network of wide roads "in a remarkably elaborate regional plan." Around these settlements, which were in place between approximately 1250 and 1400 A.D., the Xinguanos built "bridges, artificial river obstructions and ponds, raised causeways, canals, and other structures . . . a highly elaborate built environment, rivaling that of many contemporary complex societies of the Americas and elsewhere." The earlier inhabitants left no trace of *terra preta;* the new villages quickly set down thick deposits of black earth. "To me," Woods said, "it looks as if someone invented it, and the technique spread to the neighbors."

One of the biggest patches of *terra preta* is on the high bluffs at the mouth of the Tapajós, near Santarém. First mapped in the 1960s by the late Wim Sombroek, director of the International Soil Reference and Information Center in Wageningen, the Netherlands, the *terra preta* zone is three miles long and half a mile wide, suggesting widespread human habitation— exactly what Orellana saw. The plateau has never been carefully excavated, but observations by geographers Woods and Joseph McCann of the New School in New York City indicate that it is thick with ceramics. If the agri- culture practiced in the lower Tapajós were as intensive as in the most complex cultures in precontact North America, Woods told me, "you'd be talking something capable of supporting about 200,000 to 400,000 people"— making it at the time one of the most densely populated places in the world.

Woods was part of an international consortium of scientists studying *terra preta.* If its secrets could be unraveled, he said, it might improve the expanses of bad soil that cripple agriculture in Africa—a final gift from the peoples who brought us tomatoes, maize, manioc, and a thousand different ways of being human.

"Betty Meggers would just die if she heard me saying this," Woods told me. "Deep down her fear is that this data will be misused." In 2001, Meggers charged in an article in *Latin American Antiquity* that archaeolo- gists' claims that the Amazon could support intensive agriculture were effectively telling "developers [that they] are entitled to operate without restraint." These researchers had thus become unwitting "accomplices in the accelerating pace of environmental degradation." Centuries after the conquistadors, she lamented, "the myth of El Dorado is being revived by archaeologists."

Doubtless her political anxieties are not without justification, although— as some of her sparring partners observed—it is difficult to imagine greedy plutocrats "perusing the pages of *Latin American Antiquity* before deciding to rev up the chainsaws." But the new picture doesn't automatically legitimate burning down the forest. Instead it suggests that for a long time clever people who knew tricks that we have yet to learn used big chunks of Amazonia non-destructively. Faced with an ecological problem, the Indians *fixed* it. Rather than adapt to Nature, they *created* it. They were in the midst of terraforming the Amazon when Columbus showed up and ruined everything.

❊ 10 ❊

The Artificial Wilderness

A THOUSAND KUDZUS EVERYWHERE

Until about 200 million years ago Eurasia and the Americas were lashed together in a single landmass that geologists call Pangaea. Pangaea broke into pieces, sending the continents drifting like barges across the ocean floor. For millions of years, the separate fragments of Pangaea had almost no communication. Evolution set their species spinning off on separate trajectories, and the flora and fauna of each land diverged so far from each other that the astounded Columbus remarked that "all the trees were as different from ours as day from night, and so the fruits, the herbage, the rocks, and all things."

Columbus was the first to see the yawning biological gap between Europe and the Americas. He was also one of the last to see it in pure form: his visit, as Alfred Crosby put it, initiated the process of knitting together the seams of Pangaea. Ever since 1492, the hemispheres have become more and more alike, as people mix the world's organisms into a global stew. Thus bananas and coffee, two African crops, become the principal agricultural exports of Central America; maize and manioc, domesticated in Mesoamerica and Amazonia respectively, return the favor by becoming staples in tropical Africa. Meanwhile, plantations of rubber trees, an Amazon native, undulate across Malaysian hillsides; peppers and tomatoes from Mesoamerica form the culinary backbones of Thailand and Italy; Andean potatoes lead Ireland to feast and famine; and apples, native to the Middle East, appear in markets from Manaus to Manila to Manhattan. Back in 1972 Crosby invented a term for this biological ferment: the Columbian Exchange.

By knitting together the seams of Pangaea, Columbus set off an ecological explosion of a magnitude unseen since the Ice Ages. Some species were shocked into decline (most prominent among them *Homo sapiens,* which in the century and a half after Columbus lost a fifth of its number, mainly to disease). Others stumbled into new ecosystems and were transformed into environmental overlords: picture-book illustrations of what scientists call "ecological release."

In ecological release, an organism escapes its home and parachutes into an ecosystem that has never encountered it before. The majority of such escapees die rapidly, unable to thrive or reproduce in novel surroundings. Most of the survivors find a quiet niche and settle in, blending inconspicuously with the locals. But a few, finding themselves in places with few or none of their natural enemies, look around with the hopeful incredulity of juvenile delinquents who discover the mall's security cameras are broken— and wreak havoc. In their home ecosystems these species have, like all living things, a full complement of parasites, microbes, viruses, and insect predators to shorten and immiserate their lives. Suddenly free of this burden, they can burst out and overwhelm the landscape.

The Japanese grind the roots of a low vine called kuzu *(Pueraria lobata)* into a white powder that thickens soup and is alleged to have curative properties; they also plant the species on highway shoulders as erosion-preventing ground cover. In the 1930s the U.S. Civilian Conservation Corps planted millions of kuzu seedlings to fight soil loss, a major fear in the era of the Dust Bowl. Renamed "kudzu," the vine prevented so much erosion that villages across the U.S. Southeast celebrated kudzu festivals and crowned kudzu queens. People harvested it like hay and fed it to cows; entrepreneurs marketed kudzu cereal, kudzu dog food, and kudzu ketchup. In the early 1950s rural areas suddenly awoke from their trance and discovered that kudzu was eating them alive. Without its natural enemies the plant grew so fast that southerners joked they had to close their windows at night to keep it out. Worse, the plants themselves grew bigger than is usual in Japan—nobody knows why. Engulfing fields in dense mats of root and vine, kudzu swarmed over entire farms, clambered for miles along telephone lines, wrapped up trees, barns, and houses like a green Christo. The roots sank so deep that the vine was nearly impossible to remove. In 1996 the federal government estimated that kudzu had swallowed seven million acres. The figure is now much larger.

What happened after Columbus was like a thousand kudzus everywhere. Throughout the hemisphere ecosystems cracked and heaved like winter ice. Echoes of the biological tumult resound through colonial manuscripts. Colonists in Jamestown broke off from complaining about their Indian neighbors to complain about the depredations of the rats they had accidentally imported. Not all the invaders were such obvious pests, though. Clover and bluegrass, in Europe as tame and respectable as accountants, in the Americas transformed themselves into biological Attilas, sweeping through vast areas so quickly that the first English colonists who pushed into Kentucky found both species waiting for them. Peaches, not usually regarded as a weed, proliferated in the southeast with such fervor that by the eighteenth century farmers feared that the Carolinas would become "a wilderness of peach trees."

South America was hit especially hard. Endive and spinach escaped from colonial gardens and grew into impassable, six-foot thickets on the Peruvian coast; thousands of feet higher, mint overwhelmed Andean valleys. In the pampas of Argentina and Uruguay, the voyaging Charles Darwin discovered hundreds of square miles strangled by feral artichoke. "Over the undulating plains, where these great beds occur, nothing else can now live," he observed. Wild peach was rampant in South America, too. Peachwood, Darwin discovered, had become "the main supply of firewood to the city of Buenos Ayres." Some invasions cancel each other out. Peru's plague of endive may have been checked by a simultaneous plague of rats, which the sixteenth-century writer Garcilaso de la Vega reported "bred in infinite numbers, overran the land, and destroyed the crops."

A phenomenon much like ecological release can occur when a species suddenly loses its burden of predators. The advent of mechanized fishing in the 1920s drastically reduced the number of cod from the Gulf of Maine to the Grand Banks. With the cod gone, the sea urchins on which they fed had no enemies left. Soon a spiny carpet covered the bottom of the gulf. Sea urchins feed on kelp. As their populations boomed, they destroyed the area's kelp beds, creating what icthyologists call a "sea urchin barrens."

In this region, cod was the species that governed the overall composition of the ecosystem. The fish was, in ecological jargon, a "keystone" species: one "that affects the survival and abundance of many other species," in the definition of Harvard biologist Edward O. Wilson. Keystone species have disproportionate impact on their ecosystems. Removing them, Wilson explained, "results in a relatively significant shift in the composition of the [ecological] community."

Until Columbus, Indians were a keystone species in most of the hemisphere. Annually burning undergrowth, clearing and replanting forests, building canals and raising fields, hunting bison and netting salmon, growing maize, manioc, and the Eastern Agricultural Complex, Native Americans had been managing their environment for thousands of years. As Cahokia shows, they made mistakes. But by and large they modified their landscapes in stable, supple, resilient ways. Some *milpa* areas have been farmed for thousands of years—time in which farmers in Mesopotamia and North Africa and parts of India ruined their land. Even the wholesale transformation seen in places like Peru, where irrigated terraces cover huge areas, were exceptionally well done. But all of these efforts required close, continual oversight. In the sixteenth century, epidemics removed the boss.

American landscapes after 1492 were emptied—"widowed," in the historian Francis Jennings's term. Suddenly deregulated, ecosystems shook and sloshed like a cup of tea in an earthquake. Not only did invading endive and rats beset them, but native species, too, burst and blasted, freed from constraints by the disappearance of Native Americans. The forest that the first New England colonists thought was primeval and enduring was actually in the midst of violent change and demographic collapse. So catastrophic and irrevocable were the changes that it is tempting to think that almost nothing survived from the past. This is wrong: landscape and people remain, though greatly altered. And they have lessons to heed, both about the earth on which we all live, and about the mental frames we bring to it.

ONE OUT OF EVERY FOUR BIRDS

When passenger pigeons drank, they stuck their heads beneath the surface of the water until they were eye deep. When they walked, their heads bobbed awkwardly and they looked around from side to side. Passenger pigeons were greedy eaters with terrible manners; if they found some food they liked just after finishing a meal, they would vomit what they had previously eaten and dig in. Gobbling their chow, they sometimes twittered in tones musical enough that people mistook them for little girls. They gorged on so many beechnuts and acorns that they sometimes fell off their perches and burst apart when they hit the ground. But in flight they were angelic: they cut through the air with such speed and grace that they were called "blue meteors."

When passenger pigeons found an area with grain or nuts to eat, they formed a long, linear front that advanced forward, heads peck-peck-pecking at the ground. Acorns, beechnuts, and chestnuts; strawberries, huckleberries, and blackberries; wheat, oats, and maize—all went down the pigeons' iridescently feathered gullets. To grab their share, the pigeons at the rear constantly fluttered over the heads of their compatriots and landed at the leading edge of the front. Then the birds in the back flew over *them*. The line of birds advanced in a continuous swirl, the conservationist John Muir recalled, "revolving something like a wheel with a low buzzing wing roar that could be heard a long way off."

Passenger pigeons traveled in massive assemblies, billions strong, that rained enough excrement to force people indoors. As a boy Muir saw a mob of birds sweep "thousands of acres perfectly clean of acorns in a few minutes." Pigeons destroyed farm fields so often that the bishop of Quebec formally excommunicated the species in 1703. A hundred and ten years later the artist and naturalist John J. Audubon saw a flock passing overhead in a single cloud for three whole days. "The air," Audubon wrote later, "was literally filled with Pigeons; the light of noon-day was obscured as by an eclipse." When he visited their roost, the "dung lay almost two inches deep" for miles.

> The Pigeons, arriving by thousands, alighted everywhere, one above another, until solid masses as large as hogsheads were formed on the branches all round. Here and there the perches gave way under the weight with a crash, and, falling to the ground, destroyed hundreds of the birds beneath, forcing down the dense groups with which every stick was loaded. It was a scene of uproar and confusion. I found it quite useless to speak [over the roar of wings], or even to shout to those persons who were nearest to me.

According to Arlie W. Schorger, author of a definitive study on the bird, in Audubon's day at least one out of every four birds in North America was a passenger pigeon.

In colonial times, the Haudenosaunee celebrated pigeon roostings by gathering around the birds for a massive feast. Horatio Jones, captured as a teenager by the Seneca (one of the six nations in the alliance), participated around 1782 in a mass pigeon hunt near the Genesee River. The birds, roosting on low branches, were too full and too stupid to flee. Men knocked them down with poles or toppled the trees they were sitting on. Children wrung the birds' necks while women stewed them in pots, smoked them over fires, and dried them to preserve in storehouses. Sometimes the Seneca ate half a dozen squabs at a time, necks tied together in a carnivorous sculpture. "It was a festival season," Jones later recalled. "Even the meanest dog in camp had his fill of pigeon meat." In Haudenosaunee lore, the birds represented nature's generosity, a species literally selected by the spirit world to nourish humankind.

Non-Indians, too, saw the pigeon as a symbol of the earth's richness— "the living, pulsing, throbbing, and picturesque illustration of the abundance of food, prepared by bountiful Nature, in all her supreme ecstasy of redundant production of life and energy," one businessman/pigeon enthusiast gushed. Colonists grilled the birds, stewed them with salt pork, and baked them into pies; they plucked their feathers to stuff mattresses, pickled them in barrels as a winter treat, and fed them to livestock. Incredibly, hunters in the countryside captured tens of thousands of pigeons in nets and sent the living birds to urban hunting clubs for target practice.

Then, suddenly, the passenger pigeon vanished—the last bird, Martha, named after Martha Washington, died on September 1, 1914. The passenger pigeon remained an emblem of natural bounty, but now it also represented the squandering of that bounty. In 1947 the conservationist Aldo Leopold dedicated a monument to the pigeon near the site of its greatest recorded nesting, at which hunters slaughtered 1.5 million birds. The plaque read: "This species became extinct through the avarice and thoughtlessness of man."

The pigeon should indeed stand as a rebuke and warning. But if archaeologists are right it should not be thought of as a symbol of wilderness abundance.

Passenger pigeons' diet centered on mast, the collective name for acorns, beechnuts, hazelnuts, chestnuts, and the like; they also really liked maize. All were important foods to the Indians of eastern North America. Thus passenger pigeons and Native Americans were ecological competitors.

What would be the expected outcome of this rivalry? asked Thomas W. Neumann, a consulting archaeologist in Atlanta. Neumann noted that Indians had also vied for mast and maize with deer, raccoons, squirrels, and turkeys. Unsurprisingly, they hunted all of them with enthusiasm, as documented by the bones found in archaeological sites. Indeed, as Neumann noted, Indians actually sought out pregnant or nursing does, which hunters today are instructed to let go. They hunted wild turkey in spring, just before they laid eggs (if they had waited until the eggs hatched, the poults could have survived, because they will follow any hen). The effect was to remove competition for tree nuts. The pattern was so consistent, Neumann told me, that Indians must have been purposefully reducing the number of deer, raccoons, and turkeys.

Given passenger pigeons' Brobdingnagian appetites for mast and maize, one would expect that Indians would also have hunted them and wanted to keep down their numbers. Thus their bones should be plentiful at archaeological sites. Instead, Neumann told me, "they almost aren't there—it looks like people just didn't eat them." Pigeons, roosting en masse, were easy to harvest, as the Seneca hunt showed. "If they are so easy to hunt, and you expect people to minimize labor and maximize return, you should have archaeological sites just filled with these things. Well, you don't." To Neumann, the conclusion was obvious: passenger pigeons were not as numerous before Columbus. "What happened was that the impact of European contact altered the ecological dynamics in such a way that the passenger pigeon took off." The avian throngs Audubon saw were "outbreak populations—always a symptom of an extraordinarily disrupted ecological system."

Intrigued by Neumann's arguments, William I. Woods, the Cahokia researcher, and Bernd Herrmann, an environmental historian at the University of Göttingen, surveyed six archaeological studies of diets at Cahokia and places nearby. All were not far from the site of the huge pigeon roost that Audubon visited. The studies examined household food trash and found that traces of passenger pigeon were rare. Given that Cahokians consumed "almost every other animal protein source," Herrmann and Woods wrote, "one must conclude that the passenger pigeon was simply not available for exploitation in significant numbers."

Some archaeologists have criticized these conclusions on the grounds that passenger pigeon bones would not be likely to be preserved. If so, their absence would reveal nothing about whether Indians ate the species. But all six Cahokia projects found plenty of bird bones, and even some tiny bones from fish; one turned up 9,053 bones from 72 bird species. "They found a few passenger pigeon bones, but only a few," Woods told me. "Now, these were hungry people who were very interested in acquiring protein. The simplest explanation for the lack of passenger pigeon bones is a lack of passenger pigeons. Prior to 1492, this was a rare species."

Passenger pigeons were but one example of a larger phenomenon. According to the naturalist Ernest Thompson Seton, North America at the time of Columbus was home to sixty million bison, thirty to forty million pronghorns, ten million elk, ten million mule deer, and as many as two million mountain sheep. Sixty million bison! The imagination shrinks from imagining it. Bison can run for hours at thirty miles per hour and use their massive, horned skulls like battering rams. Mature animals weigh up to a ton. Sixty million of them would have been more than sixty billion pounds of grouchy, fast-moving mammal pounding the plains.

Seton made his estimate in 1929, and it is still widely quoted today. Ecologists have since employed more sophisticated theoretical tools to produce new, lower population estimates; ethologist Dale Lott put the number of bison in "primitive America" at twenty-four to twenty-seven million in 2002. Nonetheless, most continue to accept Seton's basic thesis: the Americas seen by the first colonists were a wildland of thundering herds and forests with sky-high trees and lakes aswarm with fish. Increasingly, though, archaeolo-

The Indian impact on American ecosystems was transformative, subtle, and persistent, as suggested by these photographs of remnant Native American maize hills in the outskirts of Northampton, Massachusetts, in the 1920s. Maize had not grown in these abandoned pastures for centuries, but the handiwork of the land's original inhabitants remained for those with eyes to see it.

Agricultural terraces like these in Peru's Colcha Valley still cover thousands of square miles in Mesoamerica and the Andes, mute testimony to Native Americans' enduring success in managing their landscapes.

This grand Indian irrigation system near Pisco, a coastal town south of Lima, fell to developers' bulldozers—the photograph dates from 1931.

gists demand a caveat. The Americas seen by the first colonists *were* teeming with game, they say. But the continents had not been that way for long. Indeed, this Edenic world was largely an inadvertent European creation.

At the time of Columbus the Western Hemisphere had been thoroughly painted with the human brush. Agriculture occurred in as much as two-thirds of what is now the continental United States, with large swathes of the Southwest terraced and irrigated. Among the maize fields in the Midwest and Southeast, mounds by the thousand stippled the land. The forests of the eastern seaboard had been peeled back from the coasts, which were now lined with farms. Salmon nets stretched across almost every ocean-bound stream in the Northwest. And almost everywhere there was Indian fire.

South of the Río Grande, Indians had converted the Mexican basin and Yucatán into artificial environments suitable for farming. Terraces and canals and stony highways lined the western face of the Andes. Raised fields and causeways covered the Beni. Agriculture reached down into Argentina and central Chile. Indians had converted perhaps a quarter of the Amazon forest into farms and agricultural forests—an area the size of France and Spain taken together.

All of this had implications for animal populations. As Cahokia grew, Woods told me, so did its maize fields. For obvious reasons its farmers did not relish the prospect of buffalo herds trampling through their fields. Nor did they want deer, moose, or passenger pigeons eating the maize. They hunted them until they were scarce around their homes. At the same time, they tried to encourage these species to grow in number farther away, where they would be useful. "The net result was to keep that kind of animal at arm's length," Woods told me. "The total number of bison, say, seems to have gone down quite a bit, but they wanted to have them available for hunting in the prairie a couple days' journey away."

When disease swept Indians from the land, this entire ecological *ancien régime* collapsed. Hernando De Soto's expedition staggered through the Southeast for four years in the early sixteenth century and saw hordes of people but apparently didn't see a single bison. (No account describes them, and it seems unlikely that chroniclers would have failed to mention sighting such an extraordinary beast.) More than a century later the French explorer La Salle canoed down the Mississippi. Where De Soto had found prosperous cities La Salle encountered "a solitude unrelieved by the faintest trace of man," wrote the nineteenth-century historian Francis Parkman. Everywhere the French encountered bison, "grazing in herds on the great prairies which then bordered the river." When Indians died, the shaggy creatures vastly extended both their range and numbers, according to Valerius Geist, a bison researcher at the University of Calgary. "The post-Columbian abundance of bison," in his view, was largely due to "Eurasian diseases that decreased [Indian] hunting." The massive, thundering herds were pathological, something that the land had not seen before and was unlikely to see again.

The same may have held true for many other species. "If elk were here in great numbers all this time, the [archaeological] sites should be chock-full of elk bones," Charles Kay, a wildlife ecologist at Utah State, told me. "But the archaeologists will tell you the elk weren't there." In middens around Yellowstone National Park, he said, they first show up in large numbers about five hundred years ago, the time of the great epidemics. Until European contact the warm coastline of California was heavily populated, according to William S. Preston, a geographer at California State Polytechnic University in San Luis Obispo. After Columbus everything changed. The Indian population collapsed. Clams and mussels exploded in number; they also grew larger. Game overran the land. Sir Francis Drake sailed into San Francisco's

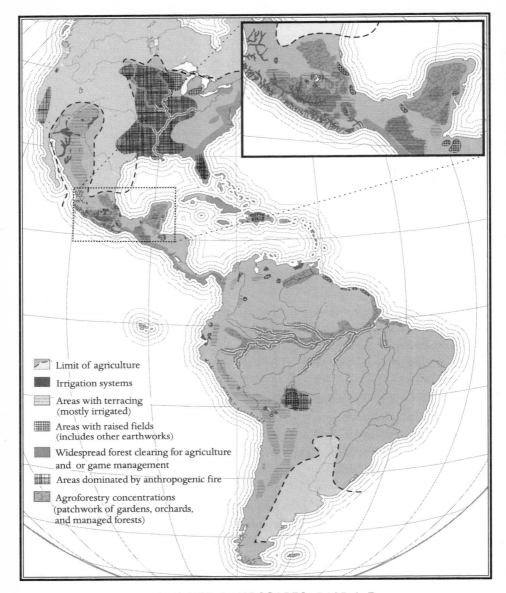

HUMANIZED LANDSCAPES, 1491 A.D.

Limit of agriculture

Irrigation systems

Areas with terracing
(mostly irrigated)

Areas with raised fields
(includes other earthworks)

Widespread forest clearing for agriculture
and or game management

Areas dominated by anthropogenic fire

Agroforestry concentrations
(patchwork of gardens, orchards,
and managed forests)

Complex as it is, this map of Indian effects on the environment is incomplete; no single map could possibly do justice to the subject. The most important omission is fire. I have highlighted some areas where fires deliberately set by Indians effectively controlled the landscape, but this practice played an important ecological role throughout the hemisphere as well, except in wettest Amazonia and northeastern North America. Similarly, scattered clearing, burning, and earth movement for drainage occurred in all agricultural areas—the map indicates only where these factors were especially concentrated. (My depiction of fire-dominated regions in the southern Amazonian highlands is highly speculative, unlike the rest of this map. Researchers have not established where such burning occurred—only where it seems likely.)

harbor in 1579 and saw a land of plenty. "Infinite was the company of very large and fate Deere," he announced. How could he have known that just a century before the shoreline had been thickly settled and the deer much more scarce?

Not all of these claims have been endorsed enthusiastically. Kay's work on elk has drawn especially heavy fire. Elk are big and Indians may have butchered them where they fell, meaning that few elk carcasses would appear in middens. Nonetheless, ecologists and archaeologists increasingly agree that the destruction of Native Americans also destroyed the ecosystems they managed. Throughout the eastern forest the open, park-like landscapes observed by the first Europeans quickly filled in. Because they did not burn the land with the same skill and frequency as its previous occupants, the forests grew thicker. Left untended, maize fields filled in with weeds, then bushes and trees. My ancestor Billington's great-grandchildren may not have realized it, but the impenetrable sweep of dark forest admired by Thoreau was something that Billington never saw. Later, of course, Europeans stripped New England almost bare of trees.

When the newcomers moved west, they were preceded by a wave of disease and then a wave of ecological disturbance. The former crested with fearsome rapidity; the latter sometimes took more than a century to tamp down, and it was followed by many aftershocks. "The virgin forest was not encountered in the sixteenth and seventeenth centuries," wrote historian Stephen Pyne, "it was invented in the late eighteenth and early nineteenth centuries." Far from destroying pristine wilderness, that is, Europeans bloodily *created* it.

By 1800 the hemisphere was thick with artificial wilderness. If "forest primeval" means woodland unsullied by the human presence, Denevan has written, there was much more of it in the nineteenth century than in the seventeenth.

The product of demographic calamity, the newly created wilderness was indeed beautiful. But it was built on Indian graves and every bit as much a ruin as the temples of the Maya.

NOVEL SHORES

I once visited Santarém, in the central Amazon, during the river's annual flood, when it wells over its banks and creeps inland for miles. Forest paths become canals and people boat through the trees. Farmers in the floodplain build houses and barns on stilts. Stir-crazy cattle in the barns stick their heads out the windows and watch pink dolphins sporting on their doorsteps. Acre-size patches of bobbing vegetation, the famous "floating islands" of the Amazon, drift by. Ecotourists are taken in motorboats through the drowned forest. Kids in dories chase after them, trying to sell sacks of incredibly good fruit.

In the center of Santarém, telephone poles are made of cement, as is usual in tropical countries that can afford them. (Wooden ones get eaten.) At the edge of town, the authorities create poles by cutting down trees and propping them wherever needed; in a display of lethargy, town workers do not lop off branches, strip away bark or vines, or even remove termite mounds. After maybe a mile they stop using logs and just string the lines on tree branches. A little further the lines stop altogether. Beyond this the river is occupied only by hamlets on the bluffs at the water's edge. The biggest building always seems to be the Pentecostal or Adventist church. After ser-vices whooping kids fill the red-dirt churchyard and fly kites. Sometimes they attach razor blades to the sides of the kites and in a war of all against all try to cut each other's strings. Rural Brazil is the only place I have ever seen attack kites.

Between communities water traffic continually darts, hopscotching back and forth with the speed of gossip even though many boats are still powered by pushing a long pole against the bottom. At the river's edge during flood season are small trees inundated to the tips of their branches. Thirty feet above them dangles the red fruit of tall kapok trees, each scarlet bulb reflected perfectly in the still water. People make shortcuts through narrow tunnels in the vegetation called *furos*. When I visited an old plantation called Taperinha, site of an earlier Anna Roosevelt dig, the man at the tiller abruptly turned the boat straight into the forest. We shot through a *furo* two thousand feet long and six feet wide. Some *furos* have existed for centuries, I was told. There have been water highways in the forest since before Columbus.

All of this is described as "wilderness" in the tourist brochures. It's not, if the new generation of researchers is correct. Indeed, some believe that fewer people may be living there now than in 1491. Yet when my boat glided into the *furo* the forest shut out the sky like the closing of an umbrella. Within a few hundred yards the human presence seemed to vanish. I felt alone and small, but in a way that was curiously like feeling exalted. If what was around me was not wilderness, how should one think of it? Since the fate of the for-est is in our hands, what should be our goal for its future?

European and U.S. environmentalists insist that the forest should never be cut down or used—it should remain, as far as possible, a land without peo-ple. In an ecological version of therapeutic nihilism, they want to leave the river basin to its own devices. Brazilians I have encountered are usually less than enthusiastic about this proposal. Yes, yes, we are in favor of the environment, they say. But we also have many millions of desperately poor people here. To develop *your* economy, *you* leveled your forests and carpeted the land with strip malls. Why can't *we* do the same? If *you* now want more forest, why don't *you* tear down some of *your* strip malls and plant trees? Yes, yes, we are in favor of helping the poor, environmentalists respond. But if you cut down the tropical forest, you won't be creating wealth. Instead you will only destroy the soil. Turning Amazonia into a wasteland will help nobody.

These dialogues of the deaf have occurred so often that the participants can almost recite their lines by rote. In a way, the words are curiously weightless, for the environmentalists tend to live in, or at least reflect views from, rich places like London, Berlin, or San Francisco. And the advocates of development are often from São Paulo, Rio de Janeiro, or Brasilia, cities that are thousands of miles away from the Amazon and culturally almost as remote as environmentalists' cities. "You should see people's faces here [in Amazonia] when we tell them we're from São Paulo," Eduardo Neves told me. "It's like New Yorkers coming to southern Illinois, only worse. 'My God, aliens have invaded! Kill them before they infect us all!' "

At the same time, the clash between environmentalist and developer cannot be dismissed. At stake, after all, is the world's greatest forest. And similar arguments play out in a hundred or a thousand other places that need protection. Beneath the entangling personal motives, the debate is one of the oldest in the Western philosophical tradition, between *nomos* and *physis*. The ancient Greeks saw existence as a contest between *nomos* (rationality / order / artifice) and *physis* (irrationality / chaos / nature). In environmental terms, Thoreau, who saw the landscape as imbued with an essential wildness that could be heedlessly destroyed, embodies *physis*. *Physis* says, Let Nature be our guide; step out of the way of the environment, and it will know how to keep itself healthy. *Nomos* is the postmodern philosopher who argues that the entire landscape is constructed—that it has no essential, innate qualities, but is simply a reflection of chance and human action. *Nomos* says that no one ecological state is inherently preferable to any other, but that all of them are a product of human choices (even the ones with no people, since we will have made the choice not to go there).

Accepting the magnitude of the Indian impact on the landscape seems to push us toward the *nomos* side. In 1983 Cronon laid out the history of the New England countryside in his landmark book, *Changes in the Land*. In it he observed that wilderness as it was commonly understood simply did not exist in the eastern United States, and had not existed for thousands of years. (A few years later, Denevan referred to the belief in widespread wilderness as "the pristine myth.") When Cronon publicized this no-wilderness scenario in an article for the *New York Times*, environmentalists and ecologists attacked him as infected by relativism and postmodern philosophy. A small academic brouhaha ensued, complete with hundreds of footnotes. It precipitated one of the only books attacking postmodern philosophy ever written largely by biologists. Another book, *The Great New Wilderness Debate*, published in 1998, was edited by two philosophers who earnestly identified themselves as "Euro-American men . . . whose cultural legacy is patriarchal Western civilization in its current postcolonial, globally hegemonic form."

It is easy to tweak academics for their earnestly opaque language, as I am doing. Nonetheless the philosophers' concerns are understandable. The trees closing over my head in the Amazon *furo* made me feel the presence of something beyond myself, an intuition shared by almost everyone who has walked in the woods alone. That something seemed to have rules and resistances of its own, ones that did not stem from me. Yet the claim that the forest was shaped by people does not seem to leave room for anything else, anything bigger and deeper than humankind.

Understanding that nature is not normative does not mean that anything goes. The fears come from the mistaken identification of wildness with the forest itself. Instead the landscape is an arena for the interaction of natural and social forces, a kind of display, and one that like all displays is not fully under the control of its authors.

Native Americans ran the continent as they saw fit. Modern nations must do the same. If they want to return as much of the landscape as possible to its state in 1491, they will have to create the world's largest gardens.

Gardens are fashioned for many purposes with many different tools, but all are collaborations with natural forces. Rarely do their makers claim to be restoring or rebuilding anything from the past; and they are never in full control of the results. Instead, using the best tools they have and all the knowledge that they can gather, they work *to create future environments*.

If there is a lesson it is that to think like the original inhabitants of these lands we should not set our sights on rebuilding an environment from the past but concentrate on shaping a world to live in for the future.

Coda

II

The Great Law of Peace

Fleeing the Nazi conquest of Europe, the writer Vladimir Nabokov and his family took a ship to the United States in the spring of 1940. Although Nabokov was the scion of a Russian noble family, he detested the class-bound servility ubiquitous in the land of his birth. He was delighted when the lowly U.S. customs officers on the Manhattan dock failed to cringe at his aristocratic bearing and pedigree. Indeed, he reported, "when they opened my suitcase and saw two pairs of boxing gloves, two officers put them on and began boxing. The third became interested in my collection of butterflies and even suggested one kind be called 'captain.' When the boxing and the conversation about butterflies finished, the customs men suggested I close the case and go." Their straightforward, even brash demeanor, with its implicit assumption that everyone was on the same social level, enchanted him.

Nabokov was hardly the first emigré to be surprised by the difference between Americans and Europeans—a cultural divide that Henry James, like many others, attributed to the former's "democratic spirit." As has been widely noted, this spirit has consequences both positive and negative. The sense that anyone is as good as anyone else fuels entrepreneurial self-reliance, but also can lead to what outsiders view as political know-nothingism. For better and worse, though, this spirit is widely identified as one of the Americas' great gifts to the world. When rich stockbrokers in London and Paris proudly retain their working-class accents, when audiences show up at La Scala in track suits and sneakers, when South Africans and Thais complain that the police don't read suspects their rights as they do on *Starsky & Hutch* reruns, when anti-government protesters in Beirut sing "We Shall Overcome" in Lebanese accents—all these raspberries in the face of social and legal authority have a distinctly American tone, no matter where they take place. To be sure, apostles of freedom have risen in many places. But an overwhelming number have been inspired by the American example—or, as it should perhaps be called, the *Native American* example, for among its fonts is Native American culture, especially that of the Haudenosaunee.

A loose military alliance among the Seneca, Cayuga, Onondaga, Oneida, Mohawk, and, after about 1720, the Tuscarora, the Haudenosaunee were probably the greatest indigenous polity north of the Río Grande in the two centuries before Columbus and definitely the greatest in the two centuries after. The evidence is unclear, but the ancestors of the Five Nations, neighboring bands of gatherers and hunters, may have lived in their homeland since the glaciers retreated from the Finger Lakes—the eleven deep, narrow lakes that lie like cat scratches across central New York State. Some time around 1000 A.D., the Indian agricultural trinity of maize, beans, and squash appeared in the area. Taking up agriculture, the Finger Lakes people, by now consolidated into five main groups, lined the region's hills with farms. Population rose, as has happened time and time again when human societies make the transition from foraging to farming. The burgeoning cultures took to fighting with each other. Because the abduction, injury, or death of a family member had to be revenged, every violent incident led to a spiral of brutal, tit-for-tat skirmishes. From this brutal environment a heroic figure emerged: Deganawidah, the Peacemaker.

So little is known about Deganawidah's life that archaeologists disagree about whether he actually walked the earth or belongs entirely to the realm of legend. Various traditions provide different accounts of his background, but most say that Deganawidah was not a member of the Five Nations. He was a shamanic outsider who was born to a virgin girl in a village far to the north. Abjuring his past, he floated from his home village in a canoe made from white stone and wandered the Adirondack and Allegheny forests, then a place of constant violence and, apparently, intermittent cannibalism.

Deganawidah had a message of peace. He couldn't easily promulgate it, though, because he had a tragic flaw: a severe speech impediment, perhaps a stutter. Somehow he connected with Ayenwatha, an Onondaga who was a famous orator. (As "Hiawatha," this man became the protagonist of the historically confused epic poem of that name by Henry Wadsworth Longfellow.) With Ayenwatha as Deganawidah's spokesman, the two men confronted Tododaho, the powerful leader of the Onondaga, a shaman in his own right, and a warrior-leader who was so deeply locked into the logic of prideful violence that he regarded the thought of peace as a betrayal. In the ensuing conflict Tododaho killed Ayenwatha's three daughters, nearly derailing the quest for peace. Other versions have the girls killed in a raid by another group. Whatever the circumstances, Ayenwatha vowed that no parent would ever experience such a loss again and rededicated himself to spreading Deganawidah's ideas.

Over the years Deganawidah and Ayenwatha persuaded the Seneca, Cayuga, Oneida, and Mohawk to form an alliance instead of constantly fighting. Tododaho and Onondaga continued to refuse. In a parley, Deganawidah took a single arrow and invited Tododaho to break it, which he did easily. Then he bundled together five arrows and asked Tododaho to break the lot. He couldn't. In the same way, Deganawidah prophesied, the Five Nations, each weak on its own, would fall into darkness unless they all banded together.

Soon after Deganawidah's warning, a solar eclipse occurred. The shaken Tododaho agreed to add the Onondaga to the nascent alliance. But he drove a hard bargain, demanding that the main Onondaga village, now buried under the present-day city of Syracuse, New York, become the headquarters for the confederacy. Despite all the convulsions of history, the Onondaga have kept the council fire burning for Haudenosaunee to this day. And Tododaho has remained the title for the alliance's main speaker.

Deganawidah laid out the new alliance's rules of operation in the Haudenosaunee constitution: the Great Law of Peace. When issues came up before the alliance, the Tododaho would summon the fifty sachems who represented the clans of the Five Nations. Different nations had different numbers of sachems, but the inequality meant little because all decisions had to be unanimous; the Five Nations regarded consensus as a social ideal. As in all consensus-driven bodies, though, members felt intense pressure not to impede progress with frivolous objections. The heads of clans, who were all female, chose the sachems, all male. As a rule, sachems were succeeded by their nephews, but the system was not entirely hereditary—sachems could be impeached if they displeased their clan, and if their nephews were not deemed fit for office, someone outside the family could take over.

Striking to the contemporary eye, the 117 codicils of the Great Law were concerned as much with establishing the limits on the great council's powers as on granting them. Its jurisdiction was strictly limited to relations among the nations and outside groups; internal affairs were the province of the individual nations. Although the council negotiated peace treaties, it could not declare war—that was left to the initiative of the leaders of each of Haudenosaunee's constituent nations. According to the Great Law, when the council of sachems was deciding upon "an especially important matter or a great emergency," its members had to "submit the matter to the decision of their people" in a kind of referendum.

In creating such checks on authority, the league was just the most formal expression of a region-wide tradition. The sachems of Indian groups on the eastern seaboard were absolute monarchs in theory. In practice, wrote colonial leader Roger Williams, "they will not conclude of ought . . . unto which the people are averse." The league was predicated, in short, on the consent of the governed, without which the entire enterprise would collapse. Compared to the despotic societies that were the norm in Europe and Asia, Haudenosaunee was a libertarian dream.

In the same sense, it was also a feminist dream: the Five Nations were largely governed internally by the female clan heads, and the Great Law explicitly ordered council members to heed "the warnings of your women relatives." Failure to do so would lead to their removal. The equality granted to women was not the kind envisioned by contemporary Western feminists—men and women were not treated as equivalent. Rather, the sexes were assigned to two separate social domains, neither subordinate to the other. No woman could be a war chief; no man could lead a clan. Like other "separate-but-equal" arrangements, one side was less equal than the other. Still, the women of the Five Nations under this regime were so much better off than their counterparts in Europe that nineteenth-century U.S. feminists like Lucretia Mott, Elizabeth Cady Stanton, and Matilda Joslyn Gage, all of whom lived in Haudenosaunee country, drew inspiration from their lot.

According to Haudenosaunee tradition, the alliance was founded centuries before Europeans arrived. Non-Indian researchers long treated this claim to antiquity with skepticism. The league, in their view, was inherently fragile and fissiparous; if it had been founded a thousand years ago, it would have broken up well before the Pilgrims. And there was little archaeological evidence that the league had existed for many centuries. But both traditional lore and contemporary astronomical calculations suggest that Haudenosaunee dates back to between 1090 and 1150 A.D. The former date was calculated by Seneca historian Paula Underwood, who based her estimate on the tally of generations in oral records. The latter came from astronomer Barbara Mann and historian Jerry Fields of Toledo University, in Ohio. The Five Nations recorded the succession of council members with a combination of pegs and carved images on long wooden cylinders called Condolence Canes. (Iroquois pictographs could convey sophisticated ideas, but functioned more as a mnemonic aid than a true writing system. The symbols were not conventionalized—that is, one person could not easily read a document composed by another.) According to Mohawk historian Jake Swamp, 145 Tododahos spoke for the league between its founding and 1995, when Mann and Fields made their calculation. With this figure in hand, Mann and Fields calculated the average tenure of more than three hundred other lifetime appointments, including popes, European kings and queens, and U.S. Supreme Court justices. Multiplying the average by the number of Tododahos, the two researchers estimated that the alliance was probably founded in the middle of the twelfth century. To check this estimate, Mann and Fields turned to astronomical tables. Before 1600, the last total solar eclipse observable in upstate New York occurred on August 31, 1142. If Mann and Fields are correct, this was the date on which Tododaho accepted the alliance. The Haudenosaunee thus would have the second oldest continuously existing representative parliaments on earth. Only Iceland's Althing, founded in 930 A.D., is older.

Scholars debate these estimates, but nobody disputes that the Haudenosaunee exemplified the formidable tradition of limited government and personal autonomy shared by many cultures north of the Río Grande. To some extent, this freedom simply reflected North American Indians' relatively recent adoption of agriculture. Early farming villages worldwide were much less authoritarian places than later societies. But the Indians of the eastern seaboard institutionalized their liberty to an unusual extent—the Haudenosaunee especially, but many others, too. ("Their whole constitution breathes nothing but liberty," said colonist James Adair of the Tsalagi [Cherokee].) Important historically, these were the free people encountered by France and Britain—personifications of democratic self-government so vivid that some historians and activists have argued that the Great Law of Peace directly inspired the U.S. Constitution.

Taken literally, this assertion seems implausible. With its grant of authority to the federal government to supersede state law, its dependence on rule by the majority rather than consensus, its bicameral legislature (members of one branch being simultaneously elected), and its denial of suffrage to women, slaves, and the unpropertied, the Constitution as originally enacted was sharply different from the Great Law. In addition, the Constitution's emphasis on protecting private property runs contrary to Haudenosaunee traditions of communal ownership. But in a larger sense, the claim is correct. The framers of the Constitution, like most colonists in what would become the United States, were pervaded by Indian ideals and images of liberty.

In the first two centuries of colonization, the border between natives and newcomers was porous, almost nonexistent. The two societies mingled in a way that is difficult to imagine now; Europeans had close-up views of their indigenous neighbors. In a letter to Thomas Jefferson, the aging John Adams recalled the Massachusetts of his youth as a multiracial society. "Aaron Pomham the Priest and Moses Pomham the King of the Punkapaug and Neponsit Tribes were frequent Visitors at my Father's House," he wrote nostalgically. "There was a numerous Family in this Town [Quincy, Massachusetts, where Adams grew up], whose Wigwam was within a Mile of this House." They frequently visited Adams, "and I in my boyish Rambles used to call at their Wigwam, where I never failed to be treated with Whortle Berries, Blackberries, Strawberries or Apples, Plumbs, Peaches, etc." Benjamin Franklin was equally familiar with Native American life; as a diplomat, he negotiated with the Haudenosaunee in 1744. Among his closest friends was Conrad Weiser, an adopted Mohawk, and the Indians' unofficial host at the talks. And one of the mainstays of Franklin's printing business was the publication of Indian treaties, then viewed as critical state documents.

As Franklin and many others noted, Indian life—not only among the Haudenosaunee, but throughout the Northeast—was characterized by a level of personal autonomy unknown in Europe. Franklin's ancestors may have emigrated from Europe to escape oppressive rules, but colonial societies were still vastly more coercive and class-ridden than indigenous villages. "Every man is free," the frontiersman Robert Rogers told a disbelieving British audience, referring to Indian villages. In these places, he said, no other person, white or Indian, sachem or slave, "has any right to deprive [anyone] of his freedom." As for the Haudenosaunee, colonial administrator Cadwallader Colden declared in 1749, they had "such absolute Notions of Liberty, that they allow of no Kind of Superiority of one over another, and banish all Servitude from their Territories." (Colden, who later became vice governor of New York, was an adoptee of the Mohawks.)

Rogers and Colden admired these Indians, but not every European did. "The Savage does not know what it is to obey," complained the French explorer Nicolas Perrot in the 1670s. Indians "think every one ought to be left to his own Opinion, without being thwarted," the Jesuit Louis Hennepin wrote twenty years later. The Indians, he grumbled, "believe what they please and no more"—a practice dangerous, in Hennepin's view, to a well-ordered society. "There is nothing so difficult to control as the tribes of America," another Jesuit unhappily observed. "All these barbarians have the law of wild asses—they are born, live, and die in a liberty without restraint; they do not know what is meant by bridle and bit."

Indian insistence on personal liberty was accompanied by an equal insistence on social equality. Northeastern Indians were appalled by the European propensity to divide themselves into social classes, with those on the lower rungs of the hierarchy compelled to defer to those on the upper. The French adventurer Louis Armand de Lom d'Arce, Baron of Lahontan, lived in French Canada between 1683 and 1694 and frequently visited the Huron. When the baron expatiated upon the superior practices of Europe, the Indians were baffled. The Huron, he reported in an account of his American years, could not understand why

> one Man should have more than another, and that the Rich should have more Respect than the Poor. . . . They brand us for Slaves, and call us miserable Souls, whose Life is not worth having, alleging, That we degrade ourselves in subjecting our selves to one Man [a king] who possesses the whole Power, and is bound by no Law but his own Will. . . . [Individual Indians] value themselves above anything that you can imagine, and this is the reason they always give for't, *That one's as much Master as another, and since Men are all made of the same Clay there should be no Distinction or Superiority among them.* [Emphasis in original.]

The essayist Montaigne had noted the same antiauthoritarian attitudes a century earlier. Indians who visited France, he wrote, "noticed among us some men gorged to the full with things of every sort while their other halves were beggars at their doors, emaciated with hunger and poverty. They found it strange that these poverty-stricken halves should suffer [that is, tolerate] such injustice, and that they did not take the others by the throat or set fire to their houses."

I asked seven anthropologists, archaeologists, and historians if they would rather have been a typical citizen of Europe or the Haudenosaunee in 1491. None was delighted by the question, because it asked them to judge the past by the standards of today—a fallacy disparaged as "presentism" by social scientists. But every one of the seven chose the Indians. Some early colonists gave the same answer. The leaders of Jamestown tried to persuade Indians to transform themselves into Europeans. Embarrassingly, almost all of the traffic was the other way—scores of English joined the locals despite promises of dire punishment. The same thing happened in New England. Puritan leaders were horrified when some members of a rival English settlement began living with the Massachusett Indians. My ancestor's desire to join them led to trumped-up murder charges for which he was executed—or, anyway, that's what my grandfather told me.

> When an Indian Child has been brought up among us [Franklin lamented in 1753], taught our language and habituated to our Customs, yet if he goes to see his relations and makes one Indian Ramble with them, there is no perswading him ever to return. [But] when white persons of either sex have been taken prisoners young by the Indians, and lived a while among them, tho' ransomed by their Friends, and treated

with all imaginable tenderness to prevail with them to stay among the
English, yet in a Short time they become disgusted with our manner of
life . . . and take the first good Opportunity of escaping again into the
Woods, when there is no reclaiming them.

Influenced by their proximity to Indians—by being around living, breath-
ing role models of human liberty—European colonists adopted their insub-
ordinate attitudes, which "troubled the power elite of France," the historian
Cornelius J. Jaenen observed. Baron d'Arce was an example, despite his noble
title; as the passage he italicized suggests, his account highlighted Indian freedoms as an incitement toward rebellion. In Voltaire's *Candide,* the eponymous hero is saved from death at the hands of an imaginary group of Indians
only when they discover that he is not, as they think, a priest; the author's
sympathy with the anticlerical, antiauthoritarian views of Indians he called
"Oreillons" is obvious. Both the clergy and Louis XIV, the king whom Baron
d'Arce was goading, tried to suppress these dangerous ideas by instructing
French officials to force a French education upon the Indians, complete with
lessons in deferring to their social betters. The attempts, Jaenen reported,
were "everywhere unsuccessful."

In the most direct way, Indian liberty made indigenous villages into competitors for colonists' allegiance. Colonial societies could not become too
oppressive, because their members—surrounded by examples of free life—
always had the option to vote with their feet. It is likely that the first British
villages in North America, thousands of miles from the House of Lords,
would have lost some of the brutally graded social hierarchy that characterized European life. But it is also clear that they were infused by the democratic, informal brashness of Native American culture. That spirit alarmed
and discomfited many Europeans, toff and peasant alike. But it is also clear
that many others found it a deeply attractive vision of human possibility.

Historians have been puzzlingly reluctant to acknowledge this contribu-
tion to the end of tyranny worldwide. Think of I. Bernard Cohen claiming
that Enlightenment philosophers derived their ideas of freedom from New-
tonian physics, when a plain reading of their texts shows that Locke, Hume,
Rousseau, and Thomas Paine took many of their illustrations of liberty from
native examples. So did the Boston colonists who held their anti-British Tea
Party dressed as "Mohawks." When others took up European intellectuals'
books and histories, images of Indian freedom exerted an impact far
removed in time and space from the sixteenth-century Northeast. For much
the same reason as their confreres in Boston, protesters in South Korea,
China, and Ukraine wore "Native American" makeup in, respectively, the
1980s, 1990s, and the first years of this century.

So accepted now around the world is the idea of the implicit equality and liberty of all people that it is hard to grasp what a profound change in human society it represented. But it is only a little exaggeration to claim that everywhere that liberty is cherished—Britain to Bangladesh, Sweden to Soweto—people are children of the Haudenosaunee and their neighbors. Imagine—here let me now address non-Indian readers—somehow meeting a member of the Haudenosaunee from 1491. Is it too much to speculate that beneath the swirling tattoos, asymmetrically trimmed hair, and bedizened robes, you would recognize someone much closer to yourself, at least in certain respects, than your own ancestors?

APPENDIX A

Loaded Words

Anyone who attempts to write or even speak about the original inhabitants of the Americas quickly runs into terminological quicksand. And the attempt to extricate writer and reader by being logical and sensitive often ends with both parties sucked deeper into the mire. The difficulties fall into two broad categories: names for individual groups of Indians, and names for social categories used to classify those groups. Most well known among the former is "Indian," a term so long recognized as absurd that in the 1960s and 1970s social scientists moved to change it to "Native American" or, sometimes, "Amerindian."

The change was well meaning, but not entirely successful. On a literal level, the replacement name is as problematic as the original. "Native American" is intended to refer to the peoples who inhabited the Americas before Columbus arrived and their descendants today. Literally, though, it means something else: as the activist Russell Means has complained, "Anyone born in the western hemisphere is a Native American." Worse, the term introduces an entirely new set of confusions. "Indian" does not refer to the Inuit, Aleut, and other peoples of the far north, whose cultures, languages, and even physical appearance are so different from their neighbors to the south that researchers generally argue they must have come to the Americas in a separate, much later wave of migration (though still many centuries ahead of Columbus). But all of them are Native Americans, which eliminates a distinction found useful by both scholars and indigenous peoples themselves.

In conversation, every native person whom I have met (I think without exception) has used "Indian" rather than "Native American." One day I said "Native American" when speaking to a Bolivian graduate student of indigenous descent. She shook her head dismissively at the phrase. "Aquí somos indios," she explained. "Los 'americanos nativos' viven solamente en los Estados Unidos." *We are Indians here. "Native Americans" live only in the United States.* "I abhor the term Native American," Means declared in 1998. Matching his actions to his words, Means had joined and become prominent in an indigenous-rights group called the American Indian Movement. "We were enslaved as American Indians," he wrote, "we were colonized as American Indians, and we will gain our freedom as American Indians, and then we will call ourselves any damn thing we choose." (At the same time, the common British usage of "Red Indian" to distinguish American natives from "East Indians" is unwelcome.)

Historically speaking, both "Indian" and "Native American" are remote from the way America's first peoples thought about themselves. Much as the inhabitants of the tenth-century Carolingian Empire did not describe themselves as "Europeans," a name coined in the seventeenth century, the inhabitants of the Western Hemisphere in that same era did not think in terms of "Indians," "Native Americans," or any other collective hemispheric entity. Instead they regarded themselves as belonging to their immediate group—the Patuxet village in the Wampanoag confederation, for instance.

To a considerable extent, the same holds true today. When Russell Thornton, the UCLA anthropologist, kindly sent me some copies of his work, he enclosed his curriculum vitae, which identified him as a "registered member of the Cherokee Nation," not as an Indian, Native American, Amerindian, or indigenous person. When I mentioned this to Thornton, he responded that only one experience united the diverse peoples of the Americas: being flattened by European incursions. "'Indians' or 'Native Americans' as a category both owe their existence to Europe," he said.

For all these reasons, this book uses "Indian" and "Native American" interchangeably, with the latter serving mainly to avoid repetition.

Note, though, that I use these terms as cultural and geographical categories, not racial ones. "Indian" is the Western Hemisphere's equivalent to "European," not to "white" or "Caucasian." Racial categories are inevitably problematic, because they are ostensibly biological—that is, they are supposed to be based on heritable physical characteristics like skin color—but in fact are heavily cultural, as demonstrated by the infamous "one drop" rule in the nineteenth-century southern United States, which proclaimed that men and women were Negroes, even when they could not be distinguished by whites from appearance, if any of their ancestors, no matter how remote, were African. Avoiding such inconsistency and ambiguity is easier if one eschews categorizing by race, which I have tried to do, except for the occasional rhetorical flourish.

In referring to particular groups of Indians—the Wampanoag or the Maya—I use a simple rule of thumb: I try to call groups by the name preferred by their members. This approach, which seems only courteous, is sometimes attacked as condescending. After all, the argument runs, people in the United States use the English labels "French" and "German" rather than *français* and

Deutsch. To insist on using "proper" names for Indians is thus to place them in a special category of fragility. But this objection is not well thought out. Although English-speakers do speak of "Germans" rather than *Deutscher,* "French people" rather than *les français,* they tend to avoid insulting terms like "Kraut" and "Frog." Many common names for Indian groups are equally insulting, or descended from such insults. Unsurprisingly, they are slowly being changed.

My "simple" rule of thumb to call people by the name they prefer is more complex than it may seem. The far north, for example, is home to a constellation of related societies generally known as "Eskimo," but in the 1980s this term was replaced by "Inuit" in Canada, where most of these groups live, after complaints that "Eskimo" came from a pejorative term in Algonquian language that meant "eater of raw flesh." Why this would be bothersome seems unclear, because raw meat is a preferred part of northerners' diet, much as sushi is favored by the Japanese. In any case, linguists believe that "Eskimo" actually stems from the Algonquian terms for "snowshoe netter" or "people who speak a different language," neither of which seems especially derogatory. Worse for contemporary purposes, "Inuit" is also the name of a specific subgroup of Arctic societies, to which such northern indigenous peoples as the Aleutiiq in the Aleutian Islands and Innu in Labrador do not belong. If that weren't enough, the Inupiat in Alaska, who belong to the Inuit subgroup but speak a different language than their cousins in Canada, have generally resisted the term "Inuit" in favor of "Alaska Native" or, sometimes, "Eskimo."

An additional source of confusion occurs when indigenous languages have different romanization schemes. Runa Simi (Quechua), the group of languages spoken in the former Inka empire, has several; I have tried to follow the one promulgated by the Peruvian Academia Mayor de la Lengua Quechua in 1995, which seems to be slowly gaining popularity. The choice is more difficult for the three dozen languages grouped as "Maya." As an example, the name of the ruler slain at the beginning of Chapter 8 has been rendered as, among other things, Toh-Chak-Ich'ak, Chak Toh Ich'ak, and Chak Tok Ich'aak; his title, "lord," has been romanized as *ahau, ahaw, ajau, ajaw,* and even *axaw.* In 1989 the Ministry of Culture and Sports in Guatemala published a standardized orthography for Maya. Unfortunately, Mexico has a different one. Indeed, it has *several.* Various Mexican agencies have issued putatively official orthographies, most based on Alfredo Barrera Vásquez's classic *Diccionario Maya Cordemex,* all intended to "help save these languages from extinction." In this book, I throw up my hands and spell Maya names as they appear in the most authoritative recent source I have come across: *Chronicle of the Maya Kings and Queens,* by the epigraphers Simon Martin and Nikolai Grube. (None of this is to say that I have not made mistakes or sometimes failed to follow my own rules. I'm sure I have done exactly that, though I tried not to.)

The second type of problem, that of categorization, is equally knotty. Take the word "civilization"—"a saltpeter of a word, often triggering explosive arguments," Alfred Crosby has written. The arguments occur when cultures are deemed not to be civilizations; are they therefore "uncivilized"? Archaeologists and anthropologists have proposed dozens of definitions and argue about whether the existence of a written language is essential. If it is, there may have been no Indian civilizations outside Mesoamerica. Yet other parts of the Americas are filled with ruins (Tiwanaku, Marajó, Cahokia) that would be described as the product of a civilization if they were anywhere else in the world. The distinction seems to me unhelpful. Like Crosby, I use the word "not in moral comment, but simply in reference to peoples settled in cities, villages, hamlets, and to the kinds of political, economic, social, and military structures associated with such populations."

Sometimes researchers attempt to avoid the whole debate by substituting the term "complex society." Not much is gained thereby, because it implies that hunters and gatherers have simple lives. A century ago, anthropologist Franz Boas demonstrated the contrary as he struggled to fathom the mind-bogglingly elaborate patterns of Northwest Coast Indian life. Still, the term has some resonance. As societies grow larger, their members become more encrusted by manufactured goods, both standardized for the mass consumer and custom-made for the elite. Along with this growth comes a growth in the size and variety of the technological infrastructure. It is in this material sense that I use the words "complex" and "sophisticated."

In this book I tend to marshal terms like "king" and "nation" rather than "chief" and "tribe." Supposedly the latter refer mainly to kin-based societies whereas the former are for bigger societies based on a shared group identity. In practice, though, "chief" and "tribe" have historically been used to refer disparagingly to frontier cultures conquered by larger societies. In textbooks the Roman emperors, heroic custodians of Greco-Roman civilization, are always fighting off the "barbarian chiefs" of the "Germanic tribes." But these "tribes" had rulers who lived in big palaces, held sway over sizable domains, and had to abide by written codes of law. The Burgundian "tribe" even conquered Rome and set up its own puppet Roman emperor in the fifth century. (He was killed by another "tribe," which installed its own emperor.)

Maps of fifth- and sixth-century Europe usually depict the "Celtic kingdoms," "Kingdom of the Lombards," and so on, their borders marked by the solid lines we associate with national frontiers. But entities of equal or greater size and technological sophistication in the Western Hemisphere are routinely called "chiefdoms" and "tribes," implying they are somehow different and of smaller scale. And fuzzy lines mark their borders, as if to indicate the looseness with which they were organized and defined. " 'Tribe' and 'chiefdom' are not neutral scientific terms," archaeologist Alice Beck Kehoe has declared. "They are politically loaded." I have mostly avoided them.

In general, I have tried to use the terms that historians of Europe or Asia would use to describe social and political entities of similar size and complexity. This approach risks obliterating the real differences between, to cite one example, the court in Qosqo and the court in Madrid. But it supports one of the larger aims of this book: to explain in lay terms researchers' increasing recognition that the Western Hemisphere played a role in the human story just as interesting and important as that of the Eastern Hemisphere.

A final note: throughout the text, I use the European terminology of B.C. and A.D. Many researchers object to them as ethnically bound. In truth, it is a little odd to be talking about "years before Christ" in reference to people whose cultural traditions have nothing to do with Christianity. But no plausible substitutes are available. Some historians use B.C.E. to mean "before the Christian era," but this still places past events in reference to Christianity, the main objection. Besides, in some parts of South America and Mesoamerica there never *has* been a Christian era. One could switch to a neutral calendar, like the Julian calendar used by astronomers (the latter at least doesn't get tripped up by zero—it is the first European calendar as sophisticated as the Mesoamerican Long Count). This doesn't seem useful; to discharge their informational content, readers will have to translate Julian dates back into what they know, the familiar A.D. and B.C. It seems only kind to save them the bother.

APPENDIX B

Talking Knots

All known written accounts of the Inka were set down after the conquest, most by Spaniards who had, of course, never experienced the empire in its heyday. Because many of the chroniclers tried to do their job conscientiously, most scholars use their reports, despite their deficiencies, as I do in this book. For obvious reasons historians of the Inka have never liked being forced to rely exclusively on postconquest, non-native written sources, but there seemed to be no avoiding it.

Recently, though, some researchers have come to believe that the Inka did have a written language—indeed, that Inka texts are displayed in museums around the world, but that they have generally not been recognized as such. Here I am referring to the bunches of knotted strings known as *khipu* (or *quipu,* as the term is often spelled). Among the most fascinating artifacts of Tawantinsuyu, they consist of a primary cord, usually a third to a half an inch in diameter, from which dangle thinner "pendant" strings—typically more than a hundred, but on occasion as many as 1,500. The pendant strings, which sometimes have subsidiary strings attached, bear clusters of knots, each tied in one of three ways. The result, in the dry summary of George Gheverghese Joseph, a University of Manchester mathematics historian, "resembles a mop that has seen better days."

According to colonial accounts, *khipukamayuq*—"knot keepers," in Ruma Suni—parsed the knots both by inspecting them visually and by running their fingers along them, Braille-style, sometimes accompanying this by manipulating black and white stones. For example, to assemble a history of the Inka empire the Spanish governor Cristóbal Vaca de Castro summoned *khipuka-mayuq* to "read" the strings in 1542. Spanish scribes recorded their testimony but did not preserve the *khipu;* indeed, they may have destroyed them. Later the Spanish became so infuriated when *khipu* records contradicted their version of events that in 1583 they ordered that all the knotted strings in Peru be burned as idolatrous objects. Only about six hundred escaped the flames.

All known writing systems employ instruments to paint or inscribe on flat surfaces. *Khipu,* by contrast, are three-dimensional arrays of knots. Although Spanish chronicles repeatedly describe *khipukamayuq* consulting their *khipu,* most researchers could not imagine that such strange-looking devices could actually be written records. Instead they speculated that *khipu* must be mnemonic devices—personalized memorization aids, like rosaries—or, at most, textile abacuses. The latter view gained support in 1923, when science historian L. Leland Locke proved that the pattern of knots in most *khipu* recorded the results of numerical calculations—the knotted strings were accounting devices. *Khipu* were hierarchical, decimal arrays, Locke said, with the knots used to record 1s on the lowest level of each string, those for the 10s on the next, and so on. "The mystery has been dispelled," archaeologist Charles W. Mead exulted, "and we now know the quipu for just what it was in prehistoric times . . . simply an instrument for recording numbers."

Based on such evaluations, most Andeanists viewed the Inka as the only major civilization ever to come into existence without a written language. "The Inka had no writing," Brian Fagan, an archaeologist at the University of California in Santa Barbara, wrote in *Kingdoms of Gold, Kingdoms of Jade,* his 1991 survey of Native American cultures. "The quipu was purely a way of storing precise information, a pre-Columbian computer memory, if you will."

But even as Fagan was writing, researchers were coming to doubt this conclusion. The problem was that Locke's rules only decoded about 80 percent of *khipu*—the remainder were incomprehensible. According to Cornell archaeologist Robert Ascher, those *khipu* are "clearly non-numerical." In 1981, Ascher and his mathematician wife, Marcia, published a book that jolted the field by intimating that these "anomalous" *khipu* may have been an early form of writing—one that Ascher told me was "rapidly developing into something extremely interesting" just at the time when Inka culture was demolished.

The Aschers slowly gained converts. "Most serious scholars of khipu today believe that they were more than mnemonic devices, and probably much more," Galen Brokaw, an expert in ancient Andean texts at the State University of New York in Buffalo, said to me. This view of *khipu* can seem absurd, Brokaw admitted, because the scientists who propose that Tawantinsuyu was a literate empire also freely admit that no one can read its documents. "Not a single narrative khipu has been convincingly deciphered," the Harvard anthropologist Gary Urton conceded, a situation he described as "more than frustrating."

Spurred in part by recent insights from textile scholars, Urton has been mounting the most sustained, intensive attack on the *khipu* code ever performed. In *Signs of the Inka Khipu* (2003), Urton for the first time systematically broke down *khipu* into their grammatical constituents, and began using this catalog to create a relational *khipu* database to help identify patterns in the arrangement of knots. Like cuneiform marks, Urton told me, *khipu* probably did begin as the kind of accounting tools envisioned by Locke. But by the time Pizarro arrived they had evolved into a kind of three-dimensional binary code, unlike any other form of writing on earth.

The Aschers worked mainly with *khipu* knots. But at a 1997 conference, William J. Conklin, a researcher at the Textile Museum, in Washington, D.C., pointed out that the knots might be just one part of the *khipu* system. In an interview, Conklin, perhaps the first textile specialist to investigate *khipu*, explained, "When I started looking at khipu . . . I saw this complex spinning and plying and color coding, in which every thread was made in a complex way. I realized that 90 percent of the information was put into the string *before* the knot was made."

Building on this insight, Urton argued that *khipu* makers were forced by the very nature of spinning and weaving into making a series of binary choices, including the type of material (cotton or wool), the spin and ply direction of the string (which he described as "S" or "Z," after the "slant" of the threads), the direction (recto or verso) of the knot attaching the pendant string to the primary, and the direction of the main axis of each knot itself (S or Z). As a result, each knot is what he called a "seven-bit binary array," although the term is inexact because *khipu* had at least twenty-four possible string colors. Each array encoded one of $2^6 \times 24$ possible "distinct information units"—a total of 1,536, somewhat more than the estimated 1,000 to 1,500 Sumerian cuneiform signs, and more than twice the approximately 600 to 800 Egyptian and Maya hieroglyphic symbols.

If Urton is right, *khipu* were unique. They were the world's sole intrinsically three-dimensional written documents (Braille is a translation of writing on paper) and the only ones to use a "system of coding information" that "like the coding systems used in present-day computer language, was structured primarily as a binary code." In addition, they may have been among the few examples of "semasiographic" writing—texts that, unlike written English, Chinese, and Maya, are not representations of spoken language. "A system of symbols does not have to replicate speech to communicate narrative," Catherine Julien, a historian of Andean cultures at Western Michigan University, explained to me. "What will eventually be found in *khipu* is uncertain, but the idea that they have to be a representation of speech has to be thrown out."

Writing and reading are among the most basic methods of transmitting information from one person to another. In cultures throughout the world, this procedure is fundamentally similar. One reads a parade of symbols, taking up information with the eyes; emphasis and context is provided visually, by changing the size and form of the symbols (printing in italics or boldface, increasing or diminishing the font size, scattering words or characters around the page). All European and Asian cultures share the common experience of reading—sitting in a chair, the book in one's lap, wagging the head from side to side (Europe) or up and down (Asia).

Because Tawantinsuyu existed only for a few centuries, it is widely assumed that the Inka *khipu* built on other, earlier forms of writing that had been developed in the region. And these cultures were unique, if Urton is right. Their books were loose bundles of string—more practical, in some ways, than paper scrolls or books, because less susceptible to water damage and physical pressure. They were read both tactilely, by running the fingertips along the knots, and visually, by looking at the colors of the strings. And whereas the choice of letters and words at the beginning of a sentence or paragraph exercise little constraint on physical connection to those at the end, the choices made by the *khipu* maker at the beginning of a string could not be undone halfway through. As a result, each *khipu* pendant provided a burst of information at the beginning that was refined further down the string.

However anomalous to European eyes, this form of writing has deep roots in Andean culture. Knotted-string communication was but one aspect of these societies' exploration of textile technology (see Chapter 3). In these cultures, Heather Lechtman, of MIT, has argued, cloth "was the most important carrier of status, the material of choice for the communication of message, whether religious, political, or scientific." Similarly, Urton told me, binary oppositions were a hallmark of the region's peoples, who lived in societies "typified to an extraordinary degree by dual organization," from the division of town populations into complementary "upper" and "lower" halves (moieties, in the jargon) to the arrangement of poetry into dyadic units. In this environment, he said, "*khipu* would be familiar."

As this book went to press, Urton and Carrie Brazine, a software developer/weaver/mathematician at Harvard's Peabody Museum, were creating an online database characterizing most of the surviving *khipu*, a more sophisticated successor to a pioneering database created by Robert and Marcia Archer. The hope is that computerized analysis will be able to spot patterns that thus far have eluded human researchers.

At the same time, Urton and other *khipu* specialists have been searching for an Inka Rosetta stone—a colonial translation of an extant *khipu*. One candidate exists—maybe. In 1996, Clara Miccinelli, an amateur historian from the Neapolitan nobility, caused a stir by announcing that she had unearthed in her family archives both a *khipu* and its Spanish translation (it encoded a folk song). But because the putative *khipu* isn't made the same way as other surviving *khipus* and the same documents also claim that Pizarro conquered the Inka empire by poisoning its generals with arsenic-adulterated wine, many

U.S. scholars have questioned their authenticity. Angered by the doubts, Miccinelli has thus far refused to let non-Italian researchers examine the documents, although she did allow an Australian laboratory to evaluate their age with a mass spectrometer. (The results, published in 2000, suggest that they are from the fifteenth century.) Because of the controversy, most researchers have been, according to Brokaw, "strategically ignoring" the Italian documents, at least for the present.

More widely accepted are the thirty-two *khipu* found in a tomb in the Peruvian Amazon in 1996, one of which Urton tentatively deciphered as a census record for the area in late pre-Hispanic times. With the help of a MacArthur fellowship he received in 2001, he has been searching Peruvian archives for something with more narrative content to match against the other *khipu*—a quest, according to Julien, that "has a chance of bearing fruit." If Urton's quest or others like it are successful, she told me, "We may be able to hear the Inkas for the first time in their own voice."

I asked what she thought that voice might sound like—the voice of people attuned to tension and cloth, people who saw the stones of the world charged with spirit, people who had never seen animals larger than a llama, people who broke the world into complementary halves and thought more in terms of up and down than north and south, people who took in information about the world through their fingers.

"Foreign," she said.

APPENDIX C

The Syphilis Exception

No one doubts today that European bacteria and viruses had a ruinous effect on the Americas. So, too, did African diseases like malaria and yellow fever when *they* arrived. The question inevitably arises as to whether there were any correspondingly lethal infections from the Americas, payback to the conquistadors. One candidate was long ago nominated: syphilis.

Syphilis is caused by *Treponema pallidum,* a wormlike bacterium that writhes in corkscrew spirals on microscope slides. The disease occurs in four different forms, and syphilis researchers disagree about whether the various forms are caused by different subspecies of *Treponema pallidum* or whether *Treponema pallidum* is not actually a single species but a brace of slightly different species, each responsible for a different set of symptoms. One form of infection is bejel, which creates small, coldsore-like lesions inside and around the mouth; it mainly afflicts the Middle East. The second, yaws, found in tropical places worldwide, infects cuts and abrasions and causes long-lasting sores. Neither disease spreads to bone or nerves, and they rarely kill their victims. Syphilis, the third form, is another matter. Passed on mainly by sexual contact, it inflicts genital rashes and sores before it apparently disappears, relieving sufferers but silently—and often fatally—infecting their hearts, bones, and brains. (The fourth form, which exists mainly in Mesoamerica, is pinta, a mild skin infection.)

The first recorded European epidemic of syphilis erupted in late 1494 or early 1495. In the former year, Charles VIII of France led fifty thousand vagabond mercenaries from every alley of Europe to attack Naples, which he desired to rule. (He used mercenaries because even at the dawn of the sixteenth century most European states did not have the resources to support a standing military.) Charles conquered the city only to learn after he had occupied it for a few months that the various Italian statelets were massing against him, aided by a big contingent of Spanish troops. Struck with fear, the king ignominiously fled with his men in the spring of 1495. Both entry and exit were accompanied by sack, pillage, wanton slaughter, and mass rape. Somewhere along the way *Treponema pallidum* wriggled into the bloodstream of Charles's retreating mercenaries. The most widely suggested source is their Spanish attackers, with transmission occurring via the women violated by both sides. Whatever the case, Charles's army disintegrated as it fled, shedding companies of venereal soldiers along the way. A more effective means for spreading syphilis over a large area is hard to imagine. Within a year cities throughout Europe were banishing people afflicted with the disease.

Did Columbus bring the disease from the Americas, as the timing of the first epidemic suggests? There are three main arguments to support an affirmative answer to this question and an equal number against it. The first on the pro side is the sheer deadliness of the disease—early records indicate that syphilis then was even more ghastly than it is now. Green, acorn-size boils filled with stinking liquid bubbled everywhere on the body. Victims' pain, one sixteenth-century observer noted, "were as thoughe they hadde lyen in fire." The fatality rate was high. Such deadliness fits in with the notion that *Treponema pallidum* was new to Europe. Orthodox Darwinian theory predicts that over time the effect of most transmissible diseases should moderate—the most lethal strains kill their hosts so fast they cannot be passed on to other hosts. Thus syphilis, then wildly virulent and lethal, acted like a new disease.

A second argument is that Europeans at the time believed that the disease had "its origin and its birth from always in the island which is now named Española [Hispaniola]," as the prominent Spanish doctor Ruy Díaz de Isla put it in 1539. Díaz claimed that he had observed and tried to treat syphilis in the crew from Columbus's first voyage, including, it seems, the captain of the *Pinta*. Apparently the man picked up the parasite in Hispaniola, brought it back to Europe, and died within months—but not before passing it on to some luckless bedmate. Díaz de Isla's testimony was backed by the pro-Indian cleric Bartolomé de Las Casas, who was in Seville when Columbus returned.

Syphilis seems to have existed in the Americas before 1492—the third argument. In the mid-1990s Bruce and Christine Rothschild, researchers at the Arthritis Center of Northeast Ohio, in Youngstown, inspected 687 ancient Indian skeletons from the United States and Ecuador for signs of syphilitic disease. Up to 40 percent of the skeletons from some areas showed its presence. To nail down the chain of transmission, they subsequently discovered—working in concert with researchers from the Dominican Republic and Italy—that syphilis was equally common in Hispaniola when Columbus arrived. Indeed, the disease seemed to date back about two thousand years—it may have originated as a mutated form of yaws on the Colorado plateau.

The three main counterarguments against the America-as-origin theory are, first, that *Treponema pallidum* may have existed in Europe before Columbus. Archaeologists have turned up a few medieval skeletons, most of them in Britain, carrying what look like the marks of syphilis. Although pre-1492 syphilitic skeletons exist in the Americas, even a few European exemplars would undermine the Columbus-as-Typhoid-Mary case. Indeed, some medical researchers propose that syphilis has always existed worldwide, but manifested itself differently in different places. Second, the 1495 outbreak may not have been the introduction of a new disease but the recognition of an old one, which until then had been confused with Hansen's disease (or, as it was known, leprosy). Descriptions of syphilis during and after the 1494–95 epidemic and Hansen's before it are surprisingly similar; both were "treated" with mercury. In 1490 the pope abolished all of the leprosaria in Europe, allowing hordes of sick people to return home. Could that humanitarian gesture also have unleashed a storm of syphilis? At least some researchers think it likely.

The third counterargument is psychological. In part, as Alfred Crosby admitted, he initially devoted attention to the possible American origin of syphilis "because I was uneasy about so many diseases crossing west over the Atlantic and none going east." He thought there must be some sort of "epidemiological-geographical symmetry." Other historians followed suit. Later Crosby realized that examining the evidence in the hope of redressing the infectious balance was a mistake. "They want pox in Europe to balance the scales for smallpox in Mexico," Vine Deloria Jr. told me. "They're all hoping to find there's a real Montezuma's Revenge."

Yet even if syphilis *did* originate in the New World, the scales would not be balanced. Syphilis is fascinating, "like all things venereal," Crosby wrote in 2003, "but it was not a history-maker" like smallpox. *Treponema pallidum,* awful as it was and is, did not help topple empires or push whole peoples to extinction. "There was little symmetry in the exchange of diseases between the Old and the New Worlds," Crosby said, "and there are few factors as influential in the history of the last half millennium as that."

Calendar Math

Dictionaries define the calendar almost as if it were a machine: "a system for fixing the beginning, length, and divisions of the civil year." But in every society calendars are much more than that. People experience time as both linear and circular. On the one hand, it marches remorselessly from birth to death, a vector with fixed endpoints and a constant velocity. On the other hand, time is cyclical, with the wheel of the seasons endlessly spinning, and no clear end or beginning. Calendars are records of a culture's attempt to weight and reconcile these different visions.

In early European societies, the end of the year was regarded as dangerous: a period when the calendar literally runs out of days, the landscape is blanketed by night and cold, and nobody can be truly certain that the heavens would usher in a new year. Embodying that mysterious time when the end of the calendar somehow looped round and rejoined itself at the beginning, Romans celebrated Saturnalia, an upside-down week when masters served their servants and slaves held the great offices of state. The Christian calendar bracketed the strange, perilous final days of the year on one end with the birth of Christ, symbol of renewal, on December 25, and on the other with Epiphany, the day when the three kings recognized the infant Jesus as the Savior, another symbol of renewal, on January 6. Christmas and Epiphany bridge the dangerous gap between the end of one year and the beginning of the next.

The Mesoamerican calendar also tied together linear and cyclical time, but more elaborately. In its most fully developed form, at the height of Maya power, it consisted of three separate but interrelated calendars: a sacred tally known as the *tzolk'in;* the *haab,* a secular calendar based, like the Western calendar, on the rotation of the sun; and the Long Count, a system that, among other things, linked the other two.

The sacred calendar is both the calendar most dissimilar to Western calendars and the most important culturally. Each day in the *tzolk'in* had a name and a number, in somewhat the same way that one might refer to, say,

"Wednesday the 15th." In the Western calendar, the day names (e.g., Wednesday) run through cycles of seven, making weeks, and the day numbers (e.g., the 15th) run through cycles of 28, 30, or 31, making months. The *tzolk'in* used the same principle, but with less variation in the lengths of the cycles; it had a twenty-day "week" of named days and a thirteen-day "month" of numbered days. The analogy I am drawing is imprecise; what I am describing as the *tzolk'in* "week" was longer than the "month." But just as Thursday the 16th follows Wednesday the 15th in the Christian calendar, 10 Akbal would follow 9 Ik in the *tzolk'in*. (The Maya had a twenty-day "week" in part because their number system was base-20, instead of the base-10 in European societies.)

Because the *tzolk'in* was not intended to track the earth's orbit around the sun, its inventors didn't have to worry about fitting their "weeks" and "months" into the 365 days of the solar year. Instead they simply set the first day of the year to be the first day of the twenty-day "week" and the thirteen-day "month," and let the cycle spin. In the language of elementary school mathematics, the least common multiple (the smallest number that two numbers will divide into evenly) of 13 and 20 is 260. Hence, the *tzolk'in* had a length of 260 days.

In the Western calendar, a given combination of named and numbered days, such as Wednesday the 15th, will occur a few times in a calendar year. For instance, in 2006 the 15th of the month falls on Wednesday three times, in February, March, and November; in 2007 Wednesday the 15th occurs just once, in August. The irregular intervals are due to the differing lengths of the months, which throw off the cycle. In the *tzolk'in*, every "month" and every "week" are the same length. As a result, "Wednesday the 15th"—or 1 Imix, to give a real example—in the *tzolk'in* recurs at precise intervals; each is exactly 13 × 20 or 260 days apart.

Many researchers believe the movements of Venus, which Mesoamerican astronomers tracked carefully, originally inspired the *tzolk'in*. Venus is visible for about 263 consecutive days as the morning star, then goes behind the sun for 50 days, then reappears for another 263 days as the evening star. It was a powerful presence in the heavens, as I noted in Chapter 8, and a calendar based on its celestial trajectory would have shared some of that power. Within the sacred year, every day was thought to have particular characteristics, so much so that people were often named after their birth dates: 12 Eb, 2 Ik, and so on. In some places men and women apparently could not marry if they had the same name day. Days in the *tzolk'in* had import for larger occasions, too. Events from ceremonies to declarations of war were thought to be more likely to succeed if they occurred on a propitious day.

Because people also needed a civil calendar for mundane purposes like knowing when to sow and harvest, Mesoamerican societies had a second, secular calendar, the *haab:* eighteen "months," each of twenty days. (Unlike the *tzolk'in,* which counted off the days from 1, the *haab* months began with 0; nobody knows why the system was different.) Simple arithmetic shows that eighteen twenty-day months generates a 360-day year, five days short of the requisite 365 days. Indians knew it, too. Rather than sprinkling the extra five days throughout the year as we do, though, they tacked them onto the end in a special "month" of their own. These days were thought to be unlucky—it was as if the year ended with five straight days of Friday the 13th. Although the ancient Maya knew (unlike their contemporaries in Europe) that the solar year is actually 365¼ days, they did not bother to account for the extra quarter

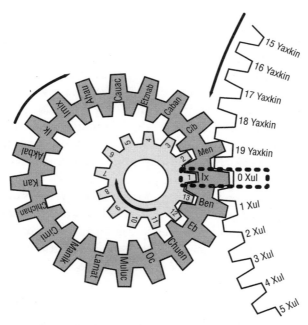

The Mesoamerican calendar was both more complex and more accurate than the European calendars of the same period. It consisted of a 365-day secular calendar, the *haab* (right), much like contemporary European calendars. The *haab* was tied to the second, sacred calendar, the *tzolk'in* (left), which was unlike any Western calendar. With a "week" of twenty named days and a "month" of thirteen numbered days, the *tzolk'in* produced a 260-day "year." Mesoamerican societies used both simultaneously, so that every date was labeled with two names (1 Ix 0 Xul in the drawing). I have not rendered the *haab* as a wheel-within-wheel like the *tzolk'in,* even though it, too, had perfectly regular "weeks" and "months." This is because the *haab* had to fit the 365-day solar year, which forced Maya calendar designers to spoil their system by tacking on an irregular, extra-short month at the end.

day; there were no leap years in Mesoamerica. The failure to do so seems surprising, given that their astronomers' mania for precision had led them to measure the length of the lunar month to within about ten seconds.

With two calendars, every day thus had two names, a sacred *tzolk'in* name and a civil *haab* name. Usually the Maya referred to them by both at once: 1 Ix o Xul. The two different calendars, each perfectly regular (but one more regular than the other), marched in lockstep, forming what is now called the Calendar Round. After one 1 Ix o Xul, there would not be another 1 Ix o Xul for 18,980 days, about fifty-two years.

By describing dates with both calendars Mesoamerican societies were able to give every day in this fifty-two-year period a unique name. But they couldn't distinguish one fifty-two-year period from its predecessors and successors—as if the Christian calendar couldn't distinguish 1810, 1910, and 2010. To avoid confusion and acknowledge time's linear dimension, Mesoamerican societies invented the Long Count, which counts off the days from a starting point that is believed to have been in mid-August, 3114 B.C. Long Count dates consisted of the number of days, 20-day "months," 360-day "years," 7,200-day "decades," and 144,000-day "centuries" since the beginning. Archaeologists generally render these as a set of five numbers separated by dots. When Columbus landed, on Tuesday, October 11, 1492, the Maya would have marked the day as 11.13.12.4.3, with the "centuries" first and the days last. In the *tzolk'in* and *haab,* the day was 2 Akbal 6 Zotz.

Although extant Long Count dates have only five positions for numbers, the Maya knew that eventually that time would pass and they would have to add more positions. Indeed, their priestly mathematicians had calculated *nineteen* further positions, culminating in what is now called the *alautun,* a period of 23,040,000,000 days, which is about 63 million years. Probably the longest named interval of time in any calendar, the *alautun* is a testament to the grandiosity of Mesoamerican calendries. Just as the *tzolk'in* is one of the most impeccably circular time cycles ever invented, the Long Count is among the most purely linear, an arrow pointing straight ahead for millions of years into the future.

❄ ACKNOWLEDGMENTS ❄

In putting together this book I worked under the shadow of great travelers, scientists, and historians ranging from William H. Prescott, Francis Parkman, and John Lloyd Stephens in the nineteenth century to (I cite only a sampler) William Cronon, Alfred W. Crosby, William M. Denevan, Francis Jennings, John Hemming, Claude Lévi-Strauss, Roderick Nash, and Carl Sauer in the twentieth and twenty-first. The comparison is daunting. Luckily, I have been able to benefit from the advice, encouragement, and criticism of many scholars, beginning with Crosby and Denevan themselves. A number of researchers read the draft manuscript in part or whole, a great kindness for which I thank Crosby, Denevan, William Balée, Clark Erickson, Susanna Hecht, Frances Karttunen, George Lovell, Michael Moseley, James Petersen, and William I. Woods. Although they helped me enormously, the book is mine in the end, as are its remaining errors of fact and balance.

I am grateful to all the researchers who were kind enough to put aside their doubts long enough to help a journalist, but in addition to those mentioned above I would especially like to thank—for favors, insights, or just the gift of time—Helcio Amiral, Flavio Aragon Cuevas, Charles Clement, Michael Crawford, Winifred Creamer, Vine Deloria Jr., Henry F. Dobyns, Elizabeth Fenn, Stuart Fiedel, Susan deFrance, Jonathan Haas, Susanna Hecht, Charles Kay, Patricia Lyon, Beata Madari, David Meltzer, Len Morse-Fortier, Michael Moseley, Eduardo Neves, Hugo Perales, Amado Ramírez Leyva, Anna C. Roosevelt, Nelsi N. Sadeck, the late Wim Sombroek, Russell Thornton, Alexei Vranich, Patrick Ryan Williams, and a host of Bolivian, Brazilian, Canadian, Mexican, and U.S. graduate students. My gratitude to the editors of the magazines in which bits of 1491 first appeared: Corby Kummer, Cullen Murphy, Sue Parilla, Bill Whitworth, and the late Mike Kelly at *The Atlantic Monthly;* Tim Appenzeller, Elizabeth Culotta, Colin Norman, and Leslie Roberts at *Science;* David Shipley and Carmel McCoubrey at the *New York Times;* Nancy Franklin at *Harvard Design Magazine;* and George Lovell at *Journal of the Southwest.*

For library access, travel tips, withering critiques, friendly encouragement at psychologically critical times, and a daunting list of other favors I owe debts to Bob Crease, Josh D'Aluisio-Guerreri, Dan Farmer (and all the folks on the fish.com listservs), Dave Freedman, Judy Hooper, Pam Hunter (and Carl, too, of course), Toichiro and Masa Kinoshita, Steve Mann, Cassie Phillips, Ellen Shell, Neal Stephenson, Gary Taubes, Dick Teresi, and Zev Trachtenberg. Newell Blair Mann was a boon traveling companion in Bolivia and Brazil; Bruce Bergethon indulged me by coming to Cahokia; Peter Menzel went with me to Mexico four times. Jim Boyce helped get me to Oaxaca and CIMMYT. Nick Springer provided a design for the rough maps that Tim Gibson and I put together. Stephen S. Hall was really, really patient and really, really helpful about the immune system. Ify and Ekene Nwokoye tried at various times to keep me organized. Brooke Childs worked on photo permissions. Mark Plummer provided me with far too many favors to list. The same for Rick Balkin (the fifth book for which he has done so). June Kinoshita and Tod Machover allowed me to finish Chapter 4 in their carriage house in Waltham. My deepest gratitude to Faith D'Aluisio and Peter Menzel, who let my family and me stay in their guesthouse in Napa, where Chapters 6 through 8 emerged into the world. Caroline Mann read an early draft and provided many useful comments. Last-minute help from Dennis Normile and the Foreign Correspondents Club of Tokyo is hereby recognized and thanked.

I am lucky in my publishers, Knopf in the United States and Granta in the United Kingdom. In this, our third book together, Jon Segal at Knopf demonstrated his mastery of not only the traditional pencil skills of the classic editor but also the new techniques the times require to send a book on its way. In addition, I must doff my beret in Borzoi land to Kevin Bourke, Roméo Enriquez, Ida Giragossian, Andy Hughes, and Virginia Tan. At Granta, Sara Holloway gave excellent advice and tolerated repeated auctorial meddling and procrastination. So many other people in so many places pulled strings on my behalf, tolerated repeated phone calls, arranged site visits, edited or checked manuscripts, and sent me hard-to-find articles and books that I could not possibly list them all. I hope that in the end this book seems to them worth the trouble.

❄ NOTES ❄

Every book is built on other books, the adage says, and this one is an exemplary case. Think of the list of texts below as the architect's specifications for 1491. Except that this list is more selective, consisting as it does only of the works consulted necessary to make a particular point, not everything used in the construction of the book. If at all possible, I have cited printed, English-language versions of each source; many texts can be found online, too, but URLs change so fast that I have avoided listing them whenever possible. Texts available on the Web as of early 2005 are indicated by a star (★); most can be found through search engines or in such collections as Early English Books Online, Project Gutenberg, the Foundation for the Advancement of Mesoamerican Studies, the University of Virginia's Electronic Text Center, the University of Maryland's Early American Digital Archive, and the Virtual Cervantes Library.

Perhaps paradoxically, some works were so important to this book that my notes give short shrift to them; they are in the background everywhere, but rarely summoned to make a specific point. For the first section, these would include Terence d'Altroy's *The Incas;* William Cronon's *Changes in the Land;* Alfred W. Crosby's *Columbian Exchange* and *Ecological Imperialism;* John Hemming's *Conquest of the Incas;* Karen Ordahl Kuppermann's *Indians and English;* María Rostworowski de Diez Canseco's *History of the Inca Realm;* and Neal Salisbury's *Manitou and Providence.*

As I stitched together the second section, books that kept my keyboard constant company included Ignacio Bernal's *The Olmec World;* Jared Diamond's *Guns, Germs, and Steel;* Brian Fagan's *Ancient North America;* Stuart Fiedel's *Prehistory of the Americas;* Nina Jablonski's edited collection, *The First Americans;* the special issue of the *Boletín de Arqueología PUCP* edited by Peter Kaulicke and William Isbell; Alan Kolata's *The Tiwanaku;* Mike Moseley's marvelous *Incas and Their Ancestors;* and the historical writings of David Meltzer, which I hope he will someday combine into a book, so that people like me won't have to keep piles of photocopies.

The third section sometimes seems like an extended riff on the three *Cultural Landscapes* books assembled by William Denevan and written by Denevan; Thomas M. Whitmore and B. L. Turner II; and William E. Doolittle. But I depended also on the special September 1992 issue of the *Annals of the Association of American Geographers* edited by Karl Butzer; the essays in *The Great New Wilderness Debate,* edited by J. Baird Callicott and Michael P. Nelson; Michael Coe's sturdy sourcebook, *The Maya;* Melvin Fowler's *Cahokia Atlas;* Shepard Krech's *Ecological Indian;* the amazing *Chronicles of the Maya Kings and Queens,* by Simon Martin and Nikolai Grube; and two books on *terra preta* (and much else besides), *Amazonian Dark Earths: Explorations in Space and Time,* edited by Bruno Glaser and William Woods, and *Amazonian Dark Earths: Origin, Properties, Management,* edited by Johannes Lehmann et al. (Full citations are in the Bibliography.)

Even a book of this length must leave out many things, given the magnitude of the subject matter. Thus I ignored the inhabitants of the Americas' northern and southern extremes and barely touched on the Northwest Coast. The most painful decision, though, was to omit, after it had been written, a section on the North American West. My qualms were soothed by the recent appearance of Colin Calloway's *One Vast Winter Count,* a magnificent synthesis of practically everything known about the subject.

1 / A View from Above

3 Erickson and scope of Beni earthworks: Erickson 2005, 2001, 2000b, 1995; see also Denevan 2001:chap. 12.

4 Old view of Indians: Ward Churchill, a professor of ethnic studies at the University of Colorado in Boulder, mockingly summed the paradigm: "How many Indians were there?—One million; Where did they come from?—Across the Bering Strait land bridge; When did they come?—15,000 years ago (plus or minus 15 minutes); How did they live?—They were squalid Stone Age hunter-gatherers wandering nomadically about the landscape at the bare margins of subsistence, waiting hopefully, millennium after millennium, for Europeans to show up and improve their quality of life" (Churchill 2003:44).

4 Smithsonian-backed archaeologists: Dougherty and Calandra 1984 (small numbers needed for causeways, 180; natural origins of mounds, 182–85). Their discussion has been dismissed as "improbably interpreted" (Myers et al. 1992:87). Roughly similar conclusions appear in Langstroth 1996.

4 Snow's critiques: Interviews, Snow.

5 Pristine myth: Denevan 1992a, 1996b.

5 Wilderness Act: P.L. 88–577, 3 Sept. 1964 ("untrammeled," section 2c); Callicott 1998:349–50 (act embodies "the conventional understanding of wilderness").

5 Obligation to restore natural state: Cronon 1995a:36.

5 Fish weirs: Erickson 2000a.

5 Future options for Beni: Interviews, Erickson, Balée, CIDDEBENI. By leasing their land to loggers and miners, the Kayapó in the southeast Amazon basin demonstrated how Indians can disappoint environmentalists (Epstein 1993; the article is reproduced and discussed in Slater 1995:121–24). Some environmentalists propose tucking the eastern Beni into a nearby UNESCO biopreserve, one of the 350 such preserves the agency sponsors worldwide.

6 Devil tree: Interviews and email, Balée. I found no published work on this specific form of obligate mutualism, but see, generally, Huxley and Cutler eds. 1991.

6 Ibibate and pottery: Interviews, Balée, Erickson; Erickson and Balée 2005; Balée 2000; Erickson 1995; Langstroth 1996.

7 Holmberg's view of Sirionó: Holmberg 1969:17 ("brand," "culturally backward"), 37 ("sleepless night"), 38–39 (clothing), 110 (lack of musical instruments), 116 ("universe," "uncrystallized"), 121 (count to three), 261 ("quintessence," "raw state"). After Holmberg's death, Lauriston Sharp introduced *Nomads* as a study of "lowly but instructive" "survivors" who "retained a variety of man's earliest culture." The book, he said, "discovered, described, and thus introduced into history a new and in many respects extraordinary Paleolithic experience" (Sharp 1969:xii–xiii). *Nomads* was a widely used undergraduate text for decades (Erickson, pers. comm.).

8 Holmberg's work and career: Interviews, Henry Dobyns; Doughty 1987; Stearman 1987 (account of his blind walk, Chap. 4).

8 Lack of study of Beni and Langstroth: Interviews, Erickson, Langstroth; Langstroth 1996.

9 Sirionó epidemics: The chronology is uncertain. Holmberg (1969:12) describes smallpox

and influenza epidemics that forced the "decimated" Sirionó into mission life in 1927. Citing other sources, Swedish anthropologist Stig Rydén, who visited the Sirionó briefly ten years after Holmberg, reports epidemics in 1920 and 1925, which he interprets as episodes in a single big flu epidemic (Rydén 1941:25). But such heavy casualties are less likely from a single source.

9 Sirionó population: Holmberg 1969:12 (fewer than 150 during his fieldwork). Rydén (1941:21) estimated 6,000–10,000 in the late 1920s, presumably a pre-epidemic count. Today there are 600–2,000 (Balée 1999; Townsend 1996:22). Stearman (1986:8) estimated 3,000–6,000.

9 Stearman returns, bottleneck, abuse by army and ranchers, Holmberg's failure to grasp: Stearman 1984; Stearman 1987; author's interviews, Balée, Erickson, Langstroth. Holmberg (1969:8–9) noted the incidence of clubfoot and ear marks, but made little of it.

10 Migration of Sirionó: Interviews, Balée; Barry 1977; Priest 1980; Pärssinen 2003. A Spanish account from 1636 suggests that they had arrived only a few decades before (Métraux 1942:97), but this is not widely accepted.

10 First Beni research and Denevan thesis: Nordenskiöld 1979a; Denevan 1966.

10 Bauré culture and Erickson's perspective: Interviews, Erickson; Erickson 1995, 2000b, 2005; Anon. 1743.

12 Las Casas ethnography: Casas 1992a; Wagner 1967:287–89 (publication history).

13 "lyve in that goulden": Arber ed. 1885:71 (letter, Martire, P., to Charles V, 30 Sept. 1516).

13 "Indian wisdom": "[W]e cannot know truth by contrivance and method; the Baconian is as false as any other, and with all the helps of machinery and the arts, the most scientific will still be the healthiest and friendliest man, and possess a more perfect Indian wisdom" (Thoreau 1906 [vol. 5]:131).

13 Crying Indian campaign: Krech 1999:14–16.

13 Indians without history: "In North America, whites are the bearers of environmental original sin, because whites alone are recognized as laboring. But whites are thus also, by the same token, the only real bearers of history. This is why our flattery . . . of 'simpler' peoples is an act of such immense condescension. For in a modern world defined by change, whites are portrayed as the only beings who make a difference" (White 1995:175). The phrase "people without history" was popularized in an ironic sense in Wolf 1997.

13 "unproductive waste": Bancroft 1834–76 [vol. 1]:3–4.

14 Kroeber on warfare and agriculture: Kroeber 1934:10–12 (all quotes).

14 Conrad on Indian dyspepsia: Conrad 1923:vi.

14 "pagans expecting": Morison 1974:737.

14 "chief function": Trevor-Roper 1965:9. To be fair, the baron was dismissing *all* indigenous peoples around the world, not singling out Indians.

14 Fitzgerald survey: Fitzgerald 1980:89–93 ("resolutely backward," 90; "lazy," 91; "few paragraphs," 93). See also, Axtell 1992.

14 Views have continued to appear: Examples, listed alphabetically by author, include Bailey et al. 1983:9 (the "vast and virgin continent . . . was so sparsely populated by Indians that they could be eliminated or shouldered aside. Such a magnificent opportunity for a great democratic experiment would never come again"), quoted in Axtell 1992:203; Bailyn et al. 1977:34 ("But the Indians' hold upon the land was light. . . . Nowhere was more than one percent of the land available for horticulture actually under cultivation"; editions of this textbook appeared, essentially unaltered, into the 1990s); Berliner 2003 ("Prior to 1492, what is now the United States was sparsely inhabited, unused, and undeveloped. . . . There was virtually no change, no growth for thousands of years"); Billard 1975:20 ("To a virgin continent where prairie grass waved tall as a man and vast forests

perfumed the air for miles offshore came Spanish adventurer, French trapper, Dutch sailor, and doughty Englishman"); Fernández-Armesto 2001:154 (many Amazonian Indians' lives were "unchanged for millennia" and the rainforest was "still a laboratory of specimen peoples apparently suspended by nature in a state of so-called underdevelopment"—the key word here being "suspended," as in fixed in place, motionless); McKibben 1989:53 (Wilderness Society founder Robert Marshall concluding a currently unpopulated part of the United States was "as it existed outside human history"); Sale 1990:315–16 ("the land of North America was still by every account a lush and fertile wilderness . . . [which] gave off the aspect of an untouched world"); Shabecoff 1993:23 (Lewis and Clark traveling through land "unchanged by humans"); Shetler 1991:226 ("Pre-Columbian America was still the First Eden, a pristine natural kingdom. The native people were transparent in the landscape, living as natural elements of the ecosphere. Their world, the New World of Columbus, was a world of barely perceptible human disturbance").

14 "For thousands": Current, Williams, and Brinkley 1987:1. Such statements are often due less to prejudice than to European and American historians' continuing uncertainty about how to think about non-European and non-American societies. Thus on the next page Current et al. describe Indians both as establishing some of "the world's most dazzling cultures" and "lack[ing] some of mankind's most basic tools and technologies" (2)—the latter state assuming, ethnocentrically, that European technologies are "basic" whereas indigenous technologies are inessential. See Chaps. 2 and 3.

15 New perspectives and techniques: Crosby ed. 1994 ("faint smudges," 7).

15 "replaced": Vale 1998:231.

16 Growth of Bering Strait theory and fight over Chilean site: See Chap. 5.

17 Deloria index entries: Deloria 1995:284.

17 Invention of agriculture: See, e.g., Lev-Yadun, Gopher, and Abbo 2000.

17 Neolithic Revolution: I am simplifying here. Sumerian villages were growing wheat and barley by about 6000 B.C. Around 4000 B.C. the villages became hierarchically organized towns or cities. Early forms of writing date to at least 3000 B.C. Five centuries later, the writing had become a unified system and the city of Uruk had a population of forty thousand.

17 "The human career": Wright 2005:45. Sumer was the first to develop agriculture, laying the foundation for later civilizations in Egypt, Greece, India, and Mesopotamia. China apparently invented farming on its own, but borrowed mathematics, writing, art, and much else from Sumer. This last claim is fiercely debated, though, and some believe China to have been as independent of Sumer as Peru and Mesoamerica.

18 Maize and early American domestications, Olmec accomplishments: See Chaps. 6, 7.

19 "one of the greatest": Dantzig 1967:35. I am grateful to Dick Teresi for introducing me to this terrific book.

19 History of zero: Kaplan 1999:11–57; Teresi 2002:22–25, 86–87, 379–82.

20 "bleak, frigid land": von Hagen, V., commentary, in Cieza de León 1959:272.

20 Tiwanaku: See chap. 7.

22 Populations of Tiwanaku and Paris: Kolata 1993:204–05; Bairoch, Batou, and Chévre 1988:28. Metropolitan Paris reached a quarter million in about 1400.

22 Wari: See chap. 7.

22 Glacial evidence of dust storms: Thompson, Davis, and Mosley-Thompson 1994. More than a few archaeologists are skeptical of this evidence (Erickson, pers. comm.).

22 Mega-Niños: Schimmelmann, Lange, and Meggers 2003; Meggers 1994.

23 Climate and Tiwanaku, Wari decline: Kolata 2000; Binford et al. 1997; Thompson, Davis, and Mosley-Thompson 1994.

23 Little Ice Age: Lamb 1995:Chaps. 12, 13; Fagan 2001.

23 Maya: See Chap. 8.

24 Toltecs and Yucatán: Diehl 1983 (basic history); Coe 1999:165–80 (favoring invasion scenario); Schele and Mathews 1998:198–201, esp. fn. 13 (arguing against). The Schele-Mathews arguments center on disputed radiocarbon dates and interpretations of artworks' styles that to my mind seem all but to ignore their content.

25 Mississippians: See Chap. 8.

25 Plains Indians rock rings: Teresi 2002:107–09.

25 Lake Superior copper: S. R. Martin 1999.

26 Newly discovered Acre sites: Pärssinen et al. 2003. See also Erickson 2002.

26 Amazon: See Chap. 9.

26 Early world histories: E.g., Otto I 1966; Dinawari 1986.

2 / Why Billington Survived

31 Massasoit, Samoset, and Tisquantum: Bradford 1981:87–88; Winslow 1963b:37, 43–59 ("tall proper men," 53); Deetz and Deetz 2000:61–62. In quotations I have modernized the use of "f" and "v."

32 Negotiations: Bradford 1981:87–89; Winslow 1963b:50–59 ("very lusty," 57); Deetz and Deetz 2000:61–62; Kuppermann 2000:7.

34 "A friendly Indian": Wood et al. 1971:73.

34 Tisquantum's life: I have relied greatly on Salisbury 1989. See also Adams 1892–93 (vol. 1): 22–44; Foreman 1943:20–21; Humins 1987; Kinnicutt 1914; Shuffelton 1976.

34 Tisquantum, and fish fertilizer: Accounts of Squanto and fish fertilizer include Winslow 1963a:81–82 ("increase," 82); Bradford 1981:94–95; Morton 1632:89. Skepticism about the aboriginality of fish fertilization dates back to 1939, but the question was first raised forcefully in Rostlund 1957a and then still more strongly in Ceci 1975a, 1975b, 1990b. Ceci's conclusions were disputed (Nanepashemet 1991; Russell 1975, 1980:166–67; Warden 1975), but much of the critique boiled down to refuting the charge that the Indians were too stupid to figure out the use of fertilizer, an argument Ceci did not make. Instead Ceci suggested that the added productivity would not have been worth the added trouble, given the alternative of fallowing. Because Europeans had much less land per person and less mobility, they had to resort to fertilization. In the early 1990s Stephen A. Mrozowski, an archaeologist at the University of Massachusetts in Boston, unearthed evidence on Cape Cod suggesting that fish were used there as fertilizer a few decades before the *Mayflower,* but he has not yet published it (interview, Mrozowski). The fish may have been ordinary household waste, though. Incidentally, fish fertilizer was common in Peru (Denevan 2001:35–36).

35 Pilgrims' lack of curiosity about Indian motives: The early chroniclers did explore Tisquantum's motives, especially when they accused him of scheming to better his station. But they did not, in modern terms, try to put themselves in his place, which is what is at issue here. Nor did the colonists puzzle over why they never suffered a sustained attack, to judge by the lack of discussion by Bradford, Winslow et al. Here one cannot charge the colonists with special insensitivity. Compared to later historians, Pilgrim writers were more likely to see Indians as independent actors with their own beliefs and goals (Kuppermann 2000:2–4).

35 "Divine providence": Gookin 1792:148.

35 Dissatisfied historians: For a survey of ethnohistory's origins, see Axtell 1978.

35 Explosion of research: Author's interviews, Axtell, Neal Salisbury; Chaplin 2003:esp. 1445–55 ("No other field," 1431).

36 Squanto as devil: Shuffelton 1976. Tisquantum, according to a Massachusett dictionary, is a variant of *musquantum*, "he is angry." When Indians had accidents, according to Roger Williams, the minister and linguist who founded Rhode Island, "they will say, God was angry and did it; *musquantum manit,* God is angry" (cited in Shuffelton 1976:110).

37 Norumbega: D'Abate 1994; Parkman 1983 (vol. 1):155. The term referred vaguely to a mythical city, the river that supposedly reached it, and the region around the river, all somewhere in the Northeast.

37 Patuxet population: A vexing question. Tisquantum is said to have claimed it had two thousand souls (James ed. 1963:29). According to the most widely cited colonial observer, Daniel Gookin, the Wampanoag federation, of which Patuxet was a member, "could raise, as the most credible and ancient Indians affirm, about three thousand men" (Gookin 1792:148). If the federation were able to muster three thousand adult males, then typical population estimates for the whole would be on the order of twelve to fifteen thousand. The Wampanoag had about a dozen settlements, which would suggest that Patuxet may have had a thousand inhabitants, or maybe a few more. Countering this, anthropologist Kathleen Bragdon argues the available archaeological evidence suggests that individual coastal settlements like Patuxet held "probably no more than two hundred people" (Bragdon 1996:58). I have accepted Gookin's figure because it was apparently derived from contemporaneous Indians themselves, and because the archaeological traces, as Bragdon herself notes, are difficult to interpret.

37 Names and distribution of Indian groups: Most historical accounts rely on Gookin (1792:147–49), including the standard reference, Salwen (1978:160–76). See also Bragdon 1996:20–25; Russell 1980:19–29; Salisbury 1982:13–30 passim; Vaughan 1995:50–58.

37 Dawnland: Stewart-Smith 1998:49.

38 Slow movement into New England: Bragdon 1996:57–58 (salt marshes, 1000 B.C.); Wilkie and Tager eds. 1991:10–11 (maps of distribution through time of known paleo-Indian archaeological sites); Fagan 2000:101–04 (low carrying capacity of postglacial areas); Petersen 2004. On a continental scale, the New England indigenous groups were so small that one conscientious continental survey doesn't even mention them (Fagan 1991).

38 Patchwork environment: Cronon 1983:19–33 ("tremendous variety," 31).

38 Glottochronology: Glottochronology was invented in the 1960s by U.S. linguist Morris Swadesh, a controversial figure who spent much of his career in Mexico after his colorful political views cost him his passport during the McCarthy period. The technique was the subject of his posthumously printed magnum opus, *The Origin and Diversification of Language* (Swadesh ed. 1971). Glottochronology tries to ascertain how long ago two languages diverged from a common ancestor language, as French and Italian did from Latin. To accomplish this, Swadesh drew up a list of one hundred basic terms, such as "ear," "mother," and "vomit." When two languages are closely related, Swadesh argued, their words for these terms will resemble each other. For example, the French and Italian for "ear" are *oreille* and *orecchio,* terms similar enough to suggest that these languages split off from each other relatively recently. On average, Swadesh claimed, the words on the Swadesh list change at a rate of 14 percent every one thousand years. Thus if two languages have similar entries for seventy-nine of the hundred words on the Swadesh list, they broke off from a common ancestor about 1,500 years ago. Unsurprisingly, Swadesh's ideas have been criticized. Especially implausible is the notion that linguistic change occurs at a constant, universal rate. Nonetheless researchers use glottochronology, partly because of the lack of alternatives, and partly because the basic idea intuitively seems correct (Swadesh 1971, 1952; Hymes 1971, 1960:5–6).

38 Glottochronological analysis of Algonquian languages: Fiedel 1987; Goddard 1978; Mulholland 1985.

39 Diverse New England communities: This description relies on the surveys of evidence in Petersen and Cowrie 2002; Bragdon 1996:55–79 ("no name," 58–59). Bragdon (1996:39) adopts the term "conditional sedentism" for the coastal communities (coined in Dunford 1992). For the growth of coastal communities, see Robinson 1994. In the past, some have argued that coastal Indians practiced little agriculture (Ceci 1990a), but Petersen and Cowrie assemble evidence to refute this.

39 Coastal diet: Little and Schoeninger 1995; Kavasch 1994.

39 Description of Patuxet: Author's visit; James ed. 1963:7 ("Pleasant for air," alewives), 75–76; Winslow 1963b:8–43; Anon. ed. 1963:xx–xxi (map of area in 1613 by Champlain). In these years big areas along the coastline had neatly planted maize fields, traces of which survived even into the twentieth century (Delabarre and Wilder 1920:210–14).

40 *Wetus,* meals, and domestic style: Morton 1637:24–26; Wood 1977:86–88, 112 ("warmer," 112); Bragdon 1996:104–07; Gookin 1792:149–51 ("so sweet," 150–51). "The best sort" of *wetus,* Gookin said, were "covered very neatly, tight, and warm, with barks of trees"— "warm as the best English houses" (150). Clearly, the homes of the wealthy in England were not leaky or drafty, but in that deforested land even the rich could not afford the plentiful fires that kept Indians warm (Higginson 1792:121–22).

40 2,500 calories/day: Bennett 1955:table 1; Braudel 1981–84 (vol. 1):129–45 (European calorie levels).

41 Indian and European views on children: Kuppermann 2000:153–56; Williams 1936:29 (spoiling); Denys 1908:404; Ariés 1962 (European views).

41 Games: Wood 1977:103–06.

41 Character, training, and *pniese:* Salisbury 1989:229–31; Wood 1977:91–94 ("He that speaks," 91; "Beat them," 93 [I have modernized "winch," an obsolete form of "flinch"]); Winslow 1624:55–56; James ed. 1963:77; Kittredge ed. 1913:151, quoted in Axtell 1981:44.

42 Sachems: Wood 1977:97–99; Winslow 1624:56–60; Gookin 1792:154–55; Salisbury 1982:42–43; Dunford 2001:32–37; Johnson 1993:chap. 3. To the north, sachems were called sagamores, a distinction I am ignoring.

42 Population increase, attendant social change, and rise of political tensions: On the one hand, there is surprisingly little archaeological evidence for coastal agriculture (Ceci 1990a); on the other, there are multiple colonial reports that the seacoast was thick with farms. This scenario is an attempt to reconcile the apparently contradictory evidence (Bragdon 1996:146–53). See also Johnson 1993:chap. 3; Thomas 1979:24–44 ("The political scene," 30); Metcalf 1974; and esp. Petersen and Cowrie 2002.

43 Indigenous warfare as less bloody: Hariot 1588:36–37; Williams 1936:188 ("farre less"); Hirsch 1988; Kuppermann 2000:106–09; Russell 1980:187–94; Vaughan 1995:37–41. One reason for the low casualties, Williams observed, was that Indians fought "with [so much] leaping and dancing, that seldome an Arrow hits." (Evidently, the games of archery dodgem paid off.) Some activists have claimed that scalping was actually invented by white colonists. But European visitors witnessed the practice in the 1530s and 1540s, before any colonies existed north of Florida. "Hanging, disemboweling, beheading, and drawing and quartering were commonplace" in Europe, James Axtell observed, but not scalping. Each continent had its own forms of mutilation, and "it hardly seems worth arguing" which was worse (Axtell 1980:463).

43 Early European exploration: Some of the vast literature includes Kuppermann 1997a; Bourque and Whitehead 1994; Quinn 1974:chap. 1; Salisbury 1982:51–54; Axtell 1994:154–55 (Corte-Real).

44 Verrazzano as first visitor: In his popular book, *1421: The Year the Chinese Discovered America,* Gavin Menzies, a British ex–naval officer, argues that in that year a huge fleet led by warrior eunuchs sailed from China to the Americas. After the fleet lost many ships to

Caribbean reefs, it had to leave off "several thousand men and concubines" in Rhode Island. They were supposed to be picked up by subsequent expeditions, but the emperor who sponsored the expedition died, and his successor was not interested in globetrotting. The stranded Chinese melted into the local population. Verrazzano noted that the peoples of Rhode Island were more "beautiful" than other Indians, which to Menzies is evidence that they were not Indians. So enchanting is the image of 500-foot-long Chinese junks in New England that I am sorry to report that few researchers other than Menzies believe it (Menzies 2003:281–96 ["several thousand," 291]).

44 Verrazzano's account: Wroth ed. 1970:71–90, 133–43 ("densely populated," 137; "little bells," 138; "irksome clamor," 139; "showing," "barbarous," 140); Axtell 1992:156–57.

44 Indians' physical appearance: Gookin 1792:152–53 ("one part," 153); Higginson 1792:123; Morton 1632:32 ("as proper"); Wood 1977:82–83 ("more amiable," 82, "torture," 83); Russell 1980:30–32. See also the drawings of Algonquians further south by John White (Hulton 1984). Differences between colonial and native ways of treating the body are explored in Kuppermann 2000:chap. 2 (bow string, 55–56), and Axtell 2000:154–58.

46 Popularity of Indian hairstyles: Kuppermann 1997b:225 ("lovelocks"); Higginson 1792:123.

46 Indian views of Europeans: Jaenen 2000 (weak, 76; ugly, 77; sexually untrustworthy, 83; Micmac, 85; dirty, handkerchiefs, 87); Axtell 1988; Stannard 1992:5 (Indian cleanliness).

46 Two hundred British ships: Cell 1965.

48 Champlain's exploration: Biggar ed. 1922–36 (vol. 1):349–55, 397–401. See also, Salisbury 1982:62–66, and the enjoyable Parkman 1983 (vol. 1):191–93, 199.

48 Gorges and Maine: Gorges 1890a:204–07; Salisbury 1982:92–94. I have followed Salisbury rather than wholly accept Gorges's account, which is confused and confusing. Unlike Plymouth colony, the Maine expedition did not land in winter with no food. It lost only two members the first winter, whereas death and illness so beset the Pilgrims that in their first few months ashore they usually had only a few functioning people.

48 Pring: Pring 1905:51–63.

48 Smith and Pocahontas: The best retelling of the Pocahontas story I have come across is Gunn Allen 2003. A similar, briefer account is Richter 2001:70–78. An enjoyable nonscholarly account of Smith and Virginia is Milton 2000.

48 Smith in New England, Hunt kidnaps Tisquantum: Arber and Bradley eds. 1910 (vol. 1):192–205, 256–57 ("great troupes," "fortie," 205); (vol. 2):697–99; Bradford 1981:89–90; Winslow 1963b:52; 1963c:70; Gorges 1890a:209–11 ("worthlesse," 209; "warre," 211).

50 French sailors killed or enslaved: Winship 1905:252 (shipwreck); Winslow 1963c:27–28 (finding body); Bradford 1981:92; Hubbard 1848:54–55; Adams 1892–93:6–10.

50 Billington: Bradford 1981:259–60 (hanging, "profanest"), 97 (runaway), 173–74; Bradford 1906:13 ("knave"); Winslow 1963b:31 (shooting gun in ship); Winslow 1963d:69–72 (runaway); Prince 1855:291 (contempt charge); A. C. Mann 1976; Dillon 1975:203 ("troublesome").

50 Framing my ancestor: My grandfather told me that Billington was an excellent hunter and trapper. With this independent source of food, he could ignore colonial edicts. To take him down a peg, my grandfather claimed, the powers that be sent men to rob his traps. Billington caught on. He lay in wait and discovered a thief in the act. The thief shot at him. My ancestor, a much better shot, returned fire, with predictably lethal consequences. This story is unlikely but not impossible. The Billingtons were among the few families to survive the first winter intact, suggesting that John may indeed have been a fine hunter. And the Pilgrims' contemporary reputation for ridding themselves of religiously unsympathetic people was so widespread that in 1664 the poet Samuel Butler mocked the practice in his popular satire *Hudibras:* "Our brethren of NEW ENGLAND

use / Choice malefactors to excuse, / And hang the guiltless in their stead, / Of whom the Churches have less need" (Canto II, lines 409–12).

51 Actual first executions: During the catastrophic "starving time" (winter 1609–10) in Jamestown, according to colony governor George Percy, "one of our Colline murdered his [pregnant] wyfe Ripped the childe outt of her woambe and threw itt into the River and after chopped the Mother in pieces and salted her for his foode." Percy had the man tortured and executed (Percy 1922:267). In March 1623 a man at Wessagusset, a rival Massachusetts colony, was hanged for stealing maize from an Indian family (Morton 1632:108–10; Bradford 1981:129). Bradford calls Billington's execution "the first" in Plymouth (259), so my family can claim that our ancestor was the first person of European descent hanged in the Cape Cod area.

51 No idea where they were heading: According to Bradford, their intended destination was "some place about Hudson's River" (Bradford 1981:68), an assertion backed up by the diplomat John Cory, who surveyed Plymouth in 1622 on behalf of British investors (James ed. 1963:5–6). But they had earlier tried to obtain permission to settle in what is now New England, so some historians have argued that it is possible that they were going there. One theory is that the Dutch, who then had possession of the Hudson, bribed the *Mayflower*'s captain to steer them away (Morton 1669:11–12). In any case, they gave little evidence of knowing where they were going (Rutman 1960). Smith's claims, which seem to be true, are reported in Arber and Bradley eds. 1910 (vol. 2):891–92.

51 Pilgrim incompetence: Most of this catalog of error is lifted from Bates 1940:112–13.

51 Half the Pilgrims died: Accompanied by about 30 crew members, 102 people set sail. One died en route, but a child was born before landfall, the wonderfully named Oceanus Hopkins, making the party 102 again. Of these, 44 died before spring. Among them was Bradford's wife, Dorothy, thought to have drowned herself by leaping off the *Mayflower* rather than face the unknown continent (Deetz and Deetz 2000:39, 59–60).

51 Robbing Indian graves and houses: Bradford 1981:73–75; Winslow 1963b:19–29 ("providence," 26). Later the Pilgrims did try to compensate the Indians for the theft (Winslow 1963c:61–62).

51 English vs. continental financing for colonies, British colonists' flakiness and helplessness: Kuppermann 2000:3–4, 11–15, 148 ("utterly," 13); Cell 1965.

52 Inability to understand climate: The confusion is especially surprising given that a number of British visitors had kept careful track of the weather (e.g., Anon. 1979).

52 Time of drought: Stahle et al. 1998.

52 Thoreau's disdain: Thoreau 1906 (vol. 4):295–300 ("A party," 300).

52 Tisquantum's travels in New England: Baxter 1890:103–10 ("appears to," 106); Gorges 1890a:212–25; 1890b:26–30; Dermer 1619 ("void," 131). The line from *The Tempest* is in act 2, scene 2.

53 "Indians themselves": Panzer 1995:118–19 (text of *Sublimis Deus,* Paul III).

53 Slany: Cell 1965:615.

55 Epidemic: Morton 1637:22–24 ("died," 23; "Golgotha," 23); Hubbard 1848:54–55 (French sailor's curse); Spiess and Spiess 1987; Snow 1980:31–42; Snow and Lanphear 1988. Salisbury (1982:103–05) suggests that the disease was the plague, but Snow and Lanphear point out that this requires a chain of transmission that would have trouble getting established. According to John Smith, "where I had seene 100 or 200 Salvages [in 1614], there is scarce ten to be found [in 1620]" (Arber and Bradley eds. 1910 [vol. 2]:259). The Pilgrims may have seen evidence of the original disease carrier. One of the corpses they exhumed on Cape Cod had blond hair and was buried in a wrap of sailor's canvas (Winslow 1963b:27–28).

55 "The idea": Gunn Allen 2003:30.

55 Mather's experiment: Mather 1820 (vol. 1):507.

56 Wampanoag spiritual and political crises: Salisbury 1989:235–38 ("their deities," 236).

56 Plymouth and more than fifty villages: Pyne 1982:45–48; Cronon 1983:90.

56 Bradford and Gorges quotes: Anon. 1792:246 (attrib. to Bradford); Gorges, 1890b:77. From today's point of view, these opinions were both unfortunately sanguine and unfortunately common. Viz., John Winthrop, first governor of the rival colony in Massachusetts Bay, describing in May 1634 the legal implications of the loss of many natives to smallpox: "The Lord hathe cleared our title to what we possess" (Winthrop 1976:116); or Cotton Mather calmly explaining that the land had been swept free "of those pernicious creatures [Indians], to make room for better growth [Europeans]" (quoted in C. F. Adams 1892–93 [vol. 1]:12).

56 "Could make [the] English": Pratt 1858:485.

58 "He thinks we may": Winslow 1963b:58.

58 Indians and guns: Chaplin 2001:111–12; Percy 1905–07:414 (all Jamestown quotes).

58 Indian technology: Rosier 1605:21 (canoes); Kuppermann 2000:166–68 (shoes); Bourque and Whitehead 1994:136–42 (Indian shallops). To some readers, the notion that European technology did not determine the outcome of the culture clash may seem absurd. Compare, though, the difference between the colonial histories of the Americas and Africa. The indigenous inhabitants of both places had technology that is often described as wildly inferior. And both places were the target of sustained colonial enterprises by the same nations. In the Americas, though, the Indians were rapidly defeated. "The Indians die so easily that the bare look and smell of a Spaniard causes them to give up the ghost," a missionary commented in 1699 (quoted in Crosby 2003b:37). Yet the majority of Africa—which had, if anything, an even more "inferior" technological base—did not fall until the late nineteenth century. Technology was not a dominant factor.

59 Massasoit's negotiations: Winslow 1963b:43–59; Deetz and Deetz 2000:61–62.

59 Tisquantum's machinations, death: Bradford 1981:108–09 ("came running," "and he thought," "all was quiet"), 125–26 (Tisquantum's death); Morton 1637:103–05; Winslow 1963a:82 (thanksgiving); Humins 1987; Salisbury 1989; Shuffelton 1976.

61 Massasoit's son and war in 1675: The best short account I have encountered is the first section of Schultz and Tougias 1999. See also Richter 2001:90–109; Vaughan 1995:308–22; Salisbury 1982:Chap. 7.

61 1633 epidemic: Snow and Lanphear 1998.

3 / In the Land of Four Quarters

62 Pizarro's body: Maples and Browning 1994:213–19.

63 Ezell thesis: Ezell 1961.

63 Dobyns in Peru and Mexico: Interviews, Dobyns; Dobyns 2004.

63 Prescott as first full history: As opposed to colonial-era accounts.

64 Politicization of Andean studies: Beyers 2001. Among the better known examples (and actually a pretty good book) is Baudin 1961.

64 Dobyns's 1963 article: Dobyns 1963.

64 Comparison of Inka realm to other states in 1491: Fernández-Armesto 2001:390–402 ("imperial potential," 395).

65 Inka realm as empire: Peruvian historian María Rostworowski de Diez Canseco has argued that because the term "empire" has "Old World connotations"—it implies a sophisticated center that dominates "barbarians" on the periphery, as was the case for Rome—it should not be applied to the Inka, who overran societies bigger and more cosmopolitan than themselves (Rostworowski de Diez Canseco 1999:x). Although one can see what she means, the word is now used loosely to describe a situation in which "a

core polity gains control over a range of other societies" (D'Altroy 2002:6). And the Inka did exactly that.

65 Inka goals, methods: "The Inkas were coolly pragmatic, efficient, and totalitarian in their policies toward conquered nations, [attempting to impose] a restrictive area wide standardization of politics, religion, customs, and language. . . . They maintained order by instilling fear and using force rather than by encouraging knowledgeable participation" (Dobyns and Doughty 1976:48–49).

65 Inka road system: Hyslop 1984:esp. 215–24, 342–43. The network appears to have been planned carefully (Jenkins 2001:655–87).

65 "not with the Wars": Rowe 1946:329.

65 "where millions": Quoted in Lechtman 1996a:15. My next sentence is a revamped version of Lechtman's sentence following the quotation.

67 Steepest street: Filbert Street. I am grateful to Wade Roush for checking this comparison.

67 "a wide range": Diamond 1997:140.

67 20 of 34 lifezones: Burger 1992:12. Only 2 percent of Peru is today considered suitable for agriculture (ibid.).

68 "vertical archipelagoes": Murra 1967.

68 Inka origin accounts: Cobo 1979:103–07 ("extreme ignorance," 20; "ridiculous," 103).

69 Betanzos: Betanzos 1996 ("thirty small," 13; "two hundred," 19). For a discussion of his value as a source, see Fossa 2000.

69 Inkas vs. Chankas, Wiraqocha Inka vs. Inka Yupanki: Betanzos 1996:19–43 ("To this," 33; "crazy impulse," 36); Cieza de León 1998:317 (Pizarro sees skins); Cobo 1979:130–33 ("valiant prince," 130); Pachacuti Yamqui Salcamayhua 1879:270–73; D'Altroy 2002:62–65; Rostworowski de Diez Canseco 2001:78–119; Santa 1963. Three of the fifteen Spanish accounts of Inka history claim that Wiraqocha Inka, not Inka Yupanki, fought the Chankas and then his father. Among them is Cobo, who confusingly attributes what seem to be the same events to both. Rostworowski de Diez Canseco (1999:28–34) convincingly argues against Wiraqocha. Pachakuti literally means "he who remakes the world" or "he who turns over time and space," but I have followed Michael Moseley in an attempt to suggest how the name might have struck Inka ears (Moseley 2001:14).

69 Inka chronology: John H. Rowe laid out the timeline of the empire in an influential article (Rowe 1946:203). Rowe relied on the calculation in a manuscript from 1586, still not published in its entirety, by Father Miguel Cabello Balboa (Cabello Balboa 1920). A Swedish historian, Åke Wedin, fiercely criticized Rowe's use of this and other sources (Wedin 1963, 1966). An insurmountable problem with the accounts, Wedin insisted, was that they were not drawn from interviews with the elite record keepers who actually kept track of events. The implication was that most other Indians were as reliably informed about their society's history as, say, average U.S. citizens are about their society's history. Since Wedin's work historians have come to place a little more trust in Spanish chronicles, which although not taken from record keepers tended to be drawn from interviews with the educated elite. In addition, radiocarbon dating seems generally to support the chronology (Michczynski and Adamska 1997). Rowe's chronology is now typically viewed as roughly correct, though subject to debate.

70 Fall of Chincha: Castro and Ortega Morejón 1974:91–104 ("son of the Sun," 93; "Everything," 95). My thanks to Robert Crease for obtaining this article for me. See also Santillán 1879:14; Sarmiento de Gamboa 2000:113–14, 135 (brother left in command). As Sarmiento de Gamboa notes, Chincha was a minor incident in a much larger campaign against the bigger polity of Chimor (see Chap. 6). The rising claim on local labor both reflected a deliberate strategy by the Inka state of gradually increasing control and a rise in labor demand in the Inka state itself (Morris 1993:36–50).

71 Luttwak's book: Luttwak 1976.

71 Inka as hegemonic empire: D'Altroy 1987; Hassig 1985.

71 Austere, contemporary feel of Inka art and architecture: Paternosto 1996:219–22 (influence on twentieth-century art); Thomson 2003:60–62, 86–87, 246–49.

71 Qosqo and Awkaypata: Rowe 1991, 1990. I thank Patricia Lyon for sending me a copy of these articles. Descriptions of the structures are in Sarmiento de Gamboa 2000:85–91.

72 "point of a pin": Pizarro 1969:272–73. He was describing Saqsawaman fortress, at the edge of town, but the same is true of the structures in central Qosqo. Sancho was similarly impressed (Sancho 1917:156–57). One viceroy wrote in 1571 that an Inka fortress was "the work of the devil . . . for it does not seem possible that the strength and skill of men could have made it" (quoted in Wright:2005:57).

73 Zeq'e and Wak'a: D'Altroy 2002:155–67 ("otherwise diligent," 156 [D'Altroy closed his remark by wryly noting "(see below)"]). He relied on Bauer 1998, which I have also done. The classic colonial account is from Cobo 1990:51–84 ("more than a thousand," 9). But as a *Booknews* reviewer dryly noted, Cobo "based his account of [Inka] religion almost entirely on previous literature (his employer having eradicated his subject)."

73 Calendar: The Inka calendar and their means of reckoning time were so complex that I have basically ducked and avoided them. See instead Aveni 1995:278–304.

73 Inka economics and labor system: Cobo 1979:189–93, 211–34; La Lone 1982:312–36; Murra 1980; Rostworowski de Diez Canseco 2001:182–201; D'Altroy 2002:263–86.

74 Absence of money in Europe: Braudel 1981–84 (vol. 1):467–68.

74 "managed to eradicate": Vargas Llosa 1992:26.

74 Population reshuffling: Cieza de León 1959:59–63; Cobo 1979:189–93; D'Altroy 2002:248–49; Rowe 1946:269–70.

75 Disproportionate size of conquest: The contrast between the tiny Spanish force and the vast Inka empire was noted as early as 1534, in the first narrative of the conquest, *Verdadera relación de la conquista del Perú*, by Francisco de Xerez. "When in ancient times have such few [triumphed] against so many?" he crowed. "And who has equaled those of Spain? Certainly not the Jews nor the Greeks nor Romans, about whom most is told." Although the Romans subjugated many lands, Jerez said, "it was with equal or greater numbers of people, in known territories, provided with the usual sustenance, and with paid captains and armies. But our Spaniards . . . were never more than two or three hundred, sometimes a hundred or even less. . . . And the many times they traveled, they were neither paid nor forced but went of their own will and at their own cost" (Xerez 1938:16–17).

76 Inka "crown" and clothes, saving of waste: Pizarro 1969:222–26 (clothing and headband); Cobo 1979:244–47; Ruiz de Arce 1933:361 (spittle), cited in Hemming 2004:51; Rowe 1946:258–59.

76 Thupa Inka's grandeur, military career: Sarmiento de Gamboa 2000:112–19, 122–23 ("worshiped and adored," 112); D'Altroy 2002:67–74. The description of the litter is from Thupa Inka's successor, but seems to apply in general (Pachacuti Yamqui Salcamayhua 1879:79).

76 Thupa Inka's marriage(s): Betanzos 1996:119–20; Cobo 1979:142; D'Altroy 2002:103–06. As Rowe notes, multiple sister-marriages were embedded in Inka culture—the leader of the four brothers who arrived in Qosqo married his four sisters (Rowe 1946:317–18). In addition, Andean societies traditionally recognized that a man owed obligations to his sister's son. By ensuring that his nephew was also his son, the Inka tried to reduce the potential for intrafamilial conflict (Rostworowski de Diez Canseco 2001:103–04).

76 Troubled accession of Wayna Qhapaq: Sarmiento de Gamboa 2000:133–38; Pachacuti Yamqui Salcamayhua 1879:293–97; Rostworowski de Diez Canseco 2001:104–05. According to one report, Wayna Qhapaq was sixteen (Anello Oliva 1998:77). See also, Peñaherrera de Costales and Costales Samienego 1964.

76 Makework projects: Cieza de León 1959:77 ("mountain"), 137–38.
77 Ecuador campaign: Cobo 1979:155–60 ("commanded," 155, "prepared himself," 156); Betanzos 1996:182–83; Cieza de León 1959:46–50, 77–78; Cabello Balboa 1920:84–108; Niles 1999:97–105. Betanzos, but not Cobo, mentions Atawallpa's disgrace; Cobo, but not Betanzos, describes Wayna Qhapaq's discomfiture; omissions are consonant with the chroniclers' biases.
78 "When his captains": Pizarro 1969:198–99, 228 (vampire-bat wool).
78 Wayna Qhapaq's death, succession battle: Cieza de León 1959:78–87; 1998:187–93; Pachacuti Yamqui Salcamayhua 1879:309–24; Sarmiento de Gamboa 2000:144–60; Cabello Balboa 1920:113–21, 128–72; Anello Oliva 1998:87–92. A clear summary is D'Altroy 2002:76–83; see also, Rostworowski de Diez Canseco 2001:110–25. Betanzos's narrative, though useful, is understandably biased; his wife was Atawallpa's sister (Betanzos 1996:183–234). Pedro Pizarro's version of events interestingly highlights the internal politics of Qosqo (Pizarro 1969:198–206). Garcilaso de la Vega says that Wayna Qhapaq's death followed omens and prophecies of the collapse of the empire, which seems unlikely. If true, though, it may account for a certain fatalism toward the Spanish among the Inka elite (Gheerbrant ed. 1962:284–89). He also suggests that the war occurred after Wayna Qhapaq split up Tawantinsuyu in a Lear-like fashion, giving Atawallpa a rump kingdom to the north. Most ethnographers and historians disagree. Garcilaso's description of the war itself as consisting in essence of a single big engagement outside Qosqo is at variance with other accounts.
79 Washkar's marriage and his mother's marriage: Pachacuti Yamqui Salcamayhua 1879:308; Cabello Balboa 1920:120–21 ("begging," 121).
80 Cieza de León casualty estimates: Cieza de León 1959:84 (16,000), 87 (35,000).
80 Skull cup: "I saw the head with the skin, the dried flesh, and its hair, and it had the teeth closed, and between them was a silver straw, and attached to the top of the head was a gold cup [with a hole in the bottom that entered the skull], from which he drank when memories of [Atawallpa's] war against his brother came to mind; he put *chicha* in the cup, from which it came out through the mouth, and he drank through the straw" (Mena 1930:250–53). The cup is also mentioned in Cieza de León 1959:84.
80 Pizarro and Atawallpa at Cajamarca: I draw mainly on Hemming 2004:30–85. See also, Sancho 1917:9–19; Mena 1930:231–81; Pizarro 1969:171–221 ("made water," 179–80); Ruiz de Arce 1933:363 ("mounds"), cited in Hemming 2004:42.
81 Spaniards and gold: Restall 2003:22–23 ("nonperishable," 23), 34–37, 65–67.
82 "What could," "No amount": Hemming 2004:115, 158. See also the vigorously argued Guilmartin 1991.
82 Marveling at failure to develop steel: "It is worthy of remark, that . . . the Peruvians, in their progress towards civilization, should never have detected the use of iron, which lay around them in abundance" (Prescott 2000:810).
82 Andean metallurgy: Burger and Gordon 1998; Lechtman 1996b ("hardness," 35; "plasticity," 37); 1993 ("eminent scholar," 253); 1984.
83 Different contexts of technology: Interviews, Lechtman ("people solved"), Conklin, Leonard Morse-Fortier (force of sling projectiles); Ihde 2000.
84 Inka ships: Cieza de León 1998: 75–76; Heyerdahl 1996; Hemming 2004:25; Prescott 2000:854–55; interview, Vranich (replica boat created for documentary). See the account of the new ship at http://www.reedboat.org.
84 "without endangering themselves": Sancho 1917:62.
84 Importance and fineness of textiles in Tawantinsuyu: Murra 1964 (stripping soldiers, 718); Lechtman 1993:254–59 (five hundred threads per inch, 257). "The [cotton] clothes they made were so fine that we [Spaniards] thought they were made of silk, worked with figures of beaten gold, beautifully made" (Mena 1930:225).

84 Cloth armor: Lechtman 1993:256; Murra 1964:718 (stripping of soldiers); Rowe 1946:274–75; Montell 1929:Fig. 21.

84 "with enough force": Enríquez de Guzmán 1862:99.

84 Inka rebellion with flaming missiles: Hemming 2004:193–94; Prescott 2000:1021–23.

84 Inka armies and horses: Hemming 2004 ("Even when," 111–12; "dreaded," 158).

85 Inka roads and horses: Letter, Pizarro, H., to Oidores of Santo Domingo, 23 Nov. 1533, quoted in Hemming 2004:31 ("so bad"); Prescott 2000:954. On one steep road "all made of steps of very small stones," Pedro Sancho wrote, Pizarro's "horses toiled so much that, when they had finished going up, the greater part of them had lost their shoes and worn down the hoofs of all four feet" (Sancho 1917:63).

86 Inka military techniques: Sancho 1917:67; Hemming 2004:195 (bolas); Prescott 2000:922, 984.

87 Historians ignore disease: Interviews, Crosby, Denevan, Dobyns. According to Dobyns, "the published works focused on New World historic epidemiology could be counted on the fingers of one hand" at that time (Dobyns 1995). Actually, Dobyns's own count is eighteen articles prior to 1964. Still, most researchers in the field did not "seem to be paying much attention" (ibid.), e.g., the claim that "not until 1720 did any great losses through pestilence occur in Peru" (Kubler 1946:336). Peruvian researchers noted the epidemics (Patrón 1894 [proposing that Wayna Qhapaq died of bartonellosis, not smallpox]), but others were like U.S. researchers in failing to grasp the impact of disease (Vellard 1956). I am grateful to Robert Crease for helping me obtain a copy of this last article.

87 Cieza de León: Cook and Cook 1998 (bio); Cieza de León 1959:52 ("great plague").

87 Elite losses to smallpox: Sarmiento de Gamboa 2000:144–45; Pachacuti Yamqui Salcamayhua 1879:307 ("scabs," "millions"); Murúa 1962–64 (vol. 1):136 ("infinite"), quoted in Crosby 2003b:53; Pizarro 1969:196–97; Cobo 1979:160; Poma de Ayala 2001:114, 141, 288; Hopkins 1983:208–11. For a dissenting view, see McCaa, Nimlos, and Hampe-Martínez 2004.

88 Evolution of smallpox: Baxby 1981; Gubser and Smith 2002.

88 "virgin soil": Crosby 1976.

88 India smallpox study: Rao 1972:37, cited in Fenn 2001:21.

88 "may well have been halved": Dobyns 1963:497.

88 Thucydides' account of epidemic: Thucydides 1934:109–14.

89 Not in a European language: Crosby 2003b:xxii.

89 Royal mummies: Pizarro 1969:202–04, 251–54 ("the greater part," 203); Estete, M.d., untitled narrative of journey to Pachacamac, quoted in Hemming 2004:127 ("seated"); Sancho 1917:159, 170, 195, 200; Rowe 1946:308; D'Altroy 2002:96–99, 141–42. Sarmiento de Gamboa matter-of-factly describes Inka methods of storing bodies after death, though he only uses the word "mummy" once (Sarmiento de Gamboa 2000:120–23, 135–36, 145–46).

89 Burning of Thupa Inka: Sarmiento de Gamboa 2000:121, 159; Betanzos 1996:74–79; D'Altroy 2002:108.

90 Atawallpa execution: Rowe 1997. I thank Patricia Lyon for sending me this article.

91 "win the land": Pizarro 1969:199. See also, Sancho 1917:171–72; Wright 1992:72–75.

91 European failures without epidemics, factions: Restall 2003:70–72 (Mexico, Florida); Hemming 1978:69–84 (Brazil); White 1991: esp. Chap. 4 (France).

92 Additional smallpox epidemics: Hopkins 1983:212–13 ("They died by scores," quoted on 213).

92 Typhus, flu, etc., 90 percent death toll: Dobyns 1963. Dobyns's argument was supported almost two decades later in Noble David Cook's book-length survey, which argued that

six main epidemics hit Tawantinsuyu between 1524 and 1614, reducing the population by an estimated 93 percent (N. D. Cook 1981).

92 Smallpox in Hispaniola: The first evidence of smallpox's arrival is in a letter of 10 January 1519 by the Hieronymite Fathers, then entrusted with ruling Hispaniola. At the time, the disease had killed a third of the island's inhabitants and spread to Puerto Rico (Henige 1986:17–19). Smallpox may not have been the first Caribbean epidemic. Francisco Guerra, a medical historian at the Universidad de Alcalá de Henares, in Spain, makes a strong case for a swine influenza epidemic in 1493 that "was responsible for the disappearance of the American Indians in the Antilles" (Guerra 1988:305). Noble David Cook suggests the epidemic was smallpox (N. D. Cook 2003).

93 Smallpox hits Mexico: The evidence is examined carefully in McCaa 1995. See also, Hopkins 1983:204–08 and the sources in Chap. 4.

93 "Debated since": Denevan ed. 1976:xvii. Denevan was far from alone in his interest. At about the same time, for instance, Wilbur Jacobs, a historian at the University of California in Santa Barbara, described the puzzle of native numbers as "truly one of the most fascinating number games in history" (Jacobs 1974:123).

94 Mooney: Mooney 1928; Ubelaker 1976, 1988. Mooney's article was posthumous.

94 Kroeber's estimates: Kroeber 1934 ("sharply localized," 25); 1939:31, 134, 166. Greenland is included in Kroeber's population density figure, lowering it somewhat.

94 Sauer, Cook, and Borah: Among their many works are Sauer 1935; Cook and Simpson 1948; Borah and Cook 1964; Cook and Borah 1963, 1979. See also, Denevan 1996c.

94 "Historians and anthropologists": Dobyns 1995.

94 World population in 1500: United Nations Population Division 1999:5.

94 "greatest destruction": Lovell 1992:426. See also, Crosby 1986:208–09; Porter 1998:163; Jacobs 1974:128.

95 Dobyns's 1966 article, Denevan's book: Dobyns 1966; Denevan 1976.

95 Dobyns's ideas attacked: Author's interviews, Dobyns, Russell Thornton, Shepard Krech. See also Thornton 1987:34–36; Krech 1999:83–84; Henige 1998, 1990, 1978b.

95 Dobyns revises figures: Dobyns 1983:42. The new figure was for North America only.

95 Henige bio, critiques: Interview, Henige; Henige 1998 (bio, 4–5; "Suspect," 314); 1978b (Hispaniola); Osborne 1998.

95 "You always hear": Interview and email, Stiffarm. The unconscious persistence of the view that before Columbus the Americas were uninhabited, or almost so, is amazing. As late as 1986 Bernard Bailyn, past president of the American Historical Society, published a book called *The Peopling of British North America: An Introduction* (Bailyn 1986). The book is about British immigration. But the title also suggests that before Europeans the land was not peopled. Indeed, Indians are almost not to be found in the text.

95 "crater": Interview, Wilson; Wilson 1999.

4 / Frequently Asked Questions

97 De Soto: Duncan 1995; Mena 1930:264–66 (Challcochima). De Soto, Hemming observed, was "as brutal as any other conquistador. He [led] the force that raped the mamaconas [nuns, more or less] of Cajas during the march toward Cajamarca. His reputation among some modern writers of being more humane than his companions is undeserved" (Hemming 2004:555).

97 De Soto expedition: The numbers of men and animals differ somewhat in different accounts. I use Ramenofsky 1987:59. The basic sources are "Gentleman of Elvas" 1922 and its apparent predecessor, Fernández de Biedma 1922. These and other documents are collected in Clayton, Knight, and Moore eds. 1993. The state of scholarly knowledge

is assayed in Galloway ed. 1997. Popular accounts include Wilson 1999:134–37; Morgan 1993:72–75; Parkman 1983 (vol. 1):28–31.

97 Hudson's reconstruction of route: Interview, Hudson; Hudson 1993. For a fierce debate on the reliability of these reconstructions, see Henige 1993; Hudson, DePratter, and Smith 1993; Hudson et al. 1994.

97 De Soto's passage over Mississippi: "Gentleman of Elvas" 1922 (vol. 1):112–17 (all quotes, 113); Fernández de Biedma 1922 (vol. 2):25–28. See also Rollings 1995:39–40.

98 La Salle expedition: Parkman 1983 (vol. 1):920–30.

98 Contrast between De Soto and La Salle's experiences: Author's interviews, Galloway, Hudson, Ramenofsky; Ramenofsky 1987:55–63; Burnett and Murray 1993:228.

98 Pigs as source for epidemic: Ramenofsky and Galloway 1997:271–73; Crosby 1986:172–76, 273; Crosby 2003b:77 (importance of pigs to Spanish).

99 Indian lack of domesticated animals, lactose intolerance: Crosby 1986:19, 27; Ridley 2000:192–94. Francisco Guerra notes that the Philippines did not experience epidemics from colonization, though its inhabitants were as isolated as Indians. The critical difference, he suggests, was the existence of domesticated animals, especially pigs, in the Philippines (Guerra 1988:323).

99 Caddo and Coosa: Perttula 1993, 1991:512–14; M. T. Smith 1994:264–65; M. T. Smith 1987.

99 Mass graves in the Southeast: M. T. Smith 1987:60–68.

100 1918 flu epidemic: Crosby 2003a.

100 Plague origin, losses: Epidemiologists increasingly question whether the Black Death was bubonic plague. Rats and fleas carry bubonic plague, but the Black Death spread faster—and over colder land—than these animals usually travel. And *Y. pestis* has never been shown to be as contagious as the Black Death. The epidemic may instead have been of a hemorrhagic fever like Ebola (Scott and Duncan 2001). I am grateful to David Henige for drawing this discussion to my attention. For losses, see, e.g., Wrigley 1969:63.

100 Population nadir: Ubelaker 1992:169–76, table 3. The 1890 U.S. census listed the Native American population as 237,000 (United States Bureau of the Census 1937:3, table 2). But it is widely believed that the Census Bureau undercounted, both because it did not accurately survey many native areas and because its definition of "Indian" was too restrictive. Most demographers double the reported number.

100 Zambardino critique: Zambardino 1980 ("the errors multiply," 8; "meaningful," 18).

101 "no better than": Crosby 1992:175.

101 Skepticism: Interviews, Ubelaker, Snow; Snow 1995 ("no support," 1604); 1992; Snow and Lanphear 1988. I believe David Henige coined "Low Counter" and "High Counter."

101 Historians' reluctance: Calloway 2003:415–16 ("boggle," 415); McNeill 1998:19–23.

102 1967 measles epidemic: Interviews, Napoleon Chagnon, Thomas Headland, Francis Black, Patrick Tierney; Neel et al. 1970; Neel 1977:155–68. The epidemic became the subject of controversy when U.S. journalist Patrick Tierney accused Neel and his anthropologist coauthor, Chagnon, of exacerbating and perhaps even causing it in the course of an unethical experiment on the effects of vaccination (Tierney 2000). After a furor, researchers generally agreed that the likelihood that Neel and Chagnon had spread measles was negligible (Mann 2000a, 2001; Neel et al. 2001); as the main text indicates, the epidemic apparently originated with the Tootobi missionaries (Headland 2000). The Yanomamo are also known as Yanomami, Yanoama, and Yanomamö, the different terms coming from different dialects.

103 Distribution of blood types: Crosby 2003b:22–30. For a more complete explanation, see Crawford 1998:95–101.

103 Relative lack of genetic disease: Author's interviews, Black, Crosby, Dobyns (cystic

fibrosis, Huntington's chorea); Black 2004:155 (asthma and autoimmune diseases); Hurtado, Hurtado, and Hill 2004:185 (diabetes). Dobyns stressed that the evidence is weak. Because Europeans recorded "things like the lack of beggars and madmen in city streets," he told me, "you can assemble a sketchy picture" of societies with little genetic disease. "But as Henige would say," Dobyns remarked of his fiercest critic, "it's an argument from silence."

104 Black and HLA types: Author's interviews, Black, Stephen S. Hall; Black 1992, 1994, 2004; Crawford 1998:131–34. HLA classes are succinctly explained in Hall 1997:368–69. My thanks to Steve Hall for walking me through this material.

105 "Europeans' capacity": Jennings 1975:22.

105 Russian fur trade: Standard histories include Fisher 1943; Lincoln 1994.

105 1768–69 epidemic: Bril 1988:238 ("No one knows"); Samwell 1967:1252–59 ("Ruins," 1252); Sauer 1802:306–08. Sauer's death tally of 5,368 is identical to that of the writer William Coxe (Coxe 1780:5) and reasonably congruent with the estimate that "three fourths" of the populace died by French consul Jean Baptiste Barthelemy Lesseps, who was traveling in Kamchatka at the time (Lesseps 1790:128–29 ["three fourths," 128]). I am grateful to Elizabeth Fenn for providing me with her notes on these references, from which I have taken the material from Lessep and Sauer.

105 "As soon as": Füch 1988:169–70. Again I thank Prof. Fenn.

107 Helper-T cell hypothesis: Hurtado, Hurtado and Hill 2004.

107 Revolutionary War epidemic: Interviews, Fenn; Fenn 2001 (start of Boston epidemic, 46; ten to thirty a day, 47; one day before the Declaration, 53–54; "Ethiopian regiment," 57–61; Quebec, 62–71; Adams, 79).

108 Mexico City epidemic: Calloway 2003:417–19 ("It seems likely," 561); Fenn 2001:138–40 (Fenn suggests that a third epidemic, which moved west from New Orleans, may have "collided" with the Mexico City epidemic in the Southwest).

108 Hopi-Nermernuh-Shoshone-Blackfoot connection: Thompson 1916:318–25, 336–38 ("with our sharp," 336–37); Calloway 2003:419–21 (Sioux, 421); Fenn 2001:211–22. See also, Ewers 1973. "Blackfoot" usually refers to groups in Canada; "Blackfeet," to those in the United States.

109 "winter counts": Sundstrom 1997; Calloway 2003:424. In Sundstrom's survey of winter counts, all but one of the fifteen that cover 1780–82 characterized at least one of the years with the symbol for an epidemic, though some called it measles instead of smallpox (many groups initially did not distinguish them). Plains Indians defined a year as the period between the first snowfall of one winter and the first snowfall of the next, so it was not the same as a European year.

110 Pox in Northwest: Calloway 2003:421–23; Fenn 2001:224–32 ("great preponderance," 227), 250–58; Harris 1994; Boyd 1999:esp. 21–39.

110 Vancouver expedition: Vancouver 1984 (vol. 2):516–40 and passim ("promiscuously scattered," 516); Puget 1939:198 ("pitted").

110 Quarantine: Braudel 1981–84 (vol. 1):86–87; Salisbury 1982:106 ("could only"); Cronon 1983:88.

110 Wider impact of epidemics: Crosby 1992; Calloway 2003:419–26; Stannard 1991:532–33; Thornton 1987; Hopkins 1994:48 ("my people"); Salisbury 1982: 105–06.

110 Death of Hawaiian king and queen: Kuykendall 1947:76–81.

111 Montreal peace negotiations: Havard 2001:49, 65 (Haudenosaunee losses), 130–02 (epidemic and Kondiaronk's death).

111 Former Haudenosaunee captives: Brandão 1997:72–81.

111 Fates of Cree, Shoshone, Omaha: Calloway 2003:422–26 ("The country," 422). See also, Campbell 2003.

112 1524 meeting: Sahagún 1980; Klor de Alva 1990. See also, Motolinía 1950:37–38, 174–86 (de Valencia's life).

112 "bishops and pampered prelates": Prescott 2000:637.

112 Franciscan-Mexica debate: Sahagún 1980:lines 109, 115, 117, 217–18, 223–29, 235–37, 759–63, 1054 ("gods were not powerful," 54 [summary]). See also, León-Portilla 1963:62–70.

115 Teotihuacán and its influence: Often-cited works include Cowgill 1997; Carrasco, Jones, and Sessions eds. 2000; Berlo ed. 1993.

116 Mexica arrival date: Smith 1984.

116 Tezozómoc's account: Quoted in Sullivan and Knab eds., trans. 1994:98–100.

117 Tlacaélel: Chimalpahin Quauhtlehuanitzin 1997 (vol. 1):41–53, 135–45; (vol. 2):33–37, 89, 109; León-Portilla 1992a:xxxvii–xli ("It is not fitting," xxxviii); 1963:158–66. As Chimalpahin put it, Tlacaélel "was the instigator, the originator, through wars [of the system] by which he made the great city of México Tenochtitlán eminent and exalted" (35; trans. slightly altered for readability).

118 "In this Sun": Anon. 1994:66.

119 "tortillas": Durán 1994:231.

119 "moral combat": León-Portilla 1963:216.

119 Cortés on sacrifice: Cortés 1986:35–36 (both quotes). See also, Durán 1994:406 (excitedly, raising the toll to "2,000, 3,000, 5,000, or 8,000 men" a day on special occasions).

119 Denial of sacrifice: Hassler 1992; Moctezuma and Solis Olguín 2003 (indigenous images of sacrifice). The anthropologist Michael Harner argued (1977) that the human sacrifice and cannibalism of the Mexica were "natural and rational," "the only possible solution" (both 132) to supply protein to a dense population with no domesticated animals. But the Mexica lived on a lake with abundant fish and aquatic life and also obliged conquered peoples to ship them food (Ortiz de Montellano 1978). See also, Graulich 2000.

119 European executions: Braudel 1981–84 (vol. 2):516–18 (Tyburn, "the corpses," 518); Pepys 1970 (vol. 5):21 Jan 1664 ("at least").

119 English executions, population: Gatrell 1994:6–15; Wrigley 1983:121.

120 Nahuatl corpus: Frances Karttunen, pers. comm.

120 *Tlamatinime:* León-Portilla 1963:9–24, 62–81, 136 (quotes, 12–13).

120 Nezahualcóyotl poems on mortality: Peñafield 1904, quoted in Sullivan and Knab eds. 1994:163 ("Truly"—I slightly altered the first line to scan better); León-Portilla 1963:6 ("Do flowers"); 1992:81 ("Like a painting"); Nabokov 1989:19 ("brief crack").

121 Nahuatl rhetoric: Author's interviews, Karttunen; Garibay 1970:115.

121 Art and truth: León-Portilla 1963:71–79 ("nothing is 'true,' " 73; "He goes," 75; "From whence," 77).

123 Northwest Coast art: Jonaitis 1991:chaps. 1, 8.

123 Spanish reactions to Tenochtitlán: Díaz de Castillo 1975:214–19; Cortés 1986:102–12 ("can there," 108–09; "obliterate," 88).

123 Conquest of alliance and disease's role: Thomas 1995. Crosby (1986:200) calls Cortés's victory "a triumph of the [smallpox] virus."

129 Postconquest population decline: Borah 1976; Borah and Cook 1964; Cook and Borah 1963 (25.2 million, 88); Borah 1951; Cook and Simpson 1948. For postconquest epidemics in Mexico and New Spain, see the thorough discussions in Prem 1992; N. D. Cook and Lovell 1992; the other articles in N. D. Cook and Lovell eds. 1992; Malvido 1973. Cook and Borah's estimate was a best guess; more confidently, they argued that the precontact population was between eighteen and thirty million.

129 "We Christians": Cieza de León 1959:62.

129 Holocaust and moral capital: Examples include Thornton 1987; Stannard 1992; Churchill 1997. To be clear: Many of the books and articles that employ the term "holocaust," such

as Russell Thornton's *American Indian Holocaust and Survival* (1987), are careful works of scholarship. But their authors wish also to make a political point, one that in their view flows directly from their research. Sensitive to language, they have selected a charged term to convey that point. For discussions of the moral capital that is the reward of mass victimhood, see Stannard 2001; Alexander 1994:esp. 195.

129 "Very probably": Katz 1994 (vol. 1):20 (emphasis in original).

130 "economic depression": Borah 1951:27.

130 Holmes: Quoted in Stannard 1992:244.

131 Inadvertent subjugation: I made this argument myself in Chap. 2.

131 Siege of Kaffa: O'Connell 1989:171.

131 "And what was": Churchill 2003:53.

131 "the Spaniards are": Klor de Alva 1992:xx–xxi.

132 Díaz de Castillo: This line is not in any recent English translation, all of which are abridged; it is the last sentence of chapter 174 in the Spanish original.

132 Argument in Spanish court: Detailed in Pagden 1990: Chap. 1.

132 Spanish view of sickness: Porter 1998; interviews, Crease, Denevan, Lovell.

132 Salomon: Salomon 1993.

132 Las Casas: Las Casas 1992b:28 ("beehive"), 31 ("twelve million"). See also, Motolinía 1950:38–40.

133 Colonial accounts came to seem exaggerated: "Modern students commonly have been inclined to discount early opinions of native numbers, but rarely specified their reasons for doing so" (Sauer 1935:1). Responding to Sauer, the anthropologist Alfred L. Kroeber simply said, without further explanation, "I am likely to reject most [sixteenth- and seventeenth-century documents] outright" (Kroeber 1939:180). See also, Cook and Borah 1971 (vol. 1):376–410 ("Sixteenth-century," 380).

133 Numbers creep down: Jennings 1975:16–20.

133 Forty or fifty million: Spinden 1928:660 (50 to 75 million "souls" lost); Rivet, Stresser-Pean, and Loukotka 1952 (40 to 45 million).

133 "Most of the arrows," Henige's estimate: Author's interviews, Denevan, Henige.

133 "a very high population": Zambardino 1978. Henige responded in Henige 1978a.

5 / *Pleistocene Wars*

137 Discovery of Lagoa Santa skeletons: Calogeras 1933 (reproducing Lund's initial letters of discovery); Mattos 1939. Lund and his successors did not well document their initial location (Soto-Heim 1994:81–82; Hrdlička et al. 1912:179–84).

137 Fifteen thousand years: Laming-Emperaire 1979. Other researchers got even older dates, e.g., Prous 1986. Other very early Brazilian dates include Beltrão et al. 1986.

137 Morphology of skulls: Neves, Meyer, and Pucciarelli 1996; Soto-Heim 1994:86–103; Neves and Pucciarelli 1991; Beattie and Bryan 1984; Mattos 1946.

138 North American scoffing: One example: "These claims [of great antiquity] have long been shown to be erroneous, although the proponents of early glacial humans in the area remain vociferous" (Bruhns 1994:62). No citation for the refutation is provided.

138 Botocudos history: Wright and Carneiro de Cunha 2000; Paraíso 1999 (*botoques*, 423–24); Paraíso 1992:esp. 240–43 ("just war," 241).

138 Botocudos' purported similarity to Lagoa Santa Man: Interview, Pena; Soto-Heim 1994:84.

139 Two genomes: I borrow the phrase from Margulis and Sagan 2001. Margulis pioneered the contemporary theory of the origin of mitochondria.

139 Human genome project: Genome International Sequencing Consortium 2001; Venter et

al. 2001. The announcement was in June 2000; publication followed seven months later. These genome maps were preliminary; biologists put together a 99.9 percent complete picture only in 2003.

139 Mitochondrial genome project: Anderson et al. 1981.

139 Mitochondria in sperm: Gyllensten et al. 1991.

139 History of mtDNA research: Richards and Macaulay 2001.

139 Four haplogroups: Schurr et al. 1990; Horai et al. 1993; Torroni and Wallace 1995; Bandelt 2003. In 1998 scientists reported a fifth, very rare haplogroup. Also found in Europe, it may be a legacy of Genghis Khan's incursion (Brown et al. 1998).

140 Disdain for amateurs: As far back as 1893, William J. McGee reported with satisfaction that the Anthropological Section of the American Association for the Advancement of Science was refreshingly free "of those pseudoscientific communications which tend to cluster about every branch of science in its formative period . . . anthropology is rapidly taking form as an organized body of knowledge no less definite than the older sciences" (McGee 1900:768).

141 Taino Letter, Columbus, C., to Santangel, L.D., 14 Mar. 1493, trans. A. B. Hart and E. Channing, in Eliot ed. 1909–14, online at http://www.bartleby.com/43/2.html.

142 Test of divinity: Benzoni 1857:77.

142 Motecuhzoma and Spanish "gods": Restall 2003:108–20. For an example of the story, see Prescott 2000:171–73; Tuchman 1984:11–14 ("wooden," 14).

142 Northeast and supernatural powers: Trigger 1991.

142 Choctaw and Zuñi origins: Cushman 1999:199; Bunzel 1932.

143 "mountains of Ararat": Genesis 8:4 (King James version).

143 Christian befuddlement: Hallowell 1960.

143 José de Acosta wrestles with question: Acosta 2002:51–74 ("contradict Holy Writ," "Europe or Asia," 61; "must join," 63; refutation of Lost Tribes theory, 71–72).

143 Candidate ancestors: Wauchope 1962:3. The full list of candidates is even longer, but some pride of place should be given to the Welsh, who have had a widespread following for two hundred years. As Lewis and Clark began their journey across the continent, Thomas Jefferson tried to put them in contact with a man who had come from Wales to search for errant bands of Welsh-speaking white Indians (Letter, Jefferson, T., to Lewis, M., 22 Jan. 1804, available from the Library of Congress at http://memory.loc .gov/cgi-bin/query/r?ammem/mtj:@field(DOCID+@lit(je000060)). See also, Williams 1949a, 1949b. In an earlier article (Mann 2002c), I incorrectly wrote that Jefferson himself had instructed them to look for Welsh Indians.

143 Most widely accepted answer: Hrdlička 1912 ("the most widespread theory, and one with the remnants of which we meet to this day, was that the American Indians represented the so-called Lost Tribes of Israel," 3); Kennedy 1994:225–31 (Mormons); Hallowell 1960:4–6 (Penn, Mather). See also, Parfitt 2002.

143 Lost Tribes of Israel: II Kings 17:4–24, 18:9–12 ("So was Israel," 17:23); II (or IV) Esdras 13:39–51 ("a distant land," 42–48); Ezekiel 37:15–26 ("take the children," 21); Jeremiah 13:11, 33:7–8. All quotes except Esdras from King James version; Esdras is from *New English Bible,* as it is not in the King James version.

144 Ussher's calculation: Ussher 1658:1 (23 Oct. 4004); 68 (721 B.C.).

144 Ussher's authority: White 1898:Chap. 6 ("his dates"). One modern history says that although few endorsed "the exact detail" of Ussher's chronology, its precepts ruled "general thought about man's past" (Daniel and Renfrew 1986:22).

144 Discovery of European Pleistocene remains: Grayson 1983. I have simplified the story somewhat. In 1858 British geologists, Sir Charles Lyell among them, unearthed tools and Pleistocene fossils in an English cave. Twenty-one years before, Jacques Boucher de

Crèvecoeur de Perthes, a French customs officer and amateur scientist, had made a similar but larger find near Abbéville, in northern France. His announcement was met with ridicule, some of it from Lyell. A year after the British discovery, Lyell and other scientists went to Abbéville, decided that Boucher de Perthes had been right all along, and issued gracious public apologies. From that point on, the scientific consensus was in favor of an early origin of humankind.

145 Abbott's finds, proselytizing: Abbott 1876 ("driven," 72); 1872a ("so primitive," 146); 1872b.

146 Bureau of American Ethnology: Meltzer 1994; 1993:chaps. 3, 5; Judd 1967. The Smithsonian's brief history of the Bureau of American Ethnology is at http://www.nmnh .si.edu/anthro/outreach/depthist.html.

146 Holmes critique: Interview, Meltzer; Meltzer 1992; 1994:9–11; Hough 1933.

147 Abbott, McGee, and the Paleolithic Wars: Abbott 1892a ("'The stones are inspected," 345); 1892b ("scientific men of Washington," 270); 1883a ("high degree," 303); 1883b ("more 'knowing,'" 327); 1884 ("neither among," 253); Meltzer 2003; 1994:11–12; 1993:41–50; Cultural Resource Group 1996.

148 Hrdlička's life work: Meltzer 1994:12–15; 1993:54 ("respectable antiquity"); Montagu 1944; Loring and Prokopec 1994:26–42.

149 "favorable cave": Quoted in Deuel 1967:486.

149 Folsom: Meltzer 1994:15–16; 1993:50–54; Roberts 1935:1–5; Kreck 1999.

151 Brown's announcement: Anon. 1928; Chamberlin 1928.

152 Whiteman: Anon. 2003; McAlavy 2003; Cotter and Boldurian 1999:1–10.

152 "driving mania": Eiseley 1975:99.

152 Howard at Clovis: Cotter and Boldurian 1999:11–20 ("EXTENSIVE BONE," 11; "One greenhorn," 14; 130°F, 15); Anon. 1932; Howard 1935 (I thank Robert Crease for helping me obtain this article).

153 Discovery of Clovis culture: Cotter 1937; Roberts 1937.

154 "So far": Hrdlička 1937:104. Other skeptics were less careful. Writing in 1933, Walter Hough, of the U.S. National Museum, flatly claimed that "archaeologists now agree that there are no American paleolithic implements" (Hough 1933:757).

154 Lack of skeletons: Interview, Petersen; Steele and Powell 2002 (ten skeletons); Preston 1997:72 (interview with Owsley).

154 More than eighty Clovis and Folsom sites: Hannah Wormington lists ninety-six sites in the 1957 edition of her well-regarded *Ancient Man in North America*. But she describes some as small and uncertain, so I have hedged and said "more than eighty" (Wormington 1957). Grayson and Meltzer (2002) tally seventy-six paleo-Indian sites in the continental United States.

155 Cosmic-ray race: Crease and Mann 1996:Chap. 10.

155 Detection of organic C^{14} and halflife: Anderson et al. 1947a, 1947b; Engelkemeier et al. 1949.

155 First radiocarbon dates: Arnold and Libby 1949 ("seen to be," 680); Marlowe 1999.

155 "You read books": Libby 1991:600.

155 UA C^{14} lab and Haynes's background: Author's interview, Haynes; Feldman 1998.

155 Consistency of C^{14} dates: Haynes 1964.

155 13,500 and 12,900 years ago: I use the calibrations in Stuiver et al. 1998 (online at http:// depts.washington.edu/qil/datasets/intcal98_14c.txt.). These calibrations are essentially applied to Clovis and Folsom in Fiedel 1999b:102. They have been attacked as based on unreliable data (Roosevelt, Douglas, and Brown 2002; Roosevelt 1997).

156 Beringia: For a general physical description, see Fiedel 1992:46–47. Although now a little dated, Fiedel's book remains one of the best expositions of the basic issues.

156 Beringia insects: Elias 2001; Elias et al. 1996; Alfimov and Berman 2001; Colinvaux 1996.

156 Temperature rise: Alley 2000.

157 Ice-free corridor and 1950s investigations: E.g., Elson 1957.

157 "ice-free" and "700 years": Haynes 1964:1412. The potential relevance of the ice-free corridor was first described in Johnston 1972:22–25, 44–45. I am grateful to Josh d'Aluisio-Guerreri for helping me obtain this book.

158 Pleistocene bestiary: Anderson 1984; Kurtén and Anderson 1980.

158 11,500 and 10,900 B.C.: Corrected radiocarbon dates from unpublished data provided to the author by Stuart Fiedel.

158 "zoologically impoverished": Wallace 1962 (vol. 1):149–50.

158 Martin's overkill thesis: Martin 1984, 1973 ("thoroughly superior predator," "swift extermination," 972), 1967.

160 Other extinctions: Wilson 1992:244–53.

160 "Paradigmatic image": Fiedel 1992:63–84. The image is summed in Easton 1992 ("stout-hearted," 31).

161 Northwest Coast salmon wars: Wilkinson 2000. The treaty language at issue ("right of taking") is in Article 3, http://www.nwifc.wa.gov/tribes/treaties/tmedcreek.asp.

162 Hrdlička in Larsen Bay: Denny's story can be augmented with the essays in Bray and Killion eds. 1994. Larsen Bay was not an anomaly. In 1902 Hrdlička visited Sonora, Mexico, where Yaqui Indians were fighting the Mexican army. On a battlefield Hrdlička found sixty-four fresh Yaqui corpses—men, women, and children. He lopped off their heads and shipped them to the Smithsonian (Hrdlička 1904:65–66).

164 Fifty shot down: Cited in Meltzer 1995:22. "The shelf-life of pre-Clovis claims seems little more than a decade," Meltzer wrote (ibid.).

164 "Clovis police," new Hrdlička: Author's interviews, Meltzer, Haynes, Thomas Dillehay; Pringle 1999 (police); Alsoszatai-Petheo 1986:18 (new Hrdlička); Meltzer 1989:478–79. Clovis-firsters were attacked as the "Clovis Mafia" (Koppel 2003:147–50). Fiedel (2000:42–43) marshals evidence against the charges.

164 Landmark article: Greenberg, Turner, and Zegura 1986 ("the three," 479; "we are dealing," "28 key," "dental clusters," 480; "widely held," 484; "tripartite division," 487).

165 Languages of California: Mithun 1997 (fifteen families); Kroeber 1903 (five families).

165 180 language families: This rough figure for the linguistic state of the art in 1986 is created by adding together two then-recent tallies: Campbell and Mithun 1979 (62 families in North America) and Loukokta 1968 (118 in South and Central America).

165 Critiques of three-migrations paper: Campbell 1986 ("Neither," "should be," 488); Morrell 1990b ("zero"). See also, Campbell 1988; Laughlin 1986.

166 Geneticists pursued the question: Reviewed in Merriwether 2002.

166 Mitochondrial DNA indicates multiple migrations: Schurr et al. 1990; Horai et al. 1993.

166 Wallace and Neel timing estimate: Torroni et al. 1994.

167 Haplogroup A study: Bonalto and Bolzano 1997.

167 Size of founding groups: Schurr et al. 1990 (little mtDNA diversity, small group); Ward et al. 1991 (much diversity, big group).

167 Diverse possible origins: Merriwether et al. 1996 (Mongolia); Karafet et al. 1999 (Lake Baikal); Torroni et al. 1993 (east Asia); Lell 2002 (southern middle Siberia and Sea of Okhkotsk, in two major migrations).

168 "only one thing": Cann 2001:1746.

168 Monte Verde: Meltzer 1997; Dillehay ed. 1989–97 (summary of dig history, vol. 2:1–24). See also Dillehay 2001; Gore 1997; Wilford 1998b, 1997b.

168 Dates: Dillehay ed. 1989–97 (vol. 1):18–19, 133–45, esp. Table 6.1. Dillehay did not use calibrated radiocarbon dates; I use the calibration in Stuiver et al. 1998. Fiedel says the likely occupation date is 13,500–14,100 years ago, if the data are correct (Fiedel 2000:50).

168 Hostility: Interviews, Crawford, Dillehay, Fiedel, Meltzer; Morrell 1990a:1.

168 Site visit to Monte Verde: Meltzer 1997; Adovasio and Page 2003:Chap. 9 (according to Meltzer, an accurate account [interview, Meltzer]); Gibbons 1997; Wilford 1997b ("ball game"). See also, Haynes 1999.

169 Fiedel's critique: Author's interviews, Fiedel; Fiedel 1999a ("virtually every," 1); Pringle 1999. See also, in general, Haynes 2003.

169 Haynes's misgivings: Haynes 1999 ("further testing").

169 Corridor critics: Levson and Rutter 1996; Burns 1996; Catto 1996; Jackson, Phillips, and Little 1999.

169 Lack of evidence in corridor: Driver 2001.

169 Critique of overkill: Grayson and Meltzer 2003 ("lives on," 590).

170 Clovis-firsters in minority: Roosevelt, Douglas, and Brown 2002 ("[T]he tide of public and scholarly opinion has definitely turned against Clovis as the earliest culture," 159); Lynch 2001 ("Some of our," 39; "blow the whistle," "political correctness," 41).

171 Three other pre-Clovis sites: Meadowcroft Rockshelter, in Pennsylvania, excavated mainly by James Adovasio; Cactus Hill, in Virginia, excavated by Joseph McAvoy; and Topper, in South Carolina, excavated by Allan Goodyear. See Adovasio and Page 2003.

171 Kennewick Man: Chatters 2001; Thomas 2001. The European connection links to Smithsonian archaeologist Dennis Stanford's idea that the Clovis culture descended from the Solutrean culture in Pleistocene Era France and Spain. Because Solutrean spear points resemble Clovis points, Stanford has speculated that they wandered across a northern arch of ice from Ireland to Greenland to northeast Canada, in an Atlantic version of the passage through Beringia. Stanford's Solutrean proposal was never published in scholarly journals, though it was adumbrated in *Newsweek* and the *New Yorker*. Specialists in Solutrean culture have not greeted these ideas with equal warmth (Stanford and Bradley 2002; Straus 2000; see also, Preston 1997; Begley and Murr 1999).

172 Baja skulls: González-José et al. 2003; Dillehay 2003.

172 Australians into Brazil: Mattos 1939:105–07.

172 Fladmark and coastal route: Fladmark 1979 (see references therein to earlier papers); Mason 1894 (early proposal); Easton 1992; Koppel 2003:68–74; Powledge 1999; Hall 1999.

172 "Even primitive": Quoted in Chandler 2002.

173 (Re)settlement of Europe: Tolan-Smith 1998; Rozoy 1998. Before the Ice Age, northern Europe was populated, but there was no cultural continuity between the earlier and later inhabitants.

6 / Cotton (or Anchovies) and Maize

174 "weft-twining": My thanks to Nobuko Kajitani and Masa Kinoshita for helping me with textile terminology.

174 Huaricanga dig: Author's interviews, Haas, Creamer, Ruiz, Gerbert Asencios, Dan Corkill, Luis Huaman, Kit Nelson.

175 Discovery of Norte Chico: The ruins were first written up by Max Uhle (1856–1944), a German researcher who is often called the "father of South American archaeology" (Uhle 1925). For Uhle's life and work, see Menzel 1977; Rowe 1954.

177 Among the world's biggest buildings: Huaricanga was built before the Egyptian pyramids, at a time when the only other structures that could be called monumental were in the city-states of Sumer. But at the time even these were smaller than the Huaricanga pyramid, so far as archaeologists can tell. The other main Eurasian culture centers—the Indus Valley, the Nile Delta, and the Shang homeland in China—did not even have cities then. Later the ziggurats of Mesopotamia and the pyramids of Egypt surpassed the Peruvian temples in size.

177 McNeill book: McNeill 1967.

177 High-school textbook: Stearns 1987 ("four initial centers," 16; Indian history, 203–12). It was better than some other histories. *A World History,* by Mazour and People, gave the Americas just five pages (281–86). R. J. Unstead's *History of the World* devoted three and a half pages to Indians: one and a half in the chapter "Other Cultures," and two pages in the chapter "Europeans in America" (Unstead 1983:58–59, 200–02).

177 Maize as most important crop: The 2001 maize harvest was 609 million metric tons, whereas rice and wheat were 592 million mT and 582 million mT respectively. Statistics from the FAO agricultural database are online at http://apps.fao.org/default.htm.

177 Three-fifths of the crops: Weatherford 1988:204.

178 Olmec as founder of Peruvian societies: This idea was common in the 1920s and 1930s (Wells 1920 [vol. 2]:189–90). Later it fell out of favor, though it continued to be mooted until at least the 1960s (Coe 1962).

178 Sumer as world's oldest city: Some densely populated settlements were older, notably Çatalhöyük, in central Turkey, and 'Ain Ghazal, in Jordan. But archaeologists believe that these were not true cities, because they show little evidence of public architecture, strong social hierarchy, and division of labor (Balter 1998; Simmons et al. 1988).

178 Eurasian trade in ideas: Examples lifted from Teresi 2002.

179 Pan-American Highway: The roadless gap in Panama and Colombia, once quite large, has shrunk to about fifty miles. Still, the road is so bad that the Lonely Planet guidebook describes the Pan-American Highway as "more of a concept than an actual route."

179 Atacama as model for Mars: Navallo-González et al. 2003.

179 Pizarro's pilot's advice: Quoted in Thomson 2003:139.

180 Possible Paleo-Indian routes to coast: Arriaza 2001.

180 Two *Science* reports: Sandweiss et al. 1998; Keefer et al. 1998; deFrance et al. 2001. See also, Pringle 1998b; Wilford 1998a.

180 Different early adaptations: A fine summary is provided in Moseley 2001:91–100.

180 First finding of mummies: Max Uhle found the same mummies but didn't further excavate there (Uhle 1917). I am grateful to the librarians at Pontificia Universidad Católica del Perú who hunted down this article for me.

180 Chinchorro diet: Aufderheide and Allison 1995. My thanks to Joshua D'Aluisio-Guerreri for helping me obtain this article.

180 Chinchorro mummies: Arriaza 1995 (1983 find, chap. 2); Allison 1985; Pringle 1998a.

180 Anemia in child mummies: Focacci and Chacón 1989.

181 Tapeworm eggs: Reinhard and Urban 2003.

181 Import of Norte Chico: Author's Interviews, Haas, Creamer, Ruiz, Mike Moseley. Haas and Creamer 2004 ("The complex of sites," 36); Haas, Creamer, and Ruiz, 2004.

181 Aspero: Willey and Corbett 1954 ("knolls," 254); Moseley and Willey 1973 ("excellent, if embarrassing," "temple-type," 455); Feldman 1985; 1980:246 (rejecting older dates), cited in Haas, Creamer, and Ruiz, 2004.

183 Caral: Shady Solis, Haas, and Creamer 2001; Shady Solis and Leyva eds. 2003; Shady Solis, pers. comm. See also, Pringle 2001; Sandweiss and Moseley 2001; Fountain 2001; Bower 2001; Ross 2002.

184 Dating of other Norte Chico sites: Haas, Creamer, and Ruiz 2004.

184 Egypt: For dates and sizes I have relied on Algaze 1993 and Spence 2000 (which dates construction on the Great Pyramid of Khufu to begin in 2485–75 B.C.).

185 Invention of government: Author's interviews, Haas, Petersen; Haas, Creamer, and Ruiz 2004.

185 Cotton domestication: Sauer 1993.

186 Cotton in Europe and the Andes: Braudel 1981–84 (vol. 1):325–27; (vol. 2):178–80 (bans, prostitutes), 312–13; Murra 1964.

187 MFAC hypothesis: Moseley 2005, 1975b. See the critiques in Wilson 1981, Raymond 1981.

188 Work parties and music: Author's Interviews, Haas, Creamer; Shady Solis 2003a, 2003b.

189 Champ de Mars: Schama 1989:504–09.

189 Early Staff God: Author's interviews, Creamer; Makowski, pers. comm.; Haas and Creamer, forthcoming; Spotts 2003; Makowski 2005.

190 Norte Chico as foundation: In the past anthropologists have sometimes tried to describe Peruvian societies in terms of *lo Andino,* a being whose special characteristics have uniquely defined those societies throughout time. I am arguing something different, that people who have solved problems in one way will often return to those proven methods to solve new ones.

191 Domestication of tobacco: Winter 2000.

191 Itanoní description, plans, history: Author's interviews, Ramírez Leyva.

192 Uniqueness of Itanoní: Small tortillerías using local maize persist in rural Mexico, although they are threatened by the industrial production of Maseca, the large, state-affiliated maize and tortilla firm. By contrast, Itanoní is a boutique operation that sells as many as eight different varieties of tortillas, each made from a separate local cultivar. The difference is akin to the difference between an Italian village café that sells liters of unlabeled local wine and an *enoteca,* a fine wine store featuring the carefully labeled production of the region.

194 Millet as first cereal: Callen 1967.

194 Genetic similarity of cereals: Gale and Devos 1998.

194 Productivity of wild cereals: Zohary 1972; Harlan and Zohary 1966.

194 Teosinte: Author's interview, Wilkes; Wilkes 1972, 1967 (I am grateful to Dr. Wilkes for giving me copies of his work); Crosby 2003b:171 (nutritional value).

194 Wheat and barley nonshattering mutation: Zohary and Hopf 2000:29–30, 59–60; Hillman and Davies 1990.

194 Maize history: Warman 2003; Anon. 1982 ("not domesticated," 5).

194 Paleo-Indian agricultural development and MacNeish's work: MacNeish 1967, 1964; Flannery and Marcus 2002. MacNeish died in 2001.

195 Long debate over origin of maize: Kahn 1985:3–82; Galinat 1992.

195 Mangelsdorf theory: Mangelsdorf, MacNeish, and Galinat 1964. Mangelsdorf first proposed the extinct-wild-ancestor theory in Mangelsdorf and Reeves 1939. I am grateful to Dr. Wilkes for lending me a copy of this document. See also, Mangelsdorf 1986.

195 Beadle's theory: Beadle 1939.

195 Caustic letters: E.g., the exchanges between Beadle and another Nobel-winning biologist, Barbara McClintock, in 1972 (McClintock Papers, "Searching for the Origins of Maize in South America, 1957–1981: Documents," letters of 22 Jan.–24 Feb. 1972, available online at http://profiles.nlm.nih.gov/LL/Views/Exhibit/documents/origins.html).

195 Iltis theory: Iltis 1983.

195 Teosinte-gamagrass theory and critiques: Eubanks 2001b (McClintock quotes, 509), 1997; Bennetzen et al. 2001.

196 Teosinte mutations: The development of three of these mutations is elucidated in Jaenicke-Després 2003. See references therein for the discoverers of the genes.

196 Maize in a decade: Eyre-Walker et al. 1998. Essentially the team argued that in ten years breeders with exactly the right teosinte variants could have created maize if they were as systematic as modern breeders. One assumes that the actual development time was longer.

196 Locus and timing of development of maize: MacNeish went back to his early maize cobs with new tools and decided they dated to about 3500 B.C. (Farnsworth et al. 1985). Subsequently, researchers did the same for early maize cobs from nearby Oaxaca, pushing

back the date to about 4200 B.C. (Piperno and Flannery 2001; Benz 2001). Both of these sites contained fully domesticated maize (Benz and Iltis 1990). Pope et al. found teosinte pollen grains as early as 5100 B.C. in a wet Gulf Coast site where teosinte is not native, suggesting that it was moved there from the highlands. By 4000 B.C. the pollen is dominated by modern maize (Eubanks 2001a; MacNeish and Eubanks 2000; Pope et al. 2001).

196 "arguably man's": Federoff 2003.

196 Diversity of maize: Doebley, Goodman, and Stuber 1998. The reason for the diversity is that the ancestor species were hyperdiverse (Eyre-Walker et al. 1998).

197 Aragón Cuevas research: Author's interviews, Aragon Cuevas. The number of landraces varies from study to study, because the term is not precisely defined. It is often claimed that more than two hundred exist in Latin America (e.g., Wellhausen et al. 1957, 1952).

197 Five thousand cultivars: Author's interview, Wilkes. This is a widely cited guess by a distinguished researcher with long experience in the field.

197 Chamula statistics: Anon. ed. 1998a. The data are from 1991, the most recent year for which census results are available.

197 Perales's study: Author's interview, Perales.

197 *Milpa:* Here I describe the Mesoamerican variant of an ideal. *Milpa*-style agriculture occurs in much of South America, though centered often on potatoes or manioc instead of maize. Even in Mesoamerica, plenty of actual *milpas* are nothing more than maize fields, especially where farmers grow maize for the market. Subsistence-farm *milpas* I have seen tend to be more diverse. *Milpa* cultivation is often described—incorrectly, according to Wilkes (author's interview)—as synonymous with "slash-and-burn," in which farmers clear small areas for short times and then let them go fallow (e.g., the otherwise useful Ewell and Sands 1987). Slash-and-burn, though, is generally a modern innovation (see chap. 9). A good description of the *milpa* is Wilken 1987. A classic early study is Cook 1921.

198 Green Revolution and *milpa:* Author's interviews, Denevan, Hallberg, Perales, Wilkes ("most successful"), James Boyce; Mann 2004.

199 Abundance of wild wheat and barley: Harlan and Zohary 1966 ("square kilometers," "Over many thousands," 1078).

200 "the key": Coe 1968:26.

200 Kirkby's estimate: Kirkby 1973.

200 Maize iconography: Fields 1994.

201 Maize in Europe: Crosby 2003b:180–81.

201 Pellagra in Europe, Goethe: Roe 1973; McCollum 1957:302; Goethe 1962:33–34.

201 Maize and slavery: Author's interviews, Crosby; Crosby 2003b:186–88; 1994:24.

202 Oaxaca data: Anon. ed. 1998b:532–68. The data are from 1991, the most recent year for which census results are available.

202 Estimated productivity of Green Revolution maize in Oaxaca: Author's interviews, Aragon Cuevas, James Boyce. The estimate is roughly confirmed by the calculations of Ackerman et al. (2002:36) that "a 1 percent increase in use of improved varieties was typically associated with an increase in yield of 0.037 tons/ha" and hence a 100 percent switchover is a jump of 3.7 tons/ha.

202 Economic problems of landrace maize in Oaxaca: Author's interviews, Aragón Cuevas, Bellon, Boyce, Hallberg, Ramírez Leyva, Wilkes.

7 / *Writing, Wheels, and Bucket Brigades*

204 Stirling's find of dated stela: Stirling 1939 ("knees," "hurried," 213), 1940a; Coe 1976b. Stirling's position was held previously by William Henry Holmes, scourge of amateur "relic

hunters." In his *National Geographic* article, Stirling says the first giant head was discovered in 1858; others put the find at 1862 (Bernal 1969:29). Following an earlier, mistaken understanding of the Mesoamerican calendar, Stirling believed that the stela was earlier than now thought; I use the modern date. Because carbon-dating had not yet been invented, he had the dates of Maya emergence wrong, too. Still, he was right to be puzzled by the Olmec.

205 Second Veracruz trip, first Olmec article: Stirling 1940b ("designed," " 'The ticks,' " 312; "basic civilization," 333; "mysterious," 334).

207 The Olmec: Among the few general book-length overviews are Coe 1996 (especially valuable for its illustrations of Olmec art); Pina Chan 1989; and Bernal 1969 (1968), the last still surprisingly useful despite its age. All espouse the "mother culture" view, which has come under increasing fire.

207 "enigmatic people": Baird and Bairstow 2004:727. Similar language can be found in the *Eyewitness Travel Guide: Mexico* (New York: Dorling Kindersley, 2003), 254. These characterizations are common in the popular press (e.g., Stuart 1993a ["the Olmec stand for many as a kind of 'mother culture' to all the civilizations that came after, including the Maya and the Aztec," 92]; Lemonick 1996 ["More than 1,500 years before the Maya . . . , the mysterious Olmec people were building the first great culture of Mesoamerica," 56]).

207 Olmec emerge abruptly: Some researchers have hypothesized that Olmec society was stimulated into existence by a migration from the Pacific coast, but recent ceramics research in Veracruz casts doubt on this idea (Arnold 2003).

207 "quantum change": Meggers 1975:17.

207 "There is now little doubt": Coe 1994:62.

207 Bad name: Bernal 1969:11–12. Actually, the name is even worse than I indicated. "Olmec" doesn't refer to a people, but to the political phenomenon that began and ended with their cities. The people in those cities may still be around, but called something else.

207 Mixe-Zoquean: Campbell and Kaufman 1976.

208 Olmec rubber: Hosler, Burkett, and Tarkanian 1999; Rodríguez and Ortiz 1994.

208 1800 B.C.: Rust and Sharer 1988.

208 San Lorenzo: Coe and Diehl 1980; Cyphers ed. 1997.

208 Olmec theology: Reilly 1994.

209 Thrones changed into sculptures: Porter 1989.

209 Africa-Olmec and Shang-Olmec connection: For the Africa-Olmec connection, see Barton 2001; Winters 1979; Van Sertima 1976. Van Sertima's claims are attacked in Haslip-Viera, Ortiz de Montellano, and Barbour 1997. For the Shang-Olmec connection, see Xu 1996; Meggers 1975; Ekholm 1969. I am grateful to Mike Xu for sending me a copy of his manuscript. Meggers was critiqued in Grove 1977 and responded in Meggers 1977.

209 Olmec sculptures of fetuses and pathological conditions: Tate and Bendersky 1999; Dávalos Hurtado and Ortiz de Zárate 1953. I am grateful to the Bancroft Library staffers who went to considerable trouble to find the second article for me.

209 Olmec appearance: Bernal 1969:76–79.

210 Mirrors: Heizer and Gullberg 1981.

210 Destruction of sculptures: Grove 1981.

210 La Venta: Rust and Sharer 1988. A succinct description is in Bernal 1969:35–43.

211 "not only engendered," "established the pattern": Bernal 1969:188. A well-argued contemporary version of this view is Diehl 2005.

211 Competitive interaction in Mesoamerica: Flannery and Marcus 2000 ("chiefdoms in the Basin," 33). I thank Joyce Marcus for walking me through these ideas.

211 Zapotec rise: Blanton et al. 1999; Marcus and Flannery 1996; Flannery and Marcus 2003 ("virtually unoccupied," 11802; radiocarbon dates, 11804); Spencer 2003.

213 Oldest writing: Marcus pers. comm. (750 B.C.), 1976 (glyphs and translation); Flannery and Marcus 2003. See also, Serrano 2002. The reason I have called the temple carving the first "securely" dated writing is that two other candidates for the title of first written text exist, but neither can be dated accurately because their archaeological context is unknown. Both are from the Tlatilco culture north of present-day Mexico City; they may have been made as early as 1000 B.C. One seal shows three glyphs that some think resemble Olmec writing. The other, a true mystery, bears what look like letters in a script of which there are no other extant examples (Kelley 1966). A third candidate for earliest Olmec writing exists. In the 1990s a team led by Mary Pohl of the University of Florida discovered a cylindrical greenstone seal two miles from La Venta. Dated to 650 B.C., the seal bears a bas-relief bird with a comic-book speech bubble bursting from its mouth. Pohl and two colleagues identified the glyphs in the bubble as precursors to the Mayan glyphs for the date 3-Ajaw (Pohl, Pope, and von Nagy 2002; Stokstad 2002). The identification is controversial. The text cannot be Mayan, they say, because Maya civilization was not firmly set in place until centuries later. Nor can it be Olmec, because other Olmec texts seem not to be related to Maya glyphs. According to John Justeson, a linguistic anthropologist at the State University of New York in Albany who has deciphered other Olmec texts, "Although many accept the greenstone glyphs as plausibly being writing, what [Pohl's team] read as a ritual calendar date on the ceramic is scarcely accepted by anyone" (email to author).

214 Inanna temple example: Urton 2003:15–16.

215 Zero as number: Teresi 2002:79–87 (GPA example, 80).

216 Tres Zapotes date: In fact, the initial 7 (the *baktun* figure) was missing, because the stela was broken. Stirling guessed that it was a 7, a supposition that was proven correct in 1972, when the other part of the stela was discovered (Cohn 1972).

216 Tentative assignation: In *The Olmec World*, for instance, Bernal never directly says that the Olmec invented zero. He merely describes the Long Count, remarking that it "necessarily implies knowledge of the zero" (Bernal 1969:114).

216 More than a dozen systems of writing: Coe 1976a:110ff. Coe lists thirteen forms, but does not include Olmec and whatever is on the Tlatilco seals.

216 Deciphered Olmec stela: Stuart 1993a, 1993b; Justeson and Kaufman 1993; 1997; 2001 (Chiapas potsherd translation, 286).

218 Monte Albán dispute: I have borrowed the formulation in Zeitlin 1990. Some argue that not enough data exist to resolve the question (O'Brien and Lewarch 1992).

218 Slabs as slain enemies: Marcus 1983:106–08, 355–60.

218 Fight with Tilcajete: Spencer and Redmond 2001.

219 Mixtec marriage politics: Spores 1974.

219 8-Deer's story: Pohl 2002; Byland and Pohl 1994:119–60, 241–44; Caso 1977–79 (vol. 1):69–83, (vol. 2):169–84; Smith 1962; Clark 1912.

222 Wheeled toys: Stirling 1940b:310–11, 314; Charnay 1967:178–86.

223 Egypt and wheel: Wright 2005:46.

223 Moldboard plow: Temple 1998 ("so inefficient," 16). I am grateful to Dick Teresi for directing me to this book and example ("as if Henry Ford": e-mail, Teresi to author).

223 Lack of relation between technology and social complexity: I lift this point bodily from Webster 2002:77. See also Ihde 2000.

225 Osmore Valley geography: I am grateful to Mike Moseley and Susan DeFrance for guiding me through this area, and to Patrick Ryan Williams and Donna Nash for showing me Moquegua and Cerro Baúl.

225 Wari and Tiwanaku: A succinct overview is La Lone 2000. Surprisingly little has been written about Wari. Among the few recent books are Isbell and McEwan eds. 1991 and Schreiber 1992. The most widely cited recent works on Tiwanaku are Kolata 1993 and

Kolata ed. 1996–2003. William Isbell has pointed out that the two names refer simultaneously to cities, states, and religions. He has suggested that the Spanish names Tiahuanaco and Huari be used for the physical ruins and the Aymara and Ruma Suni spellings
Tiwanaku and Wari be used for these polities' political and cultural styles (Isbell 2001:
457).

225 Sixth-century climatic disaster: Fagan 1999:Chap. 7. The major apparent victims were
the Moche, who flourished in a three-hundred-mile strip along the northern coast after
100 A.D. Drought put Moche society in crisis; El Niño rains led to floods that destroyed
entire villages and canal systems. El Niño also changed ocean current patterns to deposit
river sediments on the shore. These quickly turned to dunes, which winds blew toward
the Andes, threatening farmland. The Moche tried to regroup—and failed.

225 Potato's advantages and status vis-a-vis maize: McNeill 1991, Murra 1960.

227 Wari religion: It should be emphasized that the common image of the Staff God did not
mean that the deity meant the same thing in every culture (Makowski 2001).

227 Terracing, arable land, abandonment: Peruvian ecologist Luis Masson has estimated
that 1.2 to 1.4 million acres was terraced on just the west side of the Andes, 75 percent of
which is now abandoned (pers. comm., cited in Denevan 2001:173–75); Cobo 1990:213
("flights of stairs"); Moseley 2001:230–38 ("patenting and marketing," 233; prospering of
Wari despite climatic assault, 232).

227 Isbell-Vranich article: Isbell and Vranich 2004 ("repetitive," 170).

228 Wari and Tiwanaku in Cerro Baúl: Interviews, DeFrance, Moseley, Nash, Williams;
Williams, Isla, and Nash 2001.

229 Geertz's four states: Geertz 1980:121–22.

230 Chiripa: The major recent work on Chiripa is described in Hastorf 1999. A summary is
Stanish 2003:115–17.

230 Pukara: Stanish 2003:138–48, 156–60, 283–84. Stanish suggests that a drought that began
in about 100 A.D. may have induced Pukara's collapse (157). But the drought may not
have occurred—its existence has been deduced from a study of Lake Titicaca bottom
sediments (Abbott et al. 1997). But the lake-sediment data, as the authors noted, conflicted with previous ice-core studies; in addition, the depositional processes were suffi-
ciently poorly understood that one could not judge when the putative dry periods began
and ended.

230 Rise of Tiwanaku: Stanish 2003:chap. 8, 2001.

230 Tiwanaku as predatory state: Kolata 1993:81–86, 243–52 ("predatory," 243; "lower cost,"
245).

231 Akapana: Interviews, Nicole Couture, Michael Moseley, Alexei Vranich; author's visit;
Cieza de León 1959:282 ("how human hands"); Kolata 1993:103–29. Wendell Bennett
excavated at Akapana in the 1930s, but the first major excavations at Tiwanaku in general
did not occur until the late 1960s, with the work of researchers from the Instituto
Nacional de Arqueología de Bolivia, led by Carlos Ponce Sanginés. Ponce's work has
come under fire, because he published little of his data and because he "restored"
Tiwanaku landmarks inaccurately. In the 1980s Alan Kolata of the University of Chicago
led a large team that produced the first comprehensive overview of the city and its envi-
rons.

232 Kalasasaya and Gateway of the Sun: Author's interviews, Couture, Vranich; Kolata
1993:143–49.

232 Isbell-Vranich vision of city: Isbell and Vranich 2004.

232 Lack of markets: Kolata 1993:172–76 ("a city was," "symbolically," 173).

233 Vranich picture of Tiwanaku: Interviews, Vranich; Vranich 2001; Vranich et al. 2001:
150–52; Isbell and Vranich 2004.

235 Chimor history: Sakai 1998; Moseley and Cordy-Collins eds. 1990.

235 Chimor irrigation and canal: Denevan 2001:152–57. Some scholars attribute the uphill sections to tectonic uplift; Denevan finds the regularity of the error difficult to reconcile with tectonic causes (156).

235 Layout of Chan Chan: Shimada 2000:esp. 102; Moseley 1975a.

235 Fall of Chimor and execution of Qhapaq Yupanki: Sarmiento de Gamboa 2000:102–03; Rowe 1946:206.

236 Chimor and Thupa Inka: Rostworowski de Diez Canseco 1999:72–73, 77–79; Sarmiento de Gamboa 2000:102–03, 112–15.

238 Nazca lines: The original report, which I have not seen, is Mejía Xesspe 1940. Von Däniken's claims are found in, among many other titles, Von Däniken 1969, 1998. Calendrical and astronomical theories are (to my mind) convincingly dismissed in Morrison and Hawkins 1978. The best explanation I know of the current geology-and-water hypothesis is Aveni 2000. For a variant, see Proulx, Johnson, and Mabee 2001.

239 Moche: Bawden 1996; Uceda and Mujica eds. 1993. Research on the Moche was greatly stimulated by the discovery of relatively untouched, art-filled tombs in Sipan in 1987. (Accounts of the efforts by Peruvian archaeologist Walter Alva to save the site's artifacts from looters, include Kirkpatrick 1992 and Atwood 2004.) Since Sipan, much research on the Moche has focused on their art—understandably so, given its high quality (e.g., Alva and Donnan 1993).

240 Chavín de Huantar: Author's visit; Burger 1992; Lumbreras, González, and Lietaer 1976 (roaring sounds); Lumbreras 1989; Rowe 1967.

8 / Made in America

243 Chak Tok Ich'aak's life and death: Stuart 2000; Schele and Mathews 1998:75–79; Martin and Grube 2000:28–29 (portrait reproduced on 28, "entered the water," 29); Harrison 1999:71–81. See also Stone 1989.

244 The four cities are Palenque (Martin and Grube 2000:156), La Sufricaya (Estrada-Belli 2002), El Perú and Uaxactun (Martin and Grube 2000:28–29).

246 "No words": Webster 2002:7.

246 Morley's theory: Morley 1946:262. The earliest version of the ecological-overshoot theory I know of is Cooke 1931. Cooke claimed that overexpansion of agriculture had caused erosion that filled up Maya water reservoirs.

246 Pollen studies: Vaughan, Deevey, and Garett-Jones 1985; Deevey et al. 1979.

246 Environmental degradation, deforestation, floods: Binford et al. 1987; Abrams and Rue 1988; Woods 2003. I am grateful to Prof. Woods for sending me a copy of his article.

246 Deforestation-induced spiral to collapse: Santley, Killion, and Lycett 1986.

246 Drought: Curtis and Hodell 1996 ("Our findings suggest a strong relationship between times of drought and major cultural discontinuities in Classic Maya civilization," 46). See also, Hodell, Curtis, and Brenner 1995.

246 Green parable: See, e.g., Catton 1982; Lowe 1985; Lutz 2000 ("Environmentalists concerned about the rapid growth of world population repeatedly cite the Maya collapse as an example of what happens if a region's population growth exceeds its population carrying capacity," vii); Ponting 1991 ("The clearest case of environmental collapse leading to the demise of a society comes from the Maya," 78); Diamond 2004: 157–77; Wright 2005: 94–106 (Maya collapse shows that "civilizations often behave like 'pyramid' sales schemes, thriving only when they grow," 83). Part of the appeal, one assumes, is that the Maya fall (like that of Cahokia, which I cover later) was not due to Europe.

247 "were able to," "Are contemporary": Ponting 1991:83; 1990:33.

247 Examples of spiritual books: Grim 2001; Berkes 1999; McGaa 1999; Durning 1992.

247 Five Great Values: Derived from Reiten 1995. Reiten, an administrator in a Bureau of Indian Affairs school in New Mexico, gave her list to Tony Sanchez, of Oakland State University, who revised it to broaden the values' applicability from the Lakota to all Indians—implicitly, and one assumes benevolently, asserting that all indigenous peoples thought alike, thus denying their intellectual and cultural diversity. I quote from Dr. Sanchez's revised version (Sanchez 2001:420–21).

248 Van der Donck: Shorto 2004; Van der Donck 1841 ("all free by nature," 207; "They remark," 210; "woods, plains and meadows," 150–51; "several hundred miles," 138).

248 "Such a fire": Van der Donck 1993:n.p. ("Of the Wood, the Natural Productions and Fruits of the Land"). I use this translation here because it is more evocative.

249 The following discussion of the natural role of fire draws from Mann and Plummer 1995:89–92; Mt. St. Helens from author's visits.

249 Nature not in lockstep: Botkin 1990; Pickett and Thompson 1978.

250 Ecological role of fire: Wright and Heinselman 1973; Komarek 1965 ("The earth," 204).

250 Fire and landscape management: Pyne 1982:71–81 (Lewis and Clark, 71–72; Jefferson, 75); Day 1953:334–39; Williams 1989:47–48; Williams 2002; Cronon 1983:48–52; Morton 1637:52–54 ("to set fire," 52). The impact of fire varied; in Martha's Vineyard, for instance, it seems to have been negligible (Foster et al. 2002).

251 Carriages in Ohio: Bakeless 1961:314, cited in Denevan 1992a:369.

251 "could be": Wroth ed. 1970:139. See also, Higginson 1792: 117–18 (reporting "thousands of acres of ground as good as need to be, and not a tree in the same").

251 Smith's gallop: Smith 1910 (vol. 1):64. He also saw Indians hunting with fire (70).

251 Bison range: Roe 1951; Mathiessen 1987:147–52; Cronon 1983: 51–52 ("were harvesting").

251 Impact of Native American burning: Pyne 1982:71–83; Little 1974; Dorney and Dorney 1989; Delcourt et al. 1986; Rostlund 1957a, 1957b.

251 Great Plains and anthropogenic fire: Axelrod 1985; Steuter 1991; Sauer 1975; Williams 1989:46–48; Lott 2002:86–88 ("When Lewis and Clark," 88).

251 Fidler's fires: Fidler 1992 ("Grass all," "Not a," "All burnt," "the grass," 13–15; "The Grass," 36; "very dangerous," 59).

252 Return of forest to Midwest: Williams 1989:46 (Wisconsin, Illinois, Kansas, Nebraska); Fisher, Jenkins, and Fisher 1987 (Wyoming); author's visit, Texas (displays of historical photographs).

252 "disastrous habit": Palliser 1983:30.

252 Raup: Raup 1937 ("have been," 84; "inconceivable," 85).

252 "It is at least": Brown and Davis 1973:116, quoted in Williams 2002:183.

252 Vale: Vale 2002 ("modest," 14); 1998. Vale was rebutted in Keeley 2002. An example of how natural scientists continue to dismiss the human presence is Hillspaugh, Whitlock, and Bartlein 2000 (examining long-term fire frequency at Yellowstone National Park, an area inhabited for thousands of years, "offers a natural 'experiment' that allows us to consider the sensitivity of fire regimes *to climate change alone*," 211 [emphasis added]).

252 Cahokia description: Author's visit; author's interviews, Woods; Dalan et al. 2003:64–78.

253 Biggest population concentration: Iseminger 1997, cited in Woods 2004:152.

253 Controversy over mound origins: Silverberg 1968 (Bancroft, 98); Garlinghouse 2001; Kennedy 1994:230–39; Jefferson 1894:query XI (excavation of "barrow").

254 Ouachita mounds: Saunders 1997; Pringle 1997 ("I know it," 1762). The mounds no longer overlook the river, which has changed its course since their construction.

256 Origins and rise of eastern North American agriculture: Smith 1993 ("the indigenous crops in question," 14), 1989. See the similar early argument in Linton 1924:349.

256 Eastern Agricultural Complex: More formally, the Eastern Agricultural Complex consists of squash *(Cucurbita pepo)*; marshelder or sumpweed *(Iva annua)*; erect knotweed

(*Polygonum erectum*); maygrass (*Phalaris caroliniana*); common sunflower (*Helianthus annuus*); little barley (*Hordeum pusillum*); and lambsquarter, aka chenopod or goosefoot (*Chenopodium berlandieri*). Marshelder, like sunflower, has an edible, oily seed. Erect knotweed is a low plant with starchy, edible seeds; it is not the invasive Japanese knotweed that is a problem in the eastern United States. The grain from maygrass and little barley, both knee-high grasses with tufted stalks, was probably dried and pounded into flour. Lambsquarter is a spinach-like green that unfortunately looks like the toxic western black nightshade.

258 Hopewell culture: Woodward and McDonald 2002; Romain 2000; Seeman 1979. For the bow and arrow, see Browne 1938. Browne's long-accepted argument that the bow and arrow arrived relatively late has recently been challenged (Bradbury 1997) and reaffirmed (Boszhardt 2002).

258 Hopewell religion: Brown 1997.

258 "stunning vigor": Silverberg 1968:280–89.

259 Cahokia chronology: There are many versions of Cahokian chronology, because the radiocarbon calibrations have been revised repeatedly, but they differ more in detail than in substance. I use the chronology in Dalan et al. 2003:69. But see also Fowler 1997: Appendix 1.

259 London population: Weinreb and Hibbert eds. 1993:630–32.

259 Cahokia not a city: Woods and Wells 2001.

260 Big Bang: Pauketat 1994:168–74. Pauketat himself did not use the term "Big Bang," though it is now in common use.

260 Synchrony and proximity of mound sites: Emerson 2002.

260 Engineering of Monks Mound: Woods 2001, 2000. My thanks to Ray Mann for help in understanding the engineering and to Dr. Woods for a copy of these and other papers.

260 Pauketat's model: Pauketat 1998; 1997:30–51; 1994:esp. chap. 7.

261 Burials in small mound: Fowler et al. 1999.

262 Slow introduction of maize: Riley et al. (1994) dated maize found near Cahokia from 170 B.C.–60 A.D.

262 Maize not important to Hopewell: interviews, Woods; Lynott et al. 1986.

262 Woods's model of Cahokia fall: Author's Interviews, Woods; Woods 2004, 2003; Woods and Wells 2001. In its basics, this scenario is similar to that in Mehrer 1995:esp. Chap. 5.

262 Widespread land clearing: Lopinot and Woods 1993.

264 Sedimentation evidence for flooding: Holley and Brown 1989, cited in Woods 2004:155; Woods 2003. See also, Holden 1996, Neumann 2002:150–51.

264 Haudenosaunee villages: Day 1953:332–34 (six square miles, Denonville, 333; "hundreds of acres," 338).

264 American chestnuts: Kummer 2003; Mann and Plummer 2002.

264 "They pound them": Bartram 1996:56. For many groups in the Southeast, milk from mast was the only kind of milk available.

265 Lack of evidence for deaths or hunger: Milner 1992.

265 Palisade: Iseminger 1990. In a novel interpretation, Pauketat argues that the Cahokians' attempt to shut themselves behind a palisade actually could have been "an offensive tactic" that let Cahokia's rulers "project a larger-than-normal armed force by freeing up people who otherwise would have guarded the capital" (Pauketat 1998:71).

266 Status gap: Trubitt 2000.

266 1811–12 earthquakes: Nuttli 1973. According to Nuttli's estimates, which are based on multiple historical accounts, the earthquake was so powerful that ten miles away from the fault it apparently kicked the ground up at a foot per second, enough to shotput people into the air (table 7). Cahokia, 140 miles away from the center of the 1811 earth-

quakes, would not have experienced such drastic shaking, but because the soft Mississippi soils readily transmit earthquake waves the impact would still have been devastating.

267 Lack of Calakmul investigation: Strictly speaking, this isn't true. Two Carnegie Institution archaeologists visited Calakmul several times after a Carnegie botanist reported its existence, but the site was so remote that they did little other than map the central area (Lundell 1934; Ruppert and Denison 1943).

267 Calakmul description: Folan 1992; Folan et al. 1995, 2001.

267 Calakmul population: Culbert et. al. (1990) estimated the population of the entire Mutal (Tikal) city-state at 425,000. Fletcher and Gann (1992) used the same methods for Calakmul, concluding that Calakmul was 37 percent bigger than its rival (see also Folan 1990:159). The resultant population would be 582,250, which I have rendered as 575,000 to maintain a similar level of approximation.

270 Stuart's work: Stuart 2000. Tatiana Prouskouriakoff and Clemency Coggins suggested the outlines of the encounter in the 1960s, but later archaeologists rejected the idea of an actual intrusion from Teotihuacán, instead arguing that the evidence suggested an influx of ideas, rather than people. Stuart marshaled enough data to convince most of his colleagues that Prouskouriakoff and Coggins were right to begin with.

270 Mutal-Kaan war: Martin and Grube 1966. I thank Prof. Grube for sending me a copy of this widely cited and influential work. A recent summary is in Martin and Grube 2000. See also, Martin 2000.

270 Beginning of Kaan: Folan et al. 1995:325–30 (discussion of chronology).

271 Views of Maya state organization: Fox 1996. The most prominent early advocate of the small-equal-state position was Morley (Morley 1946:50, 159–61). In the more recent past it was adopted by such prominent Mayanists as Peter Mathews (1991), Stephen Houston (1993), Nicholas Dunning (1992), and William Sanders and David Webster (1988). The most widely cited dissent to the small-state view that I know of came from Joyce Marcus, who argued for four dominant centers in several publications (e.g., Marcus 1973). An unpublished but widely circulated analysis by Martin and Grube (1996) changed many minds (see also, Grube and Martin 1998). I thank Prof. Grube for sending me copies of both. The most accessible summary of their views is Martin and Grube 2000:17–21.

271 Semblance of empire: This is a revamped version of a sentence in Chase, Grube, and Chase 1991:1.

271 Decipherment of *y-ahaw*: Usually credited to Houston and Mathews 1985:27; Bricker 1986:70.

271 "The political landscape": Martin and Grube 2000:21. Martin's comparison of the Maya to the Greeks comes from interviews and email.

271 Sky Witness: Martin and Grube 2000:90–92, 102–04.

271 Mutal size and population: Adams and Jones 1981:318–19; Culbert et al. 1990 (arguing for 425,000 as total size).

271 Possible motives for Kaan-Mutal war: Fahsen 2003 (trade routes); Harrison 1999:121 (commerce, dynasty); Grube, pers. comm. (ideology).

272 Landscape alteration: The literature is vast. Examples include Darch 1988; Dunning et al. 2002; Fedick and Ford 1990; Gunn et al. 2002 ("geochemically hostile," 313); Scarborough and Gallopin 1991; Sluyter 1994. See also, Scarborough 2003.

273 Oxwitza' (Caracol): Chase and Chase 2001, 1996, 1994 (population, 5).

275 *Star Wars* attack on Mutal: Harrison 1999:122; Houston 1991; Freidel 1993. The Chases are skeptical of Kaan's role, because they think it too far from Caracol and because they are skeptical about the translations by Grube and Martin (Chase and Chase 2000:63).

275 Maya way of conquest: Grube and Martin 1998.

275 Dos Pilas: Guenter 2003; Fahsen 2003. Previous attempts at decipherment include Boot 2002a, 2002b; better readings of the glyphs led to corrections. See also, Guenter 2002; Williams 2002.

275 Stairway quotes: Guenter 2002:39 (flint), 27 (skull).

276 Morley's tally of dates: Morley 1946:64. Updated in Sidrys and Berger 1979; Hamblin and Pitcher 1980. I use Sidrys and Berger. A few hard-to-read inscriptions might have been set down as late as 928.

277 Four lines of evidence: Robichaux 2002 (waterflow evidence); Gill 2000 (ethnohistorical [Gill also uses many other types of data]; "starvation and thirst," 1); Curtis, Hodell, and Brenner 1996 (oxygen data; "driest intervals," 45); Haug et al. 2003 (titanium).

278 Paradoxical survival in the north: Dahlin 2002 ("How and why," 327); Robichaux 2002. The Maya also fled west, toward Guatemala's Pacific coast, another dry area in which they thrived during the drought. I leave the western cities out of the main account solely for simplicity.

278 Chichén Itzá: Milbrath and Peraza Lope 2003.

9 / *Amazonia*

281 Orellana's expedition: The main sources are collected in Heaton ed. 1934 ("by God," 262). The best histories of the expedition that I have come across are Smith 1990:chap. 2; Hemming 1987:185–94. Still enjoyable to read, though dated, is Prescott 2000 ("Not a bark," 1075).

282 Orellana's betrayal: The case for the prosecution is summed up in Means 1934. For Pizarro's reaction, see letter, Pizarro, G., to king, 3 Sept. 1542, in Heaton 1934:245–51 ("the greatest cruelty," 248).

283 "We were eating": Heaton ed. 1934:408.

283 Angry hives: I have borrowed the simile from Smith 1990:68. The next two sentences are essentially reworkings of his sentences.

283 Carvajal on populousness, Tapajós attacks: Heaton 1934 ("farther we went," 202; "all inhabited," "five leagues," 198; "numerous and very large," 200; "Inland," 216; "more than twenty," 203).

284 Carvajal publication: Medina ed. 1894.

284 Carvajal criticism: López de Gómara 1979:131 (*"mentirosa"*); Myers et al. 1992; Denevan 1996a:661–64; see also, Shoumatoff 1986. Oddly, critics rarely mention that Orellana's account is similar to those from the second Amazon expedition. This was the Pedro de Orsua expedition of 1559–61, subject of the Werner Herzog film *Aguirre, the Wrath of God*. The basic sources are collected in González and Tur eds. 1981. It stopped at the Tapajós in 1561, but provided little further information about the region, except for the suggestive fact that the Indian towns' streets were laid out in a grid and that they had wooden temples with deities painted on the doors (González and Tur eds. 1981:111, 370).

285 Ecologists' views: Arnold 2000. For how they fit into the general Western propensity to view the Amazon as a tropical Eden, see Holanda 1996; Slater 1995; and the polemical Stott 1999. German ecologist Andreas Schimper invented "tropical rain forest" as a scientific construct in 1898 (Schimper 1903). It was an example of a new scientific category that included the living community and its nonliving environment together as a single functioning unit—an ecosystem, a term Schimper's school coined in 1935.

285 More sympathetic views of Carvajal: Author's interews, Balée, Erickson, Peter Stahl, Anna Roosevelt. See also, Porro 1994, Whitehead 1994, for contemporary treatments of early accounts.

285 Must become priority: E.g., "The time bomb of ecological, environmental, climatic and

human damage caused by deforestation continues to tick, and the problem of tropical rainforest clearance must remain a priority within international politics" (Park 1992:162).

286 "A ceaseless round": Belt 1985:184; Darwin ed. 1887 (vol. 3):188 ("best of all").

286 Richards: Richards 1952. Richards's ideas drew heavily on the idea of the natural progression of ecosystems toward a final, stable "climax" developed by ecologists Frederick E. Clements and Arthur George Tansley. In this view, the tropical forest was the climax, the ultimate vegetative destination, in hot, humid areas.

286 "wet desert": The image of the Amazon as a lush forest growing on a desert was apparently popularized in Goodland and Irwin 1975.

288 Rainforest soils: This argument is crisply stated in Wilson 1992:273–74.

288 *Counterfeit Paradise:* Meggers 1996 (orig. ed., 1971).

288 Slash-and-burn as ecologically sensitive response: Interviews, Meggers; Meggers 1996: 20–23. See also, Kleinman, Bryant, and Pimentel 1996; Luna-Orea and Wagger 1996.

288 Unchanged harmony: "In the Western imagination, more generally speaking, the Amazon has stood for centuries as the benchmark of primordial (pure) nature and as a refuge of 'primitive' peoples: our contemporary ancestors" (Heckenberger, forthcoming).

288 Yanomamo as windows into the past: E.g., Brooke 1991 ("a tribe virtually untouched by modern civilization whose ways date from the Stone Age"); Chagnon 1992. In the foreword to the latter, Harvard biologist Edward O. Wilson calls the Yanomamo "the final tribes living strong and free in the style of the preliterate peoples first encountered by Europeans five centuries ago." To Wilson, "the Yanomamö way of life gives us the clearest view of the conditions under which the human mind evolved biologically during deep history" (ix).

289 "mega-Niño events": Author's interviews, Meggers; Meggers 1994; 1979 (other climatic constraints).

289 El Niño fires: Cochrane and Schulze 1998; Pyne 1995:60–65. Fires from a big El Niño in 1925–26 were described in a short, apparently self-published monograph by Giuseppe Marchesi (Marchesi 1975) that I found in a used-book store in Manaus. According to Marchesi, the fires on the Río Negro were so intense that the smoke blocked out the sun in Manaus, hundreds of miles away.

290 Recovery time of forest: Uhl 1987; Uhl and Jordan 1984; Uhl et al. 1982.

290 Upper limit of a thousand: Meggers (1954) says that the rainforest will not permit societies to surpass the "Tropical Forest" pattern of slash-and-burn subsistence (809), which she defines as "villages of 50–1,000 pop[ulation]" (814, fig. 1). The implication is that environmental limits set the maximum village population at one thousand.

290 Meggers dismisses Carvajal: Meggers 1996:187 ("Evidence [of environmental limits] casts doubt on the accuracy of the early European descriptions of large sedentary populations along the floodplain"). Oddly, Meggers endorsed Carvajal in the same book ("These eyewitness reports of numerous large villages are substantiated by archaeological evidence," 133). See also, Meggers 1992a, 1992c.

290 Unchanged lives, population: Meggers 1992 (two thousand years, 199).

290 Meggers and Marajó: Author's interviews, Meggers; Popsin 2003; Meggers and Evans 1957. See also Schaan 2004.

291 Meggers's law: Meggers 1954 ("There is a force," 809; "level to which," 815). Meggers called the stage of slash-and-burn cultivation the "Tropical Forest" pattern. In the brackets, I have replaced references to that term. Her law drew on the environmental-determinist arguments of earlier geographers such as Ellen Churchill Semple, whose *Influences of Geographic Environment* trained two generations of researchers: "The geographic element in the long history of human development has been operating strongly and operating persistently . . . [and] is for all intents and purposes immutable in com-

parison with the other factor in the problem—shifting, plastic, progressive, retrogressive man" (Semple 1911:2).

292 Marajó as offshoot: Meggers and Evans 1957:412–18. See also, Evans and Meggers 1968. Meggers and Evans were influenced by Julian Steward, editor of the influential *Handbook of South American Indians*, who also thought that Marajóara culture originated somewhere else—the Caribbean, he suspected (Steward 1948).

292 Diminishing influence: "Few contemporary scholars accept the hypothesis of environmental limitations and lack of cultural development in the Amazon Basin" (Erickson 2004:457).

292 "Rather than admiration": Cunha 1975:1. I thank Susanna Hecht for letting me use her translation, which is from her forthcoming compilation of da Cunha's Amazonian writings. In the meantime, the original version of this marvelous book can be found at http://www.librairie.hpg.com.br/Euclides-da-Cunha-A-Margem-da-Historia.rtf.

293 Not a disaster: I paraphrase anthropologist Roland Bergman (Bergman 1980:53, quoted in Denevan 2001:60).

293 Rock paintings: Author's visit; Consens 1989.

294 Roosevelt reexcavates: Author's interviews, Roosevelt; Roosevelt 1991 ("outstanding indigenous," 29; "100,000," 2).

294 Earlier challenges to Meggers: Author's interviews, Balée, Denevan, Erickson, Peter Stahl, Woods. Donald Lathrap of the University of Illinois (1970), Michael Coe of Yale (1957), and Robert L. Carneiro of the American Museum of Natural History in New York City (1995, see refs.) mounted the most important ones.

295 Meggers reaction: Author's interviews, Meggers; Meggers 1992b ("polemical," 399; "extravagant," 403). See also Meggers 2004, 2001.

295 Montaigne: Montaigne 1991:233–36.

296 "forest animals": Condamine 1986, quoted in Myers et al. 2004:22.

296 "Where man has remained": Semple 1911:635. The ideas in *Influences of Geographic Environment* were typical for their day. "The Amazon winds its slow way amid the malarious languor of vast tropical forests in which the trees shut out the sky and the few natives are apathetic with the eternal inertia of the hot, damp tropics," Semple's Yale contemporary, Ellsworth Huntington, wrote in 1919 (Huntington 1919:49). "It is generally agreed," Huntington said, "the native races within the tropics are dull in thought and slow in action. This is true not only of the African Negroes, the South American Indians, and the people of the East Indies, but of the inhabitants of southern India and the Malay peninsula" (Huntington 1924:56). See also, Taylor 1927.

296 Meggers-Roosevelt dispute: Author's interviews, Meggers, Roosevelt, Balée, Denevan, Erickson; Meggers 1992a:37 (colonialism, elitism); Baffi et al. 1996 (CIA membership).

297 Painted Rock Cave excavations: Roosevelt et al. 1996; Fiedel et al. 1996; Haynes et al. 1997. Press coverage was unusually thorough. (Gibbons 1996; Wilford 1997a; Hall 1996). In *Science*, Roosevelt presented her estimate of initial occupation as ~11,200 to 10,500 uncalibrated radiocarbon years B.P. (380); I converted the mean, 10,600 B.P., into calendar years with Stuiver et al. 1998.

297 Contemporaneity with Clovis: This is subject to debate, with Clovis-firsters challenging Roosevelt's earliest radiocarbon dates, and Roosevelt crying foul because (in her view) the Clovisites apply more stringent standards to challengers than they do to Clovis (Haynes et al. 1997). Further confusing the issue is the participants' disagreement over the best way of calibrating raw radiocarbon dates from this period.

297 138 crops: Clement 1999a, 1999b.

298 Stone axes: Author's interviews, Denevan; Denevan 1992b. I am grateful to Prof. Denevan for sending me a copy of this article, upon which my discussion of stone axes

is based. See also the updated version of the argument in Denevan 2001:116–23. To some extent, Denevan was anticipated by Donald Lathrap, who called slash-and-burn "a secondary, derived, and late phenomenon within the Amazon Basin," which only made economic sense after the introduction of maize one or two thousand years ago (quoted in ibid.:132). Denevan argued for a much later, post-1492 introduction.

298 Experiments with stone and steel axes: Carneiro 1979a, 1979b; Hill and Kaplan 1989 (difference between hardwoods and softwoods). True, Carneiro's workers had no experience with stone axes, which one assumes unfairly magnified their inefficiency. But Carneiro also did not include the effort required to obtain the stone (often far away), make the ax, and keep it sharp, all of which were time sinks.

298 Three years: Beckerman 1987. I thank Prof. Brush for helping me get this book.

298 Yanomamo history: Author's interviews, Balée, Petersen, Chagnon.

299 Yanomami and steel tools: Author's interview, Ferguson; Ferguson 1998 (lifestyle changes, 291–97), 1995; Colchester 1984 (seventeenth-century change, 308–10). Ferguson's thesis is disputed, in part because it downplays the antiquity of Yanomamo warfare (author's interview, James Petersen).

299 Controversy on Yanomami gifts: These and other charges were publicized and amplified in Tierney 2000. Tierney's charges of exacerbating epidemics seem to have been refuted (see note to p. 102), but the furor over them obscured discussion of uncontrolled gifts of steel tools (Mann 2001, 2000a).

299 Absence of slash-and-burn in North America: Doolittle 2000:174–90 ("gossamer," 186; "once fields," 189).

300 Small farmer slash-and-burn as contributor to deforestation: Author's interviews, Clement, Fearnside; Fearnside 2001. Fearnside's figure is a step down from the estimate that slash-and-burn was responsible for 55 percent of total tropical forest clearing in the Americas in Hadley and Lanly 1983.

300 Nutrient loss: Hölscher 1997. I thank Beata Madari for giving a copy of this article to me.

301 Meggers survey: Meggers et al. 1988; Meggers 1996:183–87.

301 Central Amazon archaeology: Author's interviews, Bartone, Heckenberger, Neves, Petersen; Heckenberger, Petersen, and Neves 2004; Neves et al. 2004; Mann 2002a. I convert uncalibrated radiocarbon years as per Stuiver et al. 1988. The site discussed here is called Hatahara, after its owners.

302 Rainfall and canopy: Brandt 1988.

302 Importance of agroforestry: Interviews, Clement. See also, Denevan 2001:69–70, 83–90, 126–27; Posey 1984; Herrera 1992.

302 Bluffs as preferred sites: Denevan 1996.

303 More than half are trees: Clement 1998 (80 percent); 1999a:199. I am grateful to Dr. Clement for sending me copies of his work.

303 Uses of peach palm: Interviews, Clement; Mora-Urpí, Weber, and Clement 1997 ("only their wives," quoted on 19); Clement and Mora-Urpí 1987 (yield); Deneyan 2001:77 (saws).

304 Domestication of peach palm: Clement 1995, 1992, 1988.

304 Agricultural regression and fallows forests: Balée 2003 ("These old forests," 282); 1994.

305 Anthropogenic forests: Interviews, Balée, Clement, Erickson, Nigel Smith, Stahl, Woods; Balée 1998; 1989 (11.8 percent, 14); Erickson 1999 (I am grateful to Prof. Erickson for sending me a copy of this paper); Smith 1995; Stahl 2002, 1996.

306 "Gift from the past": I have lifted this phrase from the title of Petersen, Neves, and Heckenberger 2001.

306 *Terra preta*: Much of what follows below is taken from the excellent Lehmann et al. eds. 2004; Glaser and Woods eds. 2004; and Petersen, Neves, and Heckenberger 2001. For a popular treatment, see Mann 2002b, 2000b. Lehmann et al. argue that from a scientific

standpoint ADE (Amazonian dark earth) is a better term than *terra preta*. I use *terra preta* to avoid acronyms.

306 *Terra preta* valued: Smith 1980:562. Smith's fine early article on *terra preta* was largely ignored on publication—"I got two reprint requests for that article," he told me. "Nobody was ready to hear it."

307 *Terra preta* distribution estimates: Author's interviews, Woods, Wim Sombroek; Sombroek et al. 2004:130 (.1–.3 percent); Kern et al. 2004:52–53 (*terra preta* sites every five kilometers along tributaries).

307 Maya heartland: The Maya heartland—from Petén, Guatemala, and Belize north to southern Campeche and Quintana Roo in Mexico—covers about fifteen thousand square miles, a third or half of which was devoted to agriculture.

307 Charcoal: Glaser, Guggenberger, and Zech 2004; Glaser, Lehmann, and Zech 2002. My thanks to Prof. Glaser for giving me a copy of this article.

308 Microbial activity: Author's interview, Janice Theis; Theis and Suzuki 2004; Woods and McCann 1999 (inoculation). I thank Joe McCann for giving me a copy of this article.

308 Charcoal and global warming: Author's interview, Ogawa; Okimori, Ogawa, and Takahashi 2003.

308 Kayapó: Author's interviews, Hecht; Hecht 2004 ("low-biomass," "cool," 362–63; "To live," 364). I am indebted to Prof. Hecht for several fascinating discussions.

308 *Terra preta* experiments: Author's interview, Steiner; Steiner, Teixeira, and Zech 2004.

309 Río Negro site: Author's interviews, Bartone, Neves, Petersen; Heckenberger, Petersen, and Neves 2004, 1999.

309 Timing of *terra preta* at plantation: Neves et al. 2004:table 9.2.

309 Xingu and black earth: Heckenberger et al. 2003 ("regional plan," "bridges," 1711; "built environment," 1713). For criticism, see Meggers 2003.

310 Santarém *terra preta*: Interviews, Woods, Sombroek; author's visit; Kern et al. 2004.

310 Meggers reaction: Meggers 2001 ("without restraint," 305; "accomplices," 322). A response appears in Heckenberger, Petersen, and Neves 2001.

310 "rev up": DeBoer, Kintigh, and Rostoker 2001:327.

311 "Rather than adapt": I swipe this phrase from Erickson 2004 ("Native Amazonians did not adapt to nature, but rather they created the world that they wanted through human creativity, technology and engineering, and cultural institutions," 456).

10 / *The Artificial Wilderness*

312 "all the trees": Columbus 1963:84. I discovered this quotation, and the ideas around it, in Crosby 2003:3–16, 1986:9–12 (knitting together Pangaea).

312 Invention of Columbian Exchange: McNeill 2003:xiv.

313 Kudzu: Blaustein 2001; Kinbacher 2000.

313 A thousand kudzus everywhere: Crosby 1986:154–56 (spinach, mint, peach, endive, clover), 161 (Darwin), 191 (Jamestown, Garcilaso).

314 Cod and sea urchins: Jackson et al. 2001.

314 Keystone species: Wilson 1992:401.

315 "widowed land": Chapter title in Jennings 1975.

315 Passenger pigeons: Schorger 1955 (vomiting, 35; rain of droppings, 54; huge roostings, 10–15, 77–89; excommunication, 51; one out of four, 205).

315 Muir and pigeons: Muir 1997:78–82.

316 Audubon and pigeons: Audubon 1871 (vol. 5):115.

316 Seneca and pigeon: Harris 1903:449–51.

316 "living, pulsing": French 1919:1.

317 Leopold and monument: Leopold 1968.
317 Mast competition, lack of passenger pigeons: Interview, Neumann, Woods; Neumann 2002:158–64, 169–72; Herrmann and Woods 2003 (I thank Prof. Woods for giving me a copy of this paper).
318 Seton's estimate: Seton 1929 (vol. 3):654–56. See, in general, Krech 1999:chap. 5.
318 Lott's and other modern estimates of abundance: Lott 2002:69–76 ("primitive America," 76); Flores 1997; 1991 ("perhaps" twenty-eight to thirty million, 471); Weber 2001 ("more likely" twenty to forty-four million). Shaw (1995) and Geist (1998) suggested the number should be ten to fifteen million.
321 De Soto never saw bison: Crosby 1986:213.
321 La Salle's buffalo: Parkman 1983 (vol. 1):765.
321 "post-Columbian abundance": Geist 1998:62–63.
321 Elk begin to appear: Kay 1995.
321 California: Preston 2002 (Drake, 129).
323 "The virgin forest": Pyne 1982:46–47. See also, Jennings 1975:30.
323 "artificial wilderness": I borrow the phrase from Callicott and Nelson eds. 1998:11.
323 More "forest primeval" in nineteenth century: Denevan 1992a:377–81 ("pristine myth" article).
326 Cronon, academic brouhaha: Cronon 1995a, 1995b; Soulé and Lease eds. 1995; Callicott and Nelson eds. 1998 ("Euro-American men," 2). An abridged version of Cronon 1996b appeared in the *New York Times Sunday Magazine*, 13 Aug. 1995.
326 Making gardens: Janzen 1998.
326 Creating future environments: I have borrowed the phrase and the thought from McCann 1999a:3.

11 / *The Great Law of Peace*

329 Nabokov in New York: Boyd 1991:11–12.
330 Early history of Haudenosaunee, Deganawidah story: Fenton 1998; Snow 1994:58–65; Hertzberg 1966.
331 Rules of operation: Tooker 1988:312–17. The basic source is Morgan 1901:77ff.
331 Checks and balances: Grinde 1992:235–40; Tehanetorens 1971 ("especially important," sec. 93; impeachment grounds and procedures, secs. 19–25, 39 ("warnings," sec. 19); rights of individuals and nations, secs. 93–98). A modern translation is online at http://www.iroquoisdemocracy.pdx.edu/html/greatlaw.html.
332 "they will not conclude": Williams 1936:201.
332 Iroquois women: Wagner 2001; Parker 1911:252–53 ("Does the modern American woman [who] is a petitioner before man, pleading for her political rights, ever stop to consider that the red woman that lived in New York state five hundred years ago, had far more political rights and enjoyed a much wider liberty than the twentieth century woman of civilization?"). I thank Robert Crease for helping me obtain this source.
332 Underwood's estimate: cited in Johansen 1995:62.
332 Condolence Canes: Barreiro and Cornelius eds. 1991; Fenton 1983.
333 Age of council: Mann and Fields 1997. See also, Johansen 1995.
333 Haudenosaunee as second oldest: Some of the Swiss cantons have continuously functioning parliaments that are older, too. But I did not include them because the individual cantons seem more comparable to the individual nations of Haudenosaunee than to the league as a whole.
333 Great Law as inspiration: Grinde and Johansen 1991; Grinde 1977; Johansen 1987; Wright 1992:94 ("Their whole").

333 Differences between Constitution and Great Law: Venables 1992:74–124 (Adams's reminiscences, 108).

334 Franklin: Johansen 1987:40–42.

334 Indian freedoms: Josephy ed. 1993:29.

334 "Every man": Quoted in Venables 1992:235.

334 "such absolute": Colden 1747:100.

334 Perrot, Hennepin, Jesuit on Indian liberty: Quoted in Jaenen 1976:88 (Jesuit), 89 (Perrot), 92 (Hennepin).

334 Lahontan: Lahontan 1703 (vol. 2):8.

335 Montaigne: Montaigne 1991:233.

335 Greater attractiveness of native lives: Axtell 1975; Wilson 1999:67 (fleeing Jamestown). Axtell's conclusions were sharply critiqued in Vaughan and Richter 1980; Axtell's response (1981:351) was convincing, at least to me. See also Calloway 1986; Treckel and Axtell 1976.

335 Pilgrims dismayed by renegades: Salisbury 1982:128–33.

335 "When an Indian": Quoted in Axtell 1975:57.

335 "troubled the power elite": Jaenen 1976:95.

Appendixes

339 "I abhor": Quoted at http://www.russellmeans.com/russell.html.

340 Insulting names: This is a separate issue from the use of Indian references on geographical features and U.S. sports teams, some of which have long annoyed Indians. Various efforts have been made to ban the use of "squaw," for example, as in Squaw Valley, home of a big ski resort in California, on the grounds that the word is a vulgar term for the vagina used to demean native women. Most linguists do not believe this is true. Still, the use of specific terms for the women of an ethnic group rings oddly these days—one can't imagine a resort called Jewess or Negress Valley. Redskin, as in the Washington Redskins, the football team of the U.S. capital, also seems unhappily anachronistic. According to the team, the name is intended to celebrate Indians' warrior spirit, a good quality, and is therefore not derogatory. But it seems like calling a dance troupe the New York Pickaninnies and saying the name is intended to extol African Americans' innate sense of rhythm, a good quality.

341 "snowshoe," "people who": Goddard 1984; Mailhot 1978.

342 Crosby on civilization: Crosby 2002:71. See also, Wright 2005:32–33.

343 " 'Tribe' and 'chiefdom' ": Kehoe 2002:245.

345 *Khipu:* For a brief overview, see Mann 2003.

345 "resembles a mop": Joseph 1992:28.

345 Governor consults *khipu:* Collapiña, Supno et al. 1921.

345 *Khipu* are banned: Urton 2003:22, 49.

346 Locke and Mead on *khipu:* Mead 1923 ("the mystery", n.p.). Locke (1923:32) shared Mead's view: "*The evidence is intrinsically against the supposition that the quipu was a conventional scheme of writing*" (italics in original). For another early attempt at decipherment, see Nordenskiöld 1979.

346 "Inka had no writing": Fagan 1991:50.

346 Urton and *khipu* writing: Urton 2003.

346 Aschers' work: Interview, R. Ascher ("clearly non-numerical"); Ascher and Ascher 1997:87 ("rapidly developing").

347 Breakdown of *khipu* meaning units: Urton 2003:chaps. 2–5 ("system of coding information . . . binary code," 1; comparison with Sumer, Maya, Egypt, 117–18).

348 Miccinelli documents: Laurencich-Minelli 2001; Laurencich-Minelli et al. 1998, 1995; Zoppi 2000.

349 Tentative decipherment: Urton 2001.

351 Charles VIII and European syphilis epidemic: Baker and Armelagos 1988:708.

351 "Iyen in fire": Quoted in Crosby 2003:125–26.

352 Darwinian predictions about diseases: Ewald 1996:chap. 3. More precisely, nonvector-borne microorganisms evolve toward moderate malignity.

352 Díaz and Las Casas: Williams, Rice, and Lacayo 1927:690 ("origin"). My thanks to June Kinoshita for helping me obtain this article. On the origin of syphilis, Las Casas was unequivocal: "From the beginning, two things did and do afflict the Spanish on this island [Hispaniola]: the first is the sickness of the bubas [pustules], which in Italy is called the French disease. And I know for the truth that it came from this island or from when the first Indians came here, when Admiral Christopher Columbus returned with the news of the discovery of the Indies, which I saw in Seville, and they were stuck rotting in Spain, infecting the air or some other route, or else there were some Spanish with the disease among the first returnees to Castille." Las Casas also says the epidemic began during the war in Naples (Las Casas 1992 [vol. 6]:361–62).

352 Recent syphilis findings: Rothschild and Rothschild 2000 (Colorado); 1996 (U.S. and Ecuador); Rothschild et al. 2000b (Caribbean). See also, Rogan and Lentz 1994, cited in Arriaza 1995:78.

352 Evidence for early European syphilis: E.g., Pearson 1924 (suggesting that Bruce's recently excavated skeleton and deathmask support a diagnosis of syphilis, rather than leprosy); Power 1992 (I am grateful to Robert Crease for making it possible for me to obtain this source); Stirland 1995:109–15. News reports indicate that other such skeletons exist, too, though some have not yet appeared in the scholarly literature (e.g., Studd 2001; Barr 2000). In the past, though, few of "the numerous cases of pre-Columbian Old World syphilis . . . have withstood reexamination" (Baker and Armelagos 1988:710).

353 Universal presence of syphilis: Hudson 1965a, 1965b.

353 Confusion with Hansen's disease: Baker and Armelagos 1988:706–07.

353 Historians' motives: Crosby, "Preface to the 2003 Edition," in 2003b:xix.

❋ BIBLIOGRAPHY ❋

ABBREVIATIONS

AA *American Anthropologist*
AmAnt *American Antiquity*
AJHG *American Journal of Human Genetics*
AAAG *Annals of the Association of American Geographers*
CA *Current Anthropology*
HE *Human Ecology*
JAH *Journal of American History*
JAR *Journal of Archaeological Research*
JB *Journal of Biogeography*
LAA *Latin American Antiquity*
NH *Natural History*
NYT *New York Times*
PNAS *Proceedings of the National Academy of Sciences*
QI *Quaternary International*
QR *Quaternary Research*
QSR *Quaternary Science Reviews*
WA *World Archaeology*
WMQ *William and Mary Quarterly*

Abbott, C. C. 1892a. "Paleolithic Man: A Last Word." *Science* 20:344–45.
———. 1892b. "Paleolithic Man in North America." *Science* 20:270–71.
———. 1884. "The Intelligence of Snakes." *Science* 3:253–56.
———. 1883a. "The Intelligence of Birds." *Science* 2:301–03.
———. 1883b. "The Intelligence of Fish." *Science* 1:327–28.
———. 1876. "Indications of the Antiquity of the Indians of North America, Derived from a Study of Their Relics." *American Naturalist* 10:65–72.
———. 1872a, and 1872b. "The Stone Age in New Jersey." *American Naturalist,* part 1, 6:144–60; part 2, 6:199–229.
Abbott, M. B., et al. 1997. "A 3500 14C yr High-Resolution Record of Water-Level Changes in Lake Titicaca, Bolivia/Peru." *QR* 47:169–80.
Abrams, E., and R. Rue. 1988. "The Causes and Consequences of Deforestation Among the Prehistoric Maya." *HE* 14:377–99.
Ackerman, F., et al. 2002. "Environmental Impacts of the Changes in US-Mexico Corn Trade Under NAFTA." Unpub. ms., 15 May.
Acosta, J. D. 2002. *Natural and Moral History of the Indies.* Trans. F. M. López-Morillas. Durham, NC: Duke University Press (1590).
Adams, C. F. 1892–93. *Three Episodes of Massachusetts History.* 2 vols. Boston: Houghton Mifflin. (★)

Adams, R. E. W., and R. C. Jones. 1981. "Spatial Patterns and Regional Growth Among Classic Maya Cities." *AmAnt* 46:301–22.

Adovasio, J. M., and J. Page. 2003. *The First Americans: In Pursuit of Archaeology's Greatest Mystery.* New York: Modern Library.

Alexander, E. 1994. *The Holocaust and the War of Ideas.* New Brunswick, NJ: Transaction.

Alfimov, A. V., and D. I. Berman. 2001. "Beringian Climate During the Late Pleistocene and Holocene." *QSR* 20:127–34.

Algaze, G. 1993. *The Uruk World System: The Dynamics of Expansion of Early Mesopotamian Civilization.* Chicago: University of Chicago Press.

Alley, R. B. 2000. "Ice-Core Evidence of Rapid Climate Changes." *PNAS* 97:1331–34.

Allison, M. J. 1985. "Chile's Ancient Mummies." *NH* (October):74–81.

Alsoszatai-Petheo, J. 1986. "An Alternative Paradigm for the Study of Early Man in the New World," in Bryan 1986, 15–23.

Alva, W., and C. B. Donnan. 1993. *Royal Tombs of Sipan.* Los Angeles: University of California Press.

Anderson, E. 1984. "Who's Who in the Pleistocene: A Mammalian Bestiary," in Martin and Klein 1984, 40–89.

Anderson, E. C., et al. 1947a. "Natural Radiocarbon from Cosmic Radiation." *Physical Review* 72:931–36.

———. 1947b. "Radiocarbon from Cosmic Radiation." *Science* 105:576–77.

Anderson, S., et al. 1981. "Sequence and Organization of the Human Mitochondrial Genome." *Nature* 290:457–65.

Anello Oliva, G. 1998. *Historia del Reino y Provincias del Perú y Vidas de los Varones Insignes de la Compañía de Jesús.* Lima: Pontificia Universidad Católica del Perú (1631).

Anon. 2003. "Whiteman, James" (obituary). *Clovis* (N.M.) *News Journal,* 23 Sep.

———. 1994. "Leyenda de los Soles." Trans. T. Sullivan. In Sullivan and Knab 1994, 62–81.

———. 1982. *El Maíz, Fundamento de la Cultura Popular Mexicana.* Mexico City: Museo Nacional de Culturas Populares.

———. 1979. "Occurents in Newfoundland," 1 Sep. 1612–1 Apr. 1613, in D. B. Quinn, ed., *New American World: A Documentary History of North America to 1612.* New York: Arno, 4:157–78.

———. 1932. "Arrowheads Found with New Mexican Fossils." *Science* 36:12a–13a.

———. 1928. "Trace American Man Back 15,000 Years." *NYT,* 23 Sep., N1.

———. 1743. "Extract of a Spanish Relations Containing the Life and Death of Father Cypriano Baraze of the Society of Jesus, Founder of the Mission of Mojos in Peru," in J. Lockman, ed., *Travels of the Jesuits into Various Parts of the World.* London: John Noon, 2:437–68 (1703).

Anon., ed. 1998a. *Anuario Estadístico del Estado de Chiapas.* Aguascalientes, Ags.: Instituto Nacional de Estadística, Geografía e Informática.

———. 1998b. *Anuario Estadístico del Estado de Oaxaca.* Aguascalientes, Ags.: Instituto Nacional de Estadística, Geografía e Informática.

———. 1963. *Mourt's Relation: A Journal of the Pilgrims at Plymouth.* Bedford, MA: Applewood (1622). (★)

Arber, E., ed. 1885. *The First Three English Books on America, [?1511]–1555 A.D.* Birmingham, UK: Turnbull & Spears.

Arber, E., and A. G. Bradley, eds. 1910. *Travels and Works of Captain John Smith: President of Virginia and Admiral of New England, 1580–1631.* 2 vols. Edinburgh: John Grant.

Ariés, P. 1962. *Centuries of Childhood: A Social History of Family Life.* New York: Knopf.

Arnold, D. 2000. " 'Illusory Riches': Representations of the Tropical World, 1840–1950." *Singapore Journal of Tropical Ecology* 21:6–18.

Arnold, J. R., and W. F. Libby. 1949. "Age Determinations by Radiocarbon Content: Checks with Samples of Known Age." *Science* 110:678–80.

Arnold, P. J., III. 2003. "Early Formative Pottery from the Tuxtla Mountains and Implications for Gulf Olmec Origins." *LAA* 14:29–46.

Arriaza, B. T. 1995. *Beyond Death: The Chinchorro Mummies of Ancient Chile.* Washington, DC: Smithsonian.

Arriaza, B. T., et al. 2001. "The Peopling of the Arica Coast During the Preceramic: A Preliminary View." *Chungará* (Arica, Chile) 33:31–36.

Ascher, R., and M. Ascher. 1997. *Code of the Quipu.* New York: Dover (1981).

Audubon, J. J. 1871. *The Birds of America, from Drawings Made in the United States and Their Territories.* 5 vols. New York: G. R. Lockwood.

Aufderheide, A. C., and M. J. Allison. 1995. "Chemical Dietary Reconstruction of North Chile Prehistoric Populations by Trace Mineral Analysis," in *Proceedings of the First World Congress on Mummy Studies, February 3–6, 1992.* Cabildo de Tenerife: Museos Arqueológico y Etnográfico de Tenerife, 1:451–61.

Aveni, A. 2000. *Between the Lines: The Mystery of the Giant Ground Drawings of Ancient Nasca, Peru.* Austin, TX: University of Texas Press.

———. 1995. *Empires of Time: Calendars, Clocks, and Cultures.* New York: Kodansha (1989).

Axelrod, D. A. 1985. "Rise of the Grassland Biome, Central North America." *Botanical Review* 51:164–201.

Axtell, J. 2000. *Natives and Newcomers: The Cultural Origins of North America.* New York: Oxford University Press.

———. 1994. "The Exploration of Norumbega: Native Perspectives," in Baker 1994, 149–65.

———. 1992. "Europeans, Indians, and the Age of Discovery in American History Textbooks," in *Beyond 1492: Encounters in Colonial North America.* New York: Oxford University Press, 197–216.

———. 1988. "Through Another Glass Darkly: Early Indian Views of Europeans," in *After Columbus: Essays in the Ethnohistory of Colonial North America.* New York: Oxford University Press, 125–43.

———. 1980. "The Unkindest Cut, or Who Invented Scalping?" *WMQ* 37:451–72.

———. 1978. "The Ethnohistory of Early America: A Review Essay." *WMQ* 35:110–44.

———. 1975. "The White Indians of Colonial America." *WMQ* 32:55–88.

Axtell, J., ed. 1981. *The Indian Peoples of Eastern America: A Documentary History of the Sexes.* New York: Oxford University Press.

Baffi, E. I., et al. 1996. Letter. *SAA Bulletin* 5:5.

Bailey, T. A., et al. 1983. *The American Pageant.* Lexington, MA: D. C. Heath, 7th ed.

Bailyn, B. 1986. *The Peopling of British North America: An Introduction.* New York: Knopf.

Bailyn, B., et al. 1977. *The Great Republic: A History of the American People.* Lexington, MA: D. C. Heath.

Baird, D., and L. Bairstow. 2004. *Frommer's Mexico 2005.* New York: Frommer's.

Bairoch, P., J. Batou, and P. Chévre. 1988. *La Population des Villes Européennes, 800–1850: Banque de Données et Analyse Sommaire des Résultats.* Geneva: Droz.

Bakeless, J. 1961. *The Eyes of Discovery: The Pageant of North America as Seen by the First Explorers.* New York: Dover (1950).

Baker, B. J., and G. J. Armelagos. 1988. "The Origin and Antiquity of Syphilis: Paleopathological Diagnosis and Interpretation." *CA* 29:703–37.

Baker, E. W., et al., eds. 1995. *American Beginnings: Exploration, Culture and Cartography in the Land of Norumbega.* Lincoln, NE: University of Nebraska Press.

Balée, W. 2003. "Native Views of the Environment in Amazonia," in H. Selin, *Nature Across Cultures: Views of Nature and the Environment in Non-Western Cultures.* The Netherlands: Kluwer Academic.

———. 2000. "Elevating the Amazonian Landscape." *Forum for Applied Research and Public Policy* 15:28–32.

———. 1999. "The Sirionó of the Llanos de Mojos, Bolivia," in R. B. Lee and R. Daly, eds., *The Cambridge Encyclopedia of Hunters and Gatherers*. New York: Cambridge University Press, 105–09.

———. 1998. "Historical Ecology: Premises and Postulates," in Balée ed. 1998, 13–29.

———. 1994. *Footprints in the Forest: Ka'apor Ethnobotany: The Historical Ecology of Plant Utilization by an Amazonian People*. New York: Columbia University Press.

———. 1989. "The Culture of Amazonian Forests," in D. A. Posey and W. Balée, eds., *Resource Management in Amazonia: Indigenous and Folk Strategies*. New York: New York Botanical Garden, 1–21.

Balée, W., ed. 1998. *Advances in Historical Ecology*. New York: Columbia University Press.

Balée, W., and C. L. Erickson, eds. 2005. *Time and Complexity in Historical Ecology: Studies in the Neotropical Lowlands*. New York: Columbia University Press.

Balter, M. 1998. "Why Settle Down? The Mystery of Communities." *Science* 282:1442–45.

Bancroft, G. 1834–76. *History of the United States, from the Discovery of the American Continent*. 7 vols. Boston: Little, Brown.

Bandelt, H.-J., et al. 2003. "Identification of Native American Founder mtDNAs Through the Analysis of Complete mtDNA Sequences: Some Caveats." *Annals of Human Genetics* 67:512–24.

Barr, R. 2000. "Tracing Syphilis: Medieval English Skeletons Had Syphilis Before Columbus." Associated Press, 29 Aug.

Barreiro, J., and C. Cornelius, eds. 1991. *Knowledge of the Elders: The Iroquois Condolence Cane Tradition*. Ithaca, New York: Cornell University Press.

Barry, I. 1977. "The Sirionó of Eastern Bolivia: A Reexamination." *HE* 5:137–54.

Barton, P. A. 2001. *A History of the African-Olmecs: Black Civilizations of America from Prehistoric Times to the Present Era*. Bloomington, IN: 1stBooks.

Bartram, W. 1996. *Travels and Other Writings*. New York: Library of America (1791).

Bates, E. S. 1940. *American Faith: Its Religious, Political, and Economic Foundations*. New York: Norton.

Baudin, L. 1961. *A Socialist Empire: The Incas of Peru*. Trans. K. Woods. Princeton, NJ: Van Nostrand.

Bauer, B. 1998. *The Sacred Landscape of the Inca: The Cusco Ceque System*. Austin, TX: University of Texas Press.

Bawden, G. 1996. *The Moche*. Cambridge, MA: Blackwell.

Baxby, D. 1981. *Jenner's Smallpox Vaccine: The Riddle of Vaccinia Virus and Its Origin*. London: Heinemann.

Baxter, J. P. 1890. "Memoir," in Baxter ed. 1890, 1:1–198.

Baxter, J. P., ed. 1890. *Sir Ferdinando Gorges and His Province of Maine*. 3 vols. Boston: Prince Society.

Beadle, G. 1939. "Teosinte and the Origin of Maize." *Journal of Heredity* 30:245–47.

Beattie, O. B., and A. L. Bryan. 1984. "A Fossilized Calotte with Prominent Brow Ridges from Lagoa Santa, Brazil." *CA* 25:345–46.

Beckerman, S. 1987. "Swidden in Amazonia and the Amazon Rim," in Turner and Brush 1987, 55–94.

Begley, S., and A. Murr. 1999. "The First Americans." *Newsweek*, 26 Apr., 50–57.

Belt, T. 1985. *The Naturalist in Nicaragua*. Chicago: University of Chicago Press (1874).

Beltrán, C. L. 1937. "Informe del Director de la Escuela Indigenal de Guacharecure." *La Patria* (Oruro, Bolivia), 19 Mar.

Beltrão, M. C. de M. C., et al. 1986. "Thermoluminescence Dating of Burnt Cherts from the Alice Boer Site, Brazil," in Bryan 1986, 203–13.

Bennett, M. K. 1955. "The Food Economy of the New England Indians, 1605–75." *Journal of Political Economy* 63:369–97.

Bennetzen, J., et al. 2001. "Genetic Evidence and the Origin of Maize." *LAA* 12:84–86.

Benson, E. P., ed. 1981. *The Olmec and Their Neighbors: Essays in Memory of Matthew W. Stirling.* Washington, DC: Dumbarton Oaks.

Benz, B. F. 2001. "Archaeological Evidence of Teosinte Domestication from Guilá Naquitz, Oaxaca." *PNAS* 98:2104–06.

Benz, B. F., and H. H. Iltis. 1990. "Studies in Archaeological Maize I: The 'Wild' Maize from San Marcos Cave Reexamined." *AmAnt* 55:500–11.

Benzoni, G. 1857. *History of the New World, by Girolamo Benzoni, of Milan: Showing His Travels in America from A.D. 1541 to 1556.* Trans. W. H. Smyth. London: Hakluyt Society (1572).

Bergman, R. W. 1980. *Amazon Economics: The Simplicity of Shipibo Indian Wealth.* Ann Arbor, MI: University Microfilms.

Berkes, F. 1999. *Sacred Ecology: Traditional Ecological Knowledge and Resource Management.* London: Taylor and Francis.

Berliner, M. 2003. "On Columbus Day, Celebrate Western Civilization, Not Multiculturalism." Cybercast News Service, 14 Oct. Online at http://www.cnsnews.com/View Commentary.asp?Page=%5CCommentary%5Carchive%5C200310%5CCOM20031013c.html.

Berlo, J. C., ed. 1993. *Art, Ideology, and the City of Teotihuacán: A Symposium at Dumbarton Oaks 8–9 October 1988.* Washington, DC: Dumbarton Oaks.

Bernal, I. 1969. *The Olmec World.* Trans. D. Heyden and F. Horcasitas. Berkeley, CA: University of California Press.

Betanzos, J. D. 1996. *Narrative of the Incas.* Trans. R. Hamilton and D. Buchanan. Austin, TX: University of Texas Press (1557).

Beyers, C. 2001. "Directions in Ethnohistorical Research on the Inca State and Economy." CERLAC Occasional Papers. Online at http://www.yorku.ca/cerlac/papers/pdf/Beyers.pdf.

Biggar, H. P., ed. 1922–36. *The Works of Samuel de Champlain.* 6 vols. Toronto: Champlain Society.

Billard, J. B. 1975. *National Geographic Atlas of the World.* Washington, DC: National Geographic, 4th ed.

Binford, M. W., et al. 1997. "Climate Variation and the Rise and Fall of an Andean Civilization." *QR* 47: 235–48.

———. 1987. "Ecosystems, Paleoecology, and Human Disturbance in Tropical and Subtropical America." *QSR* 6:115–28.

Black, F. M. 2004. "Disease Susceptibility Among New World Peoples," in Salzano and Hurtado 2004, 147–63.

———. 1994. "An Explanation of High Death Rates Among New World Peoples When in Contact with Old World Diseases." *Perspectives in Biology and Medicine* 37:295.

———. 1992. "Why Did They Die?" *Science* 258:1739–40.

Blanton, R., et al. 1999. *Ancient Oaxaca.* New York: Cambridge University Press.

Blaustein, R. J. 2001. "Kudzu's Invasion into Southern United States Life and Culture," in J. A. McNeeley, ed., *The Great Reshuffling: Human Dimensions of Invasive Species.* Cambridge: World Conservation Union, 55–62.

Bonatto, S. L., and F. M. Salzano. 1997. "A Single and Early Migration for the Peopling of the Americas Supported by Mitochondrial DNA Sequence Data." *PNAS* 94:1866–71.

Boot, E. 2002a. "The Life and Times of B'alah Chan K'awil of Mutal (Dos Pilas), According to Dos Pilas Hieroglyphic Stairway 2." Online at http://www.mesoweb.com/features/boot/DPLHS2.pdf.

———. 2002b. "The Dos Pilas–Tikal Wars from the Perspective of Dos Pilas Hieroglyphic Stairway 4." Online at http://www.mesoweb.com/features/boot/DPLHS4.pdf.

Borah, W. W. 1976. "The Historical Demography of Aboriginal and Colonial America: An Attempt at Perspective," in Denevan ed. 1976, 13–34.

———. 1951. *New Spain's Century of Depression.* Berkeley, CA: University of California Press.

Borah, W. W., and S. F. Cook. 1964. *The Aboriginal Population of Central Mexico on the Eve of Spanish Conquest.* Berkeley, CA: University of California Press.

Boszhardt, R. F. 2002. "Contracting Stemmed: What's the Point?" *Midcontinental Journal of Archaeology* 27:35–67.

Botkin, D. B. 1990. *Discordant Harmonies: A New Ecology for the Twenty-First Century.* New York: Oxford University Press, rev. ed.

Bourne, E. G., ed. 1922. *Narratives of the Career of Hernando de Soto.* New York: Allerton (1544).

Bourque, B., and R. H. Whitehead. 1994. "Trade and Alliances in the Contact Period," in Baker et al. 1994, 131–47.

Bower, B. 2001. "Peru Holds Oldest New World City." *Science News* 159:260.

Boyd, B. 1991. *Vladimir Nabokov: The American Years.* Princeton, NJ: Princeton University Press.

Boyd, R. 1999. *The Coming of the Spirit of Pestilence: Introduced Infectious Diseases and Population Decline Among the Northwest Coast Indians, 1774–1874.* Seattle: University of Washington Press.

Bradbury, A. P. 1997. "The Bow and Arrow in the Eastern Woodlands: Evidence for an Archaic Origin." *North American Archaeologist* 18:207–33.

Bradford, W. 2002. *Governor William Bradford's Letter Book.* Boston: Applewood (1906).

———. 1981. *Of Plymouth Plantation, 1620–1647.* New York: Modern Library (1856). (★)

Bragdon, K. J. 1996. *Native People of Southern New England, 1500–1650.* Norman, OK: University of Oklahoma Press.

Brandão, J. E. 1997. *"Your Fyre Shall Burn No More": Iroquois Policy Toward New France and its Native Allies to 1701.* Lincoln, NE: University of Nebraska Press.

Brandt, J. 1988. "The Transformation of Rainfall Energy by a Tropical Rain Forest Canopy in Relation to Soil Erosion." *JB* 15:41–48.

Braudel, F. 1981–84. *Civilization and Capitalism, 15th–18th Century.* Trans. S. Reynolds. 3 vols. New York: Harper & Row (1979).

Bray, T., and T. Killion, eds. 1994. *Reckoning with the Dead: The Larsen Bay Repatriation and the Smithsonian Institution.* Washington, DC: Smithsonian.

Bricker, V. 1986. *A Grammar of Mayan Hieroglyphs.* New Orleans, LA: Tulane University Press.

Bril, A. 1988. "A Report from Adam Bril, Governor of Irkutsk, Describing the Native Peoples of Kamchatka and the Nearby Islands in the North Pacific Ocean," in Dmytryshan, Crownhart-Vaughan, and Vaughan 1988, 2:236–44.

Brooke, J. 1991. "Brazil Creates Reserve for Imperiled Amazon Tribe." *NYT,* 19 Nov.

Brown, A. A., and K. P. Davis. 1973. *Forest Fire: Control and Use.* New York: McGraw Hill, 2nd ed.

Brown, J. A. 1997. "The Archaeology of Ancient Religion in the Eastern Woodlands." *Annual Review of Anthropology* 26:465–85.

Brown, M. D., et al. 1998. "MtDNA Haplogroup X: An Ancient Link between Europe/Western Asia and North America?" *AJHG* 63:1852–61.

Browne, J. 1938. "Antiquity of the Bow." *AmAnt* 3:358–59.

Bruhns, K. O. 1994. *Ancient South America.* New York: Cambridge University Press.

Bryan, A. L., ed. 1986. *New Evidence for the Pleistocene Peopling of the Americas.* Orono, ME: Center for Early Man Studies.

Bunzel, R. L. 1932. "Zuñi Origin Myths." *Forty-Seventh Annual Report of the Bureau of American Ethnology, 1929–1930.* Washington, DC: Government Printing Office, 545–609.

Burger, R. L. 1992. *Chavín and the Origins of Andean Civilization.* New York: Thames and Hudson.

Burger, R. L., and R. B. Gordon. 1998. "Early Central Andean Metalworking from Mina Perdida, Peru." *Science* 282:1108–11.

Burnett, B. A., and K. M. Murray. 1993. "Death, Drought, and De Soto: The Bioarchaeology of Depopulation," in Young and Hoffman 1993, 227–36.

Burns, J. A. 1996. "Vertebrate Paleontology and the Alleged Ice-Free Corridor: The Meat of the Matter." *QI* 32:107–12.

Byland, B. E., and J. M. D. Pohl. 1994. *In the Realm of 8 Deer: The Archaeology of the Mixtec Codices.* Norman, OK: University of Oklahoma Press.

Cabello Balboa, M. 1920. "Bajo la dominación de los Incas," in H. H. Urteaga, ed., *Colección de Libros y Documentos Referentes a la Historia del Perú.* Lima: Sanmarti, vol. 2 (1586).

Callen, E. O. 1967. "The First New World Cereal." *AmAnt* 32:535–38.

Callicott, J. B. 1998. "The Wilderness Idea Revisited: The Sustainable Development Alternative," in Callicott and Nelson eds. 1998, 337–66.

Callicott, J. B., and M. P. Nelson. 1998. "Introduction," in Callicott and Nelson eds. 1998, 1–20.

Callicott, J. B., and M. P. Nelson, eds. 1998. *The Great New Wilderness Debate.* Atlanta: University of Georgia Press.

Calloway, C. G. 2003. *One Vast Winter Count: The Native American West before Lewis and Clark.* Lincoln, NE: University of Nebraska Press.

———. 1986. "Neither White nor Red: White Renegades on the American Indian Frontier." *Western Historical Quarterly* 17:43–66.

Calogeras, J. P. 1933. "O Dr. Peter Wilhelm Lund." *Revista do Instituto Historico e Geografico Brasiliero,* n.v., 85–93.

Campbell, G. R. 2003. " 'We Believed the Good Spirit Had Forsaken Us': The Cultural Impact of European Infectious Disease Among Indigenous Peoples of the Northwestern Plains." Paper at the Confluence of Cultures Conference, Missoula, MT, 28–30 May.

Campbell, L. 1997. *American Indian Languages: The Historical Linguistics of Native America.* New York: Oxford University Press.

———. 1988. "Language in the Americas" (review). *Language* 64:591–615.

———. 1986. "Comment." *CA* 27:488.

Campbell, L., and T. Kaufman. 1976. "A Linguistic Look at the Olmecs." *AmAnt* 41:80–89.

Campbell, L., and M. Mithun. 1979. "North American Indian Historical Linguistics in Current Perspective," in *The Languages of Native America: Historical and Comparative Assessment.* Austin, TX: University of Texas Press, 3–69.

Cann, R. L. 2001. "Genetic Clues to Dispersal in Human Populations: Retracing the Past from the Present." *Science* 291:1742–48.

Carneiro, R. L. 1995. "History of Ecological Interpretations of Amazonia," in L. E. Sponsel, ed., *Indigenous Peoples and the Future of Amazonia: An Ecological Anthropology of an Endangered World.* Tucson: University of Arizona Press, 46–52.

———. 1979a. "Forest Clearance Among the Yanomamö, Observations and Implications." *Antropológica* 42:39–76.

———. 1979b. "Tree Felling with the Stone Axe: An Experiment Carried Out Among the Yanomamö Indians of Southern Venezuela," in C. Kramer, ed., *Ethnoarchaeology: Implications of Ethnography for Archaeology.* New York: Columbia University Press, 21–58.

Carrasco, D., L. Jones, and S. S. Sessions, eds. 2000. *Mesoamerica's Classic Heritage: From Teotihuacán to the Aztecs.* Boulder, CO: University of Colorado Press.

Caso, A. 1977–79. *Reyes y Reinos de la Mixteca.* 2 vols. Mexico City: Fondo de Cultura Económica.

Castro, C. D., and D. D. Ortega Morejón. 1974. "La Relación de Chincha (1558)." *Historia y Cultura* (Lima) 8:91–104 (1558).

Catto, N. R. 1996. "Richardson Mountains, Yukon–Northwest Territories: The Northern Portal of the Postulated 'Ice-Free Corridor.' " *QI* 32:3–19.

Catton, W. R., Jr. 1982. *Overshoot: The Ecological Basis of Revolutionary Change.* Urbana, IL: University of Illinois Press.

Ceci, L. 1990a. "Radiocarbon Dating 'Village' Sites in Coastal New York: Settlement Pattern Changes in the Middle to Late Woodland." *Man in the Northeast* 39:1–28.

———. 1990b. "Squanto and the Pilgrims: On Planting Corn 'in the Manner of the Indians,' " in Clifton 1990, 71–89.

———. 1975a. "Indian Corn Cultivation" (letter). *Science* 189:946–50.

———. 1975b. "Fish Fertilizer: A Native North American Practice?" *Science* 188:26–30.

Cell, G. T. 1965. "The Newfoundland Company: A Study of Subscribers to a Colonizing Venture." *WMQ* 22:611–25.

Chagnon, N. 1992. *Yanomamö: The Last Days of Eden.* San Diego: Harcourt Brace.

Chamberlin, J. 1928. "New Evidence on Man in America." *NYT*, 30 Sep.

Chandler, J. C. 2002. "The Baja Connection." *Mammoth Trumpet* (March). Online at http://csfa.tamu.edu/mammoth.

Chaplin, J. E. 2003. "Expansion and Exceptionalism in Early American History." *JAH* 89:1431–55.

———. 2001. *Subject Matter: Technology, the Body, and Science on the Anglo-American Frontier, 1500–1676.* Cambridge, MA: Harvard University Press.

Charnay, D. 1967. "Wheeled 'Toys,' " in L. Deuel, ed., *Conquistadors Without Swords: Archaeologists in the Americas.* New York: St. Martin's Press, 178–86.

Chase, A. F., and D. Z. Chase. 2001. "Ancient Maya Causeways and Site Organization at Caracol, Belize." *Ancient Mesoamerica* 12:273–81.

———. 2000. "La Guerra Maya del Periodo Clásico desde la Perspectiva de Caracol, Belice," in S. Trejo, ed., *La Guerra entre los Antiguos Mayas: Memoria de la Primera Mesa Redondada de Palenque.* Mexico City: Instituto Nacional de Antropología e Historia y Consejo Nacional para la Cultura y las Artes, 55–72.

———. 1996. "More than Kin and King: Centralized Political Organization Among the Late Classic Maya." *CA* 37:803–30.

———. 1994. "Details in the Archaeology of Caracol, Belize: An Introduction," in *Studies in the Archaeology of Caracol, Belize.* San Francisco: Precolumbian Art Research Institute, 1–11.

Chase, A. F., N. Grube, and D. Z. Chase. 1991. *Three Terminal Classic Monuments from Caracol, Belize.* Washington, DC: Center for Maya Research.

Chatters, J. C. 2001. *Ancient Encounters: Kennewick Man and the First Americans.* New York: Simon and Schuster.

Chimalpahin Quauhtlehuanitzin, D.S.A.M. 1997. *Codex Chimalpahin: Society and Politics in Mexico Tenochtitlán, Tlatelolco, Texcoco, Culhuacán, and Other Nahuatl Altepetl in Central Mexico: The Nahuatl and Spanish Annals and Accounts.* Ed., trans. A. J. O. Anderson and S. Schroeder. 2 vols. Norman, OK: University of Oklahoma Press. (~1620).

Churchill, W. 2003. "An American Holocaust? The Structure of Denial." *Socialism and Democracy* 17:25–76.

———. 1997. *A Little Matter of Genocide: Holocaust and Denial in the Americas, 1492 to the Present.* San Francisco: City Lights.

Cieza de León, P. D. 1998. *The Discovery and Conquest of Peru.* Trans. A. P. Cook and N. D. Cook. Durham, NC: Duke University Press (~1553).

———. 1959. *The Incas.* Trans. H. D. Onis. Norman, OK: University of Oklahoma Press (~1553).

Clark, J. C. 1912. *The Story of "Eight Deer" in Codex Colombino.* London: Taylor and Francis.

Clayton, L. A., V. J. K. Knight Jr., and E. C. Moore, eds. 1993. *The De Soto Chronicles: The Expe-*

dition of Hernando de Soto to North America in 1539–1543. 2 vols. Tuscaloosa, AL: University of Alabama Press.

Clement, C. R. 1999a and 1999b. "1492 and the Loss of Amazonian Crop Genetic Resources." *Economic Botany,* part 1, 53:188–202; part 2, 53:203–16.

———. 1998. "Human Impacts on Environments of Brazilian Amazonia: Does Traditional Ecological Knowledge Have a Role in the Future of the Region?" Paper at the Centre for Brazilian Studies, Oxford, 5–6 June.

———. 1995. "Pejibaye *Bactris gasipaes* (Palmae)," in J. Smartt and N. W. Simmonds, eds., *Evolution of Crop Plants.* London: Longman, 2nd ed., 383–88.

———. 1992. "Domesticated Palms." *Principes* 36:70–78.

———. 1988. "Domestication of the Pejibaye Palm (*Bactris gasipaes*): Past and Present," in M. J. Balick, ed., *The Palm: Tree of Life.* New York: New York Botanical Garden, 155–74.

Clement, C. R., and J. Mora-Urpí. 1987. "Pejibaye Palm (*Bactris gasipaes,* Arecaceae): Multi-Use Potential for the Lowland Humid Tropics." *Economic Botany* 41:302–11.

Clifton, J. A., ed. 1990. *The Invented Indian: Cultural Fictions and Government Policies.* New Brunswick, NJ: Transaction.

Cobo, B. 1990. *Inca Religion and Customs.* Trans. R. Hamilton. Austin, TX: University of Texas Press (1653).

———. 1979. *History of the Inca Empire.* Trans. R. Hamilton. Austin, TX: University of Texas Press (1653).

Cochrane, M. A., and Schulze, M. D. 1998. "Forest Fires in the Brazilian Amazon." *Conservation Biology* 12:948–50.

Coe, M. D. 1999. *The Maya.* New York: Thames and Hudson, 6th ed.

———. 1996. *The Olmec World: Ritual and Rulership.* Princeton, NJ: Art Museum at Princeton.

———. 1994. *Mexico: From the Olmecs to the Aztecs.* New York: Thames and Hudson, 4th ed.

———. 1976a. "Early Steps in the Evolution of Maya Writing," in H. B. Nicholson, ed., *Origins of Religious Art and Iconography in Preclassic America.* Los Angeles: UCLA Latin American Center, 107–22.

———. 1976b. "Matthew Williams Stirling, 1896–1975." *AmAnt* 41:67–73.

———. 1968. *America's First Civilization: Discovering the Olmec.* New York: American Heritage.

———. 1962. "An Olmec Design on an Early Peruvian Vessel." *AmAnt* 27:579–80.

———. 1957. "Environmental Limitation on Maya Culture: A Reexamination." *AA* 59:328–35.

Coe, M. D., and R. A. Diehl. 1980. *The Archaeology of San Lorenzo Tenochtitlán.* Austin, TX: University of Texas Press.

Cohn, V. 1972. "Missing Part of Mystery Tribe's Calendar Is Found." *Washington Post,* 16 Feb., A8.

Colchester, M. 1984. "Rethinking Stone Age Economics: Some Speculations Concerning the Pre-Columbian Yanomama Economy." *HE* 12:291–314.

Colden, C. 1922. *The History of the Five Indian Nations of Canada Which Are Dependent on the Province of New York.* London: T. Osborne, 1747. (★)

Colinvaux, P. 1996. "Low-Down on a Land Bridge." *Nature* 382:21–22.

Collapiña, Supno, et al. 1921. "Discurso Sobre la Descendencia y Gobierno de los Incas," in H. H. Urteaga, ed., *Informaciones Sobre el Antiguo Perú.* Lima: Sanmartí y Cía, 1–53 (1542/1608).

Columbus, C. 1963. *Journals and Other Documents on the Life and Voyages of Christopher Columbus.* Trans. S. E. Morison. New York: Heritage Press.

Condamine, C. M. d. l. 1986. *Viaje a la América Meridional por el Río de las Amazonas.* Barcelona: Editorial Alta Fulla (1743).

Conrad, J. 1923. "Introduction," in *A Handbook of Cookery for a Small House.* Garden City, NY: Doubleday Page, i–viii.

Consens, M. 1989. "Arte rupestre no Pará: Análise de Alguns Sítios de Monte Alegre." *Dédalo* (São Paulo) 1:265–78.

Cook, A. P., and N. D. Cook. 1998. "Introduction," in Cieza de León 1998, 5–35.

Cook, N. D. 2003. "¿Una Primera Epidemia Americana de Viruela en 1493?" *Revista de Indias* 43:49–64.

———. 1993. "Disease and the Depopulation of Hispaniola, 1492–1518." *Colonial Latin American Review* 2:213–45.

———. 1981. *Demographic Collapse: Indian Peru, 1520–1620*. New York: Cambridge University Press.

Cook, N. D., and W. G. Lovell. 1992. "Unraveling the Web of Disease," in Cook and Lovell eds. 1992, 213–42.

Cook, N. D., and W. G. Lovell, eds. 1992. *"Secret Judgements of God": Old World Disease in Colonial Spanish America*. Norman, OK: University of Oklahoma Press.

Cook, O. F. 1921. "Milpa Agriculture: A Primitive Tropical System," in *Annual Report of the Board of Regents of the Smithsonian Institution, Showing the Operations, Expenditures and Condition of the Institution for the Year Ending June 30, 1919*. Washington, DC: Government Printing Office, 307–26.

Cook, S. F., and W. W. Borah. 1979. "Royal Revenues and Indian Population in New Spain, ca. 1620–1646," in *Essays in Population History: Mexico and California*. Berkeley, CA: University of California Press, 3:1–128.

———. 1971. "The Aboriginal Population of Hispaniola," in *Essays in Population History: Mexico and the Caribbean*. Berkeley, CA: University of California Press, 1:376–410.

———. 1963. *The Indian Population of Central Mexico*. Berkeley, CA: University of California Press.

Cook, S. F., and L. B. Simpson. 1948. *The Population of Central Mexico in the Sixteenth Century*. Berkeley, CA: University of California Press.

Cooke, C. W. 1931. "Why the Mayan Cities of the Peten District, Guatemala, Were Abandoned." *Journal of the Washington Academy of Sciences* 21:283–87.

Cortés, H. 1986. *Letters from Mexico*. Trans. A. Pagden. New Haven, CT: Yale University Press, (1520–26).

Cotter, J. L. 1937. "The Significance of Folsom and Yuma Artifact Occurrences in the Light of Typology and Distribution," in D. S. Davidson, ed., *Twenty-Fifth Anniversary Studies*. Philadelphia: University of Pennsylvania Press, 27–35.

Cotter, J. L., and A. T. Boldurian. 1999. *Clovis Revisited: New Perspectives on Paleoindian Adaptations from Blackwater Draw, New Mexico*. Philadelphia: University of Pennsylvania Press.

Cowgill, G. L. 1997. "State and Society at Teotihuacán, Mexico." *Annual Review of Anthropology* 26:129–61.

Coxe, W. 1780. *Account of the Russian Discoveries Between Asia and America*. London: T. Cadell.

Crawford, M. H. 1998. *The Origin of Native Americans: Evidence from Anthropological Genetics*. New York: Cambridge University Press.

Crease, R. P., and C. C. Mann. 1996. *The Second Creation: Makers of the Revolution in 20th-Century Physics*. New Brunswick, NJ: Rutgers, rev. ed.

Cronon, W. 1995a. "Introduction," in Cronon ed. 1995, 23–56.

———. 1995b. "The Trouble with Wilderness; or, Getting Back to the Wrong Nature," in Cronon ed. 1995, 69–90.

———. 1983. *Changes in the Land: Indians, Colonists, and the Ecology of New England*. New York: Hill and Wang.

Cronon, W., ed. 1995. *Uncommon Ground: Rethinking the Human Place in Nature*. New York: Norton.

Crosby, A. W. 2003a. *America's Forgotten Pandemic: The Influenza of 1918*. New York: Cambridge University Press, 2nd ed.

————. 2003b. *The Columbian Exchange: Biological and Cultural Consequences of 1492*. Westport, CT: Praeger, rev. ed.

————. 2002. *Throwing Fire: Projectile Technology Through History*. New York: Cambridge University Press.

————. 1994. "The Columbian Voyages, the Columbian Exchange, and Their Historians," in *Germs, Seeds, and Animals: Studies in Ecological History*. London: M. E. Sharpe.

————. 1992. "Hawaiian Depopulation as a Model for the Amerindian Experience," in T. Ranger and P. Slack, eds., *Epidemics and Ideas: Essays on the Historical Perception of Pestilence*. New York: Cambridge University Press, 175–202.

————. 1986. *Ecological Imperialism: The Biological Expansion of Europe, 900–1900*. New York: Cambridge University Press.

————. 1976. "The 'Virgin-Soil' Epidemic as a Factor in the Aboriginal Depopulation in America." *WMQ* 33:289–99.

Culbert, T. P., et al. 1990. "The Population of Tikal, Guatemala," in T. P. Culbert and D. S. Rice, eds., *Precolumbian Population History in the Maya Lowlands*. Albuquerque, NM: University of New Mexico Press, 103–21.

Cultural Resource Group. 1996. "Abbott Farm: A National Historic Landmark" (brochure). East Orange, NJ: Louis Berger and Associates.

Cunha, E. D. 1975. *Á Margem da História*. São Paulo: Editora Cultrix (1909).

Current, R. N., H. T. Williams, and A. Brinkley. 1987. *American History: A Survey*. New York: Knopf, 7th ed.

Curtis, J. H., D. A. Hodell, and M. Brenner. 1996. "Climate Variability on the Yucatán Peninsula (Mexico) During the Past 3,500 Years, and Implications for Maya Cultural Evolution." *QR* 46:37–47.

Cushman, H. B. 1999. *History of the Choctaw, Chickasaw, and Natchez Indians*. Norman, OK: University of Oklahoma Press (1899).

Cyphers, A., ed. 1997. *Población, Subsistencia y Medio Ambiente en San Lorenzo Tenochtitlán*. Mexico City: Universidad Nacional Autónoma de México.

D'Abate, R. 1994. "On the Meaning of a Name: 'Norumbega' and the Representation of North America," in Baker et al. 1994, 61–88.

Dahlin, B. H. 2002. "Climate Change and the End of the Classic Period in Yucatán: Resolving a Paradox." *Ancient Mesoamerica* 13:327–40.

Dalan, R. A., et al. 2003. *Envisioning Cahokia: A Landscape Perspective*. Dekalb, IL: Northern Illinois Press.

D'Altroy, T. N. 2002. *The Incas*. Malden, MA: Blackwell.

————. 1987. "Introduction." *Ethnohistory* 34:1–13.

Daniel, G., and C. Renfrew. 1986. *The Idea of Prehistory*. Edinburgh: Edinburgh University, 2nd ed.

Dantzig, T. 1967. *Number: The Language of Science*. New York: Macmillan.

Darch, J. P. 1988. "Drained Field Agriculture in Tropical Latin America: Parallels from Past to Present." *JB* 15:87–95.

Darwin, F., ed. 1887. *The Life and Letters of Charles Darwin, Including an Autobiographical Chapter*. 3 vols. London: John Murray.

Dávalos Hurtado, E., and J. M. Ortiz de Zárate. 1953. "La Plástica Indígena y la Patología." *Revista Mexicana de Estudios Antropológicos* 13:95–104.

Day, G. M. 1953. "The Indian as an Ecological Factor in the Northeastern Forest." *Ecology* 34:329–46.

DeBoer, W. R., K. Kintigh, and A. Rostoker. 2001. "In Quest of Prehistoric Amazonia." *LAA* 12:326–27.

Deetz, J., and P. S. Deetz. 2000. *The Times of Their Lives: Life, Love, and Death in Plymouth Colony*. New York: Random House.

Bibliography

Deevey, E. S., et al. 1979. "Mayan Urbanism: Impact on a Tropical Karst Environment." *Science* 206:298–306.

DeFrance, S. D., et al. 2001. "Late Paleo-Indian Coastal Foragers: Specialized Extractive Behavior at Quebrada Tacahuay, Peru." *LAA* 12:413–26.

Delabarre, E. B., and H. H. Wilder. 1920. "Indian Corn-Hills in Massachusetts." *AA* 22:203–25.

Delcourt, P. A., et al. 1986. "Holocene Ethnobotanical and Paleoecological Record of Human Impact on Vegetation in the Little Tennessee River Valley, Tennessee." *QR* 25:330–49.

Deloria, V., Jr. 1995. *Red Earth, White Lies: Native Americans and the Myth of Scientific Fact.* New York: Scribner's.

Denevan, W. M. 2003. "The Native Population of Amazonia in 1492 Reconsidered." *Revista de Indias* 43:175–88.

———. 2001. *Cultivated Landscapes of Native Amazonia and the Andes.* New York: Oxford University Press.

———. 1996a. "A Bluff Model of Riverine Settlement in Prehistoric Amazonia." *AAAG* 86:652–81.

———. 1996b. "Pristine Myth," in D. Levinson and M. Ember, eds., *Encyclopedia of Cultural Anthropology.* New York: Holt, 3:1034–36.

———. 1996c. "Carl Sauer and Native American Population Size." *Geographical Review* 86:385–97.

———. 1992a. "The Pristine Myth: The Landscape of the Americas in 1492." *AAAG* 82:369–85.

———. 1992b. "Stone vs. Metal Axes: The Ambiguity of Shifting Cultivation in Prehistoric Amazonia." *Journal of the Steward Anthropological Society* 20:153–65.

———. 1966. *The Aboriginal Cultural Geography of the Llanos de Mojos of Bolivia.* Berkeley, CA: University of California Press.

Denevan, W. M., ed. 1976. *The Native Population of the Americas in 1492.* Madison, WI: University of Wisconsin Press.

Denys, N. 1908. *The Description and Natural History of the Coasts of North America.* Trans. W. F. Gannong. Toronto: Champlain Society (1672).

Dermer, T. 1619. Letter to S. Purchas, in Purchas 1905–07, 19:129–34.

Deuel, L. 1967. *Conquistadors Without Swords: Archaeologists in the Americas.* New York: St. Martin's.

Diamond, J. 2004. *Collapse: How Societies Choose to Fail or Succeed.* New York: Viking.

———. J. 1997. *Guns, Germs, and Steel: The Fates of Human Societies.* New York: Norton.

Díaz del Castillo, B. 1963. *The Conquest of New Spain.* Trans. J. M. Cohen. New York: Penguin (1532).

Diehl, R. A. 2005. "Patterns of Cultural Primacy." *Science* 307:1055–56.

———. 1983. *Tula: The Toltec Capital of Ancient Mexico.* London: Thames and Hudson.

Dillehay, T. D. 2003. "Tracking the First Americans." *Nature* 425:23–24.

———. 2001. *The Settlement of the Americas: A New Prehistory.* New York: Basic Books.

Dillehay, T. D., ed. 1989–97. *Monte Verde: A Late Pleistocene Settlement in Chile.* 2 vols. Washington, DC: Smithsonian.

Dillon, F. 1975. *The Pilgrims.* Garden City, NY: Doubleday.

Dinawari, A. H. A. 1986. *Min kitab al-Ahkbar al-tiwal: Li-Abi Hanifah al-Dinawari; ikhtar al-nusus wa-allaqa alayha wa-qaddama laha Yahya Abbarah.* Damascus: Al-Jumhuriyah al-Arabiyah al-Suriyah, Manshurat Wizarat al-Thaqafah (895?).

Dmytryshan, B., E. A. P. Crownhart-Vaughan, and T. Vaughan, eds. 1988. *To Siberia and Russian America: Three Centuries of Russian Eastward Expansion.* 3 vols. Portland, OR: Oregon Historical Society Press.

Dobyns, H. F. 2004. Statement, in W. G. Lovell, et al., "1491: In Search of Native America." *Journal of the Southwest,* 46:443–47.

———. 1995. "Epilogue," in *Tubac Through Four Centuries: An Historical Resume and Analysis.*

Tucson, AZ: Arizona State Museum Library (1959). Online at http://www.library.arizona.edu/images/dobyns.

————. 1983. *Their Number Become Thinned: Native American Population Dynamics in Eastern North America*. Knoxville, TN: University of Tennessee Press.

————. 1966. "Estimating Aboriginal American Population: An Appraisal of Techniques with a New Hemispheric Estimate." *CA* 7:395–416.

————. 1963. "An Outline of Andean Epidemic History to 1720." *Bulletin of the History of Medicine* 37:493–515.

Dobyns, H. F., and P. L. Doughty. 1976. *Peru: A Cultural History*. New York: Oxford University Press.

Doebley, J. F., M. M. Goodman, and C. W. Stuber. 1998. "Isoenzymatic Variation in Zea (Gramineae)." *Systematic Botany* 9: 203–18.

Doolittle, W. E. 2000. *Cultivated Landscapes of North America*. New York: Oxford University Press.

Dorney, C. H., and J. R. Dorney. 1989. "An Unusual Oak Savanna in Northeastern Wisconsin." *American Midland Naturalist* 122:103–13.

Dougherty, B., and H. A. Calandra. 1984. "Prehispanic Human Settlement in the Llanos de Mojos, Bolivia." *Quaternary of South America and Antarctic Peninsula* 2:163–99.

Doughty, P. L. 1987. "Preface," in Stearman 1987, ix–xii.

Driver, J. C. 2001. "Paleoecological and Archaeological Implications of the Charlie Lake Cave Fauna, British Columbia, 10,500 to 9,500 BP," in S. C. Gerlach and M. S. Murray, eds., *People and Wildlife in Northern North America: Essays in Honour of R. Dale Guthrie*. Oxford: British Archaeological Reports, 13–21.

Duncan, D. E. 1995. *Hernando de Soto: A Savage Quest in the Americas*. New York: Crown.

Dunford, F. J. 2001. *Ceramic Style and the Late Woodland Period (1000–400 B.P.) Sachemships of Cape Cod, Massachusetts*. PhD diss. University of Massachusetts, Amherst, MA.

————. 1992. "Conditional Sedentism: The Logistical Flexibility of Estuarine Settlements in Circumscribed Environments." Unpub. ms.

Dunning, N. P., et al. 2002. "Arising from the *Bajos*: The Evolution of a Neotropical Landscape and the Rise of Maya Civilization." *AAAG* 92:267–83.

————. 1992. *Lords of the Hills: Ancient Maya Settlement in the Puuc Region, Yucatán, Mexico*. Madison, WI: Prehistory Press.

Durán, D. 1994. *The History of the Indies of New Spain*. Trans. D. Heyden. Norman, OK: University of Oklahoma Press.

Durning, A. T. 1992. *Guardians of the Land: Indigenous Peoples and the Health of the Earth*. Washington, DC: Worldwatch Institute.

Easton, N. A. 1992. "Mal de Mer Above Terra Incognita, or, What Ails the Coastal Migration Theory?" *Arctic Anthropology* 29(2):28–42.

Eiseley, L. 1975. *All the Strange Hours: The Excavation of a Life*. New York: Scribner's.

Ekholm, G. H. 1969. "Transpacific Contacts," in J. D. Jennings and E. Norbeck, eds., *Prehistoric Man in the New World*. Chicago: University of Chicago Press, 489–510.

Elias, S. A. 2001. "Mutual Climatic Range Reconstruction of Seasonal Temperatures Based on Late Pleistocene Fossil Beetle Assemblages in Eastern Beringia." *QSR* 20:77–91.

Elias, S. A., et al. 1996. "Life and Times of the Bering Land Bridge." *Nature* 382:60–63.

Eliot, C. W., ed. 1909–14. *American Historical Documents, 1000–1904*. New York: P. F. Collier & Son.

Elson, J. A. 1957. "Lake Agassiz and the Mankata-Valders Problem." *Science* 126:999–1002.

Emerson, T. E. 2002. "An Introduction to Cahokia 2002: Diversity, Complexity, and History." *Midcontinental Journal of Archaeology* 27:127–48.

Engelkemeier, A. G., et al. 1949. "The Half-Life of Radiocarbon (C^{14})." *Physical Review* 75:1825–33.

Enríquez de Guzmán, A. 1862. *The Life and Acts of Don Alonzo Enríquez de Guzmán: A Knight of*

Seville, of the Order of Santiago, A.D. *1518 to 1543*. Trans. C. R. Markham. London: Hakluyt Society (1518–43).

Epstein, J. 1993. "Battle Over Rich Brazilian Lands." *San Francisco Chronicle,* 29 Dec.

Erickson, C. L. 2005. "The Domesticated Landscapes of the Bolivian Amazon," in Balée and Erickson eds. 2005.

———. 2004. "Historical Ecology and Future Explorations," in Lehmann et al. 2004, 455–500.

———. 2002. "Large Moated Settlements: A Late Precolumbian Phenomenon in the Amazon." Paper at the Second Annual Meeting of the Society for the Anthropology of Lowland South America, 6–7 June, Annapolis, MD.

———. 2001. "Pre-Columbian Roads of the Amazon." *Expedition* 43:21–30.

———. 2000a. "An Artificial Landscape-Scale Fishery in the Bolivian Amazon." *Nature* 408:190–93.

———. 2000b. "Los caminos prehispánicos de la Amazonia boliviana," in L. Herrera and M. H. de Schrimpff, eds., *Caminos precolombinos: Las vías, los ingenieros y los viajeros.* Bogotá: Instituto Colombino de Antropología e Historia, 15–42.

———. 1995. "Archaeological Methods for the Study of Ancient Landscapes of the Llanos de Mojos in the Bolivian Amazon," in P. W. Stahl, ed., *Archaeology in the Lowland American Tropics: Current Analytical Methods and Applications.* New York: Columbia University Press, 66–95.

Erickson, C., and W. Balée. 2005. "Origins and Development of Ibibate Mound Complex in the Bolivian Amazon," in Balée and Erickson eds. 2005.

Estrada-Belli, F. 2002. "Archaeological Investigations at Holmul, Petén, Guatemala: Preliminary Results of the Third Season, 2002." Online at http://www.famsi.org/reports/01009/section19.htm.

Eubanks, M. W. 2001a. "An Interdisciplinary Perspective on the Origin of Maize." *LAA* 12:91–98.

———. 2001b. "The Mysterious Origin of Maize." *Economic Botany* 55:492–514.

———. 1997. "Molecular Analysis of Crosses Between *Tripsacum dactyloides* and *Zea diploperennis* (Poaceae)." *Theoretical and Applied Genetics* 94:707–12.

Evans, C., and B. J. Meggers. 1968. *Archaeological Investigations on the Río Napo, Eastern Ecuador.* Washington, DC: Smithsonian.

Ewald, P. 1996. *The Evolution of Infectious Disease.* New York: Oxford University Press.

Ewell, P. T., and D. M. Sands. 1987. "Milpa in Yucatán: A Long-Fallow Maize System and Its Alternatives in the Maya Peasant Economy," in Turner and Brush 1987, 95–129.

Ewers, J. C. 1973. "The Influence of Epidemics on the Indian Populations and Cultures of Texas." *Plains Anthropologist* 18:104–15.

Eyre-Walker, A., et al. 1998. "Investigation of the Bottleneck Leading to the Domestication of Maize." *PNAS* 95:4441–46.

Ezell, P. H. 1961. *The Hispanic Acculturation of the Gila River Pima.* Menasha, WI: American Anthropological Association.

Fagan, B. H. 2001. *The Little Ice Age: How Climate Made History, 1300–1850.* New York: Basic Books.

———. 2000. *Ancient North America: The Archaeology of a Continent.* New York: Thames & Hudson, 3rd ed.

———. 1999. *Floods, Famines, and Emperors: El Niño and the Fate of Civilizations.* New York: Basic Books.

———. 1991. *Kingdoms of Gold, Kingdoms of Jade: The Americas Before Columbus.* New York: Thames & Hudson.

Fahsen, F. 2003. "Rescuing the Origins of Dos Pilas Dynasty: Salvage of Hieroglyphic Stairway #2, Structure L5-49." 16 Jun. Online at http://www.famsi.org/reports/01098/index.html.

Farnsworth, P., et al. 1985. "A Re-Evaluation of the Isotopic and Archaeological Reconstructions of Diet in the Tehuacán Valley." *AmAnt* 50:102–16.

Fearnside, P. M. 2001. "Effects of Land Use and Forest Management on the Carbon Cycle in the Brazilian Amazon." *Journal of Sustainable Forestry* 12:79–97.

Federoff, N. V. 2003. "Prehistoric GM Corn." *Science* 302:1148–59.

Fedick, S. L., and A. Ford. 1990. "The Prehistoric Agricultural Landscape of the Central Maya Lowlands: An Examination of Local Variability in a Regional Context." *WA* 22:18–33.

Feldman, E. 1998. Interview with Paul Damon, 29 Oct. Online at http://www.agu.org/history/sv/proxies/damon_interview.html.

Feldman, R. A. 1985. "Preceramic Corporate Architecture: Evidence for the Development of Non-Egalitarian Social Systems in Peru," in C. B. Donnan, ed., *Early Ceremonial Architecture in the Andes*. Washington, DC: Dumbarton Oaks, 71–92.

———. 1980. "Aspero, Peru: Architecture, Subsistence Economy and Other Artifacts of a Preceramic Maritime Chiefdom." PhD diss. Department of Anthropology, Harvard University.

Fenn, E. 2001. *Pox Americana: The Great Smallpox Epidemic of 1775–82*. New York: Hill and Wang.

Fenton, W. N. 1998. *The Great Law and the Longhouse: A Political History of the Iroquois Confederacy*. Norman, OK: University of Oklahoma Press.

———. 1983. *Roll Call of the Iroquois Chiefs*. Ohsweken, Ontario: Iroqrafts (1950).

Ferguson, R. B. 1998. "Whatever Happened to the Stone Age? Steel Tools and Yanomami Historical Ecology," in Balée ed. 1998, 287–312.

———. 1995. *Yanomami Warfare: A Political History*. Santa Fe: School of America Research.

Fernández-Armesto, F. 2001. *Civilizations: Culture, Ambition, and the Transformation of Nature*. New York: Touchstone.

Fernández de Biedma, L. 1922. "Relation of the Conquest of Florida Presented by Luys Hernandez de Biedma in the Year 1544 to the King of Spain in Council." Trans. B. Smith. In Bourne 1922, 2:1–41 (1544).

Fidler, P. 1992. *Journal of a Journey over Land from Buckingham House to the Rocky Mountains in 1792 &3*. Lethbridge, Alberta: HRC (1793).

Fiedel, S. J. 2000. "The Peopling of the New World: Present Evidence, New Theories, and Future Directions." *Journal of Archaeological Research* 8:39–103.

———. 1999a. "Artifact Provenience at Monte Verde." *Discovering Archaeology* (November/December):1–12.

———. 1999b. "Older Than We Thought: Implications of Corrected Dates for Paleo-Indians." *AmAnt* 64:95–115.

———. 1992. *Prehistory of the Americas*. Cambridge: Cambridge University Press, 2nd ed.

———. 1987. "Algonquian Origins: A Problem in Archaeological-Linguistic Correlation." *Archaeology of Eastern North America* 15:1–11.

Fiedel, S. J., et al. 1996. "Paleoindians in the Amazon" (letters). *Science* 274:1820–25.

Fields, V. M. 1994. "The Iconographic Heritage of the Maya Jester God," in Robertson and Fields eds. 1991, 167–74.

Fisher, R. F., M. J. Jenkins, and W. F. Fisher. 1987. "Fire and the Prairie-Forest Mosaic of Devils Tower National Monument." *American Midland Naturalist* 117:250–57.

Fisher, R. H. 1943. *The Russian Fur Trade, 1550–1700*. Berkeley, CA: University of California Press.

Fitzgerald, F. 1980. *America Revised: History Schoolbooks in the Twentieth Century*. New York: Vintage.

Fladmark, K. 1979. "Routes: Alternate Migration Corridors for Early Man in North America." *AmAnt* 44:55–69.

Flannery, K. V., and J. Marcus. 2003. "The Origin of War: New C¹⁴ Dates from Ancient Mexico." *PNAS* 100:11801–05.

————. 2002. "Richard Stockton MacNeish." *Biographical Memoirs of the National Academy of Sciences* 80:200–25.

————. 2000. "Formative Mexican Chiefdoms and the Myth of the 'Mother Culture.' " *Journal of Anthropological Archaeology* 19:1–37.

Fletcher, L. A., and J. Gann. 1992. "Calakmul, Campeche: Patrón de Asentamiento y Demografía." *Antropológicas* (Mexico City), 2:20–25.

Flores, D. 1997. "The West That Can Be, and the West That Was." *High Country News,* 18 Aug.

————. 1991. "Bison Ecology and Bison Diplomacy: The Southern Plains from 1800 to 1850." *Journal of American History* 78:465–85.

Flores, R. 1974. "Marital Alliance in the Political Integration of Mixtec Kingdoms." *AA* 76:297–311.

Focacci, G., and S. Chacón. 1989. "Excavaciones Arqueológicas en los Faldeos del Morro de Arica, Sitios Morro 1/6 y 2/2." *Chungará* (Arica, Chile) 22:15–62.

Folan, W. J. 1992. "Calakmul, Campeche: A Centralized Administrative Center in the Northern Peten." *WA* 24:148–68.

Folan, W. J., et al. 2001. *Las Ruinas de Calakmul, Campeche, México: Un Lugar Central y su Paisaje Cultural.* Campeche, Mexico: Universidad Autónoma de Campeche.

————. 1995. "Calakmul: New Data from an Ancient Maya Capital in Campeche, Mexico." *LAA* 6:310–34.

Foreman, C. F. T. 1943. *Indians Abroad, 1493–1938.* Norman, OK: University of Oklahoma Press.

Fossa, L. 2000. "La *Suma y narraçion* . . . de Betanzos: Cuando la Letra Hispana Representa la Voz Quechua." *Revista de Crítica Literaria Latinoamericana* 26:195–214.

Foster, D. R., et al. 2002. "Cultural, Environmental and Historical Controls of Vegetation Patterns and the Modern Conservation Setting on the Island of Martha's Vineyard, USA." *JB* 29:1381–400.

Fountain, H. 2001. "Archaeological Site in Peru Is Called Oldest City in Americas." *NYT,* 27 Apr. (correction, 30 Apr.).

Fowler, M. L. 1997. *The Cahokia Atlas: A Historical Atlas of Cahokia Archaeology.* Urbana, IL: University of Illinois Press, rev. ed.

Fowler, M. L., et al. 1999. *The Mound 72 Area: Dedicated and Sacred Space in Early Cahokia.* Springfield, IL: Illinois State Museum.

Fox, J. W., et al. 1996. "Questions of Political and Economic Integration: Segmentary Versus Centralized States Among the Maya." *CA* 37:795–801.

Freidel, D. 1993. "Krieg-Mythos und Realitat," in Reiss-Museum der Stadt Mannheim, *Die Welt der Maya.* Mainz am Rhein: Verlag Phillip Von Zabern, 158–76. (English version, online at http://maya.csuhayward.edu/yaxuna/warfare.html.)

French, J. C. 1919. *The Passenger Pigeon in Pennsylvania: Its Remarkable History, Habits and Extinction, with Interesting Side Lights on the Folk and Forest Lore of the Alleghenian Region of the Old Keystone State.* Altoona, PA: Altoona Tribune Co. (★)

Füch, H. V. 1988. "An Eyewitness Account of Hardships Suffered by Natives in Northeastern Siberia during Bering's Great Kamchatka Expedition, 1735–1744, as Reported by Heinrich von Füch, Former Vice President of the Commerce College, Now a Political Exile," in Dmytryshan, Crownhart-Vaughan, and Vaughan 1988, 2:168–89.

Gale, M. D., and K. M. Devos. 1998. "Comparative Genetics in the Grasses." *PNAS* 95:1971–74.

Galinat, W. C. 1992. "Maize: Gift from America's First Peoples," in N. Foster and L. S. Cordell, eds., *Chilies to Chocolate: Foods the Americas Gave the World.* Tucson: University of Arizona Press, 47–60.

Galloway, P., ed. 1997. *The Hernando de Soto Expedition: History, Historiography, and "Discovery" in the Southeast.* Lincoln, NE: University of Nebraska Press.

Garibay, A. M. 1970. *Llave del Náhuatl.* Mexico City: Porrua.

Garlinghouse, T. S. 2001. "Revisiting the Mound-Builder Controversy." *History Today* (September): 38–44.

Gatrell, V. A. C. 1994. *The Hanging Tree: Execution and the English People, 1770–1868.* Oxford University Press.

Geertz, C. 1980. *Negara: The Theatre State in Nineteenth-Century Bali.* Princeton, NJ: Princeton University Press.

Geist, V. 1998. *Buffalo Nation: History and Legend of the North American Bison.* Stillwater, MN: Voyageur Press.

Genome International Sequencing Consortium. 2001. "Initial Sequencing and Analysis of the Human Genome." *Nature* 409:860–921.

"Gentleman of Elvas." 1922. "True Relation of the Vicissitudes That Attended the Governor Don Hernando de Soto and Some Nobles of Portugal in the Discovery of the Province of Florida Now Just Given by a Fidalgo Of Elvas." Trans. B. Smith. In Bourne 1922, 1:1–223 (1557).

Gheerbrant, A., ed. 1962. *The Incas: The Royal Commentaries of the Inca, Garcilaso de la Vega, 1539–1616.* Trans. M. Jolas. New York: Orion (1609, 1617).

Gibbons, A. 1997. "Monte Verde: Blessed but Not Confirmed." *Science* 275:1256–57.

———. 1996. "Archaeology: First Americans: Not Mammoth Hunters, but Forest Dwellers?" *Science* 272:346–47.

Gill, R. B. 2000. *The Great Maya Droughts: Water, Life, and Death.* Albuquerque: University of New Mexico Press.

Glaser, B., G. Guggenberger, and W. Zech. 2004. "Organic Chemistry Studies on Amazonian Dark Earths," in Lehmann et al. 2004, 227–41.

Glaser, B., J. Lehmann, and W. Zech. 2002. "Ameliorating Physical and Chemical Properties of Highly Weathered Soils in the Tropics with Charcoal—A Review." *Biology and Fertility of Soils* 35:219–30.

Glaser, B., and W. I. Woods, eds. 2004. *Amazonian Dark Earths: Explorations in Space and Time.* New York: Springer-Verlag.

Goddard, I. 1984. "Synonymy," in D. Damas, ed., *Handbook of North American Indians*, vol. 5: *Arctic.* Washington, DC: Smithsonian, 5–7.

———. 1978. "Central Algonquian Languages," in Trigger 1978, 15:70–77.

Goethe, J. W. V. 1962. *Italian Journey* Trans. W. H. Auden and E. Mayer. London: Collins (1786–88).

González, E. M., and N. E. Tur, eds. 1981. *Lope de Aguirre: Crónicas, 1559–1561.* Barcelona: Ediciones 7½.

González-José, R., et al. 2003. "Craniometric Evidence for Paleoamerican Survival in Baja California." *Nature* 425:62–65.

Goodland, R. J. A., and H. S. Irwin. 1975. *Amazon Jungle: Green Hell or Red Desert?* New York: Elsevier Scientific.

Gookin, D. 1792. *Historical Collections of the Indians in New England*, in *Collections of the Massachusetts Historical Society*, 1: 141–227 (1674).

Gore, R. 1997. "The Most Ancient Americans." *National Geographic* (October):92–99.

Gorges, F. 1890a. "A Briefe Relation of the Discovery and Plantation of New England," in Baxter 1890, 1:203–40 (1622).

———. 1890b. "A Briefe Narration of the Originall Undertakings of the Advancement of Plantations into the Parts of America," in Baxter ed. 1890, 2:1–81 (1658).

Graulich, M. 2000. "Aztec Human Sacrifice as Expiation." *History of Religions* 39:352–71.

Grayson, D. K. 1983. *The Establishment of Human Antiquity.* New York: Academic.

———. 2003. "A Requiem for Overkill." *Journal of Archaeological Science* 30:585–93.

Grayson, D. K., and D. K. Meltzer. 2002. "Clovis Hunting and Large Mammal Extinction: A Critical Review of the Evidence." *Journal of World Prehistory* 16:313–59.

Greenberg, J. H., C. G. Turner II, and S. L. Zegura. 1986. "The Settlement of the Americas: A Comparison of the Linguistic, Dental, and Genetic Evidence." *CA* 27:477–88.

Grim, J. 2001. *Indigenous Traditions and Ecology: The Interbeing of Cosmology and Community.* Cambridge, MA: Harvard University Press.

Grinde, D. A., Jr. 1992. "Iroquois Political Theory and the Roots of American Democracy," in O. Lyons, et al., *Exiled in the Land of the Free: Democracy, Indian Nations, and the U.S. Constitution.* Santa Fe: Clear Light, 235–40.

———. 1977. *The Iroquois and the Founding of the American Nation.* San Francisco: Indian Historian.

Grinde, D. A., Jr., and B. E. Johansen. 1991. *Exemplar of Liberty: Native America and the Evolution of Democracy.* Los Angeles: American Indian Studies Center.

Grove, D. C. 1981. "Olmec Monuments: Mutilation as a Clue to Meaning," in Benson ed. 1981, 49–68.

———. 1977. "Olmec Origins and Transpacific Diffusion: Reply to Meggers." *AA* 78:634–37.

Grube, N., and S. Martin. 1998. "Política Clásica Maya dentro de una Tradición Mesoamericana: Un Modelo Epigráfico de Organización Política 'Hegemónica,'" in S. Trejo, ed., *Modelos de Entidades Políticas Mayas: Primer Seminario de Mesas Redondas de Palenque.* Mexico City: Instituto Nacional de Antropología e Historia, 131–46.

Guaman Poma de Ayala, F. 2001. *El Primer Nueva Crónica y Buen Gobierno.* Copenhagen: Kongelige Bibliotek. Online at http://www.kb.dk/elib/mss/poma/index-en.htm (1615–16).

Gubser, C., and G. L. Smith. 2002. "The Sequence of Camelpox Virus Shows It Is Most Closely Related to Variola Virus, the Cause of Smallpox." *Journal of General Virology* 83:855–72.

Guenter, S. 2003. "The Inscriptions of Dos Pilas Associated with B'ajlaj Chan K'awiil." Online at http://www.mesoweb.com/features/guenter/DosPilas.pdf.

———. 2002. "A Reading of the Cancuén Looted Panel." Online at http://www.mesoweb.com/features/cancuen/Panel.pdf.

Guerra, F. 1988. "The Earliest American Epidemic: The Influenza of 1493." *Social Science History* 12:305–25.

Guilmartin, J. F., Jr. 1991. "The Cutting Edge: An Analysis of the Spanish Invasion and Overthrow of the Inca Empire, 1532–1539," in K. J. Andrien and R. Adorno, eds., *Transatlantic Encounters: Europeans and Andeans in the Sixteenth Century.* Berkeley, CA: University of California Press, 40–69.

Gunn, J. D., et al. 2002. "Bajo Sediments and the Hydraulic System of Calakmul, Campeche, Mexico." *Ancient Mesoamerica* 13:297–315.

Gunn Allen, P. 2003. *Pocahontas: Medicine Woman, Spy, Entrepreneur, Diplomat.* San Francisco: HarperSanFrancisco.

Gyllensten, U., et al. 1991. "Paternal Inheritance of Mitochondrial DNA in Mice." *Nature* 352:255–57.

Haas, J., and W. Creamer. 2004. "Cultural Transformations in the Central Andean Late Archaic," in Silverman 2004, 35–50.

———. Forthcoming. "Possible Early Representations of the Andean Staff God." *Latin American Antiquity.*

Haas, J., W. Creamer, and A. Ruiz. 2004. "Power and the Emergence of Complex Polities in the Peruvian Preceramic." *Archeological Papers of the American Anthropological Association* 14:37–52.

———. 2004. "Dating the Late Archaic Occupation of the Norte Chico Region in Peru." *Nature* 432:568–71.

Hadley, M., and J. P. Lanly. 1983. "Tropical Forest Ecosystems." *Nature and Resources* 19:2–19.

Hall, D. A. 1999. "Charting the Way into the Americas." *Mammoth Trumpet* 14(1). Online at http://csfa.tamu.edu/mammoth.

————. 1996. "Discoveries in Amazon Cave Suggest Clovis Wasn't First." *Mammoth Trumpet* 11(3). Online at http://csfa.tamu.edu/mammoth.

Hall, S. 1997. *A Commotion in the Blood: Life, Death, and the Immune System.* New York: Holt.

Hallowell, A. I. 1960. "The Beginnings of Anthropology in America," in F. de Laguna, ed., *Selected Papers from the American Anthropologist, 1888–1920.* Elmsford, NY: Row, Peterson, 1–23.

Hamblin, R. L., and B. L. Pitcher. 1980. "The Classic Maya Collapse: Testing Class Conflict Hypotheses." *AmAnt* 45:246–67.

Hariot, T. 1588. *A Briefe and True Report of the New Found Land of Virginia.* London. (★)

Harlan, J. R., and D. Zohary. 1966. "Distribution of Wild Wheats and Barley." *Science* 153:1074–80.

Harner, M. 1977. "The Ecological Basis for Aztec Sacrifice." *American Ethnologist* 4:117–35.

Harris, C. 1994. "Voices of Disaster: Smallpox Around the Strait of Georgia in 1782." *Ethnohistory* 41:591–626.

Harris, G. H. 1903. "The Life of Horatio Jones." *Publications of Buffalo Historical Society* 6:328–526.

Harrison, P. 1999. *Lords of Tikal: Rulers of an Ancient Maya City.* New York: Thames and Hudson.

Haslip-Viera, G., B. Ortiz de Montellano, and W. Barbour. 1997. "Robbing Native American Cultures: Van Sertima's Afrocentricity and the Olmecs." *CA* 38:419–41.

Hassig, R. 1985. *Trade, Tribute and Transportation: The Sixteenth Century Political Economy of the Valley of Mexico.* Norman, OK: University of Oklahoma Press.

Hassler, P. 1992. "The Lies of the Conquistadors: Cutting Through the Myth of Human Sacrifice." *World Press Review* (December):28–29.

Hastorf, C. 1999. *Early Settlement at Chiripa, Bolivia: Research of the Taraco Archaeological Project.* Berkeley, CA: University of California Press.

Haug, G. H., et al. 2003. "Climate and the Collapse of Maya Civilization." *Science* 399:1731–35.

Havard, G. 2001. *The Great Peace of Montreal of 1701: French-Native Diplomacy in the Seventeenth Century.* Trans. P. Aronoff and H. Scott. Montreal: McGill-Queen's University.

Haynes, C. V. 1999. "Monte Verde and the Pre-Clovis Situation in America." *Discovering Archaeology* (November/December):17–19.

————. 1964. "Fluted Projectile Points: Their Age and Dispersion." *Science* 145:1408–13.

Haynes, C. V., et al. 1997. "Dating a Paleoindian Site in the Amazon in Comparison with Clovis Cuture" (letters). *Science* 275:1948–52.

Haynes, G. 2003. *The Early Settlement of North America: The Clovis Era.* New York: Cambridge University Press.

Headland, T. 2000. "When Did the Measles Epidemic Begin Among the Yanomami?" 9 Dec. Online at http://www.sil.org/~headlandt/measles1.htm.

Heaton, H. C., ed. 1934. *The Discovery of the Amazon According to the Account of Friar Gaspar de Carvajal and Other Documents.* Trans. B. T. Lee. New York: American Geographical Society.

Hecht, S. 2004. "Indigenous Soil Management and the Creation of Amazonian Dark Earths: Implications of Kayapó Practices," in Lehmann et al. 2004, 355–71.

Heckenberger, M. J. Forthcoming. "Xinguano History and Social Hierarchy: Modes of Temporality and Perspective in Amazonia," in C. Fausto and M. Heckenberger, eds., *When Time Matters: History, Memory, and Identity in Indigenous Amazonia.* Tucson, AZ: University of Arizona Press.

Heckenberger, M. J., J. B. Petersen, and E. G. Neves. 2004. "Historical and Socio-Cultural Origins of Amazonian Dark Earths," in Lehmann et al. 2004, 29–50.

————. 2001. "Of Lost Civilizations and Primitive Tribes: Amazonia. Response to Meggers." *LAA* 12:328–33.

———. 1999. "Village Size and Permanance in Amazonia: Two Archaeological Examples from Brazil." *LAA* 10:353–76.

Heckenberger, M. J., et al. 2003. "Amazonia 1492: Pristine Forest or Cultural Parkland?" *Science* 301:1710–14.

Heizer, R. F., and J. E. Gullberg. 1981. "Concave Mirrors from the Site of La Venta, Tabasco: Their Occurrence, Minerology, Optical Description, and Function," in Benson 1981, 109–16.

Hemming, J. 2004. *The Conquest of the Incas.* New York: Harvest (1970).

———. 1978. *Red Gold: The Conquest of the Brazilian Indians.* Cambridge, MA: Harvard University Press.

Henige, D. 1998. *Numbers from Nowhere: The American Indian Contact Population Debate.* Norman, OK: University of Oklahoma Press.

———. 1993. "Proxy Data, Historical Method, and the De Soto Expedition," in Young and Hoffman eds. 1993, 155–72.

———. 1990. "Their Number Became Thick: Native American Historical Demography as Expiation," in Clifton 1990, 169–91.

———. 1986. "When Did Smallpox Reach the New World (and Why Does It Matter)?" in P. E. Lovejoy, ed., *Africans in Bondage: Studies in Slavery and the Slave Trade.* Madison, WI: University of Wisconsin African Studies Program, 11–26.

———. 1978a. "David Henige's Reply." *Hispanic American Historical Review* 58:709–12.

———. 1978b. "On the Contact Population of Hispaniola: History as Higher Mathematics." *Hispanic American Historical Review* 58:217–37.

Herrera, L. F. 1992. "The Technical Transformation of an Agricultural System in the Colombian Amazon." *WA* 24:98–113.

Herrmann, B., and W. I. Woods. 2003. "Between Pristine Myth and Biblical Plague: Passenger Pigeons, Sparrows and the Construction of Abundances." Paper at Annual Meeting of American Society for Environmental History, Providence, R.I., Mar. 27.

Hertzberg, H. W. 1966. *The Great Tree and the Longhouse.* New York: Macmillan.

Heyerdahl, T. 1996. *La Navegación Marítima en el Antiguo Perú.* Lima: Instituto de Estudios Histórico-Marítimos del Perú.

Higginson, F. 1792. "New-Englands Plantation," in *Collections of the Massachusetts Historical Society* 1:117–24 (1629). (★)

Hill, K., and H. Kaplan. 1989. "Population and Dry-Season Subsistence Strategies of the Recently Contacted Yora of Peru." *National Geographic Research* 5:317–34.

Hillman, G. C., and M. S. Davies. 1990. "Measured Domestication Rates in Wild Wheats and Barley Under Primitive Cultivation, and Their Archaeological Implications." *Journal of World Prehistory* 4:157–222.

Hillspaugh, S. H., C. Whitlock, and P. J. Bartlein. 2000. "Variations in Fire Frequency and Climate over the Past 17,000 yr in Central Yellowstone National Park." *Geology* 28:211–14.

Hirsch, A. J. 1988. "The Collision of Military Cultures in Seventeenth-Century New England." *JAH* 74:1187–212.

Hodell, D. A., J. J. Curtis, and M. Brenner. 1995. "Possible Role of Climate in the Collapse of Classic Maya Civilization." *Nature* 375:391–94.

Holanda, S. B. D. 1996. *Visão do Paraíso: Os Motivos Edênicos no Descobrimento e Colonização do Brasil.* São Paulo: Editora Brasiliense (1959).

Holden, C. 1996. "The Last of the Cahokians." *Science* 272:351.

Holley, G. R., and A. J. Brown. 1989. "Archaeological Investigations Relating to the Glen Carbon Interceptor Sewer Line, Divisions 3 Through 7, Madison County, Illinois." Southern Illinois University–Edwardsville Archaeology Program Research Report No. 1.

Holmberg, A. R. 1969. *Nomads of the Long Bow: The Sirionó of Eastern Bolivia.* New York: Natural History Press (1950).

Hölscher, D., et al. 1997. "Nutrient Input-Output Budget of Shifting Agriculture in Eastern Amazonia." *Nutrient Cycling in Agroecosystems* 47:49–57.

Hopkins, D. R. 1983. *Princes and Peasants: Smallpox in History.* Chicago: University of Chicago Press.

Hopkins, S. W. 1994. *Life Among the Paiutes: Their Wrongs and Claims.* Reno, NV: University of Nevada Press (1883).

Horai, S., et al. 1993. "Peopling of the Americas, Founded by Four Major Lineages of Mitochondrial DNA." *Molecular Biology and Evolution* 10:23–47.

Hosler, D., S. D. Burkett, and M. J. Tarkanian. 1999. "Prehistoric Polymers: Rubber Processing in Ancient Mesoamerica." *Science* 284:1988–91.

Hough, W. 1933. "William Henry Holmes." *AA* 35:752–64.

Houston, S. D. 1993. *Hieroglyphs and History at Dos Pilas: Dynastic Politics of the Classic Maya.* Austin, TX: University of Texas Press.

———. 1991. "Appendix: Caracol Altar 21," in Robertson and Fields eds. 1991, 38–42.

Houston, S. D., and P. Mathews. 1985. *The Dynastic Sequence of Dos Pilas, Guatemala.* San Francisco: Pre-Columbian Art Research Institute.

Howard, E. B. 1935. "Evidence of Early Man in North America—Based on Geological and Archaeological Work in New Mexico." *Museum Journal* (University of Pennsylvania Museum) 24:55–171.

Hrdlička, A. 1937. "Early Man in America: What Have the Bones to Say?" in G. G. MacCurdy, ed., *Early Man: As Depicted by Leading Authorities at the International Symposium, the Academy of Natural Science, Philadelphia, March 1937.* Philadelphia: Lippincott, 93–104.

———. 1912. "Historical Notes," in J. W. Fewkes, et al. "The Problems of the Unity or Plurality and the Probable Place of Origin of the American Aborigines." *AA* 14:1–59.

———. 1904. "Notes on the Indians of Sonora, Mexico." *AA* 6:51–89.

Hrdlička, A., et al. 1912. *Early Man in South America.* Washington, DC: Smithsonian.

Hubbard, W. 1848. *A General History of New England.* Boston: Little, Brown, 2nd ed.

Hudson, C. M. 1993. "Reconstructing the De Soto Expedition Route West of the Mississippi River," in Young and Hoffman eds. 1993, 143–54.

Hudson, C. M., C. DePratter, and M. T. Smith. 1993. "Reply to Henige," in Young and Hoffman eds. 1993, 255–69.

Hudson, C. M., et al. 1994. "De Soto in Coosa: Another Reply to Henige." *Georgia Historical Quarterly* 68:716–34.

Hudson, E. H. 1965a. "Treponematosis in Perspective." *Bulletin of the World Health Organization* 32:735–48.

———. 1965b. "Treponematosis and Man's Social Evolution." *AA* 67:885–901.

Hulton, P. 1984. *America 1585: The Complete Drawings of John White.* Chapel Hill, NC: University of North Carolina Press.

Humins, J. H. 1987. "Squanto and Massasoit: A Struggle for Power." *New England Quarterly,* 60:54–70.

Huntington, E. 1924. *Civilization and Climate.* New Haven, CT: Yale University Press, 3rd ed.

———. 1919. *The Red Man's Continent: A Chronicle of Aboriginal America.* New York: United States Publishers Association.

Hurtado, A. M., I. Hurtado, and K. Hill. 2004. "Public Health and Adaptive Immunity Among Natives of South America," in Salzano and Hurtado 2004, 167–90.

Hutten, U. V. 1539. *Of the Wood Called Guaiacum That Healeth the French Pockes.* Trans. T. Paynel. London: Thomae Bertheleti. (★)

Huxley, C. R., and D. F. Cutler, eds. 1991. *Ant-Plant Interactions.* New York: Oxford University Press.

Hymes, D. H. 1971. "Morris Swadesh: From the First Yale School to World Prehistory," in Swadesh 1971:228–70.

―――――. 1960. "Lexicostatistics So Far." *CA* 1:3–44.

Hyslop, J. 1984. *The Inka Road System.* New York: Academic.

Ihde, D. 2000. "Why Don't Europeanss Carry Mayan Calendar Calculators in their Filo-faxes?" *Nature* 404:935.

Iltis, H. H. 1983. "From Teosinte to Maize: The Catastrophic Sexual Transmutation." *Science* 222:886–94.

Isbell, W. H. 2001. "Reflexiones Finales," in Kaulicke and Isbell 2001, 455–79.

Isbell, W. H., and A. Vranich. 2004. "Experiencing the Cities of Wari and Tiwanaku," in Silverman 2004, 167–82.

Isbell, W. H., and G. McEwan, eds. 1991. *Huari Administrative Structure: Prehistoric Monumental Architecture and State Government.* Washington, DC: Dumbarton Oaks.

Iseminger, W. R. 1997. "Culture and Environment in the American Bottom: The Rise and Fall of Cahokia Mounds," in A. Hurley, ed., *Common Fields: An Environmental History of St. Louis.* St. Louis, MO: Missouri Historical Society.

―――――. 1990. "Features," in W. R. Iseminger, et al., *Archaeology of the Cahokia Palisade: The East Palisade Investigations.* Springfield, IL: Illinois Historic Preservation Agency, 18–38.

Jablonski, N. G., ed. 2002. *The First Americans: The Pleistocene Colonization of the New World.* San Francisco: California Academy of Sciences.

Jackson, J. B. C., et al. 2001. "Historical Overfishing and the Recent Collapse of Coastal Ecosystems." *Science* 293:629–37.

Jackson, L. E., Jr., F. M. Phillips, and E. D. Little. 1999. "Cosmogenic Cl^{36} Dating of the Maximum Limit of the Laurentide Ice Sheet in Southwestern Alberta." *Canadian Journal of Earth Sciences* 36:1347–56.

Jacobs, W. 1974. "The Tip of an Iceberg: Pre-Columbian Indian Demography and Some Implications for Revisionism." *WMQ* 31:123–32.

Jaenen, C. J. 2000. "Amerindian Views of French Culture in the Seventeenth Century," in P. C. Mancall and J. H. Merrell, eds., *American Encounters: Natives and Newcomers from European Contact to Indian Removal, 1500–1850.* New York: Routledge, 68–95.

―――――. 1976. *Friend and Foe: Aspects of French-Amerindian Cultural Contact in the Sixteenth and Seventeenth Centuries.* New York: Columbia University Press.

Jaenicke-Després, V., et al. 2003. "Early Allelic Selection in Maize as Revealed in Ancient DNA." *Science* 302:1206–08.

James, S. V., Jr., ed. 1963. *Three Visitors to Early Plymouth: Letters about the Pilgrim Settlement in New England During Its First Seven Years.* Plymouth, MA: Plimoth Plantation (1622–28). (★)

Janzen, D. 1998. "Gardenification of Wildland Nature and the Human Footprint." *Science* 279:1312.

Jefferson, T. 1894. *Notes on the State of Virginia.* Brooklyn, NY: Historical Printing Club (1786). (★)

Jenkins, D. 2001. "A Network Analysis of Inka Roads, Administrative Centers, and Storage Facilities." *Ethnohistory* 48:655–87.

Jennings, F. 1975. *The Invasion of America: Indians, Colonialism and the Cant of Conquest.* Chapel Hill, NC: University of North Carolina Press.

Johansen, B. E. 1995. "Dating the Iroquois Confederacy." *Akwesasne Notes* 1:62–63. (★)

―――――. 1987. *Forgotten Founders: How the American Indian Helped Shape Democracy.* Boston: Harvard Common Press (1982). (★)

Johnson, E. S. 1993. *"Some by Flattery and Others by Threatening": Political Strategies Among Native Americans of Seventeenth-Century Southern New England.* PhD diss. University of Massachusetts, Amherst.

Johnston, W. A. 1972. "Quaternary Geology of North America in Relation to the Migration of Man," in D. Jenness, ed., *The American Aborigines, Their Origin and Antiquity; a Collection of Papers by Ten Authors.* New York: Russell and Russell, 11–45 (1933).

Jonaitis, A. 1991. *From the Land of the Totem Poles: The Northwest Coast Indian Art Collection at the American Museum of National History.* Seattle, WA: University of Washington Press.

Joseph, G. G. 1992. *The Crest of the Peacock: The Non-European Roots of Mathematics.* New York: Penguin (1991).

Josephy, A., ed. 1993. *America in 1492: The World of the Indian Peoples Before the Arrival of Columbus.* New York: Vintage

———. 1968. *The Indian Heritage of America.* Boston: Houghton Mifflin.

Judd, N. M. 1967. "The Bureau of American Ethnology: A Partial History." Norman, OK: University of Oklahoma Press.

Justeson, J., and T. Kaufman. 1997. "A Newly Discovered Column in the Hieroglyphic Text on La Mojarra Stela 1: A Test of the Epi-Olmec Decipherment." *Science* 277:207–10.

———. 2001. "Epi-Olmec Hieroglyphic Writing and Texts." Online at http://www.albany.edu/anthro/maldp/EOTEXTS.pdf.

———. 1993. "A Decipherment of Epi-Olmec Writing." *Science* 259:1703–11.

Kahn, E. J. 1985. *The Staffs of Life.* Boston: Little, Brown.

Kaplan, R. 1999. *The Nothing That Is: A Natural History of Zero.* New York: Oxford University Press.

Karafet, T. M., et al. 1999. "Ancestral Asian Source(s) of New World Y-Chromosome Founder Haplotypes." *AJHG* 64:817–31.

Katz, S. T. 1994–2003. *The Holocaust in Historical Context.* (2 vols.) New York: Oxford University Press.

Kaulicke, P., and W. H. Isbell, eds. 2001. *Huari y Tiwanaku: Modelos vs. Evidencias,* part 2: *Boletín de Arqueología PUCP,* no. 5.

Kavasch, B. 1994. "Native Foods of New England," in Weinstein 1994, 5–29.

Kay, C. E. 1995. "Ecosystems Then and Now: A Historical-Ecological Approach to Ecosystem Management," in W. D. Wilms and J. F. Domaar, eds., *Proceedings of the Fourth Prairie Conservation and Endangered Species Workshop.* Edmonton, Alberta: Provincial Museum of Alberta, 79–87.

Kay, C. E., and R. T. Simmons, eds. 2002. *Wilderness and Political Ecology: Aboriginal Influences and the Original State of Nature.* Salt Lake City, UT: University of Utah Press.

Keefer, D. K., et al. 1998. "Early Maritime Economy and El Niño Events at Quebrada Tacahuay, Peru." *Science* 281:1833–35.

Keeley, J. 2002. "Native American Impacts on Fire Regimes of the California Coastal Ranges." *JB* 29:303–20.

Kehoe, A. B. 2002. *America Before the European Invasions.* Harlow, UK: Longman/Pearson Education.

Kelley, D. H. 1966. "A Cylinder Seal from Tlatilco." *AmAnt* 31:744–46.

Kennedy, R. G. 1994. *Hidden Cities: The Discovery and Loss of Ancient North American Civilization.* New York: Free Press.

Kern, D. C., et al. 2004. "Distribution of Amazonian Dark Earths in the Brazilian Amazon," in Lehmann et al. 2004, 51–75.

Kinbacher, K. E. 2000. "The Tangled Story of Kudzu." *Vulcan Historical Review* 4:45–69.

Kinnicutt, L. N. 1914. "The Plymouth Settlement and Tisquantum." *Proceedings of the Massachusetts Historical Society,* 48:103–18.

Kirkby, A. V. T. 1973. *The Use of Land and Water Resources in the Past and Present, Valley of Oaxaca, Mexico.* Ann Arbor, MI: University of Michigan Museum of Anthropology.

Kirkpatrick, S. S. 1992. *Lords of Sipan: A True Story of Pre-Inca Tombs, Archaeology, and Crime.* New York: Morrow.

Kittredge, G. L., ed. 1913. "Letters of Samuel Lee and Samuel Sewall Relating to New England and the Indians." *Transactions of the Colonial Society of Massachusetts* 14:142–86.

Kleinman, P. J. A., R. B. Bryant, and D. Pimentel. 1996. "Assessing Ecological Sustainability of Slash-and-Burn Agriculture Through Soil Fertility Indicators." *Agronomical Journal* 88:122–27.

Klor de Alva, J. J. 1992. "Foreword." In León-Portilla ed. 1992a, xi–xxii.

———. 1990. "Sahagún's Misguided Introduction to Ethnography and the Failure of the Colloquios Project," in J. J. Klor de Alva, H. B. Nicholson, and E. Q. Keber, eds., *The Work of Bernardino de Sahagún: Pioneer Ethnographer of Sixteenth-Century Aztec Mexico*. Albany, NY: State University of New York at Albany Press, 83–92.

Kolata, A. L. 2003. "The Proyecto Wila Jawira Research Program," in Kolata ed. 2003, 3–18.

———. 2000. "Environmental Thresholds and the 'Natural History' of an Andean Civilization," in G. Bawden and R. Reycraft, eds., *Environmental Disaster and the Archaeology of Human Response*. Albuquerque, NM: University of New Mexico Press.

———. 1993. *The Tiwanaku: Portrait of an Andean Civilization*. Cambridge: Blackwell.

Kolata, A. L., ed. 1996–2003. *Tiwanaku and Its Hinterland: Archaeology and Paleoecology of an Andean Civilization*. 2 vols. Washington, DC: Smithsonian.

Komarek, E. V. 1965. "Fire Ecology: Grasslands and Man," in *Proceedings of the Tall Timbers Fire Ecology Conference No. 4*. Tallahassee, FL: Tall Timbers Research Station, 169–220.

Koppel, T. 2003. *Lost World: Rewriting Prehistory—How New Science Is Tracing America's Ice Age Mariners*. New York: Atria.

Krech, S. 1999. *The Ecological Indian: Myth and History*. New York: Norton.

Kreck, C. 1999. "Out of the Shadows: George McJunkin was the Forgotten Man at the Center of the Century's Most Startling Archaeological Find." *Empire: Magazine of the West* (*Denver Post*), 25 Feb.

Kroeber, A. L. 1939. *Cultural and Natural Areas of Native North America*. Berkeley, CA: University of California Press.

———. 1934. "Native American Population." *AA* 36:1–25.

———. 1903. "The Native Languages of California." *AA* 5:1–26.

Kubler, G. 1946. "The Quechua in the Colonial World," in Steward 1946, 2:331–410.

Kummer, C. 2003. "A New Chestnut." *Atlantic Monthly* (June): 93–101.

Kuppermann, K. O. 2000. *Indians & English: Facing Off in Early America*. Ithaca, NY: Cornell University Press.

———. 1997a. "A Continent Revealed: Assimilation of the Shape and Possibilities of North America's East Coast, 1524–1610," in J. L. Allen, ed., *North American Exploration*. Lincoln, NE: University of Nebraska Press, 1:344–99.

———. 1997b. "Presentments of Civility: English Reading of American Self-Presentation in the Early Years of Colonization." *WMQ* 54:193–228.

Kurtén, B., and E. Anderson. 1980. *Pleistocene Mammals of North America*. New York: Columbia University Press.

Kuykendall, R. S. 1947. *The Hawaiian Kingdom, 1778–1854: Foundation and Transformation*. Honolulu, HI: University of Hawaii Press.

Lahontan, L. d. 1703. *New Voyages to North-America*. 2 vols. London: H. Benwicke. (★)

La Lone, D. 2000. "Rise, Fall, and Semiperipheral Development in the Andean World-System." *Journal of World-Systems Research* 6:68–99.

———. 1982. "The Inca as a Non-Market Economy: Supply on Command versus Supply and Demand," in J. Ericson and T. Earle, eds., *The Contextual Analysis of Prehistoric Exchange*. New York: Academic, 312–36.

Lamb, H. H. 1995. *Climate, History, and the Modern World*. New York: Routledge, rev. ed.

Laming-Emperaire, A. 1979. "Missions Archéologiques Franco-brésiliennes de Lagoa Santa, Minas Gerais, Brésil: Le Grand Abri de Lapa Vermelha (P.L.)." *Revista de Prehistoria* (São Paulo) 11:53–89.

Langstroth, R. 1996. *Forest Islands in an Amazonian Savanna of Northeastern Bolivia.* PhD diss. University of Wisconsin, Madison.

Las Casas, B. d. 1992a. *Apologética Historia Sumaria,* in V. A. Castelló, et al., eds., *Obras Completas de Fray Bartolomé de Las Casas.* Madrid: Alianza Editorial, vols. 6–8 (1560).

———. 1992b. *The Devastation of the Indies: A Brief Account.* Trans. H. Briffault. Baltimore: Johns Hopkins University Press (1552).

Lathrap, D. W. 1970. *The Upper Amazon.* New York: Praeger.

Laughlin, W. S. 1986. "Comment." *CA* 27:489–90.

Laurencich-Minelli, L. 2001. *Il Linguaggio Magico-Religioso die Numeri, dei Fili e della Musica Presso gli Inca.* Bologna: Società Editrice Escualpio.

Laurencich-Minelli, L., C. Miccinelli, and C. Animato. 1998. "Lettera di Francisco de Chaves alla Sacra Cattolica Cesarea Maestá: Un Inedito del Sec. XVI." *Studi e Materiali di Storia delle Religioni* 64:57–92.

———. 1995. "Il Documento Seicentesco Historia et Rudimenta Linguae Piruanorum." *Studi e Materiali di Storia delle Religioni* 61:365–413.

Lechtman, H. 1996a and 1996b. "The Andean World" and "Cloth and Metal: The Culture of Technology," in E. H. Boone, ed., *Andean Art at Dumbarton Oaks.* Washington, DC: Dumbarton Oaks, 1:15–32, 33–43.

———. 1993. "Technologies and Power: The Andean Case," in J. S. Henderson and P. J. Netherly, eds., *Configurations of Power: Holistic Anthropology in Theory and Practice.* Ithaca, NY: Cornell University Press, 244–80.

———. 1984. "Andean Value Systems and the Development of Prehistoric Metallurgy." *Technology and Culture* 25:1–36.

Lehmann, J., et al., eds. 2004. *Amazonian Dark Earths: Origin, Properties, Management.* The Netherlands: Kluwer Academic.

Lell, J. T. 2002. "The Dual Origin and Siberian Affinities of Native American Y Chromosomes." *AJHG* 70:192–206.

Lemonick, M. D. 1996. "Mystery of the Olmec." *Time,* 1 Jul., 56–58.

León-Portilla, M. 1963. *Aztec Thought and Culture: A Study of the Ancient Nahuatl Mind.* Norman, OK: University of Oklahoma Press.

León-Portilla, M., ed. 1992a. *The Broken Spears: The Aztec Account of the Conquest of Mexico.* Trans. L. Kamp. Boston: Beacon, 2nd ed.

———. 1992b. *Fifteen Poets of the Aztec World.* Norman, OK: University of Oklahoma Press.

Leopold, A. 1968. "On a Monument to the Pigeon," in *A Sand County Almanac, and Sketches Here and There.* New York: Oxford University Press, 108–12 (1948).

Lesseps, J. B. B. 1790. *Travels in Kamchatka During the Years 1787 and 1788.* London: J. Johnson.

Lev-Yadun, S., A. Gopher, and S. Abbo. 2000. "The Cradle of Agriculture." *Science* 288:1602–03.

Levson, V. M., and N. W. Rutter. 1996. "Evidence of Cordilleran Late Wisconsonian Glaciers in the 'Ice-Free Corridor.' " *QI* 32:33–51.

Libby, W. F. 1991. "Radiocarbon Dating," in Nobel Foundation, ed., *Nobel Lectures, 1901–1970: Chemistry.* Singapore: World Scientific, 3:593–610 (1960).

Lincoln, W. B. 1994. *The Conquest of a Continent: Siberia and the Russians.* New York: Random House.

Linton, R. 1924. "The Significance of Certain Traits in North American Maize Culture." *AA* 26:345–49.

Little, E. A., and M. J. Schoeninger. 1995. "The Late Woodland Diet on Nantucket Island and the Problem of Maize in Coastal New England." *AmAnt* 60:351–68.

Little, S. 1974. "Effects of Fire on Temperate Forests: Northeastern United States," in T. T. Kozlowski and C. E. Ahlgren, eds., *Fire and Ecosystems.* New York: Academic, 225–50.

Locke, L. L. 1923. *The Ancient Quipu or Peruvian Knot Record.* New York: American Museum of Natural History.

Lopinot, N. H., and W. I. Woods. 1993. "Wood Overexploitation and the Collapse of Cahokia," in C. M. Scarry, ed., *Foraging and Farming in the Eastern Woodlands*. Gainesville: University Press of Florida, 206–31.

López de Gómara, F. 1979. *Historia General de las Indias y Vida de Hernán Cortés*. Caracas: Biblioteca Ayacucho (1552).

Loring, S., and M. Prokopec. 1994. "A Most Peculiar Man: The Life and Times of Aleš Hrdlička," in Bray and Killion 1994, 26–42.

Lott, D. F. 2002. *American Bison: A Natural History*. Berkeley, CA: University of California Press.

Loukokta, Č. 1968. *Classification of South America Languages*. Los Angeles: University of California Latin American Center.

Lovell, W. G. 1992. " 'Heavy Shadows and Black Night': Disease and Depopulation in Colonial Spanish America." *AAAG* 82:426–43.

Lowe, J. W. G. 1985. *The Dynamics of Apocalypse: A Systems Simulation of the Classic Maya Collapse*. Albuquerque, NM: University of New Mexico Press.

Lumbreras, L. 1989. *Chavín de Huantar en el Nacimiento de la Civilización Andina*. Lima: Ediciones Instituto Andino de Estudios Arqueológicos.

Lumbreras, L., C. González, and B. Lietaer. 1976. *Acerca de la Función del Sistema Hidráulico de Chavín*. Lima: Museo Nacional de Antropología y Arqueología.

Luna-Orea, P., and M. G. Wagger. 1996. "Management of Tropical Legume Cover Crops in the Bolivian Amazon to Sustain Crop Yields and Soil Productivity." *Agronomical Journal* 88:765–76.

Lundell, C. L. 1934. "Ruins of Polol and Other Archaeological Discoveries in the Department of Peten, Guatemala." *Carnegie Institution Contributions to American Archaeology* 11:173–86.

Luttwak, E. N. 1976. *The Grand Strategy of the Roman Empire from the First Century A.D. to the Third*. Baltimore, MD: Johns Hopkins University Press.

Lutz, W. 2000. "Introduction: Understanding Complex Population-Environment Interactions," in W. Lutz, L. Prieto, and W. Sanderson, eds., *Population, Development, and Environment on the Yucatán Peninsula: From Ancient Maya to 2030*. Laxenburg, Austria: International Institute for Applied Systems Analysis.

Lynch, T. F. 2001. "On the Road Again . . . Reflections on Monte Verde." *Review of Archaeology* 22:39–44.

Lynott, M. J., et al. 1986. "Stable Carbon Isotopic Evidence for Maize Agriculture in Southeast Missouri and Northeast Arkansas." *AmAnt* 51:51–65.

MacNeish, R. S. 1967. "A Summary of the Subsistence," in D. S. Byers, ed., *The Prehistory of the Tehuacán Valley*. Austin, TX: University of Texas Press, 1:290–309.

———. 1964. "Ancient Mesoamerican Civilization." *Science* 143:531–37.

MacNeish, R. S., and M. W. Eubanks. 2000. "Comparative Analysis of the Río Balsas and Tehuacán Models for the Origins of Maize." *LAA* 11:3–20.

Madari, B. E., W. G. Sombroek, and W. I. Woods. 2004. "Research on Anthropogenic Dark Earth Soils: Could It Be a Solution for Sustainable Agricultural Development in the Amazon?" in Glaser and Woods eds. 2004, 169–81.

Mailhot, J. 1978. "L'étymologie de 'Esquimau' Revue et Corrigée." *Etudes/Inuit/Studies* 2:59–69.

Makowski, K. 2005. "Royal Statues, Staff Gods, and the Religious Ideology of the Prehistoric State of Tiahuanaco." Paper presented at the Tiwanaku Symposium, Denver Art Museum, Jan. 14–15.

———. 2001. "Los Personajes Frontales de Báculos en la Iconografía Tihuanaco y Huari: ¿Tema o Convención?" in Kaulicke and Isbell eds. 2001, 337–73.

Malvido, E. 1973. "Cronología de las Epidemias y Crisis Agrícolas de la Época Colonial." *Historia Mexicana* 89:96–101.

Mangelsdorf, P. C. 1986. "The Origin of Corn." *Scientific American* 254:80–86.

Mangelsdorf, P. C., and R. G. Reeves. 1939. "The Origin of Indian Corn and Its Relatives." *Texas Agricultural Experiment Station Bulletin* 74:1–315.

Mangelsdorf, P. C., R. S. MacNeish, and W. C. Galinat. 1964. "Domestication of Corn." *Science* 143:538–45.

Mann, A. C. 1976. *My Father and Other Manns*. Brattleboro, VT: Privately printed.

Mann, B., and J. L. Fields. 1997. "A Sign in the Sky: Dating the League of the Haudenosaunee." *American Indian Culture and Research Journal* 21:105–63.

Mann, C. C. 2005. "The Americas' Oldest Civilization Revealed." *Science* 307:34–35.

———. 2004a. "Unnatural Abundance." *New York Times*, 24 Nov.

———. 2004b. Statement. In W. G. Lovell, et al. "1491: In Search of Native America." *Journal of the Southwest* 46:453–56.

———. 2004. *Diversity on the Farm*. New York: Ford Foundation.

———. 2003. "Cracking the Khipu Code." *Science* 300:1650–51.

———. 2002a. "The Forgotten People of Amazonia." *Science* 297:921.

———. 2002b. "The Real Dirt on Rainforest Fertility." *Science* 297:920–23.

———. 2002c. "1491." *Atlantic Monthly* (April):41–53.

———. 2001. "Anthropological Warfare." *Science* 290:416–17.

———. 2000a. "Misconduct Alleged in Yanomamo Studies." *Science* 289:2251–53.

———. 2000b. "The Good Earth: Did People Improve the Amazon Basin?" *Science* 287:788.

Mann, C. C., and M. L. Plummer. 2002. "Can Genetic Engineering Help Restore 'Heritage' Trees?" *Science* 295:1628.

———. 1995. *Noah's Choice: The Future of Biodiversity*. New York: Knopf.

Maples, W. R., and M. Browning. 1994. *Dead Men Do Tell Tales: The Strange and Fascinating Cases of a Forensic Anthropologist*. New York: Doubleday.

Marchesi, G. 1975. *Tra Fiumi e Foreste: Con le Tribú del Rio Negro d'Amazzonia*. Manaus, Brazil: Privately printed.

Marcus, J. 1983. "The Conquest Slabs of Building J, Monte Albán," in J. Marcus and K. V. Flannery, eds., *The Cloud People: Divergent Evolution of the Zapotec and Mixtec Civilizations*. New York: Academic, 106–08.

———. 1976. "The Oldest Mesoamerican Writing." *Annual Review of Archaeology* 5:35–67.

———. 1973. "Territorial Organization of the Lowland Classic Maya." *Science* 180:911–16.

Marcus, J., and K. V. Flannery. 1996. *Zapotec Civilization: How Urban Society Evolved in Mexico's Oaxaca Valley*. New York: Thames and Hudson.

Margulis, L., and D. Sagan. 2001. "The Beast with Five Genomes." *NH* (June):38–41.

Marlowe, G. 1999. "Year One: Radiocarbon Dating and American Archaeology, 1947–1948." *AmAnt*, 64:9–32.

Martin, P. S. 1984. "Prehistoric Overkill: The Global Model," in Martin and Klein 1984, 354–403.

———. 1973. "The Discovery of America." *Science* 179:969–74.

———. 1967. "Prehistoric Overkill," in P. S. Martin and H. E. Wright Jr., eds., *Pleistocene Extinctions: The Search for a Cause*. New Haven, CT: Yale University Press, 75–120.

Martin, P. S., and R. G. Klein, eds. 1984. *Quaternary Extinctions: A Prehistoric Revolution*. Tucson, AZ: University of Arizona Press.

Martin, S. 2000. "Los Señores de Calakmul." *Arqueología Mexicana* 7:40–45.

Martin, S., and N. Grube. 2000. *Chronicle of the Maya Kings and Queens: Deciphering the Dynasties of the Ancient Maya*. New York: Thames and Hudson.

———. 1996. "Evidence for Macro-Political Organization Among Classic Maya Lowland States." Unpub. ms.

Martin, S. R. 1999. *Wonderful Power: The Story of Ancient Copper Working in the Lake Superior Basin*. Detroit: Wayne State University Press.

Mason, O. T. 1894. "Migration and the Food Quest: A Study in the Peopling of America." *AA* 7:275–92.

Mather, C. 1820. *Magnalia Christi Americana, or, the Ecclesiastical History of New-England*. Hartford, CT: Silus Andrus (1702).

Mathews, P. 1991. "Classic Maya Emblem Glyphs," in T. P. Culbert, *Classic Maya Political History: Hieroglyphic and Archaeological Evidence*. New York: Cambridge University Press, 19–29.

Mathiessen, P. 1987. *Wildlife in America*. New York: Viking.

Mattos, A. 1946. "Lagoa Santa Man," in Steward 1946, 1:399–400.

———. 1939. *Peter Wilhelm Lund no Brasil: Problemas de Paleontologia Brasiliera*. São Paulo: Companhia Editora Nacional.

Mazour, A. G., and J. M. Peoples. 1968. *A World History: Men and Nations*. New York: Harcourt Brace.

McAlavy, D. 2003. "Tales of 91 Years in Clovis as a Family." *Clovis* (N.M.) *News Journal*, 10 Sep.

McCaa, R. 1995. "Spanish and Nahuatl Views on Smallpox and Demographic Catastrophe in Mexico." *Journal of Interdisciplinary History* 25:397–431.

McCaa, R., A. Nimlos, and T. Hampe-Martínez. 2004. "Why Blame Smallpox? The Death of the Inca Huayna Capac and the Demographic Destruction of Tawantinsuyu (Ancient Peru)." Paper at American Historical Association Annual Meeting, 9 Jan. Online at http://www.hist.umn.edu/~rmccaa/aha2004.

McCann, J. 1999a and 1999b. "Before 1492: The Making of the Pre-Columbian Environment." *Ecological Restoration*, part 1, 17:15–30; part 2, 17:107–19.

McCollum, E. V. 1957. *A History of Nutrition: The Sequence of Ideas in Nutrition Investigations*. Cambridge, MA: Riverside.

McGaa, E. 1999. *Mother Earth Spirituality: Native American Paths to Healing Ourselves and Our World*. San Francisco: HarperCollins.

McGee, W. J. 1900. "Anthropology at Baltimore." *AA* 2:765–84.

McKibben, B. 1989. *The End of Nature*. New York: Anchor.

McNeill, W. H. 2003. "Foreword," in Crosby 2003, xi–xv.

———. 1998. *Plagues and Peoples*. New York: Anchor. 2nd ed.

———. 1991. "American Food Crops in the Old World," in Viola and Margolis eds. 1991, 43–59.

———. 1967. *A World History*. New York: Oxford University Press.

Mead, C. W. 1923. "Foreword," in L. L. Locke, *The Ancient Quipu or Peruvian Knot Record*. New York: American Museum of Natural History, 1.

Means, P. A. 1934. "Gonzalo Pizarro and Francisco de Orellana." *Hispanic American Historical Review*, 14:275–95.

Medina, J. T., ed. 1894. *Descubrimiento del Río de las Amazonas Según la Relación hasta Ahora Inédita de Fr. Gaspar de Carvajal, con Otros Documentos Referentes a Francisco de Orellana y sus Compañeros*. Seville: E. Rasco.

Meggers, B. J. 2004. "Numbers from Nowhere Revisited: Response to Stahl." *Review of Archaeology* 25:31–29.

———. 2003. "Revisiting Amazonia Circa 1492" (letter). *Science* 302:2067.

———. 2001. "The Continuing Quest for El Dorado: Round Two." *LAA* 12:304–25.

———. 1996. *Amazonia: Man and Culture in a Counterfeit Paradise*. Washington, DC: Smithsonian, rev. ed.

———. 1994. "Archaeological Evidence for the Impact of Mega-Niño Events in Amazonia During the Past Two Millennia." *Climatic Change* 28:321–38.

———. 1992a. "Amazonia: Real or Counterfeit Paradise?" *Review of Archaeology* 13:24–40.

———. 1992b. "Moundbuilders of the Amazon: Geophysical Archaeology on Marajó Island, Brazil" (review). *Journal of Field Archaeology* 19:399–404.

———. 1992c. "Prehistoric Population Density in the Amazon Basin," in Verano and Ubelaker 1992, 197–205.

———. 1979. "Climatic Oscillation as a Factor in the Prehistory of Amazonia." *AmAnt* 44:252–66.

————. 1977. "Yes If By Land, No If By Sea: The Double Standard in Interpreting Cultural Similarities." *AA* 78:637–39.

————. 1975. "The Transpacific Origin of Mesoamerica Civilization: A Preliminary Review of the Evidence and Its Theoretical Implications." *AA* 77:1–27.

————. 1954. "Environmental Limitations on the Development of Culture." *AA* 56:801–24.

Meggers, B. J., and C. Evans. 1957. *Archaeological Investigations at the Mouth of the Amazon.* Washington, DC: Smithsonian.

Meggers, B. J., et al. 1988. "Implications of Archaeological Distributions in Amazonia," in W. R. Heyer and P. E. Vanzolini, eds., *Proceedings of a Workshop on Neotropical Distribution Patterns.* Rio de Janeiro: Academia Brasiliera de Ciencias, 275–94.

Mehrer, M. W. 1995. *Cahokia's Countryside: Household Archaeology, Settlement Patterns, and Social Power.* Dekalb, IL: Northern Illinois University Press.

Mejía Xesspe, T. 1940. "Acueductos y Caminos Antiguos de la Hoya del Río Grande de Nazca," in *Actas y Trabajos Científicos del XXVII Congreso* (1939). Lima: Congreso Internacional de Americanistas, 1:559–69 (1927).

Meltzer, D. J. 2003. "In the Heat of Controversy: C. C. Abbott, the American Paleolithic, and the University Museum, 1889–1893," in D. D. Fowler and D. R. Wilcox, eds., *Archaeology and Archaeologists in Philadelphia.* Tuscaloosa, AL: University of Alabama Press, 48–87.

————. 1997. "Monte Verde and the Pleistocene Peopling of the Americas." *Science* 276:754–55.

————. 1995. "Clocking the First Americans." *Annual Review of Anthropology* 24:21–45.

————. 1994. "The Discovery of Deep Time: A History of Views on the Peopling of the Americas," in R. Bonnichsen and D. G. Steele, eds., *Method and Theory for Investigating the Peopling of the Americas.* Corvallis, OR: Center for the Study of First Americans, 7–25.

————. 1993. *Search for the First Americans.* Washington, DC: Smithsonian.

————. 1992. "Introduction," in D. J. Meltzer and R. C. Dunnell, eds., *The Archaeology of William Henry Holmes.* Washington, DC: Smithsonian.

————. 1989. "Why Don't We Know When the First People Came to North America?" *AmAnt* 54:471–79.

Meltzer, D. J., et al. 1997. "On the Pleistocene Antiquity of Monte Verde." *AmAnt* 62:659–63.

Mena, C. d. (attrib.). 1930. "The Anonymous *La Conquista del Peru.*" *Proceedings of the American Academy of Arts and Sciences* 64:177–286 (1534).

Menzel, D. 1977. *The Archaeology of Ancient Peru and the Work of Max Uhle.* Berkeley, CA: R. H. Lowie Museum.

Menzies, G. 2003. *1421: The Year That China Discovered America.* New York: Morrow.

Merriwether, D. A. 2002. "A Mitochondrial Perspective on the Peopling of the New World," in Jablonski ed. 2002, 295–310.

Merriweather, D. A., et al. 1996. "MtDNA Variation Indicates Mongolia May Have Been the Source for the Founding Population for the New World." *AJHG* 59:204–12.

Metcalf, P. R. 1974. "Who Should Rule at Home? Native American Politics and Indian-White Relations." *JAH* 61:651–65.

Métraux, A. 1942. *The Native Tribes of Eastern Bolivia and Western Matto Grosso.* Washington, DC: Smithsonian.

Michczynski, A., and A. Adamska. 1997. "Calibrated Chronology of the Inca State." Paper at Sixteenth International Radiocarbon Conference, Groningen University, 16–20 June. Online at http://www.maa.uw.edu.pl/polski/AndyDB/MICH_ADA.HTM.

Milbrath, S., and C. Peraza Lope. 2003. "Revisiting Mayapán: Mexico's Last Maya Capital." *Ancient Mesoamerica* 14:1–46.

Milner, G. R. 1992. "Health and Cultural Change in the Late Prehistoric American Bottom, Illinois," in M. L. Powell, ed., *What Mean These Bones? Studies in Southeastern Bioarchaeology.* Tuscaloosa, AL: University of Alabama Press, 52–69.

Milton, G. 2000. *Big Chief Elizabeth: The Adventures and Fates of the First English Colonists in America*. New York: Farrar, Straus and Giroux.

Ministerio de Fomento (Spain), ed. 1879. *Tres Relaciones de Antigüedades Peruanas*. Madrid: M. Tello.

Mithun, M. 1997. *The Languages of Native North America*. New York: Cambridge University Press.

Moctezuma, E. M., and F. Solis Olguín. 2003. *Aztecs*. London: Royal Academy of Arts.

Montagu, M. F. A. 1944. "Ales Hrdlička, 1869–1943." *AA* 46:113–17.

Montaigne, M. d. 1991. "On the Cannibals," in *The Essays of Michel de Montaigne*. Trans. M. A. Screech. New York: Penguin, 233–36 (1595). (★)

Montell, G. 1929. *Dress and Ornaments in Ancient Peru: Archaeological and Historical Studies*. Trans. M. Leijer and G. E. Fuhrken. Göteborg: Elanders Boktryckeri Aktiebolag.

Mooney, J. M. 1928. *The Aboriginal Population of America North of Mexico*. Washington, DC: Smithsonian.

Mora-Urpí, J. 1994. "Peach Palm *Bactris gasipaes*," in J. E. Hernando Bermejo and J. León, eds., *Neglected Crops: 1492 from a Different Perspective*. Rome: United Nations Food and Agriculture Organization, 211–21.

Mora-Urpí, J., J. C. Weber, and C. R. Clement. 1997. *Peach Palm*: Bactris gasipaes *Kunth*. Rome: Gatersleben/International Plant Genetic Resources Institute.

Morgan, L. H. 1901. *The League of the Ho-dé-no-sau-nee or Iroquois*. 2 vols. New York: Burt Franklin (1851).

Morgan, T. 1993. *Wilderness at Dawn: The Settling of the North American Continent*. New York: Simon and Schuster.

Morison, S. E. 1974. *The European Discovery of America: The Southern Voyages, 1492–1616*. New York: Oxford University Press.

Morley, S. G. 1946. *The Ancient Maya*. Stanford, CA: Stanford University Press.

Morrell, V. 1990a. "Monte Verde Archaeologist Prevails in Dispute over Settlement's Age." *Scientist*, 20 Jan., 1.

———. 1990b. "Confusion in Earliest America." *Science* 248:439–41.

Morris, C. 1993. "The Wealth of a Native American State: Value, Investment, and Mobilization in the Inka Economy," in J. S. Henderson and P. J. Netherly, eds., *Configurations of Power: Holistic Anthropology in Theory and Practice*. Ithaca, NY: Cornell University Press, 36–50.

Morrison, T., and G. S. Hawkins. 1978. *Pathways to the Gods: The Mystery of the Andes Lines*. New York: Harper and Row.

Morton, N. 1669. *New-Englands Memoriall, or, A Brief Relation of the Most Memorable and Remarkable Passages of the Providence of God Manifested to the Planters of New-England in America*. Cambridge, MA: John Usher. (★)

Morton, T. 1637. *New English Canaan, or New Canaan*. London: Charles Green. (★)

Moseley, M. E. 2005. "The Maritime Foundations of Andean Civilization: An Evolving Hypothesis," in P. Trillo, ed. *Perú y el Mar: 12000 Años del Historia del Pescaría*. Lima: Sociedad Nacional de Pesquería.

———. 2001. *The Incas and the Ancestors: The Archaeology of Peru*. New York: Thames and Hudson, rev. ed.

———. 1975a. "Chan Chan: Andean Alternative of the Preindustrial City." *Science* 187:219–25.

———. 1975b. *The Maritime Foundations of Andean Civilization*. Menlo Park, CA: Cummings.

Moseley, M. E., and G. R. Willey. 1973. "Aspero, Peru: A Reexamination of the Site and Its Implications." *AmAnt* 38:452–68.

Moseley, M. E., and A. Cordy-Collins, eds. 1990. *The Northern Dynasties: Kingship and Statecraft in Chimor*. Washington, DC: Dumbarton Oaks.

Motolinía, T. 1950. *The History of the Indians of New Spain*. Trans. E. A. Foster. Berkeley, CA: Cortés Society (1541).

Muir, J. 1997. "The Story of My Boyhood and Youth," in J. Muir, *Nature Writings*. New York: Library of America, 1–146 (1913).

Mulholland, M. T. 1985. *Patterns of Change in Prehistoric Southern New England: A Regional Approach*. PhD diss., University of Massachusetts, Amherst.

Murra, J. V. 1980. *The Economic Organization of the Inca State*. Greenwich, CT: JAI Press.

———. 1967. "El 'Control Vertical' en un Máximo de Pisos Ecológicos en la Economía de las Sociedades Andinas," in *Visita de la Provincia de León de Huánuco en 1562*. Huánuco, Peru: Universidad Nacional Hermilio Valdizán, 2:427–76.

———. 1964. "Cloth and Its Functions in the Inca State." *AA* 64:710–28.

———. 1960. "Crop and Rite in the Inca State," in S. Diamond, ed., *Culture in History*. New York: Columbia University Press, 393–407.

Murúa, M. d. 1962–64. *Historia General de Perú*. 2 vols. Madrid: Instituto Gonzalo Fernández de Oviedo, Consejo Superior de Investigaciones Científicas (1613).

Myers, T. P., et al. 2004. "Historical Perspectives on Amazonian Dark Earths," in Lehmann et al. 2004, 15–28.

———. 1992. "Agricultural Limitations of the Amazon in Theory and Practice." *WA* 24:82–97.

Nabokov, V. 1989. *Speak, Memory: An Autobiography Revisited*. New York: Vintage (1967).

Nanepashemet. 1991. "It Smells Fishy to Me: An Argument Supporting the Use of Fish Fertilizer by the Native People of Southern New England," in P. Benes, ed., *Algonkians of New England: Past and Present*. Boston: Boston University Press, 42–50.

Navallo-González, R., et al. 2003. "Mars-Like Soils in the Atacama Desert, Chile, and the Dry Limit of Microbial Life." *Science* 302:1018–21.

Neel, J. V. 1977. "Health and Disease in Unacculturated Amerindian Populations," in Anon., ed., *Health and Disease in Tribal Societies*. Amsterdam: Elsevier, 155–68.

Neel, J. V., R. J. Biggar, and R. I. Sukernik. 1994. "Virologic and Genetic Studies Relate Amerind Origins to the Indigenous People of the Mongolia/Manchuria/Southeastern Siberia Region." *PNAS* 91:10737–41.

Neel, J. V., et al. 1970. "Notes on the Effect of Measles and Measles Vaccine in a Virgin-Soil Population of South American Indians." *American Journal of Epidemiology* 91:418–29.

Neel, J. V., Jr., et al. 2001. "The Yanomamo and the 1960s Measles Epidemic" (letter). *Science* 292:1836–38.

Neumann, T. W. 2002. "The Role of Prehistoric Peoples in Shaping Ecosystems in the Eastern United States: Implications for Restoration Ecology and Wilderness Management," in Kay and Simmons 2002, 141–78.

Neves, E. G., et al. 2004. "The Timing of *Terra Preta* Formation in the Central Amazon: Archaeological Data from Three Sites," in Glaser and Woods eds. 2004, 125–34.

Neves, W. A., and H. M. Pucciarelli. 1991. "Morphological Affinities of the First Americans: An Exploratory Analysis on Early South American Human Skulls." *Journal of Human Evolution* 21:261–73.

Neves, W. A., D. Meyer, and H. M. Pucciarelli. 1996. "Early Skeletal Remains and the Peopling of the Americas." *Rivista de Antropologia* (São Paulo), 39:121–27.

Niles, S. A. 1999. *The Shape of Inca History: Narrative and Architecture in an Andean Empire*. Iowa City, IA: University of Iowa Press.

Nordenskiöld, E. 1979a. *The Ethnography of South-America Seen from Mojos in Bolivia*. New York: AMS Press (1924).

———. 1979b. *The Secret of the Peruvian Quipus*. New York: AMS Press (1925).

Nuttli, O. W. 1973. "The Mississippi Valley Earthquakes of 1811 and 1812: Intensities, Ground Motion and Magnitudes." *Bulletin of the Seismological Society of America* 63:227–48.

O'Brien, M. J., and D. E. Lewarch. 1992. "Regional Analysis of the Zapotec Empire, Valley of Oaxaca, Mexico." *WA* 23:264–82.

O'Connell, R. 1989. *Of Arms and Men: A History of War, Weapons, and Aggression.* New York: Oxford University Press.

Okimori, Y., M. Ogawa, and F. Takahashi. 2003. "Potential of CO_2 Emission Reductions by Carbonizing Biomass Waste from Industrial Tree Plantation in South Sumatra, Indonesia." *Mitigation and Adaptation Strategies for Global Climate Change* 8:261–80.

Ortiz de Montellano, B. R. 1978. "Aztec Cannibalism: An Ecological Necessity?" *Science* 200:611–17.

Osborne, L. 1998. "The Numbers Game: These Days Historians Are Measuring Everything. But Do Their Numbers Add Up?" *Lingua Franca* (September):50–58.

Otto I, Bishop of Freising. 1966. *Chronicon: The Two Cities; a Chronicle of Universal History to the Year 1146 A.D.* New York: Octagon Books (1150?).

Owen, B., and P. S. Goldstein. "Tiwanaku en Moquegua: Interacciones Regionales y Colapso," in Kaulicke and Isbell eds. 2001, 169–88.

Pachacuti Yamqui Salcamayhua, J. d. S. 1879. "Relación," in Ministerio de Fomento ed. 1879, 231–328.

Pagden, A. 1990. *Spanish Imperialism and the Political Imagination: Studies in European and Spanish-American Social Political Theory, 1513–1830.* New Haven, CT: Yale University Press.

Palliser, J. 1983. *Papers Relative to the Exploration by Captain Palliser of That Portion of British North America Which Lies Between the Northern Branch of the River Saskatchewan and the Frontier of the United States; and Between the Red River and Rocky Mountains.* Ottawa: Canadian Institute for Historical Microreproductions (1859).

Panzer, J. 1995. "The Popes and Slavery." *Dunwoodie Review* 18:1–125.

Paraíso, M. H. B. 1999. "Os Botocudos e sua Trajetória Histórica," in M. Carneiro de Cunha, ed., *História dos Indios no Brasil.* São Paulo: Fundação de Amparo à Pesquisa do Estado de São Paulo, 2nd ed., 413–30.

———. 1992. "Repensando en la Política Indigenista para los Botocudos en el Siglo XIX," in J. N. Sánchez, ed., *Culturas y Pueblos Indigenas.* Quito: Editora Nacional, 233–58.

Parfitt, T. 2002. *The Lost Tribes of Israel: The History of a Myth.* London: Weidenfeld and Nicolson.

Park, C. C. 1992. *Tropical Rainforests.* New York: Routledge.

Parker, A. C. 1911. "Woman's Place Among the Indians." *Annual Report of the American Scenic and Historic Preservation Society.* New York: American Scenic and Historic Preservation Society, 252–53.

Parkman, F. 1983. *France and England in North America.* 2 vols. New York: Library of America (1865–92).

Parry, J. H. 1969. *The Age of Reconnaissance, Discovery, Exploring, and Settlement, 1450–1650.* New York: Praeger (1963).

Pärssinen, M. 2003. "When Did the Guaraní Expansion Toward the Andean Foothills Begin?" in Pärssinen and Korpisaari eds. 2003, 73–90.

Pärssinen, M., et al. 2003. "Geometrically Patterned Ancient Earthworks in the Rio Branco Region of Acre, Brazil: New Evidence of Ancient Chiefdom Formation in Amazonian Interfluvial Terra Firme Environment," in Pärssinen and Korpisaari eds. 2003, 97–134.

Pärssinen, M., and A. Korpisaari, eds. 2003. *Western Amazonia—Amazônia Ocidental: Multidisciplinary Studies on Ancient Expansionistic Movements, Fortifications, and Sedentary Life.* Helsinki: Renvall Institute.

Paternosto, C. 1996. *The Stone and the Thread: Andean Roots of Abstract Art.* Trans. E. Allen. Austin, TX: University of Texas Press.

Patrón, P. 1894. "La Enfermedad Mortal de Huayna Capac." *Crónica Médica* (Lima) 11:179–83.

Pauketat, T. R. 1998. "Refiguring the Archaeology of Greater Cahokia." *JAR* 6:45–89.

———. 1997. "Cahokian Political Economy," in T. R. Pauketat and T. E. Emerson, eds., *Cahokia: Domination and Ideology in the Mississippian World*. Lincoln, NE: University of Nebraska Press, 30–51.

———. 1994. *The Ascent of Chiefs: Cahokia and Mississippian Politics in Native North America*. Tuscaloosa, AL: University of Alabama Press.

Pearson, K. 1924. "King Robert the Bruce, 1274–1329, His Skull and Portraiture." *Biometrika* 16:252–72.

Peñafield, N. 1904. *Colección de Cantares Mexicanos*. Mexico City: Privately printed.

Peñaherrera de Costales, P., and A. Costales Samienego. 1964. *Huayna Capac*. Cuenca, Ecuador: Núcleo del Azuay de la Casa de la Cultura Ecuatoriana.

Pepys, S. 1970. *The Diary of Samuel Pepys*. R. Latham and W. Matthews, eds. Berkeley, CA: University of California Press (1660–69, 10 vols.). (★)

Percy, G. 1922. " 'A Trewe Relacyon': Virginia from 1609 to 1612." *Tyler's Quarterly Historical and Genealogical Magazine* 3:259–82. (★)

———. 1905–07. "Observations Gathered Out of a Discourse of the Plantation of the Southerne Colonie in Virginia by the English," in Purchas 1905–07, 18:403–19 (1606). (★)

Perttula, T. K. 1993. "The Long-Term Effects of the De Soto Entrada on Aboriginal Caddoan Populations," in Young and Hoffman 1993, 237–54.

———. 1991. "European Contact and Its Effects on Aboriginal Caddoan Populations Between A.D. 1520 and A.D. 1680," in Thomas ed. 1989–91, 3:501–18.

Petersen, J. B. 2004. "Foreword," in R. E. Funk, *An Ice Age Quarry Workshop: The West Athens Hill Site Revisited*. Albany, NY: New York State Museum.

Petersen, J. B., and E. R. Cowrie. 2002. "From Hunter-Gatherer Camp to Horticultural Village: Late Prehistoric Indigenous Subsistence and Development," in J. P. Hart and C. B. Rieth, eds., *Northeast Subsistence-Settlement Change: A.D. 700–1300*. Albany, NY: New York State Museum, 265–87.

Petersen, J. B., E. Neves, and M. Heckenberger. 2001. "Gift from the Past: *Terra Preta* and Prehistoric Cultivation in Amazonia," in C. McEwen, C. Bareto, and E. Neves, eds., *Unknown Amazon: Culture in Nature in Ancient Brazil*. London: British Museum Press.

Pickett, S. T. A., and J. T. Thompson. 1978. "Patch Dynamics and the Design of Nature Reserves." *Biological Conservation* 13:27–37.

Pina Chan, R. 1989. *The Olmec: Mother Culture of Mesoamerica*. New York: Rizzoli.

Piperno, D. R., and K. V. Flannery. 2001. "The Earliest Archaeological Maize (*Zea mays* L.) from Highland Mexico: New Accelerator Mass Spectrometry Dates and Their Implications." *PNAS* 98:2104–06.

Pizarro, P. 1969. *Relation of the Discovery and Conquest of the Kingdoms of Peru*. Trans. P. M. Means. New York: Kraus Reprint (1571).

Pohl, J. M. D. 2002. *The Legend of Lord Eight Deer: An Epic of Ancient Mexico*. New York: Oxford University Press.

Pohl, M. E. D., K. O. Pope, and C. von Nagy. 2002. "Olmec Origins of Mesoamerican Writing." *Science* 298:1984–86.

Pollard, H. P. 2003. "The Tarascan Empire," in *The Postclassic Mesoamerican World*, M. E. Smith and F. F. Berdan, eds., Salt Lake City: University of Utah Press, 79–86.

Ponting, C. 1991. *A Green History of the World: The Environment and the Collapse of Great Civilizations*. New York: Penguin.

———. 1990. "Historical Perspectives in Sustainable Development." *Environment* 32:4–9, 31–33.

Pope, K. O., et al. 2001. "Origin and Environmental Setting of Ancient Agriculture in the Lowlands of Mesoamerica." *Science* 292:1370–73.

Popsin, C. P. 2003. "First Lady of Amazonia." *Archaeology* (May/June):26–31.

Porro, A. 1994. "Social Organization and Political Power in the Amazon Floodplain: The Ethnohistorical Sources, " in Roosevelt ed. 1994, 79–94.

Porter, J. B. 1989. "Olmec Colossal Heads as Recarved Thrones: 'Mutilation,' Revolution, and
Recarving." Res 17/18:23–30.

Porter, R. 1998. The Greatest Benefit to Mankind: A Medical History of Humanity. New York: Norton.

Posey, D. 1984. "A Preliminary Report on Diversified Management of Tropical Forest by the
Kayapó Indians of the Brazilian Amazon." Advances in Economic Botany 1:112–26.

Power, C. 1992. "Medieval Waterford: A Possible Case of Syphilis." Archaeology Ireland 6:20–21.

Powledge, T. M. 1999. "The Riddle of the Ancient Mariners." California Wild (Summer):28–33.

Pratt, P. 1858. "A Declaration of the Affairs of the English People That First Inhabited New
England." Collections of the Massachusetts Historical Society 4:474–91 (1662).

Prem, H. J. 1992. "Disease Outbreaks in Colonial Mexico During the Sixteenth Century," in
Cook and Lovell, eds. 1992, 20–48.

Prescott, W. H. 2000. History of the Conquest of Mexico and History of the Conquest of Peru. New
York: Cooper Square (1843, 1847). (★)

Preston, D. 1997. "The Lost Man." New Yorker, 16 Jun., 70–81.

Preston, W. S. 2002. "Post-Columbian Wildlife Irruptions in California: Implications for Cultural and Environmental Understanding," in Kay and Simmons 2002, 111–40.

Priest, P. N. 1980. Estudios Sobre el Idioma Sirionó. Riberalta, Bolivia: Instituto Lingüístico de
Verano.

Prince, T. 1855. "New England Chronology," in N. Morton, New England's Memorial. Boston:
Congregational Board of Publication, 285–320.

Pring, M. 1905. "A Voyage Set Out from the Citie of Bristoll at the Charge of the Chiefest
Merchants and Inhabitants of the Said Citie with a Small Ship and a Bark for the Dis-
couerie of the North Part of Virginia," in G. P. Winship, ed., Sailors' Narratives of Voyages
Along the New England Coast, 1524–1624. Boston: Houghton Mifflin, 51–63.

Pringle, H. 2001. "The First Urban Center in the Americas." Science 292:621.

———. 1999. "New Questions About Ancient American Site." Science 286:657–59.

———. 1998a. "The Sickness of Mummies." Discover (December):74–83.

———. 1998b. "Traces of Ancient Mariners Found in Peru." Science 281:1775–77.

———. 1997. "Oldest Mound Complex Found at Louisiana Site." Science 277:1761–62.

Proulx, D., D. Johnson, and S. Mabee. 2001. "Beneath the Lines: A New Interpretation of the
Nasca Geoglyphs." Discovering Archaeology (Summer).

Prous, A. 1986. "Os Mais Antigos Vestigios Arqueológicos no Brasil Central (Estados de
Minas Gerais, Goias e Bahía)," in Bryan 1986, 173–82.

Puget, P. 1939. "The Vancouver Expedition: Peter Puget's Journal of the Exploration of Puget
Sound, May 7–June 11, 1792." Pacific Northwest Quarterly 30:117–217.

Purchas, S. 1905–07. Hakluytus Posthumus, or Purchas His Pilgrimes: Contayning a History of the
World in Sea Voyages and Lande Travells by Englishmen and Others. 20 vols. Glasgow: J. MacLe-
hose and Sons (1625).

Pyne, S. 1995. World Fire: The Culture of Fire on Earth. Seattle: University of Washington Press.

———. 1982. Fire in America: A Cultural History of Wildland and Rural Fire. Princeton, NJ:
Princeton University Press.

Quinn, D. B. 1974. England and the Discovery of America, 1481–1620. New York: Knopf.

Ramenofsky, A. 1987. Vectors of Death: The Archaeology of European Contact. Albuquerque, NM:
University of New Mexico Press.

Ramenofsky, A., and P. Galloway. 1997. "Disease and the Soto Entrada," in P. Galloway, ed.,
The Hernando de Soto Expedition: History, Historiography, and "Discovery" in the Southeast.
Lincoln, NE: University of Nebraska Press, 259–79.

Rao, A. R. 1972. *Smallpox*. Bombay: Kothari Book Deposit.

Raup, H. M. 1937. "Recent Changes of Climate and Vegetation in Southern New England and Adjacent New York." *Journal of the Arnold Arboretum* 18:79–117.

Raymond, J. S. 1981. "The Maritime Foundations of Andean Civilization: A Reconsideration of the Evidence." *AmAnt* 46:806–21.

Reinhard, K., and O. Urban. 2003. "Diagnosing Ancient Diphyllobothriasis from Chinchorro Mummies." *Memorias do Instituto do Oswaldo Cruz* 98 (supp.):191–93.

Reilly, F. K., III. 1994. "Enclosed Ritual Spaces and the Watery Underworld in Formative Period Architecture: New Observations on the Function of La Venta Complex A," in V. M. Fields, ed., *Seventh Palenque Round Table, 1989*. San Francisco: Pre-Columbian Art Research Institute. Online at http://www.mesoweb.com/pari/publications/RT07/EnclosedSpaces.pdf.

Reiten, G. 1995. "Five Great Values of the Lakota Sioux," in C. I. Bennett, ed., *Comprehensive Multicultural Education: Theory and Practice*. Boston: Allyn and Bacon, 3rd ed., 367–71.

Restall, M. 2003. *Seven Myths of the Spanish Conquest*. New York: Oxford University Press.

Richards, M., and V. Macaulay. 2001. "The Mitochondrial Gene Tree Comes of Age." *AJHG* 68:1315–20.

Richards, P. 1952. *The Tropical Rain Forest: An Ecological Study*. New York: Cambridge University Press.

Richter, D. K. 2001. *Facing East from Indian Country: A Native History of Early America*. Cambridge, MA: Harvard University Press.

Ridley, M. 2000. *Genome: Autobiography of a Species in 23 Chapters*. New York: HarperCollins.

Riley, T. J., et al. 1994. "Accelerator Mass Spectrometry (AMS) Dates Confirm Early *Zea mays* in the Mississippi River Valley." *AmAnt* 59:490–98.

Rivet, P., G. Stresser-Péan, and Č. Loukotka. 1952. "Langues américaines," in A. Meillet and M. Cohen, eds., *Les Langues du Monde*. Centre National de la Recherche Scientifique, 2:943–1198.

Roberts, F. H. H. 1937. "The Folsom Problem in American Archaeology," in G. G. MacCurdy, ed., *Early Man: As Depicted by Leading Authorities at the International Symposium, the Academy of Natural Science, Philadelphia, March 1937*. Philadelphia: J. B. Lippincott, 153–62.

————. 1935. *A Folsom Complex: Preliminary Report on Investigations at the Lindenmeier Site in Northern Colorado*. Washington, DC: Smithsonian.

Robertson, M. G., and V. M. Fields, eds. 1991. *Sixth Palenque Round Table, 1986*. Norman, OK: University of Oklahoma Press.

Robichaux, H. 2002. "On the Compatibility of Epigraphic, Geographic, and Archaeological Data with a Drought-Based Explanation for the Classic Maya Collapse." *Ancient Mesoamerica* 13:341–45.

Robinson, P. 1994. "A Narragansett History from 1000 B.P. to the Present," in Weinstein 1994, 75–90.

Rodríguez, C., and P. Ortiz. 1994. *El Manatí, un Espacio Sagrado de los Olmeca, Jalapa*. Veracruz: Universidad Veracruzana.

Roe, D. A. 1973. *A Plague of Corn: The Social History of Pellagra*. Ithaca, NY: Cornell University Press.

Roe, F. G. 1951. *The North American Buffalo*. Toronto: University of Toronto Press.

Rogan, P., and S. Lentz. 1994. "Molecular Genetic Evidence Suggesting Treponematosis in Pre-Columbian, Chilean Mummies." *American Journal of Physical Anthropology* (supp.) 18:171–72.

Rollings, W. H. 1995. "Living in a Graveyard: Native Americans in Colonial Arkansas," in J. Whayne, ed., *Cultural Encounters in the Early South: Indians and Europeans in Arkansas*. Fayetteville, AR: University of Arkansas Press, 38–60.

Romain, W. F. 2000. *Mysteries of the Hopewell: Astronomers, Geometers, and Magicians of the Eastern Woodlands*. Akron, OH: University of Akron Press.

Roosevelt, A. C. 1997. "Dating a Paleoindian Site in the Amazon in Comparison with Clovis Cuture" (letter). *Science* 275:1948–52.

———. 1994. "Amazonian Anthropology: Strategy for a New Synthesis," in Roosevelt ed. 1994. 1–33.

———. 1991. *Moundbuilders of the Amazon: Geophysical Archaeology on Marajó Island, Brazil*. San Diego, CA: Academic.

Roosevelt, A. C., ed. 1994. *Amazonian Indians from Prehistory to Present: Anthropological Perspectives*. Tucson, AZ: University of Arizona Press.

Roosevelt, A. C., J. Douglas, and L. Brown. 2002. "The Migrations and Adaptations of the First Americans: Clovis and Pre-Clovis Viewed from South America," in Jablonski ed. 2002, 159–223.

Roosevelt, A. C., et al. 1996. "Paleoindian Cave Dwellers in the Amazon: The Peopling of the Americas." *Science* 272:373–84.

Rosier, J. 1605. *A True Relation of the Most Prosperous Voyage Made this Present Yeere 1605, by Captaine George Weymouth, in the Discovery of the Land of Virginia Where He Discovered 60 Miles Up a Most Excellent River; Together with a Most Fertile Land*. London: Geor. Bishop. (★)

Ross, J. F. 2002. "First City in the New World?" *Smithsonian* (August):57–64.

Rostlund, E. 1957a. "The Evidence for the Use of Fish as Fertilizer in Aboriginal North America." *Journal of Geography* 56:222–28.

———. 1957b. "The Myth of a Natural Prairie Belt in Alabama: An Interpretation of Historical Records." *AAAG* 47:392–411.

Rostworowski de Diez Canseco, M. 2001. *Pachacutec: Inca Yupanqui*. Lima: Instituto de Estudios Peruanos (1953).

———. 1999. *History of the Inca Realm*. Trans. H. B. Iceland. NY: Cambridge University Press (1988).

Rothschild, B. M., and C. Rothschild. 2000. "Occurrence and Transitions among the Treponematoses in North America." *Chungará* (Arica, Chile) 32:147–55.

———. 1996. "Treponemal Disease in the New World." *CA* 37:555–61.

Rothschild, B. M., C. Rothschild, et al. 2000. "First European Exposure to Syphilis: The Dominican Republic at the Time of Contact." *Clinical Infectious Diseases* 31:936–41.

Rouse, I. 1993. *The Tainos: Rise and Decline of the People Who Greeted Columbus*. New Haven, CT: Yale University Press.

Rowe, J. H. 1997. "How Francisco Pizarro Took Over Peru." Unpub. ms.

———. 1991. "Los monumentos perdidos de la plaza mayor del Cuzco Inkaico." *Revista del Museo e Instituto de Arqueología* (Cuzco) 24:83–100.

———. 1990. "El plano más antiguo del Cuzco; dos parroquias de la ciudad vistas en 1643." *Histórica* (Lima) 16:367–77.

———. 1967. "Form and Meaning in Chavin Art," in J. H. Rowe and D. Menzel, eds., *Peruvian Archaeology: Selected Readings*. Palo Alto, CA: Peek Publications, 72–103.

———. 1954. "Max Uhle, 1856–1944: A Memoir of the Father of Peruvian Archaeology." *University of California Publications in American Archaeology and Ethnology* 46(1):1–134.

———. 1946. "Inca Culture at the Time of the Spanish Conquest," in Steward 1946, 2:183–330.

Rozoy, J.-G. 1998. "The (Re-)population of Northern France Between 13,000 and 8000 B.P." *QI* 49/50:69–86.

Ruiz de Arce, J. 1933. "Relación de servicios; Advertencias que hizo el fundador del vínculo y mayorazgo a los sucesores en el." *Boletín de la Real Academia de Historia* (Madrid) 102:327–84 (1545).

Ruppert, K., and J. H. Denison Jr. 1943. *Archaeological Reconnaissance in Campeche, Quintana Roo, and Peten*. Washington, DC: Carnegie Institution.

Russell, H. S. 1980. *Indian New England Before the Mayflower*. Hanover, NH: University Press of New England.

———. 1975. "Indian Corn Cultivation" (letter). *Science* 189:944–46.

Rust, W. F., and R. J. Sharer. 1988. "Olmec Settlement Data from La Venta, Tabasco, Mexico." *Science* 242:102–04.

Rutman, D. B. 1960. "The Pilgrims and Their Harbor." *WMQ* 17:164–82.

Rydén, S. 1941. *A Study of the Sirionó Indians.* Göteborg, Sweden: Elanders Boktryckeri Aktiebolag.

Sahagún, B. d. l. 1993. "Book XII of the Florentine Codex," in J. Lockhart, ed. trans., *We People Here: Nahuatl Accounts of the Conquest of Mexico.* Berkeley, CA: University of California Press.

———. 1980. "The Aztec-Spanish Dialogues of 1524." Trans. J. J. Klor de Alva. *Alcheringa: Ethnopoetics* 4:52–193.

Sakai, M. 1998. *Reyes, Estrellas y Cerros en Chimor: El Proceso de Cambio de la Organización Espacial y Temporal en Chan Chan.* Lima: Editorial Horizonte.

Sale, K. 1990. *The Conquest of Paradise: Christopher Columbus and the Columbian Legacy.* New York: Knopf.

Salisbury, N. 1989. "Squanto: The Last of the Patuxets," in D. G. Sweet and G. B. Nash, *Struggle and Survival in Colonial America.* Berkeley, CA: University of California Press, 228–45.

———. 1982. *Manitou and Providence: Indians, Europeans, and the Making of New England, 1500–1643.* New York: Oxford University Press.

Salomon, J.-C. 1993. "The Cancer Journal," September/October. Online at http://www.tribunes.com/tribune/edito/6-5a.htm.

Salwen, B. 1978. "Indians of Southern New England and Long Island: Early Period," in Trigger 1978, 15:160–76.

Salzano, F. M., and A. M. Hurtado, eds. 2004. *Lost Paradises and the Ethics of Research and Publication.* New York: Oxford University Press.

Samwell, D. 1967. "Some Account of a Voyage to the South Sea's [sic] in 1776–1777–1778," in J. C. Beaglehole, ed., *The Journals of Captain James Cook on His Voyages of Discovery.* Cambridge: Hakluyt Society, 3(2):987–1300.

Sanchez, T. R. 2001. " 'Dangerous Indians': Evaluating the Depiction of Native Americans in Selected Trade Books." *Urban Education* 36:400–25.

Sancho, P. 1917. *An Account of the Conquest of Peru.* Trans. P. A. Means. New York: Cortés Society (1543).

Sanders, W., and D. Webster. 1988. "The Mesoamerican Urban Tradition." *AA* 90:521–26.

Sandweiss, D. H., and M. E. Moseley. 2001. "Amplifying Importance of New Research in Peru" (letter). *Science* 294:1651–53.

Sandweiss, D. H., et al. 1998. "Quebrada Jaguay: Early South American Maritime Adaptations." *Science* 281:1830–32.

Santa, E. D. 1963. *Viracocha: L'empereur-dieu des Incas.* Brussels: Privately printed.

Santillán, H. D. 1879. "Relación del origen, descendencia, política y gobierno de los Incas," in Ministero de Fomento ed. 1879, 3–135 (~1563).

Santley, R., T. Killion, and M. Lycett. 1986. "On the Maya Collapse." *Journal of Anthropological Research* 42:123–59.

Sarmiento de Gamboa, P. 2000. *History of the Incas.* Trans. C. Markham. Cambridge, Ontario: In Parentheses Publications. Online at http://www.yorku.ca/inpar/sarmiento_markham.pdf (1572).

Sauer, C. 1993. *Historical Geography of Crop Plants.* Boca Raton, FL: CRC Press.

———. 1975. "Man's Dominance by Use of Fire." *Geoscience and Man* 10:1–13.

———. 1935. *The Aboriginal Population of Northwestern Mexico.* Berkeley, CA: University of California Press.

Sauer, M. 1802. *An Account of a Geographical and Astronomical Expedition to the Northern Parts of Russia.* London: T. Cadell.

Saunders, J. W., et al. 1997. "A Mound Complex in Louisiana at 5400–5000 Years Before the Present." *Science* 277:1796–99.

Scarborough, V. L. 2003. "How to Interpret an Ancient Landscape." *PNAS* 100:4366–68.

Scarborough, V. L., and G. G. Gallopin. 1991. "A Water Storage Adaptation in the Maya Lowlands." *Science* 251:658–62.

Schaan, D. P. 2004. "The Camutins Chiefdom: Rise and Development of Social Complexity on Marajó Island, Brazilian Amazon." Unpub. Ph.D. thesis, University of Pittsburgh.

Schama, S. 1989. *Citizens: A Chronicle of the French Revolution.* New York: Knopf.

Schele, L., and P. Mathews. 1998. *The Code of Kings: The Language of Seven Sacred Maya Temples and Tombs.* New York: Scribner.

Schimmelmann, A., C. A. Lange, and B. J. Meggers. 2003. "Paleoclimatic and Archaeological Evidence for a 200-yr Recurrence of Floods and Droughts Linking California, Mesoamerica, and South America over the Past 2000 Years." *The Holocene* 13:763–78.

Schimper, A. F. W. 1903. *Plant-Geography Upon a Physiological Basis.* Trans. W. R. Fisher, P. Groom, and I. B. Balfour. Oxford: Oxford University Press (1898).

Schorger, A. W. 1955. *The Passenger Pigeon: Its Natural History and Extinction.* Madison, WI: University of Wisconsin Press.

Schreiber, K. 1992. *Wari Imperialism in Middle Horizon Peru.* Ann Arbor, MI: University of Michigan Press.

Schultz, E. B., and M. J. Tougias. 1999. *King Philip's War: The History and Legacy of America's Forgotten Conflict.* Woodstock, VT: Countryman Press.

Schurr, T. G., et al. 1990. "Amerindian Mitochondrial DNAs Have Rare Asian Mutations at High Frequencies, Suggesting They Derived from Four Primary Maternal Lineages." *AJHG* 46:613–23.

Scott, S., and C. Duncan. 2001. *Biology of Plagues: Evidence from Historical Populations.* New York: Cambridge University Press.

Seed, P. 1991. " 'Failing to Marvel': Atahualpa's Encounter with the Word." *Latin American Research Review* 26:7–32.

Seeman, M. F. 1979. *The Hopewell Interaction Sphere: The Evidence for Interregional Trade and Structural Complexity.* Indianapolis, IN: Indiana Historical Society.

Semple, E. C. 1911. *Influences of Geographic Environment on the Basis of Ratzel's System of Anthropo-Geography.* New York: Holt.

Serrano, J. U. 2002. *Zapotec Hieroglyphic Writing.* Washington, DC: Dumbarton Oaks.

Seton, E. T. 1929. *The Lives of Game Animals.* 3 vols. Garden City, NJ: Doubleday, Doran.

Shabecoff, P. 1993. *A Fierce Green Fire: The American Environmental Movement.* New York: Hill and Wang.

Shady Solis, R. 2003a. "Flautas de Caral: El Conjunto Musical más Antiguo de América," in Shady Solis and Leyva 2003, 289–92.

———. 2003b. "Las Flautas de Caral-Supe: Aproximaciones al Estudio Acústico-Arqueológico del Conjunto de Flautas más Antiguo de América," in Shady Solis and Leyva 2003, 293–300.

Shady Solis, R., and C. Leyva, eds. 2003. *La Ciudad Sagrada de Caral-Supe: Los Orígenes de la Civilización Andina y la Formación del Estado Prístino en el Antiguo Perú.* Lima: Instituto Nacional de Cultura.

Shady Solis, R., J. Haas, and W. Creamer. 2001. "Dating Caral, a Preceramic Site in the Supe Valley on the Central Coast of Peru." *Science* 292:723–26.

Sharp, L. 1969. "Introduction," in Holmberg 1969:iii–xix.

Shaw, J. H. 1995. "How Many Bison Originally Populated Western Rangelands?" *Rangelands* 17:148–50.

Shetler, S. 1991. "Three Faces of Eden," in Viola and Margolis eds. 1991, 225–47.

Shimada, I. 2000. "The Late Prehispanic Coastal States," in L. Laurencich-Minelli, ed., *The Inca World: The Development of Pre-Columbian Peru, A.D. 1000–1534.* Norman, OK: University of Oklahoma Press, 2000.

Shorto, R. 2004. *The Island at the Center of the World: The Epic Story of Dutch Manhattan and the Forgotten Colony That Shaped America.* New York: Doubleday.

Shoumatoff, A. 1986. "A Reporter at Large (The Amazons)." *New Yorker,* 24 Mar., 85–107.

Shuffelton, F. 1976. "Indian Devils and Pilgrim Fathers: Squanto, Hobomok, and the English Conception of Indian Religion." *New England Quarterly* 49:108–16.

Sidrys, R., and R. Berger. 1979. "Lowland Maya Radiocarbon Dates and the Classic Maya Collapse." *Nature* 277:269–77.

Silverberg, R. 1968. *The Mound Builders of Ancient America.* New York: Graphic Society.

Silverman, H., ed. 2004. *Andean Archaeology.* Malden, MA: Blackwell.

Silverstein, J. E. 1998. "A Study of the Late Postclassic Aztec-Tarascan Frontier in Northern Guerrero, Mexico: The Oztuma-Cutzamala Project, 1998." FAMSI. Online at http://www.famsi.org/reports/97014/.

Simmons, A. H., et al. 1988. "'Ain Ghazal: A Major Neolithic Settlement in Central Jordan." *Science* 240:35–39.

Slater, C. 1995. "Amazonia as Edenic Narrative," in Cronon ed. 1995, 114–31.

Sluyter, A. 1994. "Intensive Wetland Agriculture in Mesoamerica: Space, Time, and Form." *AAAG* 84:557–84.

Smith, A. 1990. *Explorers of the Amazon.* New York: Viking.

Smith, B. D. 1992. *Rivers of Change: Essays on Early Agriculture in Eastern North America.* Washington, DC: Smithsonian.

———. 1989. "Origins of Agriculture in Eastern North America." *Science* 246:1566–71.

Smith, J. 1910. *A Map of Virginia, with a Description of the Countrey, the Commodities, People, Government, and Religion,* in Arber and Bradley 1910, 41–173 (1612).

Smith, M. E. 1984. "The Aztlan Migrations of the Nahuatl Chronicles: Myth or History?" *Ethnohistory* 31:153–86.

———. 1962. "The Codex Columbino: A Document of the South Coast of Oaxaca." *Tlalocán* 4:276–88.

Smith, M. T. 1994. "Aboriginal Depopulation in the Post-Contact Southeast," in C. Hudson and C. C. Tesser, eds., *The Forgotten Centuries: Indians and Europeans in the American South, 1521–1704.* Athens, GA: University of Georgia Press, 257–75.

———. 1987. *Archaeology of Aboriginal Culture Change in the Interior Southeast: Depopulation During the Early Historic Period.* Gainesville, FL: University Presses of Florida.

Smith, N. L. 1995. "Human-Induced Landscape Changes in Amazonia and Implications for Development," in B. L. Turner II, et al., eds., *Global Land Use Change: A Perspective from the Columbian Encounter.* Madrid: Consejo Superior de Investigaciónes Científicas, 221–51.

———. 1980. "Anthrosols and Human Carrying Capacity in Amazonia." *AAAG* 70:553–66.

Snow, D. R. 1995. "Microchronology and Demographic Evidence Relating to the Size of Pre-Columbian North American Indian Populations." *Science* 268:1601–05.

———. 1994. *The Iroquois.* New York: Blackwell.

———. 1992. "Disease and Population Decline in the Northeast," in Verano and Ubelaker 1992, 177–86.

———. 1980. *The Archaeology of New England.* New York: Academic.

Snow, D. R., and K. M. Lanphear. 1988. "European Contact and Indian Depopulation in the Northeast: The Timing of the First Epidemics." *Ethnohistory* 35:5–33.

Sombroek, W., et al. 2004. "Amazonian Dark Earths as Carbon Stores and Sinks," in Lehmann et al. 2004, 125–39.

Soto-Heim, P. 1994. "Les Hommes de Lagoa Santa (Brésil): Caractères Anthropologiques et

Position parmi d'autres Populations Paléoindiennes d'Amérique." *L'Anthropologie* (Paris) 98:81–109.

Soulé, M. E., and G. Lease, eds. 1995. *Reinventing Nature? Responses to Postmodern Deconstruction*. Washington, DC: Island.

Spence, K. 2000. "Ancient Egyptian Chronology and the Astronomical Orientation of Pyramids." *Nature* 408:320–24.

Spencer, C. S. 2003. "War and Early State Formation in Oaxaca, Mexico." *PNAS* 100:11185–87.

Spencer, C. S., and E. S. Redmond. 2001. "Multilevel Selection and Political Evolution in the Valley of Oaxaca, 500–100 B.C." *Journal of Anthropological Archaeology* 20:195–229.

Spiess, A. E., and B. D. Spiess. 1987. "New England Pandemic of 1616–1622: Cause and Archaeological Implication." *Man in the Northeast* 34:71–83.

Spinden, H. J. 1928. "The Population of Ancient America." *Geographical Review* 28:641–60.

Spores, R. 1974. "Marital Alliance in the Political Integration of Mixtec Kingdoms." *AA* 76:297–311.

Spotts, P. N. 2003. "Religion in the Americas Began in 2250 B.C." *Christian Science Monitor*, 17 Apr.

Stahl, P. W. 2002. "Paradigms in Paradise: Revising Standard Amazonian Prehistory." *Review of Archaeology* 23:39–51.

———. 1996. "Holocene Biodiversity: An Archaeological Perspective from the Americas." *Annual Review of Anthropology* 25:105–26.

Stahle, D. W., et al. 1998. "The Lost Colony and Jamestown Droughts." *Science* 280:564–67.

Stanford, D., and B. Bradley. 2002. "Ocean Trails and Prairie Paths? Thoughts About Clovis Origins," in Jablonski ed. 2002, 255–71.

Stanish, C. 2003. *Ancient Titicaca: The Evolution of Complex Society in Southern Peru and Northern Bolivia*. Berkeley, CA: University of California Press.

———. 2001. "Formación Estatal Temprana en la Cuenca del Lago Titicaca, Andes Surcentrales," in Kaulicke and Isbell eds. 2001, 189–215.

Stannard, D. E. 2001. "Uniqueness as Denial: The Politics of Genocide Scholarship," in A. S. Rosenbaum, ed., *Is the Holocaust Unique? Perspectives on Comparative Genocide*. Boulder, CO: Westview, 2nd ed., 245–90.

———. 1992. *American Holocaust: The Conquest of the New World*. New York: Oxford University Press.

———. 1991. "The Consequences of Contact: Toward an Interdisciplinary Theory of Native Responses to Biological and Cultural Invasion," in Thomas 1989–91, 3:519–39.

Stearman, A. M. 1987. *No Longer Nomads: The Sirionó Revisited*. New York: Hamilton.

———. 1986. "Territory Folks." *NH* (March):6–10.

———. 1984. "The Yuquí Connection: Another Look at Sirionó Deculturation." *AA* 86:630–50.

Stearns, P. N. 1987. *World History: Patterns of Change and Continuity*. New York: Harper and Row.

Steele, D. G., and J. F. Powell. 2002. "Facing the Past: A View of the North American Human Fossil Record," in Jablonski ed. 2002, 93–122.

Steiner, C., W. G. Teixeira, and W. Zech. 2004. "Slash and Char: An Alternative to Slash and Burn Practiced in the Amazon Basin," in Glaser and Woods eds. 2004, 183–93.

Steuter, A. 1991. "Human Impacts on Biodiversity in America: Thoughts from the Grassland Biome" (letter). *Conservation Biology* 5:136–37.

Steward, J. H. 1948. "Culture Areas of the Tropical Forests." *Bulletin of the Bureau of American Ethnology* 143:883–89.

Steward, J. H., ed. 1946. *Handbook of South American Indians*. Washington, DC: Government Printing Office, 7 vols.

Stewart-Smith, D. 1998. *The Pennacook Indians and the New England Frontier, Circa 1604–1733.* PhD diss. Union Institute, Cincinnati, OH.

Stirland, A. 1995. "Evidence for Pre-Columbian Treponematosis in Europe (England)," in O. Dutour et al., eds., *The Origin of Syphilis in Europe.* Toulon, France: Centre Archéologique du Var, 109–15.

Stirling, M. W. 1940a. *An Initial Series from Tres Zapotes, Veracruz, Mexico.* Washington, DC: National Geographic.

———. 1940b. "Great Stone Faces of the Mexican Jungle." *National Geographic* (September):309–34.

———. 1939. "Discovering the New World's Oldest Dated Work of Man." *National Geographic* (August):183–218.

Stokstad, E. 2002. "Oldest New World Writing Suggests Olmec Innovation." *Science* 298:1872–73.

Stone, A. 1989. "Disconnection, Foreign Insignia, and Political Expansion: Teotihuacán and the Warrior Stelae of Piedras Negras," in R. A. Diehl and J. C. Berlo, eds., *Mesoamerica After the Decline of Teotihuacán, A.D. 700–900.* Washington, DC: Dumbarton Oaks, 153–72.

Stott, P. 1999. *Tropical Rain Forest: A Political Ecology of Hegemonic Mythmaking.* London: Coronet.

Straus, L. G. 2000. "Solutrean Settlement of North America? A Review of Reality." *AmAnt,* 65:219–26.

Stuart, D. 2000. " 'The Arrival of Strangers': Teotihuacán and Tollán in Classic Maya History," in D. Carrasco, L. Jones, and S. Sessions, eds., *Mesoamerica's Classic Heritage: From Teotihuacán to the Aztecs.* Boulder, CO: University of Colorado Press, 465–513.

Stuart, G. E. 1993a. "New Light on the Olmec." *National Geographic* (November):88–115.

———. 1993b. "The Carved Stela from La Mojarra, Veracruz, Mexico." *Science* 259:1700–01.

Studd, H. 2001. "Essex Girl Claims an Historic First: Syphilis." *Times* (London), 31 May.

Stuiver, M., et al. 1998. "INTCAL98 Radiocarbon Age Calibration, 24,000-0 cal BP." *Radiocarbon* 40:1041–83.

Sullivan, T. D., and T. K. Knab, eds., trans. 1994. *A Scattering of Jades: Stories, Poems, and Prayers of the Aztecs.* Tucson, AZ: University of Arizona Press.

Sundstrom, L. 1997. "Smallpox Used Them Up: References to Epidemic Disease in Northern Plains Winter Counts, 1714–1920." *Ethnohistory* 44:305–43.

Swadesh, M. 1971. "What Is Glottochronology?" in Swadesh ed. 1971, 271–84.

———. 1952. "Lexicostatistic Dating of Prehistoric Ethnic Contacts." *Proceedings of the American Philosophical Society* 96:152–63.

Swadesh, M., ed. 1971. *The Origin and Diversification of Language.* Chicago: Aldine Atherton.

Tate, C., and G. Bendersky. 1999. "Olmec Sculptures of the Human Fetus." *Perspectives in Biology and Medicine* 42:303–33.

Taylor, T. G. 1927. *Environment and Race: A Study of the Evolution, Migration, Settlement and Status of the Races of Man.* London: Oxford University Press.

Tehanetorens. 1971. *The Great Law of Peace of the Longhouse People.* Rooseveltown, NY: White Roots of Peace.

Temple, R. 1998. *The Genius of China: 3,000 Years of Science, Discovery, and Invention.* New York: Prion.

Teresi, D. 2002. *Lost Discoveries: The Ancient Roots of Modern Science—from the Babylonians to the Maya.* New York: Simon and Schuster.

Theis, J., and K. Suzuki. 2004. "Amazonian Dark Earths: Biological Measurements," in Lehmann et al. 2004, 287–332.

Thomas, D. H. 2001. *Skull Wars: Kennewick Man, Archaeology, and the Battle for Native American Identity.* New York: Basic Books.

Thomas, D. H., ed. 1989–91. *Columbian Consequences.* 3 vols. Washington, DC: Smithsonian.

Thomas, H. 1995. *Conquest: Cortés, Montezuma, and the Fall of Old Mexico.* New York: Touchstone, 1993.

Thomas, P. A. 1979. *In the Maelstrom of Change: The Indian Trade and Cultural Process in the Middle Connecticut River Valley: 1635–1665.* PhD diss. University of Massachusetts, Amherst.

Thompson, D. 1916. *David Thompson's Narrative of His Explorations in Western America, 1784–1812.* Toronto: Champlain Society.

Thompson, L. G., M. E. Davis, and E. Mosley-Thompson. 1994. "Glacial Records of Global Climate—a 1,500-year Tropical Ice Core Record of Climate." *HE* 22:83–95.

Thomson, H. 2003. *The White Rock: An Exploration of the Inca Heartland.* Woodstock, NY: Overlook.

Thoreau, H. D. 1906: *Works: The Writings of Henry David Thoreau.* Boston: Houghton Mifflin, vol. 4, *Cape Cod,* 1–273 (1865); vol. 5, "Natural History of Massachusetts," 103–31 (1842).

Thornton, R. 1987. *American Indian Holocaust and Survival: A Population History since 1492.* Norman, OK: University of Oklahoma Press.

Thucydides. 1934. *History of the Peloponnesian War.* Trans. R. Crawley. New York: Modern Library. (★)

Tierney, P. 2000. *Darkness in El Dorado: How Scientists and Journalists Devastated the Amazon.* New York: Norton.

Tolan-Smith, C. 1998. "Radiocarbon Chronology and the Lateglacial and Early Postglacial Resettlement of the British Isles." *QI* 49/50:21–27.

Tooker, E. 1988. "The United States Constitution and the Iroquois League." *Ethnohistory* 35:305–36.

Torroni, A., and D. C. Wallace. 1995. "MtDNA Haplotypes in Native Americans." *AJHG* 56:1234–36.

Torroni, A., et al. 1994. "Mitochondrial DNA 'Clock' for the Amerinds and Its Implications for Timing Their Entry into North America." *PNAS* 91:1158–62.

———. 1993. "Asian Affinities and Continental Radiation of the Four Founding Native American mtDNAs." *AJHG* 53:563–90.

Townsend, W. R. 1996. *Nyao Itõ: Caza y Pesca de los Sirionó.* La Paz: Instituto de Ecología, Universidad Mayor de San Andrés: FUND-ECO.

Treckel, P. A., and J. Axtell. 1976. "Letters to the Editor." *WMQ* 33:143–53.

Trevor-Roper, H. R. 1965. *The Rise of Christian Europe.* London: Thames and Hudson.

Trigger, B. G. 1991. "Early Native North American Responses to European Contact: Romantic versus Rationalistic Interpretations." *JAH* 77:1195–215.

Trigger, B. G., ed. 1978. *Handbook of North American Indians.* Washington, DC: Smithsonian, 14 vols.

Trubitt, M. B. 2000. "Mound Building and Prestige Goods Exchange: Changing Strategies in the Cahokia Chiefdom." *AmAnt* 65:669–90.

Turner, B. L., and S. B. Brush, eds. 1987. *Comparative Farming Systems.* New York: Guilford Press.

Ubelaker, D. H. 1992. "North American Indian Population Size: Changing Perspectives," in Verano and Ubelaker 1992, 169–76.

———. 1988. "North American Indian Population Size, A.D. 1500 to 1985." *American Journal of Physical Anthropology* 77:289–94.

———. 1976. "The Sources and Methodology for Mooney's Estimates of North American Indian Populations," in Denevan 1976, 243–88.

Uceda, S., and E. Mujica, eds. 1993. *Moche: Propuestas y Perspectivas.* Lima: Universidad Nacional de Trujillo.

Uhl, C. 1987. "Factors Controlling Succession Following Slash and Burn Agriculture in Amazonia." *Journal of Ecology* 75:377–407.

Uhl, C., and C. F. Jordan. 1984. "Succession and Nutrient Dynamics Following Forest Cutting and Burning in Amazonia." *Ecology* 65:1476–90.

Uhl, C., et al. 1982. "Ecosystem Recovery in Amazon Caatinga Forest after Cutting, Cutting and Burning and Bulldozer Treatments." *Oikos* 38:313–20.

Uhle, M. 1925. "Report on Explorations at Supe," in A. L. Kroeber, "The Uhle Pottery Collections from Supe." *University of California Publications in American Archaeology and Ethnology* 21:257–63.

———. 1917. "Los aborígenes de Arica." *Publicaciones del Museo de Etnología y Antropología de Chile* 1:151–76.

Underwood, P. 1993. *The Walking People: A Native American Oral History.* San Anselmo, CA: A Tribe of Two.

United Nations Population Division. 1999. *The World at Six Billion.* New York: United Nations.

United States Bureau of the Census. 1937. *Fifteenth Census of the United States, 1930: The Indian Population of the United States and Alaska.* Washington, DC: Government Printing Office.

Unstead, R. J. 1983. *A History of the World.* London: A&C Black.

Urton, G. 2003. *Signs of the Inka Khipu: Binary Coding in Knotted-String Records.* Austin, TX: University of Texas Press.

———. 2001. "A Calendrical and Demographic Tomb Text from Northern Peru." *LAA* 12:127–47.

Ussher, J. 1658. *The Annals of the World.* London: E. Tyler. (★)

Vale, T. R. 2002. "The Pre-European Landscape of the United States: Pristine or Humanized?" in T. R. Vale, ed., *Fire, Native Peoples, and the Natural Landscape.* Washington, DC: Island, 1–39.

———. 1998. "The Myth of the Humanized Landscape: An Example from Yosemite National Park." *Natural Areas Journal* 18:231–36.

Vancouver, G. 1984. *A Voyage of Discovery to the North Pacific Ocean and Around the World, 1791–1795.* Ed. W. K. Lamb. London: Hakluyt Society.

Van der Donck, A. 1993. *A Description of the New Netherlands.* Trans. C. Gehring. Albany, NY: State Museum of New York (1656).

———. 1841. "Description of the New Netherlands." Trans. J. Johnson. *Collections of the New-York Historical Society* 1:125–242 (1656).

Van Sertima, I. 1976. *They Came Before Columbus: The African Presence in Ancient America.* New York: Random House.

Vargas Llosa, M. 1992. "Question of Conquest." *American Educator* (Spring):25–27, 47–48.

Vaughan, A. T. 1995. *New England Frontier: Puritans and Indians 1620–1675.* Norman, OK: University of Oklahoma Press, 3rd ed.

Vaughan, A. T., and D. K. Richter. 1980. "Crossing the Cultural Divide: Indians and New Englanders, 1605–1763." *Proceedings of the American Antiquarian Society* 90:23–99.

Vaughan, H., E. Deevey, and S. Garett-Jones. 1985. "Pollen Stratigraphy of Two Cores from the Peten Lake District, with an Appendix on Two Deep-Water Cores," in M. D. Pohl, ed., *Prehistoric Lowland Maya Environment and Subsistence Economy.* Cambridge, MA: Harvard University Press.

Vellard, J. 1956. "Causas Biológicas de la Desparición de los Índios Americanos." *Boletín del Instituto Riva-Agüero* (Lima) 2 (supp.):1–16.

Venables, R. W. 1992. "American Indian Influences on the America of the Founding Fathers," in O. Lyons, et al., *Exiled in the Land of the Free: Democracy, Indian Nations, and the U.S. Constitution.* Santa Fe, NM: Clear Light, 74–124.

Venter, J. C., et al. 2001. "The Sequence of the Human Genome." *Science* 291:1304–51.

Verano, J. W., and D. H. Ubelaker, eds. 1992. *Disease and Demography in the Americas.* Washington, DC: Smithsonian.

Viola, H. J., and C. Margolis. 1991. *Seeds of Change: A Quincentennial Commemoration.* Washington: DC, Smithsonian.

Von Däniken, E. 1998. *Arrival of the Gods: Revealing the Alien Landing Sites of Nazca.* London: HarperCollins.

———. 1969. *Chariots of the Gods? Unsolved Mysteries of the Past.* Trans. M. Heron. New York: Putnam.

Vranich, A. 2001. "La Pirámide de Akapana: Reconsiderando el Centro Monumental de Tiwanaku," in Kaulicke and Isbell 2001, 295–308.

Vranich, A., et al. 2001. "Informe de los trabajos arqueológicos realizado por el Proyecto Arqueológico Pumapunku-Akapana." Unpub. ms.

Wagner, H. R., with H. R. Parish. 1967. *The Life and Writings of Bartolomé de Las Casas.* Albuquerque, NM: University of New Mexico Press.

Wagner, S. R. 2001. *Sisters in Spirit: Haudenosaunee (Iroquois) Influence on Early American Feminists.* Summertown, TN: Native Voices.

Wallace, A. R. 1962. *The Geographical Distribution of Animals: With a Study of the Relations of Living and Extinct Faunas as Elucidating the Past Changes of the Earth's Surface.* New York: Hafner, 2 vols. (1876).

Ward, R. H., et al. 1991. "Extensive Mitochondrial Diversity Within a Single Amerindian Tribe." *PNAS* 88:8720–24.

Warden, G. B. 1975. "Indian Corn Cultivation" (letter). *Science,* 189:946.

Warman, A. 2003. *Corn and Capitalism: How a Botanical Bastard Grew to Global Dominance.* Trans. N. L. Westrate. Chapel Hill, NC: University of North Carolina Press (1988).

Wauchope, R. 1962. *Lost Tribes and Sunken Continents: Myth and Method in the Study of the American Indians.* Chicago: University of Chicago Press.

Weatherford, J. 1988. *Indian Givers: How the Indians of the Americas Transformed the World.* New York: Fawcett Columbine.

Weber, K. T. 2001. "Historic Bison Populations: A GIS Estimate." Proceedings of the 2001 Intermountain GIS Users' Conference. Online at http://giscenter.isu.edu/Research/Projects/BisonPaper.pdf.

Webster, D. 2002. *The Fall of the Ancient Maya: Solving the Mystery of the Maya Collapse.* New York: Thames and Hudson.

Wedin, Å. 1966. *El Concepto de lo Incaico y las Fuentes: Estudio Crítico.* Uppsala: Akademiförlaget.

———. 1963. *La Cronología de la Historia Incaica: Estudio Crítico.* Madrid: Insula.

Wegner, R. 1932. "Ostbolivianische Urwaldstämme." *Ethnologisches Anzeiger* 2:331.

Weinreb, B., and C. Hibbert, eds. 1993. *The London Encyclopedia.* London: PaperMac, 2nd ed.

Weinstein, L., ed. 1994. *Enduring Traditions: The Native Peoples of New England.* Westport, CT: Bergin and Garvey.

Wellhausen, E. J., et al. 1957. *Races of Maize in Central America.* Washington, DC: National Academy of Sciences.

———. 1952. *Races of Maize in Mexico: Their Origin, Characteristics, and Distribution.* Jamaica Plain, MA: Bussey Institution.

Wells, H. G. 1920. *The Outline of History: Being a Plain History of Life and Mankind.* 2 vols. New York: Macmillan.

White, A. D. 1898. *A History of the Warfare of Science with Theology in Christendom.* New York: D. Appleton. (★)

White, R. 1995. "Are You an Environmentalist or Do You Work for a Living?" in Cronon ed. 1995, 171–85.

Whitehead, N. L. 1994. "The Ancient Amerindian Polities of the Amazon, the Orinoco, and the Atlantic Coast: A Preliminary Analysis of Their Passage from Antiquity to Extinction," in Roosevelt ed. 1994, 33–54.

Wilford, J. N. 1998a. "In Peru, Evidence of an Early Human Maritime Culture." *NYT*, 22 Sep., F3.

———. 1998b. "Chilean Field Yields New Clues to Peopling of Americas." *NYT*, 25 Aug., F1.

———. 1997a. "Anna Roosevelt: Sharp and to the Point in Amazon Archeology." *NYT*, 22 Apr., C1.

———. 1997b. "Excavation in Chile Pushes Back Date of Human Habitation of Americas." *NYT*, 11 Feb., A1.

Wilken, G. C. 1987. *Good Farmers: Traditional Agricultural Resource Management in Mexico and Central America*. Berkeley, CA: University of California Press.

Wilkes, H. G. 1972. "Maize and its Wild Relatives." *Science* 177:1071–77.

———. 1967. *Teosinte: The Closest Relative of Maize*. Cambridge, MA: Bussey Institution.

Wilkie, R. W., and J. Tager, eds. 1991. *Historical Atlas of Massachusetts*. Amherst, MA: University of Massachusetts Press.

Wilkinson, C. 2000. *Messages from Frank's Landing: A Story of Salmon, Treaties, and the Indian Way*. Seattle, WA: University of Washington Press.

Willey, G. R., and J. M. Corbett. 1954. *Early Ancón and Early Supe Culture: Chavin Horizon Sites of the Central Peruvian Coast*. New York: Columbia University Press.

Williams, A. R. 2002. "A New Chapter in Maya History: All-Out War, Shifting Alliances, Bloody Sacrifices." *National Geographic* (October):xii–xvi.

Williams, D., 1949a and 1949b. "John Evans' Strange Journey." *American Historical Review*, part I, 54:277–95; part 2, 54:508–29.

Williams, G. W. 2002. "Are There Any 'Natural' Plant Communities?" in Kay and Simmons 2002, 179–214.

Williams, H. U., J. P. Rice, and J. R. Lacayo. 1927. "The American Origin of Syphilis, with Citations from Early Spanish Authors Collected by Dr. Montejo y Robledo." *Archives of Dermatology and Syphilology* 16:683–96.

Williams, M. 1989. *Americans and Their Forests: A Historical Geography*. Cambridge: Cambridge University Press.

Williams, P. R., J. A. Isla, and D. J. Nash. 2001. "Cerro Baúl: Un Enclave Wari en Interacción con Tiwanaku," in Kaulicke and Isbell 2001, 69–87.

Williams, R. 1936. *A Key into the Language of America*. Providence, R.I.: Roger Williams Press (1643).

Wilson, D. J. 1981. "Of Maize and Men: A Critique of the Maritime Hypothesis of State Origins on the Coast of Peru." *AA* 83:93–120.

Wilson, E. O. 1992. *The Diversity of Life*. Cambridge, MA: Belknap Press.

Wilson, J. 1999. *The Earth Shall Weep: A History of Native America*. New York: Atlantic Monthly.

Winslow, E. 1963a. "A Letter Sent from New England to a Friend in These Parts, Setting Forth a Brief and True Declaration of the Worth of That Plantation; as Also Certain Useful Directions for Such as Intend a Voyage into Those Parts," in Anon. ed. 1963, 81–87 (1622).

———. 1963b. "A Relation or Journal of the Proceedings of the Plantation Settled at Plymouth in New England," in Anon. ed. 1963, 15–59 (1622).

———. 1963c. "A Journey to Pokanoket, the Habitation of the Great King Massasoit; as Also Our Message, the Answer and Entertainment We Had of Him," in Anon. ed. 1963, 60–68 (1622).

———. 1963d. "A Voyage Made by Ten of Our Men to the Kingdom of Nauset, to Seek a Boy That Had Lost Himself in the Woods; with Such Accidents as Befell Us on That Voyage," in Anon. ed. 1963, 69–72 (1622).

Winslow, E. 1624. *Good Newes from New-England: or A True Relation of Things Very Remarkable at the Plantation of Plimoth in New-England*. London: William Bladen and John Bellamie. (★)

Winter, J. C. 2000. "Botanical Description of the North American Tobacco Species," in J. C. Winter, ed., *Tobacco Use by Native North Americans: Sacred Smoke and Silent Killer.* Norman, OK: University of Oklahoma Press, 87–127.

Winters, C. A. 1979. "Manding Writing in the New World: Part I." *Journal of African Civilizations* 1:81–97.

Winthrop, J. 1976. Letters to N. Rich (22 May 1634) and S. D'Ewes (21 July 1634), in E. Emerson, ed., *Letters from New England: The Massachusetts Bay Colony, 1629–1638.* Amherst, MA: University of Massachusetts Press.

Wolf, E. R. 1997. *Europe and the People Without History.* Berkeley, CA: University of California Press (1982).

Wood, L. C., et al. 1971. *America: Its People and Values.* New York: Harcourt Brace.

Wood, W. 1977. *New England's Prospect.* Amherst, MA: University of Massachusetts Press (1634).

Woods, W. I. 2004. "Population Nucleation, Intensive Agriculture, and Environmental Degradation: The Cahokia Example." *Agriculture and Human Values* 21:151–57.

———. 2003. "Soils and Sustainability in the Prehistoric New World," in B. Bensing and B. Herrmann, eds., *Exploitation and Overexploitation in Societies Past and Present.* Munich: LIT-Verlag, 143–57.

———. 2001. "Monks Mound: A View from the Top." Paper at the 66th Annual Meeting of the Society for American Archaeology, 19 Apr., New Orleans.

———. 2000. "Monks Mound Revisited," in N. Sterry, ed., *Terra 2000: 8th International Conference on the Study and Conservation of Earthen Architecture.* London: James and James Ltd., 98–104.

Woods, W. I., and J. M. McCann. 1999. "The Anthropogenic Origin and Persistence of Amazonian Dark Earths." *Yearbook Conference of Latin Americanist Geographers* 25:7–14.

Woods, W. I., and C. L. Wells. 2001. "Bubble Boys and Powerscapes." Paper presented at the 66th Annual Meeting of the Society for American Archaeology, 20 Apr., New Orleans.

Woodward, S. L., and J. N. McDonald. 2002. *Indian Mounds of the Middle Ohio Valley: A Guide to Mounds and Earthworks of the Adena, Hopewell, Cole, and Fort Ancient People.* Granville, OH: McDonald and Woodward.

Wormington, H. M. 1957. *Ancient Man in North America.* Denver, CO: Denver Museum of Natural History, 4th ed.

Wright, H. E., Jr., and M. L. Heinselman. 1973. "Ecological Role of Fire: Introduction." *QR* 3:319–28.

Wright, R. 2005. *A Short History of Progress.* Toronto: Anansi.

———. 1992. *Stolen Continents: The Americas Through Indian Eyes Since 1492.* Boston: Houghton Mifflin.

Wright, R. M., and M. Carneiro de Cunha. 2000. "Destruction, Resistance and Transformation: Southern, Coastal, and Northern Brazil (1580–1890)," in F. Salomon, and S. B. Schwartz, eds., *The Cambridge History of the Native Peoples of the Americas,* vol. 3, *South America,* part 2:340–45.

Wrigley, E. A. 1983. "The Growth of Population in Eighteenth-Century England: A Conundrum Resolved." *Past and Present* 98:121–50.

———. 1969. *Population and History.* New York: McGraw Hill.

Wroth, L. C., ed. 1970. *The Voyages of Giovanni da Verrazzano, 1524–1528.* New Haven, CT: Yale University Press.

Xerez, F. d. 1938. *Verdadera Relación de la Conquista del Perú,* in H. H. Urteaga, *Les Cronistas de la Conquista.* Paris: Desclée, de Brouwer, 15–115 (1534).

Xu, H. M. 1996. *Origin of the Olmec Civilization.* Edmond, OK: University of Central Oklahoma Press.

Young, G. A., and M. P. Hoffman, eds. 1993. *The Expedition of Hernando de Soto West of the Mississippi, 1541–1543.* Fayetteville, AR: University of Arkansas Press.

Zambardino, R. A. 1980. "Mexico's Population in the Sixteenth Century: Demographic Anomaly or Mathematical Illusion?" *Journal of Interdisciplinary History* 11:1–27.

————. 1978. "Critique of David Henige's 'On the Contact Population of Hispaniola: History as Higher Mathematics,'" *Hispanic American Historical Review* 58:700–08.

Zeitlin, R. N. 1990. "The Isthmus and the Valley of Oaxaca: Questions About Zapotec Imperialism in Formative Period Mesoamerica." *AmAnt* 55:250–61.

Zohary, D. 1972. "The Progenitors of Wheat and Barley in Relation to Domestication and Agricultural Dispersal in the Old World," in P. J. Ucko, R. Tringham, and G. W. Dimbleby, eds., *Man, Settlement, and Urbanism.* London: Duckworth, 47–66.

Zohary, D., and M. Hopf. 2000. *Domestication of Plants in the Old World.* New York: Oxford University Press, 3rd ed.

Zoppi, U., et al. 2000. "AMS and Controversies in History: The Spanish Conquest of Peru." *Nuclear Instruments and Methods in Physics Research B* 172:756–60.

❄ INDEX ❄

Italicized page numbers indicate illustrations; page numbers 362 and higher refer to endnotes

MAP CREDITS

Map designs by Nick Springer, Springer Cartographics. Maps on pages 37, 47, 65, 75, and 159 by Timothy William Gibson and author; maps on pages 21, 125, 184, 212, 229, 257, 263, 274, 287, 322, and frontispiece by the author.

21 data from Diehl, 1983; Martin and Grube, 2000; Flannery and Marcus, 2000, 2003; MacEwan, Barreto, and Neves, 2001; Heckenberger et al., 2003; Pärssinen, 2003; Denevan pers. comm.; Erickson pers. comm.; Petersen pers. comm.; Woods pers. comm.

37, 47 after Salisbury, 1982; Vaughan, 1995; Plimoth Plantation Education Dept.

65 after Hyslop, 1984; Moseley, 2001; Pärssinen, 2003

75 data from Rowe, 1946; Moseley, 2001; D'Altroy, 2002; Pärssinen, 2003

125 data from Berdan and Anawalt, 1997; Townsend, 2000; Pollard, 2003

159 after Haynes, 1964

184 after Haas, Creamer, and Ruiz, 2004

212 data from Flores, 1974; Bernal, 1969; Coe, 1994, 1999; Martin and Grube, 2000; Flannery and Marcus, 2000, 2003; Pohl, Pope, and von Nagy, 2002; FAMSI, n.d.

229 after Owen and Goldstein, 2001; Stanish, 2003

257 data from Brown, 1992; Saunders et al., 1997; Petersen pers. comm.; Woods pers. comm.; U.S. National Park Service, n.d.

263 after Fowler, 1997

274 data from Martin and Grube, 1996, 2000; Guenter, 2003; Fahsen, 2003

287 after Denevan, 1996; MacEwan, Barreto, and Neves, 2001; Heckenberger et al., 2003

322 data from Doolittle, 2000; Denevan, 2001; Whitmore and Turner, 2001; MacEwan, Barreto, and Neves, 2001; Denevan pers. comm.; Petersen pers. comm.; Pyne pers. comm.; Roosevelt, pers. comm.; Woods pers. comm. (The author is extremely grateful to Steven Pyne, Jim Petersen, Bill Woods, and especially William Denevan for putting aside their entirely justified misgivings and helping him with this map.)

ILLUSTRATION CREDITS

(★) Image digitally altered by author, usually to remove dust, scratches and bleed-through

11 (t) Martti Pärssinen, University of Helsinki; (b) Clark L. Erickson, University of Pennsylvania Museum of Archaeology and Anthropology (★)

41, 73, 175, 182, 226, 231, 233 (b), *319* (b), *357* Author's collection

464

45 (t) Library of Congress, Prints and Photographs Division (hereafter LOC), Reproduction No. LC-USZ62-53338; (b) LOC, Reproduction No. LC-USZ62-54015

57 LOC, Reproduction No: LC-USZ62-54018

67, 91 Julia Chambi and Teo Allain Chambi, Archivo Fotográfico Martín Chambi, Cusco, Peru

72 LOC, Reproduction No. LC-USZ62-97754

77 Royal Library, Copenhagen, facsimile with transcription from Guamán Poma Web site, www.kb.dk/elib/mss/poma (*)

85 Rutahsa Adventures, www.rutahsa.com (photo by Ric Finch)

116–17, 193, 198, 202, 269 (t), 289 Peter Menzel, www.menzelphoto.com

127 Instituto Nacional de Antropología e Historia, Mexico City (painting by Miguel Covarrubias)

128 (t) Bibliothèque Nationale de France, MS Mex. 385 (Codex Telleriano-Remensis, folio 45v.) (*); (b) Museum of Indian Arts and Culture, Santa Fe, N.M. (Fray Bernardino de Sahagún, Historia General de las Cosas de Nueva España, vol. 4, book 12, plate 114)

146 (l) Peabody Museum, Harvard University, Photo N25826; (r) Smithsonian American Art Museum, Washington, D.C. / Art Resource, N.Y. (Painting by Nicholas R. Brewer [1857-1949])

149 National Anthropological Archives, Smithsonian Institution (hereafter NAA), Photo MNH 31,213

154 Pete Bostrom, Lithic Casting Lab (*)

157 University Photo Center, University of Arizona, Tucson, Ariz.

168 Vanderbilt University (photo by Steve Green)

190 Proyecto Arqueológico Norte Chico

206 National Geographic Image Collection (photo by Mathew W. Stirling)

217 Joyce Marcus, University of Michigan (originally printed in Marcus 1976) (*)

221 Mount Holyoke College Archives and Special Collections (Codex Zouche-Nuttall, 1902, facsimile, original at British Museum)

233 (t) Paul Harmon, QalaYampu Project, www.reedboat.org

236 Library, American Museum of Natural History (hereafter AMNH), Neg. no. 334876 (photo by Shippee-Johnson Expedition)

239 AMNH, Neg. no. 334611 (photo by Shippee-Johnson Expedition)

244–5 University of Pennsylvania Museum, Tikal Project Neg. No. 64-5-29, Vessel 10E-52

255 Southeast Archaeological Center, National Park Service (painting by Martin Pate)

261 Cahokia Mounds State Historic Site ([t] painting by Lloyd K. Townsend; [b] painting by Michael Hampshire)

269 (b) Courtesy Gabriel González Maury, www.campeche.com

276 James Porter (*)

277 Justin Kerr

283 Araquém Alcântara

292 NAA, Photo Lot 83-15

295 Academic Press

296 Anna C. Roosevelt

309 (l) Museum of World Culture, Göteborg, Sweden (photo by Hakan Berg); (r) Museu de Arqueologia e Etnologia da Universidade de São Paulo (photo by Wagner Souza e Silva)

319 (r, l) Harris H. Wilder Papers, Smith College Archives, Smith College

320 AMNH, Neg. no. 334717 (photo by Shippee-Johnson Expedition)